ECONOMIC PRINCIPALS

ALSO BY DAVID WARSH

THE IDEA OF ECONOMIC COMPLEXITY

Economic
PRINCIPALS

Masters and Mavericks
of Modern Economics

David Warsh

THE FREE PRESS
A Division of Macmillan, Inc.
New York

Maxwell Macmillan Canada
Toronto

Maxwell Macmillan International
New York   Oxford   Singapore   Sydney

The Free Press
A Division of Macmillan, Inc.
866 Third Avenue, New York, N.Y. 10022

Maxwell Macmillan Canada, Inc.
1200 Eglinton Avenue East
Suite 200
Don Mills, Ontario M3C 3N1

Macmillan, Inc. is part of the Maxwell Communication Group of Companies.

Printed in the United States of America

printing number
1   2   3   4   5   6   7   8   9   10

Library of Congress Cataloging-in-Publication Data
Warsh, David.
    Economic principals: masters and mavericks of modern
economics/ David Warsh.
      p. cm.
    Most of the articles were previously published in the *Boston Globe.*
    ISBN 0-02-933996-0
    1. Economists—Biography. 2. Economists—United States—
Biography. 3. Economics—History—20th century. I. Title.
HB76.W37   1993
330'.092'2—dc20
  [B]   92-32152
                                         CIP

The articles in this book were previously published by the *Boston Globe*, with the exception of "Alsager's Heirs," which was previously published in slightly different form in *Nieman Reports*; "The *New* New Economics," which was previously published in *Sloan Management Review*; and the Introduction.

Acknowledgment is made of permission to quote from the following poems:

Robert Frost, "Why Wait for Science?" *The Poetry of Robert Frost*, edited by Edward Connery Lathem. Copyright © 1947, © 1969 by Holt, Rinehart and Winston; copyright © 1975 by Lesley Frost Ballantine. Reprinted by arrangement with Henry Holt and Company, Inc.; also by arrangement with the Estate of Robert Frost and Jonathan Cape, Ltd.

Marya Mannes, "Time, Gentlemen, Please." *Reporter Magazine*, July 5, 1962. Copyright © 1967 by Marya Mannes. Reprinted by permission of David J. Blow.

FOR ROBERT H. PHELPS

Contents

3. The Younger Generation

4. Engineers

5. Critics

6. Neighbors

7. Practitioners

Introduction

THE SOCIAL WORLD OF ECONOMICS IS WHAT THIS BOOK IS ABOUT. IT IS A SURVEY OF the field and its neighboring disciplines, in the form of snapshots taken at weekly intervals over the last nine years, and published in the *Boston Globe*. Taken as a whole, these may add up to a panoramic view of life among the economists—not a thesis but rather a record of how during the 1980s the profession saw its past, present and future.

After they leave school, people get their ideas about economists in funny ways. They follow columnists for a magazine. They read *The Worldly Philosophers*. They listen to a succession of presidential advisers, Alfred Kahn giving way slowly over time to Michael Boskin. They tune in occasional public television series built around figures like John Kenneth Galbraith or Milton Friedman. They read best-selling authors—Lester Thurow, for instance. They observe the parade of talking heads on the *MacNeil-Lehrer News Hour*, and puzzle over the annual anointing of a Nobel laureate.

What people don't see is the apparatus that creates this edifice. The college courses. The great research university departments. The talent searches among each year's crop of applicants to graduate school. The summer camps for the best and brightest. The textbook-writing competitions. The international scramble for the attention of politicians. The slow evolution of ideas over time. The sudden challenges to authority from outside the field, the interplay of politics and economics, the fierce arguments spanning many generations, the struggles for the top of the hill, the dramatic sanctions against renegades, the almost imperceptible (at least in the short run) rise and fall of respect accorded a partial truth.

All this creates a community with its own distinct subject matter, its many different hierarchies of competence and its own particular appeal to outsiders. In terms of the reliability and consensibility of its lore, economics seems to fall somewhere between organic chemistry and, say, professional baseball. To say that someone is an economist—or, more likely, that "economists think"—is thus to begin a perfectly reasonable statement. It is just that the opinion that follows doesn't necessarily tell you all you need to know. When a baseball manager says that "it ain't over 'til it's over," he implies one degree of precision. When a chemist says that all compounds of a certain class are chiral, he implies another. And when an economist says that investment depends on savings, it is likely to mean something else again. As with chemistry and baseball, the trick in economics is to know something about the rules of the game.

Surely the most striking aspect of what is striking about the recent history of economics is the turn to mathematics that the discipline made in the years during and after World War II. The oldest story in the book concerns the drunk who looks for his keys under the lamp, not because he lost them there, but because that was where the light was; increasing evidence suggests that this was the case with mathematical technique and game theory in economics, at least to some degree. Economists tackled the problems that the math made easy—and neglected the topics for which the math didn't exist. Unfortunately, the latter were largely problems of growth and development, the very issues that have dominated our politics for the last twenty years. It is clear now that people who listened least to economists did best during this period—the Japanese, in particular.

Yet it also seems likely that much clarity has been gained by the adoption of mathematical language by economics, and that the way to go is straight ahead. Scientific communities often find themselves trapped temporarily in box canyons; usually they quickly climb out. Look for example at the remarkable progress of chemistry in the years after the phlogiston ("the inflammatory principle") hypothesis was discarded, in favor of the idea that matter might be composed of elemental building blocks, one of which was oxygen. But just as the wise outsider wouldn't have been surprised by the failure of chemistry to make sense of everything within its purview in 1790, he wouldn't have wanted to walk away from the field in disgust just as Lavoisier, Priestley and the rest were beginning to make sense of the process of combustion. Economists are quite capable of finding their way to relevance without being beaten bloody by outsiders; it has been a remarkable 25 years in their field. What is desirable now mainly is to pay attention to what they are saying.

I should firmly state here my conviction that economics is not everything—despite its claims to be a "universal" social science, despite the joke that economists like to make that there really need be only two Nobel prizes, one for economics and the other for fiction. Yes, everything has its economic aspect. But there is a good deal more to life than "choice under conditions of uncertainty." At the same time that economics has been moving into law, economics has come under assault from philosophy and linguistics and, for that matter, from law itself. Schools of business and management have become hives of interesting activity. Historical disciplines have much to contribute to our understanding of evolution of the division of labor. Anthropology has become especially promising. Some of the likeliest new conceptual tools are coming into economics from biology, and so on. It is an incautious gambler who as a seeker of wisdom bets only on departmental knowledge.

Moreover, there is nothing sacrosanct about the university in these matters. The university may be where knowledge migrates once it has become established, but academies have no monopoly on the creation of knowledge in economics, any more than they do in any field where there exists a large body of commercial technology. Jude Wanniski and George Gilder are journalists, not economists, but if you think they didn't change the way technical economics was written in the 1980s, you have another thing coming. If you want to learn how Alfred Cowles, a wealthy stockbroker disappointed by his failure to foresee the coming of the Great Depression, returned to his college and eventually called into being the whole bewildering array of modern econometrics, turn to page 63. In much the same way, businessmen who went looking for answers in the 1980s have become a force in economics as well. And of course there were plenty of people who just went ahead and *did* things without the benefit of theory, like the business strategists who created the great airline reservation systems, or the traders who turned the old Butter and Egg Exchange in Chicago into the world's biggest market for risk—largely without understanding the whys and wherefores of what they were doing.

Hence the architecture of this book has been determined by the landscape of the economics "beat." When the time came for putting the book together, I found that the people I have written about over the last decade tend to fall into one of several categories. There are the "Greats," of course, those thinkers who have created the broad outlines of the field. There is an older generation in present-day economics, defined largely by Keynes and John Kennedy and by hopes for the new mathematical economics. There is a younger generation, those for whom Vietnam—and a retreat from Keynes of one sort or another—are the watershed events. There are those I tend to think of as engineers, persons concerned mainly with creating markets and making them work. There is a class of critics of economics, by whom I mean those operating within the economic paradigm; and there are neighbors, meaning those who are working in some different frame of mind, who may nevertheless have something interesting to say about economics. Finally, there are practitioners, persons whose main success has come in the art of making money, or helping others make it, who nevertheless hope to isolate or at least pass on some aspect of their knowledge. These people, too, have a claim on our attention.

The political scientist James David Barber once said of the division of labor between the universities and the newspapers, "We do the kids, you do the adults." This book falls somewhere in between—it is for the Wise Young and the Youthful Old. For students, it is no substitute for a text; it is a complementary good, as the economists say, a little cream for the coffee. For adults, in truth it is more likely to be a substitute; not many grownups have the faith and patience necessary to haul down an elementary principles text when they want to know a little more about economics. And for economists, perhaps the best that can be said is that its perusal may offer a good way to retain a little skepticism about their business. A cat can look at a king—in fact, often it is an interesting spectacle.

FIRST PRINCIPALS

The Sex Lives
of Great Economists

ONE OF THE CARDINAL RULES OF SCIENCE IS, "THOU SHALT NOT GET PERSONAL," AND
scientific etiquette is designed to remove controversy from the sphere of the
individual. Hence the impersonal tone and passive voice of technical papers, the complete absence of resort to anecdote and personal experience.
Even first names are omitted; initials are enough. "Ad hominem" arguments—those that respond not to the merits of a claim, but rather to the fact
that it comes from such-and-such a person—are strictly out of bounds. This
principle is especially important in economics, where arguments can get
personal all too easily.

So it is unusual, to say the least, that two major biographies of John
Maynard Keynes have appeared recently, and both dwell at some length on
his bisexuality. This is partly in reaction to Sir Roy Harrod's lengthy
hagiography of his friend, published in 1951, which omitted any mention
of it. Dozens of books on Keynes have rolled off the presses since then
without so much as hinting at the fact.

But mostly, today's attention to Keynes' sexual makeup represents a
determined attempt to come to grips with the man, to finally figure him out,
to assign him to his proper place in the intellectual firmament of the
century.

To be sure, Keynes is not exactly yesterday's child. He was born 101
years ago, the son of a prominent economist father and a mother who would
eventually become mayor of Cambridge, England. It was nearly half a
century ago, in 1936, that he launched—with the publication of his *General
Theory of Money, Interest and Employment*—the intellectual "revolution"
that bears his name. And it was just 10 years after the publication of that
difficult book that he died. Yet his claim on our attention has hardly relaxed
over the years; if anything, it has grown. All the talk about "needing a new
Keynes" notwithstanding, the old one is all we've got.

Charles H. Hession's book—*John Maynard Keynes: A Personal Biography of the Man Who Revolutionized Capitalism and the Way We Live,*—is

"addressed to the very question" of his bisexuality, the author says. It is a workmanlike job in which Hession occasionally lays aside the biographer's mantle to speculate on the relationship among homosexuality, androgyny and creativity.

The first volume of Robert Skidelsky's biography, *John Maynard Keynes: Hopes Betrayed 1883-1920*, is by far the more painstaking effort, though. It was published last year in England, and when the second volume (*The Economist as Prince*) is completed next year, the two will be published as one in the United States by The Viking Press. The picture it paints of the young Keynes is of a fairly promiscuous, always intense denizen of a hothouse society in which homosexuality was far from shocking or even uncommon.

According to Skidelsky, Keynes loved boys at first from highest principles, then turned during World War I to dating girls (all the young men were away at the front), and eventually married the ballerina Lydia Lopokova—which led John Vincent to crack in the Sunday *London Times* that "the Higher Sodomy turned out not to be the ultimate truth but a matter of supply and demand."

Meanwhile, the disagreement over what Keynes really meant continues in full flower. For 15 years, economists have argued about whether his message was fundamentally mistaken by those neoclassical economists who were eager to bend Keynes' insights about government to their more conventional analytic purposes.

Recently, Meier Kohn, a Dartmouth theorist, has made a strong argument that the portion of the *General Theory* that was quickly assimilated was mostly methodological—and that a lengthy attempt must be made now to restore his analytic approach to the financial system. Economists are in no danger of agreeing on the real Keynes, at least any time soon.

When making ad hominem judgments about Keynes, the broader context of Cambridge university life may have been far more to the point than his bisexuality, according an essay by the late Harry Johnson, a scholar who went back and forth between England and Chicago with ease. Johnson maintained that it was crucial to understand the influence that English college life had as an economic institution on Keynes' worldview.

For one thing, the sense that the world was somehow like a college colored Keynes' attitude toward the working class, whom he thought of in terms of jolly servants deserving of plenty of fringe benefits, according to Johnson. For another, it meant he viewed entrepreneurs and businessmen as failed undergraduates. "These were people for whom some reputable non-academic, non-governmental employment should be found, but who should not be rewarded on an inordinate scale for success in their second-rate activities," he wrote.

"It would also be natural for such academics [as Keynes] to believe that the messes that the practical world of business and politics got itself into resulted from the defect of inferior intelligence or, alternatively, the lack of a system of corporate decision-taking comparable to that of a college fellowship body and its council."

Is the sex life of great economists ever relevant? Well, yes and no. Certainly not in any everyday sense, but overall, there may be an element of sexual style involved in theory choice. At least Joseph Schumpeter thought so. He never remarked on Keynes' habits, at least not publicly, but in his great history of economic analysis, published posthumously, he observed of Adam Smith, "a fact I cannot help considering relevant, not for his pure economics, of course, but more for his understanding of human nature—that no woman, excepting his mother, ever played a role in his existence. In this, as in other respects, the glamors and passions of life were just literature to him." And indeed, there is something about general equilibrium analysis, which Smith can be said to have founded, that is, well, ultimately unconsummated.

And can it be entirely beside the point that Schumpeter admired the theorizing of the highly transitive Karl Marx, a fine husband and loving father who at a certain point in his trials impregnated the family maid—and then permitted Friedrich Engels (the "Lieber Fred" of later days) to take the blame?

After all, Schumpeter himself liked to brag enigmatically that he had entertained three great ambitions in his youth—to be a great horseman, a great lover and a great economist—and that he had achieved two of them.

Keynes, too, scored on two of the three counts, then—and since he had no interest in horses, perhaps he can be judged the greater man. The fundamental point about Keynes remains undoubted. It is that he changed, probably forever, the way we think about the government's responsibility for the behavior of the economy.

As Robert Skidelsky has written, he was at first "the only professional economist in Britain and the United States who grasped the point that unemployment could be seen as a technical problem in economic analysis to be solved by economic means." Or as Michael Stewart has put it, he showed that the Great Depression was the result of ignorance too deep to be borne.

Adam Smith:
The Canniest Scot

When the 250th anniversary of his birth was celebrated quietly in 1973, Adam Smith was, by and large, an afterthought, at least in the public realm of newspapers and magazines. OPEC was in the saddle and rode mankind. Twenty years of extraordinary worldwide growth were abruptly ending, for reasons that are still not well understood today. Economics, at least as Smith had framed it, was widely said to have somehow lost its explanatory snap.

This month the 200th anniversary of Smith's death is being celebrated in Scotland with a good deal more ballyhoo and grandeur. First it was a band of businessmen and politicians who flocked to Edinburgh for a Wealth of Nations 1990 symposium that its organizers, the World Business Forum, billed as "the most important conference to be held anywhere in the world this year." It ended last week, about the same time as the Group of 7 economic summit in Houston.

This week it is the economists' turn to make the pilgrimage to Scotland. No fewer than 11 Nobel laureates are on a two-day program beginning tomorrow to honor the man who put the concepts of the free market and the "invisible hand" at the center of modern technical economics. Not all will come, but all have made a living elaborating the insights of the scholar who wrote: "Where competition is free, the rivalship of competitors . . . obliges every man to endeavor to execute his work with a certain degree of exactness. . . . Rivalship and emulation render excellency, even in the mean professions, an object of ambition, and frequently occasion the very greatest exertions."

The differing atmospheres surrounding the two meetings are instructive. Led by former British Prime Minister Edward Heath; Salomon Brothers' John Gutfreund; investment banker Lord Roll of Ipsden; Jack Kemp, the U.S. Secretary of Housing and Urban Development; and others, the celebrants of *The Wealth of Nations* tended to be veterans of the recent battles of the global Turn to the Right, fought during the 1970s and 1980s. Uppermost in the minds of participants seemed to be the sudden tilt toward markets of the

Eastern European economies. Within the hearing of Rachel Johnson of the Financial Times, for example, Jack Kemp bubbled: "More people are queuing up to buy hamburgers in Moscow than to view Lenin's tomb."

The invited economists, on the other hand, had made a much longer march to Smith's grave at Canongate Kirk. The most senior among them were men who began their journey in the early days of World War II, when in the heat of general mobilization a whole slew of probabilistic methods became the catalyst that produced a lofty new vision of a thoroughly "scientific" economics, shorn of drama and surprises. They included Paul Samuelson, who as a young man began the encoding of economics in mathematical language as a post-doc hidden away at Lincoln Labs in Cambridge; Laury Klein, the father of econometric modeling, who began his career about the same time as a committed Marxist; and Maurice Allais, who spent his war writing up an impenetrable tract on the price system that went virtually unnoticed outside of France. That is, until he was awarded the Nobel Prize in 1988 for having made simultaneously in isolation many of the same discoveries of the mathematical properties of general equilibrium systems that had occasioned great excitement when made in slightly different form in America during World War II.

These two disparate realms, the highly practical and the deeply theoretical, were emblematic of the enormous complexity of a field in which politicians and philosophers seek both to change the world and to understand it. But with the economies of the Soviet Union and Eastern Europe collapsing at the end of a disastrous 70-year experiment in central planning, a certain unavoidable pride of place now belongs to Smith, the man who identified competition as a natural and desirable state of affairs, who analyzed its ins and outs with dry wit and memorable skepticism.

Who was Adam Smith? The son of a customs inspector, born in 1723, Smith took quickly to university life at 14, traveled widely on the continent, became an admirer of Isaac Newton, a friend of David Hume and, with the publication of *The Theory of Moral Sentiments*, a principal of the Scottish Enlightenment. As a Fellow of the Royal Society in London and a private tutor in Paris, he spent his evenings with the best minds of his generation, including Samuel Johnson, Edmund Burke, Edward Gibbon and Voltaire. When *An Inquiry into the Nature and Causes of the Wealth of Nations* was published in 1776, it was at first taken simply to be a massive critique of mercantilism, as the system of close governmental regulation of economic and social affairs was then called.

Knocking mercantilism was one thing. Smith, however, offered something to put in its place, a "system of natural liberty" (his phrase for what we today routinely try to capture in the word "capitalism"). It was built on "the natural effort of every individual to better his own condition," and was capable of "surmounting a hundred impertinent obstructions with which the folly of human law too often encumbers its operations." The miracle of the "invisible hand" of competition, Smith wrote, was such that the competitive struggle among persons seeking the greatest advantage induced both capital and labor to forever move from less profitable to more profitable employment—and so regulated economic society like some smooth-running machine.

Smith lived 13 years after his masterpiece was published. But his project to analyze the effects of universal competition soon was taken up by others, notably David Ricardo. It was refined and reduced to a series of "iron laws" and dire forecasts of slowing growth and subsistence wages that soon enough earned economics the sobriquet "the dismal science" and touched off two centuries of intellectual struggle.

But competition is only part of the story of *The Wealth of Nations*. An equally important theme in Smith is the contribution of accumulation, investment and the growth of knowledge—thus, the significance of entrepreneurs, research and development, wars and systems of property rights. In recent years, interest in these mechanisms have begun to regain center stage in technical economics, as a new generation of economists have come forward to put forth formal models of earlier glimpses of the significance of imperfect competition.

In a recent paper, "Increasing Returns and New Developments in the Theory of Growth," economist Paul Romer of the University of California at Berkeley traced the history of this second, less-well-known proposition that is at the heart of the Gospel according to Smith—and that is the basis for something of a revolution among the young in technical economics today.

Romer wrote: "Ultimately . . . the factor that is most likely to move the profession toward acceptance of models with increasing returns and even departures from price-taking is the incongruity between what economists actually believe and what their models of growth predict. A very large majority of economists believe that private-sector research and development expenditure is an important determinant of long-run potential for growth and that the presence or absence of intellectual property rights is important as well. Discussions of the economics of the firm or industry typically reflect this belief. It is only in formal models of growth for the economy as a whole that these effects have been absent."

Revolution in growth theory or no, economics will go on as before, sorting through Smith's reputation and the consequences of his views. As Paul Samuelson says: "They had thought he was mainly a practical fellow with a lot of wisdom. They found out there was a complete system in there." Andrew Skinner, the University of Glasgow professor who has spent the last 20 years on Smith, editing a comprehensive edition of his works and preparing various celebrations, has said in contemplation of the end of the apparently endless festivities: "Next I'm going to take on James Steuart. He was the Scottish philosopher who wrote down some of these ideas for the first time, even before Smith." And individual researchers will, of course, go on constructing precise mathematical models of mechanisms that Smith captured in single paragraphs here and there of beautiful English prose.

So in the end, then, Adam Smith may be remembered best as a voice who warned, more persuasively than any other, against the impulse of those reformers who seek to do everything at once. "The man of systems seems to imagine that he can arrange the different members of a great society with as much ease as the hand arranges the different pieces of a chess-board; he does not consider that the pieces of a chess-board have no other principle of motion besides that which the hand impresses on them; but that, in the great chess-board of human society, every single piece has a principle of motion of its own different from that which the legislature might seem to impress on it."

That doesn't mean that Smith was a government-basher, though. "No government is quite perfect," he wrote, "but it is better to submit to some inconveniences than to make attempts against it."

JULY 15, 1990

Redeeming Karl Marx

MAY DAY HAS COME AND GONE. THE GREAT OLD INTERNATIONAL HOLIDAY OF LABOR used to be marked in Moscow by daylong parades of workers, great shows of military might beneath towering banners of Karl Marx hung from the Kremlin walls. This year the authorities rented out Red Square to foreign companies to set up billboards for the day—"to raise money for the cash-strapped municipal coffers," as Deborah Seward put it in a dispatch from Moscow for the Associated Press.

"The government declared it a day of 'spring and labor,' with an emphasis on spring," she wrote, adding that participants in the celebration planned to observe a minute of silence for the victims of industrial accidents. "The Russian Information Agency said more than 8,000 people died and 12,000 were crippled in Russian industrial facilities in 1991. About 420,000 people were injured and the agency said there have been no improvements in job safety standards."

So much for communism, Russian-style. But what has happened to Karl Marx? In the West, Earth Day has taken over some of the passion and longing once reserved for May Day. "Critical studies" of various sorts have absorbed much of the intellect that once went into Marxism. David Noble's long-awaited study of the history of science, *A World Without Women: The Christian Clerical Culture of Western Science*, is the new best-seller. You can still find the collected works of Marx and Engels in university bookstores, but it is the standard economics texts that kids are buying. Does that mean that Marx will be consigned to the intellectual scrap heap? Probably not. As a symbol, he'll be around as long as people hunger for justice—a tarnished but evocative figure, in whose name great crimes have been committed, not unlike other great religious figures, such as Jesus and Mohammed. Within social science, however, he's likely to be remembered for the introduction of the theory of punctuated equilibria.

This seems likely to turn out to be a rather central point. Perhaps the best way to understand it is to work backward from the present.

At the moment the idea of punctuated equilibrium is most familiar to those who follow evolutionary biology. At one level, punctuated equilibrium simply means that once a species evolves, it will usually not undergo great change, says Niles Eldredge of the American Museum of Natural History in New York (he invented the term in a 1972 paper he wrote with Harvard paleontologist Stephen Jay Gould). Such species stability runs counter to the usual expectation going back to Darwin, that there will be mostly gradual and continuous changes in nature, he says.

More largely, the punctuated equilibrium debate is really an argument about the fundamental nature of change. Is it "easy," or is it "hard"? In Eldredge's phrase, punctuated equilibrium offers a picture of "obdurate stability interrupted only rarely by brief spurts of change." The returns are not entirely in; you can still start an argument by bringing up the term with an evolutionary biologist.

A little closer to home, the idea of punctuated equilibrium is to be found embedded in the history of science, where physicist Thomas S. Kuhn firmly placed it when he published his famous book *The Structure of Scientific*

Revolutions in 1962. Kuhn differentiated between occasional sudden break-throughs in scientific understanding and the long periods between them of consolidation or "mopping up" of the ground that had been won—between "revolutionary" and "normal" science, as he put it.

The introduction of this idea of sharp shifts and sudden discontinuities interrupting otherwise stately seeming progress was every bit as disquieting when it was introduced to the study of the growth of knowledge in the 1960s as it had been when it was introduced to physics through the study of the quantum jump in the first decade of the century. Classical physicists had suffered the equivalent of a collective nervous breakdown as they wrestled with the "black body radiation problem," retrieving order in their world only when Einstein and others firmly introduced the concept of disconti-nuity. In each case, punctuated equilibrium seemed to strike at one of the very deepest foundations at our knowledge of the world, namely the con-viction that change would always be a matter of smooth little increments at the margin of things.

Marx apparently came to his views about punctuated equilibrium the way many other social scientists form their views; he overheard it in a neigh-boring field, then found it helped explain the pattern of the facts as he understood them. In this case, it was the geologists who were debating the concept: The "uniformitarians," who thought that climate change must have shaped the Earth's surface only gradually, vs. the "catastrophists," who thought that only a long history of change could explain the physical evi-dence.

In any event, the "punctuated equilibrium" theory of Marx is still well known today to every high school student. It was a historical view of an economic system that is prone to occasional spasms of dramatic change in its underlying principles of organization.

In its most cartoonish version, there had been antiquity; after a long period of stability, it had given way, quickly and completely, to feudalism. Feudalism had reigned in turn for several hundred years until the capitalist revolution brought it to an end. And capitalism would surely be replaced in turn by a great and worldwide paroxysm that would usher in the world of communism. "Society is no solid crystal, but is an organism capable of change, and is constantly changing," Marx wrote.

Marx's opponents recognized immediately the challenge that his views posed to their science—not only in the streets, but at the deepest intel-lectual levels. The marginalists—Jevons, Menger, Walras—answered al-most immediately with the easily mathematized concepts of marginal utility and equilibrium analysis, in which all elements are kept in place by mutual counterpoise and interaction, that inform our view of economics down to the present day. Alfred Marshall put on the frontispiece of his great textbook *Principles of Economics* a line penned by Raoul Fornier in 1627 to the effect that *Natura non facit saltum*, meaning nature does not proceed by leaps. From his Cambridge pulpit, Marshall's star pupil, John Maynard Keynes, also preached against the very concept of revolution, citing the same pieties about the impossibility of discontinuous change that had comforted Darwin 75 years before.

Looking back, it seems queer how great was the fuss about the deeper aspects of Marx's view of change—except, that whole classes of people were occasionally "liquidated" in its name. Not Max Planck, not Thomas Kuhn, not Niles Eldredge and Stephen Jay Gould would have dreamt of citing Marx as an established authority in their tradition; it would have slowed immeasurably the reception of their work if they had. Punctuated equilibrium is becoming part of the everyday vocabulary of social science through the back door, not the front.

Indeed, this view of the centrality of Marx's great insight is not widely shared in economics, even today. Take, for example, the latest edition of Paul Samuelson's famous introductory textbook (now co-authored by William Nordhaus and nearly as old and as influential as the Marshall *Principles* text that ran through 8 editions.) Here Marx is represented in the familiar "family tree" of the history of economic thought only as a break-away strut from David Ricardo, leading off to the failed experiments of the command economies, having no influence whatsoever on mainstream modern economics. Economics scholars are only now bringing discontinuities into a central place in their field, mainly through the study of increasing returns to scale. Economics is finally moving slowly toward becoming a history of technology and institutions, as Marx had wanted.

But you don't need even a smattering of recondite economics to understand Marx's enduring place in the modern world. His memorial is the word "revolution," meaning not so much the bullet in the eye of an Eisenstein movie, as the relatively sudden development, generally unanticipated but quick to spread until people "accept the new as unthinkingly as they once opposed it," as Cyril Stanley Smith once put it.

We talk without controversy about the automotive, computer, the birth control revolutions, and so on. This first great glimpse into our understanding of punctuated equilibrium is Marx's legacy to the world. It is this that will never go away.

MAY 3, 1992

Keynes:
Yes, He Was a Genius,
but Was He Right?

ON NEW YEAR'S DAY IN 1935, JOHN MAYNARD KEYNES CONFIDED IN A LETTER TO
his friend George Bernard Shaw, "I believe myself to be writing a book on
economic theory which will largely revolutionize—not, I suppose, all at
once but in the course of the next 10 years—the way the world thinks about
economic problems."

It was like Babe Ruth pointing to the wall in Chicago's Wrigley Field just
before he hit The Homer. The next year Keynes published his *General
Theory of Money, Interest and Employment*, and sure enough, within 10
years, the world had come round to him. Keynes' name became synonymous with government "pump-priming"—heavy spending designed to get a
stalled economy moving again—and economics hasn't been the same since.

Born 100 years ago this summer, John Maynard Keynes died nearly 40
years ago. Can we see him clearly yet?

Certainly he was a genius—that much was clear in his lifetime. A
thoroughly practical man, he was at the elbow of statesmen from the 1919
Peace Conference at Versailles, after which he wrote a famous protest, to
the 1944 Monetary Conference at Bretton Woods, where he designed the
International Monetary Fund and the World Bank.

A disciple from college days of the philosopher G.E. Moore, he was a
card-carrying member of the Bloomsbury literary set, which included Virginia and Leonard Woolf, Clive and Vanessa Bell, Lytton Strachey and
Duncan Grant. His skill as a speculator was legendary—though he is said
to have once filled the chapel at Kings College with sacks of grain for three
days when he was forced to take delivery on a futures contract.

He amassed a famous collection of Isaac Newton's manuscripts. He
employed a great tailor. He married a beautiful Russian ballerina (a pundit
wrote, "Was there ever such a union of beauty and brains/ as when Lydia

Lopokova married John Maynard Keynes?"). And he had a long string of male lovers, too.

But how good an economist was he?

This week, a couple dozen of the world's most prominent economists are meeting in Cambridge, England, to assay the man's significance in a meeting marking the centenary of his birth. Axel Leijonhuvud, James Tobin, Paul Samuelson, Luigi Pastinetti, Nicholas Kaldor, Allan Meltzer, Frank Hahn, Edmond Malinvaud, Donald Flemming and Rudiger Dornbusch are among those who will present papers and critiques.

Nicholas Kaldor, a Hungarian who received his degree from the London School of Economics in 1930, was one of the brightest pupils involved in the spread of Keynesian economics—and he is perhaps the oldest to be still deeply involved in the field. In a telephone interview from his home in Cambridge, England, last week, Kaldor recalled happily the early 1930s, when Friedrich Hayek and Keynes were dueling over the role of monetary policy, and the word began to spread slowly that Keynes was onto something.

"People were ready for it, they were tired of waiting," Kaldor said. "The *General Theory* had such a big effect because it appeared in 1936, which was seven years after the Great Depression began.

"By that time, people were thoroughly fed up with both the Depression and with all the remedies which people were passing around, saying you must tighten your belt, you must consume less. All this made things worse instead of better."

Keynes' message, rendered in almost impenetrable technical argument spiked with his lucid prose, was that the Depression had been caused by too much saving, not too little. The answer, therefore, was to pump up demand by government spending, even if it meant big deficits.

In America, of course, President Franklin Roosevelt was already engaged in such "pump-priming," on the basis of instinct and public pressure. And in any event, the government's policy didn't seem to do much good until World War II came along with its mega-stimulus.

But after the war, governments in all the industrial nations retained a good part of the economic role that they had acquired during it. The long, broad and deep postwar boom was thus laid, at least by many Keynesian economists, to the good sense of governments in following Keynesian policies. Lord Kaldor, a man still much given to laughing, retains much of the sense of boundless efficacy that, as much as any particular doctrine, is the mark of a "Keynesian."

"I'm really furious about Mrs. Thatcher. We've got this wonderful oil discovery here. We saved ourselves any number of billions of pounds in imports, and started exporting. At that moment, you see, she should have pursued an expansionary policy. She needed to suck in additional imports in order to enable our foreign customers to pay for the oil which they bought from us.

"But instead, she embarked on austerity. The pound was driven up so high that our manufacturing nearly collaped. We had three million unemployed in manufacturing, and the sector shrank by 20 percent. That shrinkage destroyed the same amount of wealth as the oil created, but it was worse than that, for oil doesn't create as many jobs.

"We could have done wonderful investments, modernized British industry. It would be quite a different country now," Kaldor said.

Mrs. Thatcher, of course, has just been re-elected by a landslide.

The conventional wisdom these days is that while Keynes was great for the 1930s, he is irrelevant—and worse—today. As expressed by, say, Martin Feldstein, the Harvard professor now serving as chief economic adviser to Ronald Reagan, the thinking goes like this:

"A major revolution in economic thinking is underway—a retreat from Keynesian ideas," Feldstein wrote a couple of years ago. "Although scholars will continue to debate whether Keynes' ideas and prescriptions were actually correct for the 1930s, it has become very clear that those ideas were not appropriate for the U.S. economy of the 1960s and 1970s when they achieved their greatest acceptance and influence."

Feldstein singled out three broad areas where he thought Keynes' opinions had been reversed by the modern tide. Keynes' view had been that unemployment was due to inadequate demand for labor, Feldstein said. But the present-day consensus was that the ranks of the jobless were full of people entering and leaving the labor force, who were waiting to be called back or waiting until their unemployment benefits ran out to seek work. "It is a picture that stands in sharp contrast to the image of a stagnant pool of job losers who must remain out of work until there is a general increase in the demand for goods and services."

Moreover, Keynes had been almost afraid of saving, Feldstein wrote, since he wrote in the middle of a Depression, when people should have been spending their money instead of locking it away in banks. The result was Keynes paid no attention to the significance of capital accumulation—and designed policies to discourage savings. The result of following Keynesian policies, Feldstein said, has been a dangerously low level of savings and investment.

Finally, according to Feldstein, Keynes placed unwarranted faith in the ability of government to meliorate social problems through spending, and the business cycle through taxing. Excessive fine tuning and the expensive programs of the Great Society were the result of rampant Keynesian economics, wrote Feldstein, eyes all but rolling in disgust.

It would be the work of a generation to put things straight, he concluded.

Thus the economists meeting in Cambridge this week find themselves at the end of a tradition, that has been, if not discredited, at least rebuffed. They are waiting, as they say, for a new Keynes.

JULY 12, 1983

Marx, Keynes and . . . Who?

HE WAS BORN JUST 100 YEARS AGO, BUT WHILE HE CUT A FAIRLY WIDE SWATH IN HIS lifetime, he was quickly forgotten by the public after he died in 1950.

Joseph Schumpeter was finance minister of the Austrian Republic in 1919, lost a fortune five years later in banking, then emigrated and as a world-famous scholar at Harvard became the first foreign-born American to be elected president of the American Economic Association.

He wrote a monumental study of business cycles. And he schooled a generation of Harvard students in continental style. (He boasted that he had wanted to be a great horseman, a great lover and a great economist, but that he had managed only two of the three.)

And finally, he wrote a prescient book called *Capitalism, Socialism and Democracy*. In it, he argued that modern capitalism was producing the very agents of its eventual destruction in the form of risk-averse managers and hostile intellectuals. But today he is remembered mostly for a history of economic thought pulled together by his widow from boxes full of notes after his death.

Yet there is a persistent tendency on the part of some modern economists to claim Schumpeter's mantle. He was soft on Kondratieff waves, for one thing. He praised Marx lavishly, for another. He was interested in entrepreneurs and technology as engines of economic change, for a third.

So last week, MIT's Paul Samuelson took to the lectern in Boston to restore some lost glory to Schumpeter, his teacher—but to observe that the scholar was sometimes oversold, too. Samuelson, the first American to win the Nobel Prize for economics, told the annual convention of the Eastern Economic Assn. that Schumpeter's claim on modern attention had little to do with Kondratieff waves, those 50-year cycles that are supposed to contain the technologically driven rhythm of capitalism. That was "folderol" and "moonshine," he said.

In a paper called "Marx, Keynes and Schumpeter," Samuelson noted that both Keynes and Schumpeter had been born in 1883, the year Karl Marx died. "The cloth of history is written with an endless seam. I myself knew a man who knew a man who had known Napoleon," he said.

"Which of the three was the greatest economist? That is a naive question. But if you insist on asking it, my considered response would have to be that John Maynard Keynes was scientifically the greatest economist of this century. Only Adam Smith and Leon Walras can be mentioned in the same breath with him.

"Karl Marx can be measured in the same breath with Mohammed and Jesus, but it is with scientific scholarship that we are concerned here tonight and not with political movements and ideology.

"Without Joseph Schumpeter, valuable insights into the laws of motion of political change would be lost to us, and perhaps one strand of business cycle theorizing. Without Schumpeter, we would know less about economic history. Still, the 1983 corpus of economic science would not be qualitatively different from what it is now" had Schumpeter not lived, Samuelson said. It was Keynes who changed the way economists think.

Instead, "the very greatest contribution" that Schumpeter had made was in the melancholy formulation of the problems facing unfettered capitalism. Capitalism would end in stagnation, Schumpeter wrote in *Capitalism, Socialism and Democracy*, a victim of its own contradictory forces.

According to Samuelson, "the book reads better 40 years after its publication than it did in 1942 or 1950. It is a great book," he said, "and this despite the fact that its main thesis does not quite convince."

Schumpeter defined capitalism too narrowly, Samuelson said; he had defined socialism too broadly. He had failed to forsee the staying power of the modern mixed economy.

Yet the book anticipated the most imposing work on the subject that has been done since. Mancur Olson, a Harvard-trained economist of unusual depth, has for 20 years emphasized the way groups seeking their own self-interest will collude with government to foul up laissez-faire equilibrium.

"Although Mancur Olson came to Harvard years after Schumpeter died," Samuelson said, "Olson's recent *The Rise and Decline of Nations* is very much in the Schumpeter vein." Everybody knows Keynes. And everybody knows Marx. But what about Schumpeter?

Joseph Alois Schumpeter (pronounced Chum-pate'-er) was born in Moravia in February 1883. His father, a textile manufacturer, died when he was 4. His mother, then only 26, married a lieutenant-general in the Austro-Hungarian army. Ever after, Schumpeter was given to military metaphors in his writing.

In Vienna at the turn of the century, he proved to be a brilliant student in a brilliant circle. He assimilated the fervent admiration of mathematical precision that was in the air then.

He spent crucial months in England in 1906 and 1907, according to Arthur Smithies, the Harvard professor from whose account of Schumpeter's life most of these details are drawn. Smithies thought the "upstairs-downstairs" life of the time had a lasting impact on Schumpeter, and that Edwardian age seemed to him "the apotheosis of the civilization of capitalism."

Schumpeter married (a woman 12 years older than he) and went to Egypt in 1907, where, according to Smithies, he practiced law and managed the financial affairs of an Egyptian princess. "He performed the financial miracle of cutting rents on the princess' estates by half and doubling her income," Smithies wrote, a feat that has so far escaped the notice of modern-day Laffer curve enthusiasts. He left Egypt two years later and took up teaching in Austria. His marriage ended in divorce.

By 1912, he had become famous. In *The Theory of Economic Development*, he argued that rate of interest in a stationary state would be zero, a conjectural exercise that is the source of vast significance to economists and of almost no interest to everyone else. In short order he wrote another book, a history of economic theory, and got himself an honorary degree from Columbia University in New York, at the age of 30.

World War I was a hard time for Schumpeter, according to Smithies, and 1918 saw him publish a pessimistic book called *The Crisis Of The Tax State*. It led to a fiasco. He was named finance minister of Austria under a coalition government in 1919, then quickly had to quit. Inflation took over. Schumpeter refused to talk about the episode in later days.

For a time, he was president of a private bank. It went bust in 1924, costing Schumpeter a substantial personal fortune. He went back to scholarship. In 1932, he left Europe permanently for Harvard.

In the 1920s, Schumpeter regarded himself in a race with Keynes to publish a theory of money. He shelved the project after Keynes published his *Treatise on Money* in 1931. "And the reception of Keynes' *General Theory* [in 1936] put his nose permanently out of joint," MIT's Samuelson said last week.

So Schumpeter went to work on the business cycle, and here it is that he is most tantalizing to modern readers. He was looking for an explanation of development. Why did capitalism continue to grow, rather than settle down in a nice stable equilibrium? The answer had to do with the drive of entrepreneurs, and "the will to conquer, the impulse to fight, to prove oneself superior to others, to succeed for the sake not of the fruits of success, but of success itself."

But in Schumpeter's system, the innovations on which these entrepreneurs depended came not continuously, but in "swarms." The pattern of innovation and investment set up not one but three separate "waves" in the process of capitalist development—the longest being the 50-year cycle named for the Russian economist D. Kondratieff. And the Great Depression, which Keynes had blamed simply on too little spending, owed to all three waves slamming down at once.

To most modern economists, this is so much nonsense. Said Samuelson last week: "Among us professionals, the recent revival of Kondratieff moonshine—in its disparate Rostow, Forrester, Shonihara, and David Freedman reincarnations—does not make us look back more kindly on Schumpeter's Ptolemaic epicycles."

Yet in the end, Samuelson said, it was in the field of economic development that Schumpeter had made his mark. The process might not be as neat and simple as he had thought, but there was something to what he had said. The idea of growth as a process of periodic development, "driven by oscillatory impulses from the side of innovation" should be the criterion by which we know a modern Schumpeterian.

MARCH 15, 1983

Emerson:
The Philosopher of
the Business Class

RALPH WALDO EMERSON WAS THE PHILOSOPHER PAR EXCELLENCE OF AMERICAN business, and when he died, 100 years ago this month, *The New York Times* ran the news across three columns of its front page. For 50 years thereafter, bosses quoted him, workers read him, economics teachers cited him and his books made a small fortune for Boston publishers. The author of "Compensation" and "Self-reliance" was as much a part of the folklore of American commerce as Henry Ford, Thomas Edison and Andrew Carnegie, who a couple of generations later would quote his words.

Emerson was invoked to teach that sorrows were superficial, that short-term sacrifice was necessary to achieve long-time gain. He was consulted as a pastoral psychologist, his work a kind of American *Thoughts of Chairman Mao*. And the sort of doctrines likely to be quoted would explain an assault at Anzio as much as the determination to recapitalize a failing venture: "Nothing great was ever accomplished without enthusiasm"; "An institution is the lengthened shadow of one man"; "A foolish consistency is the hobgoblin of little minds"; "Insist on yourself; never imitate"; "Trust thyself; every heart vibrates to that iron string"; "In all my lectures I have taught but one doctrine, namely the infinitude of the private man."

Then, seemingly suddenly, the bottom dropped out of the Emerson market. Although the shrewd had seen it coming, a wave of revision of Emerson's reputation in the popular press hit broadside, starting in 1930 with a famous essay in the *Atlantic Monthly* by James Truslow Adams.

Adams wrote: "As the ordinary unimportant man, such as most of us are, reads Emerson, his self-esteem begins to glow and grow." He wasn't entitled to feel good, wrote Adams; reading Emerson just made men "drunk and drivelling." The Concord sage made life too easy.

Today, instead of Emerson, the "ordinary unimportant man" depends on

United Technologies advertisements and books like *Winning Through Intimidation,* Vince Lombardi videos and songs like "The Impossible Dream" to make him feel good. Emerson is on the shelf. Yale president A. Bartlett Giamatti, in a speech to undergraduates last year, described his writing as "about as appealing as a piece of barbed wire." Meanwhile, at Harvard's Fogg Museum, the statue of Emerson by Daniel Chester French is in dead storage.

The story of what happened to Emerson is a saga that casts some light on the changing ethical environment of American capitalism. Businessmen who wonder whatever happened to good old American stick-to-it-iveness would be well advised to read not Emerson but the volumes of criticism that have been collected in his wake.

The simple facts are that Waldo Emerson was born in Boston in 1803, came to influence in Boston as pastor of the Unitarian Second Church in 1829. The two high-caste religions of the day had been described by Oliver Wendell Holmes as "white-handed Unitarianism and ruffled-shirt Episcopalianism," and Emerson belonged in neither tradition.

He quit the Second Church in 1832 and moved to Concord. His book *Nature* appeared in 1836, and in 1838 he blasted the Unitarian clergy in an address at the Harvard Divinity School. His break with the church was complete, and within a few years he was known across the nation as the sage of Concord, the Transcendentalist philosopher who exhorted the common man to disintermediate, to think for himself. Though he fulminated gently against Boston, the city made him its sage, too, and for 30 years he lived gracefully in the glory that the intellectual labors of his middle years had won him.

The corpus he left behind was relatively thin: *Nature,* two volumes of *Essays, Representative Men,* his *Poems.* The message is almost impossible to sum up; it was sturdy, hopeful, gracious, intensely interested and open to life—a constellation of virtues that businessmen and, indeed, leaders ever since have valued highly. No wonder Emerson was a philosopher for the quarterdeck.

Yet, above all, there was a psychology: "A man is a method, a progressive arrangement; a selecting principle, gathering his like to him wherever he goes. He takes only his own out of the multiplicity that sweeps and swirls around him." Matthew Arnold called him "the friend and aider of those who would live in the spirit."

The problem of Emerson, it was thought, was that he didn't look on the dark side of life. The spirit wasn't enough. He had missed something. James Truslow Adams: "Concord in 1840 was an idyllic moment in the history of the race. That moment came and passed, like a baby's smile. Emerson lived in it." That Emerson could be incautiously optimistic was a discovery that didn't escape his contemporaries. For example, Charles Eliot Norton confided to his journal in 1874, "But such an inveterate and persistent optimism . . . is a dangerous doctrine for a people. It degenerates into fatalistic indifference to moral considerations, and to personal responsibilities; it is at the root of much of the irrational sentimentalism in our American politics, of our national disregard of honor in our public men, of our unwillingness to accept hard truths, and of much of the common tendency to disregard the distinctions between right and wrong, and to excuse guilt on the plea of good intentions or good nature."

Perhaps not surprisingly, in the wake of World War I, there was hell to pay. D.H. Lawrence in particular turned on the Transcendentalist. Emerson had written, "Shall I not treat all men as gods?" and D.H. Lawrence replied, "If you like, Waldo, but we've got to pay for it when you've made them feel that they're gods. A hundred million American godlets is rather much for the world to deal with."

There remains something astonishingly modern about the way Lawrence tore into Emerson. Emerson was merely of "museum-interest," he wrote; he was beside the point. Things had changed. "We've got to have a different sort of sardonic courage. And the sort of credentials we are due to receive from the god in the shadow would have been real bones out of hell-broth to Ralph Waldo."

After Lawrence, the criticism came in torrents. Yvor Winters called Emerson "a fraud and a sentimentalist." Another writer labeled him "a monument to an insufficient way of life." Still another said he had been a fool, incapable of coherent thought.

By the 1960s, the diminished Emerson had become the established version, and by the 1970s, he had become a convenient villain. Columbia professor Quentin Anderson described Emerson as the inventor of the "imperial self," the over-extender of the claims of the individual against society, the hippie, the American soldier in Vietnam. "We are stuck with the parents we've got, the children we get, the cultural moment in which we find ourselves," Anderson wrote—and the trouble was that Emerson denied it. The closer the nation came to Civil War, the more Emerson exhalted the primacy of the individual.

Even so, says Anderson, the Sage of Concord was too clever not to see the fundamental problem. He describes Emerson's "terrible clairvoyance"; the awful truth was that "the idea of community was dying in him and his fellows."

Nowadays, there is something of an Emerson revival. Harvard University Press, which has been publishing a new volume of Emerson's journals every couple of years since 1960, is now turning out his collected works. A couple of new titles on Emerson appear every year from university presses around the country. Gay Wilson Allen has a new biography out (Viking Press, $25). In the amorphous, but widespread, "new thought" religious movement, Emerson is a powerful prophet. Even some forms of "supply-side economics" owe a debt to Emerson—author George Gilder is a direct (intellectual) descendent of the sage.

"I find he is gradually reacquiring the stature and influence he had 100 years ago," said Milton R. Konvitz, a professor of law and of labor and industrial relations at Cornell University, who edited an anthology of Emerson criticism a few years ago. "He influenced me while still in high school . . . I read a few pages of *Nature* and I was hooked. I think this is not unusual. It happens to lots of people, even today."

APRIL 20, 1982

Aldo Leopold: The Common Vision of Economics and Ecology

IN PREPARATION FOR THE AVALANCHE OF REPORTS THAT WE MUST READ ABOUT THE "conference of the century" next month in Rio de Janeiro, I have been making my way slowly through a pair of absorbing biographies of Aldo Leopold (*Aldo Leopold* by Curt Meine, a University of Wisconsin paperback; and *Thinking Like a Mountain* by Susan Flader, University of Missouri Press). This gentle man, who was born in 1887 and died in 1948, had much to do with putting scientific ecology on the map of 20th-century American consciousness, both in the popular mind and in the universities. Leopold's story is important to understanding ecology's insistent claim on our attention. In a way, Leopold's story also tells something about the rise of the other science that rose in the 20th century as a key to the 21st, economics—and even something about the relationship between ecology and economics.

Leopold was a well-born Iowa youth, a Lawrenceville School preppie, a Yale Forest School graduate who joined the U.S. Forest Service in 1909. By age 25, he was managing a million acres of national forest in Colorado on the heavily lumbered upper reaches of the Rio Grande River. In 1933 he became professor of game management in the department of agricultural economics at the University of Wisconsin. Through his writings on the delicate and surprising interrelationships between animals and plants in their habitats, Leopold became known as the man who turned "game" into "wildlife" in the United States—a man of vast influence on the conservation movement, on a par with Henry David Thoreau and John Muir.

The crucial experiences of Leopold's life had to do with with his early attempts as a forest ranger to maintain stable deer populations in the wild for hunting purposes. To the young Leopold, the problem seemed simple: Get rid of the mountain lions and wolves that preyed on the deer. These hunters were "vermin," "varmints" deserving only to be hunted and killed—or preserved in zoos as tokens of biological diversity.

But experience on Michigan's Huron Mountain and Arizona's Kaibab Plateau with the odd phenomenon known as deer irruptions convinced Leopold otherwise. Irruptions were episodes in which deer populations suddenly overbred, overgrazed, then suffered drastic reductions in their numbers as thousands starved to death.

Leopold found that while there might be no simple "cause" of deer irruptions (changes in the use of land, protection from human hunters played a role), the predators he had been blithely killing played a crucial part in maintaining balance in wild populations. As Leopold put it, describing the death of a wolf he had shot, "I was young then, and full of trigger-itch; I thought that because fewer wolves meant more deer, that no wolves would mean a hunters' paradise. . . .

"Since then I have lived to see state after state extirpate its wolves. I have watched the face of many a newly wolfless mountain, and seen the south-facing slopes wrinkle with a new maze of deer trails. I have seen every edible bush and seedling browsed, first to anemic desuetude, and then to death. I have seen every edible tree defoliated to the heighth of a saddlehorn. . . . In the end, the starved bones of the hoped-for deer herd bleach with the bones of dead sage, or moulder under the high-lined junipers."

The moral of the story was that man ought to leave complex natural systems alone as much as possible. He began writing passionately about the need for a "new ethic," an ethic of conservation. This was genuinely hard to fathom when Leopold began; today it seems simple common sense.

Leopold thereby contributed to a profound change in the image we have of humankind's relationship to nature (as noted nearly 20 years ago by the philosopher John Passmore), supplanting the image of humankind as a free-floating despot, who could do pretty much as he or she pleased, with the image of humankind as a steward, who serves best when cooperating with nature.

In the 1930s Aldo Leopold was a little-known figure working in an unproven field. Even today his greatest fame rests on the posthumous publication of *A Sand County Almanac* in 1949. (He died of a heart attack after helping a Wisconsin neighbor extinguish a grass fire.) The book quickly became a classic on the responsible use of land—a prescient warning that prepared the way for our present-day preoccupations with pollution, climate change, resource depletion and species destruction.

But all the while, ecology was maturing in departments of biology, botany and zoology, moving beyond the sermons and homilies of the early days, beyond the relatively simple discoveries like those of Leopold, to real science. A survey of the origins of the field—*Foundations of Ecology*, for example, a collection of classic papers published by the University of Chicago Press for the American Ecological Association—discloses an increasingly arcane field built by specialists of whom you have never heard.

Then came the explosion. As recently as the 1950s humorist Stephen Potter (*Gamesmanship*) could still joke that a nice long boring discussion of "oikology" was a perfect strategy for terminating a romantic relationship. By the late 1960s it was not a bad strategy for starting one—at a rock concert or in a bar, even. Since then the field has acquired its own abstruse mathematical models.

But what to do with economics? Well, aside from the obvious fact that the words are cognates—from the Greek, meaning household—both concern behavior of intricate, interdependent systems of enormous diversity, natural and man-made. Both rely on a toolbox of nearly interchangeable concepts, including equilibrium, competition and optimization. True, ecology has a healthy concern with levels of organization that is lacking in economics; the stubborn facts of the natural world impose a robust empiricism on ecologists, while economists continue to operate cheerfully with their mathematical axioms. But their new-found proximity surely will bring the fields closer together. Promising work on organizational ecology has begun to appear.

Moreover, just as the dependability of ecological knowledge was borne in upon us by a series of "natural experiments," so too the overwhelming significance to our lives of economics has been established in a similar way.

The collapse of the planned economies is, in its way, rather like the deer irruptions—unmistakable evidence of good intentions gone awry. The bursts of inflation and collapsing productivity that followed the breakdown of the international monetary system in the early 1970s may yet turn out to be seen as having been a little like the eutrophication of Lake Erie—a near-disaster reversed by stringent, well-conceived policies. Governments' responsibility for regulating markets are coming to be seen as resembling the responsibility of ecologists for overseeing biota: a matter of letting natural processes have their way as much as possible, with sophisticated and light-handed intervention as a last resort, not the first response. As the mainspring of the system, the concept of "profits" may not have taken on quite the rosy glow of "wildlife," but at least it no longer shares the connotation of "vermin," that is, of being a category whose eradication devoutly is to be desired.

Wildlife management is relatively easy, Leopold liked to say; human management is the problem. In this, the ecologists have more to learn from the economists than vice versa. *Development and the Environment*, the World Bank's annual World Development Report, timed to anticipate the circus-like meeting next month in Rio, lays out the economics of development and the environment with admirable restraint and clarity.

But even here, the influence between economics and ecology works both ways. Recently the World Bank has been circulating an important new paper by a Berkeley professor of energy and resources named Richard Norgaard. Norgaard argues that economists should abandon their cherished practice of discounting the cost of current developments over the life of the investment, because such thinking tacitly assumes that all the rights to the riches of the earth belong to the present generation.

Not so, argues the author of "Sustainability and the Economics of Assuring Assets for Future Generations." Norgaard believes that distribution of resources between generations should be equal, as a matter of course. It is a point worth pondering from an evolutionary standpoint—something like what Leopold meant when he wrote in 1944, "Only the mountain has lived long enough to listen objectively to the howl of the wolf."

MAY 24, 1992

Frederic Bastiat:
For the Provisioning
of Moscow

A STANDARD COCKTAIL PARTY REMARK TODAY GOES LIKE THIS: TO BETTER UNDERSTAND the problems facing the world of 1992, read *The Federalist Papers*. These 85 short essays in defense of the Constitution, written by Alexander Hamilton, James Madison and John Jay, were published in New York City newspapers in the two years leading up to the agreement's ratification by the 13 colonies. They are indeed great essays, and Madison's argument that it is more difficult to maintain liberty in a small territory than a large one is relevant to the former Soviet Union.

But with a Big Bang of price decontrol ushering in 1992, you might just as well counsel puzzled Muscovites to read Frederick Bastiat instead. To the extent that there is any protection against the backlash accompanying the end of 74 years of price controls, it lies in the better understanding of what economists like to call "the price system." And Bastiat, according to Joseph Schumpeter, was "the most brilliant economic journalist who ever lived."

Not that you'll be likely to know him. (Where to get the original Bastiat? Robert Heilbroner devotes a few well-considered pages to him in *The Worldly Philosophers*, his still-indispensable introduction to the lives of the great economists. Otherwise, the French sage has been kept in print by libertarian economists. Several titles are available at bargain prices from the Foundation for Economic Education in Irvington-on-Hudson, New York 10533.)

Born in 1801, Bastiat died in 1850. He was unsuccessful in following his father and his uncle as merchants and instead became a gentleman farmer. But as R.F. Hebert says in *The New Palgrave Dictionary of Economics*, Bastiat "showed no more aptitude for agriculture than he had for commerce.

So he became a provincial scholar, establishing a discussion group in his village and reading voraciously."

It was the turmoil of the 1840s that brought Bastiat into his own. That state of affairs is accessible to 20th-century Americans chiefly through the prism of Victor Hugo's *Les Miserables*. Bastiat was moved by the formation of the Anti-Corn Law League in England to defend free trade in France, issuing a furious stream of pamphlets against government intervention in bourgeoning international trade. Savagely funny, Bastiat is sometimes described as being "a combination of Voltaire and Franklin." A Gallic George Gilder is more like it.

At one point, for example, he wrote cleverly of the need for a law against sunlight, the better to promote the interests of French manufacturers of candles, streetlamps and everything else connected with lighting. At another point, he suggested that, because the citizens of Bordeaux wanted a gap in the railway there, the better to enrich its merchants, that similar gaps be established at every other city between London and Madrid. The resulting "negative railway" would make France the richest country in the world. Amid the general enthusiasm for socialism, culminating in the publication of *The Communist Manifesto*, Bastiat propounded the equal and opposite doctrine of "harmonization," an argument common to Adam Smith, Francois Quesnay, J.B. Say and Schumpeter that mutual interests among the social classes greatly outweigh their antagonisms—and that a certain amount of convergence would be the result.

At his best, Bastiat penned passages that remain wonderfully clear insights into the overall workings of an economic order. "Upon entering Paris which I had come to visit, I said to myself, here are a million human beings who would all die in a short time if provisions of every sort ceased to go towards this great metropolis. Imagination is baffled when it tries to appreciate the multiplicity of commodities which must enter tomorrow through the barriers in order to preserve the inhabitants from falling prey to all the convulsions of famine, rebellion and pillage.

"And yet all sleep at this moment, and their peaceful slumbers are not disturbed for a single instant by the prospect of such a catastrophe. On the other hand, eighty departments have been laboring today, without concert, without any mutual understanding, for the provisioning of Paris."

What Bastiat was delineating here recently has come to be called the "self-organizing" quality of market economies. It was this that Adam Smith had described 75 years earlier as an "invisible hand" that led individuals, through the pursuit of private profit, to promote an orderly society "which was no part of [their] original intention."

The rest of economics is relatively simple, at least at an intuitive level. It has to do with the interplay of the forces of supply and demand, of selling and buying, of effort and desire. The theory is that the rising bread prices in Moscow are supposed to persuade more people to go into the baking business. As more bread reaches the stores (and more people cut their consumption because of high prices), the price will fall back toward "normal" levels—and the lines that are ubiquitous in Moscow today will fade to an unpleasant memory.

There are imperfections in markets, of course. Often businessfolk seek to circumvent their smooth operation (a fact oft-noted by Adam Smith). Governments will always retain far-reaching economic responsibilities. But a belief that this nearly miraculous order will materialize through the simple act of deregulation is what is necessary now in Moscow—and Beijing, for the matter.

It won't be easy: experience with market processes is simply in the air in the Western democracies. But it may not be as hard to develop as is widely expected in the newly emerging market economies, either— especially if Americans are empowered to render aid in various forms. Certainly citizens of the newly democratizing nations will need all the help that they can get in understanding what is happening to them—including, one hopes, not a few home-grown Bastiats.

Now the really interesting thing is the opposition between Bastiat and the economic theorists, both of his day and those who came after. Schumpeter described him as "a bather who enjoys himself in the shallows and then goes beyond his depth and drowns." Alfred Marshall said he understood economics hardly better than the socialists against whom he inveighed. And, indeed, the extensive theory of value that Bastiat devised made scarcely a dent on technical economics, as formulated by David Ricardo, Leon Walras, W.S. Jevons and other 19th-century thinkers.

Present-day theorists, Ricardo's heirs, met last week in New Orleans at the annual convention of the American Economic Association. They've come a long way since then. And their concerns are vital as today's headlines, though their interests are often concealed from laymen by inaccessible mathematics and opaque titles.

But the truth is that technical economists are not very good explainers for the most part. Economics has progressed a good deal in its understanding of certain aspects of its world. But more and better financial journalism, from economists and others, is what the world needs now.

JANUARY 5, 1992

The Search for Kondratieff's Wave

NICOLAI DIMITRIYEVITCH KONDRATIEFF WAS A BRILLIANT RUSSIAN ECONOMIST WHO thought he had deciphered the secret rhythm of capitalism—but he died in obscurity in the early 1930s in a Siberian prison camp, the victim of political commissars who thought his prognosis for the West too favorable.

Fifty years later, however, economists are still debating the existence of the "long wave" Kondratieff said he detected in the history of capitalism. And they argue whether the severe crash that this Kondratieff wave predicts really lies ahead.

A variety of pundits, including Geoffrey Barraclough of Brandeis University, Jay Forrester of MIT and W.W. Rostow of the University of Texas at Austin, have predicted a dolorous depression in 1983 or 1984 as a result of a deep structural wave.

Last month, at a session of the American Economic Association (AEA), a half-dozen top experts in the field considered the evidence for different mechanisms that might explain the observed pattern: institutional innovation, technological innovation, relative price shifts.

Their colleagues' conclusions, expressed privately and taken away to colleges and universities across the land, seemed for the most part a variant on the old Scottish verdict: not proven, and, for the most part, not interested.

Most economists continue to view the construction which "long-wave analysts" put on events as mere speculation, as nonsense and worse. Certainly the 50-year "Kondratieff wave" is in no danger of supplanting the mainstream concern of economics, which focuses on the business cycle, the 4- to 7-year dance of money, prices, business investment and consumption.

Indeed, the very existence of the session owed heavily to the efforts of Sir Arthur Lewis, the development economist and Nobel laureate who was president-elect of the AEA. He loaded the convention program with interesting and unusual sessions on productivity growth and economic development—and personally put together the Kondratieff session.

"We probably wouldn't be here but for Shuman and Rosenau's book," grumped Martin Bronfenbrenner, naming a popular book about the Kondratieff wave of a few years back as he opened the session. Then Edwin Mansfield of the University of Pennsylvania and Nathan Rosenberg of Stanford University, perhaps the foremost American experts on the history of technical change, dismissed the evidence for long waves as almost totally lacking.

On its surface, the idea of Kondratieff is simple. It is to be seen most clearly in the history of the American consumer price index, but the same wave appears, suitably lagged or leading, in other economic variables. There does indeed appear to be a pattern. Three times in the last 180 years, the price level has drifted slighty upward for 20 years or so.

Then, usually during a war, it has shot up sharply to a fever spike, only to be broken by a fall—a "primary recession," in Kondratieff parlance. Then, after a brief attempt to resume its upward progress, it falls again—a "secondary depression," the Kondratieff analysts say.

The obvious questions are: will it happen again? Why did it happen before? Economists ordinarily explain such trends on the basis of mundane factors like wars and bad harvests, but Kondratieff thought he discerned a deeper reason for the cycle in the erratic pace of technological progress.

A cluster of innovations would turn up, followed by a binge of investment and good times. Then there would be overbuilding, and finally a crash. Depressions occur when high-powered innovations mature—like steam engines in the 1870s, electric utilities in the 1930s, or automobiles and jet airplanes in the 1980s.

The idea probably would have died with its inventor but for Joseph Schumpeter, the thoroughly respectable Harvard economist, who took Kondratieff to his bosom and elaborated his ideas. Schumpeter, who loved cycles of all sorts, divided the recent history of the world into periods of Kondratieff "upswings" and "downswings," alternating 25-year periods of boom and bust, which it was relatively powerless to escape.

According to present-day analysis, the first Kondratieff upswing began in Europe in the 1780s, with the spread of steam power, and a host of lesser inventions. It ended 30 years later, with a series of crashes following the Napoleonic Wars. Wars often occur toward the end up an upswing, Kondratieff said.

The second upswing coincided with the extension of railroads in Europe, England and the United States, and with the extension of steam power to shipping, which in turn fueled a world export boom in textiles. A collapse again occurred—this time after the American Civil War. Stagnation ensued, until the age of electricity and cheap steel came along to rescue the world from economic depression in the 1890s.

The third Kondratieff upswing, according to its believers, rode on the wave of both the internal combustion engine and cheap electricity in the first two decades of the 20th century. By the mid-1920s it was pretty well spent, and it came to an end with the great crash of 1929.

The fourth Kondratieff upswing is the one which began in the heat of World War II. Based on plastics and consumer durables, it saw the world through more than two decades of banner growth, before giving way, in the mid-1970s, to the first tremors presaging a later shock.

To be sure, there are almost as many variations on the timing of these cycles as there are believers in them. MIT's Paul Samuelson has said, for example, "One believer almost annihilates the other. If the Rostow explanation works, there is nothing left for Forrester to latch onto, and vice versa." Samuelson was referring to the two most widely known proponents of the Kondratieff view, both mavericks. Walt Rostow has argued that the Kondratieff wave is generated by periodic shifts in raw material and food prices. MIT's Forrester, on the other hand, has argued that the logic of the wave turns on technological innovation.

Rostow, an economic historian widely admired by his colleagues, attended last month's session at the economists' convention, but Forrester, a pioneering computer engineer held in high esteem by businessmen, didn't turn up.

Perhaps the greatest excitement was occasioned by a paper prepared by three well-know radicals who argued the Kondratieff wave from a Marxist perspective. Samuel Bowles of the University of Massachusetts at Amherst, presenting the paper, said it is the famous "falling rate of profit, not inventions, that drives the wave."

"Long waves require the bunching of something," said Bowles, "but it is the bunching of institutions, not inventions."

Bowles said eras in the history of capitalism fell neatly into periods along the peaks and valleys of the wave, with periods of contraction following waves of expansion. Each time real wages climb high enough to impair profitability, Bowles said, institutional forces bring about a depression to knock them back down, a sort of cyclical "emiseration" of the worker. It is just such an attempt to make the cycle work again that is under way now, Bowles said.

"I'm not a Marxist, but their interpretation suggests a much more political, social way to view the cycle," says Robert Zevin, a Boston economist who was one of the discussants at the session. "Many of us felt we always knew that intuitively, but I thought they did a very persuasive job."

In the end, however, the real test of the Kondratieff wave comes on the numbers. Do you expect prices to fall? Most economists now believe the conditions are now in place for a normal expansion of the economy. Yet most long-wave fans believe the computer-driven economy of the future will represent a fifth Kondratieff expansion.

So if we go much longer without a depression, the Kondratieff wave will be, once and for all, just one more great-sounding economic idea that didn't work out. Not that it will cease to have its devotees, for people are always able to find excuses for why their pet ideas didn't work out exactly as expected.

But next time they will have an even harder time getting onto the program at the American Economic Association.

JANUARY 16, 1983

The New Palgrave: Smelly Cheese for Roquefort Addicts

ECONOMISTS ARE DIFFERENT FROM THE REST OF US. TO BE SURE, THEY ARE DIFFERENT from one another, too. An article by David Colander and Arjo Klamer in the new journal, *Economic Perspectives*, is causing something of a stir in the profession. They report a survey of graduate students in six top universities; their results reveal some significant differences of opinion among young economists about what they have learned and its relevance—this division into technique-driven schools being a slightly scandalous situation, in the authors' view.

But from the outside of economics (and most often from the inside, too), these differences of opinion are less interesting than the enduring similarities that make the collective analytic standpoint of economics distinctive among all other attempts to parse the human condition. Practical men and women can shrug off the doctrinal disputes among "new Keynesians" and "new classicals" with jokes. Idealists may take the inability to achieve quick consensus perhaps more seriously than it deserves. But those working hard inside the field must expect that one after another, the differences of opinion will be resolved some day—and therefore stick to their guns in the meantime.

A wonderful place to glimpse both the tension and the underlying unity of economic thought is *The New Palgrave, A Dictionary of Economics* to be published in America by the Stockton Press next month.

What's wrong with the old *Palgrave?* Nothing, except that the last attempt to survey economics whole was published over a 20-year span beginning just 100 years ago. A good deal has changed since R.H. Inglis Palgrave and the eminent Victorian economists who were his contributors surveyed the field from "abatements" to "workmen's insurance" and thereby put an enduring stamp on the way economics was taught. Palgrave's dictionary turned out to be a series of snapshots of enduring value of a discipline just on the threshold of professionalization; 50 years after its last revision, the best economists were still using it as a benchmark against which to measure change.

The New Palgrave is the product of the stylish imaginations of three economics professors—Cambridge University's John Eatwell, Harvard's Murray Milgate, Peter Newman of The Johns Hopkins University—who organized nearly 1,000 contributors with a view to showing what had changed since then (and how) and what has not. It includes 655 biographies, and 1,261 subject entries, ranging from "absorption approach to the balance of payments" to "zero sum games." (Michael Bacharach begins, "Zero sum games are to the theory of games what the 12-bar blues is to jazz: a polar case and a historical point of departure.") The essays are technically sophisticated, but, in general, they are pitched for the ear of the intelligent layman, accessible and concise.

Best of all, they are (courteously) contentious; paeans to monetarism exist side-by-side with wry dismissals of the dogma; great men are praised and then damned by different authors on the same page. "Our one stricture was that there be no surveys," says editor John Eatwell. "We were very much against the pseudo-Olympian style. Every article has a definite point of view." For anyone really interested in the field, the result is about as addictive as smelly cheese.

At $650 for the four-volume set, *The New Palgrave* may not be an appropriate New Year present for the struggling graduate student or the businessman-beginner with Something To Say. But it belongs in the library of any organization where economic advice is dispensed or consumed; and a thorough acquaintanceship with it should be part of any economist's kit of tools.

The old *Palgrave* was the product of a somewhat lonely labor, despite the fact that it was only Palgrave's editorship of *The Economist* magazine that enabled him to corral a high-quality stable of contributors. His three-volume work achieved its reputation for being a comprehensive, high-quality picture of the state of the art despite certain idiosyncracies.

Left out altogether was Alfred Marshall, for example, the Cambridge don who completely dominated the late Victorian age. And the only living economist whom Palgrave included was Leon Walras—a wise pick, you might think, says editor Eatwell, but in fact included mainly as a vehicle for writing about the (spurious) triumphs of his illustrious father.

The New Palgrave hopes to make no such mistakes. Paul Samuelson is there, in a very sober and restrained essay by Stanley Fischer. Milton Friedman is included, in an effusive article by Alan Walters. Kenneth Arrow, born in 1921, doesn't get an entry (only those 72 and older are included—some 75 living economists in all) but there are more than 20 entries under Arrow's name in the extensive index. For the rest, the dictionary is the equivalent of an all-star team writing about members of the hall of fame. Among the locals: Cary Brown on Evsey Domar, J. Fred Weston on David Durand, Donald McCloskey on Charles Kindleberger, Paul Streeten on Thomas Balogh and Gunnar Myrdahl, Gustav Papanek on Edward Mason, Robert Bishop on Sir E.H. Phelps Brown.

There is William Baumol, the actor, on performance arts; Hendrick Houthakker on futures trading; Dale Jorgenson on production functions and vintages; Harrison White and Robert Eccles on producers' markets; Alicia Munnell and Joseph B. Grolnic on indexed securities; Laurence Kotlikoff on Social Security; Andreu Mas-Colell on collective equilibrium; Peter Diamond on search costs. A number of entries from the original *Palgrave* are retained, many by F.Y. Edgeworth and P.H. Wicksteed. And, of course, there is a great deal of mathematics, including a serene essay by Gerard Debreu that is every bit as accessible as are forbidding the articles on gauge functions, saddle points and Bayesian inference.

Certainly, *The New Palgrave* reflects the political tastes of its editors. Chief editor Eatwell is economic adviser to Labor Party leader Neil Kinnock, and the Macmillan Publishing Co., which conceived the project, long has been associated both with publishing and politicizing John Maynard Keynes. (The late Harold Macmillan, former prime minister, was chairman of the firm that today his grandson Alexander runs.) Certainly, the Analytic Left is well-represented in *The New Palgrave:* Robert Heil-broner writes on capitalism and wealth; John Roemer on Marxian value analysis; Stephen Marglin on investment and accumulation; Francis Bator on fine tuning and functional finance; John Cornwall on inflation and growth, long cycles, stagflation and total factor productivity. And certainly the conservative new classicals are under-represented: there is but one piece by Thomas Sargent on rational expectations and none by Robert Lucas or Robert Barro. Neither did Harvard's Martin Feldstein nor Stan-ford's Robert Hall have anything to say about the considerable conservative revolution that they and their friends have made in the past 20 years. The Palgrave's contributors' list may not be much of a predictor of the future course of the Nobel Prize in economics.

But in general, the tugs-of-war of the past are well-limned; take the K-section, for example, on either side of Don Patinkin's article on John Maynard Keynes: there is Luigi Pasinetti on Roger Kahn and Adrian Wood on Nicholas Kaldor (both well-to-the-left of center) —but a few pages later, there is George Stigler on the Chicagoan Frank Knight followed by David Belsley on the late Edwin Kuh, the computer pioneer who served as con-sultant to George McGovern's presidential campaign. As John Eatwell says, "part of the pleasure is the wonderful juxtapositions."

It's clear *The New Palgrave* is already a great success in its own terms; it includes in one way or another most of the best economists in the world—80 percent by the editors' reckoning. It seems to be a commercial success: 1,000 sets sold in Japan, 2,000 in the United States, another 2,000 in the U.K. and Europe. (When will it become available in paper-back? Macmillan says its 20-volume *Grove Encyclopedia of Music*, pub-lished in 1980, is still selling well in hard-cover.) What remains to be seen is what has been overdrawn, and what has been left out. This will come about through the slow process of scholarly opinion-making. And the early candidate for the Oops Award is surely Benoit Mandelbrot, the maverick IBM mathematician whose discovery of fractals stemmed from some early work on cotton prices. But in a sense it doesn't matter in the least. Eco-nomics is almost sure to change in the coming years, but for many years to come, *The New Palgrave* is likely to be the best record of where it has been.

DECEMBER 27, 1987

Alsager's Heirs

IN A LITTLE ESSAY CALLED "GROUND UNDER OUR FEET," RICHARD ELY RECOUNTS how he and others founded the American Economic Association in 1886. It was a spirited meeting: its real business had to do with cutting out the conservative advocates of *laissez faire* in favor of more "progressive" scholars, excluding the religiously motivated investigators in favor of practitioners of a more "disinterested" economics, and with long-range plans to insulate economists from the general public. Long years later, Ely was still circumspect about these aspects of the occasion; they are described in detail only in Thomas Haskell's excellent account, *The Emergence of Professional Social Science.*

With the ink barely dry on the charter, however, Ely and E.R.A. Seligman tramped through the rain to the office of the Associated Press in Saratoga, "to see that we had such publicity as we both felt we deserved." Economists and those whom they have excluded have been arguing with the press ever since about exactly what each subsequent story is worth.

What is a reader—or his proxy, the reporter—to do when confronted with the vast array of double-domes and number-crunchers who can't agree on anything in the world worth knowing? The deficit is going up or down, productivity is a problem or it isn't, the savings rate a disaster or maybe not, the United States is in dire peril or else it has never been stronger. It is one thing when desk sergeants and community activists tell differing stories about what happened last night in the 18th precinct. They are expected to disagree. So are colonels, diplomats, politicians, lawyers and land salesmen.

But what are we to make of the myriad voices of the economic and financial commentary community? There are Wall Street touts and Washington policy jocks, self-taught businessmen and gifted politicians, Nobel finalists and interesting gadflies, textbook authors and left-field visionaries—all vying for our attention. Amid the constant stream of chatter from the stands and the bench, and often irrespective of it, the world constantly is going forward powerfully in the hands of businesspeople, practitioners who are reflective and otherwise, inventors, bankers, corporate planners, magnates, organizers, investors, regulators. Conflicting views, anyone? At least Americans don't have a Likud GNP and a Labor GNP, as they do in Israel.

At bottom, reporting economics is no different from reporting anything else. The cast of characters is just a little more complicated, that's all. The reporter's tools, as Stanley Karnow once described them, are nothing more than background knowledge and skepticism. In the name of background knowledge, I will sketch here a few things worth knowing about the production and distribution of economic knowledge.

Technical economics, as we know it, appeared on the scene a little more than 200 years ago. Indeed, *The Wealth of Nations* was published in 1776, the same year that the American colonies cut loose from England.

To be sure, there were plenty of beginnings before that. On the one hand there were politically-motivated students of trade like Barbon and Cantillon who sought to advise kings on the best way to raise taxes or otherwise compete successfully among nations. These thinkers were then known as mercantilists; today they tend to identify themselves as political economists—with an emphasis on the political.

On the other hand, there was the tradition of "political arithmetic," associated with Gaunt, Petty and King. Begun in frank imitation of the successes of early physicists like Issac Newton and Robert Boyle and physiologists like William Harvey, this school aspired to create a truly "scientific" economics—hence its concern with objectivity and empirical inquiry.

Technical economics burst decisively on top with the work of Adam Smith and his less-appreciated contemporary Sir James Steuart. The galvanizing concept at the heart of *The Wealth of Nations* was the idea of the economy as a big interdependent system, in which everything was dependent on everything else, rather like celestial mechanics. To convey the working of this system, Smith conjured up the famous metaphorical "invisible hand," which led every individual, pusuing his own self interest, to promote the greater good of all, giving rise to a order "which was no part of his intention." Lowly porters, rich landlords and everybody in between would come together to contribute their unique skills in the self-organizing system of the market.

To put it slightly differently, the fundamental idea in *Wealth* was the concept of negative feedback, the notion that the price of tea in China—and every other price—was somehow self-regulating, that if its price might rise, less of it would be demanded and more would be supplied, until the price returned to its normal level, and the system that supplied it—tea plantations, sailing ships, merchant bankers, warehousers and jobbers and retail shops—returned to "equilibrium." This glimpse of a systematic, predictable interdependence among individuals organized in markets was quickly seized upon and rendered more precise by David Ricardo. It has been the indispensable core of economics ever since.

In a second vital turn, just a little over a hundred years ago, economics went professional—that is, it ceased being a field for talented amateurs and became a self-selecting community which aped the social organization of science. This is the movement described so well in Thomas Haskell's book. Economists came to be those who taught in colleges and universities. They learned from texts, published in journals. They freely gave advice to politicians and business but they relied on one another for credentials and advancement. About the same time, their field underwent a considerable deepening, which gave a distinct psychological cast to their investigations. The central tenet of this "marginal revolution's" new emphasis on the psychology of value has been summed up this way: pearls are expensive not because men dive deep for them; rather men dive deep for them because they are expensive. Economists have been talking about the "utility" of pearls ever since.

(Largely left out in this transformation were the political economists, those enthusiasts for policy who sought to ground their prescriptions in some theory of how the world works that has not been submitted to economists. When you meet someone like, say, Jude Wanniski or Robert Reich, who identifies himself as a political economist in the pre-Marshallian sense, what he means is that he dissents from all that has happened in economics these last 100 years. He simply is operating in a different tradition.)

The rest is simple. From the 1870s until 1945, the world capital of economic understanding was Cambridge, England. Alfred Marshall gave way to John Maynard Keynes; his smooth Victorian confidence as propounded in the 24 editions of his *Principles* yielded to Keynes' preoccupation with the central role of government in everyday economic affairs, described in *The General Theory of Employment, Interest and Money.*

With the end of World War II, however, the center of intellectual inquiry shifted to Cambridge, Massachusetts, and, in time, a couple of counter-revolutions occurred—launched mostly from Chicago. Keynes, having been widely diffused, was rolled back on the topic of money by Milton Friedman, on interest by Robert Lucas, on employment by Martin Feldstein. All the while the field of technical economics itself has only grown. The number of economists employed in goverment, industry and finance since World War II has simply exploded.

Business and financial journalism grew up from quite other roots than these. For at least a couple of centuries, neither reporters nor their editors were very interested in economists. After all, it wasn't economists who built the modern world; it was businesspersons, investors and inventors and salesmen and empire-builders who created the far-flung and intricate international economy. It was these movers and shakers and their stock touts and lawyers and press agents that the financial press covered, from the beginning of the modern industrial economy. For a long time, most journalists paid relatively little attention to the economists. They were interested in the markets themselves.

The key event in the emergence of financial journalism probably was the shift during the Napoleonic Wars of the center of world finance to London from Amsterdam, according to Richard Fry's essay in *The New Palgrave: A Dictionary of Economics*. In London there was, for the first time, a large middle class interested in opportunities for investment. The newspapers were not slow to attempt to shed some light. Thomas Massa Alsager, a cultured businessman, was appointed the first financial editor of the *London Times* in 1817. He set a pretty good example, according to Fry. "For some years he stood alone in warning investors that the great boom in railway collections was bound to collapse. The Times lost a great deal of adverstising but the proprietors were high minded and Alsager was proved right."

In economic journalism, the signal event probably was the founding of *The Economist* magazine in London in 1843, and the appointment of the great Walter Bagehot as its editor in 1857. Bagehot was perhaps the first man to write about economics as a modern science writer might; that is, he reported the views of some leaders of the field as though they were most probably correct; he was honest about disagreements between experts when they arose; he mixed in liberally his own convictions. Ever since, *The Economist* has reported on professional debates with distinction, though never flinching from imposing its own journalistic convictions on events. Oscar Hobson's brief but extremely influential tenure as editor of the *Financial Times* in the early 1930s should be noted, as well as the rise to prominence of the *Neue Zurcher Zeitung*.

In the United States, there probably has been a good deal more action from the magazines than the newspapers. The New York papers had for many years covered Wall Street aggressively. The long boom of the 1920s persuaded Henry Luce to launch *Fortune* and the McGraw family to start *Business Week* to compete with more personal magazines like *Forbes* and *Barrons* and *Duns*. Barney Kilgore built *The Wall Street Journal* into a national business daily in the years following World War II, utterly eclipsing the daily *Journal of Commerce*. The founding of the McGraw-Hill economics department by journalist-turned-economist Dexter Keezer deserves special mention; it contributed a steady stream of talent to *The New York Times*, notably its great economics columnist, Leonard Silk. The *Times*, in turn, has greatly influenced the television networks.

Today, a remarkable array of reporters and editors for the daily and electronic press, financial magazines, trade journals and newsletters track developments in the global economy—in the U.S., Europe and Japan. Coverage is not as good as it could be; it never is: but certainly there is plenty of it.

The degree to which technical, university-based economics informs our view of the world shouldn't be underestimated, but it shouldn't be overstated, either. Today, bright kids go from classroom training at the London School of Economics to doing narrative and news on the money wires and soon leave their formal training far behind. Wall Street economists have PhDs, but they wear them lightly. Business schools see to it that their graduates have only a smattering of managerial economics, lest they come to think that they know more than they really do. All this community is loosely yoked in a great but fuzzy hierarchy at whose uppermost reaches are the great university departments.

But economics is not the only explanatory game in town. Lawyers, historians, political scientists, sociologists, anthropologists, social psychologists, linguists all have something to contribute. A good many independent thinkers and gadflys dwell on the outskirts of the field as well, latter-day mercantilists with strong positions on the issues but few ties to the academic traditions.

These persons tend to obey Paul Samuelson's dictum: over time, they either grow closer and are assimilated into economics or they grow much farther away and are forgotten. But at any given moment, they—and not the professoriat—may be right. A prime example is Jane Jacobs, whose insights into the economies of cities have been for the most part slowly confirmed and adopted by technical economists. Other major heterodox thinkers, from Henry George to Thorstein Veblen to Walter Isard to Jay Forrester can expect similar treatment. And of course the "supply side" thinkers who raised a ruckus over taxes in the late 1970s are a prime example of how grassroots, outside challengers can have a major influence on the field.

Indeed, for journalists and political types, who need right answers to serious problems in real time, the lesson from the constant tension between insiders and outsiders is a sobering one. It is that the lost key is often to be found some distance from the lamplight. The economists are at all times full of certainty. But a little knowledge, excessively depended upon, can be a very dangerous thing—a fact that is, happily, well known to most practicing politicians.

For all these reasons, there is a vast difference in point of view between the successful journalist and the good economist. Economists are those who have been "hit by the meatball" (as Robert Crumb once described the experience of conversion); reporters will take a more agnostic stance towards economic knowledge, as it is communicated by the texts and in the seminar rooms. The basic distinction here is between those who see the story as being somehow *entailed* by the theory they have learned and those who don't embrace the theory. For economists, the outlines of the map are already known; in some sense they already know the answers. Good journalists are good precisely because they don't.

So professors will continue to stream down to the AP office with their press releases. Wise journalists will continue to scratch their heads and finally ask each other (and *not* their academic advisers), What's this story worth?

SEPTEMBER 1991

On "Tech-ing It Up"

ARE YOU INTERESTED IN THE WAY THE WORLD WORKS? PICK UP A JOURNAL OF technical economics and you will be confronted with impenetrable prose and abstruse mathematics that is quite beyond the ability of businessmen, investors or even most economists to read. The recent blocking of the nomination of Harvard political scientist Samuel P. Huntington by members of the National Academy of Sciences is a reminder of a long-simmering dispute about the social sciences that takes place at every level of debate. For all the window-dressing, how scientific are they, anyway? A prime suspect is economics, which has undergone a tremendous high-tech revolution since World War II, with advances in technique coming so fast nowadays that the current crop of theorists has left most of the rest of the profession behind, in their rhetoric at least. Is all this formalization desirable? Is it necessary?

The answer, it will come as no surprise, seems from the boundaries of the professions to be both yes and no. It is always difficult to discriminate between the significance of criticism that arises from within an institution and criticism that is directed at it from outside. The great preponderance of criticism from outside economics probably is unmerited—despite the fact that there is always some Marxist, Austrian or journalist ready to denounce the field as a wild-goose chase or even as wholesale fraud. But there is a constant chorus of criticism from within the field that bends it, shapes it and keeps it a living, changing discipline. The National Academy of Sciences furor probably belongs in the former category, despite the credentials of the luminaries who administered the snub.

The National Academy of Sciences is a largely honorary organization designed to single out the nation's top scientists in five classes: the physical sciences and mathematics, the biological sciences, engineering and the applied sciences, medical sciences, and behavioral and social sciences. Each year sections within these classes nominate 90 persons, then poll members, who pick 61. Their election is nearly automatic, unless their nomination is challenged at the annual meeting and a third of the membership subsequently vote a one-year blackball. This was the case with Huntington. He probably will be elected in the next year or so, as his sponsors press the issue. But his defeat this year was widely advertised as a blow to the prestige of the social sciences.

One key to understanding the Huntington rejection is to recall that it was a Yale mathematician, Serge Lang, who led the charge against the nomination, just as it was a group of mathematicians who fought a successful action 10 years ago against the appointment of sociologist Robert Bellah to the faculty of the Institute for Advanced Study at Princeton on similar grounds, and chased director Carl Kaysen out of town for good measure. It is not that mathematicians are politically of a single point of view, but rather that they have an exaggerated sense of personal efficacy that somehow makes them professionally closer than any other group. They have greater solidarity. They can operate as a phalanx, and can achieve the same sort of effects that Birchers used to manage at school board meetings.

Another key is to understand that Huntington's nomination was a natural magnet for the opposition. The Harvard government professor has always been fairly political, for one thing, and during the 1960s he consulted to the government on Vietnam. He was head of Hubert Humphrey's task force on Vietnam and urged the senator to campaign on a bombing-halt platform—unsuccessfully, until near the end of the campaign. But to have been pro-Humphrey meant being a certain kind of hawk. So fighting Huntington's nomination was a means of carrying on opposition to the war by other means.

Moreover, as a political scientist, Huntington is at the top of a pinnacle all right (the Social Science Citation Index shows that he was the single most-frequently quoted authority in international relations in the early 1980s) but in a fairly loosely-defined field. Of all the social sciences, perhaps the least satisfying—and certainly the least high-tech—is political science, which has never made a satisfactory settlement with philosophy. The rap of pseudo-science is relatively easy to hang on a man who once wrote, "The overall correlation between instability and frustration was .50." But the irony is that Huntington has always operated far more in the literary than in the quantitative mode, in books *The Soldier and the State* and *Political Order in Changing Societies*.

The class of social scientists to which Huntington's entry was blocked was added to the National Academy of Sciences only in 1971—in the same general wave of prestigification as the Nobel Award in economics. Today it includes undisputed stars such as Paul Samuelson, Robert Solow, David Landes, Hendrick Houthakker, Dale Jorgenson, David Landes and Peter Diamond among economists; linguists such as Noam Chomsky; psychologists such as B.F. Skinner; sociologists such as James Coleman. Huntington is of roughly similar caliber as a political scientist, a fluent scholar who has done his share to maintain high standards; by common consent among social scientists, he is well above the cut necessary to make the list. "It is not my problem," says Huntington. "It's their problem."

Recently, there has been a wave of criticism within economics of the tendency to overstate the precision and certainty of results. Donald McCloskey and Edward Leamer especially have gone out of their way to tackle those who "tech it up" without regard for underlying uncertainties. One of the more interesting critiques to appear is *What's Wrong With Formalization in Economics*, by Henry K.H. Woo, chairman of the Hong Kong Institute of Economic Science. Woo gently argues for the superiority of natural language to rigid formal mathematization when it comes to describing and analyzing complex economic events. He may be right. But inside the social sciences, it is fair to say that there is more demand for high levels of abstraction and deep structures of analysis than ever before. Moreover, there's some reason to think there is today an outpouring of really high quality work being done; it may not be too much to call it an explosion.

This is not to say that the worries about "teching it up" are unjustified. But to suspend the search because it has not produced totally satisfactory answers is the wrong approach. It is tantamount to having wished to pull the plug on 18th-century chemistry because it was having trouble figuring out why things burn. The proper stance is to treat the claims to certainty of social scientists with great skepticism; to be highly tolerant of other ways of knowing; but to continue to place the preponderance of our bets on scientific methods.

MAY 10, 1987

Sand Sketches
and Skyscrapers

ONE OF THE CONSEQUENCES OF MODERN SPECIALIZATION IS THAT IT IS OFTEN HARD TO judge competing claims to competence. The world is organized in an intricate hierarchy of different and sometimes competing domains; people who have been successful in a particular discipline sometimes seek out the large sphere of the common culture to submit their claims to wisdom, often with surprising results. It is here that businessmen and politicians and journalists vie with economists for the public's attention—and the results are often exasperating to the experts. MIT's Paul Krugman put it memorably once when he said that Wisconsin's John Culbertson getting ink in the newspapers for his support of protectionism was analogous to the man who works on the power of prayer on plants getting equal billing with molecular biologists.

A pair of lively books are out, each concerned with predicting a terrible economic depression in the next few years. Each presents some great truth of its own. Mega-politics, the interplay of impersonal forces in history, is the subject of *Blood In The Streets: Investment Profits in a World Gone Mad* by James Dale Davidson and Sir William Rees-Mogg. It is the "law of social cycles" that foredooms the world to the fate which is described in *The Great Depression of 1990: Why It's Going to Happen and How to Protect Yourself* by Ravi Batra.

At the same time, a slender book by a couple of university professors has appeared, also offering a potentially far-reaching new method of using the patterns of the past to predict the future. *Dynamic Fiscal Policy*, by Alan J. Auerbach and Laurence J. Kotlikoff, addresses many of the same concerns about how tax reform, investment incentives, security prices, social security and deficit spending are connected over the really long haul. But instead of a new law of cycles, *Dynamic Fiscal Policy* offers the same old insight of economics, namely that all prices and quantities are related to each other through the interplay of supply and demand. What is new is the choice of tools: an extensive computer simulation model.

The authors of the pop books are no dummies. James Dale Davidson founded the National Taxpayers Union; Rees-Mogg, his partner, was editor of the *Times* of London until Rupert Murdoch kicked him out. Batra is a technical economist and, once upon a time, at least, a leading trade theorist; Lester Thurow wrote the forward to his book. Each of these authors has strong views of what is likely to happen next; each felt compelled to write it down, take it to a publisher who would hire a publicist to promote his views.

Batra says that a growing disparity between rich and poor will trigger the next depression; the only thing that can help is an immediate draconian redistribution. Davidson and Rees-Mogg say we are in "the twilight of a major phase of history"; there is enormous turbulence ahead. Their theory is cloaked in the form of investment advice, and they roam with crisp intelligence over an extraordinary range of topics.

No such grand schemes or colorful bits of detail are to be found in Kotlikoff and Auerbach's book, however. In fact it is a little hard to read. There are no jokes and more than a few equations. At every crucial juncture, though, the authors use a simple two-period model to illustrate the principles of the big 55-period model; these illustrations can be worked through by anyone with a little patience and a knack for algebra. The payoff is a glimpse of a world seen whole; push it here or there and everything else changes accordingly over time.

At the heart of the economists' model is, of course, the life-cycle, the deceptively simple idea for which Franco Modigliani was awarded the Nobel Prize in economics two years ago, that people tend to spend and save differently over the course of their lifetimes. Before the authors have gone a dozen pages, the work of 50 celebrated scholars over 50 years has been invoked in an ever-tightening web, until the book arrives in the vicinity of what is modern public finance. The authors then build dense links between their work and the work of the 40 or 50 other economists who together more or less define the interesting questions. This is what is sometimes called "the tapestry of economics," but when you come on it in the guise of a book, it more nearly resembles an act of architecture, a combination of vision and craft, a huge analytic skyscraper, whose turrets, towers and even fundamental underpinnings are forever susceptible to reorganization.

It is the level of its reorganization of a great deal of previously existing material that makes this book attractive to its technical readers. It incorporates into the Keynesian tradition of scrutinizing the effects of fiscal policy most of the criticisms of the "rational expectations" school—that is, its actors learn from their mistakes and change their behavior over time, switching their bets from sector to sector as opportunities arise—just like real people. It is for the reasoning-out the consequences of these choices that the authors need their computer. In their phrase, the simulation is "macroeconomics taken beyond the blackboard to where only the computer can see."

Economists who have read the book say it is full of surprises. Deficits may actually lower interest rates at first and "crowd in" investment as a result. Consumption taxes may be the best way to tax inherited wealth. Tax breaks for business investment may be self-financing. The effects of adopting the framework can be almost dizzying; Kotlikoff argues that because of arbitrary accounting conventions, the significance of the deficits of the Reagan years has been wildly overstated. The administration's fiscal policy may even have generated a small economic surplus so far, he says. But the long-term decline in savings that are associated with Social Security and other intergenerational transfers probably are creating unreported deficits over time that are truly dangerous, he adds.

Given the verdict on the Great Depression that began in 1929—that the U.S. government aggravated the contraction severely by misapprehending the money supply and by failing to exercise global leadership—you would think there might be a premium on this sort of attempt to see economic relationships as they really are. And indeed there is: Kotlikoff and Auerbach are both impressive figures in university economics; they each consult to the government at high levels.

But they don't go on talk shows, like the authors of the depression books. They are not household words. And almost inevitably the author of some pop book is going to get credit for predicting the future, whatever happens next. Compared to the skyscraper-like edifice that is technical economics, they are just sketches in the sand, soon to be washed away. What accounts for their popularity is that given the dispersion of opinion, some of them are bound to be right.

JULY 12, 1987

Short-term Sacrifices and Long-term Gains

HEADLINES IN THE NEWSPAPERS READ, "MANY STUDENTS FAIL QUIZ ON BASIC ECO-nomics." And indeed, a report prepared by the Joint Council on Economic Education showed that when a multiple choice test was administered to 8,000 high school students last spring, as many as 75 percent were unable to correctly identify definitions of terms like inflation and budget deficit and profits.

So there was more than a little wistfulness in the hall Thursday when Northwestern University's Robert Eisner rose to the lectern to deliver his presidential address to a meeting of the American Economic Association—and promptly tore into the terms in which technical discussion of the deficit is framed. Conventional measures of investment, capital and private and public saving were conceptually flawed, he said, to the point of being seriously misleading. They have often given the wrong reading on whether the American government is in surplus or deficit.

Make some basic adjustments to bring measurement in line with funda-mental theory, Eisner said, and the dreaded "twin deficits" more or less disappear. Merely by marking to their current market price the value of U.S. holdings abroad and of gold held in reserve at home (it is on the books now at $42 an ounce, less than one-tenth its present value) would be enough to counterbalance the entire American debt to foreigners; so much for being "the greatest debtor nation in the world." And further adjusting government accounts to identify capital expenditures and the effects of inflation "makes such a huge difference in the federal government budget as to wipe out the much decried 'budget deficit.' "

"To put matters bluntly," Eisner said, "Many of us have literally not known what we were talking about, or have confused our listeners—and ourselves—into thinking what we were talking about was directly relevant to the matters with which we are concerned."

This was the 103d annual meeting of the AEA, 8,000 professional economists parachuted into New York between Rockefeller Center and Times Square for three days of meetings, job interviewing and gossip. It was in part just bad luck—a stochastic shock, in the lingo of the trade—that it was Eisner's turn to talk as president. It had to happen sometime. For years, he has been part of a running controversy among senior economists over the meaning of deficits. It is just one of many disagreements that have divided the profession in recent years.

To be sure, professional economics has come a long way from 1972. That was the year when Wassily Leontief denounced the science as a near fraud in his presidential address, when radicals and dissidents threatened disruptions of the meetings, and when Harvard University led by, among others, Hendrick Houthakker, defenestrated several of its young Marxist professors who were in line for tenure.

Accepting an award this week (along with Bell Labs' Roy Radner) as a distinguished fellow of the association, Houthakker said, "I feared that 1972 might have barred me from any further role in the Association. I'm glad to see it was not so." Meanwhile, the exiled radicals, no longer young, are publishing econometric critiques of capitalism in the top technical journals from a comfortable and lively bastion at the University of Massachusetts at Amherst. So civility has returned to economics.

But underneath, there continues to be a deep division of how to think about economic events in time. Princeton's Alan Blinder, praising MIT's Robert Solow at a festive luncheon in honor of his Nobel Prize, compared "the great civil war" of macroeconomics in which Solow has been a leading skirmisher to the American Civil War. Joking aside—it was the funniest lunch the association had seen in a long time—the continuing stand-off between the two leading schools of economic theorizing still causes a great deal of pain to the people in its trenches, "New Keynesians" and "New Classicals" alike.

What triggered the war? It was the recognition—discovery is too strong a word—of the central part in economics played by information and expectations formed by individuals about future events. The suspicion that growing sophistication on the part of financial market participants at all levels will defeat easy manipulation by fiscal and monetary authorities has all but paralyzed discourse in the higher realms of theory, reducing it (in the view of many theorists) to the kind of Does! Does Not! Does Too! Does Not! Does Not! exchange that is more characteristic of the playground than

the seminar room. A second insight, that motives don't have to be pecuniary in order to be self-aggrandizing, has sowed its share of mischief too,
calling into question the motives of would-be policymakers and reformers.

How complicated are these issues? The editorialists at the *Wall Street
Journal* last week found a charming illustration of their deep, deep roots:
among the questions that the high school students last spring were asked to
answer in the investigation of their economic literacy was this one: "To
promote economic growth, a developing country must (a) increase investment, (b) increase consumption, (c) use the market system or (d) use
central economic planning." The people who graded the test, mainstream
Keynesians and new Keynesians, figured that (a) was the correct answer.
The *Wall Street Journal*, presumably along with most New Classical economists, preferred (c). There is a world of difference between the two.

There was, however, a far simpler argument at the heart of Robert
Eisner's views on the relative insignificance of the deficit as a policy issue.
His critique was no more hard to fathom than the argument that just
because a house costs $200,000 today instead of $10,000 ten years ago
doesn't mean its real cost has gone up. Just as inflation wipes out the value
of money, it also wipes out the value of debt; you can either mark liabilities
down, or mark assets up, but either way you ought to systematically restate
government accounts to reflect the results of inflation.

Fine, say Eisner's critics, as long as you are as assiduous in the hunt for
liabilities as for assets; "I'll bet there's no $100 billion for nuclear weapons
cleanup in his estimates, much less a contingent liability for our defense of
Western Europe," says Harvard's Lawrence Summers, who has consistently
argued that it is important to reduce the budget deficit. It is true that
inflation has diminished the value of the government's past-tense obligations, its bonds, in other words; but it has also greatly increased the price
of its future consumption and investment.

On the whole, there was a great deal of promise in the meeting, of events
more clearly understood, of "a society more busily engaged than ever in
trying to know itself," as Hugh Heclo has put it. For example, Federal
Reserve chairman Alan Greenspan told a meeting that, "The severity of the
crash of Oct. 19, 1987, was in a sense the outcome of a confrontation
between dramatically advancing computer and telecommunications technology on the one hand and ingrained human speculative psychology on the
other." Assar Lindbeck and Dennis Snower reported on the investigations
of insider-outsider relationships in European labor markets, where incumbent employees whose jobs are protected by the high cost of replacing them
are subtly arrayed against the unemployed and the easily replaced.

Sheldon Dantziger, Peter Gottschalk and Eugene Smolensky reported on the changing distribution of income—including their surprising finding that the nuclear family "rich," meaning those whose incomes are nine times the poverty line (about $95,000 for a family of four), actually doubled their numbers during the Reagan years, from around 3.5 percent to about 7.0 percent of the population, thanks mainly to the increase in working wives.

And MIT's Rudiger Dornbusch turned up with a new promising 10-year plan for the rescheduling of Mexico's debt, calling for 55 percent of its debt service to be paid in pesos, 25 percent to be capitalized as a kind of equity kicker designed to give lenders a share of any big gains, and 20 percent to continue to be paid in dollars. Hopes rose somewhat after Paul Volcker, long an opponent of more imaginative forms of debt relief, declined to dismiss the plan when Dornbusch brought it up before a crowded session. The need to come up with some new form of financing to replace the bridge loan that was hastily arranged by George Bush just before the election lent plausibility to the notion that a breakthrough may be near.

But when all was said and done, it was Eisner who dominated the meetings by his bold dissent from the conventional wisdom. Murray Weidenbaum, a former Reagan adviser who is one of the architects of the view that the diminution of the deficits is a top priority, was asked, "Has he made life much more difficult?" He answered, "For himself, yes." Perhaps.

But for generations yet to come, whose discussions will be illuminated by the "total income system of accounts" (with their separate governmental capital accounts) on which Eisner has been working for years, he will have made life considerably better, and ultimately easier to understand. As he said last week, "Fuller and more appropriate measures of investment and productivity might make clear that the best and perhaps the only feasible way to provide the sustenance of our future aged is to develop our public, social infrastructure and endow our young with all the education, training, research output and good health that our society is capable of offering."

JANUARY 1, 1989

The Wizard of Ec?

READERS SOMETIMES NOTE THE OLYMPIAN TONE AFFECTED BY THIS COLUMN: THE confident judgments, the frequent demurrers from conventional wisdom, the offhand references to arcane information, which are all designed to buttress the impression of an effortless mastery of the field of economics in the vicinity of politics with which it is concerned. As my colleague Chris Black once said about a column, which depended on certain parallels between the life and times of Warren G. Harding and Ronald Reagan to make the point that George Bush probably would be elected easily in 1988, "Gee, it made you sound like you know all that stuff." Exactly.

Into this comforting murmur punctuated by "of course" and "to be sure" is injected from time to time a clinker. A ferocious one occurred last week, when in the course of remarking the importance to Massachusetts of Silvio Conte's seniority as ranking minority member on the House's Appropriations Committee, I mentioned casually the Speaker of the House, Edward J. McCormack.

Now the man who represented what was then the 9th Congressional District for 42 years, who served as Speaker for eight years in the 1960s, was John W. McCormack; his brother was Edward J. (Knocko); Edward J., the former attorney general turned real estate developer, is his nephew, as was John W. (Jocko), the vending machine representative, who died in 1982. Nor was this all. In the same column, I suggested that McCormack served as Speaker before, not after Sam Rayburn. And more subtly, the explanation of how Conte went to the Appropriations Committee from day one in the Congress left out the vital link of former House Speaker and Minority Leader, Joe Martin, who was beaten in a primary by Margaret Heckler in 1966.

Fiorello LaGuardia said that when he made a mistake it was a beaut. This one was a corker, especially in Boston, where I hold down a day job as a newspaperman. I failed to be reminded of the basic fact of the matter by the spelling on two major downtown office buildings, and in my newspaper's own neighborhood, of an institute at the University of Massachusetts, a middle school, and a small park on Columbia Road where the man his friends called Uncle Jawn used to live (to say nothing of the housing project around the corner that is named for his mother.)

Nor is this ancient history: McCormack died only in 1980 at 88; his career was a symbol of the power of old Boston, from his election in 1928 to his crucial vote to save the draft on the eve of World War II and the period after President John F. Kennedy's assassination when he was de facto vice president to Lyndon Johnson. John W. McCormack was Boston before John Kennedy, before Route 128 and the Miracle. As much as Cardinal Cushing or Mayor Curley or Joe Welch or Ted Williams, he symbolized the city to the nation.

In other words, it is serious business to confuse him with his nephew. It is perhaps reasonable to dig a little beneath the surface, to inquire how it happens—and what it is that's lost—when details like these don't jibe.

Surely one of the more striking attributes of this column is the voice in which it is written. This I take to stem in large part from the two magazines where I once worked, *Forbes* and *Newsweek*. Tough Henry Luce invented this omniscient (all knowing) magazine voice, but it is the London *Economist* that refined it to the purest state of hyperconfidence. Thousands of journalists speak it in varying degrees. Note that it is almost the opposite of the standard Associated Press style, in which everything is attributed, and the newsman seeks to appear as passive transmitter. In the omniscient voice, almost nothing is attributed, and the anonymous newswriter is the authority.

This omniscient voice is designed to convey several messages, the most important of which is that life is, if not actually under control, at least susceptible to understanding. The authorities may have conflicting opinions, it seems to say, but the tacit presupposition is that the intelligent layman can listen to debate and form a firm opinion as to who is right—at least provisionally. The magazine voice thus serves the deep human need for narrative order; its structure has to do with "before," "during" and "after." Deep down, this column is really about what constitutes a satisfactory explanation.

The omniscient voice emphatically doesn't work without reporting, and plenty of it. Underneath the voice is a method of beat checks, of phone calls, of an ongoing conversation among a loose group of sources and friends and readers about what matters. It is not necessarily contributed to directly. The meditation on Silvio Conte was sparked by reporter David Rogers' observation in the *Wall Street Journal* that Conte was the last of Massachusetts' Big Three to leave its delegation, Edward Boland and Tip O'Neill having preceded him.

Above all, the voice must seek to be an expression of a coherent frame-work; it must attempt to see the world whole. Magazines each have their standpoints, so do columns. This column in particular is interested in scouting out the connections among technical economics, folk economics and politics. It is a regular Chinese box of predispositions, in part an effort to do science reporting, to see events from the point of view of corporate and government managers, and to be fair-minded to leaders and followers alike.

There are pathologies of the omniscient voice: The bigger disorders include tendencies to Panglossian optimism or Spenglerian doom-mongering. The oracular mode, with no quotations or sometimes even any information, is to be avoided; so is the ingratiating tense. Indirection, in which it is not clear whose interest is being served, is also a significant shortcoming. Perhaps the most common failings involve sins of omission, of leaving out factors better included.

But there is nothing worse than simply being wrong, as when I once identified Robert Maxwell, the famous bouncing Czech, as an Australian, or wrote of Daniel (not Danforth) Quayle. In moments like these, it can seem that there is something of the Wizard of Oz about the column, of the reporter huffing and puffing away to produce an authoritative voice, while the dog pulls away the curtain to reveal his shabby resources, a lopsided list of names, a pile of old clips. (L. Frank Baum had a point about authority, after all.) So destructive are these sloppy errors that magazines have staffs of fact checkers to avoid them. Columnists, lacking the appa-ratus, make occasional elaborate corrections.

So what was it that went wrong when I typed Edward J. McCormack into the computer last week instead of John? It was not a failure of reporting so much as a failure of background knowledge. John McCormack would have loomed large in the mind of anyone who had done Boston neighborhood newspapering; I did mine in Chicago. The name would have been a big deal in anyone who covered the Hill in the 1960s; I covered Vietnam. The right name would have been on the tip of the tongue for anyone coming out of the tradition of political reporting; I came out of business and economics. Something failed; newsmen are trained to check out facts when they have the slightest doubt of them; they are supposed to know when they are skating on thin ice and to do something about it.

Does it mean I don't know what I am talking about? Well, yes, in the sense that I don't possess all the knowledge that, in the course of a few days, I collect and fashion into a column. But the fundamental proposition on which the column rests week after week is correct, I'm convinced. It is that we know a great deal about ourselves, though it is often less than we wish.

The world can be understood. Its sudden and unexpected events can be apprehended and fit into enduring interpretations. There are answers to our questions and some of them are more correct than others. I made a mistake; forgive and remember, as the surgeons say, of the mistakes their colleagues make. The moving finger writes—and having writ and erred—moves on.

FEBRUARY 17, 1991

Scientists See Vast Changes

FOR THOSE WHO ARE TEMPTED TO BE HARD ON ECONOMISTS, IT IS WORTH REFLECTING on a headline in *The New York Times* last week. The story was about a big meeting of geochemists, ecologists, paleontologists and the like in Worcester to consider the climatological and other effects of recent economic development. "Scientists see vast changes in earth," said the headline; "But little consensus about what they might mean," said the deck beneath it.

Certainly there is a great deal of skepticism in the air these days about the economic consequences of U.S. government budget deficits, even as Congress meets with the administration in search of a compromise. It is said almost ritually now that deficits caused the crash. America has been living beyond its means, the story goes; the markets, in their infinite wisdom, realized it and tried to escape the future, all at once. The only answer now is to balance the budget.

You get the feeling that even if the economists have the general direction right, the map of economic reality is not yet a very good one.

Take Robert Eisner, a Nortwestern University economist, for example. "If large budgets caused the market to crash," Eisner writes, "why did the market roar along when the deficits were at their greatest and tumble only after the deficit fell by 33 percent?" It was rising interest rates that caused the crash, according to Eisner; looser money now is the answer, not higher taxes.

Eisner says, "The conventional wisdom of lowering the deficit, either by raising taxes or by cutting government expenditures—whatever the merits on other grounds of reducing certain swollen budgets, such as those of the Pentagon and farm problems—threatens economic disaster" to an already weak economy that needs stimulus, not contraction. "It is a mindless throwback to the economics of Herbert Hoover. We must not forget where that led."

Forget about the deficits, says Lawrence Kotlikoff, chairman of the economics department at Boston University. They are an artifact of the accounting system, which makes trivial and misleading distinctions between Social Security "contributions," federal taxes and debt. If you take a broader view of receipts and payments, Kotlikoff says—especially a view that focuses on the intergenerational balance sheet—U.S. fiscal policy in the 1980s has been tighter than in the 1970s, he says; it doesn't need to be tighter still.

Robert Barro goes even further. The Harvard economist has been arguing since the early 1970s that it makes little difference whether the government finances its activities by debt or by taxes. Borrowings today imply taxes tomorrow; smart citizens realize it and make adjustments. It is the overall size of government, not the particular distortions in the economy occasioned by its revenue-raising efforts that is of interest. The deficits are only a minor crisis, Barro says.

These sentiments are especially troubling because the authors are not peripheral guys. Eisner is president this year of the 19,000-member American Economic Association. Barro and Kotlikoff are among the smartest and most influential theorists of the generation of economists under 40.

Nor is there any comforting unity in their dissent. Eisner is a Keynesian economist who believes that government is in a position to actively manage the economy; Barro and Kotlikoff are "new classicals," who believe that markets ordinarily outwit those who seek to manipulate them, and who depend on a series of intergenerational "life-cycle" models to make their points.

Yet a large chorus of voices in the mainstream of economics disparages these arguments that the deficit is really not a problem. Harvard's Lawrence Summers is typical. "The fact is that with a national savings rate of around 2 percent, we finance what little investment we do by borrowing from abroad. We need to cut consumption and increase investment and all the fancy accounting won't change that."

These are the sentiments that have the politicians locked in a room in Washington, and in the end, they will probably elicit a significant budget deal. Even if it involves a combination of tax increases and spending cuts far in excess of the $23 billion mandated by the Gramm-Rudman approach, it is unlikely to have a major effect on the $4 trillion US economy, the conventional wisdom says; instead it will be symbolic of an American willingness to resume saving more than it spends.

Such arguments between experts are a common feature of life in the 20th century. Usually the science goes forward in due course. Citizens who must make decisions on the basis of what they know, who can't wait for the resolution of such doctrinal disputes, may take comfort from Robert Frost's poem, "Why Wait for Science?"

> Sarcastic Science, she would like to know,
> In her complacent ministry of fear,
> How we propose to get away from here
> So she had made things so we have to go
> Or be wiped out. Will She be asked to show
> Us how by rocket we may hope to steer
> To some star off there say a half light-year
> Through temperature of absolute zero?
> Why wait for science to supply the how
> When any amateur can tell it now?
> The way to go should be the same
> As fifty million years ago we came—
> If anyone remembers how that was.
> I have a theory, but it hardly does.

NOVEMBER 8, 1987

part two

THE OLDER
GENERATION

The Original

THERE WAS A CERTAIN AMOUNT OF JOLLITY THAT EVEN THE HEAT COULDN'T STIFLE AS another carload of economists arrived for the meeting. One said to another, joking, "you must arrange to have yourself banned in Boston, " and a third looked out the window and said quietly, without bitterness, "I actually was banned here, you know. "

It was Prof. Lorie Tarshis, of the College of the University of Toronto, one of the modern profession's originals, as he arrived in Boston for the convention of the Eastern Economic Association that began yesterday.

Roughly speaking, Tarshis enjoys the sort of place in economics that Samuel Huntington (not to be confused with the political scientist, his present-day descendent) does in American history. Huntington, the first American president, had the bad timing to serve in Congress under the Articles of Confederation, before the states were united under the Constitution. Tarshis is also a forgotten first.

More than a thousand other economists turned up for the meeting, too. Insiders called it one of the liveliest in years, and with the best of timing, the *Harvard Crimson* announced yesterday that, for the 11th year in a row, economics was the preferred concentration of freshmen, this time by a wider measure than ever before. (Some 177 freshman chose it, compared with 142 in second-place biology.)

Tarshis, who as a Canadian graduate student spent Monday evenings in the early 1930s drawing numbered slips of paper out of the fist of Roger Kahn to see in what order he would discuss that evening's paper at the Political Economy Club of Mr. John Maynard Keynes ("One was bad because it was dangerous to go first and five was bad because by that time everything had been said ") came to Tufts University in Medford as an instructor in 1936.

He was perhaps the second man to bring Keynes' new message to the New World. He was the first to put it in textbook form, in 1947, and the first to draw the fire of critics.

The result was that, whatever advantage a year's headstart had given him on economist Paul Samuelson was lost. Tarshis' text, published by

Houghton Mifflin, was clobbered by right-wing critics who disliked the Keynesian message.

Thus, Samuelson, Alvin Harris, even John Kenneth Galbraith, are thought of as Keynes' principal evangelists, while Tarshis is largely forgotten by the profession at large. "I took Samuelson and I never heard of the guy," a former student says fairly typically.

"They called it communist, put together a regular crusade against it," Tarshis recalled yesterday. "Principally it was a man named Merwin K. Hart, so far to the right it was hard to tell him from the fascists.

"He had a newsletter out of Washington where he called himself the 'National Economic Council' and his editor, a woman named Rose Wilde Lane, she wrote books for women, an early sort of Ayn Rand, wrote that universities which had ordered the book were canceling their orders.

"They did. "

"Then William Buckley cited it as evidence that God was gone from Yale. It didn't do my royalties any good, " he recalled.

But by that time, Tarshis had left Tufts for Stanford University, where he helped design and build one of the nation's leading departments of economics. He left Stanford for Toronto in 1974.

Yesterday, as he moved through the knots of economists meeting at the Park Plaza Hotel, however, Tarshis was the very picture of the well-led life of science. Former students, at least the better of them, sidled up to him to recall teething on his texts (he wrote two others) and colleagues took him aside to make him tell stories. While his wife, Inge, toured Boston's art galleries, Tarshis sat for newspaper photographers, and described the book he would write this summer with Tibor Scitovsky that will set the record straight on Keynes.

MAY 11, 1979

How Economics
Went High-Tech

IF THERE IS A SINGLE STRIKING FEATURE OF THE DEVELOPMENT OF ECONOMICS IN THE past 50 years, surely it is the increasing use of mathematics and statistics. Deliberate mathematization is not unheard of in science; when Copernicus published *De Revolutionibus Orbium Coelestium* in 1543, he encoded his argument in geometry as obscurely as possible, in order to not provoke the attention of the Church. Astronomy is for astronomers, he wrote.

But when John Maynard Keynes published his *General Theory of Employment, Interest and Money* in 1936, he addressed a general audience in elegant (if not especially easy to follow) English, and the mathematics was confined to an appendix. Yet just a few years later, mathematics had become the *lingua franca* of economics.

If it wasn't Keynes, who did it?

No irony in modern economics is greater than the saga of how, in the 1930s and 1940s, one of the proprietors of the then-archconservative *Chicago Tribune* bankrolled from an office in the Tribune Tower the diffusion of the Keynsian Revolution in the universities, sponsoring a generation of European refugees at the University of Chicago—including a half a dozen who would later win the Nobel Prize. All the while on the floors below, the newspaper inveighed bitterly against such "un-American activities," thoroughly unaware of the significance of events as they took place.

It began, for practical purposes, with Col. Robert R. McCormick's contemporary and silent partner, Alfred Cowles, Jr., a stockbroker in Colorado Springs who was the second-biggest shareholder in the Trib (his grandfather had been founder Joseph Medill's bookkeeper). He remained a director of the Tribune Company until 1968.

Cowles may have been one of the most scrupled advisers in stock market history. He folded his forecast service in 1931, telling subscribers he didn't know enough to predict the economic future and would try to find out more before resuming. By 1932, Cowles' doubts had compounded; he wasn't sure that anyone knew very much about economic prediction. He had begun an ambitious survey of other forecasters' track records during the period of the Great Crash. Could they forecast reliably? "It is doubtful," he concluded.

In the course of his investigation, however, Cowles stumbled across Harold T. Davis, a Unversity of Indiana mathematician and charter member of the then newly-formed (and struggling) Econometric Society. Cowles simply called Davis one day and asked if he could perform an analysis on a problem with 24 variables. Davis responded that he couldn't imagine why anyone would want to do such a thing, but, yes, he supposed it could be done . . . there was, in fact, a new way of doing such work, using Hollerith punch cards. Hollerith eventually became IBM and Cowles, for a time, became econometrics.

Davis put Cowles in touch with Irving Fisher, a celebrated Yale mathematical economist, who, like Cowles, had embarrassed himself recently by calling the market wrong, highly publicly. The businessman and the economist hit it off, with the result that Cowles offered to bankroll the society, to publish its journal *Econometrica*, and, most important, to start a foundation, the Cowles Commission, to support the work. Pausing only to make sure Cowles wasn't a crank, Fisher and his colleagues took him up on it. The seed money: $12,000 a year.

During the 1930s, the Commission's main activity was an annual, two-week, summer seminar in the Rocky Mountains. For several years, the best mathematical economists in the world, European leaders such as Jan Tinbergen and Ragnar Frisch (they won the first Nobel Prize in economics) and bright young Europeans such as Abba Lerner and Abraham Wald, were attracted to Colorado.

Then, in 1939 Cowles' father died. He had to return to Chicago, and he resolved to take the Commission with him. He arranged with Col. McCormick for space for himself in the Tribune Tower and with Robert Hutchins for a suite of offices for the Commission at the University of Chicago. That move set the stage for the econometric revolution.

That revolution really began when Cowles hired Jacob Marschak to head the project as research director in 1942. Marschak, a Russian exile (he had been a boy member of the Kerensky government during the Revolution) by way of Germany and Oxford, was a brilliant mathematician and statistician. Already renowned for his ability to spot talent, he quickly assembled a list of extraordinary young scientists after he arrived at Cowles in Chicago. Among them were four especially promising young men:

• Tjalling Koopmans, a Norwegian trained as a theoretical physicist, who had run into Frisch and Tinbergen along the way;

• Kenneth Arrow, a smart up-and-comer from New York's City College whose dissertation at Columbia was almost rejected by his professors because it didn't seem to be economics at all;

• Lawrence Klein, MIT's first PhD, freshly trained by Paul Samuelson, whose dissertation was called "The Keynesian Revolution"; and,

• Herbert Simon, an assistant professor from down the street at the Illinois Institute of Technology, who was forever bringing news about new "computing machines" that would someday replace the hand-operated calculators the Cowles staff used.

If the names sound familiar, it's because all four have been awarded Nobel Prizes in economics, for work they pursued at Cowles. [Subsequently Trygve Haavelmo and James Tobin have been recognized as well.]

What the four of the Cowles Commission had in common was partly a style of approach, and partly an idea. The style flowed from the leader, Marschak. "Marschak was the very model of a pure economic scientist," said MIT's Paul Samuelson, himself a Nobel laureate. "He always picked up each new thing so he was not just a leader, he was a worker, too."

Simon, now at Carnegie-Mellon University, said, "We learned some very high standards. There were plenty of hard exchanges, and never a soft idea."

The big idea the Cowles scholars shared was a notion of the economy "in equilibrium," in which the world hung together because the endless variety of economic actions taken by individuals worked to cancel one another out. With everything thus connected to everything else, the entire economic order could be described in a series of simultaneous equations, a model.

As Koopmans put it, the statistical studies the Cowles Commission undertook—its "estimations" of economic relationships—were always in the form of "If . . . then . . ." statements. The "model" consisted of a lot of "ifs." The "then" it produced was called—"usually but inaccurately"—its "findings."

Another important consequence of the econometric idea: If everything is connected to everything else, economists can't study each relationship separately. They have to do it all in a grand sweep. They can't do just one thing at a time.

Keynes aside, economics at the beginning of the '40s was much as Alfred Marshall had taught it for 20 years on either side of the turn of the century. It was full of familiar talk about firms and industries and the exciting possibility of "imperfect" competition. For Marschak, however, Marshallian economics was dangerously close to philosophical moralizing. The trick would be, he said, "to replace fast mumbling with a slow but sure use of an articulate language of symbols." And in 1942 mathematics was slow because it was done with slide rules.

Later, one prominent econometrician, Carl Christ, would say that one couldn't exactly state that the Cowles group had invented the idea of econometrics; Leon Walras, the great French journalist-turned-economist, had done that 75 years before. And the theory of correlation and regression was built in the last quarter of the 19th century. Marschak and company, "realizing that traditional statistical methods were inadequate, designed new ones," said Christ.

In some sense, then, the econometric revolution provided new high-tech bottles for old wine, a revolution of rhetoric. Instead of familiar tables of numbers, there were equations. Instead of hypotheses, models. Instead of dusty volumes, data banks (thanks to the wonders of time-sharing). Instead of hit-and-miss planning, the certainties of a host of mathematical tools. But the "laws" of supply and demand remained unchanged. It was a revolution in rigor, not content, or so said its protagonists, and it was only because of the advent of the computer that it was able to proceed at its lightning pace.

Three of the Cowles Nobel laureates went on to other things. Arrow, having concentrated at Cowles on developing the mathematical and logical properties of the idea of general equilibrium, went on to revolutionize his colleagues' thinking about risk. Koopmans, having contributed a battery of statistical techniques to Klein's model-building, moved on to devise the technique of linear programming, which was developed originally to pick the optimum path for ships crisscrossing the Atlantic with war cargo. Linear programming (then often called "activity analysis") has become one of the analytic rocks on which is built the new field of "decision sciences," a marriage of computers and decision-theory of which Simon is the acknowledged father. Only Klein stayed strictly within the confines of econometrics.

There were several other potential Nobel Prize winners in the crew, who are less thoroughly identified with the Cowles group, but who nevertheless were there and heavily influenced: Leonid Hurwicz, Gerard Debreu, Edmond Malinvaud, Arnold Harberger, Donald Patinkin, James Tobin, Franco Modigliani, Hendrick Houthakker, names that mean much to economists.

"I think it was one of the more exciting moments in the intellectual history of economics," said Arrow, now at Stanford. "There's never been a center comparable to it," said Prof. James Tobin of Yale, who directed the Cowles Commission during the 1950s and 1960s.

Yet it almost never got off the ground, for political reasons. As Klein remembers it, "When Marschak was at All Souls [College at Oxford], he had come over to one of the summer conferences in Colorado Springs and he was offered the job of research director. He turned it down because he said the senior people were all so dead set against Roosevelt. They were very conservative people."

Indeed, McCormick's *Tribune* at the time was editorializing vehemently against the Lend-Lease Act and the New Deal. During the '30s, the paper, which 80 years earlier almost singlehandedly had convinced Abraham Lincoln to run for president, set the standard for an isolationist reaction to world events.

Five years later, Marschak changed his mind. Soon after his arrival, the Cowles Commission offices in the Social Sciences building were the scene of serious seminars by day—"You could hear English spoken in 10 or 12 different accents," recalled Herbert Simon—and innocent revels by night.

The folks in the Tribune Tower stayed away. "They were very tolerant of us," said Klein. "There was never any input but dividends from the Cowles foundation," former director Tobin said. Simon didn't know about the *Tribune* connection until he learned about it in the course of preparation of this article.

The *Tribune*'s tendencies towards witch-hunting (the paper was a staunch supporter of Sen. Joseph McCarthy to the end) were never permitted to extend to Cowles' economic protégés. It is a good thing, for there would have been fine hunting; it was during his days at the Cowles Commission that Klein took up briefly with the Communist party in Hyde Park.

The Keynesian model, with its emphasis on the role of government demand in macroeconomic affairs, was controversial in some quarters for 20 years. But it was introduced into econometric calculations almost effortlessly, right from the start. Klein recalls the European statisticians in the crew "were well disposed to the point of view, but they weren't advocates. When I came, I came straight out of Paul Samuelson's class and so I sort of brought the ideas."

There was nothing single-handed about the propagation of Keynesian ideas, but most Cowles alumni agreed it was fair to say that the influence Alvin Hansen and Samuelson had on one wing of the profession, Klein had on the other. Klein won the Nobel Prize this year, heralded by many as "The Father of Econometrics."

The resistance with which the Keynesian revolution was met is well-known. Less well-known is the resistence to econometric revolution, not the anti-intellectual grousing of magazine writers, but the serious methodological dispute it triggered. The major indictment of econometrics from inside economics came from Milton Friedman, the modern-day personification of "The Chicago School."

Friedman had arrived at the University of Chicago in 1947 to join the Economics Dept., which was recovering from considerable disarray. The disorder he could stand, but the competition from Cowles he didn't much like: In a famous article in 1949, Friedman wrote that in their pursuit of "photographic descriptions of reality," the econometricians had gone off on a wild goose chase. He complained that "abstractness, generality and mathematical elegance have in some measure become ends in themselves."

Friedman, who worked just down the hall from the Commission offices, said he represented an alternative tradition, "Marshallian," he called it, contrasted with the "Walrasian" approach of the Cowles bunch. His tradition, he said, offered plenty of connection between theory and empirical work, instead of castles in the air. It produced policy recomendations to boot.

Marschak returned the fire: He told students that *ceterus paribus*—Latin meaning roughly "if you change one thing and let all the rest remain unchanged"—which was at the heart of Friedman's approach was "a refuge for lazy irresponsibles." Change one thing and everything changes, Marschak said.

Enough was, finally, enough. In 1953, after six years of increasingly bitter intellectual scuffling, the Cowles Commission picked up in 1953 and moved to Yale and James Tobin, after Tobin had declined to move to Chicago. Koopmans, the planner, in particular couldn't stand Chicago; by most accounts he couldn't stand Friedman, the free marketeer, either. The great flowering was over, but the resulting scattering of econometricians vastly advanced the state of the art.

But instead of turning his back on the Commission and the econometric techniques it represented—an altogether human failing of his predecessor Frank Knight—Friedman immediately moved to beef up the university's quantitative capability. A string of successful appointments were the result, culminating in Henri Theil, author of a most influential modern econometrics textbook. The econometrics revolution pulled the level of mathematical economics up with it. And eventually, the remarkable Robert Lucas, who as an undergraduate had majored in history at the University of Chicago in the 1950s, returned to the Department of Economics in 1974 and quietly brought the "Walrasian," or general equilibrium, approach back to stay through sheer force of argument. Friedman left quietly for the Hoover Institution at Stanford University a few years later.

Meanwhile, though, Friedman went on to win the Nobel Prize himself, as did Theodore Schultz, who had welcomed the Commission in 1941 and who hired Friedman in 1946. Six of the nine American Nobel laureates were thus working in the Social Sciences Building at the University of Chicago between the end of the war and 1950, during important phases of their work. That doesn't count Samuelson, who did his undergraduate work there during the late 1930s. Only Wassily Leontief and Simon Kuznets were altogether untouched by the Chicago tradition.

But the tension between the two schools—"Marshallian" mathematical economics on the one hand, "Walrasian" econometrics on the other—is still there, according to Yale's Tobin. In appointments, honors, classes, the distinctions are sharp and important. Proponents of each school can still be heard questioning the other's relevance, and there is a broad and very respectable segment that says, in effect, a pox on both houses.

"Economists don't like to collect facts," explained Leontief, the Nobel laureate responsible for input-output analysis. "They build giant statistical inference models instead."

Sidney Schoeffler, head of the Profit Impact of Marketing Strategy project, who has spent the last 20 years collecting raw economic data, agrees: "The Cowles Commission did admirable work in advancing the technology of economic analysis. Perhaps the thing to do now, before pushing ahead further with rarefied theory, is to obtain a somewhat firmer grasp of the empirical phenomena."

So far, what has econometrics got to show?

Some achievements are so concrete they aren't arguable: linear programming, for example, and other sorts of resource allocation techniques. Royal Dutch Shell uses them to dispatch its fleet of tankers; BBD&O uses them to determine what mix of advertising to buy for customers; Dupont Co. uses them to decide how many salesmen should call in a particular area, and Eastern Airlines uses them to schedule airplanes.

Other undertakings, macroeconomic forecasting, for example, finally are becoming concrete enough to be defensible. Stephen McNees, the Boston Federal Reserve Bank economist who has become an unofficial arbiter of forecasters' track records, said: "I spend my time making sure people don't go to extremes. These days the extreme to which they are likely to go is to say the macro forecasts are worthless. That is ridiculous. If you have to do a lot of forecasting, as most people do, macro models are indispensable. It's just incredible the extent to which they are used. There is just one thing: They all require judgment. Models don't make forecasts. People do."

On the minus side, the technical emphasis in economics is acting as a filter of sorts, keeping some types of people out and encouraging others to become economists.

Fr. William Neenan, dean of Arts and Sciences at Boston College and an economist who has taught in several major university departments, said, "A generation ago, the people who went into economics seemed to come out of social concern, concern with unemployment and the Depression. Even in the late 1950s and 1960s, it was fine-tuning and all that. As things have become more and more technical and mathematically demanding, it seems to me there are people getting it who are interested in technique, and who lose sight of the issues."

Whatever, the science has come a long way from the beginnings of the honest investment adviser's search for a more reliable method of forecasting the economic future. Cowles is still alive, although incapacitated. Until the early 1970s, he put in appearances at Commission offices at Yale, recalls Prof. Herbert E. Scarf, who was then director. "There was great respect when he would visit. He knew that he was getting old," said Scarf. "And he could no longer keep up with all the technical developments. But he knew, I think, that he had done something significant in the history of economic thought."

Marschak? He died in 1977, in the year in which he was to have served as president of the American Economic Assn. He never won the Nobel Prize, though many felt he might have. His best-known contribution was as a chief author in 1950 of the report that launched nuclear power as a commercial venture. He spent much of the rest of his life writing a "theory of teams," adapting game theory to the analysis of social organization.

[In June 1983, when some 65 alumni of the Cowles Commission gathered in New Haven to commemorate the founding of their research unit, talk about "Yascha" pervaded the meeting. Nearly everybody had a story or two to tell about how he had goaded a small group of young men and women into making their series of discoveries. "He was a very stubborn man," said Roy Radner. "He did not like to take no for an answer."]

The *Tribune*, having given the nation Abraham Lincoln, seems in no hurry to claim the credit for having given the world econometrics, even inadvertently. "You couldn't really say that it was the *Tribune* that did it," said John T. McCutcheon, Jr., editor of the editorial page. "We were generally sympathetic to it," he remembers, "but it was not one of our big things."

DECEMBER 2 1980—JUNE 7, 1983

Enfant Terrible—
Emeritus

WHEN PAUL SAMUELSON MARCHES IN THE MIT COMMENCEMENT PARADE TODAY, HE will be concluding his last season as an active-duty professor. Tomorrow he becomes emeritus, albeit an exceptionally undimmed emeritus.

"It's been well-known for quite a while that I was born in 1915," he says. "There won't be any change at all in my lifestyle: same office, same secretary, same committees."

Certainly there won't be changes like those that have already taken place. For a long time, Samuelson was undisputed king of the mountain in technical economics.

Then, starting in the late 1960s, just as his greatest public honors were arriving, he and his colleagues were shouldered out of the limelight in many university departments, not always politely, by students of a new generation of conservative young economists from places like Chicago and Minneapolis.

These "New Classical" economists proclaimed mathematically a subtle gospel of "don't interfere" for fear of making things worse instead of better. They accused Samuelson and his generation of hubris in their pursuit of the goal of "fine tuning" the economy and said that markets—even the job markets—worked far better than was commonly supposed. "If I were chairman of the Council of Economic Advisers," says Chicago's Robert Lucas, most influential of the New Classicals, "I'd resign."

Don't look now, but a new generation of economists whose instinct is a more sophisticated "do something" instead of "stand there," has been slowly coalescing in the universities as a coherent point of view. Two years ago, they were simply the younger generation of Keynesians; today, they are on the verge of being a real school. The cycle is swinging back toward Samuelson's point of view.

They call themselves "New Keynesians" to distinguish themselves from Samuelson's generation of "neo-Keynesians," and a mostly failed generation of "post-Keynesians." They offer a hip critique of the conservative dogma in the rarefied precincts where prefixes like these pack the wallop of an electric fence. The idea of a properly managed economy is back, they say, on a new and far more subtle level.

Moreover, events of the last few years have tended to go against conservative New Classicals. The events they predicted failed to materialize. And now, for the first time since Samuelson wrote his famous introductory text, *Economics*, nearly 40 years ago, a leading theorist has attempted a significant reformulation of economics by writing a new introductory principles text.

In a book scheduled for December publication, which is attracting considerable attention, Columbia University's Edmund S. Phelps—who did as much as anyone to undermine the old Keynesian prescriptions—has made the distinction between classicals and modernists his fulcrum.

In *Introduction to Political Economy*, Phelps describes "the two clashes occurring in economics today—the contest between the neoclassical model of the marketplace and the modernist models of imperfectly-informed markets developed in the past two decades, and the dispute between the New Classical and the New Keynesian schools over the stability, or resilience, of the market economy and the utility of 'activist' countercyclical government policies."

Phelps' book won't do for modern ideas what Samuelson's famous textbook once did for Keynes; nothing can. But in its crucial chapters it is full of talk about signalling, contracts, asymmetric information, search costs and incentive wages, all the new lingo of imperfect competition and the search for microeconomic foundations of overall economic behavior. It's the kind of talk that makes businessmen sit up and take notice.

"A very great deal has happened in the last 30 years" says Phelps.

For 50 years, Paul Samuelson has been, to all intents and purposes, the inheritor of John Maynard Keynes. As author of scientific papers that would become a formidable treatise called *Foundations of Economic Analysis*, written while still a graduate student, he established his preeminence as a theorist before World War II. Then in a series of controversies that lasted through the 1950s, he won with his MIT colleagues undisputed control of the worldwide economic mainstream with a point of view he called "neo-Keynesian."

His moral life has been as interesting as his scholarly career. He joined MIT after Harvard turned him down for tenure (because he was Jewish, it was widely believed at the time). Soon after, such barriers were a thing of the past.

He declined on principle to go to Washington to serve under President

Kennedy, whom he advised instead from a distance; rather, he stuck to his vision of making MIT's department a teaching department staffed by scientists. And, of course, he revised his textbook.

Economics, now in its 12th edition, encapsulates the spirit of its age as completely as Alfred Marshall's Victorian masterpiece had captured the certainties of that earlier time. Samuelson's book offers a smooth blend of analysis that gave confident economists a convenient bag of tools for eliminating the business cycle and driving the economy to ever greater heights through "demand management."

Starting about the time of the Vietnam War, however, this conventional wisdom—which amounted to a series of recipes for how the government should continually use monetary and fiscal instruments like tax cuts and sudden surcharges to "lean against the wind" and steer the economy—drew attacks, first from monetarists, then from a wide variety of others who emphasized the subtlety and resilience of market forms of organization.

Among the critics was Columbia's Phelps, who in 1967 challenged the analytic foundations of the Phillips Curve, the famous trade-off between unemployment and inflation that Samuelson had made his centerpiece. The blows fell faster and faster, and by 1980, the flight from Keynes was a rout. For example, Martin Feldstein, a first-rank leader in technical economics who was soon to become chief adviser to President Reagan, wrote in 1981, "A major revolution in economic thinking is under way—a retreat from the Keynesian ideas that have dominated economic policy for the past 35 years. In the decades ahead, this revolution in economic thinking is likely to have profound effects, not only on the national economy, but also on our individual lives."

Today, Feldstein teaches the introductory economics course to nearly 1,000 Harvard undergraduates. The textbook he uses, by MIT's Stanley Fischer and Rudiger Dornbusch, takes a decidedly Keynesian approach.

One of the cornerstones of New Classical economics has been the assumption of rational expectations, which is a shorthand expression for the conviction that people tend to be forward-looking, making intelligent guesses about the future, rather than essentially backward-looking, changing their minds only in response to concrete observations about errors they've already made.

This doctrine that people behave pretty much as if they had the benefit of a good course in economics can lead to some pretty strong conclusions— and has. Minnesota's Thomas Sargent argued that to end inflation, it might be enough simply to be credible, as was the German government in 1923. Rochester University's Robert Barro argued that deficits don't matter because rational taxpayers reduce consumption today when they see governments borrowing money, knowing that taxes will go up tomorrow. In other words, today's huge deficits should be accompanied by a soaring rate of savings.

In a lecture last year, Samuelson described this way some of the exasperations of the debate between the generations:

"Since the many taxpayers I knew were not cutting down on their consumption by as much of their share of the deficit in order to leave their heirs as well off as if there were to be no future public debt, I could not believe that respected economists took this argument seriously. I burst out laughing when one of the ablest young economists put it to me.

" 'You don't believe that,' I asserted.

" 'Indeed I do, and so do all the good economists under 40,' I was told. We used to expect graduate students to lose all good sense for a spell, and were not alarmed by this since we had the comfortable reassurance that later it would come back. For once, however, I felt old; the doubt kept asserting itself that maybe in this generation the loss of practical knowledge and experience might be permanent and irreversible."

Samuelson needn't have worried. Today it is the rational-expectations crowd who are on the defensive everywhere. "Events of the last few years have not been kind to the New Classical economists," says Princeton's Alan Blinder, one of the leading New Keynesians. "Economists, especially academic ones, like fads as much as everybody else. But this one didn't stand up. It doesn't give a very good account of the last 5 or 50 years."

Columbia's Phelps says, "My textbook takes the New Classicals very seriously, and it includes a good deal of their material, but I think that it is pretty clear that my heart is with the New Keynesians. I think the frictions and uncertainties of the world must be taken very seriously."

For his part, Samuelson is sublimely confident of remaining in the center of mainstream economics, if no longer exactly at the frontier. He says, "Keynesian economics is an approach, not a past doctrine. The world is constantly changing. What I would have to be is a New New New New Keynesian."

JUNE 3, 1985

A Bunch of Kids
with Adding Machines

IT WAS JUST TWO BLOCKS FROM THE UNIVERSITY OF CHICAGO FOOTBALL STADIUM where Enrico Fermi and his team started the first atomic chain reaction in 1942, but the atmosphere at the little-known Cowles Commission office two years later couldn't have been more different. At Cowles, the cradle of econometrics, there was none of the heavy security of an atomic-bomb project. There was just a bunch of kids with adding machines, led by a European exile named Jacob Marschak.

Among them: Tjalling Koopmanns, Kenneth Arrow, Herbert Simon and Lawrence Klein, all to be winners of the Nobel Prize. Klein's award, which came yesterday, was a surprise to no one.

In the traditional ceremony of champagne after breakfast, Klein stood in front of his class at the University of Pennsylvania yesterday and said he had never dreamed he could accomplish so much with mathematical models, the long chains of equations whose solutions are supposed to predict the behavior of the world's economy.

Where Klein had begun his work in Chicago 36 years before, over the door of the social sciences building, was carved a dictum of Lord Kelvin, the 19th-century English physicist: "When you can measure what you are speaking about, and express it in numbers, you know something about it; when you cannot measure it, when you cannot express it in numbers, your knowledge is of a meager and unsatisfactory kind; it may be the beginning of knowledge, but you have scarcely, in your thoughts, advanced to the stage of science."

It was for his contribution to the infusion of sophisticated modelling techniques into economics that Klein won his prize. It was the second Nobel Award to be given for econometric modeling. The other was the first award ever made in economics, in 1969 to Jan Tinbergen and Ragnar Frisch. Tinbergen constructed the first such model in 1937.

In Chicago in 1944, Klein and the others followed closely on Tinbergen's footsteps, expanding the work. Kenneth Arrow theorized and Tjalling Koopmans worked on statistical methods; but it was Klein who learned how to put the equations together in models. Herbert Simon, though not on the commission staff, was a regular visitor; he was full of ideas about new tools called "computers."

"The group was close in the form of personal contact and friendship," Koopmanns said in a telephone interview yesterday. "It wasn't that we were trying to be bohemian or anything like that. There was quite a sense of closeness, of opportunity to make a real contribution."

Down the hall from where they were working was the University of Chicago economics department, an uneasy host to the Cowles project. The department chairman was Theodore Schultz, who later won the Nobel Prize for his work in agriculture; the newest member of the faculty was Milton Friedman, who later won the Nobel for his work on monetary economics. But the university's tradition was in literature and humanities, not mathematics. Econometrics, as it was being called, didn't stick. First Klein, then Arrow and finally Koopmanns left. The Cowles foundation departed with them and found a home, with Koopmanns, at Yale.

Klein's first econometric model enabled him to predict an upsurge in post-war economic activity, instead of the depression expected by most economists, including the man who trained him—Paul Samuelson of MIT, still another Nobel winner. Klein went to England and built a model of that country's economy before returning to the United States, where he went to the University of Michigan and then to the University of Pennsylvania.

There were only slide rules when Tinbergen invented his first model; Klein was born in 1920, on the eve of the computer age. During the 1950s, he built successively more complex systems of equations to use the record of past events to predict future ones, and he cranked them into the increasingly advanced computers that were being made.

"He really did two things, each one of which is worthy of the prize," Harvard's Otto Eckstein said yesterday. "First, he brought econometric modeling to this country. He was virtually alone through the 1950s. . . . From 1945 to 1965, he was almost alone. Then other people began to come on galore. Then, in the 1970s, he went through another major round of work, on Project LINK, linking up international models, a couple of dozen of them." To be sure, Eckstein said, with the LINK model of the world economy still in its infancy, "it's harder to identify the specific scientific progress." But "linking all these models together certainly is a major scientific idea," he added.

Klein's work has been primarily non-political. In 1945, however, while at the University of Chicago, he had a minor flirtation with Marxism. In 1976, he had another brush with politics when he served as a senior adviser to Jimmy Carter when he was running for president. After Carter was elected, Klein turned down the top economic job in the administration because, he explained, in government "you're always working on yesterday's problems."

Not for Klein. A couple of years ago he was invited by the Chinese government to develop a model of its economy. Traveling to China frequently to do that, he has become, at age 60, one of the leading authorities on the Chinese macroeconomy.

OCTOBER 16, 1980

Milton Friedman's Surprising Secret

MILTON FRIEDMAN'S 80TH BIRTHDAY IS COMING UP THIS SUMMER. HE'S STILL VIGORous near the end of a remarkable career during which he won every award in sight. His new book, *Money Mischief*, has appeared, touching off amiable arguments with old friends about colorful episodes in the history of money: "the Crime of 1873," for example, when the government declined to redeem its Civil War "greenbacks" for silver and outraged the American West.

The saga of how Friedman almost single-handedly overturned the Popular Front of the Keynesian Revolution during the 1960s and 1970s through clever arguments and imaginative research is not so widely known. William Breit and Roger Ransome took the creed of the Texas Rangers as the motto of their enthusiastic profile—"Little man whip a big man every time if the little man's in the right and keeps a'comin"—and that was only 1972.

Since then, Friedman has won the Nobel Prize and turned an influential 1980 television series, *Free to Choose*, into a best-seller. His acolytes have led Chile—and in turn the rest of Latin America—in a decisive turn toward free markets; the same thing has happened in Eastern Europe. True, Friedman blunted his lance forecasting inflation in the 1980s, when he was deeply, frequently wrong. But as the animating intellectual spirit of "the Reagan Revolution," he remains a figure whose influence is of Keynesian proportions.

For all his polemical skill and energy, however, Milton Friedman's fame ultimately rests on a single idea: the famous quantity theory of money. The quantity theory says that the general level of prices is directly proportional to the quantity of money in circulation. We have talked this way about the "cost of living" and the "purchasing power of money" for centuries; Friedman is the most of recent of a long line of expositors.

The quantity theory is often written as an equation that describes the stock of money (M) and the frequency with which it changes hands (V, for its "velocity") in terms of the average price (P) and the number of transactions (T), $MV = PT$. Some variant of this framework is used by everyone, from bond traders to central bankers to the actuaries who calculate Social Security benefits, for talking about inflation. Friedman says that the equation has "the same foundation-stone role in monetary theory that Einstein's $E = MC^2$ does in physics."

There is, perhaps, a difference: circumstantial evidence suggests that the quantity theory is simply an extended analogy smuggled into economics from physics long ago, a dubious appropriation of Boyle's Law, cute, but ultimately not much more revealing than Parkinson's Law (work expands to fill the time alloted for its completion). Perhaps you remember Boyle's Law from high school physics, the first great proof that the atmosphere consisted of an "ocean" of compressible air: the greater the pressure on a fixed quantity of gas, the smaller the space it occupies; the smaller the pressure, the greater the space.

The very word "inflation," applied to prices, appears to be on loan from physics. There is a wonderful opportunity for some metaphorical archaeology here, just waiting for a properly skeptical young monetary theorist to finally get around to it.

What they will find is that the quantity theory of money rests on an ancient habit of mind, a curious assumption about the "plenitude" of the world that was inherited from the thought of Plato. Plenitude, too, can be found in early physics (among many other places): a plenum, the opposite of a vacuum, is a space completely filled with matter. More largely, a plenum is something filled with every conceivable *type* of thing; a plenary session of a convention, for example, is one that includes all the members of the meeting. In Platonic thought, it is the universe itself that is a plenum, an exhaustive gallery of possible types, complete once and for all.

The remarkable significance of the assumption of plenitude was first parsed by Arthur O. Lovejoy nearly 60 years ago in a famous book, *The Great Chain of Being*. Those who have read it usually still can recall their astonishment upon learning, from long sentences more elegant but no less convoluted than this one, just how deep a hold upon the imagination of thinkers was exercised over the centuries by the conviction that there is nothing new under the sun—because God had created everything that could possibly be. In cosmology, plenitude implied a universe that contained an infinite variety of other planets; in biology, it dictated for a time a belief that species were unchanging, until the fossil record turned biology (for a time) into a hunt for "missing links."

For the purposes of monetary thought, the assumption of plenitude seems to entail the view that, while there may be great changes on the side of money, nothing much ever changes on the side of things. This conviction is implicit in English-language formulations of the quantity theory from its earliest days: it was David Hume, for instance, who wrote, "It seems a maxim almost self-evident, that the prices of every thing depend upon the proportion between commodities and money, and that any considerable alteration on either has the same effect, either of heightening or lowering the price. Increase the commodities, they become cheaper; increase the money, they rise in their value [price]." Note how the phrase "the prices of every thing" subtly implies that there is a fixed inventory of types of thing for sale.

Now this is clearly a very useful tool for static, short-term situations, where the significant changes are occurring mainly on the side of money. The sudden discovery of a new source of precious metal; a hyperinflation of the currency, when a government finances its expenditures through printing presses: these are phenomena that can scarcely be understood *without* the quantity theory. Chronicles of episodes like these fill Milton Friedman's new book, and they are fascinating.

But the quantity theory simply is not much good for thinking about the long-term evolution of the economy, where big changes that affect the cost of living are occurring on the side of things. These changes can be technological, as, say, when electricity replaced steam or when automobiles replaced horses. They can be institutional, as, say, when the machine-driven factory system replaced old styles of "putting out," or when new roles were assigned to governments in modern mixed economies. And, up close, these changes can be nearly invisible. But there is reason to believe they can have a big impact on prices.

How? For a simple intuitive example of the relationship among money, prices and economic development, consider the familiar game of Monopoly. The game has a money supply, doled out by the banker. It has a general level of prices, meaning the average price you pay for landing on a square. And it features a great price explosion. In the course of a game, the "cost of landing" on Ventnor Avenue goes from $22 to $1,150.

But hardly anybody who plays the game would say that rising prices stemmed from an "inflation" of the money supply. Prices in Monopoly rise because monopoly blocs of properties are assembled and rents are increased accordingly, as specified by the rules. Houses and hotels are then built, and their costs, too, are bundled into prices. To be sure, the quantity of money increases steadily throughout. But it is economic development— changes in the complexity of the board, in the types of things that are created and offered for sale—that causes the price level to rise. Only because money is deliberately kept too tight does the game end at all.

Friedman came close to acknowledging the existence of this sort of mechanism in the real world last autumn in an article on health care cost "inflation." It was true that "care had become more sophisticated and expensive, and medical machines more complex," Friedman wrote. But this alone wasn't enough to explain the explosive acceleration of costs: it was the assumption by government of responsibility for hospital and medical care for the poor and elderly that really sent hospital bed prices soaring. "Anecdotal evidence suggests that increased administrative complexity played a major role in the explosion of total cost per patient day," Friedman wrote.

When you think about it, this is quite a statement from the man who gave us the mantra, "Inflation is everywhere and always a monetary phenomenon." The interplay is intricate between new goods and styles of delivering them on the one hand, and the existence of increasing money to pay for them on the other, but that's the point: it works both ways.

Health care "inflation" is by no stretch of the imagination simply a "monetary phenomenon." It tells us nothing to say that the cost of a day in the hospital exploded because the money supply increased. As in all the rest of the economy, a host of technological and institutional factors contribute to rising prices—not everywhere and always, but often. It is the assumption of plenitude, tacitly concealed in the quantity theory, that blinds the theorists among us to this fact. And that is Milton Friedman's surprising secret.

MAY 17, 1992

The Professor
of "Q"

A YALE UNIVERSITY ECONOMIST WAS AWARDED A NOBEL PRIZE YESTERDAY FOR HIS work in describing how families choose to distribute their assets in money, stocks and bonds.

James Tobin, 63, an avid Keynesian and "unsuccessful adviser" to the presidential campaign of George McGovern, was immediately hailed by peers as a kind of alternative to the conservative monetarist, Milton Friedman. In winning the $180,000 prize yesterday, Tobin became the 10th American among 18 laureates to have received the Nobel in economics since it was established in 1969.

Tobin was among those who, starting in the late 1940s, added a description of the stocks of personal wealth and business balance sheets to the Keynesian world of flows of income and expenditure. He was one of the foremost practitioners of the "new economics" of John Maynard Keynes, devised during the 1930s to counter the Great Depression. Keynesians propose relying more on tax and budget adjustments to manage the economy, while monetarists want to rely almost exclusively on controlling the supply of money and credit.

Tobin was cited by the Swedish Academy of Sciences, which awards the prize, for his analysis of "financial markets and their relations to decisions, employment, production and prices." The academy singled out his "portfolio selection theory" as his prize-winning contribution.

At his home in New Haven yesterday, Tobin described himself as "Surprised! Excited! Pleased!" In his classroom later, he described his major breakthrough as having devised a theoretical frame for the study of "not putting all your eggs in one basket."

In college departments, economists debated among themselves what the prize meant: Tobin had been a Kennedy adviser, an arch-Keynesian, "an unregenerate Democrat," as Paul Samuelson, an MIT economist, called him. In recent months he has been especially critical of the Reagan administration's mix of monetary and fiscal policies, calling tax cuts and tight money the worst of both worlds. Many economists were asking yesterday whether the award was some kind of a signal from Sweden to the world.

Tobin has been especially good at keeping track of the theorizing of Friedman, who is at the University of Chicago, over the years. If John Kenneth Galbraith was the public antagonist, Jim Tobin was the counterweight to Friedman inside the profession, associates said.

Often in the late 1950s and early 1960s, it was Tobin who dominated the defense of the Keynesian citadel—usually on narrow, technical issues—against the the monetarist counterattack that in turn was led by Friedman. In Stockholm yesterday, the economist Assar Lindbeck told the Associated Press: "Tobin is a more eclectic, more common-sense economist than Friedman, with a more complex view of the world." He added, "He does not confine his analysis solely to money but considers the range of assets and debts."

Yet Tobin is also a "supply sider," at least in the sober, professional sense of the term. A framer of the Kennedy tax cut (enacted in 1964 after the President's death), an advocate of austere fiscal policy, Tobin with his fellow members of the Council of Economic Advisers under President John F. Kennedy foreshadowed many of the programs Reaganites now claim as their own.

His interest in the financial sector led him to a position of eminence in the investment world, largely throught his design of systems of judging portfolio management. Along the way, Tobin also devised a concept called "Q" for which economists are still looking for applications. "Q" is a relatively straightforward idea of the market value of an asset divided by its replacement cost: In good times it is more than one, in bad times it is less than one. For the American economy as a whole, it is far less than one today, and has been for a decade. Some graduate students at Yale wear sweatshirts emblazoned "Q."

Economists reacted joyously to the award. "It's no surprise. It's a very good choice. It's highly welcome," said Samuelson, America's first Nobel winner in economics. Economists who read a political message in the Bank of Sweden's selection of Tobin may have read too much into it. The award was evidence of an apparent preference by the prize-givers for contributions to science rather than politics. True, Tobin, a liberal, has been among the leading critics of Reaganomics. But he fits neatly in the line the committee has been following for a decade.

Previous Nobel prizes in economics have centered on the development of mathematical economics and econometric modeling, most of which took place under the auspices of the the Cowles Commission at the University of

Chicago in the 1940s. Ragnar Frisch and Jan Tinbergen were instrumental in putting the commission together; they shared the first economics prize in 1969. In subsequent years, it was given to Herbert Simon, Kenneth Arrow, Tjalling Koopmans, Lawrence Klein, all of whom did much of their work at Cowles, and to Friedman, Theodore Schultz and Samuelson, all of whom worked nearby and who were heavily influenced by Cowles. The only Americans to win the prize who had no connection to Cowles were Simon Kuznets and Wassily Leontieff.

And Tobin? He is the man who was selected to head the Cowles Commission when it moved to Yale in 1955. He served as its director from 1955-61 and 1964-65.

Raised in Champaign, Ill., Tobin personifies the qualities known around Yale as "shoe," a '50s synonym for "cool." A summa cum laude graduate of Harvard College in 1939, he served in the Office of Price Administration and on a destroyer in the Mediterranean during the war. He went through Navy officer's training school with the author Herman Wouk, who gave him an incidental part in his novel *The Caine Mutiny*. Tobin received his PhD from Harvard in 1947 and was a Junior Fellow there for three years before accepting a professor's post at Yale in 1950.

OCTOBER 14, 1981

First Jeff, Now Mutt

IN 1946, A PAIR OF YOUNG UNIVERSITY OF CHICAGO PROFESSORS BROUGHT OUT A tract called "Roofs or Ceilings, The Current Housing Problem." In it, Milton Friedman and George Stigler argued passionately against rent control in the post-war era. The price system was infinitely preferable as a way of rationing housing space, they said.

The pamphlet touched off a terrible ruckus—not because it was a plea for deregulation, but because it was too left wing for the tastes of the conservative foundation that sponsored its preparation. Friedman and Stigler had plumped "long-term measures" to achieve more equality of incomes. The Foundation For Economic Education, which had published the booklet, insisted on a footnote disassociating itself from the professors' egalitarian sentiments.

The authors were furious. The episode contributed substantially to the tradition of the University of Chicago economics department of staying away from the right-wing money men who seek out academics to write penny-dreadful justifications of the conduct of the rich.

Yesterday, this custom of perpendicularity once again paid off, as George Stigler was named the recipient of the Nobel Memorial Award in Economic Science. At 71, Stigler joined his lifelong friend Friedman and seven other Chicago alumni, teachers, students and research fellows as winners of the prize. The committee as much as designated Stigler the intellectual Father of Deregulation. But perhaps equally significant has been his role as a kind of city-father of the community of modern technical economics: A writer of history of thought, a strong voice proclaiming the importance of tradition, a reliable guide to useful departures from it.

Stigler wasted no time proclaiming his characteristic views to wire service reporters. The old joke that a single question put to three economists would produce four answers was "nonsense," Stigler said. "I may disagree with Paul Samuelson's politics, but I won't quarrel with his theory of revealed preference."

The Swedish Academy of Sciences, in giving the $157,000 award to Stigler, cited Stigler's studies of "industrial structures, functioning of markets, and causes and effects of public regulations."

A colleague, Gary Becker, said "two contributions stand out. He pioneered the economic analysis of the role of information and decisions, and the evaluations of the causes and consequences of public policy. He is the dominant person in the field of economic organization and has influenced the research and teaching of virtually every economist in the field," said Becker.

Edward Levi, former president of the University of Chicago, a law professor who was U.S. attorney general under former President Gerald Ford, said that Stigler's work "provides a factual and intellectual framework for understanding the importance and the dimension of the tasks of deregulation, and the costs that regulation can unwittingly impose on society."

Richard N. Rosett, dean of the Graduate School of Business, said that "for a quarter of a century, George Stigler's intellectual influence has pervaded the business school." Indeed, sections of the school's faculty are in many ways an adjunct to the economics department.

Stigler said the Nobel award had made him happier and richer. He said that the country could use the money, and that he felt "my career has already paid off. I had a job all along and I hardly missed a meal."

Stigler's friendship with Friedman is a monument; the University of Chicago bookstore sells T-shirts emblazoned with pictures of the tall Stigler walking with the short Friedman down a leafy Hyde Park street, an economic Mutt and Jeff.

Also significant is Stigler's friendship with Chicago English professor Norman Mclean, author of *A River Runs Through It*. Together, Mclean and Stigler epitomize what amounts to a Chicago style: Laconic, independent and tart. As Stigler put it in the preface to a volume of essays, "I promise not to sin again, often."

OCTOBER 21, 1982

A Victory for the Pure Theory Chapter

ECONOMICS IS THE SCIENCE OF CHOICE, ITS PRACTITIONERS SAY, AND THE CHOICE ITS leaders are making about what constitutes good science became clearer yesterday. If there was ever any doubt, the award of the Nobel Prize to Gerard Debreu confirms where the mainstream of economics flows. It flows down from the uplands of high theory to the plains of measurement.

Debreu earned the award for work on the mathematical foundations of general equilibrium economics done at the University of Chicago and at Yale University, during 11 years as a research assistant at the Cowles Commission. It is the sixth time the prize has been awarded for work performed at or near the Cowles Commission. The Commission is an extraordinary research program, spanning half a century, paid for by a wealthy Chicagoan named Alfred Cowles, who was disappointed by his and others' failure to forsee the Great Depression.

Not counting Paul Samuelson, who blazed the trail of mathematical economics, Cowles alumni who are Nobel laureates include Kenneth Arrow, Tjalling Koopmans, Lawrence R. Klein, Herbert Simon and James Tobin. "They give the prize for different things," said Harvard Prof. Otto Eckstein yesterday. "George Stigler won it for applications of theory to problems of policy; Laury Klein won it for his work in economic modeling; this one went to the pure theory chapter," he said.

Other colleagues said Debreu was in a sense completing work set out by Leon Walras, a French journalist and scholar whose recognition that economies could be described by systems of siumultaneous equations, has been called the "Magna Charta of economics."

Debreu's prize was also a victory for French culture. For 30 years, one of the more interesting phenomena in the recondite world of higher mathematics has been "the Bourbaki." Depending on who you talk to, Nicholas Bourbaki was a mythical 19th-century Russian émigré mathematician or an obscure French general, but in either case, the name was taken as collective synonym by three or four French mathematicians who set out to reformulate mathematics from the ground up in a series of texts and broadsides.

"The name is an in-joke," says MIT's Samuelson. "It's how the hotshots in Paris set about showing how smart they were." Nevertheless the work is deadly serious, he says. The Bourbaki offer "a sort of modern-day Euclid," a severely axiomatic approach with little concern for pedagogy, according to Harvard's John T. Tate.

Debreu's style, colleagues say, was heavily influenced by the Bourbaki approach—austere, logical and supremely self-confident. Harvard economist Hendrick Houthakker, for example, described Debreu yesterday as being "very French, very precise, a stickler for accuracy, otherwise a very friendly guy—but someone who does not like to get his hands dirty, so to speak." Although he lived here throughout the post-war period, Debreu resisted taking U.S. citizenship until 1975. Why then? The occasion for his decision is said, at least by several of his fellow economists, to have been the successful resolution of the Watergate crisis. He wanted to be a citizen after that.

Almost as interesting, in different ways, are the stories of two researchers who didn't get the prize, Abraham Wald and Lionel McKenzie. Each made essentially the same basic breakthrough in technique as Debreu. Looking back last summer on the history of mathematical economics, Debreu himself emphasized a remarkable quartet of papers written by Wald in Vienna 20 years before he had come to the same ideas. It was a case of premature discovery. "The papers that Wald wrote in the early 1930s had received no echo for nearly two decades, but in the early 1950s the time of proofs of existence of a general economic equilibrium had clearly come."

Likewise, Debreu noted how economist McKenzie, then at Duke University, had come to a similiar method of proving the existence of equilibrium in world trade, and presented his findings at the same meetings in Chicago—just one day after Arrow and Debreu. McKenzie, now at the University of Rochester, was chosen to introduce Debreu to a reunion of the Cowles group earlier this year.

Debreu went on puzzling out the mathematical implications of the theory of supply and demand. According to Eckstein, it was probably a little book, *The Theory of Value*, that established his independence from his earlier collaborator Kenneth Arrow and set him firmly on the path to his own Nobel Prize. Debreu's work on the theory of demand and on utility functions were a major part of his career as well, McKenzie said yesterday.

Happy as was the occasion of the award announced yesterday, there was a somewhat melancholy feeling in some quarters that it should come in a year in which Piero Sraffa and Joan Robinson died (only those living can be given the award).

Both Sraffa and Robinson, writing from Cambridge University, in English instead of mathematics, sparked controversies in their lifetimes that generated much light as well as furious heat. But neither one was honored by the Swedes.

"We don't know exactly why they didn't give it to her," said McKenzie yesterday of Mrs. Robinson. And MIT's Samuelson observed, "You know, Tolstoy never got the (Nobel) prize (for literature,) and (John) Steinbeck and Pearl Buck did; you have to judge the committee on their misses as well as their hits."

OCTOBER 18, 1983

"Most Will Not
Know Who He Is"

MUCH HAS BEEN MADE BY SOME ECONOMISTS OF JOAN ROBINSON'S CLAIM TO THE Nobel Award in economics. A member of the famous Cambridge University "Circus" to which John Maynard Keynes presented his General Theory for criticism, she became a formidable critic of the American receivers of his views. Yet despite her 40 years as a fiery and productive controversialist, she died last year unhonored in Stockholm.

Yesterday the Swedes fired back a fairly straight shot—perhaps signaling a certain respect for Robinson in having waited for her departure from the scene before making the award. Sir Richard Stone, a professor at Cambridge University, was honored yesterday for his development of the social accounting matrix (SAM), which permits a detailed analysis of various parts of a national economy that is not possible in any other way.

Some significance attaches to the fact that Stone had only a brief hour in the sun as the first head of the Applied Economics Department that Keynes founded at Cambridge, before being shouldered aside by Robinson and Roger Kahn—strong left-wing Keynesians who took over and claimed the mantle of the master. He became Leake Professor of Finance and Accounting, and they became famous.

The result was that while yesterday's Nobel Award to Stone came as little news to the top of the trade, it bestowed sudden fame on a man otherwise little known even to most economists. "This is a surprise," said Arjo Klamer, a Wellesley College economist who is author of a survey of schools of economic thought. "Most will not know who he is."

Stone joins Simon Kuznets and Wassily Leontief in one skein of prizewinners, the empiricists. Another skein consists of theorists, and a third is of essentially philosophical economists. The award, established in 1969 by the Swedish Central Bank amid a certain amount of controversy, continues to gain credibility.

According to Graham Pyatt, one of Stone's leading disciples, now at the World Bank, "What Stone has done is to move away from double-entry bookkeeping to single-entry, which permits an integrated picture of the whole economy. The Leontief input-output table does for the intra-industry part of the economy, Stone's work has generalized this. It shows the fabric of the economy and not just the aggregates, in the way that Leontief showed the fabric of industry."

Hollis Chenery, a professor of economics at Harvard University, said: "A specific application is that it portrays the effects of having to go through the ringer the way Brazil has, or the Philippines or Mexico. It gives you a way to see which income recipients are being hurt by which measures. . . . Half of all the work in the field or more has been done in the last five or six years, much of it stimulated by the desire to look more at income distribution and employment rather than just aggregate GNP."

A secondary curiosity was noted yesterday by some. Apparently the citation by the Swedish Academy of Sciences didn't mention Stone's contributions to the theory of consumer demand. Many economists think that this work overshadows even his contribution to national income accounting, for under his tutelage, the modern econometric approach to modeling demand flowered. The Nobel Award committee had been fully apprised of the contribution. Yet it apparently chose not to mention it. Why?

The best guess yesterday was that the Swedes felt that to mention consumer demand would have meant that the award should have been shared. That could have opened up a field for mischief, presumably—though of what sort isn't clear. So the Swedes chose the easy way out. Meanwhile, a Festshrift volume in honor of Stone, edited by Angus Deaton of Princeton University, is in press. It should sell better than expected.

OCTOBER 19, 1984

The Architect
of the Life-Cycle

TAKE A LONG WALK ACROSS BOSTON AND OBSERVE THE GREAT INEQUALITY OF WEALTH.
See the genteel suburbs to the west, the great houses of the North Shore, the
old estates to the south, the showplaces of the Back Bay, the new apartments by the Charles River in Cambridge. Think about the claim on power
and resources that these dwellings imply.

Now observe the working-class neighborhoods of the old industrial cities, and the tumbledown buildings of Chelsea and Roxbury. This wide
disparity between rich and poor has remained much the same, decade to
decade.

Why and how does this state of affairs persist? How much of this wealth
is earned and saved during the lifetime of the well-to-do? How much of it
is inherited? How is it that the rich seem to stay rich, generation to generation? Beyond these fundamental questions lie the answers to pressing
problems of public policy: Is the current level of government borrowing
harmful to our economic future? Does Social Security impinge on investment? Are we in danger of eating our seed corn?

Franco Modigliani, who will receive the Nobel Prize for economics in
Stockholm Tuesday, is a leading specialist on how these questions are
formally asked and answered. The 67-year-old scholar at Massachusetts
Institute of Technology is the principal author of what economists call the
"life-cycle" hypothesis—itself now nearly 35 years old.

After receiving news of the award last month, he immediately rebuked
President Reagan for coining political positions that contradicted virtually
all the findings of Modigliani's 40 years of investigations.

"I think one of the big surprises of our life . . . is how a man like the
president could have started out, could have gotten elected on the grounds
that the deficit was the greatest curse that ever occurred and caused all
kinds of harm. . . . Then this man has suddenly turned around and . . .
somehow his administration explains that the deficit does not reduce sav-

ings," Modigliani said. "We are ruining (the future of our) youth, we are ruining the rest of the world, and all of that because the president says that the last thing we're going to do is raise taxes. Well, hell!" he snorted.

Modigliani told a press conference, "I sometimes think that my work on this subject was colored by the savings bank where I was banking at the time when I was working on this. Their motto was, 'Save it when you need it least, have it when you need it most.'" He paid tribute to his collaborator on the early life-cycle work, Richard Brumberg, a graduate student and close friend who died of a brain tumor at the age of 25, just as the method was being introduced.

The view that people routinely vary their savings across the trajectory of their lifetime—building up funds when they are young, drawing down when they are old—sounds commonsensical today, Modigliani said, but before he wrote, the conventional view among technical economists was that savings activity was confined mainly to the rich. His achievement was to introduce the life-cycle behavior into the austere mathematical models with which economists work.

The life-cycle approach has since proved to be a tool adopted by economists of every persuasion to study everything from retirement schemes to taxes, with a single fundamental amendment. Modigliani said that the main important addition was made by Harvard University's Martin Feldstein and Alicia Munnell of the Federal Reserve Bank of Boston, who had shown that Social Security could affect the timing of retirement, and therefore that it might have unanticipated effects on the savings rate.

The Nobel Prize citation also mentioned Modigliani's work on corporate finance, a secondary theme throughout his career. With Merton Miller of the University of Chicago, he wrote in 1961 the paper that first advanced what has become known since as the "efficient markets" hypothesis, arguing that information about the future quickly becomes incorporated in the market price of securities. And he has been a continuous contributor to the exploding literature of corporate finance ever since. (He is the only man ever to be elected president of both the American Economic Association and the American Finance Association. A university professor, he holds a dual appointment at MIT as well, as a member of both the economics department and the Sloan School of Management.)

Alas, as if to confirm the worst fears of those who think that economics is an undercooked science, the award cloaks much controversy about what exactly is implied by it. At a meeting last summer to celebrate the lifetime accomplishments of Modigliani, his friend and former close collaborator

Albert Ando (along with Arthur Kennickell of the Federal Reserve system) asked how much support there was for dominant interpretation of the life cycle in household data for the United States and Japan.

There was not much, they concluded. Attempts to use it to explain very large-scale empirical studies must be judged "a complete failure," they wrote in a survey of the published work. "We started with one of the most elegant theories in economics, and we could not find a way to fit abundant bodies of data into its neat framework," they concluded. (A cheerful Modigliani immediately set to work defending his hypothesis at the meeting, of course.)

Somewhat more generally, the University of California's Thomas Mayer wrote a decade ago, "Of all the many tests which have been undertaken by friends of the (life-cycle) hypothesis, not a single one supports it . . . I therefore conclude that the . . . hypothesis is definitely invalidated."

So, are the Swedes honoring a guy who made a bad guess? Of course not. It is well over three centuries since Francis Bacon noted that the fundamental tenet of modern science is that "truth emerges more readily from error than confusion," and if Modigliani's work did not pin down, once and for all, the reasons for observed patterns of economic growth, savings and wealth, his conceptual breakthrough did make possible the formulation of efficient questions about these topics on a new level of concreteness.

Thus the Nobel Prize "should have come sooner," says Mayer, the critic of a decade ago. "Super-well-deserved," says Harvard's Lawrence H. Summers, who perhaps has done more than any other scholar to controvert Modigliani's findings, at least on one level. "The crucial idea was that you should look at utility-maximizing through time, and that consumption-smoothing was an important part of savings decisions," says Summers.

But the funny thing is that Modigliani has got himself crosswise with most of the rest of the profession over the way this forward-looking behavior on the part of people actually works itself out in life. Modigliani thinks that most people save only for themselves—and not for their children.

"Franco thinks that the only substantial bequests that are left are left by people who are caught by surprise by the grim reaper, people who haven't yet spent all that they intended to spend," says colleague Robert Solow. "Many other economists don't think that, and there is plenty of controversy on that point."

What is the evidence? Summers lists some of the reasons for arguing that bequests are an important part of savings decisions. For one thing, he says, there was savings behavior before there was retirement. "In 1900, there was much less retirement, and life expectancy was shorter, but there was a higher savings rate," he says. The implication: that people save even when they know they'll go on earning.

Then, too, it is difficult to find evidence that wealth declines the way it is supposed to in Modigliani's view. "The key thing in the old theory is that you decumulated wealth in retirement," says Summers. "But in fact, the data tend to suggest that the savings rate among 80-year olds is positive." Still another skein of evidence involves the observation that the demand for annuities, reverse life insurance products, is far less than the life-cycle hypothesis would predict. "Circuit breaker" programs, which permit the elderly to postpone their property taxes until after they die, at which time the tax bill is paid out of proceeds of sale of a house, are not popular either.

But the most persuasive points are the most fundamental, according to Summers. One is that the inequality of wealth is very much greater than the inequality of earnings. Bequests are a natural explanation for the fact. Moreover, consumption patterns don't look the way a simple life-cycle story says they should. "It's not true that most of the earnings come early in life, and that consumption comes late in life, as the hypothesis suggests."

None of which has persuaded Modigliani. When Summers and Lawrence Kotlikoff published a paper concluding that up to 80 percent of existing wealth has been inherited, Modigliani checked their algebra, changed a few definitions and concluded that only 20 percent of wealth came in the form of bequests. His old friend Ando says Modigliani still calls up at intervals to argue that bequests are not of very great importance. Even his close associates sometimes wonder aloud why Modigliani insists on the unimportance of inheritance.

But none doubt that he is his own best exemplar. Upon learning of his Nobel award, which carries a stipend of more than $200,000, Modigliani said he would do what his theory predicted. With one eye on the time horizon of his life, he bought airplane tickets for a grand European tour for a dozen members of his family.

OCTOBER 16, 1985—DECEMBER 8, 1985

The Skeptic's Reward

James Buchanan, America's newest Nobel laureate in economics, came by his resentment of the Eastern establishment the old-fashioned way: he inherited it. The grandson of a populist Tennessee governor of the 1890s, he grew up reading yellowed old pamphlets attacking the robber barons of Wall Street. Not surprisingly, life turned out pretty much the way he expected it to be. As Buchanan told Jane Seaberry of the *Washington Post* last week, discrimination radicalized him further during the World War II years: "I went to midshipman's school in New York. It's a long story, but there was a lot of obvious discrimination against all of us who went to small southern colleges, despite our records. . . .

"They chose the cadet officers without testing, people from Harvard and Yale, and it was especially onerous in my particular case because we were allocated to platoons and companies by alphabet. I was in a platoon with As and Bs and it turned out that we had no Harvard or Yalies with an initial A or B. But they had too many down in the Rs and Ss. So they imported a Rockefeller to be the head of our company. That kind of discrimination hurts you."

Earlier this month, the Swedish Academy of Sciences took steps to salve the wound, better late than never. It awarded Buchanan the 1986 Nobel Memorial Award in Economics. In doing so, the academy did something for which the world has been waiting 18 years, ever since the prize was established in 1968. It did something controversial. It threw a slow-ticking bomb into the domestic politics of Sweden, Europe and the United States.

Buchanan, 67, professor of economics at George Mason University in Fairfax, Va., is the patron saint of monetary constitutions, tax caps, balanced budget amendments and the like. He's been involved, directly or indirectly, in nearly every significant skirmish of the American tax revolt, from Propositions 1 and 13 in California, in 1973 and 1978, to Proposition 2½ in Massachusetts, to Proposition 6 in Michigan, to the Balanced Budget Amendment. On the general desirability of these devices, professional economists are hardly united. But in acknowledging the intellectual power of the case Buchanan has made for the need to set some kind of limits on governments, the Swedes have empowered a bold voice in behalf of a class of citizens and activists who otherwise might still be leafing through the literature of the John Birch Society looking for respectable intellectual support for their intuitions. Far more than Ronald Reagan's 1980 election, Buchanan's Nobel Prize represents the ultimate triumph of the pre-analytic vision that was the 1964 presidential campaign of Sen. Barry Goldwater.

Not that Buchanan's message is altogether new to economics. The great Joseph Schumpeter, as recalled recently by Benjamin Barber, "suggested that democracy was little more than the name of a system in which elites competed via the ballot box for the support of an otherwise docile electorate, whose sole exercise of liberty was the occasional filling out of a ballot." Colin Clark, a pioneer in development economics, postulated that there was a limit of around 25 percent of GNP which could properly be spent through borrowing and taxation. Beyond that limit, he said, tax and interest burdens would become unacceptable to the citizenry, and the monetary authorities would be pressured to inflate the burden of the debt away. Clark's idea was howled out of economics.

What made Buchanan successful was his adherence to high standards of economic argument. In a stream of papers beginning in the early 1950s, Buchanan began potting away at the foundations of mainstream public finance. If we are to take economics seriously, he wrote, "we then quite naturally bring into the analysis complex as well as simple exchange, with complex exchange being defined as that contractual agreement process that goes beyond the economist's magic number two, beyond the simple two-person, two-commodity barter-setting. The emphasis shifts, directly and immediately, to all processes of voluntary agreement among persons." Despite nearly continuous squabbles with establishment authorities—Kermit Gordon of the Brookings Institution described Buchanan's intent to found a Thomas Jefferson Center at the University of Virginia to pursue his research program in the 1950s to be a "particularly objectionable" example of ideological bias—Buchanan made progress because of the sheer clarity of his views.

"Economics when Jim Buchanan came along was dominated by the idea of all these market failures," says Paul Craig Roberts, a Georgetown University professor who was among Buchanan's Virginia students. "But those analyses just assumed that the government was always a success. Look at any of the early editions of Paul Samuelson's textbook, that's the way it was written. The basic postulate of self-interest was suspended when it came to public finance. Nobody was maximizing for himself in government; there was only the public good. It was just basically silly. What happens to this person when he moves from Wall Street to the Treasury Department? He goes from being Saul to being St. Paul? You can't just suspend your basic postulate like that. They were wide open for the public choice movement."

Just because they recognized the logic of his views didn't mean the economic mainstream had to like them, however. Buchanan attracted a second-generation following among liberal economists—notably Harvard-trained Mancur Olson—but relatively few converts. Instead, he and co-author Gordon Tullock (who has been only slightly less influential than Buchanan) turned out a steady stream of well-trained graduate students, first at the University of Virginia, then at the Virginia Polytechnic Institute.

The trouble was, the new PhDs didn't find jobs in mainstream institutions either. "We were all heretics who were excluded from academic life by the pure thinkers," says Paul Craig Roberts, who more than any other single player wrote the legislation that brought about the tax cuts in 1981. "We had to make our way in policy circles instead. That's why so many of Jim Buchanan's students turned up in the Reagan administration."

Current chief presidential economics adviser James Miller is the senior Virginian in the administration today; policy think-tanks such as the Heritage Foundation and the Cato Institute are full of them.

Yet public choice theorizing still hasn't really caught on in the major centers of economic learning. At the University of Chicago, George Stigler, Sam Pelzman and Gary Becker can be said to be in some sense public choice theorists, yet Chicago never hired Buchanan out of his Virginia obscurity. The unwillingness to incorporate the public choice skepticism about government failure cannot all be blamed on an unwillingness to listen; a parallel and in many ways analogous criticism of the way that mainstream economics treated human expectations, led by Chicagoan Robert Lucas, has taken the profession by storm instead.

The experience of his lonely 40-year campaign has only added to the sense of deprivation with which Buchanan began. He now routinely takes aim at the analytic turn which economics has taken since he was a graduate student in the days after World War II. The leaders of the profession today "seem to be ideological eunuchs," he has written. "Their interest lies in the purely intellectual properties of the models with which they work, and they seem to get their kicks from the discovery of proofs of propositions relevant only for their own fantasy lands."

Now the Swedes honored the most unreconstructed cynic in economics for his formulation of irreversible "way-of-seeing." The question of rules that economic societies adopt, the reasons that they adopt them, and the superiority of some sets of rules to others: all these are on the table in economics to stay. The implications of what is now known remain to be worked out, as much in the political arena as in the seminar room. For perhaps the first time, the news from an economic laureate's December lecture in Stockholm is going to be something approaching hot stuff.

OCTOBER 26, 1986

Regulating Government

OVERSHADOWED BY THE CONTRAPRENEURS SCANDAL LAST WEEK WAS THE SPECTACLE of the Administration skirmishing with itself along quite a different axis, this one a proposal for a national insurance system to cover catastrophic illnesses of the sorts that usually lead to prohibitively expensive stays in nursing homes. President Reagan himself, in his State of the Union address last year, ordered that the plan be drawn up.

But when Dr. Otis R. Bowen, the Secretary of Health and Human Services, earlier this month proposed beefing up Medicare by offering coverage for all kinds of acute problems for an optional premium of $59 a year, with an annual deductible of $2,000, the White House promptly leaked a memo from its chief economic adviser opposing the plan on grounds that it would be costly and inefficient.

Beryl Sprinkel, the chairman of the Council of Economic Advisers, argued that Bowen's proposal would strengthen a government monopoly at the expense of evolving private markets, and that it would undermine the recent tax bill. The issue has just barely begun to be ventilated—nearly everyone agrees some new forms of widespread catastrophic loss-sharing are desirable—but some of the angles were already clear. Legislators like Sen. Edward M. Kennedy lined up behind Bowen, while others supported the administration's position. Kennedy said, "If the president and his advisers are listening, they will hear 28 million elderly Americans saying 'Thank God for Dr. Bowen.'"

Meanwhile, James McGill Buchanan of George Mason University is returning home from Stockholm, having accepted the Nobel Memorial Prize in economics for his pioneering contributions to the analysis of pork-barrel politics. Buchanan's award was given for analytically and systematically calling into question the motives of politicians and bureaucrats who plump for programs like national catastrophic health insurance, and nobody quite knows what to make of his status as America's newest Nobel economics laureate. There was very little hoopla in the press last week, and scholarly economics is in something of swivet over the award. Many people, including some senior scholars, figure Buchanan didn't deserve the prize at all. Many others figure it should have been shared.

One fellow who didn't share in the prize is Gordon Tullock, Buchanan's longtime partner, who says he firmly expected to be rewarded, too, until he woke up that morning in October and learned his name had been left off the citation. Tullock is one of many deserving people who didn't get the Nobel Prize this year, and looking at them provides an unusual glimpse at social geography of economics.

(For an introduction to the thought of Buchanan and Tullock, the layman can scarcely do better than the recently-published *Regulating Government*, by Dwight R. Lee and Richard B. McKenzie. The material is a little raw, barely cleansed of its snappy tax-revolt titles—"Malice in Plunderland," for example. But it is very lucid, and it contains all the themes with which modern-day liberals must come to grips).

Tullock, a University of Chicago-trained lawyer, spent a decade in Asia in the Foreign Service after World War II then resigned to write a book about bureaucracy. During a post-doctoral year at the University of Virginia, he hooked up with James Buchanan, another Chicagoan, and the two have been collaborating on and off ever since—most notably on a 1962 book, *The Calculus of Consent*. Where Buchanan has gravitated ever more toward philosophical issues in economics, Tullock remained interested in applied economics of all sorts—especially in the development of constitutional rules to govern economic interest groups, though his publications range from biology ("the coal tips bird as careful shopper") to criminal justice. In Mark Blaug's book on the 100 greatest economists since Keynes, his vista is described this way: "It is not always easy to see a common thread in Tullock's works: He is almost too fertile and throws off so many ideas in so many directions that the connecting links between them threaten to disappear from view."

One of Tullock's specialties is the analysis of "rent-seeking" behavior; indeed, he has a fair claim to have invented it as a heading of economic analysis. By rents, economists don't mean just what landlords collect; they mean the extra premium that the owner of any unique factor of production—a temporary monopolist—collects over the next-best form of activity. High baseball salaries are mostly economic rent in this sense, adjusting for what players might earn at the car wash. So are the hefty returns that entrepreneurs and inventors are forever seeking. It was rent that the OPEC nations were collecting. It is excessive rents that Sprinkel fears in a system that extends Medicare insurance. And it is rent that companies are seeking to avoid when they hire Washington lawyers to run interference for them with the government.

According to Tullock, a major cost in any modern economy is avoiding interference from government—in the dominant form of bribery in many societies, in the form of legal compliance in many others. The magnitude of aggregate rent-seeking is in some sense a measure of the overall "imperfection" in the competitive operation of the economy.

Rent-seeking is, therefore, a fairly sturdy framework for thinking about the deregulation of industry that swept out of the Carter and then the Reagan administrations. To the extent that he contributed to that seachange of opinion, Tullock is surely entitled to a slice of the award that Buchanan received.

Tullock, naturally, is not the only figure who has done distinguished work in the vicinity of the idea that individual interest groups will use government to try to further their own gain. There is Anthony Downs, for example, who first published *An Economic Theory of Democracy* in 1957, containing many of the insights that James Buchanan was to pursue for the next 30 years. There was Ann Krueger, who coined the term "rent-seeking" in 1974, and Jagdish Bhagwati, the distinguished international economist from Columbia University who pursued this idea of "directly unproductive activity" where it led. ("It's interesting," says Tullock, "that all three of us have had extensive experience in the Orient, where overt rent-seeking behavior is far more common than in the West.")

Indeed, if the Swedish economists who make the Nobel decision had been looking for some way to "balance" the award to the right-wing Buchanan, they could have cited Hungarian economist Janos Kornai as well. His analyses of the failures of central planning systems nicely complement Buchanan's criticisms of "government failures" in the West.

In the end it was Buchanan whom the Swedes chose, perhaps because his work told them much about their society. The talk of Stockholm last week was a survey by journalist Anders Isaksson on the ancestry of 209 Social Democratic Party functionaries. It shows an intricate pattern of intimate connection over several generations, of parents, children, brothers, sisters and spouses claiming many of the best jobs in the party hierarchy. They constitute, Isaksson argues, a "governing class" that has thrived over half a century by offering ever more social insurance of every conceivable sort to its electorate—"Swedish Kennedys" in effect. Many Swedes feel even more acutely than Americans the need for the kind of economic constitutionalism that is the distant promise of Buchanan and Tullock's work.

DECEMBER 14, 1986

The Man Who Discovered "Technical Change"

ROBERT M. SOLOW, A PROFESSOR AT THE MASSACHUSETTS INSTITUTE OF TECHNOLogy, was awarded the 1987 Nobel Prize for Economics yesterday for pioneering studies in economic growth.

Solow, 63, an unrepentant Keynesian with strong views of the desirability for government leadership in the economic sphere, immediately obliged reporters at a crowded morning press conference at MIT, criticizing President Reagan, drinking champagne and making jokes.

A man whose wit and clarity of expression are well-known, who nevertheless declined repeated pleas by publishers to write a popular book, was finally in the spotlight.

"If this is what it means to be famous, I want to go back to being just plain old Professor Solow," he said. "I had trouble getting my underwear on for the telephone ringing."

The MIT community was delighted; so was Harvard, where Solow went to college and did his graduate work; so were economists generally. Solow is an institute professor at MIT and a former president of the American Economic Association. He is the third MIT professor, the second in three years, to receive a Nobel Award in Economics. Solow's long-term research partner, Paul Samuelson, and Franco Modigliani are the others.

The citation by the Swedish Academy of Sciences zeroed in on Solow's contribution to growth theory, a highly mathematized branch of technical

economics that had a vogue after Solow published a pair of nearly impenetrable technical papers in 1956 and 1957.

Solow said yesterday: "It is easy to list things that might contribute to
economic growth. The problem is, as we say, to make a model, to understand how these things interreact, and to do it in such a way that you might
have a prayer of measuring it. . . . The surprising conclusion was that
technological change looms much larger than capital investment. . . . Silicon Valley is the sort of thing I'm talking about."

Robert Lucas, a University of Chicago theorist, said: "He influenced my
whole generation . . . with a kind of rough-and-ready style, not high statistical theory. It is a knack for choosing what kinds of economic theory you
expect to be useful."

David Colander, a professor of economics at Middlebury College, said:
"He is the most thoroughly reasonable of all economists. He exudes sensibility, and nobody better understands economics, both its limits and its
possibilities."

"After he made a fundamental contribution to the literature on growth,"
recalled Hendrick Houthakker, a Harvard professor, "he went to Washington and persuaded the Kennedy administration to set growth targets
through the Organization for Economic Cooperation and Development. Then
he served on the National Commission on Employment, which helped
persuade labor, especially George Meany, to accept technical change rather
than to resist it."

A leading Keynesian, Solow is a proponent of a school that had failed to
persuade many younger technical economists of its relevance. A central
tenet with which he is associated, the trade-off between inflation and unemployment, has been eclipsed.

And his basic theoretical insight—that pure university learning and
basic and applied research has in some sense been more instrumental in
fueling the upward climb of American industry than the capital supplied by
Wall Street and the banks—has been hijacked by supply siders who have
all but ignored the analytic tradition in which Solow has stood fast.

"The best thing you can say about Reaganomics is that it probably
happened in a fit of inattention," he said. "I would like to see the president
stop this nonsense about how 'I will never raise taxes over my dead body.'"

The Keynesians' time may come again, but the exuberance of yesterday's
press conference was undercut by the consciousness of the failure of later
generations to carry through on the promises of the New Frontier.

Deprived of a central place in the current consensus of economic theorizing, Solow instead has served to his colleagues as a model of good citizenship. James Poterba, a junior colleague, said, "He sets an impeccable example in every realm you can name."

Certainly nobody ever went more assiduously about the housekeeping tasks of the community of technical economics. "He's the softest touch there is for committees and commissions," said Princeton economist Alan Blinder, a former student.

Moreover, Solow has become a quiet Boston institution over the years. He lives with his wife, Barbara, who is also an economist, in a converted wharf on Boston's waterfront during the school year and on Martha's Vineyard in the summer. He sails avidly.

A former Junior Fellow at Harvard, Solow is said to have been on a short list for candidates for the presidency of the university before Derek Bok was selected. He is a former member of the President's Council of Economic Advisers and served for three years as chairman of the board of directors of the Federal Reserve Bank in Boston.

Frank Morris, the Boston bank's president, said yesterday: "He can operate on almost any level of abstraction that the situation requires. If you have a bunch of econometricians, throwing around algebraic equations, he can talk to them. But when it came to explaining something technical to our board, he was sensational."

OCTOBER 22, 1987

... For What
He Did
in the War

THE FATHER OF MODERN FRENCH ECONOMICS YESTERDAY WON THE NOBEL MEMORIAL
Award in Economic Science towards the end of career marked with profound ironies. Maurice Allais, 77, said he had all but given up hope of
earning the prize for a skein of work he began publishing during the Nazi
Occupation. "It was not till now that we discovered his greatness," Swedish
economist Assar Lindbeck told a Stockholm news conference. "Allais has
been studied by us for many years and we are now certain he is a giant."

Allais' fame rests partly on a couple of books, the 900-page *In Search of
an Economic Discipline* in 1943 and *Economics and Interest* in 1947. Un-
translated for the most part, the books have been little read beyond the
French-speaking world. Yet it was the rigorous grounding they offered for
the study of general equilibrium among markets and the accompanying
efficiency that was singled out yesterday by the citation accompanying the
announcement of the prize.

In fact the same discoveries had been made separately at more or less the
same time by John Hicks in England and Paul Samuelson in the United
States. Published in English, Samuelson's and Hicks' contributions swept
the English-speaking economic world and laid the foundations for modern
technical analysis. Samuelson won the Nobel Prize in 1970; Hicks in 1972.

"It is a very interesting prize," said MIT's Paul Krugman yesterday.
"You couldn't call the work seminal, because nothing changed as a result.
On the other hand, it compares favorably with Hicks' *Value and Capital*
and Samuelson's *Foundations of Economic Analysis*. It raises interesting
philosophical issues, like the proverbial tree falling unheard in the forest."

Allais also made contributions in other areas of economics as well,
including the theories of capital and of money, but it was a 1953 paper
extending his theories to the domain of risk-bearing—it was unmentioned

in the citation—that has kept Allais at the forefront of technical economics, according to Stanford's Kenneth Arrow, another Nobel laureate.

In it, Allais argued against the hypothesis of "expected utility," and backed up his thesis with a series of questionnaires designed to illuminate consumers' choices under circumstances of risk and uncertainty.

Indeed, when Allais experimented with a roomful of top-flight theoretical economists at a celebrated meeting in France in 1952, Arrow recalled, the answers given suggested the scholars wouldn't behave according to their own axioms when confronted with the certainty of short-term gain against the possibility of long-term windfalls.

The striking results weren't tabulated for 15 years, Arrow recalled, but Allais, meanwhile, won his argument utterly in Europe and eventually has seen the tide turn in his favor in America, in the work of psychologists like Stanford's Amos Tversky and Harvard's Richard Herrnstein, and of questionnaire-wielding economists like Yale's Robert Shiller.

As much as anything, Allais' award was taken to be a recogition of the spreading influence of French mathematical economists is the now tightly-integrated scholarly world. An engineer by training, Allais yesterday told the Paris news conference he had been converted to economics by a trip to the United States during the Depression. After the war, he taught a generation of students including Gerard Debreu (the 1983 Nobel laureate), Edmond Malinvaud (a likely future winner) and Marcel Boiteaux (who recently retired as head of France's electricity monopoly.)

Allais has published something like 1,500 scholarly papers, including studies in history and geophysics. "Now I can afford to continue my work," he said yesterday of the $400,000 prize." Allais has been a professor at the École Nationale Supérieure des Mines de Paris and director of the school's economic research institute since 1944.

OCTOBER 19, 1988

Gone Fishin'

WHEN THE TELEPHONE RANG AT TRYGVE HAAVELMO'S HOUSE IN OSLO YESTERDAY morning, there was none of the usual surprised-by-joy reaction of a fellow learning he had been awarded the $455,000 Nobel Economics Prize. Instead, Haavelmo was vexed about being called at home. He told the Reuter reporter: "I don't like the idea of such prizes. I'm not going to talk about this on the phone, and I haven't thought it through. Don't write anything." The 78-year-old theorist then went out and was not heard from for the rest of the day. Not even Norwegian national television could get through. The neighbors guessed that he had gone for a walk in the forest, as is his regular habit.

It was another peculiar twist in one of the strangest and most remarkable stories in modern economics. For recognition came mysteriously late to Trygve Haavelmo, at a time when the ultimate practicality of his contribution is open to question as never before—indeed, just when the tide of scholarly opinion seems to be shifting in favor of his archrival.

The story began in 1940, with Haavelmo as a 29-year-old refugee from the Nazi invasion of Norway, writing away on his doctoral thesis in the stacks of Harvard University's Widener Library, one of a handful of scholars plucked from wartime Europe as Rockefeller Fellows. His teacher, Ragnar Frisch, had been interned by the Quisling government; Haavelmo became worried and stayed close to the Norwegian mission in New York.

When he was done, Paul Samuelson of the Massachusetts Institute of Technology recalled yesterday, "being unpretentious, he simply typed up the results in blue ditto and circulated it widely." Haavelmo's title: "The Statistical Implications of a System of Simultaneous Equations."

The result, according to the citation by the Swedish Academy of Sciences that accompanied the Nobel Memorial Prize in Economic Science, quickly transformed a major branch of modern economics from a textbook enterprise to the combination of economic theory, probability analysis and empirical measurement that it is today. "He is the father of modern econometrics," Assar Lindbeck, the Nobel committee chairman, told reporters yesterday.

What Haavelmo did was to solve a problem that economists know today as the "identification" problem—meaning the scouting-out of the economic relationships underlying the welter of data about money and production that economists collect.

Before Haavelmo, economists, like other scientists, relied on a form of statistical analysis called "least squares" for calculating the significance of dependent variables. The problem, according to University of Illinois economist Roy Epstein, the author of a history of early econometrics, was that the least squares methods assumed that the direction of causation was clear, that one side of the equation clearly influenced the other.

"What Haavelmo did was to develop a mathematics, based on probability theory, for dealing with a system of equations where X influenced Y and Y influenced X and both influenced Z and vice versa," Epstein said yesterday. "That's what supply and demand are all about."

With speed as happy as it was rare in economics, at least in those days, Haavelmo's work was eagerly taken up by leading members in the field—especially during World War II by researchers of the Cowles Commission at the University of Chicago, including Tjalling Koopmans and Lawrence Klein, both future Nobel laureates. Klein was the first to use the new methods to build an econometric model; as he later put it, "The Keynesian theory was simply asking to be cast in an empirical mold."

Having decisively picked the lock, however, the pipe-smoking Haavelmo all but quit the field of econometrics, to the astonishment of his colleagues. He returned to Norway in 1947. "He would have rowed home, if he could," Samuelson remembered yesterday. Haavelmo assumed Frisch's professorship at the University of Oslo, but pursued pure theory, lecturing to the Econometrics Association as president in 1957 on the importance of better thinking about causal relationships. He published a book on investment theory in 1960 and became increasingly absorbed in the gap between the rich and poor nations.

When Harvard econometrician Zvi Griliches visited Haavelmo in 1967, he found him more interested in trout fishing than in current economics. Yesterday, economists mused on the Swedish Academy's lag in awarding the prize to Haavelmo. Frisch, his teacher, had shared the very first economics prize in 1970 with Jan Tinbergen. Koopmans had been honored in 1975, Klein in 1980. The significance of Haavelmo's contribution had been immediately clear. So why the wait?

Most answers yesterday mentioned the economist Herman Wold. Like Haavelmo, Wold was born in Norway, but he emigrated to Sweden at an early age. He spent his wartime years in Stockholm, theorizing on the most abstruse questions of economic explanation, like Haavelmo— but coming to nearly opposite conclusions. And in the years after World War II, Wold conducted an increasingly bitter rear-guard action against identification and simultaneity as suitable solutions to the problem of understanding economic causation.

Far less widely liked than Haavelmo, but more Swedish than the Swedes, the 81-year-old Wold lives in Gothenburg today. "Every time the economic Nobel committee had a meeting, there were these two guys staring them in the face," says a Cambridge economist who asks not to be identified. "Who knows why they did what they did?"

For in the strangest twist of all, the work done by Haavelmo in the 1940s has been searchingly questioned in the 1980s by a group of researchers marching under the banner of dynamic modelling. Led by "rational expectations" theorists, including the University of Minnesota's Christopher Sims and Thomas Sargent, the University of Chicago's Robert Lucas and Northwestern University's Nancy Stokey, this line of inquiry has questioned many of the optimistic presuppositions of the econometrics based on Haavelmo's statistical framework.

The result, however, as noted in an authoritative article by M. Hashem Peharan in the *The New Palgrave Dictionary of Economics*, has been a wave of disappointment in the possibilities of the old econometrics and a new wave of interest in the kind of recursive mathematical tools propounded by Herman Wold 40 years ago. [Mary Morgan dealt with many of these issues when she published *The History of Econometric Ideas* in 1991. In an attempt to make accessible the always difficult, sometimes thrilling story of the adoption of modern statistical reasoning by economists, she even devoted one chapter to a fictional exchange of letters between the early pioneers. *Then* she turned to Haavelmo and the argument about his work.]

In other words, the bright hopes that were celebrated yesterday by the Nobel committee are today in doubt—giving new meaning, perhaps, to the fundamental Baconian conviction among scientists that "truth emerges more readily from error than confusion."

None of it seemed to be very much of the moment to Haavelmo in Oslo yesterday, as he sought to escape the attention of the press. He promised to issue a written statement eventually. "The prize is quite irrelevant to the real issues," he told the Associated Press. "I'm exhausted, and I have nothing more to say."

OCTOBER 12, 1989

Finance
Comes of Age

THREE AMERICAN FOUNDERS OF MODERN CORPORATE FINANCE WON THE NOBEL PRIZE for economics yesterday for a series of contributions in the 1950s and 1960s in which they created the intellectual framework with which money managers evaluate the risks and rewards of their investments.

Everyone from newly minted MBAs and lofty pension managers to Eastern European entrepreneurs uses their tools to calculate the cost of capital and the rate of return on various investments, mainly stocks and bonds.

• Harry Markowitz, 63, of the City University of New York, was cited by the Swedish Academy of Sciences for developing the theory of portfolio choice.

• Merton Miller, 67, was honored for work on the effect of firms' capital structure and dividend policy on their market price.

• William Sharpe, 56, was hailed as the author of the capital asset pricing model, the device that gave Wall Street the concept of the "beta"—a coefficient designed to measure the riskiness and volatility of a particular stock relative to the performance of the stock market as a whole.

It was the first time that the Swedish Nobel committee cited three economists, though dual awards have been common enough in the 22 years since the prize was first awarded in 1969.

Several finance specialists said the late John V. Lintner Jr. of the Harvard Business School would have shared the prize had he lived, for having devised a capital asset pricing model in parallel with Sharpe. Lintner died in 1983.

In Stockholm, economist Assar Lindbeck, secretary to the Swedish Academy, said, "Each of them gave one building block. The theory would have been incomplete if any one of them had been missing. Together they created a complete picture of theory for the financial markets which has had great importance."

Colleagues said the three men never worked together much, but rather built on one another's work in journals, over a period of 10 years. Miller, a Boston Latin graduate and a member of the Harvard College Class of 1944, spent his war years at the Treasury Department "trying to think of new taxes."

He turned up at Carnegie Tech in Pittsburgh in 1953—it was then the center of the new wave in business schools—and immediately teamed up with Franco Modigliani, with whom he did much celebrated work in corporate finance. MIT's Modigliani won a Nobel Prize in 1985.

Markowitz, a native of Chicago, built on the earlier thinking by Yale's James Tobin about diversification of risk through balanced portfolios. Tobin was honored by the Nobel committee in 1981.

Sharpe, a Cambridge, Mass. native, published his seminal paper on the measurement of risk relative to the stock market as a whole in 1967, while he was a young assistant professor at the University of Washington. He was hired by Stanford University in 1970 and retired last year—to found an investment management firm.

"Sharpe published his model just at the beginning of the time when corporations were beginning to diversify, arguing that this was a way of minimizing risk," Stewart Myers, finance professor at the Massachusetts Institute of Technology, said yesterday. "That was at the start of the conglomerate boom, in which everyone thought diversification was a good thing. We now see that contributed very little to corporate performance. If anything, we've learned to mistrust diversification and to value focus.

"What Sharpe showed was that the financial markets . . . are only concerned with the risk that the companies can't diversify away. Today, nobody argues that you can lower the cost of capital by diversifying. It turned out that the theory was right."

Indeed, the skein of work begun by Markowitz, Miller and Sharpe has won the respect of even the hardest-headed money men of Boston's State Street and other centers of money management around the country. John C. Bogle, who heads the Vanguard Group of mutual funds in Valley Forge, Pa., put it this way, in the introduction to a recent collection of technical papers:

"While there is a lot of witchcraft in the academic lore, a certain naiveté among the practioners about what is truly susceptible to proof, and far too much reliance on the misbegotten idea that the past is inevitably prologue to the future, the most solid academic thinking, however abstruse and complex, is worth even a busy executive's persusal. For sound theory, sooner or later, will find its way into actual practice, and into the investor marketplace as well."

OCTOBER 17, 1990

The Long
Patrol

CHICAGO—A LONDON NATIVE WHO AS A YOUNG MAN IN THE 1930S TRAVELED TO America to interview corporate executives at Ford Motor Co., General Motors and Union Carbide about what they did, yesterday won the Nobel Prize in economics for the answers he garnered.

Ronald Coase, 80, a retired professor of law and economics at the University of Chicago, was cited for two classic papers that transformed the way economists and lawyers viewed the nature of corporations and the possibilities for government regulation.

Both were based on insights garnered on his early trip. Both aimed to persuade other economists to spend less time with their axioms and more time in the real world.

An acute form of microeconomics, the papers couldn't have been further apart in their methodological stance from the dominant macroeconomics of John Maynard Keynes, which were coming into vogue in the 1930s. "Friction," summed up Richard Epstein, a University of Chicago professor. "Friction, friction, friction, friction."

Coase, who was vacationing in Tunisia, could not immediately be reached for comment.

In *The Nature of the Firm*, published in 1937, Coase broached for the first time the idea of transaction costs. It was as if he had identified a new kind of "elementary particle," the Nobel citation said yesterday.

Quite aside from production costs, Coase argued, firms faced a wide variety of significant costs of preparing and monitoring various agreements—with their suppliers, their employees, their customers.

The ubiquitous existence of property rights associated with these costs is what explained the reason why firms arose in the first place: Corporations existed to economize the costs of buying and selling nearly everything under the sun, he wrote. He thereby cleared the way for economists to participate in the modern study of industrial organization, joining business historians such as Alfred Chandler who had pioneered the field.

In *The Problem of Social Cost*, published in 1960, Coase pushed his analysis much further. The reciprocal relations of property rights were the key to understanding problems as diverse as pollution control, government allocation of scarce resources and corporate governance, he said. Moreover, if the particular structure of law had profound implications for economic decision makers, then the designers of the law had an obligation to take economic incentives into consideration in framing their measures, he wrote, giving a powerful impetus to the law and economics movement.

Issues like the compensation of accident victims—which had previously been seen as a matter of yes and no, black and white, right and wrong before Coase wrote—almost overnight became a matter of costs and benefits.

(A third significant paper, on marginal cost pricing, much valued by Coase himself, wasn't mentioned yesterday by the Swedes.)

Coase's path to the prize was not altogether smooth. He began as an accountant, and published first on the economics of raising pigs. During World War II, he worked his way up to become the War Cabinet's chief statistician, then completed his doctorate at the University of London.

He emigrated to the United States at the end of the 1940s and had trouble catching on, finally landing a job at the out-of-the-way University of Buffalo. He moved in 1958 to the University of Virginia, where a heterodox interest in markets was taking root, effected a famous conversion of the leaders in his field, then switched to the University of Chicago in 1964.

Though Coase's work has a strong empirical flavor, "he never looked at a number in his life," said Epstein. As long-time editor of the *Journal of Law and Economics*, Coase encouraged others to pursue quantitative studies. But his own work retained a stong literary flavor.

"Anybody can understand it with a 10th-grade education," said Epstein. This clarity cost him with his colleagues. Even at Chicago, "they viewed him as a dinosaur," recalled a colleague.

Despite being recruited with a rush, he wound up on the faculty of the law school, and so became the first law professor ever honored by a Nobel.

Although *The Problem of Social Cost* is by far the most-cited paper in economics, according to several surveys, Coase has honorary degrees from only Yale and the University of Cologne.

If his fascination with the real world slowed Coase down on the Nobel track, it made it easier for him in the world of practical affairs. Law schools began adopting his views, and starting in the early 1960s, a steady stream of judges and lawyers flocked to summer camps in which law and economics were taught with excitement bordering on missionary zeal.

Prominent law professors like Guido Calabresi and Richard Posner in effect turned him on his head, using economics to write law and understand it. And prominent practioners like Posner and Frank Easterbrook moved onto the federal bench, enshrining Coaseian doctrines in their opinions.

As the Swedish Academy's citation put it, "it took a long time for his approach to gain a foothold. When the breakthrough finally occurred during the 1970s and 1980s, it was all the more emphatic.

Indeed. The radical extension of microeconomic analysis effected by Coase has unloosed a tidal wave of change, in everything from corporate control to tradable pollution rights. Takeover law was profoundly influenced by his work during the 1980s. The new atmospheric pollution regulations to be issued later this month by the Environmental Protection Agency draw heavily on his inspiration. And schemes to privatize socialist economies have Coaseian insights at their root.

Though a formidable debater, Coase has a reputation among his colleagues as being somewhat ill at ease in the world of common sense. "What was difficult for him personally—a lease, say, or a trip to the store—was precisely what he explained so deeply," said Epstein.

In Chicago, where he spends the winters, Coase lives far from the university at the fashionable Lake Point Tower. Summers he spends in the south of France. Yesterday, possibly forewarned, he was on the beach of a German resort in Tunisia—and quite unreachable.

OCTOBER 16, 1991

When the Revolution Really *Was* a Dinner Party

PEOPLE WHO ARE STILL MYSTIFIED BY THE TRANSFORMATION IN GLOBAL POLITICS IN favor of markets since, say, 1980 would do well to pay a little extra attention to this year's Nobel Prize in economics. A mild-mannered and scholarly Britisher, Ronald Coase achieved something a good deal more far-reaching and less partisan than the writing of *The Road to Serfdom*, the creation of the Institute for Economic Analysis, the founding of the *National Review*, the launching of the Goldwater campaign or any of the other events usually hailed as turning points in the intellectual history of present-day conservative politics.

At one remarkable dinner party in 1960, Coase converted the economics department of the University of Chicago to his views on regulation and privatization. The rest, as they say, is history. The story of that evening is one of the most wonderful episodes in scholarship; it offers lessons for liberals as well as conservatives.

A little background: As a 21-year-old graduate student in the early 1930s, Coase had become interested in why things were organized in capitalist economies as they were, with a few giant firms dominating some markets and other industries characterized by much different arrangements. A Socialist, he had called on presidential candidate Norman Thomas while on a traveling scholarship, but he had called on Ford and General Motors as well.

"Lenin had said that the economic system in Russia would be run as one big factory," Coase recalled a few years ago. ". . . Economists in the West were engaged in a grand debate on the subject of planning, some maintaining that to run the economy as one big factory was an impossibility. And yet there were factories in England and America.

"How did one reconcile the impossibility of running Russia as one big factory with the existence of factories in the West?"

The answer on which he hit to explain both cases was the idea of what he then called marketing costs, everything from finding workers to advertising products. These transactions costs, as they have come to be known—including search and information costs, bargaining and decision costs, policing and enforcing costs—are crucial to understanding both big corporations and command economies; the Nobel citation last week compared Coase's identification of them to the discovery of a new set of elementary particles in physics. But this is clearer to us now than it was then. Coase's arguments about the logic of economic organization, published in 1937, were all but ignored for 40 years.

By the 1950s, the restless Coase had moved to America and was ranging far beyond his study of the firm. If the subtle contracts implied by these ubiquitous costs were the essence of economic life, he reasoned, then attention should be paid to the laws by which those contracts were enforced. He became especially interested in broadcasting, where the theory of natural monopoly was deeply ensconced. And in 1958, he mailed a paper called "The Federal Communications Commission" to the citadel of market capitalism that was the economics department of the University of Chicago.

What Coase argued sounds unexceptionable today: That government itself could often make a market in scarce goods that otherwise would enjoy no market. Mildly, he wrote: "Whether a newly discovered cave belongs to the man who discovered it, the man on whose land the entrance to the cave is located, or the man who owns the surface under which the cave is situated is no doubt dependent on the law of property. But the law merely determines the person with whom it is necessary to make a contract to obtain the use of the cave.

"Whether the cave is used for storing bank records, as a natural gas reservoir, or for growing mushrooms, depends, not on the law of property, but on whether the bank, the natural gas corporation, or the mushroom concern will pay the most in order to be able to use the cave."

The cave, by analogy, was little different from the radio spectrum, for which a system of tradeable property rights could be devised as well. But back in 1958, this was heresy, and Chicago recognized it. Aaron Director, the celebrated Chicago economist who had founded the *Journal of Law and Economics*, invited Coase to dinner in Chicago—along with Milton Friedman, George Stigler, Lloyd Mints, Arnold Harberger, John McGee and another dozen academic stars. When the evening began, the vote against

Coase was 20 to 1, Stigler recalls, and it would have been worse if Coase hadn't been allowed to vote. At a certain point, "Milton Friedman opened fire and the bullets hit everyone but Coase," he says.

By the end of the evening, Coase had converted them all, and according to John McGee and Steven Cheung, "the debaters stumbled out into the evening air in a state of shock, mumbling to each other that they had witnessed intellectual history." (The episode is recalled in detail in a special 1983 issue of the *Journal of Law and Economics*.)

What exactly had happened in those few hours of sharp and lofty talk? Nothing less than 150 years of conventional wisdom on the role of goverment had been overturned, quickly and completely, at the level of expert debate. The Chicagoans had gone into the room believing, along with liberals, that there were certain indispensable services that goverment had to provide because markets couldn't be made to offer them. They had walked out with a new vision of what government might accomplish through the clever establishment of property rights. Over the next 30 years, they persuaded most liberal economists of the acuity of their intuition.

Practical consequences? Plenty of them. The intellectual underpinnings of everything from accident law to takeover regulation to the structuring of environmental pollution requirements have been rethought in the last 30 years as a result of the conversions that took place that night. Ironically, this "Coaseian revolution" was led by lawyers, who were quicker than most economists to see the point (though often they pushed it a bit too far). This sort of phenomenon goes right to the heart of our questions about the "scientific" status of modern economics. Is it merely dogma, manipulated according to arcane internal rules by its acolytes, as many writers have maintained? Or does it, like the incomparably more successful natural sciences, have some deep and mysterious connection to "the way the world works," a connection whose intricacy can be scouted out through careful observation and experiment?

Mao Tse-tung had opined that "a revolution is not a dinner party," meaning that the rules under which society will function must be hammered out in the rough and tumble of politics, complete with force. Certainly the story of Coase's theorem suggests the opposite possibility—that economics is capable of producing a kind of truth, which as the saying goes, can never be told in such a way as to be understood without being believed. The reception of Coase's ideas may have taken 50 years, but in the end it has been irrespective of national politics—as compelling in China as in Spain.

So why did it take so long to award Ronald Coase a Nobel Prize? The answer is that the Swedes have gone out of their way to signal their sense that mathematization was crucial to the formation of modern technical economics. Two years ago they even gave the prize to Norwegian Trgvye Haavelmo for a long-ago contribution to statistical inference.

But Coase has conducted a long and powerful rearguard action against the widespread use of mathematics, which he sees as way of empowering uniformed would-be philosopher-kings. "Blackboard economics," he calls it. The high point of this exercise was a 1974 essay on the history of the law and administration of lighthouses, which showed it to have been exactly the opposite of what economic theorists routinely had asserted to be the case: an excruciating critique of the first few Nobel laureates.

"In my youth it was said that what was too silly to be said may be sung. In modern economics it may be be put into mathematics," he has written. Now the Swedes have forcefully acknowledged the possibility that he is right, after all.

OCTOBER 20, 1991

Why You Never Heard of George Dantzig

NARENDRA KARMARKAR'S NAME IS NOT EXACTLY A HOUSEHOLD WORD, NOR WILL IT ever be. Within certain precincts, however, his immortality is already assured. He just might be rich and successful, too, but that depends.

Karmarkar is the Bell Laboratories fellow who came up with a new algorithm designed to replace the simplex method that's been used to solve a wide variety of scheduling problems since its discovery in 1947. Mathematicians can assess the novelty of this sort of thing very rapidly, and Karmarkar's breakthrough was advertised, among other places, on the front page of the New York Times last autumn.

And why not? Supplanting the simplex method is like beating an aging but powerful champ. Anyone who has made a phone call, bought a gallon of gas, taken an airplane trip or called a big city cop is beneficiary of it—and the method has hung onto its central place in the scheduler's tool kit for an unusually long time. "If you look at the way that progress is proceeding in all fields of applied math, the simplex method, which is 40 years old, should be dead. Hardly anything lasts that long," says Robert Dorfman of Harvard University.

It now turns out that Karmarkar's problem-solving recipe may not be more practical than simplex after all. The great joy of simplex is its applicability—it works, planners say, better than it should. But it is limited in the kinds of problems it can handle. "The simplex method is fine for problems with a few thousand variables, but above 16,000 or 20,000 variables, it runs out of steam," says Karmarkar—and of course that range is just where the 28-year-old Indian's method is thought to come in handy.

But some mathematicians and scientists fear that the new solution could turn out to be like a Russian discovery of a few years back, called the ellipsoid method, which was beautiful but not very useful in solving the workaday problems at which simplex excels. Indeed, applied mathematicians are somewhat polarized in their reaction to news of the discovery. Specialists will be flocking to a major session in Boston tonight on the matter, but it won't be settled there. "Mind you, any breakthrough in science gets attacked," says Richard C. Larson of MIT.

The occasion for a Karmarkar session—and for nearly 300 other meetings of varying degrees of accessibility—is a convention of the Operations Research Society of America, of which Larson is the president. Operations research was formed in the cauldron of World War II. The task of linking newly developed radar and Hurricane fighter planes was its first big problem; the results of the Battle of Britain its first big success. Suddenly there were dozens of wartime problems of unprecedented complexity to be solved: bombing patterns, merchant fleet operations, antisubmarine warfare searches all had to optimized, to say nothing of the logistical trains behind the front.

While economists, especially the bunch under William J. (Wild Bill) Donovan in the Office for Strategic Services, had as much to offer as any other set of keen professional intelligences, it was a different bunch that made the beginning that, after the war, became operations research. Philip M. Morse, the MIT physicist widely regarded as the American father of the field, noted in his presidential address in 1953 that what had begun with borrowing gave way quickly to original research.

The central figure in this process was George B. Dantzig, the discoverer of the simplex algorithm. An Air Force planner charged with figuring out how to build the best air corps at minimal cost, Dantzig wrestled with postwar problems of coordinating base construction, troop recruitment and training, equipment manufacture and so on. In 1947, he hit on an algebraic method he described as "climbing the beanpole," after the pattern it made in intuitive geometry. It turned out to be the solution to any number of problems, from calculating the cheapest combination of nine nutrients that would constitute a satisfactory diet to allocating resources in the most complicated ways.

So fundamental was his contribution that many felt that Dantzig should have shared the 1975 Nobel Award in Economics with Tjalling Koopmans and Leonid V. Kantorovitch—but was snubbed instead because he worked for the most part outside of economics. Other economists say the line between economics and all else has to be drawn someplace and that the leading edge of Danzig's wingtips is as good a place as any to start.

In any event, the successes in operations research came quickly after the war, as queuing theory, graph theory, optimal control theory and a whole range of optimization techniques, including dynamic programming, were quickly adapted for use in organizational planning. Practical applications of game theory proved elusive, and many operations research scholars are convinced that the field coasted for a time in the 1960s and 1970s, teaching mostly secondary material.

A burst of activity in the last 10 years has moved the field away from whatever tendency it had toward pretty mathematics to ever more concrete applications in the real world. The prime mover here has been technology. Where it formerly required a big mainframe computer to solve a few thousand equations, it's now possible to solve the most difficult models with a personal computer. The result is a booming science. MIT has 40 faculty members in its Operations Research Center; Stanford's department has four separate subsections. Digital Equipment Corp. has the biggest information science department in the country. The oil companies, the airlines and financial services firms have all gotten deeply into the act.

Dick Larson, 42, this year's president of the Operations Research Society, is a fairly typical practitioner. As an MIT graduate student, he invited a couple of girls he didn't know to a fraternity party. They turned out to be professional thieves and cleaned out the pocketbooks in the ladies' room. In the process of working with Boston Police to try to catch the crooks (they never found them), Larson developed an abiding interest in the allocation of police resources, and he's been with it ever since. Indeed, as a consultant to the Cambridge Police, he helped mount a hypercube queuing model into a powerful Apollo computer to provide a map of the city for police and ambulance responses.

A quick look at the candidates for the top prize for management science achievement this year shows Larson's interest in the practical side of things is no fluke. The finalists include New York City's garbage route planner, United Airlines' shift scheduler, the guy who schedules rail traffic along Western Canada's single mainline track, a lumber company's cross-cutting specialist, and a couple of hydroelectric planners, from California and Brazil.

Why did operations research develop so far apart from economics? As economist Robert Dorfman says, the two are really concerned with different realms, one with parts, the other with wholes. "Operations research is really welded to a normative, precriptive approach that emphasizes enterprises in a decoupled fashion, instead of as part of the circular flow that is a large economy," Dorfman says. Operations research can deal with any subject matter, he says, from how to run a farm to how to run a submarine, while economics is mostly concerned "with the interrelations among independent subsidiary components and with trying to analyze the logical structure that comes from that independence, rather than from hierarchical subordination."

Not that high theory has no place in the field of operations research: For example, more than 100 scientists met at Columbia University last week to argue about problems of the architecture of hierarchy and of computational difficulty. But the group that came to Boston this week gets more excited about keeping the streets clean and safe. Perhaps because they are basically engineers, they have little interest in the relationship of their field to the senior science of economics. Dick Larson laughs, "Every discipline regards every other discipline as a small subset of itself."

He's right, of course. The University of Chicago's George Stigler—who, incidentally, was the scholar who posed and failed to solve the diet problem that Dantzig cracked with his simplex algorithm—once spoke to the urge to expand the Nobel awards beyond their present array. There's no need for that, he said. There is one for economics and there is one for fiction. What more than that do we need?

APRIL 28, 1985

Planning, Hayek and the CTC

FRIEDRICH HAYEK, THE GREAT FOE OF GOVERNMENT PLANNING, LIVED A LIFE STILL not quite fully understood by his friends when he died last week at the ripe old age of 92.

On the surface, his career was a supremely, almost uniquely happy one. Late photographs show him smiling, winking, beckoning to the newly privatizing world he had relentlessly imagined. And why not? He outlived not only his antagonists but their ideas, outlived not only the Keynesian revolution but the Communist revolutions as well.

It is hard now to recall the fury that greeted the *The Road to Serfdom* when it was published in 1944, a time when John Maynard Keynes, Joseph Schumpeter, Karl Polanyi, Karl Mannheim and Harold Laski were trumpeting the death of capitalism and the inevitability of planning. Yet Hayek, who was born in Vienna in 1899, lived to be celebrated as the philosopher laureate of the administrations of Margaret Thatcher and Ronald Reagan. His collected papers, a series slated to reach 22 volumes, reveal a remarkable intelligence operating across a wide range of fields.

Deeper down, however, this is not an entirely happy story. A measure of this is that Hayek is not to be found in either of two interesting new books about the institutions in which he spent much of his working life. *Eminent Economists: Their Life Philosophies*, edited by Michael Szenberg, contains revealing autobiographical essays by 22 excellent economists of the older generation, including representatives of the right like Karl Brunner and James Buchanan. Hayek merits only three entries in the index.

Nor, despite having taught there for 12 years, does he have a place in *Remembering the University of Chicago: Teachers, Scientists and Scholars*, a collection of 47 biographical essays assembled (and in some cases written) by Edward Shils which conveys the flavor of that powerful institution.

The point is that Hayek was not a dominating part of the tapestry of either community (although he shared a Nobel Prize with Gunnar Myrdal in

1974). His more direct connection was with politicians and activists rather than his peers.

Why? A clue of sorts was provided last week in a report by a committee of that forum of the very best and brightest, the National Academies of Sciences and Engineering and the Institutes of Medicine, which called in a clear cool voice for the government to edge into . . . economic planning! This was a panel of 15 technology policy experts, all deployed on the cutting edge of industry, led by Harold Brown, former president of the California Institute of Technology (and secretary of defense under Jimmy Carter). At the same time, *Business Week* magazine renewed its quadrennial call for "industrial policy" in a cover story. But the academy survey is far deeper stuff, a shrewd survey of how and why the American market sometimes fails to achieve the commercialization of technology—and a path-breaking recommendation for a way to remedy the breakdown.

After considering—and rejecting—the idea of a Civilian Technology Agency, established within the conventional bureaucratic framework of the government, what the academy panel proposed instead is a Civilian Technology Corp. This would act as a kind of Federal Reserve system for innovations in their very earliest stages, a quasi-governmental institution with a chief executive, a board of directors, a non-civil service staff, $5 billion in public money that would be self-replenishing through equity positions, patents and license fees—and very little active congressional oversight. In giving the CTC a "civilian patina," the idea would be to insulate it as much as possible from pork-barrel politics, said Sen. Ernest Hollings (D-S.C.), chairman of the Senate Commerce Committee, a tireless worker in the technology-policy vineyards who received the report and held hearings on it.

To be sure, the academy panel was composed mainly of the sorts of managers who would be most at home in a Democratic administration. Besides Brown, included were several others who served in the Carter administration, including John Deutch, Richard Cooper, C. Fred Bergsten and William J. Perry. Its report had been summoned forth by the Democratic Congress. But the group also included Yale's Paul MacAvoy, a long-time adviser to President Bush, and it is hard to think who in the research and development community would oppose very strenuously the measure—except, perhaps, long-time venture capitalists who, remarkably, were unrepresented both on the panel and among its presenters.

That leaves the group—many professional economists among its number—who would prefer to accomplish the same end of stimulating key technologies with a research and development tax credit, especially one designed to permit American corporations to sponsor more work in universities. But as chairman Harold Brown notes, there would then be problems of excluding abuse through cunning definitions—and even then, the tax credit remains a blunt instrument. A Bush administration task force might refine the vision of a CTC, modify it—but at a price tag of $5 billion, it would be, frankly, frivolous not to take the gamble and plunge $5 billion in defense savings into the project, in hope that it would somehow galvanize American industry in the post-Cold War era.

Now the great Hayek was nothing if not opposed to projects like these. He hated planning in virtually all its forms. It was competition, not agreement, that led to progress, he liked to say. Indeed, all his life he argued against the governmental supervision of money and banks through central banking systems like the Federal Reserve. Private banks could issue currencies, form protective associations, conduct their own antitrust enforcement and the like.

But in these arguments, Hayek failed to persuade his colleagues. He had little interest in the many ways that markets sometimes fail: in monopolies, for example, or in the behavior of "externalities" of the price system, whether bad effects, like pollution, or good ones, like knowledge. So great was his faith in markets' efficacy—and so great his skepticism about governments' ability to achieve worthwhile aims—that he envisaged a kind of picturebook world, lacking in realism. His was not exactly a case of a Wegener (the "premature" discoverer of plate tectonics), a man who was brilliantly right ahead of his time with a key insight; rather, he was a master publicist, an advocate for the cause of human liberty. What a pity he is not here to see the horrendous global planning juggernaut now slowly heading towards Rio de Janeiro!

It may turn out that the government has no very useful place in the seed-capital industry, that it does best when it serves as a very exacting customer, as in the case of the Apollo space program or the Defense Advance Research Projects Agency, or DARPA. But clearly the future belongs to those who understand not just markets' strengths, but their weaknesses, too. Contra Hayek, then, look for government to become a little more involved in civilian technology, if only as the kind of experiment that he would have understood.

MARCH 29, 1992

Why Galbraith
Won't Receive
the Nobel Prize

ONE OF THE ILLUMINATING RIDDLES OF OUR TIME HAS BEEN JOHN KENNETH GAL-
braith's standing as an economist. What his friend Eric Roll says is perfectly true: "A poll among reasonable, educated people in most countries of
the world would certainly find his name better known than that of any other
contemporary writer in the field."

Yet it is a safe bet that Galbraith won't collect a Nobel Economics Prize
when it is announced Wednesday—or ever. Instead, the award will go to
another one of those remarkable but relatively unknown scholars who in the
1950s and 1960s put together the intellectual edifice that is modern technical economics.

Not that Galbraith has been neglected by his peers: He was president of
the American Economic Association in 1972, a different kind of high
honor. The story goes that Hollis Chenery got so mad at the suggestion by
a fellow officer that Galbraith wasn't an economist that he led a successful
fight to elect him. But the fact remains that Galbraith isn't what the Swedish
Academy of Sciences has in mind when it talks about the best economists
in the world.

How so? Well, chapter and verse of testimony to one of the best-lived
lives in Cambridge can be found in *Unconventional Wisdom, Essays on
Economics in Honor of John Kenneth Galbraith.*

This beautiful book contains 22 essays by Galbraith's friends, students
and allies in his half-century of dissent. It was assembled by Samuel
Bowles, Richard C. Edwards and William G. Shepard, three University of
Massachusetts economists. And instead of going on about Galbraith's style
and wit, his liberal politics, his taste in art, his years as ambassador to
India, his remarkable family and friendships, it concentrates instead on

presenting an extremely cogent picture of his economics and its relation to the profession's mainstream.

It is amazing to consider how much of Galbraith's work informs our everyday sense of how the modern economy works. There is his emphasis on status and advertising and the psychological creation and manipulation of wants. There is the attention he has paid to "the planning system," the "technostructure," the "new industrial state" as the seat of decisions about the future. There is his critique of the Cold War and the arms race and its devastating effect on Third World nations. There is his notion of countervailing power among companies, unions and government. Above all, there is the emphasis on the power of giant corporations.

It's true that much of the gospel of Galbraith didn't pan out. An age of affluence does not seem to be quite the same sure diagnosis it once seemed to be. He didn't reckon on the rise of the Asian Tigers. He didn't foresee just how powerful a force innovation and competition turned out to be among corporations. He was not very prescient on the sharp decline in inflation. But the fact is that Galbraith's underlying vision of the economy, his sense of the importance of the structure of markets, of the ubiquity of sticky processes and imperfect alternatives, of the central significance of institutions and the power that information gives them, is where economics has been going for the last 15 years.

But from where the technical economists sit, it is not enough to simply have it said, like so much poetry. To be taken seriously by the mainstream of the profession, an economist must "write it down," create a mathematic model of the process he is describing in ways that it can be measured, express his ideas in the language of the field, map them into the work done by others over decades.

Powerful intuition isn't enough, even when it's correct. Lots of writers proposed that the earth might go around the sun before Copernicus succeeded in arguing irrefutably how and why it was the case. Lucretius speculated that the genetic code might be like an alphabet, composed of a limited number of letters that could be combined in a nearly infinite variety of words, but that didn't make him the discoverer of DNA. As the physicist Richard Feynman put it once, "A very great deal more truth can become known than can be proved."

Present-day economics is full of the echoes of the concerns of critics of earlier years, not only those of Galbraith, but those of Edward Chamberlain, Joan Robinson and Thorstein Veblen. Above all, Joseph Schumpeter seems to loom above the field as an early student of the processes of "creative destruction" by which the growth of knowledge and new technology permit new economic sectors to reconstitute themselves, phoenix-like, from the ashes of the old.

When economists retrace the steps of earlier critics of received beliefs, they speak in terms of "getting Chamberlain right," as when Harvard's Michael Spence introduced to formal economic reasoning the idea of information-signaling, or of "getting Veblen right," as when Cornell's Robert Frank showed how considerations of status and rank could lead to surprising results.

There is often just a little bit of the holier-than-thou when an economist brings to market results confirming common sense. But there needn't be. It's one thing to diagnose the world and its ills in real time; it's quite another to work on a small part of the problem in the interest of being really sure. Proving things, nailing them down, is what economists do; everything else is just journalism.

There is some irony here, for down the street from the pink-shuttered Cambridge manse where Galbraith lives, a small group of technical economists labored last week to express the sweeping intuitions of Schumpeter in the tight technical language of their craft.

At the National Bureau of Economic Research, theorists and econometricians at the forefront of their field argued about monopolistic competition, protected markets, the magnitude of spillovers, the degree of the significance of new knowledge—as opposed to more capital or labor—in fomenting economic growth. Moreover, the theory of economic growth is only the latest field to which the new ideas about the significance of increasing returns to scale have been applied; they are already changing the way we think about international trade. Nobody talked about "getting Galbraith right" at the NBER last week—but that, in essence, is what they were doing.

The spectacle of technical economics—of Chicagoans, no less—closing in on testing the validity of his insights should warm the heart of the sage of Francis Avenue. But it will win him no phone calls from Stockholm. In due course, Nobel prizes will go to some of the scholars working on the new growth economics today, just as the award this year will probably go to a pioneer in some controversy whose technical aspects Galbraith shunned during the 1950s to write *The Affluent Society*.

As it happens, much of the usual guessing this year centers on the possibility that one of Galbraith's Harvard colleagues will be honored: Amartya Sen, Janos Kornai or Zvi Griliches. All are plausible candidates; none are household names.

But how deeply rewarding it must be for Galbraith to see the field going where long ago he thought it should. He cannot claim credit for having led the profession to the promised land; it followed its own internal logic to its current place. But what he saw was what was there, and if he emphasized the normal conduct of economic life at the expense of the revolutionary, he was still, for the most part, right.

OCTOBER 8, 1989

From the Chess Set
to Project Tipster

WHEN YOU USE AN AMERICAN EXPRESS CARD, THE MERCHANT SWIPES IT THROUGH A card reader and the information on the magnetic strip and the bill of sale go immediately by telephone to an enormous set of computers on the West Coast. The machine screens the data about the purchase and makes decisions based on a set of rules it has been taught: How much is being charged, where, the past pattern of purchases and payments, and the usual daily use of the card. Usually the computer approves the transaction by sending back an authorization number. If there's a problem, it's quickly referred to a human being.

While a lively debate continues at a philosophical level about whether machines actually think, an ever-growing number of companies are peddling products like these to industry and government. Eventually, these new ways of doing business promise to change a great deal of everyday life. The remarkable thing is how this infant industry grew out of the passions of a mild-mannered man and some of his friends in Pittsburgh in the winter of 1955.

Now Herbert A. Simon has published his autobiography, *Models of My Life*. And for anybody who likes to think, the story of how this wayward political scientist and economist more or less invented artificial intelligence in the mid-1950s is of value. It is among the newest of the Alfred Sloan Foundation series of scientific autobiographies, and it's hard to think of more successful publishing projects.

From the extraordinary Freeman Dyson (*Disturbing the Universe*) to the gracious biologist Salvador Luria (*A Slot Machine, A Broken Test Tube*; he died last month) to the self-centered Luis Alvarez (*Adventures of a Physicist*), these books disclose vivid insights into lives lived at the pinnacle of the research adventure.

For Simon, the story begins with a welter of interesting yarns from the wilds of Wisconsin. The son of a German engineer who emigrated to Milwaukee from Darmstadt at the turn of the century after facing down an opponent to avert a duel, Simon has much to say about life in the land of of Robert LaFollette and Aldo Leopold. Of a family friend he says, "If you scratch an engineer, you'll find a physiocrat underneath. Engineers believe in real things like machines and bridges and land."

As a student at the University of Chicago in the mid-1930s, Simon flourished. Price theory turned him on to mathematics, Charles Merriam introduced him to quantitative methods and models in the study of administrative decision-making. A liberal ("When in doubt, we could determine our policy by looking in the *Chicago Tribune* and opting for the opposite direction," he says of his circle of friends), Simon escaped—not by much— the later security crazes of the McCarthy era.

He moved to Carnegie-Mellon University in 1949 and began building the great business school there. He was all over the social science map in the early 1950s, one of many clever thinkers making a useful living off the Cold War. "I learned many things . . . ," he says at one juncture, "few more important than how to position the decimal point in a research proposal."

The story of artificial intelligence began in earnest when Simon teamed up with Alan Newell and the first generation of stored-program IBM computers. The two shared the idea of teaching a computer to play chess— chess is "the Drosophila of AI," Simon says. Then one day in October 1955, walking along the Hudson River at Morningside Heights, it occurred to him that a computer could solve geometry problems, too.

A month later, after much feverish work on the "Logic Theorist" program, Simon's computer—or his hand-written simulations of its processes —had begun proving simple theorems from the *Principia Mathematica*. Not long after New Year's Day, he walked into class and memorably proclaimed to his students, "Over the Christmas holiday, Al Newell and I invented a thinking machine." Soon the letters were flying back and forth to Bertrand Russell.

What followed Simon's discovery was a 35-year argument about whether machines really were capable of thinking, and whether the best way to build them was up from the metaphor of a maze (Simon's way) or upon the metaphor of the brain ("neural nets"). Except for occasional arguments about who would get funded by the government, both sides have been winners. The insights of the inventors of the field—Simon, Newell, Nilsson and others—once deemed to have been quickly superseded, have held up pretty well, today's graduate students agree, even in linguistics.

Simon writes: "In arguing that machines think, we are in the same fix as Darwin when he argued that man shares common ancestors with the monkeys, or Galileo when he argued that the earth spins on its axis." Holding opposing views are a long line of distinguished humanists, including Joseph Weizenbaum of MIT, Hubert Dreyfus of Berkeley and, most recently, Sherry Turkle of MIT. Simon continues, "My own posture has been this: My scientific work, and that of other artificial-intelligence researchers, will, in the long run, determine how many of Man's thinking processes can be simulated. I believe that ultimately all of them can, but feel no great urge to prove that to others who feel differently. In science, it is the facts that give us the final answers."

The rest of the book is taken up with accounts of various adventures: His visit with the writer Jorge Luis Borges in 1970 and the Borges-like short story that Simon had written 14 years before; an extraordinary account of his successful marriage (and of an unconsummated love affair with a graduate student in his early days); letters to his children; old columns; and plenty of science politics.

Today the research program in artificial intelligence is going forward as never before. The latest word is a project presumably supported by a consortium of intelligence agencies, administered by the Defense Advanced Research Projects Agency (DARPA), which is designated Tipster. It's a long step beyond what American Express is doing now.

The challenge: To devise machines that will perform two tasks—extraction, that is, pulling data out of texts and putting it into data bases; and classification, or routing potentially interesting documents to human readers. According to the prospectus, such systems should be able to operate in two languages, English and Japanese, and in two domains, microelectronics and mergers and acquisitions. Thus, such systems would be able to read the Dow Jones wire—or monitor the message traffic in phone calls and computer neworks, a billion at a time.

Yes, this ability to pick significant patterns out of otherwise incomprehensible swirl is exactly what Robert Redford was repeatedly nearly killed for in the movie *Three Days of the Condor*. Is it economically valuable? Is it artificial intelligence? You figure it out. Chances are, though, that before very long, machine reading too will have found its applications in the commercial world, and then you won't leave home without encountering it.

MARCH 17, 1991

How the PC Did in the Big Forecasters

WAS THERE IN THE 1970S A BUSINESS MORE PERFECTLY MARRIED TO ITS TIME THAN Data Resources Inc.? Every year the economy got a little worse, every year the Lexington company made a lot more money. Founded in 1969, DRI exemplified the glamor of a startup that went from a little borrowed capital to a $70 million business with a return on investment of around 40 percent a year for a decade. In 1979, founder Otto Eckstein sold out to McGraw-Hill at the very top of the market for $103 million.

Then came the age of the the microcomputer, typified by IBM's PC. The machine made the industry into quite a different business.

Today, DRI is more dominant than ever, but the industry is in the throes of change. Early this month DRI was carved up in many different pieces, and substantially embedded in McGraw-Hill's subsidiary Standard and Poor, as part of a company-wide restructuring, described as "historic."

Chase Econometrics, DRI's principal competition, is on the block; it could be sold as early as this week, probably to DRI. Wharton Econometric Forecasting Associates, the prestigious model-building group that started it all, is in danger of sinking from sight, at least as a commercial concern. The whole business is changing so fast it makes the head spin.

But the scene gives the lie to the general impression in Washington that quantitative economists are somehow fading from the scene. Instead of fewer there are more, and more sophisticated. They've been assimilated into staff positions, that's all.

DRI founder Otto Eckstein, an ebullient Harvard professor with a yen for policy, liked to say that he had learned his method from IBM; the trick was to bundle computing time, economic information and data together, and sell it ready-made to the consumer.

Thus Eckstein hired the top economists to write his model, collected the best data that money and good sense could buy, and bought Burroughs computers wholesale, in order to sell computer time retail. His custom was so good that Burroughs Corp. put him on its board; DRI research set the modern standard for excellence; but the hard-driving entrepreneurial talent that Eckstein hired was what made DRI grow as fast as it did. Eckstein patterned the style of the place on the Council of Economic Advisers on which he'd served under President Lyndon Johnson.

It is hard to say what changed first. Eckstein sold the firm to McGraw-Hill in 1979, and the firm's entrepreneurial flair began to diminish almost immediately. But it was when the personal computer came into widespread use that the results began to show up on the profit and loss statements. Sales of highly-profitable time-sharing services—"plain vanilla" computer time in the firm's jargon—lost ground as more clients learned to use the small high-powered machines, and revenues from the sale of DRI data suffered too, since the microcomputers tended to hang on to the numbers they used.

Meanwhile, there was much more competition on economic information, as new firms offered models and forecast services or developed their own. "A lot of economists have grown up," says Allen Sinai, who left DRI for Shearson Lehman American Express, built his own model there and who now buys mainly data from DRI. Says another forecaster: "I can buy a good model from Ray Fair, with not so many equations, but an even better record, for $3000, and use it whenever I want. Why pay $20,000 a year for a specific service from DRI? There are a lot of alternatives, and I don't depend on any one of them."

There is plenty of business left for DRI, if not much fast new growth. Revenues have continued to grow, topping $85 million last year, even while margins remain under pressure. Clearly the provision of data is becoming a bigger part of the future. Some of the business has dissolved in controversies over pricing that only a microeconomist could love; much of the rest is a scramble to offer services for personal computers.

Thus many economists believe that the glory days of econometrics services are over. What's left, they say, is consulting, a bitter fact, for with consulting there is no way to leverage the consultant's time beyond a certain point. Consulting is the smart guy's nightmare; or to put it better, DRI was the smart guy's dream.

The latest spate of excitement has been triggered by Chase Manhattan Bank's quiet offer late last year to sell its Chase Econometrics subsidiary—the second biggest force in the industry—to DRI. Despite sharp losses in its time-sharing business, the Chase unit is a well-regarded operation with a highly satisfied client base. So why doesn't the bank just ride it out? Presumably they were driven by their corporate strategy office. The econometrics business is not a fast-growing unit in a bank that is under pressure to grow; it is also losing money—some $5 million by the banks' accounting, according to one source. "It is just one of those good things that they haven't got the patience to support," said one analyst.

Neither Chase nor McGraw Hill spokesmen were willing yesterday to discuss the details, but the outlines of the deal so far could be pieced together from a variety of sources. The offer DRI made in December to the bank was essentially a price to be paid for its clients' business; severance pay for Chase's 250 employees would have been the bank's responsibility. Fewer than 50 workers would have made a smooth transition to McGraw-Hill, one source said. As negotiations moved toward their final stages in New York, Chase Econometrics president Lawrence Chimerine, based in Philadelphia, learned of them. Upset over plans to in effect disband his business, he asked for—and received—a short grace period in which to find a "white knight," either a bank willing to lend to employees against future earnings, or another corporation. Leveraged buyouts are very difficult to arrange for firms with no profits, and yesterday the industry felt that time was running out, perhaps as early as this week.

Chase Econometrics founder Michael Evans, who sold the company to the bank in 1979, could scarcely conceal his *schadenfreude*. "They said I ran too tight a ship when I had it, and they doubled the staff after they took over. I guess I was right, after all."

Chimerine declined to comment on the rumors of an impending sale, and the Chase Manhattan executive charged with disposing of the unit couldn't be reached for comment. McGraw-Hill noted that negotiations were continuing at a low level with the third significant factor in the industry, Wharton Econometrics Forecasting Associates, but said that no progress could be reported.

What about antitrust problems? How can the Big Three of the information business even think about combining their businesses? The answer, of course, is that they are not the Big Three any more. Says Joen Greenwood, the antitrust specialist at Charles River Associates in Boston: "It all depends on how you define the market. In these cases, they almost always talk about the very broad consulting market, and the world has changed so much that now all the investment bankers have their own forecasts. Five years ago, you would have wondered, but now it is a different world. I suppose that's what has happened to Chase and DRI's profits."

Thus some little shops thrive; others change with the times. For example, Urban Systems Research and Engineering, a small Cambridge consulting firm that two years ago wasn't even in the business, is now a significant force in the industry with its do-it-yourself Fair-Model. The

Planning Economics Group, which made headlines when it walked out of DRI a few years ago, is now defunct; the firm that bought it when it went broke preferred creating software for Dow Jones and Co. to econometrics consulting. Wharton Econometrics, which to all intents and purposes started the industry nearly 30 years ago at the University of Pennsylvania, twists slowly in the wind, having been sold to a French firm. According to Le Monde, the unit lost about $3.2 million last year.

Meanwhile, McGraw-Hill continues slicing up DRI. Its salary structure has been leveled to conform to that of its corporate parent, a process now largely completed; the more flamboyant entrepreneurial types have mostly left. President Joseph E. Kasputys has moved to New York; founder Otto Eckstein died last spring, at 56.

Chief DRI economist Roger Brinner says, "Just because we've dropped from 40 percent to 25 percent to 10 percent growth doesn't mean we're not growing. My unit set records again last year for both revenues and earnings." He's right, of course: Overall, the market will continue to grow. DRI plans to show a new line of personal computer-compatible products next month, and Brinner himself can run his forecasts more quickly on a personal computer now than on a mainframe.

But then that's the point: so can any corporate treasurer worth his salt.

JANUARY 15, 1985

The Enthusiast

THIS WEEK WAS TO HAVE BEEN THE OCCASION FOR PRESIDENT RONALD REAGAN'S speech on tax reform. There is now talk of putting it off until May 20—or even the end of the month. Meanwhile, details of the new Treasury proposal keep emerging: There may be no cap on the deduction for charitable giving after all; instead of indexation of capital gains, there may be a 40 percent exclusion, which would keep the rate about where it is.

The longer the president waits, the more watered down the proposal becomes, the more one thinks, why bother?

Well, why indeed? Aside from incentives to work harder, the reason the backers of tax reform most frequently give is that simplification would increase economic efficiency. According to the president, the current Internal Revenue Service Code is a nightmare pinball machine of quirky stumbling blocks and wacky incentives to investment. Tax reform would free up resources to go where they would be most productive. Capital would flow out of office buildings into factories, away from loophole-driven tennis courts and hospitals and expensive restaurants and into hard work.

Everyone gives lip service to this possibility, and supply-siders in particular talk glowingly about the salutary effects of removing subsidies of everything from cattle herds to cruise ships. The Claremont Institute's John Rutledge, for example, has made a strong, if not entirely persuasive, case for years that financial portfolio realignment alone might produce enough additional revenues to narrow the federal deficit to acceptable levels of borrowing.

But until last January nobody has attempted to focus attention on the measurement of these "efficiency gains." That was when this seemingly simple sentence crept into the debate: "The Reagan program (of 1981 and 1982) produced gains equivalent to 3.5 percent to 4 percent of the national wealth"—a paltry 1 percent of GNP growth greater than it would have been otherwise. So much, then, for the Reagan Revolution! And to reinforce this damning verdict, its author, Harvard economist Dale Jorgenson produced a table of the efficiency effects that would have come of various tax proposals other than those that were adopted:

• A flat tax like the Bradley-Gephardt or Kemp-Roth measures or the Treasury proposal of last November would have produced an 8 percent to 8.5 percent gain in wealth.

• The "present value" depreciation plan that Jorgenson and Alan Auerbach proposed in 1981 would have produced a 10.5 percent to 11 percent gain in wealth had it been adopted instead of the "Accelerated Cost Recovery System" and its subsequent semi-repeal.

• The cash flow or consumption tax put forward by Princeton economist David Bradford under the Ford administration would have increased wealth by 26 percent to 27 percent—equal to a whopping 10 percent to 11 percent gain in GNP.

In a world where hard numbers from competent forecasters count for much, at least among economists, this was a riveting claim. After all, if such gains were to be had, why not adopt Bradford's blueprint, a plan supported by no less a conservative than then-Treasury Secretary William Simon?

Talk in the tight little circle where the economic underpinnings of public finance are debated turned quickly to the question of efficiency and the tax system—thanks to a combination of audacity and technical proficiency from the author of the report.

Nerve comes easily to the 52-year-old Jorgenson. As a young man he invented ways of measuring capital and productivity that spread through technical economics like wildfire. Winner of the John Bates Clark Medal as the best economist of his generation under 40, he is one of a relative handful of theorists who really changed the way economics is done. Nevertheless, he has stayed close to policy questions. He now heads the Program on Technology and Economic Policy at the Kennedy School at Harvard. Among theorists perhaps only Martin Feldstein has more clout with businessmen.

What Jorgenson did was to employ the economist's oldest tool, his conceptual apparatus. But instead of the partial equilibrium approach of the big econometric models, where adjustments to change are of a strictly limited nature, Jorgenson made his calculations with a stripped-down but "forward looking" general equilibrium model, where everything depends on everything else, and the whole future of the economy unfolds in response to particular manipulations.

He explains, "You have to visualize the whole configuration of national wealth in place. Then ask yourself what happens if it's moved around to put the assets to more efficient use. Without actually changing the amount of capital on hand you can increase the social output by the equivalent of adding capital in the amount of X. What I'm trying to convince people here is that that is an important issue which has been neglected."

Models of the sort that Jorgenson used have been around for years; they are a great way of venturing how much of anything is enough. The trouble is that the simplifying assumptions necessary to make the thing tractable verge on the ludicrous for policy purposes: Nobody ever dies in this model, for example. Jorgenson wheeled out his study at a meeting at the Brookings Institution in Washington in January, and immediately used it to attack the more influential econometric studies used in the Treasury proposal, those of Wharton Econometric Forecasting Associates and Data Resources Inc. It was further scrutinized at a National Bureau Conference and a Stanford symposium.

Alas, what began as an intellectual battle with very high stakes quickly dissolved into a theoretical squabble quite remote from legislative consequence.

"It was a very good meeting at Brookings. They (the econometric firms) were pretty much cut up by the end of it," says Jorgenson. Says Joe

Pechman, the meeting's host, "I wouldn't say that Jorgenson carried the day, but there is no doubt that his model is the appropriate one."

Certainly, Jorgenson's rhetorical ploy proved to be very irritating to economists in the trenches. Roger Brinner, Data Resource's chief economist, defends his and Wharton's forecasts, which show little if any growth from tax reform. "There are a couple of very easy places to appropriately enter efficiency considerations. We found that it would be between .2 and 1 percent. Frankly, I don't know anyone who knows where Dale got his numbers."

It was irritating, too, to New Keynesian theorists. "The thing about a general equilibrium model is that it assumes no institutions," says Middlebury College's David Colander. "What good is that?" Another economist, so deeply immersed in the policy process that he declined to be quoted by name, snorted, "The approach is just so hopelessly oversold. When he gets up and talks about it, he talks about it as if it was the Second Coming, as if here we have the answer. A lot of people have made models like that one in the past. They just haven't had the nerve to call it a major tool for policy."

Jorgenson, accustomed to leading others around to his views, is undeterred. After all, 20 years ago he wrote many of the equations with which the current models are built.

The legislative process is too far under way this year for the debate of efficiency to have an effect. Lawyers are back in control at the Treasury, unlike 1981. The economists' argument that the tax code should be mainly used to collect revenues has probably seen its zenith; the alternative view, that the tax system should be used to accomplish social goals, is making a comeback. To be sure, the president's speech will feature an attack on loopholes; even Democrat Bill Bradley has acknowledged their diminution as the strategy underlying his bill. ("As laudable as all these credits and deductions may be, when you put them in the tax code, rates are higher than they would be otherwise.") But the defense of loopholes by Sen. Russell Long and Sen. Robert Packwood has begun; it promises to be a very effective rear-guard action.

MAY 12, 1985

A Theory
of Everything?

"LET US . . . TAKE UP THE FAMILIAR CASE OF A BEGGAR. A GENTLEMAN IS IMPLORED for relief by a repulsive piece of humanity, enshrouded by rags and covered with dirt. Moved by pity, he gives him a dime and passes on.

"What is the economical nature of this transaction? We reply that the transaction is one of supply and demand, belonging to the same class as the supply of and the demand for personal services. The combined willingness and ability of a number of persons in the community to give dimes to beggars constitutes a demand for beggary, just as much as if advertisement, 'Beggars wanted, liberal alms guaranteed,' were conspicuously inserted in the columns of a newspaper. . . .

"Mendacity will exist according to the same laws that govern the existence of other trades and occupations."

When Simon Newcomb, the astronomer turned proselytizing economist, published those words in 1885, he scandalized some readers who thought he was taking economics beyond its proper sphere. To put it mildly, they hadn't seen anything, yet. Economics has been pushing out the boundaries of its relevance ever since.

Consider Gary Becker of the University of Chicago, the inheritor of the mantle of Newcomb, and a modern pioneer, "an authentic genius," according to Nobel laureate George Stigler, the possessor of "a great gift, not a burden."

Becker, 54, is the practical progenitor of that branch of technical economics known as human capital, meaning the analysis of investment in the education and skills of a nation's population. He almost became a sociologist as a Princeton University undergraduate, then switched off because the discipline lacked tools. His economics thesis, something of a bombshell in the mid-1950s, examined the economics of racial discrimination. Then in the mid-1960s, *Human Capital* appeared, a work that virtually transformed the field of labor economics. And in a remarkable series of subsequent papers, Becker explored the economics of crime and punishment, of the allocation of time, of fertility, even of suicide.

He topped it in 1981 with *A Treatise on the Family*, an extraordinary book of mathematical analysis that surveyed (among other things) marriage and divorce, inequality and intergenerational mobility, polygamy and monogamy, the division of labor in households, the demand for children and even the organization of non-human families. Last spring he was elected president of the American Economic Association, this fall he'll receive the prestigious Seidman Prize in Memphis, and if this wasn't enough, he's begun to write a column for *Business Week* magazine.

This sudden widespread recognition has taken longer than it might have, for Becker has often been at odds with a majority of his colleagues, and his enthusiasm for applying economic analysis to other fields has spawned the epithet, "economic imperialism."

Indeed, his quest in getting the professional mainstream to take seriously his views was almost as long at that of his teacher, Milton Friedman, who required 20 years to persuade economists to reopen the matter of money. Donald McCloskey of the University of Iowa, another well-known price theorist who taught with Becker at Chicago, says, "He believes in economics as a general theory of human action. Before him, it was not taken very seriously that way, but he has brought it into very serious use.

"Today," says McCloskey, "Gary is the heir to Milton Friedman in microeconomics, the teaching of prices; Robert Lucas is the heir in macroeconomics. Because of his boldness in applying economics to places where it was not applied before, Becker is hated by very large numbers of economists. A great many non-Chicago economists just get furious. All you have to do is mention the name and people start screaming."

Why? Becker thinks it is some innate intellectual conservatism that protects the realm of the traditional liberal arts. Then, too, many economists resent his having complicated the traditional modes of discourse; now their findings, too, must exhibit the correct regression analyses. In any event, he is often the victim of scorn, something like sociobiologist Edward O. Wilson, whose work he much admires. There is something of the Eastern establishment vs. the Midwest about it, too. "It's not as though it were eating away at their intellectual capital," says Becker. "It's not like taking on, say, Keynesianism. Sociologists might have to retool because of this, but economists should welcome it. The generality of economic analysis should be a source of pride, not embarrassment."

What does one of these arguments look like? Well, here's how Becker sees the problem of dating, a matter of choice par excellence, in a passage from his *Treatise*: "Participants in marriage markets are assumed to have limited information about the utility they can expect with potential mates, mainly because of limited information about the traits of these mates.

"If they could search as 'cheaply' for other mates when married as when single, and if marriages could be terminated without significant cost, they would marry the first reasonable mate encountered, knowing they would gain from even a less-than-optimal marriage. They would then continue to search while married.

"Since, however, marriage does limit access to single persons, and termination can be costly chiefly because of children and other 'investments' specific to a particular marriage, participants usually do not immediately marry the first reasonable prospect encountered, but try to learn about them and search for better prospects."

To others, this is economic imperialism, pure and simple. MIT's Robert Solow, a persistent Becker critic over the years, says, "There are some things that should not be analyzed as if they were subject to being bought and sold. Let's be philosophical. Call them primary things, things that are intrinsic to themselves. There are all kinds of social circumstances that are fundamentally different from economic circumstances." Elusive or not, it's a point of view that many economists find persuasive.

What isn't open to argument, however, is the magnitude of Becker's impact. "He's responsible for a great broadening of his special field," says Iowa's McCloskey. "Gary took a program devised by two older men, Gregg Lewis and Theodore Schultz, and to some extent his colleague Jacob Mincer. He filled it in, he created the colors and brought the whole field to life. Before him, labor economists worked on not very interesting studies of trade unions. They are now going back to those fields, refreshed by their studies of price theory." Charles P. Kindleberger, the man from whom Becker inherits the presidency of the American Economic Association, put it this way: "In science, the strong stuff is the good stuff."

AUGUST 25, 1985

Janos Kornai:
The System Viewed from
the East

AT A TIME WHEN THE SOVIET SYSTEM IS VERY MUCH IN THE NEWS BUT JUST AS OPAQUE as ever, it is hard not to notice that most of a generation of scholars who are specialists on the Russian economy are missing in the West. Between the celebrated Abram Bergson, who retired from Harvard University last year, and today's crop of promising young kids, a 20- or 30-year cycle failed to develop normally—just when the economies of the Comecon nations of Eastern Europe were achieving new levels of development. Sure, there are a goodly number of solid performers among Eastern-bloc specialists, but few theorists have appeared who were capable of advancing the study to a new level.

Why? Well, the reason most often given is that for a long time the brightest young economists in America found it paid far better to learn mathematics than Russian. Even comparative economics—the branch of learning that deals with the differences between them and us—had its vogue for high theory about just-suppose worlds. The trouble is, supersophisticated algebra, even combined with statistical tools, is no substitute for a knowledge of the institutions of planned economies.

There are two broad solutions. One is to throw money at the problem, an approach that works pretty well over time. Columbia University, for example, has gotten an enormous bequest from Averell Harriman, and Harvard is preparing an ambitious program in regional studies. The other solution is to pay more attention to what economists in the socialist countries themselves have been doing.

Janos Kornai, 57, has been visiting at Harvard this year. A leading mathematical economist in Hungary, Kornai is a significant force in Western economics as well. He is unusually well-traveled even for a Hungarian, having spent years since the mid-1960s at the London School of Economics and Sussex, Stanford, Yale, Princeton, Stockholm and Munich universities. He is unusually well-honored, too: He has been president of the Econometric Society, and his works on planning are widely read—at least among economists, for Kornai's work is just as full of formulae, equations and models as that of the average Western economist. Three years ago he received the F.E. Seidman Prize, joining such other notables as Robert Solow, Albert Hirschman, James Buchanan and Gunnar Myrdal.

"Everybody agrees he's the best economist in Eastern Europe or in Russia," says Marshall Goldman at Harvard's Russian Research Center. Kornai's main work is called *The Economics of Shortage*. Published in 1980, the book is slightly deceptive: The two-volume set costs $100 and sounds deliberately narrow. In fact, Western experts have agreed, the book is far-ranging and incisive, tackling nothing less than the economics of planned economies. "Keynes Through the Looking Glass" would have been an equally good title, wrote John D. Hey of the University of York. It is like Keynes, to be sure, wrote Herbert Levine of the University of Pennsylvania—but a Keynes still in the process of development, who hasn't yet completed his *General Theory*.

In Kornai's view, the condition of shortage that pervades planned economies is the appropriate starting point for economists. Shortage is as characteristic a problem of socialist economies as overproduction is of capitalist ones, he says. Long queues, empty shelves, unwanted substitutions of one good for another are simply the counterparts of stagflation. To buy a car, to get a telephone, to find a house in Eastern Europe or the Soviet Union—all these require playing by a particular set of rules, not just occasionally, but constantly. This condition of permanent shortage doesn't happen in other types of economies.

Why? At rock bottom, it is because socialist firms are not afraid of failure, according to Kornai. Managers don't have to compete on price; they can pass their costs on. They don't have to economize their materials, either, for the government will never let their firms go broke. So the biggest, most important firms inexorably suck resources out of the consumer-goods sphere and into the manufacture of primary goods—steel mills, oil refineries, chemical plants and the like. The only constraints on these big firms are frail ones such as public opinion (hoarding is officially condemned) and lack of space in which to store spare parts.

Why are these inefficient systems tolerated? Because some good things come of them: They exhibit steady, dependable growth and maintain full employment. There are bad things, too. These systems get stuck in perpetual seller's markets; chronic shortage reinforces itself and the economy just produces more intermediate goods. The problem is not so much one of "inflation" in the financial sphere, Kornai says, as of "suction" of the rest of the economy into the goods-producing core.

Does this begin to sound a little like the world of defense contractors and public hospitals? After all, these great capitalist institutions can be talked about in terms of insatiable demand and permanent shortage, too. Kornai models in impeccable Marxist economics style but grounds his talk in the thoroughly neoclassical lingo of the budget constraint. A manager who expects to be bailed out has a soft budget constraint; a manager who shoots himself over the bankruptcy of his firm has experienced a hard constraint.

(The insight that exceeding one's budget may hold only varying degrees of terror has led Kornai to challenge one of the rocks on which neoclassical economics seems to be founded. With a single epigram in a technical paper nearly 20 year ago, Robert Clower dismissed a generation of models that treated the economy as a big system of barter. "Money buys goods and goods buy money but goods do not buy goods," said Clower forcefully, but he added a second condition. No one ever buys anything without a means to pay for it in mind. "Unless we presuppose something of the sort, we have absolutely nothing on which to build an account of individual decision processes," Clower wrote. But, in fact, there is a lot of observable behavior to indicate that there are economic actors who, not without reason, hope that "something will turn up" if they totter on the verge of failure, especially in socialist economies, but in capitalist ones, too. State subsidies, tax exemptions and easy credit are just three of the most obvious ways of softening the budget constraint. In Soviet-style economies, the bailout has simply become automatic.)

To be sure, not all economists are persuaded by the vision of a laminate, hierarchical world that underlies Kornai's work. To some, he seems insufficiently appreciative of the achievements of the neoclassical tradition. But even his critics grant, as Frank Hahn put it years ago, that "amid all the present noise" about the failures of mainstream economics, "his is one of the few grammatical voices."

Kornai's rise in the Hungarian establishment was not without drama; indeed, it proceeded in alternating waves of acceptance and condemnation. He presented his dissertation, on the somewhat risky topic of overcentralization in economic management in 1956, the year of the Hungarian Revolution—and was immediately attacked. The reaction diminished, and he rose steadily to head research teams at the Institute of Textiles and the

National Computing Center in the 1960s, before becoming a professor of economics of the Institute of Economics of the Hungarian Academy of Sciences.

Although he was among the first to introduce mathematical planning to the Hungarian economy, Kornai was a persistent skeptic of "computopia"—the vision, especially popular among the Russians, that big computers eventually would enable planners to do their work even better than the market. But, in an interesting paragraph tucked away toward the end of *Shortage*, Kornai recalls how he stuck to the belief that good planning could alleviate allocation problems through two earlier works, *Anti-Equilibrium* and *Rush vs. Harmonic Growth*, before the writing of *The Economics of Shortage* convinced him that it was institutional arrangements themselves and the resultant centralization and over-control that were the cause and not the effect of shortage.

A scholarly fellow given mostly to pure research, Kornai eschews interviews in favor of seminars and off-the-record talks. "I am strongly in favor of the reform process in Hungary," he says, "but I don't want to get involved in daily politics or tactical considerations. I would like to maintain my intellectual independence." He jokes easily. He has a deep interest in the Third World, obviously maintains lively political interests but indulges in no castanet act of his own.

"The healer-economist, with a cure for every economic disease, the apostle-economist, with a complete and detailed blueprint for ideal society, are familiar types," he says. "I feel alien to these colleagues. I am one of those who is aware of the poverty of our science: We can ask questions rather than answer them."

Of the Americans, Kornai is an often shrewd observer, with a slight and predictable bias. In the introduction to an English translation of his lighter essays on the Hungarian economy, soon to be published by the MIT Press, he writes, "Optimism is the 'official party line' in the United States, to use the language of my country. I must warn the reader: This is not an optimistic book. But neither is it pessimistic. There has been a Hungarian tradition for centuries: You are resigned or desperate or angry, and a happy outlook is uncertain or improbable—and yet, you work hard and honestly for improvement. Those who have read the classics of Hungarian drama or poetry . . . or have listened to Bartok's music will know exactly this contradictory mood. Perhaps a member of a gray and nonphilosophical profession, like that of the economist, can follow the same tradition."

Not everyone is convinced that Eastern Europeans have anything to offer Western economists. Paul Craig Roberts, for example, the noted exponent of supply-side policies, recently said, "We have wasted several decades of scholarship while academics bent over backwards to find successes in Soviet-type economies. . . . The politicization of scholarship that allowed academics to keep the failures of socialism under wraps for several decades, while they prattled on about the failures of markets, has adversely affected the lives and fortunes of large numbers of people."

But there are those who think otherwise. Albert Hirschman, for example, another social theorist, says, "Kornai is a man clearly at home in his own country, who has devoted himself to thinking about how to make the system there work more smoothly. He also has spent a great deal of time trying to make things there intelligible to us, in our own language. He is a very useful citizen, I would say."

MAY 26, 1985

The Hidden History of the National Bureau

WHO REALLY TURNED AROUND THE NATIONAL BUREAU FOR ECONOMIC RESEARCH? Did anyone? Most young economists nowadays think that it was Martin Feldstein, now chairman of the Council of Economic Advisers to the president. But they overlook the portion of that change that began with John Meyer, a Harvard professor who was present at the creation of the Boston consulting firm of Charles River Associates, served as vice chairman of the Union Pacific Railroad, helped invent "cliometrics" and ran the Bureau for a decade between Arthur F. Burns and Feldstein.

The question is interesting for two reasons. For one thing, the Bureau is a great institution, one of only a few bases in a shifting game of intellectual capture-the-flag. For another, it casts into sharp relief a pair of senior personalities in modern economics, and illuminates the difference between the center of economics and its periphery.

There is no doubt that in the mid-1960s, the Bureau was widely regarded as being something of an intellectual antique shop. It had been founded in 1920 by Wesley Clair Mitchell, the doyen of American institutionalism, as a place where economics could be pursued free from the taint of partisan politics, and for 20 years or so the bureau was in fact the vanguard of scientific economics. It was able to do things for government that government couldn't do for itself—date business cycles, for example, and make judgments in areas where government couldn't be entirely trusted.

The Bureau set the standard for cool detachment and empirical rigor in the study of business cycles. Simon Kuznets constructed his measures of the national income accounts there, and earned a Nobel Prize in the process. Moses Abramovitz, Solomon Fabricant, Frederick C. Mills and Geoffrey Moore did work there that was widely celebrated as first rate. After Arthur Burns took over from Mitchell in 1945, the Bureau continued to turn out interesting and original work.

But by the mid-1960s, the veins it had mined were pretty well played out. To understand why, it's necessary to know that the bureau was near the end of a 20-year battle—on the losing end. Tjalling Koopmans, the physicist-turned-economist who would later win the Nobel, fired the first salvo in 1944, when he reviewed Mitchell and Burns' magnum opus on business cycles under the title "Measurement Without Theory." Their fact-gathering was insufficient, Koopmans said; what was needed was a new science that combined theory and measurement.

The code word of the new movement in economics was "model." Behind it lurked a great edifice of thought in which statistical inference, probability theory and other techniques were used to actually measure the concepts dictated by theory. Economists finally had learned to estimate values for the things they talked about, to combine them in long chains of "if this, then that" statements that they called models. The new approach was called econometrics, and it emanated, at least at first, from another major intellectual base called the Cowles Commission at the University of Chicago.

When alumni of the Cowles Commission met last summer to celebrate the 50th anniversary of the founding of their field, they recalled to each other that they often thought of the Bureau as "the enemy" in a friendly sort of way. For its part, the Bureau reciprocated in those days: "We didn't follow fads," snorted Sol Fabricant last week recalling the atmosphere then. (Milton Friedman, whose work in the monetary history of the United States was often ascribed to the Bureau, under whose auspices it was published, is regarded as an anomaly. He was in the Bureau, but not of it, at least methodologically.)

By 1967, when Burns was preparing to take over the Federal Reserve system for Richard Nixon, it was clear that econometrics was the dominant tradition and that the historically-oriented institutionalism of Wesley Clair Mitchell was out. "The Bureau was like a natural history museum, full of stuffed Indians," recalls one tart-tongued scholar. "It was full of scholars who were still doing the important work of the 1920s and '30s."

Enter Meyer, a Harvard professor who had accomplished an unlikely series of feats in the 20 years he had been an economist. (He was just 40 in 1967.) For example, "To a large extent he produced a whole new field," says economist Robert Fogel, recalling a single paper on the economics of slavery that Meyer co-authored with Alf Conrad a decade earlier. Meyer wrote on the microeconomics of slave investment, Conrad worked on the demographics, they put the two parts together, made some convincing estimates of just how profitable slavery actually was (historians nearly universally assumed it was a money-losing business) and in that putting-together created the controversial displine known today as cliometrics. "Lincoln was right in the debates, it turned out; Stephen Douglas was wrong." Meyer says. "We were rather flabbergasted at the response," he adds; economic history has been done differently ever since.

Then there was Charles River Associates. Gerald Kraft, the founder, had been a student; so had Franklin Fisher. Meyer-trained econometricians formed the nucleus for a big, tough-minded, policy-oriented consulting firm. Meanwhile, Meyer was teaching econometrics, doing his research on transportation, urban studies, telecommunications.

"Apart from the cliometric paper, which was a stunner, the rest is just solid work," says MIT's Edwin Kuh, a long-time Meyer collaborator. "People who do empirical work, if they do it well, don't get the kudos because the results aren't sharp, clear, unambiguous; they are hedged, they're qualified."

It was Arthur Burns himself who asked Meyer to take over the NBER; the invitation "came more out of the blue than anything else," recalls Meyer. "I said I'd run it for between five and ten years; I did," he says. He moved to New Haven and took a job at Yale, so he could commute to Bureau headquarters in New York.

Meyer patiently opened up the Bureau to new ideas. He brought in econometricians, and asked Ed Kuh to design computer software for them. "My view of the bureau was that basically it should be a service organization to the profession. It should do things or fill voids that couldn't be done within the traditional university department's structure. So a heavy emphasis was put on computer development, on data banks, and the development of medical economics, because it was hard to imagine any university department that could afford more than one, or one-and-a-half medical economists."

Meyer is philosophical about what was involved. "Arthur was never so stodgy as people say. He wasn't anti-computer, either; computers were more expensive in those days." Meyer behaved courteously toward the old guard, altering the Bureau's scientific stance rather than its administrative system. He let the old scholars continue their work.

It was sometimes slow going. Kuh's computer shop never turned the profits that had been hoped for; a big project on water quality for the federal government ran ahead of budget. When Harvard sought to lure him back from Yale in 1973, Meyer agreed to come; he brought Bureau headquarters with him from New York.

It was in 1977 that he quit. Martin Feldstein, a John Bates Clark Medal winner (the prize is given every two years to an economist under 40) who a year earlier had been slipping copies of his papers beneath the doors of news magazine bureau chiefs in Boston, took over. He fired people, including Kuh, who took his highly regarded computational laboratory back to MIT. Feldstein made it clear that his NBER would be interested in policy-oriented research, not science for its own sake.

The rest is history. The "new" Bureau has become a big deal; the coterie of theorists and econometricians that Feldstein put together has been genuinely exciting. "Marty has really completed the change in direction that Meyer began," says Carl Christ, a director of the NBER throughout. But one of the new consensus disagrees. "Under Meyer, the Bureau was not fully brought up to the best part of modern economics. Economics is at its best when it has a question it can answer. It is not at its best when it has to build a model of a city, a system, a banana."

It is not much skin off Meyer's peach. He took time off to serve as vice chairman of Union Pacific Corp. (to see if he felt like going into business), worked on the Reagan administration's transportation transition team, and recently accepted a new appointment at the John F. Kennedy School of Government at Harvard University. He turns up on the short list each time a new transportation secretary is named. He is writing a handbook for the World Bank on urban transport, publishing books on airline deregulation, gearing up for a major study of ostensible "deindustrialization."

So what about it? Who turned the Bureau around? "It was a good deal more evolutionary than many people think," says Meyer.

DECEMBER 11, 1983

The Man
Who Wrote Books

HE WAS PERHAPS 45 WHEN INTERNATIONAL ECONOMICS TURNED MATHEMATICAL, SAIL-ing away from him toward incomprehensibility to all but a few. So his bibliography is full of books, rather than technical papers. When Charles P. Kindleberger was named president of the American Economic Association last week, it was a victory for a man of most unusual stripe. Kindle-berger is a literary and historical economist in an age in which mathematicians reign supreme. He just happens to resemble the immortal Ray Bolger.

Last week, while vector auto-regressions dominated the talk of mone-tarists and anti-monetarists ("It's just a fancy way of extrapolating data series from their past behavior," snorted Milton Friedman), Kindleberger snatched time between sessions to plan a convention next year heavy in economic history and international economics—topics that received com-paratively little attention at the sessions that ended Friday.

If economics is a republic of ideas, then the AEA is the human sub-continent across which it is arrayed, a confederation of 19,000-plus pro-fessionals, whose interests range from economics of the most mundane sorts—property and casualty insurance and mining—to the most erudite forms of theory and econometrics.

Annually, in the vicinity of the New Year, a substantial portion of the members of the AEA assemble in some faraway place for a week of schol-arly paper-presenting, job-hunting and gossip. Last week it was San Fran-cisco, next year it is Dallas. What earned Charlie Kindleberger the presidency? (The three other MIT past presidents—Paul Samuelson, Rob-ert Solow, Franco Modigliani—are all paragons of mathematical virtue.) Well, it was partly the result of a long life spent in the most interesting places. For the first third of his 50-year career, he was in government: the Federal Reserve system, the Office of Strategic Services, the Marshall Plan. Then he moved to the great economics department at MIT, where he had an unusually productive career as a teacher. Among his students were Jagdish

Bhawati, William Branson, Robert Mundell, Jaraslav Vanek and another dozen first-rank economists. (Kindleberger says, "I have a very pungent recollection of the remark of an MIT graduate, not my student, saying to me after a party, and somewhat in his cups, that MIT had done so well in international economics because my old-fashioned approach confused the students, who were forced to work the subject out independently for themselves.") Now he writes in a study at home in Lincoln, hikes the Swiss Alps and hangs around the New York Fed occasionally, chewing the fat with old pals Anthony Solomon, Henry Kaufman, Albert Wojnilower and Robert Roosa. His economic development textbook is still used, and at 71, he is completing a history of 500 years of financial innovation.

His greatest claim to fame, however, may rest on a book he published in 1978. *Manias, Panics and Crashes: A History Of Financial Crises*, is a short and often funny chronicle of financial spasms from the South Sea Bubble to the Penn Central crisis. On the one hand, the book is a quick summer read for businessmen; on the other, its publication was the occasion for a solemn review conference sponsored by the *Maison des Sciences de l'Homme* that attracted many of the best economists in the world. In short, it is probably the best book of its sort since Bagehot.

Bagehot, of course, was the English journalist who wrote the 1873 classic account of the psychology of financial markets, *Lombard Street*. The book explains more clearly than anything before or since the role of central banking in keeping a modern economy from self-destructive cycles of elation and panic. As a commentary on why otherwise reasonable men overdose first on hope, then on despair, it is still worth reading. So is *Manias, Panics and Crashes*.

In an interview last week, Kindleberger sounded worried. "At the moment, I think we're going to go through more trauma of a financial sort," he said. "I do believe the system is fragile and not robust. It is under a lot of strain in a lot of ways, and it is very hard to predict. It is rather like the case of oil. We economists all predicted the price would fall, but the dynamics of exactly when it would fall and why were very hard to foresee."

In Kindleberger's view, the period of the 1970s will go down in history as period of wild speculations. We are still working off the excesses, he says, and so far we've been lucky. "As long as the collapses are one at a time and well-spaced, it is OK. They have been in recent years: the real estate investment trusts, the 747s and so on. Drysdale scared the wits out of them, and Penn Square—why, Penn Square was hilarious, wasn't it? People would simply give out money without any idea of their chances of getting it back.

"Now it is the international liquidity question that is of most concern, the Argentine and Polish debt. But if crashes like these should pile on top of each other, that would be awful. The dynamics of predicting is very hard to do. Watchful waiting, wariness, those things are called for."

In his book, Kindleberger is much at pains to take issue with the doctrine known as "monetarism." Strictly speaking, he says, monetarism denies that unhealthy speculation and panic are even a possibility. Financial and commodity markets always work perfectly, everywhere. They can't be destabilized by individual investors. There is no need for the government or the central bank to concern itself with the pattern of boom and bust, aside from assuring a steady growth of the money supply.

On the contrary, he says, the record suggests that manias and panics—quite apart from the ebb and flow of the business cycle—are events that can be controlled, or at least moderated, by careful attention to them. The basic dynamic of boom and bust is quite simple, according to Kindleberger. In the manic phase, investors scramble to get out of money and into illiquid real things: stocks, commodities, real estate, tulip bulbs, whatever. In a panic, people of wealth and credit reverse the process and scramble to unload whatever they've bought, at greater and greater losses. Money is only part of it.

Speculative manias often get started in the most reasonable ways, he says. An opportunity is sensed, and investors respond to it by seeking a good return. Railroads are built, acres planted, minerals searched out. In a second phase, however, capital gains become the order of the day, as investors start selling their investments looking for windfall profits.

Meanwhile, monetary expansion fuels the flames. Bankers create credit, lending money beyond what their capital base and their reserves would ordinarily support. The purchasing power of individuals explodes, and prices are bid up. As trading heats up dangerously, swindles emerge, as fringe characters seek to get in on the action. Certain types of flim-flam occur across national and temporal lines: the noble gambler, the venal journalist, the foolish banker have been found in bubbles of every imaginable sort.

But it is the revelation of fraud and not the fraud itself that counts, Kindleberger notes. These dramatic disclosures, when they occur, "make known to the world that things have not been as they should have been, that it is time to stop to see how they truly are. The making known of malfeasance . . . is important as a signal that the euphoria has been overdone."

So at a critical stage, people begin to come to their senses. The limits have been overshot, they realize; they're a little like Wile E. Coyote of the

Roadrunner cartoons, just as he discovers he has run off the cliff, hanging in midair before he falls. Kindleberger identifies this stage of the cycle as "distress."

Then comes the crash. Desperate investors seek to unload on one another, prices plummet, bankruptcies multiply. The frontispiece of Kindleberger's book is a quotation from his mentor Bagehot: "One thing is certain, that at particular times a great deal of stupid people have a great deal of stupid money. . . . At intervals, from causes that are not to the present purpose, the money of these people—the blind capital, as we call it, of the country—is particularly large and craving; it seeks for something to devour and there is plethora; it finds someone and there is speculation; it is devoured, and there is panic."

Inevitably, Kindleberger says, once panic has set in the government has a choice of letting it "burn out," or of stepping in to try to shore up the crumbling system. As "lender of last resort," a central bank may sometimes head off a full-fledged panic by exhibiting pockets deep enough and timing good enough, but even then it may fail, and be swept away with the rest.

Always there is a difficult moral dilemma, he adds. Shall the lender of last resort save only its friends, the "good" banks and corporations that are members of the financial establishment? Or shall it offer help to those organizations who most likely to be in trouble—precisely because they are somewhat beyond the pale?

Where are we now? Kindleberger reaches for a copy of his book, and opens it to a passage on "financial distress." He reads: "Financial distress for a single firm means that its earning power has fallen far enough to create a nontrivial probability that it will not be able to pay interest and principal on its debt, with consequent deterioration in its credit standing. Financial distress for an economy also has a prospective rather than an actual significance, and implies financial adjustments or disturbances ahead."

He reads quickly over the list of adjectives culled from accounts of dozens of similiar episodes over 300 years: "uneasiness," "apprehension," "tension," "stringency," "pressure," "uncertainty," "ominous conditions," "fragility."

"Optimism and pessimism are matters of digestion," says Kindleberger, "and I am an optimist." Nevertheless, he quickly adds, the world economic order has fallen into a kind of disarray from which it will not be easily rescued. "My friends who are political scientists tend to use the word 'hegemony' to describe what I mean when I use the word 'leadership.' The United States has failed to exercise leadership, and the world just can't get along very well without it.

"I have a view that to be stable, the world needs a stabilizer—someone who takes responsibility for worrying about the world economy and for trimming the excesses when markets get too tight or loose. But no country is taking that responsibility. We used to do it, but now we are copping out."

JULY 13, 1982—JANUARY 1, 1984

An Economy Without a Middle?

Q: What's the one book Ken Galbraith never read?
A: The Dual Economy, by Robert Averitt.

HE TEACHES AT SMITH COLLEGE IN NORTHAMPTON, NOT A LIKELY PLACE FOR A GURU. There are no graduate students, his colleagues are not exactly the Knights of the Round Table, his office not much except a litter of textbooks and old issues of *Science* magazine. His publisher doesn't return telephone calls from reporters, and the leaders of his profession don't know his name.

What's more, he's not exactly a ball of fire either, "a curious mixture of ambition and sloth," he says. "Sometimes I wake up and I think I'm the smartest economist in America, that I understand it all. Other days I think that I don't know anything."

Robert Averitt is the unofficial proprietor of the phrase "dual economy," an appellation that has entered the vocabulary of indispensable economic terms, along with the "administered pricing" of Gardiner Means, the "managerial revolution" of James Burnham and John Kenneth Galbraith's notion of the "technostructure." It is one of those terms you don't learn as an economist, but one which to all others is a particularly useful way of describing the world of everyday experience.

Indeed, the fashionable modern distinctions between the "service sector" and an industrial core of the economy can trace their roots back to Averitt's book, *The Dual Economy*, (W.W. Norton & Co., 1968). Published just a year after Galbraith's best-selling *The New Industrial State*, it has slowly become an underground classic.

True, Averitt hasn't followed up his insight with as much vigor as Galbraith. There has been no second volume of applications, and his publication record has been lackadaisical. On the verge of 51, the Texas native is writing an introductory text in an attempt to diffuse his ideas. Yet the clarity of *The Dual Economy* is still great; its analytic premises are still firm. In certain important respects, Galbraith is as much a footnote to Averitt as the other way around.

What exactly is a dual economy? According to Averitt, it is one in which two different tiers of industrial organization exist side by side: a clutch of large, complicated industrial corporations at the "center," and a myriad of smaller firms at the "periphery." The big firms operate with a long time horizon; the little firms live for today.

"It's almost as though the 19th century were still alive there beside the 20th century," he says. "There are little, free-trading, personally-managed firms that do business in one way, and there are big multi-product companies that do business another way."

There was a time, of course, when this argument was more intuitively compelling than it is today. The idea of a few powerful firms immune to market forces, able to do exactly as they pleased through advertising and "administered pricing" was dealt a considerable blow by the spectacle of a handful of Japanese firms clobbering the big Detroit automakers in world markets.

Moreover, there has been an intellectual revolution of sorts in the branch of economics concerned with the size and shape of firms and their markets—industrial organization, it is called—that has given economists a bundle of useful new tools for dealing with the oft-observed facts of "imperfect competition."

"There're always people running around who think that somehow big corporations are different from small corporations, but they usually don't bother to say how," says Harvard's industrial organization expert, Richard Caves. "Who is Robert Averitt, anyway?" says George Borts, a professor of economics at Brown University who was editor of the *American Economic Review* for 10 years.

The point is, the idea of a dual economy has scarcely won a following among acolytes of that vast mainstream known as "the neoclassical synthesis," to whom the idea of two sets of rules is anathema.

Averitt makes a distinction between the goods that companies manufacture and the people they employ to manufacture them, of course: dual product markets are not necessarily the same thing as dual labor markets, and a lively tradition of two-track analysis of the structure of jobs has grown up more or less independently of him.

This "segmented labor markets" approach, with its emphasis on the division between rich and poor, of an economy without a middle, is a skein of analysis developed separately over the years by MIT's Michael J. Piore and others. It is used extensively by New England thinkers on the left, notably Rick Edwards of the University of Massachusetts at Amherst, Boston University's Peter Doeringer, Boston College's Barry Bluestone and MIT'S Bennett Harrison, to describe a system in which the middle class finds itself under pressure. But now a full-scale dual economy book by Bluestone and Harrison called *Deindustrializing America* is said to be among the hottest items of the coming autumn publishing season. Piore's work, particularily on the resurgence of the Italian economy, is attracting a widening audience. Sociologists have adopted the dual economy idea as their own. And even though he has spent his life in the shadow of Ken Galbraith, Averitt's book is selling better than ever before.

"It is one of the most cross-referenced books in economics," says Theresa Amott, a former student who is professor of economics at Wellesley. "It is a very sound book," says Alfred Chandler, the celebrated business historian, who notes the congruence between his work and Averitt's.

No wonder that Averitt has a following in the business schools; the major factor is the giant corporation, the kind of firm which Averitt describes as operating at the "center" of the economy. "The center firms' distinctiveness stems from size and independence—from their owners, industry, product mix and national origin; and secondly from their intense awareness of the total economy, their long-run destiny and the nature and drift of technical change." On the "periphery," Averit writes, are firms that are smaller, more concentrated geographically, more likely to market a single line of related products amid more competitive circumstances. These companies have less access to capital. "Their emphasis is on short-run problems, leaving little time for long-run planning," he wrote.

The public policy implications of the dual nature of the economy are unmistakable, argues Averitt. The government should play a large role in channeling capital, backing research and development, discriminating between "sunrise" and "sunset" industries. "Center firms, especially those imbedded in key industries, are semi-public institutions. The recognition of this fact is long overdue. They do not, will not and cannot adhere to the competitive rules of neoclassical price theory," Averitt wrote in 1968.

But then the theory of the dual economy is not so much a contradiction of economics as an adjunct to it. A walk around town can turn up plausible evidence of the existence of an economy arranged in tiers, and a look at the work of historian Fernand Braudel offers even more so. The lesson preached by Averitt—disaggregation—may have been disregarded for the most part by economists, but it is increasingly attended to by nearly everyone else.

"Who?" says John Kenneth Galbraith into the telephone. "Robert Averitt? I should know him but I don't. Are you doing an obit? He's still alive? Well, sorry I couldn't help you. I'm sure I should know him, but I don't."

JULY 4, 1982

How a Nuclear
Strategist Switched to
Climate Change

GEORGE BUSH ROUTINELY GETS BEATEN UP BY ENVIRONMENTALISTS OVER GREENHOUSE affairs because they think he should be leading the charge to do something. In fact, among the economists who study the problem, the opposition to quick action runs fairly deep—quite aside from uncertainty over the climatological models. Typical is Thomas C. Schelling, a thinker senior enough to be serving as the current president of the American Economic Association, who's leaving Harvard for the University of Maryland this week after a 30-year span. Indeed, a look at the 69-year-old Schelling's career illuminates a good bit of the origins of present-day thinking about the greenhouse effect.

In the 1960s, no academic figure exemplified the romance of Harvard in Washington better than Schelling. It was said that Robert McNamara was influenced by his thinking, more than by any other. The son of a naval officer and veteran of a long Marshall Plan stint after World War II, Schelling wrote a book on algebraic economics in his spare time during the late 1940s and turned it in for a Harvard PhD. Then, after a stint at the Rand Corp., he took up thinking seriously about nuclear war, earning a reputation as a tough-minded peacenik in the strenuous top-secret campaign against the Air Force to establish a testing treaty. (Another well-known test ban crusader, seismologist Frank Press, today heads the National Academy of Sciences, the clearinghouse where much of the most serious greenhouse study is done.)

Schelling published *The Strategy Of Conflict* in 1959 (sample chapter: "Bargaining, Communication and Limited War.") But it was in Kennedy's Camelot that Schelling really burst upon the Washington scene, commuting for his day-a-week consulting job on Friday, and during Lyndon Johnson's years the economist-cum-strategist was everywhere, advising the best and the brightest in the Defense Department and the National Security Council.

But in the wake of the U.S. decision to spread the Vietnam War to Cambodia in April 1970, Schelling led a delegation of 12 Harvard professors to Washington to call on old friend Henry Kissinger, who was then national security adviser. "We took turns speaking," Schelling recalls. "We told him that we had thought of the executive branch as our friend, of Congress as our enemy. From now on we would reverse it. Henry went gray in the face, he slumped in his chair. I thought at the time that he suffered serious depression. But there was no sign that it ever had any effect." For Schelling, the vow to perform no more work for the executive branch was an especially momentous pledge. It cost him both his audience and his information.

After a laborious intellectual retooling, there followed a trickle, then an outpouring of work on human behavior, energy and climate. There was still the garment bag on the shoulder at the airport on Thursday evenings, but now Schelling's clients included Congress, the National Academy of Science, and various foundations; the issues were fossil fuels, racial discrimination, sexual politics, drug addiction, the cigarette habit, medical ethics, climate change, even wearing mittens in your sleep to keep from scratching poison ivy. ("Treating your sometime self as though it were somebody else is a ubiquitous and familiar technique of self-management.")

At the heart of it all was game theory. Today, of course, the systematic taking account of other people's actions in your theorizing is all the rage in economics. In fact, probably nothing is being talked about more frequently among teachers of economics just now than David Kreps' new graduate microeconomics textbook, which incorporates game theory for the first time in the deep-down architecture of the field. But when Schelling began writing about strategy in the 1950s, it was news to most economists—so much so that his "theory of interdependent decision" was all but ignored by them.

In Schelling's hands, the most mundane choices are illuminated for their strategic considerations. Christmas savings clubs are seen to be a way of binding the self to save even in the face of temptation. Protective hockey helmets become an intricate exercise in collective choice, for nobody wears them voluntarily, while everbody benefits if they are mandated. It turns out to be easy to decide where to meet in New York City without making plans if you just think for a while about what places the other guy knows. (Under the Biltmore clock, of course.)

As Richard Zeckhauser says, "Those who read Schelling and participate in his games learn a general principle: in any interactive situation it is vitally important to look at matters from the side of the other party. . . . The other-people's-shoes approach is often recommended by soft-hearted promoters of compromise. The core principle, however, is that by understanding the other party's perspective you will improve your comprehension of the situation dramatically and will come out better yourself. This is an important lesson for hard hearts as well."

So what does Schelling's game-theoretic perspective suggest about the global warming debate? Not good, says Schelling, if you aim to prevent it from happening. Any nation that attempts to mitigate changes in climate through unilateral action pays the cost alone, he says, while sharing the benefits with the rest of the world, and the benefits might not be all that great. Suppose the United States decided to cut its fossil fuel use by a third over a 20-year span—at a yearly cost of something like $150 billion to $200 billion. The result would be a 10 percent decline in the world's carbon dioxide emissions; the time it would take to reach a doubling of atmospheric carbon dioxide would be reduced to 80 from 85 years. If China, Russia and the United States agreed to give up the use of coal, it might make a significant difference, but the chances of a global fuel compact are today remote, Schelling thinks.

But then he brightens. "What difference does climate change make, expecially if it comes slowly? The interesting thing is that, to a first approximation, it isn't going to make any difference, at least to advanced countries, where there's hardly any economic activity that's terribly affected by the weather. Of course agriculture is, but agriculture is only 3 percent of GNP. So if agriculture costs went up even by a third, a 1 percent reduction of real GNP, taking place over the course of a century, a period in which personal income would probably double anyhow, would scarcely be noticed. Then if you look at what it's going to do to human health and human comfort and recreation, even extinction of species, it's very hard to identify.

"That's because you probably undergo a greater climate change if you go from Boston to Washington than anybody's likely to experience by sitting still for the next 100 years. It is even hard in this country to find a bird or fish or insect or wildflower or even a tree that doesn't grow or occupy a habitat that covers a wider range of climates than the changes that are expected.

"Now this may not be true for developing countries, where they are much much more dependent on food production and where they may have much less margin for adaptability. This leads me to conclude that the countries that can afford to do something about it—maybe western Europe, the United States, Japan and a few others—probably won't be able to identify a powerful national interest, not when it's time to talk about our president putting a dollar-a-gallon tax on diesel fuel and gasoline. And the countries where probably the most might need to be done, like India and China, the countries that are already very inefficient consumers of fuel, are probably going to become bigger and bigger consumers of it. They probably won't and shouldn't do anything to curb greenhouse emissions, unless somebody else pays for it. I think eventually it will get around to that, but it will take 20 years instead of two years."

JUNE 10, 1990

Hepburn Retires and Is Not Replaced, as Tracy Soldiers On

SHE WOULD BUSTLE INTO A ROOM AND EACH PERSON IN IT WOULD SIT A LITTLE straighter, leaning slightly forward in case the first penetrating question should come to her. He would take off his shirt when trailing at squash, in hopes of unnerving the female student who was beating him. Together, Carolyn Shaw Bell and Marshall Goldman and their economist colleagues at Wellesley College taught a stream of college girls who wanted to understand something of the way the world works. The girls in turn have gone on to create the very archetype of the engaged female financial professional.

The high-compression Salomon Brothers jogger who was brutally attacked in Central Park, the Sigourney Weaver character in the movie

Working Girl, the largest contingent after Harvard grads themselves in each year's entering class at the Harvard Business School, much of the cream of the present generation of female policy economists: all are Wellesley women. For 25 years, the school has built an unparalleled record in preparing undergraduates to successfully enter a business traditionally dominated by men.

But last Friday, Carolyn Shaw Bell retired after more than 30 years of teaching, most of them as the Katherine Coman Professor of Political Economy, and Wellesley College, the institution that has produced more woman economists, bankers and MBAs than any other in America is, for the moment, slightly out of kilter.

Having achieved its results through a highly deliberate policy of equal representation of women and men at all faculty ranks, the economics department has now tipped decisively to men, 6–2. A decision by the college administration to overrule the wishes of the economics department, and grant tenure to the sixth man instead of offering a job to a woman elsewhere, or even holding a job open for one, has left some bad feelings in its wake. And Bell herself is miffed that the college is in a sense the victim of its own success.

"Beginning in the '70s," she wrote colleagues last month, "women economists found excellent opportunities in government, business and elsewhere in academia, and our department, in 15 years, lost more than a dozen women faculty, whose future here was bright, but only one man who preferred another position to Wellesley's.

"As a result, I leave a totally male-dominated department, which cannot offer present and future students the experience of seeing, as Peggy Howard put it, 'the way we want the world to be, where men and women treat each other as equals.' "

For more than 20 years, the demonstration of this desirable state of affairs began with Bell and Marshall Goldman. Neither was in the top rank of their generation of economists on strictly technical grounds, but each had a sure foothold in senior circles of a specialty. Together, they cooperated to teach economics to first-year students with unusual gusto and good cheer, and careful attention to all the little possibilities of unwitting sexism.

Thus if the celebrated economic magnates of the 1950s and '60s at MIT and Harvard could be said to have corresponded somehow to the great male actors of the movies—Gary Cooper, Humphrey Bogart, Clark Gable, Ray Bolger, Peter Lorre, Claude Rains, Randolph Scott, Cary Grant—Bell and Goldman made their mark as members of a team: Katharine Hepburn and

Spencer Tracy, stylish people (with their share of foibles) full of passionate regard for one another—energetic, self-respecting, fully-involved.

Instead of high scholarship, the Wellesley economists made their contribution with their teaching, civic and living styles. A Framingham native, Bell was graduated from Mt. Holyoke College in 1941, and from the University of London in 1949. The war and an early failed marriage to a fellow economist left her with both an enduring awareness that Americans come in something other than two-parent family units, and a right to droll comment on the strengths and weaknesses of the male phalanx that dominated the profession. A highly successful marriage to Wellesley businessman Nelson Bell set a dominating example of lives led successfully in tandem.

She raised daughters, entertained friends, chaired her department, politicked with colleagues to keep its quality and morale high. An endless parade of students came to supper, ate roast beef and Yorkshire pudding and trifle for desert, talked about Shakespeare and the minimum wage in an atmosphere where gender had nothing to do with performance.

Meanwhile, Marshall Goldman conducted his life by a similar compass: his China-scholar wife, his daughters, his commitment to Harvard's Russian Research Center were as much a part of learning economics at Wellesley as supply curves and regressions.

Bell's research style relentlessly connected the tools of economics to the real world. In *Who's Who in Economics*, Mark Blaug described her principal contributions this way: "Identifying policy areas where basic data are insufficient, e.g., unemployment, income, economic hardship, and focusing attention on persistent need for revising models to fit realities of institutional change. Identifying consumer choice area beyond spending and saving; retail distribution as an example of monopolistic competition; marketing as an information network. As a teacher and activist, helping other economists recognize sex bias within the profession, and work to overcome it. As a 'popularist,' contributing to more public understanding of economics and what economists do."

Perhaps most important, Bell started and maintained a newsletter sent to former students and friends, devoted mainly to the triumphs and adventures of Wellesley women who went into economics, business and finance. These FEMS (former economic majors) turned out to be an ever-more variegated parade of high-achievers; the chronicles of their exploits inspired new generations of undergraduates who flocked to the economics department to read back issues.

In later years, Bell's career held some disappointments. An early adviser to the Carter campaign, she was quickly shouldered aside by others. There was no presidency of the American Economics Association—perhaps because of her relentless work concentrating attention on the low status of women in the profession.

Her biggest disappointment, however, must be that her department has found no woman to replace her. Helen Ladd, a 44-year-old policy economist who was for several years her presumptive heir, left Wellesley first for Harvard, then for Duke. To be sure, there are several promotable women waiting in the wings in the economics department, in case a man should leave. And there is always the possibility of simply hiring a senior woman away from another school.

Still, the situation in the Wellesley economics department is a troubling reminder of the situation in the larger world. It is true that Wellesley College, with 37 women and 33 men among its full professors, has an overall ratio of women to men that is perhaps the most equal in the nation. In contrast, MIT has 26 women and 524 men (4.7 percent); Harvard has 35 women and 495 men (6.6 percent) Stanford has 18 women and 494 men (3.5 percent) and even Mt. Holyoke has only 27 women compared to 44 men (38 percent).

Ever the economist, Bell says, "Women have advanced much further and faster in private industry, despite the current complaints of a glass ceiling. Women in positions comparable to those of tenured faculty far outnumber their academic sisters. There are senior executives in major corporations, and some CEOs besides Joan Bok at New England Electric System.

"My own hypothesis is that private sector firms, under the stimulus of the profit motive, have more incentive to be efficient than not-for-profit organizations. When you come right down to it, what motive is there for any man in his 40s, tenured and comfortable with his male colleagues, to want to introduce an unknown and uncomfortable element in his life?"

JUNE 4, 1989

The Many Lives
of Marshall Goldman

YURI ANDROPOV HAS DISAPPEARED. IT IS TRUE THAT HE IS SAID TO HAVE A MIND LIKE a razor, but his shirt collars are two sizes too big, and he shuffles when he walks across the room—signs of possible bad health.

So here's Marshall Goldman, on the phone to France, to Washington, to Japan, piecing together bits of news from accounts of persons who have seen the Communist party chairman, thinking it over, zipping off to New York City for the *Good Morning America* show to explain the significance of Andropov's initiatives to an enthusiastic David Hartmann.

Goldman, 53, is an economist—a specialist on the economy of the Soviet Union. The craft has changed quite a lot since a Kremlinologist was someone who studied the photographs of May Day parades released by Tass. There are more students of the Russian economy now, the barriers are easier to penetrate.

Still, there are perhaps only a dozen first-rate Soviet economists practicing before the bar of scholarly opinion. Andropov is back from his brief absence last week, of course, and Marshall Goldman is busier than ever.

In his new book, *USSR in Crisis, the Failure of an Economic System* he argues for a reappraisal. If anything, the Russians are facing a worse crisis than he had earlier thought. "The Soviet Union simply isn't going in the right direction," he says.

The much-publicized gains of the economy that have come since Andropov took over? They may actually hurt the country in the long run, he says, by postponing the day of reckoning when real changes in the distribution of power and income will have to be made.

The book is dedicated to the USSR: "For making an economist's life so interesting."

Marshall I. Goldman is Class of 1919 Professor of Economics at Wellesley College and associate director of the Russian Research Center at Harvard University.

"My heart is in both places, my heart is in a lot of places, but my paycheck comes from Wellesley," he says.

So here's Marshall Goldman teaching a course in the reindustrialization of Massachusetts with colleague Karl E. Case. Case puts together the reading list. It is heavy on econometrics and location theory. Goldman puts together the course meetings.

There is a chat with Digital Equipment Corp. founder Kenneth Olson and a visit to An Wang (Mrs. Wang is a Wellesley alumna). George Kariotis, former secretary of economic development, comes to talk; so does a fellow who went broke with a high-tech start-up; so does venture capitalist Peter Brooke. "In the end," says Case, "it turned out that it was more useful to read the history of the industrial revolution—you know, why did it take place in England instead of in France—than any of the location theory. It was an awfully good course."

"I can't do the econometrics any more," says Goldman. "Who can? But I love the economics. Comparative economics. Isn't that what it is all about?" Andropov has been in office for more than a month, and the Russians have denied Goldman's application for a visa. So here's Marshall Goldman, wangling an invitation as houseguest of the U.S. ambassador in January. That way they have to let him in, under the current rules.

Goldman gives some lectures in Leningrad during his visit, but some other lectures are canceled as a sign of displeasure, because he wouldn't promise to stay away from dissidents.

"I took an eight-hour walk," he says. "I started with the stores, came back to the same ones in the evening. They probably would have done better to keep me bottled up in the lecture hall."

Goldman, whose first trip to Russia was in 1959, spent the fall of 1978 as Fulbright lecturer at Moscow State University. He was (relatively) optimistic on the Soviet economy at the time. Since then, he's turned bearish on the Bear.

Unbalanced growth with a concentration on basic industry, a recipe designed by Stalin himself, has brought the Russian economy as far as it can go, according to Goldman. The agricultural sector, deprived for half a century in order to foster the industrial buildup, is now chronically unable to deliver. And the whole thing is sunk deep in bureaucratic morass.

The kind of organizational revolution necessary to get the country moving again is entirely conceivable—but it just might get out of hand. So the leaders, almost all of them old men, sit tight, because "he who rides a tiger is afraid to dismount."

"Sure the Soviets are bad guys. They played a trick on us, they kept on with military spending in the 1970s when we relaxed. We still have got to deal with them.

"The Reagan administration scares me. The history of our relationship is like a pendulum, of swinging too far one way, then too far back. What happens if we swing to the opposite extreme?

"Certainly trying to starve them into breakdown is a big mistake. They have the tightest belt in the world," he says, "especially when somebody is out to get them."

Averill Harriman has given $11 million to Columbia University to further its Russian studies programs, and Columbia is preparing to blast past Harvard. Or so it thinks.

So here are the fathers of Harvard's Russian Research Center rallying the Harvard deans, raising money, cranking out the newsletters to alumni. In the van is Marshall Goldman—the very model of the entrepreneurial scholar. "He's indefatigable," says Edward L. Keenen, a Russian historian who is dean of the faculty of arts and sciences.

Some of the programs the center pushes involve the usual putting-out of roots into the community. Among them are a midcareer program, designed to bring businessmen, scholars and journalists to the center. Also under consideration is an "area fellows" program, designed to confer additional prestige on the very best students.

But toughest is the competition for scholars. The older generation of Russian specialists will be retiring in the next few years. The ranks of the younger generation are notoriously thin. "The gods have to strike twice to make a good Russian economist," says Goldman. They must know the language. And they must know economics.

The stakes for which the academicians of the Russian Research Center are playing are not small ones. Only Columbia and the Berkeley/Stanford parlay rival the eminence of Harvard in Soviet studies. "We had the first reunion of the Russian Research Center in Japan last year. Practically everyone in the Ministry of Foreign Affairs was trained here."

The money markets are wiggling. So here's Marshall Goldman, reading the broad tape, predicting interest rates. "My record is actually pretty good," he says.

Goldman writes a newsletter for the Century Bank and Trust Co., a well regarded Somerville bank that specializes in lending to small businesses. "It was the mid-1960s, Phil David Fine asked me to write a letter for the Commonwealth Bank and Trust Co. Then Marshall Sloane decided to break away from Commonwealth. He told me that if I came along to write a newsletter, he'd make me a director. I did. And now I'm chairman of the investments committee.

"Marshall runs it as a family business, and it does me a world of good to be around all these highly practical people. I love it. It gives me exposure to another world."

Brandeis University is looking for a president. Goldman is on the short list. He's tempted. He isn't asked.

"We had big arguments at home. Frankly it was the only job that I would have considered. I wouldn't have moved. My family was quite leery of it. I thought it would have meant giving up all of the Russian studies, and that is a lot of fun. On the other hand, I really enjoy asking people for money . . ."

Here's Marshall Goldman in China. His wife, Merle, is a professor of Chinese history at Boston University, and this time it is she who is giving the seminar, dragging Goldman around. He loves it. Sometimes they travel with their children; sometimes not.

Goldman was born in 1930 in Elgin, Ill., 35 miles northwest of Chicago. After college at the Wharton School of the University of Pennsylvania, he took up Russian studies at Harvard—only to be interrupted by the draft. At home in Wellesley, he swims in the summer, plays squash in the winter. He's celebrated among his partners for his competitive thirst. "He's a streetfighter, he loves a scrap," says one. "I live a nice life," he says. It's true. He does.

There's a napkin on the floor of the lunch room at the Russian Research Center. So here's Marshall Goldman, bending over, picking it up, throwing it away. Marshall Goldman is nothing if not efficacious.

MARCH 29, 1983

How Waltham
Lost Its Watch Trade

ANYONE WHO HAS EVER DRIVEN THROUGH WALTHAM, MASSACHUSETTS, MUST wonder what happened to the American watch business. The light and airy factory along the Charles River that was once the great center of the world trade in inexpensive watches is now home to an industrial hodgepodge of small machine shops and others struggling to survive.

Does the story of the Waltham watch industry offer cautionary tales for other industries—steel, autos, TV sets, even chips?

The answer is yes—but it isn't necessarily what you think. There were no impersonal forces of destiny. No experience curves nor industrial divides nor innate comparative advantages can explain the loss. Instead, the tale is mostly one of plain bad management and greed, according to David Landes.

Landes, 59, is perhaps the foremost among American economic historians. A Harvard University professor, he is the author of *Bankers and Pashas*, about the building of the Suez Canal, and *The Unbound Prometheus*, a history of the Industrial Revolution since 1750. Landes is no stranger to patterns of finance and technical change, nor is he a quick and glib critic of business. The "new economic history" with its systems of simultaneous equations puts him off (its motto is, "Whatever has been, had to be," he says).

Who better, then, to tell the story of clocks?

In *Revolution in Time: Clocks and the Making of the Modern World*, Landes starts from Lewis Mumford's observation that "the clock, not the steam-engine, is the key machine of the industrial age," because fairly precise timekeeping was necessary to synchronize the actions of working men in the age of the telegraph and the railway. He then writes an extraordinarily vivid history of timekeeping, a combination of anecdote and analysis that has been uniformly praised by businessmen, historians, scientists and economists.

Landes chronicles the "magnificent dead end" of horology in China, the rise of the clock in Europe, the progressive improvement of timekeeping devices from crude wooden devices to the latest vibrating sliver of quartz, and throughout, the rise and decline of national industries.

In all this, the story of Waltham is only a tiny part, but embedded in the fabric of the overall narrative it takes on special meaning.

The modern timekeeping industry began with a competition around the turn of the 19th century between the Swiss and the British to see who could tap into the growing market for watches that accompanied the early stages of the Industrial Revolution, Landes says. The British squandered an early lead, and the Swiss took over the business, producing a long series of innovations, including the stem-winder, which replaced the external key.

"The Swiss made watches to please the customers, the British made watches to please themselves," Landes writes.

Watches were still made by hand, then, with craftsmen fitting parts together, polishing them, finally signing their products. Mechanization took the European manufacturers a certain distance towards economies of scale. But making watches was still a business for artisans.

Then the Americans invented factory watchmaking. The industry grew from the manufacture of larger clocks, of course. Chauncey Jerome, a Bristol, Conn., clockmaker, learned to make clocks with brass instead of wooden movements; soon he was selling them successfully to the English. Jerome had learned how to assemble clocks from interchangeable instead of merely similar parts; the result was that he made a sturdier clock for less.

The process of mass production became know as "the American method" of manufacture.

It was in Waltham that the "American method" was applied to the manufacture of watches. "The breakthrough came in the 1850s," Landes says. A mechanic and watchmaker named Aaron Dennison assembled a talented team of designers and machinists to invent the machines necessary to the mass production of watches. It was slow and difficult work, but eventually it began to pay off—by 1859, its business had begun to take off.

In the next 75 years, the American Watch Co. rose to a position of dominance. To be sure, its success sparked dozens of competitors—Elgin, Illinois, Waterbury, Hamilton and about 60 others were companies that got into the act eventually, Landes says—and in three-quarters of a century American manufacturers turned out 120 million jeweled watches and twice as many "clock-watches." Some 40 million of them were made in Waltham.

What happened? Well, from the first, the company had been poorly managed, according to Landes; its success owed more to its new technology than to any innate concern with quality. The factory was organized into separate shops, each a little duchy, and all kinds of sloppy labor practices were tolerated: one report found that 4,000 people were employed to do what 2,000 could do. Meanwhile, the Swiss had come roaring back.

So starting in the 1920s, the company was bled to death, Landes says. At the behest of its commercial bankers (the Bank of Boston) and its investment bankers (Kidder, Peabody and Co.) the American Watch Co. was reorganized twice in the 1920s; the second time brought Frederic C. Dumaine in as its head. Dumaine "had learned his watch-making as boss of Amoskeag mills of Manchester, N.H., probably the largest cotton manufacturing plant in the world," Landes writes.

It was Dumaine who was the villain of the piece.

At Amoskeag, Dumaine had always promised that the good years would pay for the bad ones; the period of World War I had been one of extraordinary prosperity; the depression of the early 1920s had seen the company's first strike. But instead of plowing money into new machinery, instead of moving into artificial fibers, Dumaine ran the cotton mill without maintenance. Machines were cannibalized, spare parts were sold off for scrap. He even stopped painting the plant.

At the American watchworks, Dumaine did the same thing again, Landes writes. "In the two decades that he ran Waltham, he turned red ink into black, earned substantial profits, paid off just about all that debt, made a tidy sum for Kidder, Peabody and a fortune for himself. He did this by cutting wages and holding fresh investment to a minimum, by squeezing the last turn out of machines that had been running for decades and the last die out of toolmakers who had been working even longer."

Nor was there anything inevitable about it. Elgin and Hamilton continued to make money-making watches throughout the period, Landes writes, long after Waltham had given up. They did so by reinvesting profits in machinery and in education for their workers.

Landes writes, "With exquisite timing, Dumaine sold his stock in 1944, just before the end of wartime orders. The *American Watch Worker*, organ of the union labor with which he would never negotiate (he dealt only with intermediaries), lauded him as 'personifying New England Industry,' and went on: 'He represents a school of thought that built America.'

"With that kind of union, who's afraid of class conflict?"

Landes is philosophical about the lessons to be learned from the economic history of timekeeping. The Swiss triumph—like the later Japanese miracle in electronic watch-making—was a collective effort and performance, a matter, one might say, of an industrial policy, sometimes conscious, sometimes not.

Today, there is not much left of the American watch business. True, there was a resurgence when a Norwegian refugee named Joakim Lehmkuhl turned Timex into a first-rate producer of cheap watches, thanks to developments in hard-alloy steel. But even Timex is on the run now before the Swiss and the Japanese onslaughts.

In Waltham, what remains is memories. James Brown of Sudbury, a noted Waltham watch buff, will lecture Thursday night on "the industrial greatness of Waltham" at the Waltham Museum. Albert Arena, who directs the museum, notes that the Waltham watchworks is now occupied by diversified industries that "keep coming and going."

And the Dumaines? Well, the heirs of Frederic C. Dumaine are engaged in a titanic struggle over the $50 million trust the old man set up back in 1920 to preserve his fortune. It seems that several of his children and grandchildren have accused Frederic C. (Buck) Dumaine, Jr., the old man's son (he is 81 and lives in Weston) of systematically looting the trust just the way Landes says his father looted the Amoskeag mill and the Waltham Watchworks. The complex case is in the courts. A decision is expected this spring.

MARCH 20, 1984

The Economics of Journals

PHYSICISTS CONDUCT EXPERIMENTS. DOCTORS TREAT PATIENTS. LAWYERS DO BATTLE with each other in court. But what do economists do? How do they sort themselves out?

The answer is they publish short articles in scholarly journals. These "papers" are the approximate equivalent of lawyers' briefs, and, in a field noted for its politicians, publicists, quacks and cranks, the fundamental test of professional stature in economics is the publications list. True, some people achieve eminence without long vitae, but usually by nurturing people who do publish. The short publications list is the hallmark of a technologist, a fellow who makes a living writing his economics for private employers rather than in the organized search for durable economic understanding.

(There is nothing wrong with being an economic technologist—a stock market analyst, for example, or a corporate economist, a bureaucrat, a consultant, a statistician or a banker. Indeed, they are usually better paid than the scholarly sort. It is just that technologists are not at the top of the professional pecking order. They'll get their names in the newspaper, but unlike the scholars, they'll rarely be honored with the presidency of an association, and probably won't be remembered professionally the day after they're gone.)

The six journals that are often ranked together in a class at the top of the heap of several hundred scholarly economics journals that are published around the world are all American: the *Quarterly Journal of Economics* (QJE), the *Journal of Political Economy* (JPE), the *Review of Economics and Statistics* (RES), the *Review of Economic Studies*, *Econometrica* and the *American Economic Review* (AER).

Of these, the AER is probably at the top of the trade. For one thing, the QJE and RES are published by Harvard as the JPE is published by the University of Chicago, and these house journals sometimes reflect local concerns, while the AER is published by the American Economic Association; for another, the AER encourages a measure of controversy, in the form of exchanges.

This doesn't mean the best articles are those published in the AER. Often the most intriguing contributions turn up in the specialized journals, such as the *Journal of International Economics*, or the *Journal of Money, Credit and Banking*. It means the topics treated in the AER year after year are the broad concerns of modern technical economics. The 130 articles it publishes each year represent the state of professional knowledge, the frontiers of the science, such as it is. It is said, without much exaggeration, that what an economics graduate student learns in his four years is to read the AER.

All this makes the editor of the AER a fairly important person in the professional scheme of things. Last month a Brown University professor stepped down after 12 years as its editor and a Californian took over.

George H. Borts started teaching at Brown the year after he took his PhD from the University of Chicago in 1949. (He studied with the Cowles Commission there.) Midway in a fruitful career—he co-authored a landmark study in regional economics—he was tapped in 1968 to be managing editor of the AER, with a mandate to continue its mild-mannered, consensus-seeking editorial policy. Borts extended for four, three-year contracts in all, a remarkable stint in modern times.

The editor of a journal hardly does it all himself, of course. Borts depended first on a team of readers who would screen submissions, then on some 350 "referees," professional economists who anonymously read and recommended action on the 700 manuscripts received each year. Then, referee reports in hand, Borts would read each article himself and decide whether to publish it and how to play it.

"My philosophy was not to popularize the journal. . . . At the same time, though, I did invite articles on issues that were not thoroughly covered by people submitting articles. I was particularily interested in economic policy. I had the feeling that economists were very unwilling to invest the time in writing articles evaluating policy issues because of the risk that they would go out of date by the time they were refereed."

The length of time it takes journals to publish letters is a sore point in general with many economists. Borts says a year is a standard wait at the AER. Shortcuts bring scorn, however. Of a new journal called *Economic Letters* that does without much of the usual consensus-seeking process of referees, he said, "They're not publishing letters, I mean those letters are little riddles."

The new editor of the AER is Robert Clower, a UCLA professor who is widely known as a disequilibrium theorist and interpreter (or reinterpreter) of Keynes. Clower was immensely successful as editor of *Economic Inquiry*, but he's likely to be controversial at the AER because he is so opinionated. Said Borts, "I had a reputation for being slow, because I had this multi-tiered refereeing system. I think he's going to speed things up tremendously."

JANUARY 13, 1981

Was Oil Ever Really Scarce?

ONE OF THE GREAT CASUALTIES OF THE 1980S WAS THE MYTH THAT YOU COULD GET away with anything. Important unions like the air controllers, giant corporations like General Motors, oppressive governments like the Soviet Union, greedy financiers like Michael Milken and Bruce Wasserstein—or at least the First Boston Corp. that Wasserstein left behind—all were humbled by the discipline of the marketplace or occasional law enforcement or both.

Only Ronald Reagan and the American Congress, who cut taxes without cutting spending, seem to have been issued a free pass—so far.

Now keep your eye—again—on the Organization of Petroleum Exporting Countries—and on the Iraquis, the Iranians, and the Saudis, in particular. Who else do you know who aggressively raises prices into a global recession?

The world-historical significance of OPEC was one of the great certainties of the 1970s. President Carter, himself, once figured that oil might be used up by the end of the 1980s. The press, especially, relished its role assuring the world that a crisis was at hand. Oil was a scarce commodity, we intoned; they weren't making any more of it. Its price would go on rising indefinitely. That was before the price broke in 1981, and crashed in 1986.

What comes next?

Nobody has studied OPEC more assiduously than M.A. Adelman, who for many years was the premier energy economist at the Massachusetts Institute of Technology. It was Adelman who first scouted out the real nature of OPEC, in a famous *Foreign Policy* article called "Is the Oil Shortage Real? Oil companies as OPEC Tax Collectors." And he's followed the situation since with ever-increasing perspicacity. Retired now, he is working on a tight economic analysis of the events in the oil markets in the 1970s that is likely to overturn a great deal of the conventional wisdom of those days when it is finally published. He turned up last month on Capitol Hill to give testimony.

The price of oil is a study in monopoly, says Adelman, nothing more. The question of mineral depletion doesn't really enter into it. For a nearly a century, it was the early American oil companies, led by John D. Rockefeller, who kept the price the finding and developing cost of creating new reserves abroad, and so encouraged the constant discovery of new reserves. But with the discovery of huge new fields in the Middle East, they lost control after World War II. The inflation-adjusted price declined by 80 percent.

Then, 20 years ago, the OPEC nations shouldered the companies aside and took over themselves. "That made a big difference," says Adelman, understating the case.

Since then, instead of the smoothly administered pricing of the Seven Sisters (as the multinational oil companies were all-too-briefly known), consumers have suffered instead the ins and outs of Gulf politics—plus an implausibly short time horizon. World economic growth has suffered greatly as a result; indeed, many economists figure that the mysterious worldwide slowdown in productivity since 1973 owes to little more.

The way the OPEC hold-up works is this: The pain of falling real oil prices turns someone greedy and desperate. The cause of the present situation in the Persian Gulf, for example, was a glut of oil in June. At $13 a barrel, its price was far too high. But no one wanted to see prices fall, least of all Saddam Hussein, who was rebuilding his country after its ruinous war with Iran.

The underlying mechanism of the Third Oil Shock is just the same as the first two, says Adelman. Hussein threatened to cut production—invading Kuwait added credibility. That stampeded the market into massive stock-piling, for oil even at a high price is better than a shutdown loss. Then governments raised their official prices, ratifying the spot market's fears. And when demand falls off, cartel members can be expected to cut back on pumping to maintain those prices—for a time.

The secret of OPEC's short-term success—massive excess capacity, deliberately withheld—is also the secret of its ultimate failure, says Adel-man.

"They have no choice but to overbuild. A cartel member with no excess capacity gets no respect. To have bargaining power over production quotas, a member must make a credible threat: to create a nuisance or a danger, by overproducing to undermine price." This is how Iraq gained a larger quota in 1989, he explains, but the logic of the system virtually guarantees an overabundance of oil.

(Expelling the multinational companies has made it easier for govern-ments to throw their weight around, but harder for them to sustain their maneuvers, for the oil companies were highly skilled at acting as a buffer against competitive forces which subvert the administered price.)

The fundamental fact remains that prices will fall again, says Adel-man—and sooner, probably, rather than later. First, the burgeoning world-wide recession will cause demand to fall. Second, once the panic is over, oil will pour into the market as forestalling ceases and hoarders unload. Third, there will be more conservation. For a benchmark in thinking about the price today, Adelman recommends $18 a barrel—midway between what he reckons is the $30 a barrel monopoly ceiling and the $8 compet-itive price.

Above all, the key thing to understand is that the oil price is not a case study in depletion, says Adelman. True, it has been handled this way since Columbia University professor Harold Hotelling in 1931 handed econo-mists a way to think of natural resources as a fixed stock to divide between two or more periods. Such thinking about "running out of oil" dominated the thinking of the Carter administration. It even persists in the talk of resource economists today.

But, in fact, there is no "fixed stock" of oil, says Adelman; there is only an inventory we call "reserves," which we replenish with new prospecting and lifting techniques. What we don't choose to find or lift remains a secret of the earth, "unknown, probably unknowable, surely unimportant; a geological fact of no economic interest." In the "endless tug of war between diminishing returns and increasing knowledge," he says, technology wins out.

Thus, in 1977, he notes, worldwide reserves were 643 billion barrels. Through 1989, nearly half of that—295 billion barrels—was used up. But reserves now stand just over 1 trillion barrels—and worldwide stability of the development cost of new oil since 1955 shows that oil is no more scarce today than it was then. "The great shortage is like the horizon, always receding as you go toward it," says Adelman. What's left are monopolistic political high-jinks.

So this is the economic context in which to think about the American-led coalition's expedition to the Persian Gulf. As much as anything, the war that is in the offing is aimed at achieving global economic stability. (Whether it works that way is another question.) Three oil-driven recessions in 15 years are a high price to pay for Arab sovereignty over oil. Even the Russians and the Chinese apparently think so.

NOVEMBER 25, 1990

. . . In Which Japan, like Greenland, Shrinks Some

JUST 50 YEARS AFTER THE OUTBREAK OF WORLD WAR II, THE MAP OF GLOBAL rivalries is back to just about what it was in 1939. The United States once again has two great competitors in the world economy, Japan and Germany. The Russians have faded to second-rate status, except militarily. The Chinese, despite their revolution, are still only trembling on the brink of the dramatic growth that usually accompanies integration into the world economy. The Indians are better off, but their economy is still sluggish and self-contained.

True, Europe has changed—a little. The English, French and Italian roles have shifted slightly, and German reunification has replaced German expansionism as the explosive issue. But the Balkans are still fractious, the Scandinavians are still aloof, and the Eastern Europeans are still caught in the middle.

Indeed, the politically astute biologist Matthew Meselson observes that the only real difference between then and now is that the colonies of the pre-war era have become the Less Developed Countries of today. "The countries that used to be pink on the map have changed their colors, and in many cases their names," says Meselson. "Though that certainly is a salutary development, I'm not sure how big a change it is."

In these circumstances, a good deal of importance attaches to getting the numbers right—to not doing something hysterical based on a misapprehension of the changing face of trade. Hardly a day passes without some new claim being made of Japanese dominance. Public maneuvering in Washington over the "super 301" portion of the new trade act is muted for the moment, in the wake of the resignation of Noboru Takeshita, but pressure will soon resume to name Japan to the list of "unfair traders" by the May 30 deadline.

Meanwhile, the really appropriate means of comparing wealth and income among nations is languishing at the University of Pennsylvania. It shows America still comfortably ahead of the Japanese in terms of per capita wealth, ahead of the Europeans, too, although the gap is steadily narrowing—and far ahead of the Koreans.

"Despite all the hype, the nations of Asia rank poorly," says Robert Summers, one of the group of University of Pennsylvania professors who has built the accounting framework known as the Penn World Table. Along with co-author Alan Heston, Summers has spent the last decade figuring out what things really cost in 121 market economies and nine centrally planned economies. When this view of purchasing power parity is taken into account, a picture of a somewhat less threatening world emerges (but only somewhat!).

The Penn World Table is a second-generation accounting framework, built to correct the shortcomings of the remarkable system of national income accounts that was created on the eve of World War II by Simon Kuznets and Colin Clark. Richard Stone of Cambridge University collected a Nobel Prize a few years ago for his work enhancing this empirical map of the realities among nations. But even as the Swedes were preparing to honor the project, the gyrations of the world currency markets that began when the Bretton Woods agreement collapsed in the early 1970s were rendering seriously unrealistic some of its most crucial comparisons among countries.

Businessmen, bureaucrats and newsmen who travel extensively know that even the fabled Danes don't really live better than their American counterparts, that the Japanese aren't anywhere near as rich in their command over the world of things. But they are powerless to prove it with the official statistics of the World Bank, the International Monetary Fund and the United Nations.

The usual way of comparing wealth and productivity depends critically on exchange rates. Specialists take the dollar value of everything the United States produces, the yen value of everything Japan produces, and the mark value of everything that Germany produces. They divide by the population of each country. Then they make one simple calculation with exchange rates, and they produce an answer. At average market rates for 1987, for example, American output per person was valued at $18,400, compared with $18,700 in Japan and $18,300 in Germany. Presto: by the exchange rate method, Japan is number one.

The trouble is that exchange rates are volatile. Currency prices are moved as much by hopes and fears as stock markets, not necessarily reflecting any underlying reality. The dollar today buys 120 yen, Summers notes; four years ago it bought 250 yen. But no serious person believes that American incomes have fallen by half—or even fallen at all—in a few short years. Moreover, exchange rates may eventually move in such a way as to adjust the price of freely-traded goods in different countries, but they don't equalize the price of all goods equally. Summers cites the case of an airplane ticket between San Francisco and Tokyo. Buy it in Tokyo and you'll pay 169,800 yen, which is about $1,314, he says; buy it in San Francisco and it costs $796. The same thing goes for those $3 strawberries and $90 melons, he says; if you take them more fully into account, Japan is not quite so rich as it seems when its entire GNP is marked-up by the exchange rate.

The alternative method is to laboriously calculate the purchasing power of different currencies over precisely similar baskets of goods in different countries, then compare the results year after year. So Summers and Heston have priced a basket of more than 600 goods—food, clothing, shelter, as well as machinery and buildings and even the cost of government services—in order to see what can be bought in Japan with a given amount of yen compared a similar number of dollars in the United States.

It is this comparison that suggests that, in terms of the command its citizens' earnings have over goods and services, the United States is still the richest nation in the world. The per capita income of the U.S. citizen is 7 percent greater than his nearest competitor, Canada. Then come Switzerland, West Germany, France and Sweden among the major industrial nations. Japan stands 15th among 121 major market economies around the world with a per capita income of around 75 percent of the American level, says Summers, and Korea is 40th with a per capita income only slightly more than a third of Japan's.

The gap between the rich and poor nations of the world thus narrows somewhat—not dramatically, but enough to suggest that the Third World is not quite as poor as it seems in the official statistics. India, for example, is 7 percent as wealthy as the U.S. in purchasing power parity conversions, as opposed to 2 percent in exchange rate conversions.

The really interesting question is, of course, whether America can stay in the lead. Summers says the data indicate that we are losing ground. American incomes grew at an average of 1.7 percent over the last 15 years, compared with 3.4 percent in Japan and 2.4 percent in German. If this disparity keeps up, he adds, Japan will catch up with us by the year 2007 and Germany by 2015.

If it could keep growing at its amazing 6.9 percent annual rate for another 26 years, even Korea would catch up.

What might change these trajectories? Like many economists, Summers identifies the rate of savings and investment. While the United States has the world's slowest rate of income growth over 15 years, it also has the highest rate of consumption and the lowest rate of investment—something like a fifth of that of its principal competitors, and half the rate at which it used to save and invest. He says, "This ratio deserves attention if we hope to remain Number One."

In the end, the Penn World Table doesn't really change the shape of the distribution of the world's wealth and productive apparatus—it just gives a clearer picture. Summers compares the perspective of the Penn project to the new National Geographic map of the world, which doesn't change the face of the globe, but simply improves its perception. Finally, Greenland is trimmed down to size. The difference is that unlike Greenland, Japan and Germany are continually growing. Meanwhile, our hopes of achieving a happier resolution of the tension of 1989 than we achieved in 1939 depends at least in part on a clear understanding of where we are.

APRIL 30, 1989

The Possibilitarian

IN MANY MODERN SCIENCES A CENTRAL PROBLEM IS ENCOURAGING SYNTHESIS. WHILE 10,000 researchers are working away on slam-bang answers to tiny problems, too few are sifting through the evidence in search of the surprising big pattern. Gerard M. Edelman, a Nobel laureate for his brain research, last spring proposed creating more "scientific monasteries," small privately-funded institutions in the business of "refining questions," in which handfuls of people would practice science individually, instead of as members of the big teams that characterize modern biology.

And while nobody ever accused economists of shying away from the big picture, Paul P. Streeten, the distinguished development economist who five years ago left Oxford for Boston University, said something similar at Middlebury College last week, during a conference on the diffusion of economic ideas. "We've overgrazed the part of the range that has to do with pure theory . . . and undergrazed other promising areas. We need more first-rate people who make sense of economic ideas and relate them to other fields, and who interpret them to the educated public."

True, there are a handful of writers who regularly produce pithy speculative essays on economic topics for magazines like the *New York Review of Books*. Robert Heilbroner and John Kenneth Galbraith come to mind. But these are authors who have made their way mainly by retailing their views directly to the public, going over the heads of their brethren in the profession, so to speak.

For an economist who writes for other economists, try Albert O. Hirschman, perhaps the foremost virtuoso in his field (with the possible exception of Thomas Schelling.) It is relatively easy to do this, for Hirschman's major books are slim, not mathematical, not even quantitative—and available in cheap paperbacks.

Notre Dame has just published a volume of essays in his honor, *Development, Democracy and the Art of Trespassing*. (Hirschman is a self-confessed "trespasser" in several other disciplines.) More to the point, Hirschman himself has just published a new volume of collected essays,

Rival Views of Market Processes (Viking Press, $18.95), that is the perfect introduction to one of the most fruitful lives in modern economics.

What are these "rival views" of capitalism? Each is relatively familiar, at least to students of history: on the one hand, there is capitalism, the bringer of civilization and gentility, the deliverer from a warring feudal past. Hirschman quotes the French philosopher Montesquieu: "It is almost a general rule that where manners are gentle there is commerce; and wherever there is commerce, manners are gentle." Market relations make people more honest, harder-working, better-disciplined and more courteous to one another, in this view, which dominated the 18th century.

Far more familiar to modern readers, however, is the self-destruction thesis, associated with a long line of analysts from Marx to Schumpeter, from Max Weber to Daniel Bell, which holds (with varying degrees of subtlety) that the logic of piling-up wealth eventually discredits itself, that the moral underpinnings of capitalism are eaten away, and that the system must eventually lose its justification.

Which view is correct? Possibly both. Out of the opposition between these views, and from the sense of history on which they are based, Hirschman weaves a delicate two-by-two table from which nearly all forms of modern politics can be derived. Depletion and replenishment follow each other in a cycle that is never quite the same. Not the sort of thing that makes for great newspapering, perhaps, but the kind of diagnostic tool that can last for 100 years.

The history of ideas and their consequences is Hirschman's forte: In *The Passions and the Interests*, he traces the emergence of the concept of modern economic self-interest against the background of traditional society. In *Shifting Involvements*, he sketches out an alternating cycle of consensual commitments by succeeding generations, now to public virtue, now to private gain, that gives new meaning to Lewis Mumford's dictum: "The commonest axiom of history is that every generation revolts against its fathers and makes friends with its grandfathers."

But it is only recently that Hirschman has been preoccupied with the history of ideas. Throughout the 1950s and the 1960s he was one of the major forces in development economics, heavily influencing the governments of industrializing nations, especially in Latin America. And in his most important book, *Exit, Voice and Loyalty*, published in 1970, he explored the circumstances in which people would choose between two utterly fundamental everyday options.

There was always "exit," Hirschman wrote, meaning withdrawal from a relationship built up over time, whether with the corner grocery store, a giant corporation selling cars, an employer, a spouse, a political party or even a nation. And there was always "voice," meaning "the articulation and channeling of opinion, criticism and protest."

Under what circumstances do we prefer to "work within the system," or to quit it to try an alternative? Hirschman's remarkable lens has been used in a steadily widening sphere, to study everything from political action to consumer choice to adolescent psychology to divorce.

Born in Berlin in 1915, Hirschman came by his views about exit and voice the hard way, staying one step ahead of the Nazis, first in Italy, then in France. After two years in the French Army, with the French surrender he went underground in Marseilles and spent six months there forging documents for other refugees before escaping himself to the United States.

After the war, he worked for the Federal Reserve system on European reconstruction, then turned his attention to South America, moving to Colombia to advise the government on its development. In 1956 he turned to teaching, moving quickly from Columbia University to Yale to Harvard. A liberal? Certainly. You have only to look at "Against Parsimony" in the new volume of essays to discover a thorough-going alternative to the "economic imperialism" that has been taking social science by storm.

Not surprisingly, Hirschman wound up at one of those "scientific monasteries" that Gerard Edelman was talking about. After nearly 20 years of teaching, he joined the Institute for Advanced Study in Princeton, N.J., in 1974 and officially retired last year at 70, though he remains active there. He has won nearly every major prize, including the Siedman Award in Political Economy. He was in Boston last week to accept the Kalman Silvert Prize for Latin American Studies. He jokes that the working title of the new volume was *Last Essays, Volume 1*.

Hirschman exhorts social scientists to "embrace complexity." That means discarding their self-image as the next best thing to the Newtonian physicist and the civil engineer. "Instead of looking for necessary and sufficient conditions of change, we must train ourselves to be on the lookout for unusual historical developments, rare constellations of favorable events, narrow paths, partial advances that may conceivably be followed by others and the like. We must think of the possible rather than the probable."

NOVEMBER 2, 1986

part three

THE YOUNGER GENERATION

The *New* New Economics

DURING THE 1950S AND 1960S, SOMETHING CALLED THE NEW ECONOMICS ENJOYED enormous prestige in the United States. What was new about it was its bolder proponents' claim to have more or less eliminated the business cycle through the discovery of certain key relationships among economic variables and the development of various levers of monetary and fiscal policy with which the authorities might manipulate the economy, leaning this way and that, always "against the wind."

The prestige of this optimistic doctrine was worldwide, or at least trans-Atlantic. (It is not clear that the Japanese bought into it to any considerable extent.) A new Nobel Prize was established in Sweden in 1969 to celebrate the advances in knowledge, and, since the Massachusetts Institute of Technology was preeminent in the fashioning of this intellectual edifice, it was not surprising that the first American recipient of this new Nobel Prize should be Paul Samuelson. His award was followed by others to Franco Modigliani and Robert Solow, and Peter Diamond will surely follow in his turn. If anything, the MIT department was even more remarkable in the influence it exercised over the discipline than the records suggests.

But starting in the late 1960s, the consensus view of economics abruptly cracked up. Economists from the University of Chicago, then Stanford and eventually even Harvard led assaults on the behavioral assumptions upon which the New Economics had rested. People engaged in learning, it was noted; they were not easily fooled; they changed their conduct in response to government policies, and not always the way policymakers expected. As basic and unobjectionable as these observations may sound, the "rational expectations" movement that embodied them had profound implications for policy. The cheerful conviction that government easily could manage its way to stability was knocked away in seminar rooms. About the same time, as if to underscore the point, the international economy entered on a series of gyrations that have not ended yet. And of course the Vietnam War, the Cultural Revolution in China and the Russian invasion of Czechoslovakia taught a lesson about skepticism about government policies—*all* governments' policies—to a new generation around the world. Even on an intellectual plane (perhaps *especially* on an intellectual plane) this changing of minds was often a brutal business, and the cheerful confidence of the 1960s gave way to glum aggravation in the 1970s and 1980s. Today, a clear "Cambridge tendency" (as the London *Economist* describes it) persists in economics. But the MIT department is no longer the kind of dominating power it once was.

It may be this experience, rather than any other single fact, that is at the heart of a new book written by MIT economist Paul Krugman: *The Age of Diminished Expectations: U.S. Economic Policy in the 1990s.* Paul Samuelson's introduction says, "I am proud of my generation of policy economists. You know their names: Walter Heller, Milton Friedman, John Kenneth Galbraith, Arthur Okun, Herbert Stein, Peter Drucker and many more. But, as some sage said, science progresses funeral by funeral. Paul Krugman is the rising star of this century and the next, and the world beats a path to his door."

Now Paul Krugman is no Paul Samuelson. To be sure, he has been immensely productive of new ideas. Along with two or three others— Paul Romer, Jeffrey Sachs, Lawrence Summers—he is an exemplar of the diverse intellectual attainments and personal styles of the postmodern generation of economic theorists. He is one of the progenitors of the hot new field of strategic trade. He has been restoring almost single-handedly economic geography to a central place, has written deeply on currency fluctuations and has been a full participant in the attempt of the "new growth economics" to place imperfect competition at the core of economic theory. But in all of this, there is none of the world-girdling ambition and understated power of Paul Samuelson's voice; and the tone of Krugman's book is that of a specialist surveying the work of other specialists for a sophisticated lay audience.

This was, in fact, precisely Krugman's intent. He set out to write a guidebook to the state of technical economic knowledge across a broad array of policy issues—everything from the savings and loan scandal to the Third World debt crisis to the state of trade among nations to the conduct of monetary policy by the Fed. The book itself has an interesting history. He wrote it on commission for a politically astute book publishing subsidiary of the Washington Post Company that put the Post logo on the out-sized cover and sold it for $195 a copy to corporations—an advertising venture not very different from the Whittle Corporation series of short books by big-name authors paid for and distributed free to 100,000 or so opinion makers by Federal Express. Krugman's manuscript turned out to be so readable that the MIT Press bought the right to republish the book for a wider audience at a more affordable price. This edition (the one under review) hasn't done especially well, either, so now Krugman is working on a book he calls *Son of Diminished Expectations.*

The book might have been subtitled "the Bureau version," after the National Bureau of Economic Research, where Krugman, like almost every other talented economist in the United States, spends part of his time during the summer. The NBER is the old tripartite (business-labor-government) and non-partisan organization that Martin Feldstein in the late 1970s turned into a vital ground of mediation among high theory, empirical fact and policy relevance. In fact, if there is a Samuelson-like figure in the current age, a figure who changed the very manner in which economists express themselves, it is probably Feldstein of Harvard University (though no one will ever mistake one for the other in terms of their *spiritual* effect on the field), and the striking similarity between Feldstein and Krugman is a tipoff to the changing style of economics. Feldstein is a past chairperson of the President's Council of Economic Advisers; Krugman is in all likelihood a future chairperson. In contrast, the old giants of MIT almost never went to Washington.

The Age of Diminished Expectations is not a deep book, nor even deeply felt. Instead it relies on an easy grace and confidence that is very unusual in economic writing. In this, it has much in common with Lester Thurow's *Zero Sum Society* of a dozen years ago, except that it is a straighter, more reportorial account of the mainstream consensus. The tone is that of an easy professional fellow with whom you'd like to have lunch to explain your business, confident that he could get to the bottom of it and perhaps even show you something new. Every attempt is made to go easy on the claims, avoid unattractive certitude, make reasonable guesses.

Hence the Age of Diminished Expectations: don't get your hopes up that we economists are going to find the Answers any time soon, Krugman says, or even predict the future with any conviction. Of what must be the central puzzle of our time, the productivity slowdown, he says that even after 15 years' work on the problem, economists have to show "little more than sophisticated cocktail party chatter." The book ends with three scenarios for the United States in the 1990s: a hard landing, a soft landing and a middling muddling through. The last is the likeliest, he says. Toward the end of the book, Krugman writes, "Americans no longer expect much from their economy, nor from the politicians who manage it." That's true, but it is not the whole truth. We have lowered our expectations of our economists as well, and it's a good thing too.

FEBRUARY, 1991

"The Bureau,"
Feldstein's Power Base

BELMONT'S MARTIN FELDSTEIN HAS BEEN IN THE NEWS RECENTLY, STICKING TO HIS guns in the face of pressure from the president's men to quit his office as chairman of the Council of Economic Advisers rather than continue to warn publicly against the economic impact of huge federal deficits. Who is the owlish Harvard professor to resist the combined might of Larry Speakes and James Baker of the White House staff?

Feldstein's reputation is for energy, command of detail, ability to track more factors than anybody else in the room—and a resolute conservative streak. (He opposed the Massachusetts bottle bill on what he claimed were scientific grounds that it cost too much.) Only 44, he has left a long trail of effective work.

But the secret of his professional power, the key to understanding the stakes for which he's playing in his game of chicken with the White House staff is the National Bureau of Economic Research, known to most economists as simply "the Bureau." Until he went to Washington last year, Feldstein was its president.

To all outward appearances, the Bureau is nothing much. It occupies a floor in a building in Putnam Square in Cambridge. It has a relatively paltry $5.8 million budget.

Yet it is a uniquely powerful organization in technical economics. Founded in 1920 in the hopes of taking some of the politics out of economics, the Bureau has senior representatives of labor, business, government and university directors on its board. Its best-known function is to date the beginnings and ends of recessions; but it real work in consensus-building goes far beyond that modest aim. It serves as a kind of a high court of expert opinion, where many of the most agile scholars bring their most substantial findings for review.

"A substantial fraction of all the empirical research in economics is organized through the National Bureau," says Princeton's Alan Blinder, a Bureau researcher.

Feldstein is widely viewed as the man who returned the Bureau to a central place after taking over in 1977. "He was a whirling dervish of activity, always on the phone himself," recalls Burton Malkiel, a research economist who is dean of Yale's Graduate School of Management. "I'm not sure that it was as revolutionary as people say it was," says John R. Meyer, the Harvard professor whom Feldstein replaced. "It was more of a shift in technique."

In any event, Feldstein turned the Bureau into a university comprising most of the important "invisible colleges" by which the frontiers in economics work were established. He persuaded such senior scholars as Robert Lucas and Robert Fogel to take their National Science Foundation funding through the Bureau, says Carl Christ, a Johns Hopkins professor who is a Bureau director, "and he brought in young people who hadn't been discovered yet. Marty's just excellent at that."

The result was a continual flood of arcane but policy-oriented research across a fairly wide spectrum of political opinion. Papers with titles such as "Two-step Two-stage Least Squares Estimation in Models with Rational Expectations" and "A Model of Stochastic Process Switching" compete for attention with "Teenage Employment: Permanent Scars or Temporary Blemishes?" and "Corporate Financial Structure and Managerial Incentives."

One of the features of Bureau research under Feldstein has been to pick a problem and to try to solve it—or at least to say what it was. "Capital gains taxation, private pensions, youth unemployment—these are things that have been pretty exhaustively pursued by Bureau investigators," says Harvard's Lawrence Summers, another Bureau researcher who traveled to Washington with Feldstein. "And of course the whole program has been has been quite a boon to macroeconomics."

A persistent hope for the Bureau has been that it would somehow make economics more respectable. Arthur Burns, who presided over its affairs for 22 years (with a short time out to serve as chief economic adviser to President Dwight Eisenhower), recalled the circumstances of its founding this way in 1948: "Here a program of critical reasearch might actually be carried out, not just proclaimed aloud. Here empirical investigations might be undertaken, broader and yet more fundamental than any yet attempted by economists. . . . Here an investigator could subject his methods and results to the steady and searching scrutiny of skilled colleagues. . . . Here tested findings could accumulate, reinforce one another, and open up new problems, as was routine in the established sciences. Most important of all, here was an experiment in democratic action, men of many shades of political opinion joining in the undramatic enterprise of reviewing the factual findings of a technical staff."

The presence of a diverse board of directors is thus key to the Bureau—it is not just another organization sponsored by business. Rudolph Oswald, director of research for the AFL-CIO is a board member; so is Lazare Teper of the International Ladies Garment Workers Union; so is David Wasserman of the American Federation of State, County and Municipal Employees. Walter Heller, one of the most prominent of all liberal economists, is chairman of the executive committee.

To be sure, a fair proportion of its budget comes from foundations known to prefer conservative views: the Sloan, the Richardson, the Mellon. But a substantial portion comes from the National Science Foundation. And the fact is that most people agree that funding proceeds independent of political views. "We joke that every economist you've ever heard of is working for the Bureau," says Malkiel.

Of course this irritates some. Lawrence Kudlow, a well-known supply-sider who worked for a time for David Stockman in the Office of Management and Budget, complained the other day that Feldstein was "playing" to the boys on the Charles River when he warned that big deficits threaten the economy. And Lester Thurow, who himself was a candidate for the presidency of the Bureau in 1977, noting Feldstein's claim that a maharajah, receiving reports from five blind men feeling an elephant, could piece together an accurate picture, tartly compared Feldstein to a blind man suffering the delusion of believing he was a maharajah.

The point, however, is that for the past six years, Feldstein has served as ringmaster to 130 of the best economists in the business, young and old; he probably has had more to do with defining the present-day concerns of his field than any other single man. When he argues that deficits are a source of considerable danger to the economy in the years ahead, he is not so much taking a political position as he is talking economics with other economists. His professional reputation is on the line.

The executive committee of the Bureau met yesterday in Cambridge, but there were no jokes about Feldstein—at least according to MIT's Eli Shapiro, who replaced Feldstein. "He didn't take a leave; I'm not the acting president," said Shapiro. "I have very little doubt that he would be welcomed back."

DECEMBER 6, 1983

The Nobleman
Who Stooped to Trade

THE UNITED STATES OF AMERICA VS. INTERNATIONAL BUSINESS MACHINES CORP. (IBM) antitrust case has been over for nearly two years now, and the accounts of it are beginning to tumble from the presses. It is clear, in retrospect, how silly it all was.

In the first place, the government case rested on a misapprehension, that IBM wouldn't unbundle its computers and sell them separately. Then the case was overtaken by the headlines. An industry of "IBM and the seven dwarfs"—eight companies specializing in utility-like mainframe computers—had given way to a veritable zoo of minicomputer and microcomputer manufacturers, peripheral equipment makers and software vendors, long before the government folded its hand.

Finally, IBM put up a very spirited defense. The briefs have been published now, half last spring under the title *Folded, Spindled and Mutilated*, the other half last month as *IBM and the U.S. Data Processing Industry: An Economic History*. The common thread, the principal author of both books, is an owlish MIT professor named Franklin Fisher.

Early on, IBM lawyers had figured they would need a good economist to organize their economic defense, and to serve as an expert witness. They knew where to look. "IBM house lawyer Nicholas deB. Katzenbach asked MIT's Carl Kaysen, and Kaysen had recommended me," says Fisher. "Carl was my tutor when I was an undergraduate at Harvard and he was one of the few people who knew the secret that industrial organization was a serious interest of mine."

Fisher tumbled in. "There is one Section 2 [of the Sherman Antitrust Act] case every 10 years, a fresh interpretation of the law once every 25 years. So here was the biggest antitrust case of our time. I thought, It's my chance to have a serious impact on antitrust policy. It's true I'm doing it for the defense, but that's one of the ways to do it.' " He loved it. There was a year of briefings, of plant tours, of sharpening pencils. Then came the private antitrust suits, Telex and Greyhound. The deeper he got, the harder he worked.

The trouble was that Fisher was among the most talented economists in the world, a man at the very top of a science. For a decade, he edited the journal *Econometrica*. He was elected to the American Academy of Arts and Sciences in 1969. He won the John Bates Clark Medal in 1973, a prize that is awarded only every two years to the best American economist under 40. Figure that the medal had been awarded eight times since Fisher's 1956 graduation from Harvard College. That made him, by the common consent of his peers, one of the top 10 economists of his generation.

Yet in effect, Fisher forsook his relationship with the MIT economics department—a department that is fiercely proud of its scientific detachment—for a decade of bloodsports with Cravath, Swaine and Moore, IBM's white-shoe outside law firm. It cost him dearly. "I was one of the central figures in this department when this began; maybe I'm still one of the central figures, but sure in the mid-1970s I wasn't. I want to be careful about this . . . not that there is anything to be careful about, but I want to be fair. I cannot say that the MIT department in any official way treated me badly or anything like that. That's not true; in fact the contrary, they were very nice to me.

"Still, it is unquestionably true that my colleagues individually plainly disapproved of what I was doing. . . . I stepped outside the ethic. I did something that economists don't do. I did adversary work for money. I don't think most of my colleagues understand what the kind of work was, or the kind of excitments involved in it. I'm hoping that if they read this book, they'll decide, yes, maybe it was worth doing. It was a little like a nobleman going into trade."

Fisher is eloquent on the temptations of the life of action. "Life with Cravath was like nothing I'd ever seen. First, even before the case came to trial, those guys worked 12 to 16 hours a day. Those guys worked all the time. Second, they lived pretty high. One of the compensations for that was that they ate in terrific restaurants and they traveled around the country first class, sometimes in the company plane, and the strains on their personal lives were tremendous, far greater than on mine. I was involved in that, I was living off the same expense account."

More compelling, he says, was the sense of solidarity that trial work engendered. ("Someday perhaps it will be pleasing to remember these things," is the stoic line in Latin at the end of the string of acknowledgements to lawyers, executives, consultants and the rest who participated in the defense.) "It was exciting! I miss that. There was the sense that I was helping to move forward a great event. Things had to be done every day. . . . There was a sense of high drama. You had to be up. I had a certain amount of withdrawal when I woke up a couple of years ago to the fact that there was nothing that desperately had to be done."

There was the money, too: "It was less than most people thought I made. I have yet to hear a rumor that was lower than the amount I made. I did not make $1 million aggregate from the IBM case. I was on it for 12 years. There's a sense in which no amount of money could compensate me for 12 years. I did okay, less okay than most people think."

Perhaps the cruelest blow was that in the end the government simply folded its hand; it walked away from the courtroom. The case was thrown out, not decided. "The IBM trial staff of the antitrust department really did not understand basic economics and the economists who testified for them either were quite weak analytically or were simply misled," says Fisher. But the point was that the Big Casino of a courtroom victory was denied him: the Supreme Court is not going to quote his testimony, at least on the IBM case. (Thirteen of fourteen judges found for IBM on the private cases.) Fisher faced a real Hobson's choice: he could publish his testimony; or he could put it away.

He published—and the results make fascinating reading. The lawyers love it, generally; the economists are not so sure. The trouble is that the vital element of disinterest is missing. Fisher is well aware of the problem. At the beginning and end of the book, he writes movingly of the pitfalls that await the scientist who begins to think like a lawyer. Yet he has not entirely avoided those pitfalls—for example, ask him what he learned from the case and he tells you how good a company IBM is, how customer-oriented, how quality-control-conscious, how defensive it was in the wake of its 1956 consent decree—the words of an advocate, not an analyst.

There was high irony here, for there is some reason to think that the government's case against IBM was built intellectually on the epic economic case constructed by Carl Kaysen for use by the antitrust division in its successful 1950s lawsuit against United Shoe Manufacturing Corp. If so, it was a wholly inappropriate analogy, according to Kaysen. USM sold to little customers in a highly stable market, where barriers to entry were formidable. IBM operated in a fast-changing marketplace where customers had plenty of alternatives.

Frank Fisher has returned to economics. He has a new and very rarefied book on disequlibrium foundations of economics due out this fall; another work on price indices is almost ready for the press. He is a more substantial pillar of the community than ever, both as a scientist and as a citizen. He serves on many boards, has built a large and lucrative antitrust consulting practice. His stature and influence are great.

But the sad fact is that the IBM work is being received skeptically. The episode cost him something more than the dozen years. "In the middle 1970s . . . I sat there thinking what on earth am I doing here, wasting my life, straining my relations with my department, certainly not getting anything done. By the end of the 1970s, when I started writing my testimony, certainly when I started writing the book, I thought, this has really turned out very well. I've been away for a long time but I've done something really serious."

The differing satisfactions of the man of affairs and the scientist were never clearer.

OCTOBER 16, 1983

The Odd Genius Behind "Supply-Side" Economics

NOT EVERYBODY KNOWS SHERLOCK HOLMES HAD A BROTHER. MYCROFT HOLMES, who appeared only occasionally in Conan Doyle's famous stories, was smarter, subtler, faster, a better detective than Sherlock in every respect except one. Mycroft was fatally lazy. He lacked the will to work. Thus, the world remembers Sherlock, and not his older brother.

Robert Mundell is the Mycroft Holmes of supply-side economics. Indeed, he invented it, for in an age when few economic ideas are associated with specific individuals, he holds an undisputed patent on the policy regime against stagflation that is in effect today: tight money and tax cuts. It appears just once in all his writing, a single knock-out paragraph at the end of a scholarly monograph published in 1971. If the common criticism of mainstream economists with "supply-side" doctrines is that they are unspecified, uncodified, unspelled-out, then Mundell is the father of that style, too. He has never pursued his idea in print.

He could be in the White House. Instead, he's in Uruguay, courtesy of a former student. A book four-fifths completed lies unpublished in his Columbia University office—his "magnum opus," according to disciple Jude Wanniski—while Mundell consults to (some say he directs) the operations of the central bank of that placid little South American satrapy, and sets up a PhD program at the university in Montevideo. Canada-born, he owns a castle in Siena, Italy, and spends his summers there, host to an annual seminar. Friends say he drinks a great deal, but they can never tell whether he is drunk or sober; either way, they say, he speaks equally slowly and deliberately. Widely rumored to have been crossed off the Nobel Prize committee's short list for flouting the profession's norms, he no longer bothers to publish his views, which, according to friends, these days seem to center on the desirability of fixed exchange rates anchored by the gold standard, a highly controversial issue.

One of the things on which all economists apparently can agree, however, is that Mundell is one very smart guy. It was he who pursued a sweeping reformulation of international economics in the early 1960s (Nobel Prize-winner James Meade had begun it). He created models and concepts "that rapidly became the Volkswagens of the field—easy to drive, reliable and sleek," said Rudiger Dornbusch, an MIT professor who was Mundell's student and who is widely regarded as his successor. Prof. George Stigler of the University of Chicago said, "He permanently changed the way the fraternity of international economists view their problems."

Clearly, Mundell is a very interesting and complicated man. He couldn't be found with a dozen telephone calls; many of his friends complained of the same problem. But interviews with his admirers and colleagues provided enough for a sketch of the man.

Mundell was young when he began making his initial contribution to the field. MIT's Paul Samuelson said, "When Laury Klein won the Nobel Prize last year, I tried to figure out who had completed his PhD at MIT more quickly, he or Mundell. Mundell won, I think." Already in 1963, MIT's Charles Kindleberger, hardly a fan of the kind of econometrics in which Mundell specializes, had described him as the foremost international economist of his generation.

He was barely 30.

What Mundell was doing in this first phase of his career was extending Keynesian concepts and policies to the world economy. Economics at that point was used to pretending that national economies were "closed": that capital had no place to go. Mundell changed that, giving the profession a battery of tools for thinking about the flight of funds, the behavior of international asset markets, and the differences between fixed and flexible exchange rates.

Prof. Richard Caves of Harvard raises the issue of whether Mundell experienced a conversion of sorts in the early 1960s, towards the end of his work on international macroeconomics. "The early stuff was fairly orthodox Keynesian analysis, much concerned with the short term," he said. "Then it was as if he discovered classical principles and the long term." Maybe it was just Chicago; Mundell became a professor there, lured by the legendary Harry Johnson.

Together, building on Lloyd Metzler's work, Mundell and Johnson trained today's generation of leaders in tools unknown to orthodox Keynesian analysis: the monetary approach to balance of payments problems. Dornbusch says the fruits of their work—formal models of money creation, deficit finance, external imbalance, monetary interdependence and inflation—became available just in time for their use in the analysis of the collapse of the Bretton Woods international monetary system at the end of the 1960s.

He wasn't yet 40.

Then began the third phase of Mundell's career. "It all happened in 1969," said Arthur Laffer, the University of Southern California Business School professor who has been nearly universally mentioned in connection with the rise of "supply-side" analysis, mentioned as its Sherlock Holmes. Laffer was in Chicago then, too. "We would talk, oh, 20 hours a week. I wish I could take credit for it, but it was all Bob's genius."

"It" was something that can be described as the recognition of the general neglect of the substitution effects of fiscal policy, or of the "supply" side of the economists' equation. If inflation was too much money chasing too few goods, Mundell reasoned, then the thing to do was to keep money tight and cut taxes, thereby encouraging the production of goods.

In 1971, the idea made its initial—and apparently only—scholarly appearence in a Princeton University economics pamphlet called "The Dollar and the Policy Mix." About then, Laffer, who was serving as chief economist in the Nixon Office of Management and Budget, took Mundell to see Secretary of the Treasury George Shultz. Nothing happened. To all intents and purposes, formal supply-side economics in 1971 existed mostly in the form of John Hotson's note in the *American Economic Review* to the effect that the price-increasing effects of income taxes might outweigh their price-decreasing effects.

It is no wonder the idea was slow to catch on; it still has failed to sweep most of the profession. Cut taxes to fight rising prices? Ridiculous, said economists. The conventional wisdom was that the way to fight inflation was to put taxes up—a surcharge or some such. It was flying in the face of that usual prescription that got Mundell in serious trouble with his profession in 1974.

It was the autumn of President Gerald Ford's WIN campaign. Economists by the thousands were camping on the banks of the Potomac River to advise on how best to deal with double-digit inflation. At a conference sponsored by the American Enterprise Insitute, Mundell predicted a desperate world depression, led by the auto industry, would be forthcoming soon, that only a dramatic tax cut could diminish its sting. "Mundell disgraced himself," recalls a prominent editor. "Everyone was laughing at him," remembers his friend and fellow supply-sider Wanniski.

In economics, as in comedy, timing is all. That autumn President Ford and his advisers opted to send to Congress a tax increase to "fight inflation" and the rest is history. Within months, the United States was in a precipitous recession, and the White House was calling for a tax cut to get things moving again. Mundell has been remote from policy economics ever since.

To be sure, in an administration that is said to have bounced economist Tom Sowell's job application because he had difficulty balancing his checkbook, Mundell's reputation for erratic attention to detail is probably sufficient to earn cancellation of his borrower's card at the Library of Congress. Elected a fellow of the Econometric Society, he neglected to open the envelope that contained the news. As president of a hemispherical economic society, he failed to show up to deliver his presidential address. A stormy, imperious man, his stint as editor at the *Journal of Political Economy* nearly ruined that prestigious journal. He left a deskful of manuscripts and unanswered letters behind. ("The rumor is that he was sufficiently unsystematic that there was a certain amount of ill will to repair," is the way George Stigler put it.) When he quit Chicago in a huff to go to that traditional home to brilliant eccentrics, the University of Waterloo in Kitchener, Ontario, it is said that perhaps a dozen economists cracked wise with a single voice, "At last, Waterloo meets its Napoleon!"

But the constant refrain from professional economists is that Mundell was and is brilliant. "Elegant," "sharp," "acute," "sharply-focussed," "penetrating" are the words and phrases used again and again. "He has a bit of the poet about him," said MIT's Dornbusch. "Never trust a number from him. Never. But somehow what he says always comes out right, hangs together. Gold? He is fox-crazy. Tomorrow it may be silver, or platinum. He makes people think."

Colleagues in the economics department at Columbia say Mundell is a fully-functioning member of the department, critical, interested, in touch with students. Friends say he keeps to a handsome old apartment on Morningside Heights, venturing out only to teach and to shop for groceries. "He watches television incessantly," says his friend Wanniski. "He thinks that [Robert] MacNeil and [Jim] Lehrer [of the public television news show] are two of the smartest people in America."

Occasional rumors of Mundell's reentry into polite economic society make the rounds, and friends and former students question the extent to which he permits his name to be associated with extreme forms of "supply-side" doctrines. "He doesn't believe that nonsense," said Dornbusch. Even supply-siders see themselves as divided into "Mundellians," who view big government and the mixed economy as a permanent and even welcome fact of life, and "Lafferians," who think the 20th century is an aberration that can be rolled back.

Oh, incidentally, how is the Uruguayan economy doing? While not setting any records apparently, it has come a long way from the days of the Tupamaro guerrillas in the mid-1970s. And stateside supply-siders say it will serve as a laboratory for years to come, since it is one of the very few nations in the world to have no progressive income tax.

Meanwhile, what overtures from the Reagan administration? Dornbusch says Mundell used to joke about being Master of the Mint in a Reagan administration. Whatever opportunity for inside power he might have had was lost long ago, however, and as for the kind of hectoring in which Milton Friedman engages, Mundell seems to prefer not to. Today, as Wanniski says, "they don't even know he exists."

MAY 19, 1981

The Economics
of Status:
An Old Idea, Re-examined

THERE'S ALWAYS BEEN SOMETHING UNSETTLING ABOUT THORSTEIN VEBLEN, A BRIL-
liant critic, a sardonic writer, now remembered mainly as the contributor to
the common vocabulary of the notion of "conspicuous consumption." From
the late 1890s to the late 1920s, he pounded away in a series of books—
*The Theory of the Leisure Class, The Engineers and the Price System, The
Place of Science in Modern Civilization*—complaining with increasing bitterness that economists' conceptions of "economic man" were laughably
oversimplified and that the whole enterprise was condemned to sterility as
a result.

Veblen's message: "Not only is the individual's conduct hedged about
and directed by his habitual relations to his fellows in the group, but these
relations, being of an institutional character, vary as the institutional scene
varies. The wants and desires, the end and aim, the ways and means, the
amplitude and drift of the individual's conduct are functions of an institutional variable that is of a highly complex and wholly unstable character."

Most people, reflecting on their own experience with relative social
standing, think of Veblen's insights as the greatest common sense. Among
economists, however, Veblen's hold on professional imagination, never
strong, has pretty much been forgotten: His contemporaries didn't feel their
science was sterile, after all. Veblen died a pauper in 1929, and his books
slipped into the undergraduate underground, popularized by such literary
economists as John Kenneth Galbraith and Eliot Janeway, but otherwise
unread.

Now, however, a young Cornell University economist has taken Veblen's
central preoccupations with status and made them newly tractable, using
precisely the fundamental tools—the conception of rational economic
man—that Veblen hated. Robert H. Frank treats status within groups as a

good like any other that is traded in the market and gets highly illuminating results that are deeply grounded in utility-maximizing behavior.

Frank's book, *Choosing the Right Pond: Human Behavior and the Quest for Status*, is already being treated as a landmark event in a tight but quickly broadening circle of specialists across a swathe of fields. The University of Colorado's Kenneth Boulding, for example, says that "Frank has made economics less pure, but more nourishing and closer to the real world." The University of Chicago's James Coleman, a leading sociologist, says, "The book finally brings predictive power and some surprising implications to the notions . . . that sociologists have toyed with so long." Harvard's Edward O. Wilson, the sociobiologist, says, "Frank is obviously onto something fundamental in his treatment of envy and status as factors in human behavior." And Chicago's Gary Becker, perhaps the foremost modern explorer of the economic metaphor, allows that, "He's struggling with this important problem, and he's made a bit of progress on it. Not many people can claim that."

Whatever the excitement among professionals, Frank is hardly a household word, despite the fact—or perhaps because of it—that his book was designed to appeal to the widest possible audience. His first papers on the economics of status were repeatedly rejected; it was only when editor Robert Clower intervened that they came out in the *American Economic Review*. And *Choosing the Right Pond* has been a commercial failure. Published almost unnoticed last spring, it was panned by an uncomprehending Robert Lucas—he is Chicago's premier macroeconomist—in the *Wall Street Journal* last summer. Frank has been left with a $6,000 cartoon bill for the illustrations that are scattered throughout the book.

Yet not a few readers of *Pond* have come away with a mild sense of deja vu. As with James Buchanan and public choice, Becker and human capital, Michael Spence and signaling behavior, there is a sense that an old searchlight has been turned on a new area through the invention of a new analytic framing device—a lens, so to speak. In the end, the economics of status promises some day to transform much of the current discussion about psychology and economics, at least within the professional mainstream, as completely as the advent of information economics once superseded the discussion of "imperfect competition."

Meanwhile, in the interstices of half a dozen social sciences, attention to the processes of economic decision-making is percolating with unusual rapidity. Meetings last month at the University of Chicago and Middlebury College are evidence of the possibility that new departures from standard conceptions of rationality in years to come will be even more dramatic.

What makes Frank's economic approach so interesting? His insight comes in two parts. He begins by noting that in the competition for "positional goods," as the late Fred Hirsch called them, for every winner, there's also a loser. "If you want to be in the top half, you've got to get someone to be in the bottom half with you," he says. People who want high status must "buy" it somehow; people who value status least will become "sellers" by agreeing to occupy low-ranking jobs. Presto, an economic process.

Moreover, this "keeping up with the Joneses" mechanism is apt to touch off a chain reaction, a "positional treadmill," Frank says, with implications for everything from worker safety to the overall distribution of income. This leads to a lengthy and surprising discussion of why we require ethical systems to limit the role of money. From the betting limits of a poker game to laws against selling organs for transplant to basketball team salary caps to merit-oriented admissions to the best schools, social compacts designed to short-circuit the positional treadmill are omnipresent. The reason is to keep things from getting out of hand, according to Frank, for if one person goes all out for advantage, so do the rest, and nothing much is gained for the group. If everybody can sell babies, no baby will have much value.

A key finding is that the positional treadmill is apt to generate great income inequality, requiring some kind of income redistribution scheme— such as a progressive income tax—and regulation of the labor contract in every society. Robert Paul Wolff of the University of Massachusetts has argued that the book adds up to a new, tough version of Lester Thurow's *Generating Inequality*—a vigorous brief for redistributive justice.

Another striking point is Frank's resurrection of the all-but-forgotten "relative income" hypothesis of Harvard's James Duesenberry to explain why the poor save less than the rich. It happens because the poor have to invest heavily in status goods with demonstration effects if they ever want to be rich, Deusenberry argued, and Frank points out that the observation has striking results for the most important policy debate of the present day. People who care for their children won't respond to government deficits by saving more money to pay their kids' tax bills, as new classical economist Robert Barro has argued, according to Frank; they'll be too busy investing in status-goods that are more immediately required to provide for their children's future.

The simplicity of the analytic devices aside, the book is fairly overflowing with insights. There are prolonged investigations of chief-and-Indian phenomena, centering on the internal wage structures of firms, but ranging from everything from the reasons for spinning off the ailing division (to get its salary structure out of the larger firm) to the economics of a fair price—for Super Bowl tickets and beer. An extraordinary number of nooks and crannies of modern life are illuminated along the way.

Frank, 40, is not an especially likely candidate to be the progenitor of a fundamental advance in high theory. A Georgia Tech graduate, he went to Nepal for two years with the Peace Corps, before taking a Berkeley doctorate. At the end of the 1970s, he spent two years as chief economist at the Civil Aeronautics Board before returning to Cornell University. As noted, his book is shot through with *New Yorker* cartoons and breezy anecdotes in a brazen attempt to appeal to the largest possible audience—just the sort of thing to leave Chicago's Lucas cold.

But Frank's methods are as deeply rooted in modern economic methods as can be, and the task of bringing economic analysis to bear on status, first attempted by Veblen, is well and truly begun. The story illustrates once again the wisdom of going straight ahead in science, rather than blaming the tools—even when it takes three-quarters of a century to make it pay.

NOVEMBER 3, 1985

The Agency Theory in a Real World

SOME OF THE MOST INTERESTING RELATIONSHIPS IN ALL THE WORLD ARE THOSE BEtween the consumer, his supplier and the various intermediaries who exist to inform or even to make the buyer's choice. In the past, businessmen have learned little from economists about structure. Just as in the tired old joke, the economist stuck on a desert island with a can of beans who says cheerfully "first, assume a can-opener," so economists are inclined to assume the existence of something they call perfect competition. So who needs diversified corporations? Or labor contracts? Or products of differing quality? The result is that these relationships are among the most common and least well-understood in the modern world.

But in the last 15 years or so, economists have begun to find promising ways to think about the institutions they find in the workaday world. Most of this work comes under the heading of the economics of information; much of the action today is in a fascinating sub-branch called agency theory.

A series of papers from a meeting last year on agency theory, one of several sessions held to celebrate the 75th anniversary of the founding of the Harvard Business School, have now been published. *Principals and Agents: The Structure of Business* just might be the best new general book about economics of the year. It includes an essay by Nobel laureate Kenneth Arrow and a long introduction by John W. Pratt and Richard J. Zeckhauser, the conference organizers.

Pratt, 54, and Zeckhauser, 44, are typical of a new breed of economic thinkers who are extending their subject into the real world. Pratt is an applied mathematician with far-reaching interests who teaches at the Harvard Business School. Zeckhauser is a Harvard microeconomist and talented theorist who works out of the John F. Kennedy School of Government across the river. Both are accomplished bridge players, Zeckhauser is a former national champion. Zeckhauser explains his interest: "Both my parents were lawyers. They were always talking about what's enforceable when you rely on long-term relationships. It's natural that I would begin thinking about how to design incentives."

In their introduction, Pratt and Zeckhauser say, "Whenever one individual depends on the action of another, an agency relationship arises. The individual taking the action is called the agent. The affected party is the principal . . . the doctor is the agent, the patient the principal. The consultant is the agent, the client the principal. The corporate executive is the principal, his subordinates the agents. The corporate executive is in turn an agent for the shareholders; the general partner plays that role vis-a-vis the limited partners.

"Our theme is that businesses, workers, consumers and indeed all participants at large regularly struggle to deal with the intractable problems that arise in agency relationships, that organizations arise to deal with them and that, on average, the forms perform reasonably well. Although we must expect waste, slothfulness and even dishonesty to be with us always, the question is whether we can keep them to manageable proportions."

What agency theory offers, according to Zeckhauser and Pratt, is a tool kit: for monitoring performance, for structuring incentives, for writing employee contracts to assure good performance or for the provision of public services. In some cases, of course, the market itself provides effective monitoring. Everybody knows it makes sense to stop at the roadside stand where the most trucks are parked outside. "But if the owner can overcharge you while dealing fairly with his usual customers," they say, "you may be in trouble." That's why antique stores without posted prices scare away the unsophisticated buyer.

Private monitoring devices such as hobby magazines and user-friendly consultants arise easily enough, they say. But how to insure that government tries to satify parents and children who are the reason for its schools, for example, instead of the teachers? How to prevent the Defense Department from becoming handmaiden of its contractors? How to design rules to govern the conduct of corporate managements who are the targets of unfriendly takeovers? "These things are worth talking about," says Zeckhauser.

For his part, Kenneth Arrow lays out the economic theory of agents and principals, noting that the insurance industry had nurtured some of its more interesting concepts, such as moral hazard (meaning the tendency of fire insurance to make people sloppy—or even to turn them into arsonists.)

He then goes on to observe that the facts of the world are often dramatically different from what agency theory would lead us to expect. Take doctors, for example. The patient is unable to monitor performance; the outcome of treatment is somewhere between random and closely connected, yet the doctor's fee is in no way related to the results he gets. Malpractice liability is a small modification of the fee structure in the direction that theory suggests, Arrow says, but it doesn't apply to what he calls "run-of-the-mill shirking." So why not devise more complicated incentives? The answers may be that people prefer to keep their contracts simple, their judgments personal and their systems of rewards and punishments beyond the purely pecuniary, Arrow suggests.

An occasional equation notwithstanding, the book abounds in concrete details. Law professor Frank H. Easterbrook writes about insider trading as an agency problem. Mark A. Wolfson, an accounting specialist, analyzes the reputation for fairness of general partners as the crucial factor in oil and gas tax-shelter programs. Robert G. Eccles, a business professor, describes transfer pricing within corporations as an agency problem. Perhaps the most unusual contribution is that of Harrison C. White, a Harvard sociologist who considers agency relationships as a modern alternative to kinship as a means of maintaining control in large organizations.

As Zeckhauser says, "One of the things that they have going for them in Japan is that the lowest-down guy in the organization, when you ask him what he does for a living, he doesn't say I'm a janitor, he says I am a Toyota employee. He will treat the Toyota Motor Company the same way I treat the Zeckauser family."

For decades, many businessmen have been contemptuous of technical economists for being pointy-heads given to talking about an idealized world far removed from everyday reality. They can't afford to do that anymore. "When we were first starting out, I would discuss this with everybody I ran into in business, and I would say, 'Gee, tell me how you get your employees to work? How do your customers know your product is reliable? Does your board of directors really represent your shareholders?' . . . Since then, I've been amazed at the number of real world decision-makers who are perfectly happy to think of things this way. My estimation of the conceptual capability of business executives has improved dramatically."

Maybe. Maybe it is quality of economics reasoning that has improved. But illuminating as agency theory is, in the end there's a dimension of the organization of work that it still doesn't capture. Its strength is in the identification of incentive mechanisms, not in description of the architectural aspects of these arrangements. But then, that is part and parcel of economists' familiar urge to get beneath the surface, a passion- that often leads them to miss the clue hidden in plain sight—the varying degrees of complexity of the phenomenon itself.

JUNE 9, 1985

How the Bra Was Invented and Other Useful Lessons

BOSTON'S PLACE IN THE INTERNATIONAL DIVISION OF LABOR RARELY SEEMED MORE secure than last week. A celebrated Russian economist was squirreled away in a borrowed office at Harvard's Kennedy school, carving up his country's economy in hopes of winning Gorbachev's confidence, while the school's former dean Graham Allison, Harvard's most gifted publicist, scattered rose petals along his path to Washington.

Mitsubishi Electric Corp. announced it would open a basic computer science research lab at the other end of town, in the shadow of MIT, in hopes of tapping into the global conversation about artificial intelligence and computer complexity. True, Anthony Gottlieb, the *Economist's* science editor, has gone home to London, after two years of compiling the world's best science section from a remote terminal in Cambridge, but he'll be back from time to time.

In a way that New York isn't, Boston and its thriving research establishment is on the cutting edge of commercial knowledge—it figures significantly in, say, something like half the 22 technologies on the official list compiled recently by the National Critical Technologies Panel.

What is it that drives this dynamic? There's no simple answer to a question like this, but the chances are that the answer has a great deal to do with the city's diversity.

It is more than 20 years now since Jane Jacobs argued in *The Economy of Cities* that the really important thing about cities is their sheer variety, the fact that people from many different occupations and industries are packed into them, cheek by jowl. For those 20 years, Jacobs' views went almost entirely unattended by economists, though city planners, urban organizers and architects paid them heed.

Now, however, thanks to a new burst of interest among theorists in the kind of external effects they call spillovers, particularily knowledge spillovers, mainstream economists have become newly interested in economic geography. As Paul Krugman put it in his Gaston Eyskens lectures on geography and trade last year, "Regional comparisons offer a huge, almost untapped source of evidence about how our economy really works."

Now an especially interesting paper by Jose Scheinkman of the University of Chicago and Andrei Schleifer of Harvard University—and their students Edward Glaeser and Hedi Kallal—has set side by side Jacobs' basic argument on cities to two closely related and better-known views, and crudely tested them against the American evidence. The theories aren't always mutually exclusive, the authors acknowledge, but rather they offer differing views of what is most important. They conclude that Jacobs is probably the winner.

The first popular theory about cities has it that it is concentration that is important to the growth of cities—the kind of concentration exemplified by, say, Pittsburgh in the heyday of steel. Long before Berkeley's Paul Romer resurrected the economics of growth with an influential 1986 thesis on increasing returns, and before Stanford's Kenneth Arrow gave it an early formalization in a 1962 paper on the economics of learning by doing, this story about cities was associated with the great Victorian economist Alfred Marshall, the authors say.

Marshall figured that specialized knowledge somehow would be "in the air" in cities where particular businesses had taken root. Parents would teach their skills to children; spying, imitation and raiding would be easy for entrepreneurs looking to make a buck. Marshall predicted that monopoly would be better for growth than competition, because the externalities generated could be retained within the firm.

The second popular theory about cities also dwells on geographic concentration and specialization, but argues that competition among firms is the key force in growth. Michael Porter of the Harvard Business School is the most forceful proponent of this view, the authors say. Since the alternative to innovation is demise in these highly competitive situations, Porter's externalities are maximized in highly specialized, highly competitive cities—something like Silicon Valley today. Jacobs, unlike Marshall or Porter, believes that the most important knowledge transfers in cities come from outside the core industry there—whatever it happens to be. It's not generally steelmakers talking to steelmakers who come up with new applications, she argues, but rather metal-benders talking to cart makers that will give rise to a bicycle industry.

Thus in this view, "variety and diversity of geographically proximate industries rather than geographical specialization promote innovation and growth," the economists write, citing the case that Jane Jacobs made famous of how the brassiere evolved from dressmakers' innovations rather than from the underwear business. Dissatisfied with the way her dresses hung on her customers over the underwear of the 1920s—corset covers, chemises and ferris waists—Mrs. Ida Rosenthal designed the first brassiere. For a time she gave one away free with each dress she sold. Then she quit the dress business and opened a workroom devoted entirely to brassieres. Eventually she formed the Maidenform Brassiere Company and started factories, first in Hoboken and then in West Virginia. The fact that Mrs. Rosenthal hired West Virginia seamstresses who already knew how to sew and possibly even made their own underwear, Jacobs wrote in *The Economy of Cities* in 1969, "should not persuade us that therefore brassiere making developed from subsistence underwear making in West Virginia. The idea arose in the Hollywood of the clothing industry that was the Garment District of New York.

Using data on geographic concentration and competition in 168 American cities, Scheinkman and Schleifer find that measured by employment, industries grow more slowly in cities where they are more heavily represented. They also say that industries grow more rapidly where firms are smaller than the national average, supporting the view that competition rather than concentration tends to favor growth. Finally, they conclude that city-industries grow more rapidly when the rest of the city is more specialized.

If Jacobs—and Schleifer and Scheinkman—are right, what is it about Boston, then? Well, a large part of the answer would indeed seem to be its diversity. When Harvard Business School ace Porter put his consulting business, Monitor Co., to work on a strategic plan for the commonwealth, he and his analysts identified four related but quite different clusters of activity: health care, financial services, information technology and knowledge creation services.

Thus, the Russian economist Grigory Yavlinksy came to town last week with "knowledge creation" in mind. Mitsubishi is interested mainly in information technology. But the really big draw is that they know they may run into each other (or some wayward money manager) at Michela's restaurant or the Harvest or the Boston Harbor Hotel.

It may be also that the city's remarkable vitality begins in the geography of its central core, in the jewel-box arrangement of its research centers around the basin of the Charles River, and in the manufacturing and development enterprises arrayed in concentric rings stretching off to the New England countryside.

New York and Washington share this arrangement, though on a grander scale—just possibly a scale less suited to the kind of exchange among authorities from various fields that has attracted researchers to Boston in the first place. It may be that the smartest thing Washington ever did was to build that subway to connect Crystal City with Bethesda, Md.

Or as Schleifer and Scheinkman put it, "If geographical proximity facilitates transmission of ideas, then we should expect knowledge spillovers to be particularly important to cities. After all, intellectual breakthroughs must cross hallways and streets more easily than oceans and continents."

MAY 26, 1991

Welfare Reform?
Or Growth?

THE YEAR HASN'T SEEN MUCH MORE THAN LIP-SERVICE PAID TO POVERTY. IT WAS A nonissue in the presidential campaign, and compared to scenes of Ethiopia, the problem as it exists in America seems slight. Yet, poverty hasn't gone away, and there is a long cycle in these public-private issues. For the present, however, it has been relegated to the upper slopes of opinion-making where books do their work.

It was there, for example, that Archbishop Rembert G. Weakland of Milwaukee, who supervised preparation of *Catholic Social Teaching and the U.S. Economy*, put the full force of the church behind the question, "Can we try to plan so that the least-advantaged are sheltered more from economic adversity?"

There, too, Charles Murray argued in *Losing Ground* that government programs made matters worse; Michael Harrington said in *The New American Frontier* that the government didn't do nearly enough.

A good deal of sorting-out has been contributed by Harvard professors David Ellwood and Lawrence H. Summers, in a paper presented for the Institute for Research on Poverty at a conference in Williamsburg earlier this month.

The meeting, a regular summit conference attended by specialists in and out of government, probably will turn out to have charted federal policy for the coming decade. Ellwood and Summers' paper makes good holiday reading, for it represents an opinion on which two sophisticated econo-mists—one of unchallenged conservative credentials (Summers), the other a widely respected liberal (Ellwood)—can agree. It is a position that can command widespread assent among professionals, and serve as a baseline from which liberals can stage their departures.

Their conclusion: economic growth is by far the best medicine for the poverty rate. But what the government does, it does relatively well.

"Despite the haphazard evolution of these policies and their seeming lack of coherence, we find much to recommend them. Given the resources dedicated to fighting poverty, we have done about as well as we could have hoped."

Others at the conference quickly dissented from Ellwood and Summers' conclusion that economic growth will solve most problems. For example, Sheldon Danziger, director of the University of Wisconsin's Poverty Institute, was one who said that he felt its curative powers were "overemphasized," at least for some groups.

"Not everybody is moving along at the same rate," said Danziger. "We're seeing increased inequality that is not well explained, but very clearly documented. I think it is a mistake to think that everyone, especially women heads-of-household, are going to be swept along by a rising tide.

"But I think they caught the spirit of the conference," he continued. "Nobody argued that we should expand current programs. Nobody thought there was a simple way. The last time that Harvard made a foray into the field, they were optimistic that they could solve all the problems. This time they were much more limited in their hopes."

The neoconservative position, which has garnered a lot of ink recently—that government programs have simply increased the incentives to stay poor—was simply dismissed by the two Harvard economists. It is based on a misreading of the evidence, they said.

True, they allowed there are some bad side effects to disability insurance (it reduces the supply of older men); to aid for families with dependent children (it alters family structure somewhat, particularily among blacks); to welfare programs generally (they may increase unemployment among black youths.)

But in all three cases, Ellwood and Summers found the actual damage done by government transfer policies to be far less serious than is supposed. Who can believe that welfare benefits have caused a severe decline in the work ethic among young black men, for example, when a youth living alone is eligible only for food stamps worth $64 a month?

"We are led to reject out of hand the increasingly fashionable view that poverty programs are the source of poverty problems," they wrote, concluding firmly that "major reform appears both infeasible and undesirable."

Instead, their recommendations consisted of some fine-tuning, plus a reliance on growth. "There is some scope for carefully designed benefit increases that would reduce suffering without adverse side affects." It would be a bad idea to expand benefits for black youth, for example. But increasing benefit levels, especially for AFDC [Aid to Families with Dependent Children] recipients, might be a good idea, they said, concluding: "It would be tragic if narrow budgetary concerns or discouragement about the 'poverty problem' eliminated our experiments at promoting self-support."

DECEMBER 23, 1984

The Case
for Profit-Sharing

AUTO CONTRACT NEGOTIATIONS, WHOSE WAGE SETTLEMENTS WILL CREATE A CRUCIAL pattern for the rest of the economy, are proceeding slowly. The details are sketchy. But already it is clear that the talks' real impact on the nationwide bargaining process may be the growing interest in more ambitious forms of profit-sharing.

Profit-sharing is increasingly seen by businessmen as a way to escape from the paradox of reporting terrific income statements and taking a tough stance toward labor at the bargaining table. Likewise, union leaders are cautiously exploring various proposals to make some part of the paycheck contingent on good company performance, as a way of cushioning workers against layoffs.

At Ford Motor Co., for example, a proposal to peg all future wage increases to a profit sharing plan was put on the table by the company early this month. (Only a little of workers' pay is tied to profits now.) General Motors is expected to follow suit. Stanley J. Surma, a high Ford labor relations official, said, "When income growth is tied to profitability, two things happen, both of which make eminent good sense. First, the employees appropriately share in the company's profitability; and second, we are somewhat protected against incremental cost when severe downturns occur."

Unions remain leery. United Auto Worker negotiators have shrugged at the Ford proposal so far. "There's a feeling that if firms are willing to share profits, there aren't going to be very many profits," says Barry Bluestone, a Boston College economist who is an acute student of organized labor.

"Personally, I think we're going to see more of it. But it will come slowly, and with great difficulty."

Enthusiasm has been stimulated by the appearance of a new book by a leading economic theorist, which puts firm analytic foundation beneath the idea of indexing pay to some indicator of the firm's well-being. The cynosure is Martin Weitzman, whose book, *The Share Economy*, is scheduled to be published next month.

Weitzman, 42, is a mathematical economist at the Massachusetts Institute of Technology, for whom a book aimed at the general public is an unusual adventure. The appearance of *The Share Economy*, however, is widely regarded in economic circles as a major event. Some say Weitzman has simply dusted off and elaborated a 19th-century notion called "wages fund doctrine," but all agree that he has done a remarkable job of calling attention to the macroeconomic implications of some very mundane practices.

Some economists have said that not since John Maynard Keynes have such bold and imaginative policy measures been proposed.

At the heart of the book is the conviction that the world doesn't have to be the way it is. That is, people don't have to work for wages alone. Instead, they could work for a share of what they produced, a share that would fluctuate up and down with their production unit's fortunes.

At only one firm, such profit-sharing doesn't make much difference, and even can make matters worse for workers. But were most firms to operate under a share system, Weitzman says, the result would be to profoundly alter the operation of the economy.

Why? Weitzman says that making the cost of hiring an extra worker less than the average cost of employing a worker, a widespread share system would mean that firms would always be out hiring, seeking to boost production by adding staff. He offers the following example: Instead of paying $24 an hour and then choosing to hire 500,000 workers, General Motors could commit itself in advance to paying a total of $12 million per hour to be shared among all its workers over the lifetime of the contract. In effect, he says, a share system builds excess demand for labor into the system.

What would encourage the spread of a share system? A tax break, of course. Weitzman figures that as long as share income—as opposed to wages—were tax free, up to a certain point, the pressure on firms to convert to share plan would be overwhelming. Even unions would cave in. A 50 percent exemption for profit-sharing income would be enough, he calculates, to tip the balance, and the tax break would pay for itself if it reduced the unemployment rate by only 1 percent.

The result, he says, would be a world in which managers would "lavish as much attention on pleasing their workers as on satisfying their customers." Unemployment would all but disappear in such an economy, Weitzman thinks. He says: "A share system looks very much like a labor shortage economy. Share firms ever hungry for labor are always on the prowl— cruising around like vacuum cleaners on wheels, searching in nooks and crannies for extra workers."

Japan offers a laboratory of sorts for much of his plan, according to Weitzman, for Japan powered through the recessions of 1954, 1957–58, 1962, 1965, 1971, 1974–75 and 1981–83 with relatively little change in registered unemployment. The secret appears to be the fairly widespread use of a bonus system, which for "lifetime" workers adds up to around a quarter of total remuneration in good times. In bad times, it is simply not paid, but ordinarily, firms pay out more in such bonuses than they earn in pre-tax profits.

Such sharing schemes would also deal effectively with prejudice, he says. "When firms are hungry for labor, there is little place for nonfunctional discrimination . . . Rosie the Riveter had no trouble finding a well-paying job during the severe labor shortage of World War II, but she was thrown out of work after the labor market returned to more 'normal' conditions."

Most of all, he says, his plan would diminish the importance of the principal of "More" in labor-management negotiations. A share economy, Weitzman argues, "almost forces labor to accept a perspective broader than wage militancy for the benefit of one particular subgroup at the expense of others." Employees of a successful company can't get paid more than the going rate; the firm would try to hire more workers instead.

Finally, Weitzman says, a share economy would be far more resistant to "shocks," or sudden disturbances, than a wage economy. Imagine an OPEC-style price hike. In a wage economy, GM responds with layoffs, production cutbacks and higher prices. But in a share firm, the company would strive to minimize layoffs, knowing it needed to keep its workforce intact. The long-range consequences of higher relative oil prices would be similar, even in a share economy, for a permanent price increase in oil means a lower standard for consumers of it, but the short-term adjustment process would be far less costly in a share economy.

Precisely the virtues which make Weitzman's plan attractive in the seminar room—its tight logical coherence—make it seem less than immediately practical outside. Weitzman's proposal would require a federal share-plan administrator, for example, operating out of the Internal Revenue Service, to make certain that bonuses were real, and not merely disguised wages. Conservatives might resist it.

Nor would the proposal necessarily be embraced by unions, at least not at first blush: High-seniority workers don't need the anti-layoff protection it entails and high-wage unions would see their premium over the going rate eroded. (Weitzman figures union wages would fall by around 10 percent.)

Perhaps most exacting, the proposal would require broad public approval and understanding, just like, say, the pollution control movement. No more than firms could be expected to buy expensive pollution control equipment on their own can companies be expected to seek share plans without a legislative mandate, Weitzman says. If just one firm or industry undertook a share plan, the result would increase employment and output all right; but it would drive prices down and wages, too.

But if all or even most adopted bonus systems on cue from the government, a balanced expansion would take place, with increased demand from the newly employed feeding back to keep prices up, Weitzman says. Whether the economic commonweal is willing to stake its future on the possibility that economists' advice can be depended upon to produce the desired results overall is at least open to question, however.

Thus, Weitzman proposes a decade of talking about how a share economy might work. "The wage system promotes the illusion that welfare of the worker is independent of that of the firm. It isn't so," he says. "I do a lot of work in comparative economics, so I tend to look at things maybe from a little different angle. I don't take the U.S. economy as the paradigm of the whole world. I'm well aware that things could be different."

Indeed, that public policy is required to implement a widespread share system partly accounts for its absence. Limited attempts at share compensation, known usually as a "sliding scale," have been around for a long time. New England mills and Colorado mines were among those firms that once attempted to pay a fixed proportion of their revenues to their workers. Steel baron Andrew Carnegie stated, "It is the solution of the capital and labor problem because it makes them partners—alike in prosperity and adversity."

It was the big unions that pushed for profit-sharing throughout the 1950s and 1960s, and the companies, particularly the automakers, that resisted. Only in 1982 did the automakers come around, and then only as a way of ducking high-wage demands in a time of losses. A modified plan was adopted by both Ford and GM, and this year checks ranging from $400 to more than $800 were distributed to workers. (American Motors had a plan for years, but there were no profits to share.)

What's amazing, however, is how relatively little profit-sharing is a fact of everyday life. Weitzman estimates around 15 percent of big companies have some form of contingent employee payment, including Kodak; Procter and Gamble; Xerox; Sears, Roebuck; Texas Instruments; J.C. Penney; Chase Manhattan; and Safeway. But the plans average only 10 percent to 15 percent of total pay, and most are deferred compensation schemes such as pension plans, which are designed to skirt taxation at current rates. Even Japan has gone only a little way toward the state of affairs that Weitzman recommends.

Why? Economist Bluestone conjectures that "it is the capitalists' job to take risks, and workers job to work, and that is the way each prefers it. Workers don't ordinarily like to take risks." He notes the Chrysler workers, who received a handsome profit-sharing plan with the government bailout, immediately bargained it away when the company got out of the red. They took a substantial loss, amounting to thousands of dollars per worker, as a result. Weitzman likens the wage system to the gold standard, a primitive relic of past belief to be overcome through enlightenment. "The wage standard is not any kind of universal, inevitable consequence of divine forces, natural laws or even human nature." It is simply one way of dividing the pie, and not the best.

He says, "Those who clamor for an industrial policy to improve capitalism need look no further than a change in the way workers of large industrial corporations are compensated." A share system would, he says, "unleash more powerful forces for economic prosperity and social progress than are to be found in the wildest visions of national planners or cultural revolutionaries."

AUGUST 19, 1984

The Computer
Who Cried Wolf . . .

SAN FRANCISCO—It was just over a decade ago that the Club of Rome's *Limits to Growth* report and a study by MIT's Systems Dynamics Group called *World Dynamics* unloosed a double whammy of analysis on an already nervous audience.

The world was in serious danger, the experts warned: Natural resources and the environment were near the brink. The central problems were accelerating industrialization, swelling population, burgeoning malnutrition, the depletion of nonrenewable resources and a deteriorating environment. If present trends continued, the reports warned, the limits to growth would be reached sometime within the next 100 years.

There would be no soft landings, either. The result would be a worldwide economic collapse, including a sudden and uncontrollable decline in population. With a delicious shudder, some called for "lifeboat economics." One journalist compared the *Limits to Growth* study to the meeting of the Council of Nicea in 325 A.D. and Martin Luther's 95 theses nailed to the church door in 1517.

Last week a panel of analysts met in a convention jointly sponsored by the American Economic Association, the Association of Environmental and Resource Economists, and the American Association for the Advancement of Science to consider the reports in the light of a decade's experience. They weren't kind.

Yale's William Nordhaus, Harvard's Thomas Schelling, Stanford's Alan Manne, MIT's Robert Pindyck took pokes at the *Limits to Growth* report. In defense of the point of view, Herman Daly, a courtly Louisiana State professor, held out for voluntary simplicity. And the University of Colorado's celebrated Kenneth Boulding came in at the end to defend the *Limits to Growth* approach.

"I think we have to beware of the give-us-this-day-our-daily-growth argument," Boulding said. "Anybody who thinks you can double everything every generation simply doesn't know what exponential growth is all about."

But in general, the consensus was summed up by Nordhaus, who noted that Thomas Malthus developed the same critique of growth at the turn of the 19th century, "in not much less rigorous form, while arguing with his father at the breakfast table." The warning wasn't timely then, and it isn't timely now, he said.

"Some societies want to clean up the air and water, to provide food stamps and income support; other societies want to build nuclear weapons and missiles, to cut back on food stamps and income support and to increase incentives for the wealthy to bid up the price of Renoir paintings and yachts, but these fundamental choices are not driven, in my view, by resource scarcity," said Nordhaus.

Alan Manne added, "When the time comes to write the intellectual history of our time, I don't think *The Limits to Growth* will rank with the Nicene Creed or Luther's theses as the most exciting event of the decade."

Manne said that too little industrial growth and not too much had become the central problem now; population growth had slowed down; depletion was not as great a problem as had been expected, especially since it was now generally recognized that oil prices were not a problem of scarcity but of concentration; and as for malnutrition, it was a matter of argument, he said, whether a bad situation had really gotten worse.

Robert Pindyck generally agreed. "As long as we can substitute away from oil, and other nonrenewable resources, from copper and so forth, then there are no material limits to growth." It is possible to quantify the question by measuring scarcity rents, Pindyck said. They were still very small as a fraction of price.

Indeed, Harvard's Schelling argued that climate control is likely to be the lively controversy in the decades to come. "One thing we now know is that mankind has the ability to change the climate. The fact that we are doing it inadvertently is beside the point. I have a hunch that this decade will be known as the one in which anthropogenic climate change, at first inadvertent, then willful, became a very important matter of policy.

"They may love it in Siberia but not in Miami," he said.

Herman Daly remained unmoved. "An ecologically sustainable scale, like a just distribution of income, is a value to which the market is insensitive," he said.

"The scale of the economy relative to the scale of the ecosystem does not, as far as I know, trigger any cybernetic feedback and automatic controls within the market effects. So how do we design an economy which does not depend upon continued growth?"

Neither Dennis Meadows, the principal author of the *Limits to Growth* report, nor Jay Forrester, the progenitor of the Systems Dynamics Group, was at the convention. Each continues to be active in the field of economic and environmental forecasting; neither has yet published a reappraisal of his earlier work.

It was Nordhaus who surveyed the various factors threatening continued growth in an effort to weigh their likely influence on future growth. "Events in the real economy have lent some superficial weight to the *Limits to Growth* view, while economic studies have not," he said, mentioning the productivity slowdown in particular as a possible early warning of depletion. He estimated that only an eighth of the slowdown was due to the depletion of easily available resources, however.

Using a variety of models, he asked "how much less growth would there be" if a variety of dismal scenarios unfolded: If energy gets worse, if minerals give out, if carbon dioxide and other greenhouse gases continue to increase, if pollution got worse and far more expensive to contend with.

Thus calculated, he added up all the conceivable "drag" on growth and got between 6 and 19 basis points (or hundredths of a percentage point). That is, if growth were expected to be 3 percent a year for a century, instead it would be cut by depletion-drag to between 2.81 percent to 2.94 percent, if his calculations were correct.

"If technological change proceeds at anything near its historic pace, however, it should offset the effects of the drag. Suppose someone comes up with a ceramic substitute for copper, for example, that can be made from abundant materials. That would wipe a basis point off my results forever," he said.

Nordhaus acknowledged a "Murphy's Law" at work as well—if something can go wrong, it will. "Every decade we discover something new that we didn't know about. Maybe these effects are small, maybe they are very large, but they may be out there," he said.

"At this point," he concluded, "many economists have forgotten the *Limits to Growth*, except as 'the computer who cried wolf,' or 'the return to Chicken Little.' I think this neglect is unwarranted. It may not be dangerous, but it certainly is unwarranted. I think these long-run issues are significant. If you add up 10 basis points here and 10 basis points there, after a while it begins to add up to real money."

JANUARY 3, 1984

The "New Classical" School's First Textbook

THE LATE 1960S WERE A TIME OF GREAT FERMENT IN TECHNICAL ECONOMICS. OUT OF the period grew a movement called the "New Classical" economics, designed to depose the Keynesian orthodoxy. At a time when Keynesians were moving to tackle what were viewed as imperfections in markets—sticky wages in particular—the New Classicals chose to see things differently.

Just suppose, the new view went, that markets, especially labor markets, are working the way they are supposed to. Suppose that those who aren't working aren't really *involuntarily* unemployed, that they simply prefer leisure to the prevailing wage. Suppose also that because people correctly anticipate attempts by government to manage the economy, of the sort designed by Keynes and his followers, these managing efforts have little or no effect—or worse, actually contribute to instability.

If so, then the thing for government to do would be to recognize that all was almost always for the best, and to retreat into following a few simple rules, such as keep money growth steady and government spending down.

Sound like Reaganomics? Well, at a deep and satisfying level, maybe so. It was far more sweeping than monetarism, though in its defiant rejection of the conventional medicine, and in its emphasis on mind over apparent illness, it seemed a little like Christian Science to its detractors.

The New Classical economics is now reaching the textbook stage, marking a highly interesting time. Robert Barro's intermediate text, *Macroeconomics*, has been out for a year now, the first exemplar of the New Classicals' point of view. It has made a respectable beachhead, if perhaps somewhat smaller than many had expected, selling 10,000 copies last year in an American market estimated to be around 130,000 books a year at its cyclical peak.

Textbooks are big business, of course. Those who major in economics require an intermediate text as well as a principles book, and then there are the MBAs. The big sellers are the elementary texts, where the market is dominated by the University of Nebraska's Campbell McConnell, followed at a distance by MIT's Paul Samuelson and a half dozen others of roughly comparable sales. For new ideas, though, the customary approach to the principles texts is through the intermediate books. So the extent to which New Classical economics will or won't come to dominate the way economics is taught in college will be determined here—not all at once, but over time—where salesmen and editors meet college professors.

So economists are watching Barro's book with far more lively interest than they ordinarily accord a new text. How is it doing? Is it hard to teach? Do students like it? With 10,000 copies sold in its first year, the book's performance is solid to some, disappointing to others.

The two leading Keynesian texts—one by Rudiger Dornbusch and Stanley Fischer of MIT, the other by Robert Gordon of Northwestern University—are thought to roughly split between them half the market, about 55,000 to 65,000 volumes. So the Barro book seems to have vaulted firmly into third place. On the other hand, just what is third place worth in a market like that? A more eclectic book by two Stanford authors with good New Classical credentials, Robert Hall and John Taylor, is awaited with interest. Whose lunch will they eat?

Meanwhile, publisher John Wiley and Sons has poured money into the Barro text, making a beautiful job of its physical production, supporting it heavily with advertising and supplementary material. Wiley is a major force in the industry; "It is the most important economics book we've ever published," says editor Richard Esposito.

Not surprisingly, reaction to Barro's book ranges from exuberant to cautious to resentful, depending mainly on which side the reader is on. A young Duke University professor who teaches with the book emphasizes its explanatory power. "The kids really like it," he says. A Midwestern state university teacher who admires the book declines to teach from it. "This is not what they're going to hear out there in the world after they graduate," he explains. A Princeton University professor, who says he is waiting for a more "balanced" text, adds, "It is a very idiosyncratic book."

There is no doubt that the Barro book imposes unusual demands on its readers. Gordon's text makes the most painstaking attempts to locate its lessons in the world of recent experience. The Dornbusch and Fisher book has the panache expected of a pair of theorists who dominate Cambridge, the capital city of economics. But apart from a few beautiful charts, the Barro book has the detachment of a physics text. (Physics was his undergraduate field at Cal Tech.) It is Robinson Crusoe economics writ large and modeled with great clarity.

"Barro certainly has a very optimistic way of thinking about how markets work," says Wellesley College's Arjo Klamer, whose book, *Conversations with Economists*, expertly details the scope and history of the controversy between the New Classicals and everybody else. "What the Keynesians say is that, no, the constraints are much more complicated than we thought, there are all kinds of uncertainties, all kinds of shocks, things happen you cannot anticipate."

Barro, 40, says he had no wish to provide a "balanced" treatment of different approaches to macroeconomics. The market-clearing approach is simply superior to the Keynesian model on scientific grounds, he says, and will rise or fall on its own merits in the market. Says editor Esposito, "Paul Samuelson says he's going to rewrite his text to include the New Classical point of view. Well, we say it can't be done that way. You've got to tear his book up and start again."

Ironically, author Barro was a leader in developing the disequilibrium underpinnings of Keynesian economics until he converted to the New Classical point of view in the early 1970s. Educated at Harvard, he taught at Brown University and the University of Chicago before settling last year at the University of Rochester. He says he is satisfied with the book's progress so far, and also with the $5 royalty from the $34 cover price that he collects every time a new book is sold.

Meanwhile, Barro says he may be on the verge of agreeing to write an introductory principles text. "I would like to have about six or seven publishers bidding on it," he says. "That would be a nearly perfect market."

What about signaling between bidders? Barro raises an eyebrow. In the world of the New Classicals, such signaling doesn't work. In textbooks, he says, no less than in the Republic of Ideas, the free market knows best.

FEBRUARY 24, 1985

A Primer
for Democrats Seeking
Policy

WITH EACH PASSING DAY, DEMOCRATIC PARTY ECONOMICS GET A LITTLE SILLIER. A promising congressman comes back from chatting up West Coast public relations guru Regis McKenna for advice. The front-running senator throws a "Casino Society" mixer in New York—based on a magazine article he's read—and invites the press. Coming on the air moments after President Reagan's State of the Union Address, five Democrats talk pleasantly about small town values—and say next to nothing about macroeconomic policies.

The Democrats don't know where to turn.

Where's the action? Well, would-be candidates might do well to go back to school. There will always be the happy pell-mell of the demimonde, where technologists, consultants, savants, moneymen, politicians and the press all compete for attention. But university-based economics is the core around which it is all organized—and at the moment, the abstruse world of technical economics is in the early stages of a dramatic rediscovery of government's implicit powers to mitigate the undesirable effects of the operation of markets.

Today's textbooks foreshadow tomorrow's politics. A year ago, for example, Robert Barro, a University of Rochester professor who is a leader of the New Classical school of anti-Keynesian "hands-off" economists, entered the lists with an intermediate textbook. The New Classicals have dominated the high-fashion end of economics for 15 years, and there were hopes that they could extend their gospel of non-interference to college classrooms generally.

But the Barro text has failed to live up to expectations, and today it's an ambitious text by Edmund Phelps of Columbia University that crops up most often in the gossip of a certain stratum of the profession. As an exemplar of the "New Keynesian" school of thought, it is hardly taking college classrooms by storm. But as a glimpse of the shape of things to come, it has something to offer anyone who ever wondered what Democratic party economics could become.

Like Barro's book, Phelps' *Political Economy* (Norton) is a lavish production. But where Barro's *Macroeconomics* is as austere and abstract as a Cal Tech sensibility could make it, *Political Economy* is as full of the cultural world as the Upper West Side of New York. Its chapters develop economic doctrines historically; they are decorated with beautiful architectural drawings, garlanded with incisive quotations from the movies; there are lively literary questions at their ends.

But for all its high-brow appeal, *Political Economy*— like almost any economics textbook—celebrates markets from cover to cover. They have "enormous usefulness" says Phelps, "especially markets of competing private firms." But unlike Barro, Phelps has an eye for circumstances in which markets don't work, including a "a nightmarish analysis of how badly markets are apt to work without regulatory protection." If you believe that unemployment is a serious problem, for instance, then Phelps' is the book for you.

"There is an impression that Democrats have got the hearts and Republicans have got the brains," says Lawrence Summers of Harvard, who is one of the foremost admirers of Phelps' book. "This is a good example of how liberal positions can be rendered in just as tough-minded a fashion." It makes good reading, Summers says, for "a philosopher, physicist or even a Supreme Court Clerk interested in discovering what economics is about."

Not that the Democratic National Committee should rush out and buy dozens of copies for delegates. The book is "in the tradition of Alfred Marshall," says David Colander of Middlebury College, but it has none of the easy accessibility of that Victorian classic, to politicians or anyone else for that matter. Indeed, even to economists, it has turned out to be somewhat forbidding.

"I'd use it to teach our smartest 40 students," says a professor at a leading eastern university. "But it is not for the kid with a 473 on his SATs." Blurbs have piled up, but adoptions by universities have lagged. The publisher is embarrassed and Phelps is vexed. "I don't know whether it's just a reluctance to bear the risks of innovation or whether there is also some fear of its breadth," he says.

It is perhaps not surprising that hoi polloi find Phelps' explication difficult, for he sometimes goes too fast even for his fellow economists. For 20 years, Phelps has been one of the most fruitful minds in the field, a major contributor to a dozen controversies at the highest levels of theory. Like

"Milton," "Marty" and "Lester," he is known to nearly everyone by his first name, or rather its diminutive, "Ned."

He helped develop the so called "golden rule of capital accumulation," a highly technical test of whether a society is saving enough; he contributed to thinking about "dynamic consistency," the criteria by which economic reputations are judged; with Milton Friedman, he demolished the long-range Phillips Curve, demonstrating there would be no long-range trade-off between inflation and employment; and he helped puzzle out how supply shocks could be accommodated by policy.

Perhaps not as intimately involved in theoretical controversy these days, he is an active adviser to European governments, a scholar and a senior member of the scientific estate. And now he is the author of an introductory text.

Whatever its sales, Phelps' book seems destined to change the way economics is taught. For one thing, there's all the new territory that it explores, juxtaposing developments in unusual ways. Phelps writes, "In the past couple decades, economics has added a whole new vocabulary: incomplete information, transactions costs, customer markets, asymmetric information, incentive compatibility, reputation, incentive or efficiency wages and job rationing, statistical discrimination, implicit contracts, macroeconomic equilibrium and the accelerationist hypothesis, the island parable, rational expectations, the policy ineffectiveness proposition, disinflation and credibility." Most of these concepts have arisen as a result of the New Classical controversies, he notes—and most bid fair to elbow aside the enthusiasm for near-total laissez faire that was inspired by the "rational expectations revolution."

Then, too, there are some unusual policy recipes built into the book. Tax cuts are expansionary, right? Not necessarily, according to Phelps, who argues that crowding-out mechanisms could defeat their purpose. One thing that all right-thinking persons can agree on is that free trade is best, right? Not so fast—there may be some rationale for import protection, according to Phelps.

The point is that even if future Democratic policy viziers don't learn their elementary economics from Phelps' text, the book nudges the authors of all the other introductory books to stake out stronger positions. It marks an unmistakable turn toward the possibility of a sophisticated governmental activism—in long-term unemployment, in discrimination, in macroeconomic coordination—that is deserving of the sadder-but-wiser label, "New Keynesian."

Democrats are fond of pointing out that politics exhibits a 25-year or so

cycle. The funny thing is, so does economics. Indeed, the discipline follows roughly the cycle of generational dialectic of public and private pursuits that Albert Hirschman describes in *Shifting Involvements*. Having
been profoundly conservative in the 1920s and 1930s, economic dogma
turned liberal during the 1940s and 1950s, before becoming conservative
again in the late 1960s.

This conservatism still dominates in the 1980s, but the tide is already
turning—not toward a rent-control populism, not toward a dirigiste man-on-
horseback act, but toward a sophisticated stewardship of the economy and
its market mechanisms. Would-be Democratic candidates will be well-
advised to skip the magazines on these cold winter evenings and curl up
with a good textbook instead.

FEBRUARY 9, 1986

Why the Mighty Fall

ONE OF THE OLDEST STORIES IN THE HISTORY BOOKS IS "HOW THE MIGHTY HAVE
fallen." One moment an institution looks as though it will last forever—the
Portuguese, Spanish, Dutch and English empires, for example, or U.S.
Steel, the New Industrial State and the San Francisco '49ers.

But whatever it is, before the ink is dry on the latest manifesto proclaiming its invincibility, it is crumbling, and some new outfit is rising to
take its place. From football teams to foreign empires, it's hard to remain
No. 1 for any length of time.

Now there is someone who thinks he knows why.

"Economic sclerosis" is a hitherto unheard-of diagnosis that is creating
a certain amount of excitement among economists. It is the brainchild of
one of the nation's most fruitful basic economists, a University of Maryland
professor named Mancur Olson. He believes he has discovered a process by
which nations grow old economically and die.

At 50, Olson has been a star all his professional life. His dissertation,
published 20 years ago as "The Logic of Collective Action," attracted a
wide following among social scientists, if not among economists, as the first

attempt to extend economic reasoning to the diverse universe of groups larger than the company but smaller than the state.

Like a handful of other pure economic scientists—Robert Lucas, Gary Becker, James Buchanan, Robert Mundell, Douglass North, Martin Feldstein, William Baumol—he has established himself as the source of a transforming vision of his field.

But like John Kenneth Galbraith, Olson probably has had more influence on people outside his field than in it. Naming another non-traditional economist, one of Olson's friends says: "Mancur is like Albert Hirschman, only not quite as successful."

For several years, Olson has argued to an ever-widening circle of experts that special-interest groups inevitably will conspire to choke off economic growth in stable democratic societies, large and small.

When his book, *The Rise and Decline of Nations: Economic Growth, Stagflation and Social Rigidities* was published last autumn by the Yale University Press, it had already been widely circulated, reviewed and discussed. Its publishers did everything but hire the Royal Albert Hall to commemorate the event. (They did hire the National Press Club.)

The list of its godparents reads like a Who's Who of opinion-making institutions: the National Science Foundation and the Environmental Protection Agency; Stanford's Hoover Institution and Princeton's Woodrow Wilson International Institute for Scholars; the Sloan Foundation and the Lehrman Institute.

What better way to bring an idea to market? Especially one that has been written up in witty, elegant English, with its single set of equations confined to a footnote.

The trouble is, the book may be a trifle overpromoted. "It is not quite the complete explanation of everything there is that Mancur thinks it is," says Thomas Schelling, a professor at Harvard University's Kennedy School of Government and Olson's mentor, "but it comes off as a very important book."

Charles Kindleberger of MIT, who faults the book for providing no explanation of how fast sclerosis occurs, says: "I think he's really on to something." Yet others have refused altogether to review the book, rather than say unkind things about its sweeping generalities.

Replies Olson: "When you are a kid with a hammer, the whole world looks like a nail."

The argument of *Rise and Decline* goes something like this: Individuals, left to their own devices, form dense networks designed to advance their own welfare and to beggar their neighbors. When it comes to opposing economic "progress," labor unions are only the tip of the iceberg, according to Olson.

Professional associations, farm organizations, cartels and lobbies of all sorts arise like so many miniature governments. Each fights to win its members a larger slice of the pie; all stifle initiative and strangle growth.

The result, he says, is economic decline; the sclerotic society will be overtaken by the one with fewer and less powerful distributional coalitions. "The British Disease," that stalemate of high inflation and low growth that has become epidemic in the 1980s, is the inevitable fate of any nation that survives long enough to catch it, Olson says.

Conversely, he says, one of the easiest ways to beat this aging process is to see your contending lobbies emasculated or abolished by totalitarian rule or foreign occupation.

Just this sort of destruction may explain the "post-war miracles" of German and Japanese economic growth, he says, and the continual turmoil of French politics—especially of the fractiousness of its unions—may have retarded the development of the special interest groups and collusions that have elsewhere retarded economic growth.

Significantly, the implications for policy of Olson's argument are just about the precise opposite of all the current clamor for "reindustrialization" and "protectionism."

"Reindustrialization is a nice word for—how shall I say it?—the media. But I'm unaware of any substantial professional literature on the subject," says Olson. "The argument [of *Rise and Decline*] makes free trade look even better. Not only do we get comparative advantage, but we undercut the cartelizing interests that make for inefficiencies in our own economy. So I suppose that the point is," says Olson, "if the United States takes the road to progress, we'll drive there in foreign cars."

DECEMBER 26, 1982

Yes, Virginia,
There Is a Truth About
Taxes

"I CAN'T MAKE A DAMN THING OUT OF THIS TAX PROBLEM," COMPLAINED PRESIDENT Warren G. Harding to a friend. "I listen to one side and they seem right, and then—God!—I talk to the other side and they seem to be right . . . I know that somewhere there is a book that will give me the truth, but I couldn't read the book. I know somewhere there is an economist who knows the truth, but I don't know where to find him and haven't the sense to know him and trust him when I find him. God! What a job."

In those few words of an exasperated president in conversation with a friend more than 60 years ago is the timeless story of the social world of tax policy. Yes, Virginia, there is a truth about taxes—at least enough truth for now. Yes, there are economists who know it. Yes, there is a book, called *Untangling the Income Tax*, in which the Harding quotation serves as an introduction.

Written by economist David Bradford of Princeton University for the Committee for Economic Development and scheduled to be published Tuesday, the book frames the debate over tax reform with extraordinary clarity. Bradford, 47, a Princeton dean who was born and raised in Arlington, Mass., has been working on the analysis of income tax inside the Treasury and outside it for more than a decade. He is perhaps the nation's preeminent tax scholar. And yes, Virginia, the president and the Congress have disregarded most of what he has to say.

"I wonder if we'll ever have a thing that's called 'an effort to reform the income tax' again," he says. "I bet we won't. The Bureau of National Affairs and the Commerce Clearing House which sell newsletters and tax information are the only ones benefiting. What a mess!"

The reason it is all so hard, writes Bradford, has to do with defining income and measuring it in a world where purchasing power comes in a lot more forms than wages, tips and salaries, and where inflation can introduce truly amazing distortions in a fairly short period of time. For example, he notes, most people think that the mortgage-interest deduction is the big subsidy to homeowners in today's income tax. On the contrary, he says, the real break comes from exempting the income the homeowner realizes from his investment, namely shelter; from the point of view of a perfect income tax, the homeowner is not much different from the employee who enjoys the tax-free use of a company gym. By making the subsidy more widely available, the mortgage-interest deduction probably makes the system fairer, not less fair, Bradford writes.

Once you've got the concepts of income, consumption and wealth firmly in mind, you've got a choice between two quite different methods of taxing income—an accrual basis and a consumption basis. What we have now is a highly complicated combination of the two. Under a pure accrual system, all the additions to wealth during the year are taxed, whether capital gains, corporate earnings that are imputed to individuals, increases in the values of trusts, to say nothing of all kinds of perks. Cash transactions would be just the starting point. Under a pure consumption system, you simply pay tax—one way or the other—on everything you buy.

But isn't a consumption standard hopelessly harder on the poor than the rich? Not necessarily, says Bradford. Consumption taxes can be made progressive, too, with simple brackets and exemptions. He distinguishes mainly between two kinds of consumption taxes, value-added and retail sales taxes on the one hand, and personal consumption or cash-flow taxes on the other, such as the Robert Hall–Alvin Rabushka "flat tax," or the pure cash-flow tax that Bradford devised for the Treasury Department during the administration of President Gerald Ford. Such taxes tend to leave the government out of savings and investment decisions, and to adjust automatically for inflation. Bradford thinks we should move toward more consumption taxation, if for no other reason than accrual taxation is hard to administer. "There is nothing like money at stake to reveal the soft points of a definition," he writes, reciting the hit parade of recent tax dodges: "one year, tax straddles; another year, self-constructed assets; another year, installment sales; another year, discount bonds; and so on."

He acknowledges, however, that for one reason or another people just don't feel very comfortable with the consumption standard. Under Donald Regan, the Treasury Department simply brushed aside a previous Republican administration's tax plan (devised by none other than David Bradford!) and devised its own accrual plan instead, widely ballyhooed as Treasury I—and substantially watered in a dozen subsequent iterations.

Why is it that people don't like consumption taxes? Perhaps it's because people don't understand them. According to Bradford, the simplest way to move to a consumption-oriented tax would be to to phase out all the restrictions—including the age restrictions—on deposits and withdrawals from tax-sheltered savings plans, such as IRAs and Keough Plans. Then accelerate depreciation until first-year writeoff is the rule. Then phase out the interest deduction. Finally, find a transitional way to tax the retained earnings of corporations that would be distributed under such a scheme and—presto—you'd have a personal-consumption tax that dramatically changed the treatment of savings and investment, and a tax that would probably raise additional revenues to boot.

IRAs have already begun to deeply alter the way people think about their income; by the end of the 1980s, it is a program that could look politically attractive.

APRIL 13, 1986

The Thief of Baghdad, Explained

SADDAM HUSSEIN, WHO LAST WEEK STOLE KUWAIT FROM THE FAMILY THAT HAD RUN it for 250 years, has been painted as a madman, a Hitler, an irrational pirate willing to plunge himself into obloquy—and perhaps the world into a recession—just to gain access to a few oil wells.

What's needed to make him stop?

As always, a good understanding of what makes him go in the first place would be useful.

That's where Reuven Brenner comes in. Brenner is a maverick economist at the University of Montreal, who has written extensively on rivalry and uncertainty in a steady stream of books and articles since 1983. (The most recent is *Gambling and Speculation: A Theory, a History and a Future of some Human Decisions*, just published by Cambridge University Press.) He's well outside the mainstream of what university-based economists are doing, tackling topics far bigger than those with which most economists are comfortable. Brenner would put the question this way: Is Saddam Hussein really any different from any other gambler?

Brenner is interested in why people decide to undertake risky acts. In his view, it's mainly a matter of relative standing. It's when gamblers fall behind in the competition with their rivals that things get touchy, he says, for the perception of inequality is what encourages people to take risks. Each person's satisfaction depends not just on his or her wealth alone, but on the fraction of the population that is richer than him.

Moreover, Brenner says, nothing affects the distribution of wealth and opportunity more than the sudden growth of population—precisely because nothing changes the underpinnigs of wealth like an onslaught of new job-seekers. The willingness of human beings to forsake their customary habits and to bet on new ideas—all kinds of new ideas, from war and revolution to new forms of art and science—increases dramatically whenever there is a spurt in the size of the human community, Brenner says.

Do Brenner's notions fit the situation in Iraq? Pretty well. For one thing, consider the nature of the prize that is Kuwait. A British protectorate until 1961, the little state is essentially the desert fiefdom of a Mesopotamian tribe that was lopped off from the rest of Iraq by the colonials. It operates more like a family business than an independent nation, and its relations with Iraq reflect a Hong Kong-like status: It played banker to Iraq throughout its costly war with Iran, loaned something between $10 billion and $20 billion (with which Hussein bought some of the tanks that captured the city). In other words, it doesn't cost Iraq much to assimilate Kuwait. (Nor does it cost the Kuwaiti royal family much to escape; something like $100 billion in global assets are managed by its holding company based in London, far beyond the reach of Iraqi tanks—though that's small comfort to the 750,000 or so citizens who are not cousins.)

Moreover, there are the internal pressures of the Iraqi economy, where population has been growing at nearly 4 percent a year. Mindful of the chaos touched off by untrammeled economic growth in Iran, Hussein has attempted to keep a tight rein on Iraq's income distribution, raising the per capita income of the poor as quickly as he can while clamping down tightly on the spending habits of the rich, funneling the ever greater numbers of the young and unemployed into his 1-million-man army. The strategy makes for a narrowing gap between rich and poor within Iraq, all right, but also for a rapidly broadening differential between it and neighboring Kuwait, where population has been stable and economic growth robust.

But the key dimension in understanding Hussein's sudden move is probably the inter-Arab one, especially in connection with the Arab states' bitter rivalry with Israel. A Brenner-style analysis would have us look at Hussein's standing in the Arab League, and here Hussein has made no secret over the years of his ambitions. As *Forbes* magazine's Lawrence Minard wrote as long ago as 1980, "Hussein wants to be for the 1980s and 1990s what Gamal Abdel Nasser was for the 1950s and 1960s, the leader of an as-yet-unborn Third Force, telling Soviets and Americans to stay off his turf." In taking over Kuwait, then, and threatening Saudi Arabia, Hussein is bidding for leadership of the Arab world—and neither the Americans, the Israelis nor the Europeans can hope to remove him without calling down the wrath of all Islam.

This perspective on the competitive logic of Saddam Hussein's strategic moves is not the one you'd find in a standard text on development economics, much less a course in microeconomics. It isn't even a view of competition very widespread at the frontiers of present-day economic research, though Robert Frank, Tibor Scitovsky and Amartya Sen have all raised similar points about the importance of strictly positional concerns. But then, as MIT's Franklin Fisher says, "Reuven Brenner understands far better than most industrial economists that the drama of competition is not confined to the narrow state of standard theoretical models. Rather that the drama occupies a wide stage: one in which innovative personalities strive to outdo each other in a constant leap-frogging game."

Nor is it just the situation in Iraq that is illuminated by Brenner's notion of deep-seated and pervasive rivalry. The fundamental question, "Can we leapfrog?" is to be found in every human realm, from competition within companies and industries to races among nations. When Donald Trump doubles and redoubles his bets in real estate, he is trying to improve his standing at the expense of some other magnate—Warren Buffet, say—more than to simply buy another boat. When a company bets the store on the advantages of some new technology, it is making a deliberate attempt to move up sharply in the standings of its division in its industry.

When millions of ordinary persons plunk down a dollar or two in state lotteries, where a few large prizes promise to dramatically change the station of their winners, they are making a small-cost, long-shot bid to move directly to the head of the parade. And when a scientist stakes his reputation on a far-out idea—cold fusion, say—it's best seen as a bold attempt to win a new place at the table. These position-bettering gambles are the essence of human history, Brenner argues.

What, then, for those of us who like stability? Well, if each person's sense of well-being is inextricably bound up with the status and well-being of those above and below him in the pecking order, as Brenner supposes it is, then the first principle of economic order is to keep the population stable, or at least growing along predictable lines. (That will surprise no one who has ever reflected on the class underpinnings of the planned-parenthood movement.)

At least as important, however, is to keep the perception of inequality from becoming very great. Rich nations, like rich citizens, walk a tricky line when it comes to dealing with the poor, Brenner says. They can rely on geography, police, armies and burglar alarms to persuade the have-nots to leave them alone; or they can transfer wealth through charity, taxation and wages so as to diminish the relatively poor's incentive to commit crimes against them. Last week Kuwait learned that if your competition is near and desperate enough, sometimes neither one will do.

AUGUST 5, 1990

Why Bureaucrats Prefer Quotas

ALAN BLINDER, THE LIBERAL PRINCETON ECONOMIST, WAS LIVID—AND VIVID. "IMAGine a bill imposing a tax of $1.25 on every pair of shoes sold in America, with the revenue earmarked to pay $50,000 annual subsidies to shoe manufacturers for each new worker hired at the average industry wage of $14,000 per year." A few things seemed clear, he said. Shoe prices would go up. Employment in the shoe industry would be encouraged. And the bill would never pass Congress.

Yet measures with this effect are now a virtual inevitability—precisely because they don't have to pass Congress. Last May, the International Trade Commission recommended strong protection, in the form of a quota designed to save about 26,000 jobs. The recommendation is on President Ronald Reagan's desk now, being studied. You can expect his decision any day now.

But you'll never see its potential effects spelled out so clearly as this, because the measures taken—whatever they are—will be couched not as a tax on imports but as a quota on them. The consumer loss of the ITC's recommendation as the result of higher prices is estimated to be around $1.28 billion annually, says Blinder—which works out to a tax of $1.25 a pair of shoes, or $50,000 per job saved.

The growth of world trade since the end of World War II is one of the great success stories of our time, and liberalization measures have played a major part. It is the era of "the GATT," the General Agreement on Tariffs and Trade, the agency that argues out differences in commercial policy. As Robert Baldwin of the University of Wisconsin wrote in a recent survey for the National Bureau of Economic Research, 30 bilateral agreements and eight multilateral negotiations have cut tariffs steadily to about 20 percent of their 1930 levels.

But practically all the trade intervention since World War II has been in the form of quotas, the commercial equivalent of off-balance sheet borrowing, of off-budget spending. Steel, autos, textiles and a great variety of agricultural produce have been affected by some form or another of agreement over the years; the first time a quota was ever rolled back was recently, with Japanese autos.

Why do we like quotas so much? James E. Anderson, professor of economics at Boston College, has some interesting answers. One reason often given is that outside the GATT, he says, it is a little easier to negotiate—but only a little. And of course quotas and voluntary export agreements can be bilateral, not general. But, deep down, Anderson thinks that quotas are the modern remedy of choice because they work to the advantage of bureaucrats. "Middle level managers like these things, because it gives them influence," he says.

To begin with, the results of quotas are hard to quantify. To identify their economic consequences, you can do the sort of back-of-the envelope calculation that Alan Blinder devised for shoes, but any serious advocate can quarrel with your numbers. Worse, such straight "certainty equivalent" calculations don't capture the uncertain way the world works.

"It's so devilishly hard to estimate the effects," says Anderson. "Anybody who tries to do a study, no matter how careful, runs into this rejoinder, 'well, that's just an estimate.' No one can dispute what the tax rate is, though."

Besides, he notes, with a quota you buy off the people who are being hurt, at least to some extent. "If you allocate the import licenses to the people that are already in the market, you're tending to buy off some of your influential critics. Why shouldn't we know how much they're being bought off for, and for how long?

"As a small 'd' democrat, I'd really prefer that we all know what taxes we're paying. Quotas are really pernicious because they just don't have clarity. You've got hidden transfers taking place, but you can't really see how extensive they are. Quotas are obnoxious for that reason, but it's the very reason the bureaucrats love them. They give them that many more degrees of freedom to interfere."

Just one more trick of the vested interests in government and business, all but impossible to combat? Not necessarily. Anderson, 42, is a successful deep theorist in international trade. Recently he's been devising new methods of measuring the efficiency of various instruments of protection.

Not surprisingly, he finds tariffs more efficient than quotas to achieve a given level of job protection; after all, that's what the Invisible Hand theorem would suggest. On cheese and textiles, for example, a tax on imports would be 30 percent more efficient than a quota. It is too late to apply his methods to the shoe case, though, significantly, the government tried.

What's different is that Anderson's method is sophisticated and his results are robust, which is to say they are convincing. As a rhetorical tool, therefore, his method may be quite powerful. The information required to perform his calculations is readily available; he gives away his software to anyone who asks; similar methods can evaluate trade instruments on other targets, such as average output, profit or wage income. "I suspect that as the volume of case studies mounts in the next several years," he says, "a strong case for the inefficiency of quotas will develop."

In a nation generally committed to the pursuit of efficiency, observations like these can build up over time to have extraordinary force on the real world. Consider, for example, the effects of deregulation, once the intellectual case was made. Amid all the talk of protectionism today, Anderson's arguments offer more than a small ray of hope.

Still, the extraordinary strength of the dollar remains the biggest bar to a strong, competitive American economy. As Alan Blinder says, "We can't export manufactured goods because we are manufacturing high interest rates and the strong dollar."

To put shoes on an equal footing with the rest of the world—along with American-made cars, computers, chemicals, machine tools and everything else—it is better to remove the causes of a too-strong dollar by balancing the budget than to enact quotas.

AUGUST 4, 1985

Which Model
for Eastern Europe?

YUGOSLAVIA TRAVELED TO THE BRINK OF CIVIL WAR LAST WEEK AND THEN BACKED OFF a little: the Croats vs. the Serbs, an old story. Overlooked in the commotion is a new story, an interesting skirmish in the controversy over the best route from clumsily planned hierarchies of the communist countries to generally free markets.

The question has to do with how best to privatize existing businesses. The alternatives being considered are the same as those all over Eastern Europe: Various forms of decentralized LBOs—worker buyouts—versus several varieties of mutual funds and holding companies designed to let a few specialists decide which enterprises will continue and which will be closed.

It's a monumental headache, considering that the essence of the communist economies was that profitable firms were heavily taxed to keep losers in business—without the benefit of the information contained in prices to distinguish between one and the other. That's a little like America's difficulties with its failed thrift institutions, but on a far, far grander scale.

And the problem now is that what works best for East Germany may not work well at all for Yugoslavia, because of their differing political histories. The controversey is playing out in Slovenia, the little post-industrial jewel at the peaceful northwestern end of Yugoslavia, next door to Austria. Not exactly the center of the world, true. But the practical issues are similar all across Eastern Europe, and the philosophical implications are universal, one of those unexpected dividends in self-knowledge arising from the translation of the crazy-house language of the communist economies into western terms.

A little background first. When Eastern Europe "fell" in 1989 all the complicated debate about the proper sequencing of reforms that had preceded it was rendered moot. With the walls tumbling down, politicians suddenly had to free up prices, stabilize their currencies and develop plans to put state-run businesses back in private hands.

Early hopes for a smooth transition to private property were dashed. Foreign buyers didn't flock to buy; the locals had little cash. Schemes for handing companies back to those from whom they were expropriated at the end of World War II went nowhere; a lot had happened in 40 years. Politicians turned to economists, looking for ideas.

Next were developed a series of mass privatization schemes: Shares would be mailed to all citizens, which could then be traded on newly established stock markets—a style popularized by Margaret Thatcher in England. But in the absence of well-established capital markets it was quickly concluded that such "paper privatization" schemes wouldn't change the way Eastern European firms were managed.

So attention turned to great holding companies, like the German "Treuhandanstalt," that would run state enterprises until they could be sold or closed. Broadly speaking, these centralized holding company schemes are today's preferred form of reorganization.

(For a basic description of how they fit into economic thinking, you can't beat the just-published *Reform in Eastern Europe*, in which five top economists of the new generation—Olivier Blanchard, Rudiger Dornbusch, Paul Krugman, Richard Layard and Lawrence Summers—describe the lay of the land.)

The guy playing the biggest role in implementation of reforms, however, is a Harvard University economist named Jeffrey Sachs. Everybody knows Sachs, a talented theorist, an authentic liberal and a deeply engaged consultant to the economically troubled. He parlayed an engagement in Bolivia into a global role. Today he runs a non-profit consulting company of red-hot kids, crunching numbers and advising governments on their problems.

Considerably less well-known is David Ellerman, 48. Trained as a mathematician, Ellerman has written and taught economics at Boston College, Boston University and Tufts University—and for 15 years, consulted to the Industrial Cooperative Association, specializing in establishing employee-owned firms. This was far from the pinnacle of capitalism, to be sure, but the ICA group is the major player in the low-income, self-help development business, and Ellerman knew employee stock ownership programs—ESOPs—backwards and forwards. Tired of teaching, he took off for Eastern Europe and struck up a lively consulting business in Ljubljana and Prague.

Where mainstream economists preach the virtues of holding companies, run by bankers and MBAs, as the appropriate institution to borrow from the West, Ellerman touts the great "taking-private" movement of the 1980s in the United States, at least for parts of Eastern Europe. Instead of having their fates decided by financial wizards operating far "over their heads," says Ellerman, let managers and workers of successful Yugoslav firms buy their companies themselves, using money borrowed against future earnings.

Thirty years of de facto decentralization in Yugoslavia have generally permitted the best people to find their way to the tops of the firms they run, he says; the situation is just the opposite of, say, Czechoslovakia or East Germany where a high degree of political correctness was required for advancement. So what mainly is required to touch off a binge of worker buyouts is enabling legislation, much like the American Employee Retirement Income Security Act of 1974.

Indeed, just such an act was before the Slovenian parliament two weeks ago according to Ellerman—when Harvard's Sachs stormed into town, addressed the legislators, urged them to adopt a voucher-style mutual fund plan instead, and threw the process into a cocked hat.

"What's happening here is that a country that quietly developed quasi-private institutions with socialist labels over the last 30 years is now being quietly socialized with capitalist labels. The economists should trust the business managers and workers to carry the country forward, and not give it over to the centralized decision makers—even ones with MBAs. As my friends say, a few more years of this and we'll be back to Bulgaria."

Ellerman just could be right—though Sachs strongly disagrees. Slovenia may be yet another case of the economists going too far. Nations are like Tolstoy's families: Happy ones are all alike, but every unhappy one has a different story.

MAY 12, 1991

DRI's New Man
for the '80s

IT WAS THE WEEKEND BEFORE THE THANKSGIVING ADJOURNMENT OF CONGRESS. To insiders, it looked as though "the Dole thing," a plan to narrow the deficit, might go though. US Sen. Paul Tsongas and other Democrats were talking about an "economic summit meeting;" the Reagan administration was talking about putting the standby tax increase into the budget.

"We knew that if you put in a big tax increase and an important expenditure reduction that in the short term there could be negative implications for the economy and it would be very difficult to convince Congress to take such action if that was the only story you told," says Roger Brinner. So Brinner and a handful of other senior Data Resources Inc. economists locked themselves in a room for a couple of days.

Out popped a study examining the economic potential of U.S. Sen. Robert Dole's proposal to postpone 2½ percentage points of indexation on the income tax for two years—it was subtle, and, it turned out, very effective medicine. For a few days the DRI study was at the center of the storm.

"It was so clear that [Federal Reserve Chairman Paul] Volcker had signaled that the Fed would make a countervailing contribution. U.S. Rep. and leading supply-sider Jack Kemp even accused him of meddling in fiscal policy. The Dole plan does produce a situation where there is some sluggishness of a moderate nature, but you do get very quickly a snap back and a very important reorientation of the economy. Capital spending really stays alive because all the people in the executive suite are no longer really certain that there is going to be a recession."

Alas, despite the heroic present tense into which Brinner slips to describe the option, the plan is history, at least for now. The persuasive DRI stimulation notwithstanding, the attempt to reach a compromise with the White House fell through. "I don't think it came to nothing, exactly," says Brinner. "It provoked a good deal of thought."

Brinner, 36, is the new chief economist at Data Resources, succeeding

Alan Sinai. It may be the top job, but it is not always an easy one at a company where founder Otto Eckstein is still the top economist—as well as Harvard professor and political operative. Brinner takes his relationship with the master in stride, concentrating on turning out the monthly forecast while Eckstein works on major pieces of research—such as an investigation of what has happened to American manufacturing in the past four years.

Brinner has his work cut out for him. DRI is in a fast-changing business. It is a common observation that the company made its money selling computer time, not econometrics; that is, that time-sharing of main-frame computers containing DRI economic information and data banks provided a hefty portion of the company's earnings. Such leverage is what led to the sale price of $103 million, paid when McGraw-Hill bought the firm from Eckstein and his shareholders in 1980.

The advent of the small computer now threatens to dent the time-sharing business. Why pay retail prices to rent DRI's main-frame when you can get the same results with your own personal computer? The result is that Brinner and nearly everyone else at DRI is looking for ways to "unbundle" its services to appeal to those with their own hardware—and to find new products to sell. "We've got a software venture going with Visicorp designed to allow people with personal computers to access our data. You don't have to know any programming; you can be an insurance agent or a mortgage banker and you can pump it down to your personal computer with a handful of commands.

"It used to be that you paid one fee and it implicitly had in it the cost of our labor, the cost of our data bank, the cost of our software and the cost of our computers. Now you pay separately for almost each of those elements. We're more and more billing our time on an hourly basis."

Doesn't that mean the company stands to lose a big chunk of revenue as the time-sharing business drops out? "We still have growth in our main-frame business," says Brinner. "It isn't the 30 percent it used to be; it's more like 10 percent or 15 percent."

On the other hand, there has been no price increase in the last 15 months. "We've been able to slow down our deliveries; we haven't had to retire capacity. It is more that the growth has to come from these other networks and gateways," says Brinner.

Brinner faces another problem. "Chief economists" are a dime a dozen now; econometric models are proliferating, and pretty soon there will be dozens of them from which to choose, too.

For example, last week Yale professor Ray Fair was in town, peddling his model—which had previously been known among forecasters as notoriously esoteric—now on a floppy disc for personal computers for around $2,000 annually, or about a tenth of what a subscription to the DRI or the Chase econometric model would cost.

How is DRI going to do business against econometricians operating out of their briefcases with no fixed costs?

Brinner says he plans to concentrate on explaining the linkages within the DRI model—a model which is, after all, probably the most carefully thought out and persistently studied one in the business.

"Forecasting has occasionally been sold as an infallible black box. It's not. It is really a way of thinking things through. An econometric model is just like a large Visicalc [now Lotus] worksheet, where you understand each element of the relationship and the way they work together."

DECEMBER 18, 1983

The Games That Nations Play

CERTAINLY IT IS GOOD NEWS THAT PRESIDENT BUSH MET TOSHIKI KAIFU LAST WEEK in Newport Beach to help the prime minister out in his by-election. There is good news, too, on the trade balance with Japan—good news that the value of the dollar can turn up and nobody screams bloody murder.

But beneath the relatively smooth relationship of the moment, sentiment is building for some more explicit form of American industrial policy—and that promises a thicket of interesting new political problems for years to come. The newest raised voice is that of Kenneth Flamm, the widely respected semiconductor analyst at the Brookings Institution in Washington. American trade policy has come to a fork in the road, he says: The semiconductor agreement this summer is going to be a test case that will establish policy for decades to come.

"The status quo is unsustainable," Flamm says. "It is simply unacceptable for the American government to leave our high-technology firms, as individual players, at the mercy of coordinated strategic policies organized by coalitions of their foreign competitors, backed explicitly or implicitly by their national governments."

This sentiment exemplifies a subtle trend, operating at a high level in present-day economic thinking, inside universities and among business groups. It is not that economists are giving up on their long-held conviction that freer trade brings benefits to all; most aren't. Rather they are recognizing that free trade may be easier to subvert, and harder to arrange than previously thought. They are acknowledging a new wing of their studies of cooperation, coordination and competition built in the last 30 years by game theory.

Behind this search for an appropriate new role for government in the supervision of trade is not a single galvanizing book—the way that Keynes' *General Theory of Employment, Interest and Money* laid down the case for government stabilization in the 1930s.

Instead, there have been a series of theoretical and empirical developments in trade theory in the last 10 years, led perhaps by Elhanan Helpman of Tel Aviv University and Paul Krugman of MIT, opening out quickly into a host of subtleties explored by others.

In the "new" international economics, strategic trade policy is not simply a matter of picking winners and losers, of whipping up enthusiasm for big projects, but rather a matter of delicate thrusts and feints, not just in particular markets, but in macroeconomic policies, too.

Until recently, the best introduction to the implications of this new way of thinking about your opponents was a metaphoric one—mathematician Nesmith Ankeny's little classic, *Poker Strategy: Winning with Game Theory*, published in 1981. It is still a pretty good window on the world, though sadly, it is out of print.

Now, however, there is a fascinating new book, *Thinking Strategically: The Competitive Edge in Business, Politics and Everyday Life*, written by two economists who are at the very center of the game theory craze. Avinash Dixit of Princeton and Barry Nalebuff of Yale write about tennis, incentives, brinksmanship, courting, commuting, voting, cheating, bargaining and Robert Campeau in terms that can be read with real pleasure by anyone who likes business magazines. In the process, they extend the strategic point of view into every realm of policy, and make it clear why thinking about government will never be the same again.

Strategic thinking, they say, is the art of outdoing an adversary, knowing that he's trying to do the same to you. A lumberjack doesn't have to think strategically, they say, but a general does—and so does a spouse, a child, a business rival. Wise practitioners are forever thinking about their collaborators' and opponents' aims and expectations, and a great deal is known about the situations that typically arise. "Our aim is to improve your strategy IQ," they write.

The problem is, of course, that if Dixit and Nalebuff can improve your IQ, they can improve your competitor's as well—and the Japanese translation rights to their book were sold months ago. Contests between strategically sophisticated competitors quickly turn into grown-up versions of the children's game, played with fists and fingers, of scissors-paper-stone.

Which brings us back to the problems of pursuing national industrial policies that are designed to permit their implementers to prosper at the expense of others. The mischief that can arise when nations begin to play these games on an international scale can be truly monumental. Discussions of the success of Japanese industrial planning usually concentrate on the handful of unambiguous successes of the Ministry of Industry and Trade—and leave out the broken plays and outright fumbles of that legendary agency over the years. Nor do they mention that most of MITI's striking successes happened before Japan's economy grew large and complex.

And as Harvard University's Dale Jorgenson notes, industrial policy enthusiasts usually ignore altogether the factor that the Japanese themselves believe is responsible for their amazing post-war success: The blend of macroeconomic policies designed to stimulate capital formation and investment. The stewardship of the Ministry of Finance, far more than MITI, accounts for Japanese success, according to Jorgenson.

No doubt about it: The world of strategy is a rich and complicated realm. There are plenty of worthwhile skills that will enable you to see through your opponents' strategy, achieve cooperation, make credible commitments, and so forth—and they can be learned and mutually understood.

But important as technical ability is, perhaps the worst mistake a strategist can make is to think that knowledge is the beginning and end of the game. In his poker book, mathematician Ankeny identifies four attributes that are fundamental to winning any game. Knowing the rules and probabilities is only one. Discipline, judgment and hustle are the others, he says. Those proposing to prescribe an industrial policy for America should keep in mind all four.

APRIL 7, 1991

How to Stop
Cream-Skimming in
Health Care

THERE ARE A LOT OF THINGS WRONG WITH THE AMERICAN HEALTH CARE SYSTEM, MOST of them recognizable to anyone who has been near a hospital recently. There is nest-feathering, wherein parties build themselves artificially high standards of living. There is bells-and-whistles medicine, wherein high-technology care becomes routine even when it hasn't been shown to be effective. There is divide-and-conquer procurement, wherein small consumer groups pay higher rates than big ones because they lack bargaining power with providers.

The worst problem—the hardest to spot and the most important to do something about—is cream-skimming. That is the tendency of insurance companies to design their policies to attract low-risk individuals, leaving those who really need insurance outside the system.

To understand it, one must think back to the late 1970s, something of a golden age of American medicine. Physicians could practice pretty much as they pleased, hospitals grew as fast as they could borrow money, suppliers of pharmaceuticals and equipment had a field day. Insurance companies were effective middlemen; Medicare and Medicaid were growing fast. The number of uninsured people dropped to a record low.

It was in those deep-pocket days that the cream-skimming began.

At first it was the health maintainence organizations, and who could blame them? The HMOs were a revolutionary force, calling attention to wasteful practices of the old insurers, wherein procedures that could be performed in 15 minutes in a doctor's office often required a day or two of hospitalization. HMO insurance rates were so much lower than those of the "Blues" that young—and healthy—consumers switched to them in droves.

Then corporate insurance buyers sharpened up. They recognized that they could drive harder bargains with insurers who in many cases had been charging single rates for whole communities, even though different groups offered different degrees of risk (affluent white-collar workers were charged less than muffler-men in auto shops in the poor end of town). Federal insurance programs put a tighter leash on hospitals, precipitating a new round of efforts to save on costs.

Within the short space of a decade attempts to escape the soaring cost spiral have turned into a well-camouflaged and very desperate game of musical chairs, with society's most-threatened members its victims—those who figure they cannot switch jobs lest they lose insurance, those whose policies are canceled, those who take a gamble on not buying it at all.

What would help? Well, there are no fewer than 50 various plans before the public now, each designed to do something about the 35 million Americans who have no health insurance. The Democratic leadership is pressing forward with a plan to download the responsibility for health care on corporate America. But before plunging ahead it might pay to listen to a very senior MIT theorist named Peter Diamond, age 51.

It is a familiar sight, now, the economist from a prestigious university traveling off to South America or Eastern Europe to present a plan for fixing some element of the messed-up economies of those ill-governed nations. We cede authority to these youngsters because we know that there is something fundamentally architectual about the act of imagining economic reform. No amount of nuts-and-bolts knowledge of the situation "on the ground" can substitute for a clear intuition of how markets actually work together in their broadest outline. Diamond, head of an expert panel for the Advisory Council on Social Security, knows his way around the real world as well. His plan was first broached in his presidential address to the Econometric Society in Philadelphia in June.

Diamond's idea is that Congress should create a Health Care Fed, modeled fairly closely on the Federal Reserve system. Why the Fed? Because the only things more deeply connected to the local community in the United States than the provision of medical services is banking. And the decentralized model of the Federal Reserve system—with its regional banks and central offices, its tradition of semi-independence and political accountability—has been a singularly successful government institution for 80 years.

What would such a Health Fed do? Diamond's initial proposal is that it organize the U.S. population into large groups—each running from 10,000 to 100,000 persons—for the purpose of purchasing insurance. By eliminating choice and simply assigning families to large groups based mainly on geography, the Health Fed would disconnect the central cream-skimming mechanism right from the beginning. Individuals would leave their group only upon marrying or moving to another region of the country.

As the sponsor of such groups, the Health Fed would then begin to operate more or less like the insurance office of a large corporation. It would set up competitions between insurance companies for the right to sell insurance to each group. In some respects, this packaging of families in groups would be analogous to what the Federal National Mortgage Association now does when it assembles large numbers of individual mortgages into pools. Just as investors who buy Fannie Mae bonds know they are buying a statistically uniform package of debt, insurance companies who catered to Fed-organized family groups would know that they were servicing populations that contained some big risks, some extremely healthy people, and a vast majority somewhere in between. (Such a system would bear more than a passing resemblance to the German national health system, with its decentralized "sickness funds.")

Through such groups, then, individuals would buy a certain basic coverage for themselves. The Health Fed would narrow choices to a certain menu of policies; it would monitor quality and handle complaints about the insurance company. People too poor to pay for their basic coverage would have their premiums paid by Medicaid. People who preferred HMO-style coverage could choose it. Individuals who wanted to buy supplemental coverage that would entitle them to more or better care could buy it, with certain qualifications.

Diamond says, "Individuals would deal with their insurance companies much as they do now," with the Health Fed replacing the personnel office of a large firm in narrowing the range of choices for an individual.

As matters stand now, the Democratic leadership in Congress seems determined to assign the responsibility for fixing the health care system to employers, especially large corporate employers. These are shoulders on which the responsibility does not belong.

If the Democratic party is ever again to stand for the principle that there are some things that government does better than markets, the idea that overseeing health insurance is a fundamental government responsibility would be an excellent place to start.

JULY 14, 1991

First Thing We Do,
Optimize the Lawyers

Every few years someone tosses a big new stink bomb at the lawyers. Some are better than others.

A few years ago wunderkind Peter Huber—he was first in his engineering class at MIT and at Harvard Law—argued in quite a good book called *Liability* that tort law had been greatly opened up to new forms of injury and redress by a small group of legal theorists and practitioners he called "the Founders." Then *Forbes* magazine went after well-to-do plaintiffs' lawyers in a big way and incurred the wrath of Ralph Nader. Nor does the right wing have any monopoly on lawyer-bashing. Economics writer Robert Reich (who was trained as a lawyer) likes to beat them up as well.

It's a standard rap with only a few basic variations: Lawyers get in the way, they gum things up, they siphon off talent from legitimate areas like engineering, they open up whole new areas of the law and they become engines of redistribution, or "paper entrepreneurs," who destroy long-term value for short-term financial gain.

What do these critics have to say about the business cycle now ravaging the law business? Not very much. The fact is that the recession in legal services is probably as tough as in any other sector of the economy, with the possible exception of banking. There is blood in the scuppers of major firms—corporations are riding herd on their legal expenses as never before. The impersonal forces of the market are being as hard on lawyers as they are on everybody else.

But critics of the profession believe that thanks to their political acumen, lawyers are relatively immune to the market. If business dries up in one sphere—malpractice, for instance—the corps of lawyers will lobby to change the law in some other field: taxation, perhaps, or trade. These critics are doubtless right—up to a point. A new study by UCLA's Richard E. Sander and E. Douglass Williams of Carleton College published in the journal, *Law and Social Inquiry*, finds that the legal services industry has grown sixfold in real terms since 1960—from 0.5 percent of national income to 1.4 percent today. That rivals the auto industry in size.

Indeed, now an economist has estimated how much he thinks lawyers are costing America. According to Stephen P. Magee, a professor of economics at the University of Texas, American gross national product in the mid-1980s was about 10 percent lower than it should have been. This $500 billion annual penalty translates into $1 million per lawyer in foregone growth.

Naturally, Magee has got a regression analysis, boiled down to a chart showing "the negative effect of lawyers on economic activity." It is to be found on the back cover in the current issue of of *Economic Insights*, a new magazine published by Washington's Institute for International Economics. Chile, Uruguay and the United States have a lot of lawyers and slow growth since 1960. Japan has few lawyers and high growth. Magee took into account the differences in capital and labor inputs in the various countries of his survey; and still there was a difference. Sure enough, it must be the lawyers.

His solution is twofold. First, he wants to limit lawyers to 20 percent of the current law school admission rate. That will greatly increase the salaries of those who do manage to qualify for one of the rationed places. But it will save money in the long run, says Magee. "Every time another litigator is admitted to the bar, society acquires another heat-seeking negative externality that does economic damage for 40 years."

Second, Magee proposes a 20 percent federal tax on lawyers' "excessive claims." That would be the difference between what the plaintiffs asked for and what they got. If a lawsuit that asked for $1 million collected only $200,000 from a hard-hearted jury, the tax would be 20 percent on the $800,000 excess claim. By tradition, the lawyer would pay a third, the client would pay the rest—the IRS might share the swag with the unjustly accused defendant, and the litigious would think twice before going to court with a speculative claim.

Even if the ranks of lawyers were closed tomorrow, Magee says, it would be 26 years before the ratio of lawyers to white-collar workers would be the same as in Germany and 36 years to reach the low level of Japan.

Magee's analysis is neatly embedded in the theory of "rent-seeking," which has been around among economists since the mid-1970s. The idea is that economic actors are forever seeking to devise little monopolies in pursuit of a quiet life and a well-feathered nest. It is an entirely plausible analysis of how advantage-seeking can create economic "black holes" whose costs really mount up over time.

But it's just a little alarming to see calculations like these becoming a part of daily life in Washington. It's on just such an analysis that the American case against European farm subsidies rests—the magnitudes are unassailably large. But lawyers? Can anyone really say with confidence that American lawyers are the reason we're falling behind?

Lawyers do a lot of good things, too: They maintain an elaborate system of intellectual and other property rights and thus keep money flowing to investment; they oversee an intricate federal division of power that is a peculiarly American achievement; they pursue justice in mysterious ways and contribute to a general sense of empowerment. Does anyone truly want to see a reduction of American lawyer ratios become the center of the next structural impediment initiative talks with Japan—instead of waiting for the market to do its work? Does anyone really believe that economists understand the world well enough to prescribe at this micro-level?

It is true that America has more lawyers than Japan. It also has a far greater proportion of economists. The standard folk wisdom among Japanese industrialists is that their success is inversely proportional to the number of economic Nobel Prizes their countrymen have won. Might it not be that the negative effect of economists on economic activity may be even greater than that of lawyers?

FEBRUARY 24, 1991

A Bully Pulpit for Dukakis' Economist in the Bush Administration

WHAT'S THE BEST-READ AND MOST WIDELY DISCUSSED ECONOMIC POLICY DOCUMENT IN the world? Not the report of the chairman of the Council of Economic Advisers, though plenty of work goes into that—Americans simply aren't that interested in expert thinking. Not the annual report of the Bank for International Settlements, though this account by the central bankers' central bank probably has the best audience, chiefly global financiers.

Instead, it's the *World Development Report*, the annual survey that is published each July by the World Bank. Assembled by the top guns of an enormous research staff (1,000 economists work for the bank!), co-written by editors seconded from London's *Economist* magazine, it is the view from one of the citadels of world capitalism: shrewd, dry-eyed and carefully defended. As the implicit agenda for the world's largest lender to developing nations, the *WDR* makes a determined attempt to be persuasive to the widest-possible range of views, from Eastern Europe to Latin America to New York and Tokyo. Last summer, for example, it published an analysis of global poverty and what could be done about it that was the equivalent of a lay-down hand at bridge.

For the past eight years, the job of chief economist was done by Hollis Chenery, Anne Kreuger and Stanley Fischer. All were distinguished, each was representative of a distinctive tradition: a lifetime development economist, a free-market enthusiast who specialized in trade, and a well-travelled sophisticate who was co-author of a best-selling macro text, respectively.

Friday the bank named Lawrence Summers, 35, to the job—but not before the young Harvard professor had run into a flurry of opposition. The trouble was, of course, that Summers had been the principle economic adviser to Michael S. Dukakis in his failed presidential bid.

"Larry Summers is the last of the die-hard Keynesians," growled Melanie Tammen, director of the global economic liberty institute of the Cato Institute. "We could have had Alan Walters!" (Walters, a frequent consultant to the bank, was Margaret Thatcher's personal adviser for many years.) Dan Mitchell of the Heritage Foundation said, "A fiasco! They take, not just another liberal economist, but the head adviser to the guy who tried to beat them and give him one of the best jobs in Washington, $180,000-plus a year, tax free. Summers is a kind of a dinosaur, anyway, preaching theories of central planning that have been discredited. They could have appointed somebody like Richard Rahn of the Chamber of Commerce, who has been working on theories that have helped the world turn away from socialism. It's just another sign of the disintegration of the Bush administration."

Said MIT's Rudiger Dornbusch, "The Dukakis campaign gave a bad name to everybody associated with it. This is a chance for Larry to clear his name." Summers' appointment seemed untroubled until Wednesday. Chief economic adviser Michael Boskin, Federal Reserve chairman Alan Greenspan and Treasury undersecretary David Mulford were said to have signed off on it, though Mulford forcefully denied it.

At the the last moment, however, a little counterrcharge developed: Sen.

Bob Kasten, (R-Wis.) spearheaded the drive, as chairman of the appropriations subcommittee that oversees the American contribution to the bank. Treasury sources said deputy chief of staff Andrew Card and deputy personnel director Ron Kaufman were enlisted at the White House to fight the appointment, as well.

After a flurry of angry calls, the effort came to naught. World Bank president Barber Conable, who had offered Summers the job in the first place, stemmed the tide, won a vote from his board Thursday. Conable had been a longtime Republican congressional leader before being appointed by Ronald Reagan to head the bank; he knows his way around Capitol Hill. He maintained, apparently without much difficulty, the banks's tradition of insulation from partisan politics.

But the question remains, why does Reagan's man at the bank appoint Dukakis's chief adviser—with President Bush's concurrence?

Well, part of the answer is that Summers was always on the right wing of the Dukakis campaign. He fought a continual rear-guard action against a slew of other would-be lieutenants who sought to push the candidate further to the left: industrial policy buffs, heavy tax advocates and populists of all sorts. These advisers, in turn, like to beat Summers over the head with the fact that he had served for a year as a senior staff economist on Ronald Reagan's first-term Council of Economic Advisers.

Another part of the reason for his appointment is that he is clearly one of the most gifted three or four of the generation of economists that came of age during the 1970s—one of a number of leading scholars who were trained by Harvard's Martin Feldstein. A specialist in taxation, Summers had much to do with undermining traditional Keynesian views of the nature of unemployment. He holds the largest no-strings grant ever made to an economist by the National Science Foundation; he's been serving as economic adviser to the government of Lithuania in its battle to secede from the Soviet Union; and he's a champion practitioner of policy-oriented research.

But probably the factor that ultimately accounts from Summers' appointment has to with the World Bank's need to have stronger technical leadership than its sister-organization, the International Monetary Fund, if it wants to avoid being pressed into service as a mere debt collector. Jacob Frenkel, a conservative University of Chicago monetary specialist who is the IMF's chief economist, is no slouch at technical analysis, to say the least. So Conable had to reach for an equally powerful figure in order to keep his organization's edge in the fast-breaking debate over world economic integration.

Now it's true that the World Bank is a bright red flag to "supply-side" conservatives. It has rarely been a partisan of the kind of grass-roots rebellion against the center that they favor. It is true, too, that the bank is a top-heavy bastion of privilege. Its employees pay no taxes on their princely salaries, and when a senior officer recently suggested the organization try to save some money by flying its functionaries on their missions business class instead of first class, the bank negotiated an agreement with British Airways that provided for free upgrades to Concorde first class instead.

But it is also true that the bank has been an extremely persuasive advocate of free market economics throughout the 1980s, emphasizing free trade, identifying unproductive agricultural policies, calling for efficient finance sectors, advocating privatization and the down-sizing of overgrown public sectors. Its monthly newsletter, *Socialist Economies in Transition*, has effectively focused the entire debate on Eastern Europe for the last couple of years. The kind of public finance reform that the Latin American economies need so badly could be greatly facilitated by the bank, too.

Summers' appointment is not likely to appeal to the Cato Institute, nor to Vaclav Klaus, the finance minister who styles himself the Milton Friedman of Czechoslovakia, nor to the Latvian editor who said last week that since the Norwegians (under subcontract from the Swedes) had given their Nobel Peace Prize to Gorbachev this year, they should give it to Saddam Hussein the next.

Instead, it symbolizes faith on the part of the president that the mainstream economics consensus knows something, that politics is ultimately secondary to technique and the dispassionate search for truth. It is further evidence that what the Bush presidency is about, as was the Ford administration, is the rebuilding of the American establishment. This time, let's hope it sticks.

OCTOBER 28, 1990

Is a Class War in the Offing?

SUDDENLY, CONGRESSIONAL DEMOCRATS HAVE FASTENED ON TO "THE FAIRNESS IS-sue." With a large army in Saudi Arabia, with support for the expedition from Germany and Japan eroding, with the American economy tottering on the brink of what could become a serious recession, Congress has become locked in a bitter bipartisan battle over whom to tax. After all, the election is just a month away. So the analysis du jour is that class warfare is making a comeback.

Is it really?

Down beneath the partisan broadsides, what's been happening to the distribution of income in America these last 10 years? It would help to know what the numbers say.

Following economist Herbert Stein, it makes sense to start at the bottom. There is one group, he says, perhaps 1 percent of the population, who constitute an underclass. They live with little hope in urban squalor, amid crime and drug addiction, drop out of school easily and have high rates of illegitimacy.

There is another group, perhaps 10 percent of the population, says Stein, that is "poor by American standards." This fraction, after declining until about 10 or 15 years ago, has been static since.

Then there is the great middle class, some 75 or 80 percent of the population, who do all right, except that their income hasn't been growing much in the 1980s. Their wages and their pensions cover the cost of living in a certain way they think of as being vaguely middle class; they have houses, cars, televisions, food, vacations. They are worried today as never before about being able to maintain their standard of living in the future, worried too about the quality of their schools and their medical care.

Above them are those who constitute the upper middle class, another 5 percent or so, most of whom live in families that make more than $75,000 a year. With around 65 million families in the country, this adds up to around 3.5 million families; they live in the best suburbs, drive the BMWs and so forth.

Finally there are the truly rich, another 1 percent or so of the population, those who make $200,000 or more, who control vast amounts of wealth. Even more than the upper middle class, the value of their holdings soared during the 1980s.

Now ordinarily the large middle income group doesn't get decomposed very much. They are assumed to think and act pretty much as one big group, beguiled by president Ronald Reagan one year, worried about the Japanese the next, content to be "in between." But the big noise in this field for a couple of years has been the research of a couple of technical economists, Larry Katz of Harvard University and Kevin Murphy of the University of Chicago. And what they have found is that the middle class is indeed in some danger of coming apart.

What Katz and Murphy found is that a serious gap has opened up between white-collar workers and older blue-collar workers on the one hand, and new kids who went to work in the 1980s without a college degree on the other. The college wage premium rose from 1963 to 1971, they report, fell from 1971 to 1979, then rose sharply from 1979 to 1987. Meanwhile, the experience differential was widening, too, never more than in the 1980s.

The inescapable conclusion is that new blue-collar workers are not going to do as well as did their parents' generation.

Why? What turned around so abruptly the palmy atmosphere of the 1970s, when auto workers vacationed in France, and plumbers and bakers liked to joke they made as much as doctors? (They didn't!) It's a complicated story, naturally. But the Katz and Murphy findings boil down to two main themes, both of them familiar to readers of the business pages.

One has to do with the increasing demand for kids with college degrees and well-developed skills in high tech and service industries. The other has to do with sharply declining demand for unskilled workers in traditional manufacturing industries.

Why did this happen? There's no particular mystery to it, says Frank Levy of the University of Maryland, another specialist in the study of the distribution of income. He says the long borrowing spree of the Reagan administration made it difficult for manufacturers to compete on the world stage or even at home, first raising dramatically the value of the dollar, then keeping real interest rates high. Employers laid off workers, busted unions and bought automating machinery as fast as they could.

The result was to depress blue-collar wages; certain kinds of families—

the young, those with key workers unemployed, those headed by the poorly-educated—were, for a time at least, "left behind," in Katherine Bradbury's telling phrase.

"If the trade deficit had clobbered the income of newscasters, it would have been a different story," says Levy. "When it first happened, the dollar's rise, there was all this *Wall Street Journal* euphoria," he continues. "They said, my God, that just shows what a great country this is, everybody wants to be here. The first guy to say 'Wait a second,' was Commerce Secretary Malcolm Baldrige, who was getting reports from the field that said my people are getting destroyed by this."

In due course, the dollar came down; many American manufacturing firms adjusted to new competitive realities. But big government deficits are keeping the cost of capital in America high; the national savings rate has reached a dismal level. And so Congress has been urged to cut the budget deficit, as a way of increasing national savings. The disturbing little fissure between the blue-collar and white-collar earnings of the old and the young that opened up in the 1980s will probably go away, or at least cease to increase, once America's economic policy has restored its businesses to a level playing field. (Of course, those who were "left behind" for a time in the 1980s will probably never catch up to where they would have been otherwise, much like those who came of age in the Depression.)

None of this, of course, has much to do with those who bear the burden of the relatively small tax increases now contemplated by Congress. The "fairness issue," for the representatives who are now adopting every conceivable posture on it, is a scapegoat, as much as affirmative action is a red-herring for David Duke. It scarcely matters who bears the short-term pain of bringing the budget more nearly into balance. What does matter is the truly long-term hurt and humiliation that will attend a failure to get America's fiscal house in order, now.

OCTOBER 14, 1990

Economists Take
Sides on Trade

THERE IS AMONG ECONOMISTS A SORT OF MISSING GENERATION, BETWEEN THE GIANTS of the 1960s and the whippersnappers of today. The Samuelsons, Friedmans, Galbraiths, Steins and others who became brand names then are in their 70s or even 80s today. The new generation of bright kids, who look on 51-year-old Martin Feldstein of Harvard as a kind of uncle, are for the most part in their 30s.

In between are many distinguished economists: Joseph Stiglitz, Mancur Olson, Amartya Sen, Gary Becker, George Ackerlof, Elhanan Helpman and Robert Lucas, to name a few. But relatively few of this in-between generation have the kind of involvement with a single issue or a point of view, fought out in the popular press, that makes an icon, much less a household word. Harry Johnson is one, but he's dead; Jagdish Bhagwati is another, very much alive—as is Lester Thurow. Both are partisans on different sides of the single issue that is most likely to divide the economists' house in the 1990s: the question of free trade.

Johnson, of course, was a peripatetic Chicagoan—the operating arm of George Stigler and Milton Friedman, a close student of the world trading system, a dauntless foe of protectionism. As an unflagging commuter to Europe, he sometimes wrote two papers on a single transatlantic flight. When he died in 1977, of a stroke at 53, it was said that he had so many publications in the pipeline that most economists didn't know he was dead for three years. Pragmatic, monetarist, lucid, skeptical, tart-tongued, but above all, free-trade: that was Harry Johnson. Next week his pupil, Bhagwati, turns up in London to honor him with a lecture—on the current threats to the General Agreement on Tariffs and Trade and free trade generally. There is no economist better known on trade today—or better able to defend it—than Bhagwati.

Surely it's an auspicious time to pop with a defense of what is sometimes derided as the "general agreement to talk and talk." With heads of state and finance ministers of the Group of Seven leading industrial nations meeting in Houston this week, it is subsidies to farmers—and how to fairly ratchet them down—that is the leading issue on the table. But there is much more to it than that. The rules for trade in services, for the preservation of intellectual property rights, and for the tendency of the world to break itself up in trading blocs will be discussed in Houston, too. All these controversies must be resolved to some degree, then tabled, by the end of the three-year Uruguay Round of negotiations in December. But since the spring the GATT talks have been at an impasse and gloom about the future of free trade is growing. It was Thurow who said, at a symposium in Switzerland as long ago as 1988: "GATT is dead."

Can it be? After the Bank for International Settlements, GATT is surely the least-well-understood of the major international coordinating agencies. Staffed by only a hundred or so career civil servants in Geneva, GATT has eight times since World War II convened the stately paced talks known as "rounds." Mainly through a commitment to playing by the rules, these negotiations have all but eliminated the tariffs and other barriers that for a couple of centuries had plagued the trading nations; 97 nations have joined the organization, including 10 since 1982. China is negotiating and the Soviet Union is next in line. "Surely, necrophilia has not broken out!" Bhagwati cracks.

But with crass taxes banished, attention in recent years has shifted to the wide range of "non-tariff barriers" by which nations are said to be able to close themselves to key foreign goods. A stereotype of the "predatory" Japanese of the 1980s and 1990s has replaced the image of the "ugly" Americans of the 1950s and 1960s. Legislatures and newspapers are full of proposals to bring the other fellow into line.

The threats to GATT come from four different directions, Bhagwati says. First there is the the rise of the perception of unfair trade practices, he says. It was aggravated by the wide range of protectionist measures instituted in the wake of the second oil shock and amplified by the effects of flexible exchange rates. One important source of it is what he calls America's "diminished giant syndrome"—the profound nostalgia (from which Great Britain suffered in its day) for the period in which America utterly dominated a ruined, war-torn world.

Then there is the issue of "managed trade"— the conviction in some quarters that high-technology industries are so important they cannot be left to the marketplace. Non-economists are fairly standing in line to manage America's industrial policy, Bhagwati notes; many economists, whom he thinks should know better, are sharpening their pencils to prove that a philosopher-queen, with nearly perfect information, could in theory out-fox all her trading partners—in theory, at least.

Meanwhile, an aggressive and unattractive unilateralism is also breaking out, especially in the United States, where the Super 301 section of the 1988 Trade Act permits Congress to play trade cop to the world—in direct contravention to the multilateral spirit of GATT. "As 301 and Super 301 actions are undertaken, unilaterally accusing others of unfair trade practices and demanding their removal, the notion is also reinforced that others are unfair traders, creating a poisoned atmosphere which conventional protectionists can hope to exploit to their advantage," he writes.

Finally, a new emphasis on regionalism may be subtly threatening to the spirit of GATT. A North America free-trade area, Pacific free-trade area and the European Common Market are now all the rage. The liberalization of the communist regimes will surely accelerate the trend. But these regional free- trade compacts aren't antithetical to GATT unless they're used that way, as a kind of straw man with which to beat up on the over-arching plan, Bhagwati says. "This false antithesis certainly prompted Thurow's folly in calling our attention to a live corpse," he adds.

Which way out? Well, one notion now gathering steam is a Canadian proposal for a World Trade Organization, a much higher level of visibility for GATT with beefed-up responsibilities and powers. Fine in due course, Bhagwati says, but at the moment it is overreaching—a "grandiose task" that threatens the success of current negotiations. The trick is to let GATT continue to slowly evolve into an organization capable of undertaking still more ambitious tasks—not to try to kick it up to whole new levels of complexity all at once.

The controversey over GATT's future is not likely to light up the sky—at least not unless it deteriorates into a series of escalating skirmishes. But a powerful coterie of analysts exists who would prefer to replace the Cold War with the almost equally threatening specter of a trade war. Bhagwati's broadside is a powerful argument for "trade management" arrayed against a large group of advocates who feel they must "manage trade."

JULY 8, 1990

"Big Bang" vs. Evolution

THERE HAS EMERGED IN THE PAST COUPLE OF YEARS A GENERAL AGREEMENT AMONG economists that a "Big Bang" is the right way to go about fixing the command economies. The possibility of sudden success is remembered from the "German Miracle," when Ludwig Erhard abolished all rationing overnight in 1949. It gains credibility from the interventions of Jeffrey Sachs, the baby-faced Harvard professor who is surely the most powerful economic engineer since John Maynard Keynes. But the case for the "major surgery" approach has been made most forcefully by Janos Kornai, the great and valiant Hungarian economist, whose little book, *The Road to a Free Economy: Shifting From a Socialist System, The Example of Hungary*, has just appeared.

The basic idea is to pop a macroeconomic market system on a nation all at once: decontrol prices, let the exchange rate go, permit the unemployment rate to soar and the standard of living to plummet, hold back on progressive income taxation and prepare to tolerate the vast inequalities of wealth that will inevitably occur. Reforms like these have been advocated from China and Russia to Poland and Hungary.

There is, however, a dissenting view, one based on alternative vision of capitalism, advanced by Joseph Schumpeter, a remarkable theorist who 50 years ago was eclipsed by Keynes. The advent of this "Schumpeterian" approach is perhaps the most exciting development in present-day technical economics. It views economic growth and development as being a process of natural selection: successful organizations grow, less successful competitors are weeded out. It stresses institution-building, the diffusion of new products and the growth of knowledge. For the communist nations, it recommends a go-slow approach, with reliance on the technology-transferring powers of the multinational economies. Let Du Pont, General Electric, United Technologies and IBM lead the way with manufacturing subsidiaries; a skilled work force—and eventually spinoffs, startups and breakaways—will follow.

A leading exponent of this evolutionary view is Peter Murrell, a 39-year-old University of Maryland professor who is among the new generation of comparative economists. These scholars actually perform empirical studies of competing economies, instead of mastering the textbook theories and then applying them in Eastern Europe based on experiences in Bolivia and Brazil.

Morever, Murrell's observations are deeply grounded in theory and econometrically tested. His material is state of the art, and his new book, *The Nature of Socialist Economies: Lessons from Eastern European Foreign Trade*, isn't easy reading for non-economists. Nevertheless, it is important stuff; many persons figure that Big Bang policies are an invitation to disaster, and Murrell's scheme for a gradual phasing-in of capitalist institutions is perhaps the only other intellectually respectable one on the table.

For Murrell, the key advantages of capitalism are not the ones usually cited by neoclassical economists: not simply the decentralization of authority with a given set of institutions, the information-conveying wonders of the price system and the allocative efficiency. It is that nobody ever knows what is going to work. Capitalism is an evolutionary scheme, he says, built up over the years to cope with the fact that there are always going to be a few good ideas and a lot of mediocre ideas. Society needs a mechanism for favoring good organizations over the less-successful ones, says Murrell; it needs also a mechanism that forces workers to move between jobs.

For example: Last week control of the largest and best company in the international abrasives industry appeared ready to move from Massachusetts to Paris, when a giant French firm, Compagnie de Saint Gobain paid $1.9 billion for Norton. A lot of promises were made to the city of Wocester, where Norton has its headquarters, but they were mostly baloney. The Paris bourse will now chart Norton's fate. The significant fact, however, is that the decision to relocate strategic control of this small but vital industry from one nation to another was made by perhaps 100 people, executives, lawyers and bankers. Their deliberations were underpinned by an obscure court in Delaware, and removed almost entirely from politics. Politicans entered only briefly as helpless dupes. In contrast, the government of Poland hasn't been able to close its shipyards in Gdansk despite 20 years of mounting losses. And as for easily starting new enterprises in Warsaw: well, forget it.

The trouble is there are some things the big bureaucratic enterprises of Eastern Europe and the Soviet Union do well. Murrell has econometrics to suggest that, in some industries, they do as well as the oligopolies of the

West, and the yields of Czechoslovakia's 10,000-acre dairy farms rival Western levels. These enterprises grew up in the environment of central planning. Introduce a Big Bang, take away their natural mechanisms for attracting capital and keeping workers, and they could collapse, Murrell says. "We could destroy the efficiency of what exists, five or ten years before we have a working private sector in place."

What Murrell recommends instead of blanket reforms is a systematic search for promising sectors, where new styles of privatization could be introduced, coupled with a systematic reining-in on the power—and eventually, the size—of the big state-run enterprises of the East. A phase-in period would give workers a chance to choose the most promising sectors and would give them a chance to prepare for the dislocations that would affect their lives. And as the fertile macroeconomic enterprise sector grew up, more and more persons would choose to leave the security of the big enterprises for the greater opportunities of the more dynamic private sphere.

Thus, instead of the big shocks that are now being contemplated by Eastern European planners, the single most important measure might be to let the multinational corporations in—in droves. The centrality of multinationals in the Schumpeterian scheme of things is striking, Murrell says; foreign investment seems to have been the major engine of change. Thus in Spain, which is about the same size as the newly liberalizing nations, nearly 50 percent of GNP is organized by subsidiaries of multinationals, he notes. Moreover, the American capital in the new Disneyland outside of Paris alone is greater than the total of all its investment in the Soviet Union. Eliciting new foreign direct investment by big companies may be more important than installing a price system.

Meanwhile, the leading experiment in this evolutionary approach is, of course, China. The government there moved in quickly to stem the pro-democracy movement last spring, and with it the rush to pell-mell economic development. He Xin, a leading defender of Deng Xiaopeng, who wrote a memo on the eve of the Tiananmen Square massacre urging the government at once to control the demonstrations and to avoid violence, has emerged as a leading spokesman for the go-slow approach.

Like Deng, the 40-year-old He has vivid memories of the Red Guards. Deng's son was flung out a window and crippled; He Xin has handcuff marks on his wrists from his torture as a counterrevolutionary. But civil war, military coups and popular uprisings are what worry the researcher for the Academy of Social Sciences if a Big Bang were to come to China. Let economic reform proceed as it has so far, he has written in a series of influential newspaper articles over the last year, as a bottom-up, trial-and-error process from the rural provinces. Tackle the big cities last, He Xin says. "We all want a free environment in the end. But if we tried to achieve this overnight, we would only get turmoil and disaster."

APRIL 29, 1990

What We Know (and Don't Know) About the '80s

IS IT TOO EARLY TO JUDGE THE PERFORMANCE OF AMERICA IN THE 1980S? OF COURSE not; we're doing it all the time. There is a steady flow of criticism, generally from the Left, the most substantial of it in the form of books, and now it's beginning to pile up: Barbara Ehrenreich's *The Worst Years of Our Lives*, Bryan Burrough and John Helyar's *Barbarians at the Gate*, Paul Kennedy's *The Rise and Decline of Great Powers*, Kevin Phillips' *The Politics of Rich and Poor*.

Such is the clamor that *Commentary* magazine has published a symposium in its September issue, having invited 19 persons to comment on whether the decade was a triumph or a disaster. What alarms the magazine, of course, is that it speaks for the neoconservatives, whose political program, in the form of "supply side economics" and the Committee on the Present Danger (it was the Soviets), ushered in the decade.

And though the issue makes fascinating reading, what it really illustrates is the big difference between gut opinion—both Right and Left—and the serious story-telling research from which we will ultimately write our history.

Certainly the *Commentary* panelists frame the issue well enough. James Neuchterlein, editor of *First Things*, a right-wing journal of religion and public life, writes: "American liberalism has in fact never recovered from the Great Society. . . . Activist government was no longer in the public mind an unambiguous good thing; it had become, at best, uncertain and problematic, at worst the unwitting source of our deepest problems. It was

Ronald Reagan's achievement to raise all this from the level of inchoate intuition to conscious perception."

And Christopher Lasch, professor of history at the University of Rochester, speaks for the Left when he writes, "The collapse of communism represents a victory, of sorts, for the West—but not much of a victory for the United States and certainly not for the 'prevailing ideas and policies of the American '80s. The real winners, as everybody knows, are the West Germans and the Japanese, who owe their power and prosperity to a combination of circumstances having nothing to do with the 'policies of the American '80s.' While the United States and the Soviet Union were exhausting themselves in the production of armaments, West Germany and Japan, unburdened by competition in the arms race, rebuilt their shattered economies and cultivated the arts of peace."

Moreover, there are great little reminders scattered here and there of battles that the rest of us have forgotten. Robert Coles looks back on Dr. Helen Caldicott, for example, the nuclear freeze activist whose Paul Revere–like warnings that thermonuclear war was imminent in the early 1980s puzzled a generation of schoolchildren. He quotes a factory hand from Framingham who had listened to Caldicott on his car radio:

"She's half crazy, and so are some of you who hold her up as the wisest one around. You can hear it in her voice, not just her words—all that scary talk, all that screeching, it is! And if you disagree with them, they point fingers and shout and try to tell you that they're smart and you're dumb, and they're right and you're—well, you're not just wrong, you're sick!" There is a strange silence from such people now, Coles notes.

What is most striking, however, is that there are relatively few numbers in the *Commentary* exchange, and what there are have been produced mainly for rhetorical effect, not because they are agreed upon. No economist is included in the group, though there are a political scientist (Charles Murray), a lawyer (Robert Reich), a sociologist (Paul Starr) and a couple of journalists (George Gilder and Tom Bethell) who write mainly on economic topics. This alone tells you something about where the neoconservatives are coming from after a decade of debate.

But more largely, it demonstrates something worth knowing about New York intellectuals: they are usually more interested in banter—some of it rhetorically very powerful—than in pinning things down. And the *Commentary* selection offers an oil-and-vinegar array of extremes. (Only historian Eugene D. Genovese successfully seeks the center of the debate.) It is in this sense that an article by Andrei Schleifer and Robert W. Vishny on

"The Takeover Wave of the 1980s" in an August issue of *Science* magazine offers a contrast.

Schleifer and Vishny are professors at the Graduate School of Business at the University of Chicago; together with Kevin Murphy of Chicago's economics department they are jokingly known as "The Trio" by the younger generation of technical economists, the result of their collaboration on an influential series of policy-oriented articles in scholarly finance journals. They are among the cream of the crop of a generation of young economists who have stepped forward to the center of the debate over America's place in the world economy.

There can be few people in America who don't have friends or family who were affected by the merger boom of the 1980s. Hostile takeovers and leveraged buyouts, "Saturday night specials" and bust-ups were as much a part of the decade as were turn-of-the-century trusts, 1920s oligopolies or 1960s conglomerates. So what happened? A decade of unparallelled greed?

Not exactly. Schleifer and Vishny argue that, spurred by the easy availability of funds and a rethinking of the antitrust laws, the principle effect of the merger boom seems to have been to unwind the conglomerate movement of the 1960s. That movement, fostered by antitrust rules that were stringent to the point of being otherworldly (a combination that moved market share from 5 percent to 7 percent of a narrowly defined market could be nixed by the Feds), resulted in growth-oriented corporate executives buying companies in unrelated industries about which they knew nothing, instead of paying out earnings in dividends. Kraft cheese took over Eveready batteries; Revlon moved aggressively into health care. Not surprisingly, the conglomerates generally didn't prosper.

Thus the merger movement of the 1980s acted mainly to move assets out of conglomerates and toward more specialized users of capital, Schleifer and Vishny write. The presumption is that less diversified companies can manage their businesses more effectively, and so increase American competitiveness in the world economy. What's more, the three most common objections to takeovers don't really hold up, the Chicagoans say. Great concentrations of market power haven't arisen, job losses are confined mostly to white-collar employees (among whom significant lengthy employment hardly exists), and the widely-feared reductions in investment in R&D are exaggerated, they say. They take sharp issue with the MIT *Made in America* report's conclusion that pressures of debt and financial markets prevent American managers from focusing on long-term projects. Although "the jury is still out" on the merger wave, they conclude, the evidence recommends "cautious optimism."

Now it is true that Schleifer and Vishny haven't persuaded everybody of the accuracy of their critique; just the editors and referees of *Science* magazine. And it is true, too, that the merger movement is just one aspect of the American '80s. There is the matter of widening inequality, of women's entry into the workplace, of excessive debt and financial fragility.

But careful people will work these questions through—and of course the meaning of the last chapter will take on more significance as we travel more deeply into the next chapter. In the meantime, there will be more nimble posturing, intellectual skywriting and yes, well, screeching.

SEPTEMBER 23, 1990

Political Economy
of the First Amendment

NEW ORLEANS—IS THE MODERN-DAY SUPREME COURT THE BEST INSTITUTIONAL FRIEND that organized religion ever had? You wouldn't think so, not if you mull over its decisions on questions of religion in recent years.

From its stand on school prayer (it is against it) to its decisions involving contraception, abortion, illegitimacy and obscenity, the court has routinely preferred the secular point of view to the religious one. Only in matters concerning the "free exercise" of opinion has the court appeared to sanction religiosity in its diverse forms (it has forbidden states to withhold unemployment benefits from a person whose religion forbids him to work on Saturday, for example).

But if you stand back and take a slightly different view—an "economic" one—the court's thinking on religion takes on quite a different cast. The "market for ideas" in religion—and in news coverage, too, for that matter—turns out to be a market in which the justices have resolutely declined to interfere.

The result has been an easier entry for new church groups, less competition from government agencies offering essentially the same "products" aimed at producing moral behavior, and in general a continuing "deregulation" of spiritual life that may account for, among other things, the recent explosion of old-fashioned evangelical Christianity.

That is the view of Richard A. Posner, a former University of Chicago law professor, who is perhaps the leading proponent of the "law and economics" movement that for 30 years has been steadily extending its influence. Now serving as a federal judge in the U.S. Court of Appeals in Chicago, he is regarded as one of the two or three leading candidates for the next vacancy on the Supreme Court. His unusual interpretation of the First Amendment came in his lecture to the annual meeting of the American Economic Association in New Orleans last week.

"A lecture is not the place to prove a new economic theory," said Posner. He added, "No doubt the Supreme Court's casual role in all this is smaller than I have suggested. The tradition of religious diversity in the United States is very old, and the court's contribution to maintaining it may be very slight. Nevertheless, economic analysis suggests that religious leaders who denounce the course of the court's decision and the secular leaders who defend it may be arguing contrary to their institutional self-interests."

Posner argues that the Supreme Court aids religion in a number of ways. By prohibiting almost any kind of religious activity in public schools, no matter what the justification, the court increases the demand for private schools that teach religious values. In other words, it has permitted Jerry Falwell to do to the public schools what Fred Smith did to the post office with his Federal Express.

By insisting, under the clause of the First Amendment that says that Congress may establish no official religion, that the same privileges granted one religious group, no matter how dominant—Sundays off, for example—be granted to any religious group, the court avoids favoring the establishment at the expense of less powerful groups. And by declining to serve as the enforcement arm of mainstream churches on moral matters—on abortion, most notably—the court casts into sharp relief the differences between a secular and a religious system of belief. Said Posner, "If the government enforced the value system of Christianity, as it used to do, people would have less to gain from being Christian."

In this view, a lot of small religious organizations are preferable to a few big ones because small organizations are better at keeping their members in line than big ones; this is the essence of Cartel Theory, says Posner. "It may be hard to believe that the moral tone of our society has actually improved since the Supreme Court adopted its aggressively secularist stance, but economic analysis suggests that the situation might be worse than better if the court had weakened private religious organizations by allowing government to compete more effectively with them inculcating or requiring moral behavior."

This is, of course, a question that brings tears of frustration to the eyes of the wisest person. Have the last 20 years in America been decades of progress or decline in the human condition? Are we better off for the enormous increase in sophistication, complexity and freedom to choose from a wide variety of alternatives? Or was our welfare somehow greater when the United States was an extensive national collection of city machines and villages governed by a small collection of white Anglo-Saxon Protestant males?

Certainly the kind of analysis that Posner brought to bear last week on First Amendment matters is just the sort of theorizing that usually gets branded "economic imperialism." It leaves some people cold and drives others wild. Indeed, the Chicago judge spent the whole first half of his talk dealing with objections to the continuing extension of economic reasoning to a wide range of non-market behavior. He noted that today there is an economic theory of property rights, of corporations and other organizations, of government and politics, of education, of the family, of crime and punishment, of anthropology, of history, of information, of racial and sexual discrimination, of privacy, even of the behavior of animals.

There is no fixed domain to economics, he said, only an open-ended set of concepts, beginning with the assumption that, when faced with a choice, people will usually choose the option that they consider best for themselves. In this sense, said Posner, "There is nothing that makes the study of marriage and divorce less suitable . . . for economics than the study of the automobile industry or the inflation rate."

In truth, the winds of change now blowing through economics seem to come mainly from Chicago. The American Economic Association meeting here last week was dominated by sessions organized by Chicago's Gary Becker, this year's president, and led by other Chicagoans. George Stigler talked about the economics of science and the origins of financial deregulation; Douglass North led a session on the "new political economics" of interest groups; Robert Lucas set his sights on the economics of development. There were reports on new investigations into the relationship between the demand for children and the Social Security system, a question raised by Becker and Robert Barro. James Coleman, the distinguished sociologist, talked about social capital, the intricate network of relationships that surround and support the individual.

To be sure the other pole of economics whose spiritual home is Cambridge, Mass., was well represented; but in its stubborn address of the thorny problems of the modern world economy—from stopping hyperinflation to fixing exchange rates to setting national shares of income to battling inflation—it seemed more nearly like engineering than the pure theory of the Chicagoans.

A hundred years ago Easterners branded Chicago "the windy city," not for the force of its lakeshore breezes, but for the extravagance of its lofty claims. Things haven't changed much, except that Chicago has made a century of progress in refining and extending its ambitions.

JANUARY 4, 1987

A New Generation of Democratic Policy Intellects

WHEN THE CONGRESSIONAL BUDGET OFFICE WAS CREATED IN 1974 TO STREAMLINE Capitol Hill's analysis of federal spending, it was agreed that Republicans and Democrats should take turns naming its director—or so the oral tradition has it. The idea was that the office should be as non-partisan as possible, but that politics are an inescapable fact of life.

Alice Rivlin of the liberal Brookings Institution took over and in eight years created an operation whose reputation for sober and persuasive analysis surpassed expectations. Rudy Penner, of the conservative American Enterprise Institute, followed and kept the standards high during the difficult years of the big Reagan deficits.

But Penner's four-year term is running out; it's now the Democrats' turn to fill the job, subject to Republican advice and consent. Who should head the CBO?

Congressional staffers have put together a list of 10 candidates, each proposed by a legislator. Among other things, the list gives a pretty good picture of who's available to serve in a Democratic administration, should there be one. Here's how the candidates stack up.

JOE PECHMAN. He is the grand old man of liberal economics politics, a tax specialist and the only one of the Brookings pantheon (Arthur Okun, Charlie Schultze, Barry Bosworth) who hasn't served a president personally. But Pechman's age (69) and health are against him, as is the fact that he's identified perhaps too closely with old-fashioned Democratic policies. An honorary candidacy.

HENRY AARON. A tireless and eloquent advocate of social programs, Aaron, 51, is among the most influential Democratic party economic strategists. But precisely because he was on the frontlines in the Carter administration (as assistant secretary for planning and evaluation in the Department of Health, Education and Welfare), Aaron may be unacceptable to the Republicans.

NED GRAMLICH. Gramlich, 47, is the current deputy director of the CBO. He is perhaps the front-runner for the opening; not only does he have the advantage of experience, but he has served previously in Republican administrations. The trouble is he only wants the job for two years.

ISABEL SAWHILL. A macroeconomist, Sawhill, 49, is now at the Urban Institute and is familiar with a wide range of government programs, employment, poverty, welfare, demographics. True, she hasn't much government administrative experience to show for her 20 years in Washington. But the National Commission for Employment Policy, which she headed from 1977 to 1980, was not a trivial job.

ROBERT REISCHAUER. Now at the Brookings Institution, Reischauer, 45, is said to be Alice Rivlin's first choice for the job. He's well-regarded by his peers and could step into the position easily, but Republicans worry that he's too much of a Brookings loyalist.

VAN OOMS. Chief economist of the House Budget Committee, Ooms is the candidate who has been formally proposed by the House to the Senate. The CBO job is nothing if not a balancing act, however, and years of allegiance to the House seem certain to win a blackball from the Senate.

ERIC HANUSHEK. A former deputy director of the CBO under Rivlin, Hanushek is now a University of Rochester professor. A solid but unspectacular performer, with a reputation for strong administrative performance, Hanushek would work well with both houses.

JOHN PALMER. Another assistant secretary for planning and evaluation in the Department of Health and Human Services, Palmer is now at the Urban Institute. He may be the closest thing to a Republican on the list. But in many minds, at least, he is clustered along with Sawhill, Reischauer and Hanuchek at the very center of the list of candidates.

ALICIA MUNNELL. Research director of the Federal Reserve Bank of Boston, Munnell, 44, is a former Brookings staffer with plenty of experience in the nation's central banking system. Should the Congress be looking for a budget watchdog not yet infected with the Beltway mentality, Munnell could serve nicely.

ROBERT HAVEMAN. A former staffer for Sen. William Proxmire at the Joint Economic Committee, Haveman teaches economics at the University of Wisconsin. Haveman's considerable personal authority and habit of meeting Republicans half way make him a credible candidate even though he is a relative outsider.

Looking over the list, two things stand out. One is that it is an extremely middle-of-the-road group.

The other is that it is skewed heavily towards youth. The hardest thing in the world is to declare that a whole generation is over the hill, but the fact is that no one over 50 should apply for the CBO job. The Democrats' most pressing need now is for new blood and fresh recruits.

The question of who should head the Congressional Budget Office is now in the hands of two legislative committees: six Democrats and four Republicans in all. In due course, out of their alchemy, a new CBO director will be chosen.

FEBRUARY 18, 1987

Reports of the Death of the Middle Class Are Exaggerated

FOR SEVERAL YEARS NOW, THERE HAS BEEN A LIVELY DEBATE ON THE EDGE OF economics about whether we are witnessing the birth of a "dual society." The rich are getting richer, the argument goes, the poor are getting poorer, and, in the extreme form, the middle class is losing ground or even in danger of disappearing. The driving force behind this process is ascribed to a variety of mainsprings: either foreign competition in basic industry or the "femininization of poverty" or the general world Turn to the Right.

Nor is the hypothesis heard only from organizers on the political Left who are looking for a galvanizing issue. The Conference of Catholic Bishops has made the claim, as has a report of the Joint Economic Committee of Congress. It has been headlined in *Fortune* and the *Wall Street Journal*. "A surge in inequality" even was reported as unassailable fact in a lead piece earlier this year in *Scientific American* by economist Lester Thurow.

From most economists, however, there has been a continuous stream of warnings that these things do not change much over time. The shape of the income distribution—of society's wage structure—is amazingly resistant to both the ambitions of workers to change it and the avarice of the rich, they say. Now, a new book by a University of Maryland economist takes on the question of how standards of living have changed for families since World War II, sifts the evidence about as carefully as it can be sifted, and confirms the convential wisdom. *Dollars and Dreams, The Changing American Income Distribution*, by Frank Levy, shows that the middle class is alive and well and living in America. Its composition has changed, it is not quite as rich as it once hoped to be by now, it is under pressure, and it has been scrambling hard to keep up. Things could get worse. But the real villain in the story is not deindustrialization but a decade of slow economic growth, the book argues. In the process, Levy demonstrates what it is to be rhetorically powerful. It is likely that his conclusions will dominate the discussion for years to come.

The basic story is this: The mechanically-defined middle class is still doing almost exactly as well as it did 40 years ago; the same with the rich and the poor. The middle three-fifths of families got 52 percent of income in 1947, they received 53.8 percent in 1969, they got 52.4 percent in 1984. The ticket of admission to this middle 60 percent today is $12,489; you leave the group for the uppermost fifth when you start making $45,301, and the upper-reaches of the pyramid are not so far away. Some $73,200 is enough to get you in the top 5 percent of all wage-earners. (Don't get cocky, though, for aggregation masks a lot of differences. For example, if you're a young to middle-aged professional, you need $65,000 just to make it into the top quintile. On the other hand, if you didn't make $1 million this year, don't feel too bad; there are 64 million families in America, but only 10,000 households including the bachelors had income of more than $1 million.)

Indeed, the data reinforce a familiar if intuitive story about the years since World War II. The middle class has become a roomier, more complicated place—and much, much better off. Where once the wage structure was relatively compressed, today is is somewhat more spread out. A far greater diversity of jobs offers a wider range of pay. But the entire structure has shifted decisively to the right, in the direction of higher pay; most people are better off. Meanwhile, what has happened to the middle class is a little like what has happened to major league baseball in the last 40 years: What was once a simple, easy-to-understand arrangement of two leagues of eight teams each has grown by expansion into a very complicated arrangement of 26 teams embracing a multitude of new players.

The really important changes have been taking place in the composition of the big middle group. The elderly are doing far better today than they were 40 years ago, thanks to Social Security, but their traditional place at the bottom of the order has been taken by young families just starting out, especially those headed by a single person. With the change in places has gone a tremendous liberalization of lifestyles. Whereas the typical family was relatively easy to define at the end of World War II—it looked like Ozzie and Harriet with grandparents—today we deal with a far more exotic mixture of late-marriers, working wives, laid-off blue collar workers who are living in their summer homes, and so on.

What accounts for the persistent rumors of the death of the middle class? Author Levy theorizes that the stagnation of incomes since 1973 plays the leading role. Until the watershed year, he says, real wages (meaning the command over goods and services) were growing steadily by 2 percent or 3 percent, and the elevator lifted everyone; the average 40-year-old in 1953 earned $15,500 (in 1984 dollars) and the average 40-year-old in 1973 made $28,120 (in 1984 dollars.) Then the progress stopped. Had growth continued at its usual post-war rate, the average 40-year-old in 1984 would have earned about $35,000. Instead, he earned $24,600 in real terms—a 15 pay-cut from his counterpart of a decade earlier.

To put it another way, says Levy, middle-income workers have been falling behind in their ability to afford the basket of goods that makes up the middle-class dream, whatever that is. Say it takes $30,000 to buy that house in the suburbs; the proportion of families making $30,000 or more declined from 51 percent in 1973 to 45 percent in 1984, despite a vast increase in the number of working wives. The middle of the income distribution is still there, in other words, but being a member of it no longer guarantees access to a middle-class lifestyle—even if both husband and wife are working!

Important conclusions flow from this. "We really had relied on rising wages to smooth over all kinds of conflict," says Levy. "Conflict among industries that were rising and falling, among regions of the country, between generations. Suddenly most things stop growing and all these little cracks appear." His preferred solution, of course, is to get the economy growing again, by cutting the budget deficit and increasing the savings rate; but even then, there would be enormous difficulty integrating the poor and the underclass into the economy. And the risk remains that the problem of underinvestment will continue to be ignored. He writes: "There will be no great crash (the English economy has had no great crash). Our economy will simply grind down, and we will have far less of the mobility and opportunity on which we have come to depend."

Does this mean that dual society scholars—notably Barry Bluestone of the University of Massachusetts, or Thurow of MIT—are simply wrong and ought to be disregarded? No, the people who search the data for early warning signs of troubling trends are immensely valuable, and Thurow in particular is right far more often than he is wrong. But those who discern a disappearing middle class are going to have to run a little harder to keep their theories from being assigned to the heap of discarded sky-is-falling theories. For example, researcher Katherine Bradbury of the Federal Reserve Bank of Boston contributed an important new finding last year by showing that the Ozzie and Harriet family is worse off over the last 10 years. But her argument, that the middle class is shrinking, could be made to stick only by setting its upper bound at $49,000. That's not what the American middle class mentality is all about.

Indeed, Levy's book is a demonstration of what it takes to command high ground in today's debates about public policy. There is a broad awareness that, after a decade or more of impaired confidence in its authority, economics needs to be restored to a more central place in our discourse. It won't be easy. Various attempts are being made to state what is known and what is not known. *Science* magazine, for example, has been publishing a series of articles summing up professional wisdom on a variety of topics; the American Economic Association is about to introduce a new journal, *Economic Perspectives*, pitched for the sophisticated lay reader; the National Bureau of Economic Research has a variety of task forces working away on various thorny problems, attempting to build consensus on how they should be handled. The big foundations are on the prowl for ambitious new projects. All these efforts are promising; none is thoroughly satisfying.

What Levy's project suggests is that there is really no substitute for the work of the individual scholar. Thoroughly rooted in the current research consensus—it was sponsored in a collaboration of the Social Science Research Council, the Alfred P. Sloan Foundation and the Russell Sage Foundation, and extensively reviewed—it nevertheless retains a distinctive personal touch: friendly, light, but tough-minded and only 240 pages long.

Levy begins his book with a quotation from Alexis de Tocqueville, another man who sought to see the picture whole. As much as anything else, it describes the situation of the middle class. "The heart of man is not so much caught by the undisturbed possession of anything valuable as by the desire, as yet imperfectly satisfied, of possessing it, and by the incessant dread of losing it."

OCTOBER 4, 1987

Divided, Conquered

MOST EVERYBODY KNOWS THE U.S. HEALTH-CARE SYSTEM IS IN A SEVERE CRISIS. True, something like 85 percent of all Americans still have access to health care through private or government insurance. But that means more than 30 million people depend on nothing more substantial than charity. Meanwhile, desperate earthquakes are occurring throughout the insurance industry. That's because healthy people desert the Blues for private plans or little I've-got-mine-Jack HMOs, leaving those with problems to spread their soaring costs over shrinking bases. Years of confusing cost-containment fads haven't prevented the sum of resources spent on this mainstream core from rising faster than virtually any other sector of the economy.

In fact, as a percentage of gross domestic product, health-care costs in the U.S. United States soared to almost 10 percent in 1986, the latest year available, from about 7.7 percent in 1976. In a recent survey, 90 percent of those Americans sampled figured the system was broke and needed to be fixed.

Elsewhere among the industrial nations of the world, there is no such crisis. In the European nations, medical expenses aren't rising any faster than everything else. Take Germany, for example: Direct health-care expenditures have been about flat for more than a decade, rising slightly to about 7.7 percent in 1986, from nearly 7.4 pecent in 1976. Yet in Germany practically everybody is covered by broad and deep insurance. Germans choose among competing doctors with private practices, who operate at arm's-length from a hospital system with a distinctly high-tech orientation. One of the world's best pharmaceutical industries is deeply involved in the system.

And nearly everything is covered, not just hospital care, but routine doctors' services, dentists and prescription drugs. Benefits even include stays in health spas after major operations. About the only out-of-pocket spending most Germans do for healh care is for over-the-counter drugs and fancier eye-glasses than those covered by insurance.

How do to the Germans do it? The answer is relatively simple, according to Princeton University's Uwe Rheinhardt, one of the brightest lights in the medical economics community. They run their health-care sector as a "monopsony," a market with many sellers but only a few buyers, funneling all their purchasing through a few carefully coordinated financing channels. In a report prepared for the U.S. Bipartisan Commission on Health Care, Rheinhardt compares the German system to the American medical economy, where myriad uncoordinated and independent purchasers exert next to no control over the market. Divided, Americans are easily conquered financially by the well-meaning people who provide them with health care. And if the German system has not turned out to be paradise either, Rheinhardt notes, it is at the very least a good reflector of what America does and doesn't get for its money.

All modern systems of health care rest on a kind of economic triangle. Consumers pay money to insurance companies or governments, which, in turn, shoulder the risks that individual patients would otherwise face. The providers of care collect from these third-party payers, and often from the patients as well. How these relationships are set up can make all the difference in the overall cost of the system, says Rheinhardt. For example, take the difference between "actuarily fair" insurance premiums and those that ignore the health or family status of the insured person. Most Europeans, and most Americans, too, tend to think that contributions to health plans should be based on the ability to pay, and not the insurers' best guess about the health of the insured. Indeed, most American insurance plans tend to spread the risks as widely as possible, at least over the employees of a single firm.

But European health plans, in general, and German plans, in particular, take the form of taxes and premiums that are totally divorced from the health status of the individual: Everyone but the very poor pays the same. It may be, as various proponents of market-based approaches to health care insist, that actuarily fair plans build incentives to stay healthy into the system—in the form of whopping high prices for those who get sick. This after all, has been the logic behind many attempts to turn American "patients" into "consumers" by cost sharing during the 1980s. But it may be, too, that such approaches defeat the whole purpose of insurance, and wind up costing more, not less, because they are so widely perceived to be unfair.

More to the point, according to Rheinhardt, are the differing architectures of the respective payment systems. What the Germans have created over the years are regional associations of private health insurers endowed with quasi-governmental powers to collectively negotiate binding contracts with physicians' associations and hospital networks. Doctors and hospitals get paid by the "sickness funds" on a fee-for-service basis according to a binding schedule of fees that are negotiated yearly.

These aren't draconian, take-it-or-leave-it bids. Like the Diagnostic Related Grants, or DRGs, that the Reagan administration flung at the hospitals in the 1980s, but rather good faith negotiations between highly sophisticated bargainers. A series of sophisticated safeguards prevents consumers from shopping around for a favorable price-performance ratio, depending on where they are in their life cycle. Thus, this sort of adverse-risk selection currently plaguing the Blues in this country is ruled out. And the payers' associations keep a watchful eye out for the natural tendency of providers to build more capacity than is needed.

There are problems with the German system, of course. With only a few buyers of technical services, for instance, inventors and entrepreneurs who develop surprising new treatments often find it hard to break down the door. Middle-class citizens are often impatient that their money doesn't buy them any better treatment than the next guy—and envious of the well-to-do who are often permitted to supplement their insurance benefits with private cash to procure superior care in private systems. Indeed, the Europeans are constantly scouting the American system, looking for innovations— especially technical innovations—that they can adopt.

In contrast, Rheinhardt says, doctors in the United States have pursued a divide-and-conquer strategy over the years in designing a system wherein the insurers who pay their bills never have enough clout to seriously bargain for lower fees or less extravagant procedures; in this they've been abetted by their patients' yearning to be able to shop around. He writes: "Throughout their history, Americans have been fearful of concentrating economic power in the hands of a few who might be corrupt, or inept, or both. Consequently, Americans have looked askance at regulatory macromanagement of their health-care system.

"Instead of concentrating the flow of money to providers into one or a few major pipes, the American health system lets these funds flow through a myriad of small, uncoordinated money pipes originating directly from patients and from literally thousands of third-party payers that include governments at all levels, business firms, insurance companies, labor unions and countless private, voluntary agencies." One result is the kind of perfect confusion about what everything really costs that grocery store proprietors only dream about. Where German consumers know exactly how their agents are doing bargaining on their behalf with the medical establishment every year—they can read the results in the withholding column of their paycheck, after all, and follow the annual negotiations in the newspaper—the average American forks out so much in co-payments, unreimbursed expenses, premiums and taxes that he hasn't the slightest idea what he or she is actually paying altogether in the end.

Rheinhardt concludes: "The single-pipe approach probably more so than any other factor enables these countries to allocate to health care a much smaller slice of the gross national product than is being allocated in the United States. If Americans are unwilling to countenance that approach and prefer to continue with their myriad pipes, they are likely always to pay more for health care, per unit of service, and overall, than they otherwise would."

What are the chances that Americans in the next few years will rally to create the relatively controllable, centralized purchasing system that makes the European programs so much more efficient? Well, tactically speaking, the hope rests almost entirely on the corporations that now pay so much of the health-care bill; only they can possibly stiffen the spine of the insurance companies. But instead, their favorite solution for the last 10 years has been to make workers pay more in hopes of raising their consciousness. That's dropping the ball.

Strategically, however, the solution to the health-care crisis is almost entirely a political matter. It will come when and if America discovers what the Europeans already know: that unfettered, universal access to health care for all is, as Rheinhardt puts it, "part of the cement that binds a people together as a nation."

SEPTEMBER 24, 1989

The Winner's
Curse

WHAT'S WRONG WITH WALL STREET? THERE IS A GROWING SENSE THAT SOMETHING
is wrong with the latest merger boom, and not just in Hollywood or on the
campaign trail, either.

The blue-ribbon MIT Commission on Industrial Productivity, for instance, in an interim report has identified a preoccupation with short-term
financial gains along with four other factors as a prime contributor to the
American malaise. The business magazines have been promoting Warren
Buffett-mania as a way of getting back to the value-oriented roots of investing. One of Buffet's intellectual fellow-travelers, Columbia University
law profesor Louis Lowenstein, is about to publish a readable and well-
grounded analysis, *What's Wrong With Wall Street: Short-Term Gain and
the Absentee Shareholder*. And for those willing to think a little about the
accounting profession, H. Thomas Johnson and Robert S. Kaplan, have
written perhaps the most interesting book yet on what ails American corporations and how to fix it.

In *Relevance Lost, The Rise and Fall of Management Accounting*, Johnson
and Kaplan argue that American manufacturers—goaded partly by the
government-mandated drive of the 1930s for comprehensive and standard-
ized corporate disclosure—gradually abandoned an accounting system that
effectively counted widgets and adopted one that counted dollars instead,
a system that produced financial statements instead of cost and quality
control reports.

By the time industrialists found themselves locked in desperate international competition, the information they were getting about their products
and processes was "too late, too aggregated and too distorted" to be of much
use, the authors say. They make a compelling case, and offer a number of
hopeful suggestions. "We are not trying to split the atom, perform genetic
recombination or explore the solar system. All that may be required is to
return to basics, to ask what makes sense and what is important for the
organization. . . ."

But the steady stream of books, magazine articles and special reports pales in comparison to an example of the phenomenon itself—a rip-snorting takeover fight, such as the recently concluded Campeau-Macy-Federated battle. That one ended earlier this month when Canadian real estate developer Robert Campeau agreed to pay $6.6 billion for Federated Department Stores Inc., having bought Allied Stores for $3.6 billion just two years ago. Aided by battalions of investment bankers, lawyers and rich confederates, Campeau was suddenly the fourth biggest retailer in America, behind Sears, K Mart and Wal-Mart.

Do these takeover artists really know what they're doing? Are these mergers truly likely to be good for someone besides the shareholders whose palms are greased? It is here that, for sheer rhetorical power, it is hard to beat a series of experiments performed in a Boston University classroom a few years ago by a pair of economists.

What Max Bazerman and William Samuelson wanted to know was whether kids make shrewd guesses. So they sealed exactly $8 worth of coins in each of 48 bottles, then took the bottles to the microeconomics classes that they taught at the Graduate School of Management. The asked each of their classes to bid on a bottle; the winner would get to keep it, at his price; they also asked each bidder to privately estimate the value of the coins, with a $2 prize to the winner. They ran the experiment four times each in 12 classes.

The results: Private estimates were on the conservative side, with a mean of $5.13 per jar. But the winning bid was usually a wild card: its mean was $10.01, or $2.01 more than each jar was worth. The professors made about $100 fleecing their students while teaching them a valuable lesson.

This phenomenon—in which the slightly-manic guy gets the goods—is the "winner's curse." It is discussed in a recent article by Richard H. Thaler, a leading expert in behavioral economics at Cornell's Graduate School of Management, writing in the *Journal of Economic Perspectives*. Winner's curse was first identified by petroleum engineers in 1971, Thaler says. When oil companies bid on the drilling rights to a particular parcel of land, the engineers noted, the estimates are often all over the map; it isn't easy to figure out how much oil is beneath the ground, after all. Some experts' forecasts are too low, others are too high, but it is the high bidding companies that win, even those that discount somewhat their own experts' estimates.

The result is the winner's curse. Its existence has been borne out by many more experiments, including some on experts who should know better; it has been observed in many realms, from publishing to professional sports. And it can be very expensive to the would-be market wizard: as the engineers who first noted the curse pointed out, the rich oil and gas field in the Gulf of Mexico to which the oil companies had flocked paid off over a period of 20 years "at something less than the local credit union."

In the world of the professional economist, the winner's curse is an anomaly, something that is not supposed to happen. If everyone was perfectly rational, they would take into account the presence of the other bidders, and discount the expected value of the prize just enough so that they would never overpay. But as hard as they may try to be rational, people don't always succeed. Indeed, says Thaler, winner's curse may be a common phenomenon. Some people—maybe even many people—apparently make systematic errors. It is not enough to say that economic theory precludes them.

The implications of the winner's curse are, of course, enormous. When the Federal Reserve Bank of Boston last autumn assembled a collection of leading experts to think about the merger boom, opinion cleaved pretty well between those who have a generally positive view of mergers and acquisitions and those who don't, according to economist Lynn E. Brown, who summarized the meeting in the most recent issue of the *New England Economic Review*. The former were financial economists, relying on portfolio models; the latter were specialists in industrial organization, who said they felt that most mergers don't work.

But the fact is that at the Federal Reserve conference, even the economists who were most skeptical of the efficiency of the merger boom were extremely reluctant to advocate measures that would protect incumbent managers or prohibit the hefty premiums paid to shareholders by corporate raiders.

As if to underscore the possibility that takeover artists often do know what they are doing, Robert Campeau this week has announced a string of changes in management style at the Federated units he plans to keep. In many details, they resembled the sorts of recommendations that accounting professors Johnson and Kaplan made in *Relevance Lost*: less hierarchy, more attention to invisible costs, less clutter, longer views. The market may not always be right. But over the long horizon, it is usually better than the next guess.

APRIL 17, 1988

Living as a "Diminished Giant"

Just because George Bush got elected doesn't mean that protectionism has gone away. Indeed, Republican administrations are just as prone to making sweetheart deals with their constituencies as are Democratic, and sometimes more so. True, the October merchandise trade deficit dipped slightly to $8.9 billion, but there is a widespread sense that more improvement awaits a further decline in the dollar. That will benefit American exporters at the expense of Europeans and Japanese. So the world trading system goes clipping along, never far from the brink of a dangerous low-level trade war.

There is at the moment no more distinguished student of the patterns and pathologies of trade than Jagdish Bhagwati. An MIT-trained theorist and Columbia University professor, he is at 54 among a tiny handful of specialists in international economics who have had an impact beyond their field. Robert Mundell mathematized the study of the international macroeconomics, Robert Baldwin empiricized the results of protectionism, but it was Bhagwati (along with Anne Krueger) who helped restore the politics to political economy, by focusing attention on the myriad forms of "directly unproductive activity" in which businessmen and politicians team up to squeeze a little extra out of the generally-unsuspecting consumer.

A punchy writer of smooth old-boy prose, he has kept up a steady stream of criticisms of trade-limiting proposals on both sides of the Atlantic in recent years; his "diminished giant" thesis, which compares the erosion of U.S. hegemony 40 years after World War II to a similar process that eventually overtook Great Britain in the wake of its triumph in the Napoleonic Wars, has become a standard interpretation of international tensions since it appeared last year; indeed, when he published an elegant little summing-up volume entitled *Protectionism* last summer, the *Financial Times* described him as "the slickest pen in the west." In an article forthcoming in the *Journal of International Affairs*, Bhagwati surveys the trend of trade barriers since Ronald Reagan took over and spots a dangerous pattern: despite declining tariffs, protectionism has developed a large covert operation and today proceeds by stealth.

Bhagwati differentiates between two dominant forms of protection: a "high-track" form of highly visible restraints exercised by the exporting country, and a "low-track" form of countervailing taxes designed to fight alleged foreign dumping. "High-track" restraints masquerade as prudent self control, but "low-track" measures are more insidious for they are far less understood. By making "unfair trade" charges far easier to levy, the 1988 Omnibus Trade Act makes these low-ball forms of harassment far easier to undertake. Between 1980 and 1985, the United States initiated more than 500 special taxes on foreign goods suspected of being dumped illegally, everything from Kenyan carnations to Italian pads for the keys of woodwind instruments. The "super 301" section provisions of the 1988 Act, which urge the president to scout out all "unreasonable" acts by trading parters everywhere, present a field for mischief that threatened American competitors and their lawyers have just begun to exploit.

American indignation at the need to measure up to foreign competition is stoked by two processes, says Bhagwati: the "double squeeze" and the "diminished giant syndrome." The double squeeze is the more direct threat: with the newly industrializing countries threatening old "sunset" industries like steel and textiles, and with Japan offering fierce competition in high-tech "sunrise" industries, American industry seems caught in a pincer movement. The possibility that cunning rivals are moving to displace U.S. leadership in key technologies vital to the creation of the next generation of products only adds to the conviction that others are ganging up.

The paranoia engendered by the "double squeeze" is amplified by the vague sense that it used to be different. Sure enough. In 1950, America accounted for something like 40 percent of world output; by 1980 the figure had declined to about 22 percent. It was not that the United States was getting poorer, but that other nations were becoming rich; yet the results have been much the same as when Great Britain's share of world production dropped from 32 percent to 14 percent between 1870 and 1914: a stiff protectionist backlash has developed, accompanied by a fear of being eclipsed in all things.

To be sure, nothing could be more boring to most people than the world of quotas and tariffs, of CVDs and ADs and VERs. Yet these are the stuff of daily life for nearly every businessman who exports or sells imported goods. A vast international bureaucracy exists to weigh the claims of those who think the opposition is cheating, and a good thing, too, says Bhagwati, for the regime that airily denies that such cheating can take place is inviting trouble for itself. But it has become disturbingly easy to capture the fair-trade process by filing "strike" suits against successful competitors, and the process of the smooth international division of labor is in danger of bogging down in the courts. Eternal skepticism about those claims of damage are the price of an efficient trading system, he says.

DECEMBER 18, 1988

The Third Coast

FOR SOME YEARS, ECONOMISTS HAVE ENJOYED MAKING A DISTINCTION AMONG THEM-selves between "salt-water" and "fresh-water" approaches to economics. Salt-water economics is shorthand for the familiar Keynesian vision of things: The government is the inescapably dominant actor in the economy, and it has a responsibility to keep prices stable and to eliminate recessions. Salt-water economics has been taught in the leading universities on the East and West Coasts for 50 years, ever since Keynesian insights were first transmitted to this country from England.

Fresh-water economics, on the other hand, asserts generally that free markets almost always outsmart government intervention, that strategies of pump-priming and punch-bowl-hiding are apt to fail the second time around, and that the best fine-tuning is no fine-tuning. Also known as the "rational expectations school" or the "new classical economics," the fresh-water school takes its name from the fact that it is taught in universities located on or near the shores of the Great Lakes, from Minnesota to Rochester, N.Y., a 1,000-mile stretch that literally makes up a third American coast. The indisputable capital of fresh-water economics is, and has been for more than 50 years, the University of Chicago.

Relatively little newspaper ink has been spilled in recent years over how the fresh-water school, under cover of the Vietnam War, quietly captured the forefront of technical economics. The skeptical tenor of its thought, as much as its content, seemed well-suited to a generation of scholars who came of age at a time when government's claims to superior wisdom in everything from foreign policy to domestic economic management were crashing down around the presidential ears of Lyndon Johnson and Richard Nixon.

Still less attention has been paid to how completely the Chicagoans have captured the Reagan administration. Before 1984, no University of Chicago economist had ever served on the Council of Economic Advisers. Suddenly in the second term, there were three—Beryl Sprinkel, Michael Mussa and Thomas Gale Moore. Now a fourth graduate of the University of Chicago, Allan H. Meltzer, a prominent economist now teaching at Carnegie-Mellon University, has reported to Washington to unofficially replace Mussa as a member of the senior staff.

Nor is the council the only citadel of Chicago influence in the Reagan administration: there is Secretary of State George Shultz and Allen Wallis, his deputy at the State Department; economist Michael Darby at the Treasury Department; and countless less notable academicians in other Cabinet posts. James C. Miller 3d, director of the Office of Management and Budget, is an honorary Chicagoan; he was trained at the University of Virginia when it was a satellite school. Even Texas Sen. Phil Gramm is a product of the Chicago mindset.

No name connected with Chicago is better known than that of Milton Friedman, and indeed along with MIT's Paul Samuelson, the short, ex-Chicago economist (he now lives in San Francisco), is one of the two most influential economists since Keynes. Certainly the two men together typify the opposite ends of economic possibility, fresh-water and salt-water.

But there are many other persons connected with the Chicago tradition, including George Stigler who hit the front pages briefly in 1982 when as that year's Nobel laureate, he described the downturn then as a depression rather than a recession, thereby getting thrown out of the White House. Now Stigler has published an autobiography—*The Memoirs of An Unregulated Economist*—and it is a good place to encounter both the Chicago habit of thought and also to glimpse the social world of scientific economics.

Not that Stigler has anything in particular to offer in the way of resolving the fresh water–salt water controversy—as he says, the complexities of macroeconomics, meaning the behavior of the economy taken as a whole, never appealed to him. Instead, the professor offers a series of sketches of controversies in which he was involved strung together on the spine of his autobiography—from the fracas over oleomargarine at Iowa State University in 1943 to the reaction of a distinguished Harvard professor in 1960 when Gary Becker proposed in a seminar that the demand for children in families could be treated as a special case of consumer demand, like refrigerators, say.

Stigler limits himself to precisely one blast at what he takes to be a central failing of the salt-water school. "At leading centers of economic theory such as MIT, it has been the practice to ask: Is the new theory logically correct? That is a good question but not as good as a second question: Does the new theory help us to understand observable economic life? No one will deny the desirability of eventually answering the second question, but many economists prefer to leave that question for a later time and a different person to answer. That division of labor is quite proper, but until the second question is answered a theory has no standing and, therefore, should not be used as a guide to public policy."

Given the outpouring of empirical research in recent years devoted to assaying the brashest claim of fresh-water economists—that deficits don't really matter very much because citizens immediately begin saving to pay the taxes they know will surely come—the complaint may seem a little dated. But there is no denying that the Chicagoans established an empirical style that has converted most of the rest of the profession.

Stigler's book is one of a series of autobiographies by leading scientists commissioned by the Alfred Sloan Foundation (others include Luis Alvarez, Freeman Dyson, Peter Medawar, Salvador Luria, and Francis Crick). These have been widely acclaimed by scientists and Stigler's book is no exception. Beautifully written, it will appeal to anyone seeking a better understanding of what technical economics is all about. It is full of stories about powerful minds, courageous intellects and tightly focused issues.

But for that very reason, however, it is of relatively little help in understanding the larger questions of salt-water versus fresh-water economics, of liberal versus conservative intuitions of the nature of the state.

Why has the fresh-water movement carried the day so completely in recent years? Why does Gov. Michael Dukakis find himself on the defensive before a Republican party that declares, "We are the change"? The answer seems to be that there is some deep-down dialectic at work. The seeds of the policy harvest that Reagan reaped for eight years—deregulation, strong monetary policy, tax simplification and reform—were sown many years ago by a generation of economists and other scholars. To understand the triumph of the Chicago school in the 1980s, one should look to its founding in the 1940s and to its gradual evolution ever since.

If Michael Dukakis suddenly finds himself behind George Bush in the race for president, it may be because he hasn't confronted—and acknowledged—the successes of the Reagan era or their intellectual underpinnings. It's pretty late to start now.

SEPTEMBER 4, 1988

Yankees Resplendent, Celtics Rebuilding

FORGET "RUEFFIAN ECONOMICS," THE LATEST HALF-BAKED PRESCRIPTION TO EMANATE from a rootless Washington think tank and an ambitious businessman. For 100 years real economics around the world has been driven by a trio of university departments. As George Will put it the other day, only half in jest, "The Cold War is over and the University of Chicago won."

Between 1890 and 1940 it was Cambridge, England, that dominated the top of this pyramid, with Alfred Marshall and Arthur Cecil Pigou. With the beginning of World War II the capital shifted abruptly to Cambridge, Mass.—to Keynes as interpreted by Paul Samuelson and a whole generation of mathematical economists. Then starting, say, in 1969, it was Chicago that dominated, more or less under a trio of banners of monetarism, rational expectations and Coaseian law and economics.

These three periods correspond to the high conservatism of the Triple Entente and the Gold Standard, to the rise of the Welfare State and to the advent of global neoconservatism. In truth, you could have seen each wave coming—if only you had known at the outset which university to watch.

The last few years have seen an erosion of this tendency of a single center to dominate. There has been a tremendous diffusion of economists to other good departments, particularly in California. "Farm teams"—universities like Rochester, Carnegie-Mellon, Virginia and George Mason—have assumed increasing significance. So have business schools—and even the economics departments of some investment banks.

With more husband-and-wife teams in the business, good people aren't as quick to move to the single best place. A new force making itself felt is the National Bureau of Economic Research, which brings researchers from far-flung universities into contact with the center. The same can be said of computer networks. Finally, there is a generally acknowledged decline in loyalty: Every autumn, for a few weeks, there is open season on rival faculties, as good departments seek to fill in holes in their lineups.

For all of this, the departments of the great universities remain the fundamental units of economics—precisely because it is here that the highest value is placed on the deep insights that drive changes in the way economies are understood. When all their perks are factored in, the sharpest university professors outdistance and sometimes even out-earn even the brightest stars on Wall Street. Those who are able teach. For this reason, the situation in Cambridge, Mass., today bears watching.

For the Harvard University economics department, these are glory days. Martin Feldstein, once the overly independent adviser to Ronald Reagan, is now the behind-the-scenes senior economic guru to George Bush. Hendrick Houthakker is counselor to the Pope. Jeffrey Sachs is rewiring Eastern Europe; Graham Allison consults to Moscow; William Hogan does the same for the Ukraine. Lawrence Summers is chief economist at the World Bank. Dale Jorgenson and his businessmen pals are creating tax policy in Washington; Richard Cooper built the highly influential Institute for International Economics there; department chairman Benjamin Friedman often advises the Federal Reserve system. Great men come from around the world to teach at Harvard: Amartya Sen from India, Janos Kornai from Hungary. Harvard macroeconomists have a pipeline to the the *Wall Street Journal* editorial page.

Down the river at the Massachusetts Institute of Technology, the restructuring of the communist world is not quite as big a deal. Rudiger Dornbusch is influential in Japan; Stanley Fischer is a hero in Israel and Latin America; alumnus Pedro Aspe is running the Mexican economy, but he's working for Carlos Salinas de Gortari, a Harvard man. Michael Piore has a large following among political analysts in Europe; macroeconomist Olivier Blanchard cuts a formidable figure in France; alumnus Carl Christian von Weizsacker is an influential German leader. But MIT's best-known economist in America, Lester Thurow, hasn't worked in the field for many years.

True, MIT's influence on the profession is considerably greater than that of Harvard. Its industrial organization group is a major force, including Jean Tirole, Oliver Hart, Paul Joscow and Richard Schmallensee, who just returned from a hitch on the president's Council of Economic Advisers. Fischer-Dornbusch is still a leading undergraduate text. Blanchard-Fischer's *Lectures on Macroeconomics* is the most widely read introduction to latter-day Keynesian analysis—but, of course, Keynes' position in economics is still hotly debated.

It is true also that there is at least one more Nobel Prize due an MIT professor: to Peter Diamond, for his work on uncertainty in economics and the role of search. Paul Krugman, who is frequently an adviser to Democratic presidential aspirants, just won the John Bates Clark Medal as the best economist under 40. Like Blanchard and James Poterba, Krugman can be said to be a leader of the younger generation. What this means is that many of the best students still prefer to go to MIT to learn their science.

But MIT may be suffering somewhat from what alumnus Jagdish Bhagwati calls "the diminished giant syndrome": Where once the department absolutely dominated its world, like Britain in the 19th century or America in the 20th, today it has plenty of competition. Nobel laureate Samuelson, the greatest economist of a half century, is retired (though, sharp as a tack, he still participates fully, even to the point of holding court occasionally in a local Burger King). Franco Modigliani is retired as well, as is Charles P. Kindleberger. Robert Solow, youthful at 67, soldiers on, teaching and consulting to a wide range of organizations.

The great finance group at the Sloan School, which lit up the world with its discoveries in the early 1970s, is disbanded: Fisher Black to Goldman Sachs, Myron Scholes to Stanford and Salomon Brothers. Robert Merton, the Cal Tech math genius who MIT turned into a world-class economist, is teaching down the river at the Harvard Business School. In econometrics, Daniel McFadden has gone back to California, and Jerry Hausman and Franklin Fisher spend their spare time consulting. A raid on Princeton's economics department backfired last year; MIT's Henry Farber unexpectedly went to Princeton instead.

All this came to a head a few weeks ago when MIT star-citizen Poterba, 33, almost left Tech for the other end of Massachusetts Avenue. A graduate of Harvard College, Poterba had told friends he was leaning 90 percent to Harvard—then at the last minute opted to stay at MIT. You could almost hear the sighs of relief.

Now understand, the MIT department has always operated as a team— rather like the Boston Celtics, in fact. The great unit, which started when Harvard declined to promote a youthful Samuelson in 1940, built up in a great surge, then renewed itself by promoting its students. Its central figures fairly lived for economics—lunching together around a round table, taking a lively interest in one another's work, nurturing their students through school and beyond. They declined to go the Washington route, refused to take on big consulting engagements, insisted on each teaching a relatively heavy load—developing all the while a coherent and highly influential intellectual style and a policy prescription that could be summed up in two words: fine-tuning. A cagey and warmly supportive administration backed them up.

In contrast, Harvard has operated like the New York Yankees—occasionally like George Steinbrenner's Yankees. Its busy professors work in isolation from one another, hurl their thunderbolts as they please, often take long leaves away from the university. Their students often complain of feeling neglected and being left to fend for themselves.

Today Harvard is the beneficiary of its diversity. It may lack coherence, but it's got a little bit of everything that is good in economics and a lot of the currently dominant taste for the "applied" variant. MIT, if anything, is the victim of its team-style homogeneity of play. Its teachers have done relatively little grappling with the outside streams of opinion from Chicago and Minnesota that have swirled through macroeconomics the past 20 years and left it an enormous field of broken dreams. Visitors from Chicago and Stanford seldom turn up at its seminars; its professors seldom go the other way.

Whether this was a function of the continuing presence of the giants among the young economists who had to carry on their tradition is anybody's guess; it is a common problem among first-rate university departments in many disciplines, university administrators say. But where Harvard has Robert Barro as a thorny exemplar of a style of skeptical thought that many of its professors abhor, MIT has no one to hold up the other side.

For all of that, MIT remains one of the two or three best departments in the world, along with Stanford or Chicago. It may be second to Harvard in all respects but teaching, but it is well within reach of first—by its time-tested means of leap-frogging and team play. Looking for a good bet on the department whose ideas will dominate the intellectual battles of the 21st century? Don't short Harvard—its successes are real enough. But you just might want to buy some calls on MIT.

DECEMBER 15, 1991

The Self-Inventors:
Clinton's Advisers

SUPPOSE BILL CLINTON IS ELECTED, WHAT THEN? ONE OF THE BEST STORIES IN Washington will be the saga of the outsiders suddenly in charge of the government, specifically the tension between the wannabe-economists who are among Clinton's oldest friends and closest advisers, and the real liberal economists, who are not. This drama has been unfolding quietly and behind the scenes since the 1980s. In the event of a victory, it would move to center stage.

By now the story of Clinton's long march to front-runner status is fairly well known. From the photo-opportunity with President John F. Kennedy at the American Legion Boys' Nation conference to his undergraduate career at Georgetown University, from his Rhodes Scholarship experience at Oxford University to Yale Law School to the McGovern campaign, Clinton has been the formulator of an unusual network of friends dedicated to working for and perhaps serving in an eventual Clinton presidency. The innermost of this circle have for many years been known among themselves and Clinton's staff as FOBs—Friends of Bill's.

It is hard to be certain, but the closest of the FOBs seem to go back to the Oxford years, when Rhodes Scholar Clinton was agonizing over the Vietnam War and his responsibility to the draft. And among his circle then were three young men who, in a remarkable exhibition of luck and will, have risen to prominence since as economic gurus, with an audience mainly on the left. Now the scrutiny has begun, and these fellows are relatively easy targets.

Derek Shearer, a professor of public policy at Occidental College in Los Angeles, was singled out (not once but twice) last week in the *Wall Street Journal*. He is a former planning commissioner of Santa Monica, Calif., a Tom Hayden–Jane Fonda groupie in those years, a tireless pamphleteer and the author of *Economic Democracy*, a book whose opinions are left-wing even by standards of the 1970s. Shearer has told reporters that a President Clinton would establish an Economic Security Council in the White House, paralleling the National Security Council, to oversee international trade at the expense of the Council of Economic Advisers.

Ira Magaziner is a charismatic business consultant, who worked a brief stint at the Boston Consulting Group during its go-go years and now heads his own firm in Providence. As an undergraduate, Magaziner launched an effort to reform the curriculum at Brown University; after graduation he led a group in an abortive effort to take over (Santa Monica–fashion) the city of Brockton; a decade later he devised Rhode Island's ambitious "Greenhouse Compact" (which went down to an ignominious 4–1 defeat). He led the charge a couple of years ago for awarding the state of Utah huge sums to pursue cold fusion, then failed in a recent attempted turnaround at Wang Laboratories. An inveterate winner-picker (and odds-on loser-chooser), Magaziner's most recent book is *The Silent War: Inside the Global Business Battles Shaping America's Future.*

Robert B. Reich, a lecturer at the John F. Kennedy School of Government at Harvard, is far and away the nimblest intellect of the trio. He is the author of a stream of books and op-ed pieces since the early 1970s that show a steady evolution from the days when he co-authored an industrial policy tract called *Minding America's Business* with Magaziner. True, he suffered a swivet after the crash of 1987; and a recent PBS series called *Made in America* bombed. But Reich's latest book, *The Work of Nations*, is a bold and sophisticated exposition of ideas, many of them widely shared by professional economists—the importance of free trade, for instance. The fact remains that Reich is in no danger of being taken for an economist; the characteristic deep absorption with the workings of the price system just doesn't seem to be part of his make-up.

Indeed, there is a striking similarity in the approaches of candidate Clinton and author Reich to their respective fields. Both are the possessors of superb natural equipment: warm dispositions, charming manners, ready humor, quick intellect. Both are superb talkers. But both are fundamental outsiders to the organizations that are among those they most seek to affect.

There exist in American life many great habilitating organizations. People meet them young, often before they even know what they are. One of these is the US armed forces; another is the economics profession. And at the crucial time in their careers, neither Clinton nor Reich was willing to become involved. Both went from their Oxford studies straight to Yale Law, then on into the real world, each proclaiming on matters beyond his officially-certified competence, Reich at the Federal Trade Commission, Clinton as the governor of Arkansas.

In this, Clinton's trio of inside economic advisers resembles nothing so much as the "supply-siders" whose presence enlivened the early years of the Reagan administration: that is, they are essentially journalists seeking to horn in on a conversation that has been conducted with much greater subtlety (in far greater obscurity) by economists. They even seem to possess the same gift for mythmaking. Writer Sidney Blumenthal has described their attempt to persuade Americans that what they need is a leaner activist government as "The Conversation" with the same reverence previously accorded the famous cocktail napkin of Arthur Laffer.

Indeed, the existence of this extensive PR machine goes a long way in explaining the presence of Clinton at the head of his party today. Party theoreticians proclaimed him fit. Blumethall writes: "From the start, Clinton has been part of The Conversation, perhaps having more ties to more of those in it than any other elected Democrat." And if it were just PR, one might dismiss it as just so much campaign fluff—the work of writers blurbing each other's books, rather more interested in their careers than in the ideas themselves.

But in fact The Conversation has its counterpart conversations going on in other realms of discourse, from the barber chair to cloak rooms to the lecture hall. For instance, a possible role for government in choosing industrial development targets has been the subject for a great deal of discussion at high theoretical levels in technical economics for the past several years. So has the economic significance of education, which is greatly stressed by author Reich. Clinton's economic ideas aren't altogether petty, just for having been developed outside the main currents of such thought (neither were Ronald Reagan's, after all); his enthusiasms just seem to be somewhat stronger and streakier than conventionally-developed think-tank views.

Thus there exists a second, outer circle of more conventional economic advisers working on the campaign, developing positions, working out issues, responding to the thrusts and parries of the Bush campaign. Chief among them appears to be Alan S. Blinder, a Princeton University professor and senior figure in the technical economics fraternity whose book, *Hard Heads, Soft Hearts: Tough-Minded Economics for a Just Society*, blazed a trial five years ago. Others include Laura Tyson, Lawrence Katz, Rudiger Dornbusch and Paul Krugman, typical in all ways of a generation of young economists of strong liberal convictions who have nowhere else to turn. Policy enthusiasts are present, too, including Rob Shapiro of the Progressive Policy Institute and writer David Osborne (*Reinventing Government*).

There is, however, this crucial difference between the proprietors of The

Conversation and the supply-siders: Ronald Reagan did not go to Oxford with Jude Wanniski, and when the time came to cut the crazies loose, he did and fairly quickly. Clinton is one of the gang. To judge from the profiles, he really believes this stuff.

On the other hand, nothing makes you into an instant insider like getting elected. As president, Clinton probably would abandon his pals and head for the center—at least eventually. The real question is whether Americans want to go through the pain.

SEPTEMBER 13, 1992

part four

ENGINEERS

After
the Crash

IN A BEAUTIFUL LITTLE BOOK CALLED *ENGINEER'S WITNESS*, PUBLISHED A COUPLE OF
years ago, Ralph Greenhill displayed the 19th-century history of civil
engineering in America in 90 photographs with authoritative captions on
the pages opposite. There are the Chicago water cribs with their subaque-
ous tunnels; the enormous wheelpits and penstocks and generators of the
Niagara Falls hydraulic station; the great pumps of the Philadelphia wa-
terworks; a pneumatic subway in New York; a skyscraper with its newly-
invented elevators; the Capitol dome in Washington; and of course any
number of beautiful bridges and mighty engines. Each triumph is caught in
an early moment of great precariousness: primitive, fragile, incomplete,
dangerous.

It is interesting to reflect on the history of civil engineering in America
in connection with the October crash and the aftermath of analysis and
calls for reform. In all likelihood, financial engineering is in roughly the
same situation today as civil and mechanical engineering were 150 years
ago: on the verge of a dramatic takeoff into mastery of its world. Indeed,
the very phrase "financial engineering" has entered common discourse
only in the past 10 years, mostly abroad. It is not yet in the economic
dictionaries.

A computer search last week uncovered a wide variety of meanings of the
term in current usage, ranging from slick practices to marketing palaver to
dignified intellectual enterprises. In Italy financial engineering often means
manipulation just short of fraud; in Japan, the term serves as the translation
for *zaiteku*, the questionable practice of investing corporate profits in the
Japanese stock market, relying on the bull market to boost earnings where
hard selling cannot. Sometimes the phrase financial engineering connotes
the arrangements underlying corporate restructuring, as in "our firm doesn't
have much experience in financial engineering;" sometimes it means any
new technique for raising funds; and sometimes it refers to public policy
initiatives, as in "East-West trade requires some complicated financial

engineering" or "the Third World debt problem has been ameliorated somewhat by savvy financial engineering."

It doesn't seem unreasonable, then, to suggest that the term should be applied broadly to the entire field of activity by which complicated financial institutions, structures and instruments are created and maintained. Thus, the creation of the futures and options markets in Chicago was a feat of financial engineering. So was the rise of the Euromarkets in currencies and interbank dealings in London and other European capitals. The invention and perfection of the leveraged buyout and the junk bond market by investment banking firms as a means of putting the corporate investor in the driver's seat was an act of financial engineering. So was the spread outward from the mortgage markets of securitization, meaning the sale of financial assets like loans in secondary markets, that is taking many of the kinks out of the world financial system.

Mexico, in both the form of its restructuring agreements and the financial instruments involved (including Dutch auctions and "collateralized" floating rate bonds) is a pioneer in financial engineering. So is Poland: precisely because it is still burdened by massive debt, trade there requires complicated financial engineering on nearly ever deal, including barter and captive finance, and so on. As LBO specialist Ted Stolberg told *Inc.* magazine last year, "Financial engineering is a lot like building a bridge. You can build it any way you like as long as it doesn't collapse when heavy trucks run over it and you can add additional lanes when you want more traffic to go over it. And when it's all done, it should be a thing of beauty, like the Golden Gate."

Who are the people who are doing these things to us? Why are they doing them? A fair number of the new financial engineers are simply tinkerers with plenty of experience in markets and a strong entrepreneurial bent— bankers, traders, money managers of all sorts. They are driven by the same complicated array of motives as were the great engineers of the 19th century. But just as with electrical engineering, an increasing number of the new financial entrepreneurs are drawn from university departments and business schools. These professors and their best students—"quants" and "rocket scientists" in the lingo of Wall Street—are routinely pushing back the limits of what is known about the behavior of markets, creating new forms of investment technique, integrating world markets.

But are they just a bunch of gamblers and quick-buck artists, out to trim the little guy? Some are, undoubtedly. But it isn't easy to tell the benefactor from the beneficiary—especially since, as the historian Stephen Sass points out, the very idea of engineering connotes the pursuit of tensile strength—

the efficient and safe management of stress. John Roebling's Brooklyn Bridge, Cyrus Field's trans-Atlantic cable, George Westinghouse's air brakes are remembered with (fairly) unambiguous satisfaction, even though they were criticized and feared in their day. Wouldn't it be ironic if, when the smoke clears, when the public relations men and the prosecutors go home and the accumulated fortunes begin to be spent on good works, if today's leading financial innovators of the options-pricing formula, the LBO, the index fund, interest rate and currency swaps are remembered in a similarly rosy light?

What is striking in Greenhill's photographic history is the omnipresence of government's involvement. At every point, there is government facilitating, interfering, intervening, sponsoring, investigating, regulating. The government's Springfield Armory introduced the nation to a new manufacturing system based on interchangeable parts. "Boss" Tweed shut down the pneumatic subway because he was betting on the elevated railroad competition. The Commonwealth of Massachusetts took over the Hoosac tunnel from its bankrupt railroads and finished the job. Government regulators begin turning up in the photographs, along with the engineers, early in the 1840s.

Above all, government's role in 19th-century engineering was to investigate its failures. For example, when a Western Railroad train heading out of Worcester on its way to Westfield smacked up one autumn day in 1841, killing two, maiming eight and injuring nine others, there was an enormous hue and cry. Citizens inveighed against the folly of traveling at 30 miles an hour and proposals were advanced to outlaw the trains. Instead, the Western Railroad instituted a number of reforms—better signals, more safeguards, deeper planning—and they proved to be enduring institutional innovations that greatly abetted the spread, not just of the "Iron Horse," but of manufacturing enterprise generally.

It is in this context that one should think of the Brady Commission Task Force report on the October crash. For all the talk of the damage done by computerized trading strategies on Oct. 19 and 20—and there isn't the slightest doubt that these contributed to the magnitude of the market's fall—what the Brady task force said was that the system simply needed more engineering. The report didn't propose to ban, say, dynamic hedging; what it mentioned was the need for a new unified clearing system. It didn't seek to outlaw index arbitrage; instead, it called for "circuit-breakers" and experiments designed to dampen volatility.

In all likelihood, the computer poses no more fundamental threat to safety in markets than the railroad engine did to safety in transport. To be sure, there are differences in the respective social significance of civil and social engineering; when a bridge fails in Cincinnati, only those on it are deeply affected, whereas the unexpected bankruptcy of an obscure financial unit could presumably throw the entire financial world into gridlock, at least momentarily. But the very deepening and growing interdependence of markets is probably the best safeguard against their fragility. And in any event, the movement toward more safety and higher standards in financial engineering will proceed in roughly the same way as did the parallel movements in 19th-century public works: a slow and sometimes painful process of discovering new ways of doing things, unsuspected pitfalls—and the eventual technical solutions to them.

JANUARY 17, 1988

Rocket Science and Its Dilemmas Are Here to Stay

IT'S AN OLD SAW AMONG HISTORIANS OF SCIENCE THAT THERMODYNAMICS LEARNED A lot more from the steam engine than the steam engine ever learned from thermodynamics. Indeed, steam boats were chugging up and down the Thames and Seine and Hudson long before Sadi Carnot and James Joule got around to the disagreement about engines' efficiency that produced the two laws of thermodynamics. Nobody rides in steamboats any more, and not many remember the Second Law very well, but everybody is affected by fruits of the quantum revolution in physics that followed in due course. They include, among other things, nukes and chips.

The point is that practitioners, practical men and women who never went to school, can learn to do some pretty fancy things all by themselves, without much help from theorists. But sooner or later, theorists begin to unlock the riddles of the art and are able to offer some very practical suggestions of their own, at least in many fields.

That's more or less the situation in present-day financial economics, where abstruse theory has begun to make some very concrete contributions to the real world. It was underscored last week with the award of a Nobel Prize to three scholars—Harry Markowitz, William Sharpe and Merton Miller—who are far from household words, even in the homes of macro-economists.

Ordinarily, the rise of modern portfolio theory would be just another story for business fans and investment buffs. But in this case, there is a broader point that is worth considering. It has to do with understanding the post-industrial world we live in now.

Some people like to assign a central strategic role to President Reagan's Strategic Defense—Star Wars—Initiative in changing the geometry of international relations during the 1980s. The Russians were intimidated into making peace, the argument goes, when the Americans threatened to leap far ahead in computer management of a battlefield dominated from space. But in some deep sense, it was arguably American financial muscle, as much or even more than its lead in weaponry, that brought the Cold War to a decisive end. One of the reasons for this surge is the deep tradition of unfettered talk and untrammelled innovation in corporate finance.

Not that the American capital markets weren't a pretty remarkable achievement long before Harry Markowitz brought mean-variance analysis to bear on the problems of choosing an investment portfolio. The principle of diversification was intuitively well understood. Mutual funds had been invented and were beginning their phenomenal growth. Securities analysts labored to forecast earnings of various companies (and thus to implicitly calculate their rates of return).

There were elaborate rules of thumb about when corporations should issue common or preferred stock, and when they should borrow money. Futures trading as a way of hedging against uncertainty dates back to 17th-century Holland, and the Butter and Egg Exchange in Chicago had been in business since before the Civil War.

What Markowitz, Sharp and Miller did was to build a deep and solid mathematical foundation under the analysis of investments of all sorts, to bring a quantitative approach to thinking about uncertainty. Separately, their principle contributions are known among economists as portfolio theory, the capital asset pricing model and the Miller-Modigliani theorem. Together, they constitute the basis of a system for evaluating risks and the rate of return, usually against the benchmark of the performance of the overall market itself, of enormous generality and wide applicability. In the 1950s and 1960s, their ideas were written down in esoteric equations; in the 1970s and 1980s, they were systematically translated by entrepreneurs into tens of thousands of jobs, a vigorous and bountiful new sector of the economy.

"The striking thing is that their work has permeated so much of financial activity, and in a fairly direct way. Though there have been many modifications, you can recognize the original contributions in what people are doing now in practice," says the Harvard Business School's Robert Merton. "There are lots of things that great economists have done that provide a framework for thinking about something. It is much rarer where you can find a contribution that will be so recognizable in the final product."

Like what? Well, the futures and options markets in Chicago are direct descendants of these ideas, says Peter Bernstein, a New York investment advisor who is writing a social history of the development of modern finance called *Capital Ideas*. Another example: Index funds with which investors buy baskets of securities that are representatives of the market as a whole— that's 10 percent of the holdings of pension funds already. And virtually every week the authoritative *International Financing Review* brings a report of the introduction of some new-fangled security that would be completely unfathomable without an advanced grounding in finance.

To be sure, there is a pessimistic view of the rise of modern financial technology, a view that often fastens on the role played by the markets in futures and options that are now spreading from Chicago to other centers of global finance. Nobel laureate Merton Miller, a fierce defender of the industry he helped create, has distinguished between a "casino view" of markets as a zero-sum game of investors betting on price movement and an "information view" in which speculative profits are the "bribe" which societies offers investors to assimilate information and to provide insurance against unexpected developments. There's not much doubt that the information view is the more helpful.

(You don't have to be a Luddite to have concerns about the safety of the new markets, however. Portfolio insurance, a theoretical idea, was quickly translated into a financial product during the mid-1980s by a relatively small group of West Coast academics. They made a fortune, but the product is viewed in some quarters as having contributed to the seriousness of the October 1987 crash. Interest rate swaps are another esoteric new financial product; they haven't yet been tested by a serious financial panic. It's a good bet that ill-designed financial instruments can blow up on occasion, just like a poorly-built steam engine; it's reasonable to think that safety testing of the new know-how is still in its infancy.)

Moreover, as more disciples of the new quantitative approach rise toward the top of money management, one hates to see the old liberal arts crowd in eclipse. There is a sort of tough-minded, independent and plain-English gentleman, full of wisdom and good character, who typifies the old style of money management—Ben Graham, Warren Buffett, John Templeton, T. Rowe Price. The newer generation hires more quants.

As Vanguard chairman John Bogle recently wrote, reviewing a volume of technical papers: "While there is a lot of witchcraft in the academic lore, a certain naiveté among the practitioners about what is truly susceptible to proof, and far too much reliance on the misbegotten idea that the past is inevitably prologue to the future, the most solid academic thinking, however complex, abstruse and precise, is worth even a busy financial executive's perusal. For sound theory, sooner or later, will find its way into actual practice in the financial markets, and into the investor marketplace as well."

But the most interesting problem of all may have to do with new potential conflicts of interest between the universities and private enterprise that have arisen with the development of the new economic knowledge. Merton Miller, a University of Chicago professor, is a director of the Chicago Mercantile Exchange (the old Butter and Egg Exchange) and a defender against federal attempts at its regulation. William Sharpe retired early from Stanford to make money by, among other things, advising AT&T's pension fund. Harry Markowitz worked for General Electric and IBM before a brief and somewhat checkered fling on Wall Street. Private gain and public knowledge are sometimes difficult to reconcile, and redefining the ethical horizons is not going to be any easier in finance than it has been in medicine and biotechnology.

OCTOBER 21, 1990

The Money Launderers
Stay a Step Ahead

THE CHARTER PLANE FULL OF CASH FROM THE UNITED STATES LANDS IN PANAMA CITY once a week and is met by an armored car. The money goes to a no-questions-asked Panamanian bank, from which it can be wired back, whistling clean, to the United States. There is evidence suggesting that one of the owners of the charter company is Gen. Manuel Antonio Noriega, head of the army and leader of the nation in all but name.

But that is not all. Besides laundering money for American organized crime leaders, Noriega is said to be deeply involved in facilitating the drug trade, brokering shipments from Colombia's M-19 terrorists, investing in an opium factory of his own, and smuggling proscribed high-tech items to Cuba and Eastern Europe.

All this came to light in a remarkable story by Seymour M. Hersh in *The New York Times* last week. Hersh's own authority was buttressed at every turn by quotations from officials at the State Department, the White House, the Defense Intelligence Agency, the National Security Agency and the Central Intelligence Agency.

The signal was all the more pointed because Noriega was visiting in Washington when the story broke. "It's precisely because we have long-term strategic interests in Panama, with the canal, that it's important to have reliable people to deal with," a senior American diplomat told Hersh, who reported in the next sentence that National Security Adviser John M. Poindexter had been wondering aloud about alternatives to the wayward general.

As a symptom of burgeoning dissatisfaction with the government of Panama, the news story represents the latest step in an American campaign against bank secrecy of all sorts. For an administration often billed as being laissez faire to a fault, the enforcement establishment under Ronald Reagan has built a fairly striking record of prosecuting tax evasion (Marc Rich); egregious cash management practices (E.F. Hutton); money laundering

(Bank of Boston et al.); insider trading (Dennis Levine); and high-tech smuggling (Richard Mueller's Digital Equipment franchise in the Soviet Union and Eastern Europe)—to name only the most celebrated cases of the 1980s.

But the new wave of enforcement is not putting the money-launderers out of business, according to economist Ingo Walter; it is making them more inventive and more vigilant instead. "The demand for secret money vehicles and the willingness to pay for them will remain strong and perhaps grow," Walter writes.

Walter is a German finance professor with a substantial international consulting practice who now teaches at New York University. In the recently- published *Secret Money*, he surveys the illegal cash industry and finds it booming—despite tougher and more sophisticated enforcement. The book can be tough-going for the layman, particularily a chapter on the theory of secret finance. But there are enough war stories and anecdotes to keep the reader going, especially since the book is a systematic attempt to fit wrongdoing into an overall scheme of things.

Like any good economist, Walter divides the world into buyers and sellers of secrecy. The most commonly thought of demand arises from smugglers and drug peddlers, he says, but it does not stop there. "The tax evader skimming unreported income into an offshore account; the briber shuffling funds to the bribee; the violator of the securities laws squirreling away illegal profits; the insecure politician or government official building a retirement fund abroad; the businessman fleeing his creditors; the husband fleeing his wife; the law-abiding citizen fleeing exposure to political or economic risk. All are players in the global financial secrecy game," he writes.

Against this background of willing and sometimes desperate customers, Walter describes a well-differentiated variety of products, offered by shadowy bankers, lawyers and government officials in the tax and banking havens of the world. There are big commercial banks that denounce Latin American countries for permitting their loans to be recycled into numbered bank accounts in Europe—while quietly soliciting flight capital themselves. There are black-market currency brokers who offer elaborate currency transactions designed to move blocked money into dollars; real estate brokers who arrange swaps; businessmen who help out their foreign suppliers with phony invoices; helpful bankers who wire money through intricate nests of shell corporations in Liechtenstein and the Dutch Antilles.

"Like the automobile market with its Subarus, Nissans, Chevrolets, Buicks, Volvos, BMWs, Jaguars, Mercedes Benzes and Rolls Royces, there are different products for different needs," he writes. "Competition is severe and the choice is sufficiently wide."

Walter is especially illuminating on the problems of making good on profits reaped from inside knowledge, and the steady erosion of the Swiss banking laws. A numbered account in Geneva or Lugano does not confer the sort of anonymity under pressure that it used to. He identifies the St. Joe Minerals Corp. case as the dominant recent landmark: When financier Giuseppe B. Tome bought heavily on the knowledge that his friend Edgar Bronfman's Seagram Corp. was about to go after St. Joe, the Securities and Exchange Commission went after Tome, starting within days of the deal. It got him, too, after a U.S. judge threatened to fine a Swiss bank $50,000 a day unless it named the customer for whom it was trading. (Faced with the seizure of its U.S. assets, the Banca della Svizera Italiana somehow persuaded Tome to turn himself in to the SEC, according to an account of the affair by Bruce Ingersoll in the *Wall Street Journal* last week.)

What about the Bank of Boston affair last year? Walter dismisses the suggestion that the bank ever had much to do with international secret money—apart from accepting shopping bags full of crumpled bills from the Angiulo family for deposit at its North End branch. The government contended that the bank's failure to report big cash shipments to Switzerland must have been willful; he notes that the contention took a beating when C. Todd Conover, the comptroller of the currency, admitted that his regulators, too, had misunderstood the very law they were supposed to enforce— and had failed to require the reports during a special investigation of the bank. And he writes that most of the violations discovered at Bank of Boston and at dozens of other banks across the country were reporting errors and not instances of money laundering.

But he observes that the process of trial-by-headline got bankers' attention most thoroughly. "U.S. banks appear to be increasing internal controls to guard against money laundering. . . . Training programs teach tellers to identify launderers. New policies make cashiers checks available to regular customers only. Data processing software has become available that produces daily lists of accounts with cash transactions of more than $10,000," he writes.

Walter believes that the secret money business is going to continue into the future, the advent of minicomputers notwithstanding—especially when it comes to flight capital from unstable nations. He concludes: "While crackdowns on secret money that are unambiguously criminal in nature can expect at least some degree of international cooperation and even coordination, flows related to politically motivated activities cannot. . . . Unless one is able to predict a golden age of domestic and international political tranquility, this source of the demand for secret money will continue to be a vibrant one indeed."

JUNE 15, 1986

Wall Street: An Oral History

WITH THE DOW JONES INDUSTRIAL AVERAGE AT 2,500, AN ASTONISHING 30 PERCENT increase over its 1986 close, it is worth reflecting on the transformation in both the global financial system and the underlying world economy that is behind its long-term rise. Twenty years ago, Lyndon Johnson was in the White House, the United States was in Vietnam, the Dow was at 800, passbook savings accounts were paying 5 percent, and inflation was at 3 percent and rising. Boston was a city at the end of a long decline, the nations of the world were tubs pretty much on their own financial bottoms. Wall Street was the same sort of white-shoe club it had been since Alexander Hamilton was secretary of the Treasury.

Today, a booming city of Boston is aggressively borrowing in the Euromarkets to transform the last of its dusty neighborhoods, corporate America has had a shaking it never anticipated, and Wall Street—along with Tokyo, Singapore, London and Chicago—has been transformed from a sleepy village enterprise to a powerful engine of change. This financial revolution stems partly from a fundamental deregulation whose roots are in the 1960s, partly from a wave of innovation and integration that began in the 1970s, and it affects everyone. If you want a guide to meditate on what has happened, you might have a look at the 20th anniversary issue of *Institutional Investor* magazine.

II is a fan magazine for money managers. It was started by a New School for Social Research graduate student, Gilbert Kaplan. Among his original investors were Gerald Bronfman, money manager Peter Bernstein and Robert Heilbroner, the economist. His first editor was George Goodman, a/k/a Adam Smith. *II* proved to be a gusher: Kaplan sold it to the public in 1969 at about $13 a share, then bought it back a few years later at around $3 a share (Oppenheimer's Leon Levy called it the greatest short sale he had ever seen) and finally sold it again in 1984, this time to Capital Cities Communications Inc. for a price rumored to be about $50 million. Kaplan now spends much of his time hiring orchestras that will permit him to conduct Mahler's Second ("Resurrection") Symphony, which he reveres, but with his veteran editor Peter Landau he continues to run *II*, and having all that money has given him an ever-improving window on the way professional money managers operate. The magazine has remained a model of the sort—quick, hip, irreverent, enthusiastic and usually on the money. Its biggest failure, perhaps, was its extreme lethargy on the insider trading scandal until its proportions were clear to all.

To celebrate the 20th anniversary of its founding, *Institutional Investor* put together an "oral history" of the last 20 years, the sort of project in which Studs Terkel pioneered. In its fat June issue, 80 money men and two money women (Muriel Siebert, a stockbroker, and Brenda Gall, an apparel and household products analyst for Merrill Lynch) reminisce about the way it was—along with a couple of beat cops from Wall Street, three neighborhood clergymen and a newspaper reporter, Dan Dorfman. These rambling narratives, composed about equally of war stories and moralizing, are somehow far more interesting than had their stories been strung together by a hack. They are separated by handsome black and white photographs of the principals, too—good art has always been a key *II* gimmick. The combination makes for fascinating reading.

For example, there's Walter Wriston shedding light on the way big bankers make their decisions—in his case, the bank's consumer strategy. "We began by looking at the fundamentals, and that was that demand deposits of the clearinghouse banks in New York didn't increase for 10 years in nominal terms. You don't have to be too bright to know that with the nominal GNP increasing in nominal terms every year, we're out of the ball game. So the CD certificate of deposit was invented and gave the clearinghouse banks another couple of years of life. But there's a finite limit to everything. And the next thing was holding companies issuing commercial paper. That gave them another 10 years of life. What do you do after that? The answer is you go, as Willie Sutton said, where the money is. And the money is in the consumer's pocket."

Or there is Bernie Cornfeld, whose International Overseas Services failed and became a byword for the overripe market of the late 1960s, musing on how he would like to get back into the mutual fund business today. "God, I miss Ed Cowett who died in the mid-1970s. When we drove somewhere together, we'd sing in harmony. He had a beautiful voice; he had wanted to be a cantor. We were complementary. I need someone like him to get this thing off the ground."

Eugene Rotberg, associate director of the tradings and market division of the Securities and Exchange Commission, who put in motion the reports that led to the famous "Mayday" deregulation of fixed commissions on Wall Street in 1974, reflects, "We basically were not comfortable with regulation; we didn't trust how it could be turned or corrupted." With Manny Cohen and Irving Pollack as commissioners, he describes how the SEC staff took apart the antitrust exemption of the securities industry and put the industry on a highly competitive footing—before he left to become treasurer of the World Bank.

Edward Johnson 3d, the man who has built the modern mutual fund powerhouse that is Fidelity Management and Research Corp., recounts some of the details of his struggles with fund manager Jerry Tsai for "Mister Johnson's" affections in the mid-1960s. John Neff, of Wellington Management/Thorndike, Doran Paine & Lewis, describes the life of a fund manager amid the fads and fripperies of the 1970s. Dean LeBaron of Batterymarch Financial Management describes the early days of program trading, when the significance of the computer to the market was dawning.

Felix Rohatyn of Lazard Freres & Co., never slow to offer to shoulder responsibility for anything, claims he undertook to salvage New York City's finances simply in order to escape jury duty. John Loeb, former senior parter at Loeb, Rhoades & Co., expresses the old order's distaste for the new: "The fees paid now for so-called investment banking are obscene." Frederick Whittmore, long-time head of syndications for Morgan Stanley, takes a more balanced view: "I like the idea that the firms today are strong, and that they're more diverse. . . . But the old business was a fun business. It had a different origin, function and style. Life was simpler. You could shout and yell at each other. You could win or lose . . . I had a chance to shape things and to play a role that would be hard to define in today's world—it doesn't exist. But on the other hand, as a business, and as a productive business, we're better than we used to be."

The idea for the oral history issue came from *II* managing editor Cary Reich, himself a gifted journalist who wrote the book on Andre Meyer, perhaps the ultimate financier. And certainly the level of talk in the magazine presupposes a certain familiarity with Wall Street for full enjoyment. But the *II* issue shows how fascinating the talk of very competent people can be to the layman, no matter what the field. And if the underlying theme

of the project is a satisfaction—mixed with amazement—at the metamorphosis the financial system has undergone, there is also a certain persistent
sense that the boom times won't last forever.

Paul Miller, one of Philadelphia's most celebrated money men, puts it
this way: "I think Wall Street is in for a come-uppance beyond the insider
trading thing, maybe the next time the market turns down. Money is simply
not as easy to make as it has been. And if it is for this small group of people,
then there's something very wrong with the system."

JULY 19, 1987

Where Ignorant Armies Trade by Night

SO WHAT DOES THE STOCK MARKET KNOW AND HOW DOES IT KNOW IT? ON THE NEWS
that George Bush had won the American election, U.S. share prices
abruptly tumbled. Because a Bush victory was widely forecast, something
else must have happened.

Like what?

The behavior of markets in response to news has been a feverish topic
among economists and money men since the October crash in 1987.

For more than 25 years, the stock market has been said by many of its
students to be "efficient," that is, to so quickly assimilate whatever is
known about the prospects for the future that it is always "right." The crash
torpedoed the strictest version of this hypothesis, because it was itself
unforeseen.

In the absence of some dominating piece of news, in other words, the
market can't be absolutely "right" about fundamental values when between
Monday morning and Tuesday afternoon it lost something like $1 trillion.
It may have been right one day or the other, but not both. Any number of
pundits, therefore, have announced the death of efficient markets hypothesis in the wake of the crash.

A modification of the hypothesis has been suggested recently by Stewart
Myers, an MIT professor who is one of the bright lights of the efficient
markets movement. Speaking at *Institutional Investor's* Money Management

forum, Myers proposed the idea that people grope around in wide band for the right level of prices.

Instead of absolute efficiency, where everyone who can afford a newspaper stock table knows the exact level of appropriate prices, Myers proposed the notion of "fuzzy efficiency," in which no one holds a confident, exact opinion on the exact level of prices.

Fuzzy efficiency strikes at some of the more mechanical interpretations of efficient markets, Myers said, but preserves most of the important parts, especially as they relate to investment techniques.

According to Myers, modern finance does best when calculating relative prices—the appropriate price of Ford in relation to GM, of corporate bonds to T-bills, of options and futures to the underlying securities they represent. Hence the ubiquity of the capital asset pricing models of the sort that triggered the mad dash for the door in October a year ago.

But finance theory has little purchase on the question of the absolute level of the stock market, relative to the operation of the real economy, he says. The standard tool of discounted cash flow valuation modeling is old and crude; investors' expected rates of return are hard to pin down, economic uncertainty is great.

In the absence of some sure-fire reality checks, markets tend to take yesterday's prices as the correct ones, marking them up or down accordingly, based on today's news. As long as new information arrives smoothly, it doesn't trigger large discontinuous changes in fundamentals or in risk preferences, and as time passes, investors will become more and more confident that they are in the right place.

But let investors begin to lose confidence in the benchmark of yesterday's price, and a period of confused trading may set in, making for volatile times until a new benchmark is agreed upon. The new benchmark will be somewhere in a fuzzy band of possible prices, Myers says—but even after it's found, there may be random departures from it until the market again settles down to the normal process of day to day updating.

A story of the crash that fits this vision of fuzzy efficiency? Myers says, "Some important investors decided that prices were too high relative to their fuzzy estimates of fundamental values. Other investors, seeing the pessimistic fundamentalists depart, lacking confidence in their own more optimistic estimates of fundamental value, and facing unusual macroeconomic uncertainty, decided to exit. Then in the resulting confusion, the market had to grope for a new benchmark.

"In this story there is no simple speculative bubble, in which investors know the market is fundamentally overvalued, but, nevertheless, hold on, hoping to play the game just a bit longer. Even with a year's hindsight, it's not really clear whether the market was too high at the start of October 1987 or too low at the end. It was much less obvious at the time.

"Moreover, the story does not imply that the institutional portfolio managers who rushed from the exit were acting on psychological or irrational motives. Their personal rewards largely depend on the amount of money allocated to them to manage. Their clients' allocations largely depend on their performance relative to other managers. If prices are likely to fall, and intrinsic value is unclear, the rational action may be to try to get out first," Myers concludes.

Myers' fuzzy efficiency is a welcome departure from the hyperconfident insistence of efficient market theorists in the past that each days' prices are the best of all possible worlds, and for a number of reasons. For one thing, it prepares investors for occasional sharp, discontinuous shifts in prices as plates of opinion change. For another, it zeroes in on the problem of how expectations are formed—and changed. If it seems a little remote, just remember that truth emerges more readily from error than from confusion.

NOVEMBER 10, 1988

A Graduate School for Little Capitalists

CHICAGO—WHAT IS IT THAT IS SO FASCINATING TO SO MANY PEOPLE ABOUT INVESTING? Not just the money, surely, not after it starts to mount up. After a while, the kick of getting and spending is no longer enough to account for the long hours that intelligent people spend trying to beat the market. The pleasures of money management seem to stem from the sense of making judgments of the world, day in, day out; changing them or standing fast; and being sustained or reversed by subsequent events. For many people, this has all the satisfactions and frustrations of a part-time job. Almost incidentally, these investors serve as small but key cogs in the global development machine.

The job has become a good deal more complicated recently. The simple old world of certificates of deposit, a couple of mutual funds and the occasional bond is defunct. The new world includes everything from a dozen stock markets around the world to bond funds to mortgage-backed securities to index funds and a galaxy of life insurance products. The change has tossed up a wondrously diverse menu of instruction and advice for sale, running from the relatively expensive services of financial planners ($1,000 a year and up for a good one) to do-it-yourself advice from business magazines to newsletters—not to mention the constant stream of banter from brokers who sell particular instruments for a living.

From whatever vantage point, there is a constant emphasis on instruction and self-improvement: *Forbes*, it's been said, is a magazine about the big greedy for the little greedy; *Institutional Investor* is described as a fan magazine for money men. Time Inc.'s *Money* magazine is perhaps the most frankly investor-oriented of the lot: it spends more time than any other explaining how particular investments work. But as good as each is in its way, all are couched in the fleeting idiom of the news. Is there anything in between the mags and a cumbersome MBA program for those who want to know more about investing?

For a long time, the National Association of Investment Clubs was the mainstay of groups who band together for mutual support and instruction. These range from tiny homegrown mutual funds operated by Midwestern school teachers whose hobby is debating stock prospects, to relatively high-powered aggregations of "doctor money" put together by money management pros; the NAIC explores these groups' common concerns through a variety of educational services. For the last few years of the bull market, however, a new organization has been making headway, pitched to a slightly higher level of sophistication than the investment clubs and aimed at the person who wants to manage his own assets. The American Association of Individual Investors, headquartered in Chicago, is the rough equivalent of a graduate school for little capitalists.

Founded by James B. Cloonan, the AAII was designed to provide disinterested and well-informed advice to the self-reliant investor. A finance professor at DePaul University (with a University of Chicago MBA and a Northwestern marketing PhD), Cloonan had been an options trader and securities firm partner before starting the group in 1979 as a part-time flyer. When association membership soared with the stock and bond markets in 1982, he hired fellow professors to turn out a steady stream of journal articles and research; today some 10 professionals operate in tightly-packed offices above a Chinese restaurant on fashionable North Michigan Avenue in Chicago.

After eight years in the business, Cloonan, 56, is well on his way to becoming an examplar of a species that is to be found somewhere or other in most specialized fields: the arbiter, the czar deputized by the league, the incorruptible man who keeps track of the competing claims of marketers in an attempt to enforce (without any very overwhelming success) certain standards of honesty.

Today, Cloonan's association has 108,000 members. Some 40 percent of them have graduate degrees, he says; their median income is $70,000; their median portfolio is $177,000, but the variance is great. They are organized in chapters across the country—with a strict rule that no sales pitches by members are allowed at meetings. Barely 25 percent of the membership goes to meetings, anyway; the rest do their studying at home, starting with the journal that the association publishes 10 times a year, as well as an investment software guide and an annual mutual fund performance guide that is more complete than those published by *Forbes* or *Money*. There are 50 all-day seminars in different cities around the country, too, teaching everything from investment fundamentals to the fine points of real estate investment and portfolio analysis, and an annual meeting in Boston in June this year. Annual dues are $48; there is no advertising in the journal. A couple of direct mail solicitations annually are enough to keep membership growing slightly.

"We lose about half of all our new subscribers after the first year," says Cloonan. "I think we are a little like a health club, in that people make a resolution, then find they can't stick with the program." The journal articles tell the story. They tackle tougher subjects more nearly straight on than, say, *Money* magazine; they are written far more simply and clearly than treatments of similar topics in the *Journal of Portfolio Management* or the *Financial Analysts Journal*.

The articles often exhibit a certain academic grounding in modern finance theory, but they display a solid practical emphasis on explanation as well. For example: Why stock splits work as they do (capital gains differentials in the old tax law). Why mutual fund timing series aren't worth the cost (their claims are often greatly overstated). Why sector mutual funds are a waste of money (you can do it yourself more cheaply.) Why you don't need whole life insurance (it's too confusing). Why rating services don't tell you much about the likelihood of bond defaults (investment grade bonds, those rated Baa or better, hardly ever default). Why you'll never get a hot new issue (big customers of the underwriters get in first). Obviously, such debunking flies in the face of a lot of hype.

As you'd expect, the AAII is firmly oriented toward fundamental analysis and the idea that smart investors can spot bargains before others; there is not much time spent on technical analysis or attempts to assess "market psychology." There is a great deal of emphasis on diversification, and constant reference to modern portfolio theory. A key concept is a list of "shadow stocks," out-of-the-spotlight little public companies that are too small to be of much interest to professional analysts or the press. These often outperform the market, according to John Markese, director of research at AAII; doing really well is a matter of screening out the right stocks from the list.

Cloonan says he used to worry a lot about regulation, and figured that more lobbying on Capitol Hill was the answer. "I hate to see the public ripped off by some of the sleazy outfits that are around. But now I figure that more and better education is a better bet. Besides, it's a lot of fun teaching motivated adults who don't ask if they have to know this or that for the final exam."

APRIL 26, 1987

When 2 + 2 = 3

JUST BECAUSE YOU CAN THINK OF IT DOESN'T MEAN YOU HAVE TO DO IT—OR EVEN THAT it will work if you try.

That's the inescapable moral of Michael Porter's study of the 30-year record of big American corporate mergers, acquisitions, joint ventures and start-ups. The dominant strategic fad of the 1960s and the 1970s—diversification—almost never worked out as promised, he concludes.

Porter, 40, a Harvard Business School professor, is perhaps the world's foremost student of corporate strategy, having created the kind of niche that Peter Drucker occupied in an earlier age, more analytic and empirical, less avuncular than the old Austrian giant. Porter's findings are published in the current *Harvard Business Review*.

"The track record of corporate strategies has been dismal," he writes. "I studied the diversification records of 33 large, prestigious U.S. companies over the 1950–1986 period and found that most of them had divested far more acquisitions than they had kept. The corporate strategies of most companies have dissipated instead of created shareholder value."

Why has the 20-year binge of companies buying other companies occurred? Well, all sorts of reasons have been offered, some of them good. The classic rationale for diversification is to "get more legs on the stool," to smooth out the cyclicality of one particular business by complementing its profits with those of another company in a different cycle. Another often-heard management ambition is to search out inter-relationships between businesses and exploit them, the famous "2 + 2 = 5" or "synergy" of the 1960s.

Another justification is the supposedly superior ability of professional managers to spot bargains. Porter suspects that most deals have been done by bosses hungry for growth in an inflationary era, who "confused company size with shareholder value."

Time and again, corporate insiders have told of the terrific sense of power that develops in the vortex of the high-priced deal. With the fever fanned by investment bankers, consultants, lawyers and press agents, it is no wonder that bouts of takeoveritis are as common as flu.

Sometimes this is well intentioned. Among the big diversifiers, no one has been more serious and decent than Raytheon in Lexington. It places near the top in Porter's survey, along with Johnson & Johnson and Procter & Gamble, among those who kept the businesses they bought and made a go of them. But from Badger to Beech, successful acquisitions have been the exception at Raytheon rather than the rule.

And when the acquirer is less temperate, the spectacle can be grandiose. Everybody remembers William Agee and Mary Cunningham as the foremost exemplars of the hostile takeover as a form of erotic art. But the same drama has been acted out on a smaller scale at a more private level all the time. Dorman Commons, former chief executive of Natomas Corp., spelled out in gripping detail in *Tender Offer: The Sneak Attack in Corporate Takeovers* the experience of being acquired by a determined opposition. The argument that such hostile takeovers enhance the aggregate income of the nation was accurate only in the shortest of short terms, he wrote.

The worst press has been reserved for comic-strip conglomerateurs: Harold Geneen, for example, with his traveling trunks of data. And Porter writes, "Supervising dozens or even hundreds of disparate units and under chainletter pressure to add more, management begins to make mistakes" of this "management by the numbers" school. The story is almost always the same, he says: Costs mount up; return on investment deteriorates; eventually a new team comes in to sell off all the jazz and return the company to its core businesses. Gulf & Western, Consolidated Foods (now Sara Lee) and ITT are just a few comparatively recent examples, he says.

But Porter's study found those with relatively good names in the business press were among the top divestors and hence the worst diversifiers: CBS, RCA and Cummins Engine all sold off more than 80 percent of the companies they bought, he found. Xerox, Westinghouse, General Electric and W.R. Grace all divested 65 percent or more.

Sharing know-how or related activities such as the distribution chain seemed to be key to successful diversification, Porter found, but no guarantee—and going far afield from the company's core business is just asking for trouble. Even IBM seemed to stumble when it got outside its area, he noted. And even when the integration is in what is broadly speaking the same industry, as with the ill-fated would-be travel conglomerate Allegis Corp., it is likely to misfire.

Indeed, the kindest words Porter has are for the kind of restructuring tactic that has been demonstrated with great success by Laurence Tisch of Loew's Corp. and Richard Smith of General Cinema. He singles out Britain's dreaded Hanson Trust as possibly the most successful evaluator of the corporate halt and lame: Ever Ready Batteries, London Brick, SCM Corp. and Courage Breweries all benefited from their purchase by the Terrible Trust. Nor does restructuring have to come from the outside; Procter & Gamble last week reserved $800 million in the current quarter for weeding out and cleaning up its worldwide manufacturing operations. Managers should let shareholders do the diversifying, Porter says; let executives pay dividends and don't use tax rules for smokescreen.

And for diversifications that really need to be done? Porter proposes three tests. The industry chosen for diversification should be structurally attractive, or capable of being made so. The cost-of-entry should not capitalize all future profits. And the new unit, or the acquiring company, should be made better off by the deal. Porter doesn't go as far as business consultant Milt Lauenstein in proposing that boards of directors take over governance of corporations from executives—but the thrust is the same. Managers should pay more attention to building their businesses and getting results.

Porter's message has been getting plenty of attention in corporate circles; indeed, it has been gospel among the best companies now for several years. This doesn't mean that a good company will never again be chewed up and spit out by an absentee landlord, but this much is clear: Corporate strategy has come a long way from the days when dogs, cash cows and stars were all you needed to smash a multimillion-dollar business.

JUNE 14, 1987

Buy This Junk Bond! Don't Break the Chain!

RECESSIONS START IN THE NEWSPAPERS—OR RATHER IN THE PHONE CALLS, THE unadvertised little meetings, the hurried hallway consultations, the stacked-up message slips that precede the newspaper stories. In his classic study *Manias, Panics and Crashes*, Charles P. Kindleberger noted that the spark can be almost anything: a bankruptcy, a suicide, a flight, a refusal of credit, some change in views that causes a serious actor to unload a big position; anything that "snaps the confidence of the system, makes people think of the dangers of failure, and leads them to move from commodities, stocks, real estate, bills of exchange, promissory notes, foreign exchange—whatever it may be—back into cash."

There was a jolt of this sort—not enough to cause a recession presumably, but enough to remind you what it is like to be in the presence of surprising and unpleasant news—last week when a 21-page paper by a Harvard Business School trio made it out of the seminar and the conference rooms of Chicago and New York into the world. It is hard to believe that a few pages of lucid writing with a couple dozen tables at the end could have such an effect.

But there is some reason to think that a study by Paul Asquith, David W. Mullins, Jr., and Eric D. Wolff did what the indictment of Michael Milken earlier didn't—put the junk bond market into a nosedive, causing several billion dollars in value to evaporate from the surface of the $180 billion market in a few days of trading last week—merely by persuasively suggesting that the real rate of default on junk bonds was as much as 10 or 15 times higher than previously had been thought.

Other factors were at work in the junk-bond market as well, including disappointment over the Eastern Airlines debacle, the specter of an enormous crop of bonds coming to market next week, another spate of rumors about the government's case against the men who made the market, and a general fear of the effect of a recession on highly leveraged borrowers.

But even a day of economic news on Friday that included just about everything that a devotee of the "soft landing" school of no recession could hope to hear wasn't enough to prevent the junk-bond gloom from spreading to institutional portfolio managers, who began pulling out of junk-bond mutual funds, even as stocks and the rest of the bond market rallied.

Until Monday of last week, analyses of the market for high-yield or "junk" bonds nearly always rested on the contention that the undertakings financed by Mike Milken's wonderful borrowing machine—the leveraged buyouts, expansions of fast-growing smaller companies, and corporate takeovers—had a remarkably good record for paying off. The issuers of junk bonds paid higher rates than the blue chip corporate borrowers to whom the credit market had been limited in the past, but their bonds didn't seem to be much riskier than those of investment grade, at least not in comparison to their higher coupon rates. Edward Altman, a New York University professor whose work has been cited more often than any other authority, had calculated that between 1970 and 1985, the default rate on junk bonds never was higher than 2.1 percent. Several other estimates fell in the same range.

Enter Paul Asquith, a 10-year veteran Harvard Business School finance professor with an ultra-sharp Chicago PhD. Along with co-author David W. Mullins (now on leave from Harvard while an assistant secretary of the Treasury) and research assistant Eric D. Wolff (now a Justice Department official), Asquith set out 18 months ago to discover whether the incidence of forced exchanges among junk bonds—essentially work-out situations for companies in trouble—made any difference when it was factored into the failure rate along with outright defaults. It did, though the effect wasn't large. They also found that call provisions tended to work in the issuers' favor to an unrecognized extent—if a company improved its credit rating, it called in its high-yield IOUs and refinanced its debt on more favorable terms.

But before very long, Asquith & Co., had stumbled onto a fascinating wrinkle—that the junk-bond market was growing so explosively that, for all intents and purposes, ordinary calculations of the default rate amounted to a kind of pyramid scheme, in which the new money coming into the game was enough to disguise the effect of old money leaving—as long as the flow kept growing. It all had to do with the choice of denominator.

Most calculations simply took the number of defaults in a given year and divided it by the number of bonds outstanding, Asquith found. But most companies didn't run into trouble right away—indeed, the average default lay 3½ or 4 years in the future. With the market growing so fast that a majority of bonds are only one or two years old, naturally calculations were skewed by the fact that the new borrowers simply hadn't had time to become stretched too tight. Once he built some considerations of the aging of bonds into his calculations, Asquith discovered the default rate climbed sharply for bonds that had been around a while.

For example, a buy-and-hold investor who purchased a portfolio of all the high-yield bonds issued in 1977 and 1978 would have experienced a default rate of 34 percent by the end of 1988. For bonds issued between 1979 and 1983, the default rate was between 19 percent and 26 percent—so far. But bonds issued between 1984 and 1986 had default rates between 4 and 9 percent, Asquith found. Either the quality of debt had been improving handsomely with experience—or else young bonds have low default rates.

But even if it is much higher than previously was thought, the risk of default on junk bonds is only part of the story. What's missing is the rate of return. "We don't know really whether junk bonds right now are a good investment or a bad investment," says Asquith. "Obviously, the defaults are going to hurt returns somewhat. Whether they're going to hurt them enough that the yields on junks don't compensate for the risks, I'll be able to tell you in about eight to 10 months." Meanwhile, institutional money managers, who will be judged by the risk-adjusted rate of return that they earn for investors, will be making table-cloth calculations of their own, deciding whether junk-bond prices should go up or down.

Whatever the story turns out to be, it may well be that the release of study of defaults will come to be seen in time as one of the Harvard Business School's finest hours. Most of the research previously done on junk-bond performance has been only a few steps up from the sales brochure—perhaps not surprising in a market that has been growing as if touched by celestial fire. Some of the obscurity surrounding junk bond performance owes to the difficulty of getting data in the first place: unlike stock trades, bond prices aren't publicly disclosed; thus researchers depend on the willingness to cooperate of the big bond dealers who together make the markets.

And doubtless some of the murk owes to the fact that much of the academic work undertaken previously was sponsored by the firms who were growing rich underwriting the bonds. Truly, it is staggering that the analysis of the aging of junk bonds did not come into play until now.

The striking thing about the bad news that emanated from the Harvard Business School last week is that nobody in the industry wanted to hear it: not the issuers of bonds, not underwriters of bonds, nor the people who own the paper. The only people who might eventually thank the researchers for their trouble are those investors who might buy junk bonds in the future—and, of course, people interested in a general way about the soundness of the system.

APRIL 16, 1989

Weird Economics

MORNING COFFEE AT THE SANTA FE INSTITUTE: MEMBERS ARE CHUCKLING AND shaking their heads at the photographs that have appeared in the national newspapers of the Biosphere group, who have sealed themselves up in an airtight, plant-filled greenhouse with some monkeys, hummingbirds and worms in the desert in Arizona, the next state over.

The Santa Fe scientists are laughing, with good reason, at the chutzpah of the Arizona "Biospherians," who plan to charge visitors $9.50 apiece for a look at their digs. They are smiling at the Star Trek suits, at the tittering over the prospects for sex under the dome, at the dubious scientific quality of much of the work. (A big power line into the project defeats some of its point, they say.) But the New Mexicans are a little jealous, too. At $150 million, the Biosphere project is lavishly funded; Edward P. Bass of the Texas oil family is among its patrons.

In contrast, the Santa Fe Institute is getting by on a shoestring. Its scientists, too, have an artificial world, or rather a host of them, but it is a computer simulation of the real world—of an economy, or an ecosystem—that they are building, an "adaptive system" built from the ground up with techniques including genetic algorithms and object-oriented programming—more of a plan for a model than a model itself.

They have a long list of meetings scheduled—meetings whose invitation list includes some of the smartest, most restless people in the social sciences. But they have no very good place to gather, even when staffers are among themselves. Having lost the lease on the picturesque church on Santa Fe's fashionable Canyon Road where they spent their first few years, they are ensconced in a suite of rooms in an undistinguished office complex on the edge of town.

The Santa Fe Institute was founded in 1984 by a group of underemployed scientists from nearby Los Alamos, the lab where the atomic bomb was invented. George Cowan, a physicist, was its president; Robert Anderson, an oil financier and long-time organizer of the Aspen Institute, was its chairman. The idea was to provide a workshop where senior physicists, mathematicians, economists, computer scientists and biologists could mix and mingle, to talk about the newest developments in their fields, which were presumed somehow to be converging at a hectic pace. Nearly everyone wanted to come to Santa Fe for a week or two now and then, after all.

The institute got a boost in 1986 when chairman John Reed of Citibank poured in some money. David Rockefeller came to call—and left. The think-tank seems to have settled somewhere between the old Rockefeller Institute (the original model for its aspirations) and the unnamed, still-lamented Washington, D.C., institution in the social sciences whose plan collapsed when lawyer Thurman Arnold and psychiatrist Harry Stack Sullivan were unable to agree about who would get the corner office. Today, it's getting by on $1 million or so a year. "We would at least like to get an endowment for building and a permanent staff," says Kenneth Arrow of Stanford University, a prominent member of the board who is a Nobel laureate in economics.

Some of the candidates for this scientific swap-meet were an obvious fit: new developments in the analysis of time series, for instance. But the ambitions of the institute go far beyond comparing notes on methods of statistical inference. At its heart is excitement over "chaos theory," a still emerging field that promises to find order underneath behavior that would otherwise seem merely random: the turbulence of the atmosphere, a dripping faucet, perhaps the stock market. It would, of course, be no small achievement to replace celestial mechanics with the image of the weather as the central metaphor undergirding our understanding of how markets work. But it remains to be seen just how this might be done.

Certainly this is an area known to be susceptible to impenetrable fads. The applicability of "general systems theory" of Ludwig Bertalanffy proved to be something of a disappointment in the 1950s; so did "catastrophe theory" of Rene Thom in the 1970s—though each generated substantial newspaper ink. Nevertheless, the story of non-linear dynamics is of widespread interest to scientists; James Gleick's book *Chaos: Making a New Science* is still a great place to start.

A meeting last month devoted to the growth of cities was typical, if not an especially successful specimen of the type. Paul Bairoch, a distinguished Swiss historian set the tone; economists told what they knew. Institute types groused that there was not enough talk about self-organizing criticality, one of the concepts that supposedly lies at the heart of the new science. "Myself, I'm self-critical and disorganized," cracked economist Paul Krugman.

As Arrow's presence suggests, these are not marginal people. Three other Nobel laureates are involved, including physicist Philip Anderson. The people they have brought in to conduct programs are consistently interesting: Michigan's John Holland, Yale's Martin Shubik, Wisconsin's William (Buz) Brock, Harvard's Richard Herrnstein, Chicago's Jose Scheinkman, Minnesota's David Lane, Illinois' David Pines, Stanford's Brian Arthur. Thanks to John Geanakoplos of Yale, who is also head of fixed income research at Kidder, Peabody & Co., the institute's links to Wall Street's leading "quants" are real enough.

But the work of the institute itself hasn't exactly taken hold, except in the pages of *Scientific American*. Despite talk about "the Santa Fe approach," its publications record does not yet seem very remarkable. Staffers talk as if they were on the brink of some great breakthrough—but they haven't yet written it down. Backers wonder aloud if its looming program for computational social science doesn't somehow resemble "systems dynamics"—another project from the 1950s of noble scope and ambition that has failed to be widely adopted beyond MIT. Even support for the national laboratories, including Los Alamos, is fading.

So now the Santa Fe Institute is branching out into other ventures, in hopes of finding for the think-tank an independent income. There are plans to develop software for sale, for example. The legendary physicist J. Doyne Farmer, former group leader in complex systems at Los Alamos, who was among the institute's earliest members, has started a company, Prediction Co., designed to play high-powered markets in currencies, bonds, equities. The institute is hoping he strikes it rich.

Farmer is best remembered as the hero of *The Eudaemonic Pie* by Thomas Bass, a high-spirited chronicle of a group of hippie scientists and computer hackers who dreamed of breaking the bank at Las Vegas by predicting the motions of a ball in a roulette wheel—with the help of a computer chip concealed in the heel of a shoe. After many adventures, they gave up. They were $7,000 ahead of the game—but a very good deal more famous.

OCTOBER 6, 1991

Building a New Zoo

FOR UNDERSTANDING THE SPECTACLE OF THE GREAT FINANCIAL RESTRUCTURING THAT is reaching a frantic pace this summer in Washington, perhaps the most useful metaphor is the one created by Albert N. Wojnilower, the canny Wall Street economist. As recently as the 1960s, Wojnilower says, the American financial system had been like a well-ordered zoo. Different species of financial institutions were in different cages.

Here were the banks, there the securities dealers, over there the insurance companies, mutal fund managers, credit card companies and so forth. All were separated from one another functionally by the Glass-Steagall Act and geographically by the McFadden Act.

The cages were all overpopulated and competitive, at least in a narrow sense: One company occasionally swallowed another. But careful zoo-keeping preserved the pecking order in each cage. In general, the animals got enough to eat.

Now the government is about to let the animals out of the cages, with orders to eat or be eaten.

Not that this "decompartmentalization" of finance can be avoided much longer—global competition and the advent of the computer have assured that massive change must come. Rather, the necessary restructuring can be accomplished well or poorly. The cages of the old zoo are coming down, no matter what.

Something of a preview of just how badly a partial perestroika can go was afforded when the Reagan administration "deregulated" the thrift institutions in the early 1980s, while Congress simultaneously resisted any consolidation of the savings and loan associations and savings banks.

"Pushing house cats into the jungle is not liberation but murder," says Wojnilower.

The zoo keeper, in the most recent case, is the Bush administration's Treasury Department, which has drafted an extensive plan for redrawing the regulatory map. What the president's men have proposed, Congress now will dispose. The collective task is to set several vast industries, long kept apart, loose on unfamiliar terrain.

The aim is—or should be—not so much no zoo at all as a grand new zoo, one on which the forces of innovation and evolution can take their course a good deal more naturally than in the old system.

That the financial system must be thought of as a zoo at all arises from the fundamental fact of government's stewardship of modern markets. Probably no more profound lesson than this is to be gleaned from the dramatic political revolution that has convulsed the established order, East and West, for the last 15 years.

Just as elected officials must accept the responsibility for promulgating rules and laws that maintain the stability and health of the global environment, so they must superintend the equally fragile and sometimes more complicated structures of the global economy.

This responsibility for relative stability goes far beyond the bounds of particular national interests. It is the harmony of the international trading system that must be maintained.

The people undertaking this task for George Bush presumably want to create an American financial industry that will last for another 60 years. They are remarkable, among other things, for their Harvard University connections. Treasury Secretary Nicholas Brady, undersecretary for finance Robert Glauber and Federal Reserve system vice chairman David Mullins all hail from the Business School; Federal Deposit Insurance Corp. chairman William Seidman, Securities and Exchange Commission chairman Richard Breeden, Currency Controller Robert Clarke, Assistant Treasury Secretary John Robson, Treasury deputy assistant secretary for financial institutions John Dugan all attended the Law School.

Largely unrepresented on this team are the mainstream regulators of the financial system, which is to say graduates of departments of economics who have found their place in the Federal Reserve system. Newly reappointed chairman Alan Greenspan? He is remarkably able but not deeply-rooted. A lifetime of consulting and politics seems to have left him unconnected to any bureaucratic tradition beyond his economic understanding.

Thus it may be U.S. Rep. John Dingell, more than any other, who is coming to stand for the Federal Reserve's instinctive institutional position, for the old-fashioned premise that someone has got to take the responsibility.

It is Dingell, as chairman of the House Energy and Commerce Committee, who has taken up the cause of the continuing separation of banking and commerce—a position regularly espoused by Gerald Corrigan, president of the Federal Reserve Bank of New York, the senior career man in the system.

Indeed, in his gruff, authoritative manner, Dingell, like Corrigan, is a perfect exemplar of just what a certain sort of government figure is supposed to be: part animal trainer, part zoo keeper. Both are big, physically imposing men, used to imposing their will on others. The difference is that on his office walls Dingell has mounted the heads of animals he has shot as a hunter, a reminder of his legislative skills. Corrigan has the recollections of bank panics that he's stopped, written in the eyes of those who watch him as he moves across the floor.

Chances are that Dingell's and Corrigan's battle to prevent combinations of banks and industrial concerns in America will be lost. After all, as Wojnilower says, Japan and Germany have shown that cooperation between banks and industry can be a fruitful thing. The emphasis instead will likely be on "firewalls," to prevent federal deposit insurance from being abused. Hence the blueprint that seems to be entailed by the Treasury plan: A system dominated by a few giant "department stores" of finance, whose subsidiaries may rise and fall with ever-changing innovations, but whose management will seem to go on forever.

Still, you have to admire these two strongmen, Dingell and Corrigan, of Georgetown and Fordham universities, espousing a view of government as old-fashioned, and as durable as the Constitution—with, perhaps, a certain overtone of the Church as well. After all, they say, somebody has got to take the responsibility.

AUGUST 4, 1991

A "Strong" Man
for the Fed?

SUPPOSE THAT PAUL VOLCKER HAS ALREADY MADE UP HIS MIND TO LEAVE NEXT August, at the end of his second term as chairman of the Federal Reserve Board. It is well-known, after all, that a sizable faction of administration staffers are after his scalp. Suppose he has decided to quit no matter what? What happens after Volcker goes?

Well, when Warren Harding in 1923 named Daniel L. Crissinger, a schoolyard pal with whom he had played marbles, to head the central bank, leadership of the system swung to the New York bank and its president, Benjamin Strong. While Harding played poker with Crissinger in Washington, Strong in Manhattan organized the presidents of the 11 other reserve banks to take unified action, including the first attempts to intervene against recession.

It could happen again, according to a scenario circulating at high levels, both in and outside the federal system. The intensity of the speculation over Volcker's fate is testimony to the lively interest in the financial community, especially among bond traders, in the future conduct of monetary policy.

As short-term interest rates have fallen over the last few months, 30-year rates on government borrowing have remained on a higher plateau, reflecting increasing worry that a seven-member board of governors, packed by the White House with easy-money advocates eager to meet the administration's growth targets, inadvertently will spark a new round of high inflation.

President Reagan has been slowly filling the seven-member board with outsiders, naming Martha Seger, Manuel Johnson, Wayne Angell and Robert Heller as governors. Gov. Emmett Rice is quitting on Jan. 1, giving the president a fifth appointment. Gov. Henry Wallich is gravely ill. And Volcker himself is likely to quit if his chairmanship is not renewed. "It would be almost unprecedented for him to stay on," says Donald Kettl, a University of Virginia professor who has written a study of leadership at the Fed.

In the presence of an inexperienced chairman—Manuel Johnson, say—New York Federal Reserve Bank president Gerald Corrigan might become the most powerful force in the system, or so the current story goes. Together, the seven governors and a rotating coterie of five bank presidents constitute the Federal Open Market Committee, the key decision-making unit; in principle, it is possible to render the chairman captive to the majority's will.

"Corrigan would be a kind of Volcker-in-exile," is the way one insider puts it; presumably less-experienced members of the governing committees would rally to his leadership in a pinch. It mightn't be so simple, says Princeton University professor Lester Chandler, historian of the Strong years and student of the present-day system. "Corrigan is first rate. No doubt about that. But it would be hard for him to take over the system. In Ben Strong's time, there was no tradition as to who was on top. He was not bucking any clearly established authorities.

"Still, I think it is conceivable that Corrigan might take over the Federal Open Market Committee. It would be a point in his favor that new members of the Fed are so incompetent, that it might become clear early. The risk would be that it wouldn't become clear until it was too late." The conjecture illuminates just how hard it is to capture completely the nation's central bank, the regulatory authority that superintends banking institutions and charts its monetary policy. By law, the president appoints the system's seven governors, but the boards of directors of the 12 regional banks appoint their presidents, with the Fed's consent. And who are these boards of directors? Well, three are appointed by the Fed chairman in Washington, and six are appointed by the local bank president, to serve particular segments of the community.

Thus the directors of the Boston Federal Reserve Bank include a number of New England commercial bankers, as well as Joseph Baute, chairman of Markem Corp., Keene, N.H.; George Hatsopoulos, chairman of Thermoelectron Corp; former U.S. Rep. Michael Harrington, now a Salem lawyer; Richard Oster, a Providence businessman; Matina Horner, president of Radcliffe College; and Ralph Sorenson, chairman of Barry Wright Corp.

The composition of the Boston board is of more than passing interest, since the next bank president in the system to retire is none other than Boston's Frank Morris, who is 63. With the White House appointing relatively unknown persons to the board of governors, the track record of bank presidents takes on increasing importance. Corrigan, Volcker's chief protégé, now at the New York Fed, is the man who took charge during the run on the Illinois Continental Bank in 1983. Most other reserve bank presidents are Volcker loyalists as well.

So in the end, it may be the bond markets and the bank presidents, not the president, who choose the next leader of the Fed. When Volcker leaves the chair, no matter who is nominated to replace him, Corrigan will remain in the system, and where he sits, there may be the head of the table.

OCTOBER 15, 1986

At the Head of the Queue

WHAT WITH THE GASOLINE CRUNCH, IT TAKES NO WIZARD TO SEE THAT A VERY PRECISE gas gauge and a good sense of where you are going are very useful tools. Too much gas in your tank and you tie up unnecessary cash in your safety margin; too little gas, and you court the disaster of running out, waste time filling up. Of course a knowledge of gas availability in the area is helpful, too. Combined with a reliable understanding of the capacity of your tank and of your itinerary, it's all you need.

It is more or less the same with the information capacity of computers, only more so. For an ever-increasing number of big and little businesses, computers are not a little like fuel tanks, storing and dispensing information instead of gas.

The difference is partly in the price: Excess capacity can costs hundreds of thousands of dollars; undercapacity can cost even more in terms of snafus and lost business. And it is partly in the order of complexity of computers compared to cars: Imagining what the differences in capacity among 20 or 30 differently configured systems is no job for a seat-of-pants navigator with a pencil and a clean sheet of paper.

Therefore, a new technique for using advanced mathematics to model and measure the capacity of computer systems against their expected use that was developed and marketed by three aging math wizards from Harvard (average age: late 30s) is of considerable interest to the $100 billion a year computer-buying public. The service amounts, buyers say, to a customized (and cut-rate) do-it-yourself *Consumer Reports* on the whole universe of data processing gear or—to put it another way—a very precise gas gauge. This is very useful in a world in which competing computer salesman make claims that are notoriously difficult to weigh. It is the reason that sales are going through the roof at BGS Systems Inc., one of the new generation of Cambridge-born, Rte. 128-raised high technology firms "gaining rapid acceptance, " according to *Datamation* magazine. "A welcome addition," said *Auerbach Computer Technology Reports*.

For $19,000, the company peddles a consumer-oriented package of programmed advice, a super-sophisticated guide that answers questions for the information-processing consumer. "Capacity planning" is the buzzword, and the job designator of a new kind of computer specialist. The software package of fancy mathematics is known as Best/1. For example: Ever wonder "What if?" you had a Ruddynicker mainblat with a Freebosch thimbleknocker and a set of hamberverts? Feed the specs, along with a couple of "key volume indicators" to provide an outline of your usage requirements, into Best/1 and click, click, click, out comes the answer. What if all that speed tripled the demand for your product? Click, click click: you'd need to buckle on a new crob and probably a couple of weetertwoofers, that's what.

The secret of reducing all this to an intelligible model is something called queuing theory, an area of applied mathematics that developed decades ago as a way of thinking about the telephone network, but which only recently has been developed for thinking about computers by—surprise!—the founders of BGS Systems.

So what's a queue? Well, metaphorically at least, it's the line that forms at the entrance to the computer or the exit—or entrance or the exit to the disc or drum or tape or printing unit or any other piece of peripheral equipment—as dozens of users compete for the unit's services. Indeed, in some respects a computer queue is analogous to all the lines of motorists that form at the pumps of gasoline stations around the world—and if the difficulty isn't clear to you involved in forecasting the average wait for gas when the length of the average line, say, doubles, then you weren't paying attention last summer.

By the same token, thinking about the gas shortage should make clear to you just how dangerous a lack of capacity—even a slight shortfall—can be to a computer user.

It was Jeffrey Buzen, "father of computer queuing theory" and co-founder of BGS, who cut the knot where computers are concerned back in the early 1970s when he hit on a queuing model for a central server and a "convolution algorithm," or computational recipe, that allowed him to predict what would happen when multiple users do multiple things to various computer configurations.

Along with then-fellow graduate students Robert Goldberg and Harold Schwenk, Jr., Buzen persisted until the three—all working on doctoral dissertations at the time—had a computer program into which they could plug readily available data and come up with reliable estimates of computer capacity, and a capability to ask "what if" questions about the results. The result was something proprietary and eminently sellable, a far more economical and precise method than computer "benchmarking" or "simulating" that had been the alternative procedures for gauging capacity. After years of shuttling back and forth between consulting jobs, mostly with Honeywell Information Systems, the three set up BGS in late 1976.

"There was queuing theory, just like there was a general theory of combustion," says Schwenk, now president of the firm. "We figured out how to make the equivalent of a gasoline engine."

Customers apparently agree. "It's an extremely usable product, a very flexible one, and it does its work with a great deal of economy of effort," said Linard Risgin, a capacity planner for John Hancock Insurance Co., and a pioneering user of the BGS model. Other insurance companies are adapting Best/1 to their needs, and manufacturers as diverse as Chrysler, Gillette, Republic Steel and Ralston Purina are among the little company's customers.

The result for BGS is a sales curve that is apparently about to explode well into the millions of dollars. "We'd been selling packages at the rate of one a week, now it's up to two or three, we've had five this week and the week is only two days old," said Robert Goldberg in an interview yesterday. With colleague Leonard D. Lipner out on the road giving advanced seminars in the queuing model, BGS is doing a land-office business, and tripling its office space next month.

Don't get your hopes up, however. The company is privately held, and has no plans to go public or to sell out. Quite aside from being closely held, the company is virtually takeover proof. "Our autonomy is protected to a certain extent," says president Schwenk. "It is important that we be independent. After all, we are a little like a certified public accountant."

SEPTEMBER 6, 1979

How the Financial Markets Went High-Tech

THE HOLIDAY SEASON IS A FINE TIME FOR GIVING BOOKS. FOR READERS OF THIS column—fans of the narrative thread provided by the ebb and flow of money—usually there are a plethora of reading choices. This year there is an overwhelming favorite.

I refer to Peter Bernstein's *Capital Ideas: The Improbable Origins of Modern Wall Street*. Bernstein has done for the new financial technology what his old friend Robert Heilbroner did 40 years ago for economics in his classic, *The Worldly Philosophers*. That is, he has put in readable form the story of the remarkable developments that have transformed investing from a genteel art to a high-tech profession since the 1960s.

Moreover, Bernstein relied on his other great old friend, Nobel laureate Paul Samuelson, as his principle guide to these ideas, so the product is not some idiosyncratic screed, but rather a quite dependable journalistic account, more readable than Horace Judson's *The Eighth Day of Creation* (which was about the discovery of DNA) and just as central to an understanding of the modern age. This is, as John Bogle, William Simon, J. Carter Bacot, Arthur Zeikel, Richard Brealey, Dean LeBaron and Richard Zeckhauser all agree in the accompanying bumpf, a quite fantastic book. Though officially not published until January, *Capital Ideas* is in most bookstores now.

"Americans have always welcomed change," Bernstein begins; Thomas Edison, Henry Ford and Benjamin Franklin are among our heroes, after all. "But sometimes change seems to run amok and things appear to be out of control. Then fear takes over and spoils our appetite for novelty. That is what has happened in Wall Street over the last 15 or 20 years."

He's right, of course. Program trading, capital asset pricing models, index funds, currency swaps, synthetic derivatives—what are these except code words to strike terror in the heart of every individual investor and money manager who ever consulted the wisdom of Benjamin Graham and David Dodd?

Yet common sense and past experience suggest that what the financial engineers have built in the past 20 years or so is not some imponderable doomsday machine but rather a technological structure whose usefulness and desirability will become more apparent to even the smallest investor as it is better understood—analogous in most respects to the advent of steam, electricity, radio and modern medicine. And sure enough, that is the story that Bernstein tells.

Thus, he starts with Alfred Cowles, the Colorado Springs coupon clipper whose failure to foresee the Great Depression led him to bankroll the fledgling Econometric Society, which put economics on a mathematical and statistical foundation, beginning in the depths of World War II. He relates the stories of the little-known men who turned out to be great makers of the world of modern finance.

Thus Harry Markowitz, whose dissertation on portfolio theory was nearly rejected by Milton Friedman because it wasn't economics, but who later won the Nobel Prize. Or William Sharpe, who as a young graduate student working for the Air Force and Rand Corp. in the early 1960s found a way to put Markowitz's ideas into forms that would generate better investing returns. Or Eugene Fama, the volatile third-generation Sicilian from Boston who turned the investment world upside down in the early 1960s with his "efficient markets" hypothesis, which holds that no one can hope to beat the markets over a long period of time.

At every juncture, Bernstein takes pains to locate his characters in the social world. These are some very colorful people, and not just Baron Rothschild, who observed that "only three people in the world understand the meaning of money and none of them have very much of it." Franco Modigliani and Merton Miller make "bombshell assertions" that overturn corporate finance in out-of-the-way journals. Barr Rosenberg transforms pension fund investing by developing measures of risk while consulting like some flower-child Castro to the back office of the Wells Fargo Bank trust department. Fisher Black and Myron Scholes invent their options-pricing formula, "the universal financial device," while taking instruction from the youthful genius Robert Merton at MIT—and watch as a few formulas create an industry. Merton says of the nearly instant adoption of their device, "I got the biggest kick out of hearing those options traders routinely talk about hedge ratios and deltas, partial differential equations and stochastic differential equations. Who would ever think that people would be talking like that?"

Yet people had no choice, Merton continues. "They couldn't deal with it the way they had dealt with it over-the-counter. There is no other way to deal with the complexity of the option. The models made sense intuitively and seemed to work." And so the traders loaded the Black-Scholes formulas in their calculators and went back to trading as they had butter and eggs. The relentless message of the professors: "Knack, feel, whim and intuition are . . . useless relics."

Capital Ideas derives authority from the fact that Bernstein was himself once a professional money manager. As he watched the new theories emerging from the universities during the 1950s and 1960s, he says he found them "alien and unappealing," as did most other practitioners. He converted after the crash of 1974, by abandoning money management and founding instead the *Journal of Portfolio Management* under the aegis of the magazine *Institutional Investor*. So his reconnaisance then became history. And if Bernstein is just a trifle too kind to the men he so admires, often ignoring their clashes and foibles, so what? He has written a wonderful story.

DECEMBER 8, 1991

Dau!
Dau! Dau!

THERE WERE ONLY A HANDFUL OF WORDS THAT ALL SERVICEMEN WERE ISSUED UNofficially when they went to Vietnam, like the official green and white ribbons that signified their attendance at the war—no more than four or five of them.

"Please" was not among them; neither was "Thank you." They included *chau, sin loi, di di mau, ti ti, chieu hoi* and *dau! Chau* meant hello, as in *chau ba* (Hello, Mrs.), *sin loi* meant sorry (as in sorry 'bout that), *di di mau* meant get out of here, *ti ti* meant just a little bit (it was itself a corruption of a French phrase from an earlier war). *Chieu hoi* meant surrender and *dau* (pronounced *tzau*) meant liar.

It is not hard to imagine why the vocabulary consisted of just those few words: much, maybe most, of daily life and the war itself, could be discussed with them. *Dau!* (it was inevitably pronounced as an exclamation) was particularily handy, since the possibility of exaggeration, disavowal, betrayal was continually on everybody's mind, in circumstances ranging from the most intimate to the grandiose setting of the war itself.

All this comes to mind because of the story of Jeffrey Beck, a top Wall Street merger-maker, that was rolled out yesterday in the *Wall Street Journal* by reporter Bryan Burrough. Burrough is co-author, along with fellow *Journal* reporter John Helyar, of the better of two new books about the RJR Nabisco deal. *Barbarians at the Gate*, it is called. But the remarkable story in the paper yesterday isn't in the book. It comes as close to the total destruction of a man as it is possible to imagine, far more damaging than a criminal indictment.

As a senior partner at Drexel Burnham Lambert, Jeff Beck relished the nickname "Mad Dog." In the years before he turned into one of Wall Street's more visible merger-and-acquisition specialists, Beck liked to tell colleagues that he had been a Green Beret platoon leader in Vietnam. In a bitter battle in the Ia Drang valley, he had earned a Silver Star by calling in napalm on his own position. Nor was this story in any way incidental to his life. He nearly talked actor/producer Michael Douglas into filming his grunt-to-glory story.

There is, of course, just one problem. According to reporter Burrough, Beck was no Green Beret, was never even in Vietnam, wasn't even in the army, really: Mad Dog Beck was a weekend warrior. Most of the rest of his autobiography, including a huge family fortune, was a tissue of lies as well. Burrough portrays Beck confronted with the truth at lunch, growing misty-eyed, before explaining that for 20 years he'd led a double life as an intelligence agent.

(Leaving Mad Dog Beck aside, what's striking in the Burrough/Helyar account is the extent to which the argot of Vietnam has spread to Wall Street. For example, here's LBO magnate Henry Kravis on the RJR deal: "We were charging right through the rice paddies, not stopping for anything, and taking no prisoners." Like Beck, what Kravis knows about Vietnam is mainly what he'd seen in the movies: he was a rich kid at Columbia in 1968.)

Now here's the interesting thing. The guy who introduced Mad Dog Beck to a wider world was filmmaker Oliver Stone, and it was Beck in turn who introduced Stone to the world of investment banking for his celebrated movie *Wall Street*. It was Beck, for example, who talked Stone into putting the command "lock and load!" into the mouth of an investment banker preparing to do battle. And it was Stone who in turn wrote Beck into a cameo speech in *Wall Street*. Stone told an interviewer, "Jeff was on the killing edge, the front lines of the takeovers. To me, he really was the new Wall Street."

Certainly to many people, Oliver Stone really is the old Vietnam. Director of the new hit movie *Born on the Fourth of July*, he also made the highly successful *Platoon* back in 1986. No one doubts that Stone was in Vietnam. He served 15 months as a combat infantryman.

Nevertheless, *Platoon* is a profoundly meretricious movie, which passes off as truth nearly every tired cliché of combat life. *Platoon* is full of great visuals, but the best scene in it showed GIs walking downhill from a village they had just torched, carrying villagers' kids on their shoulders. Subtle? Yes. Moving? Yes. Plausible? No.

Thus the Beck-Stone connection involves a kind of double deception. Vietnam wasn't the way Stone paints it. Neither is Wall street. He and Beck were just a couple of macho braggarts spinning each other war stories, and the results are screwy in one way as the world according to Jane Fonda is in another. No one should give them any credence.

JANUARY 23, 1990

part five
CRITICS

Das
Appropriation Problem

most exciting thing that ever happened to this monthly meeting of Boston scholars of the history of economic thought was to seem to lose forever, late last year, its meeting-place in Harvard's Baker Library.

The space in question, a gracious and extensive wood-paneled reading room, was headquarters for an excellent collection of pre-1850 economics materials, an old-fashioned testament to the centrality of history in America's premier university town. The curator of the Kress Collection stayed late on the nights of seminar meetings to keep the library open.

But then, as part of the start of a library expansion, the Harvard Business School accepted the resignation of the curator of the comfortable satrapy, locked the door, buttoned up about the future of the collection and opened a new gym next door. When the historians yelped, the B-School expanded its plans to keep the collection together and announced that history was safe at Harvard.

In fact, the Kress Seminar is the point of entry into economics for some very interesting insights. It is the center of a regular little industry in which economic science is explored from the outside, as a historical phenomenon. Sometimes people bring to the Kress Seminar new versions of old products. Sometimes there is empirical work. And sometimes there are bombshells.

For example, take Todd Buchholz and his book, *New Ideas from Dead Economists: An Introduction to Modern Economic Thought*. It's a generally successful attempt to rewrite Robert Heilbroner's classic, *The Worldly Philosophers*, which was first published in 1953, to bring it more into line with what most technical economists think of as the facts of the case. What *New Ideas* lacks in style, it makes up for in fidelity to what seem to be the facts of the present day, for deep down in Heilbroner's version of history the market is a somewhat dated institution—destined to be supplanted eventually by central planning—and the economists' modern turn toward mathematics and technique has been mostly a mistake. For Buchholz, on the other hand, the history of economics is a happy progression toward its present-day triumph, and there are chapter headings such as: "Why Didn't Keynes Anticipate the Public Choice School?" A law and economics professor, Bucholz is now coordinating economic policy in the Bush administration.

In a slightly different category are Arjo Klamer and David Colander's new book, *The Making of Economists*. Klamer and Colander are concerned with getting at the nature of the competing sects that characterize modern economics. In the book's middle are lengthy conversations with graduate student novices at MIT, Harvard, Columbia University, and the University of Chicago. These interviews are sandwiched between an enlightening survey of professional education at the front of the book and two fascinating interpretive essays on the results at the back. You can quarrel with either man, but you can't doubt these two are among the brightest students of the profession around.

But for a real bombshell, there is Philip Mirowski. Intellectual stars of his magnitude (as opposed to scientific stars) don't come along very often. For five years Mirowski's work has been quietly wending its way toward publication, in the Kress Seminar and many other places. Now, in *More Heat Than Light: Economics as Social Physics, Physics as Nature's Economics*, he states a challenge that is going to haunt economists for years.

Mirowski says that because of a "natural symbiosis" of natural and social concepts, physicists and economists have borrowed concepts back and forth so freely over the years that the sciences are practically indistinguishable. This is the "appropriation problem," as Mirowski calls it, oft noted but rarely addressed by economists. With its Langrangian multipliers and Hamiltonian equations, its intricate parallel between potential energy and human utility, economics practically is physics, he says—but it is a curiously old-fashioned clockwork, 19th-century kind of physics.

The real problem is that economics hasn't yet faced up to the 20th-century experience of physics, with its emphasis on chance and discontinuity. When it does, Mirowski says, highly mathematical models will lose their persuasive power; sophisticated institutionalism such as that of Thorstein Veblen and Gunnar Myrdal will emerge, instead.

More Heat Than Light is not for the timid among the liberal arts set. It sets its arguments about those Hamiltonians out in both mathematical and scientific detail. But for people who like this sort of thing, the footnotes alone are worth the hefty price, at least to the library. For example, did you know the concept of the invisible hand, which has become economists' shorthand for the unintended social order that arises from individual human acts, first made its appearance in Adam Smith's writing on the history of ancient physics? "Heavy bodies descend, and lighter bodies fly upwards by the necessity of their own nature; nor was the invisible hand of Jupiter ever apprehended to be employed in these matters."

The bombshell effect arises because Mirowski's view is very corrosive of faith in the enterprise of economics. If modern technical economics is all "just physics," after all, it is relatively easy for a non-believer to dismiss.

At times, Mirowski's tone wavers between Marx and tabloid columnist Howie Carr. One of the most brutal sentences I've read recently is this one, which mocks Nobel laureate Paul Samuelson: "Yet it was a joy to be young and mathematically gifted once it dawned on you that you had seen this stuff before, probably in Mechanical Engineering 14a, and it was just a matter of digging out those old notes." Mirowski says he'll leave the "further sport of deconstruction of Samuelson's rhetoric" to others. It's clear that his insights will keep a generation or two of radical students busy.

In science as in politics, however, only a new candidate replaces an old one. If the theory of value has been dictated by the evolution of physical theory as Mirowski believes, and not by something that inheres in the nature of economic transactions themselves, what do you do?

Well, one alternative is to do what Stanford economist Kenneth Arrow and Princeton physicist Philip Anderson—both Nobel laureates—have done: Get a bunch of physicists and economists together in Santa Fe, knock heads and see what comes out next. Add a few biologists and computer scientists from time to time. Mirowski thinks he's seen this particular future and that it doesn't work: "Thermodynamics, general relativity, quantum mechanics, subatomic theory, chaos theory—wherever one turns, one is confronted with an unsavory and repugnant sludge."

The other alternative is to do what Mirowski does, to embrace new-fangled anthropologists such as Mary Douglas, David Bloor and Bruno Latour. For these thinkers there is simply no solid foundation for scientific knowledge in the social realm, and vice versa: They are interdependent. There is no way to really "prove" anything. So Mirowski sets out to construct, a "social theory of value"—presumably something a little like Keynes' vision of the stock market as "a beauty contest."

There are, of course, other approaches too: The most obvious is to head for the metaphorical attic of modern evolutionary biology, and plenty of people are doing just that. But these are presumably vulnerable to the same outside critique of "appropriation." Mirowski himself says it's not impossible to fashion a better understanding of the economic world; it's "just messier than anyone has heretofore anticipated, mostly because of the absence of any Archimedean point to get outside it all."

Mirowski and his ideas are about to move out of the history of economics into the wider stream. Ideas practically fly off the man; he sits, shifting in his chair, until he gets his turn at discussion. Then a slightly silly, mischievous grin appears, a riposte, the sudden sweetness of a stolen pie. Here's a hunch: A social theory of value is never going to really replace the common sense that we take as traditional economics. But Mirowski's project is going to generate plenty of heat—and light, too.

MARCH 11, 1990

What the Fuss Was About

FOR 10 YEARS, A STORM HAS RAGED HIGH IN THE STRATOSPHERE OF ECONOMICS OVER the likelihood that the government can play a useful role in "fine-tuning" the economy. Like an earlier controversy over the nature of economic growth that unfolded during the 1950s, the debate has occupied the best minds of the generation full time, and generated much heat but little light, except on the professional reputations involved.

Now a Wellesley College professor has made the so-called "rational expectations" argument if not exactly accessible, at least accessible-in-principle. Arjo Klamer has written *Conversations with Economists—New Classical Economists and Opponents Speak Out on the Current Controversy in Macroeconomics*. For those who really like economics, these long interviews are indispensable and delightful.

Klamer's conversations—there are 11 economists interviewed, including Robert E. Lucas, Jr., Thomas J. Sargent, Robert M. Townsend, James Tobin, Franco Modigliani, Robert M. Solow, Alan S. Blinder, John B. Taylor, Karl Brunner, David Gordon and Leonard B. Rapping—are by no means a complete guide to what has happened to the science during the 1970s; they say little of the technical supply-side revolution, for example. But as an explanation of the debate, they are unsurpassed and likely to remain so for a long time. If the book doesn't have the narrative drive of, say, James Watson's *The Double Helix*, it is the next best thing, the highest of the *Haute Journalisme*.

New Classicals vs. Neo-Keynesians are, roughly speaking, the positions that used to be called monetarist and "Keynesian," though even the monetarists scruple at the more ethusiastic forms of New Classical theory. The debate was transformed by the assumption that people are essentially forward-looking rather than backward-looking in their stance toward economic transactions, that their expectations are "rational" rather than "adaptive"—not a bold statement in itself, but dynamite when incorporated into formal models.

Suddenly, the New Classicals had a strict basis for arguing from their strongholds in Chicago, Minnesota, Rochester and Pittsburgh that whatever the government attempted in the way of policy would be defeated by people who would anticipate its effects. Along with a tough new stance on whether markets "cleared" or not—which amounted to the argument that all unemployment is voluntary—it was just the thing to put the fine-tuning Keynesians on the defensive in the rarefied world of the scholarly journals. The economy is always doing the best it can, the New Classicals said, for if it could do better, it would.

The world in which such things can be seriously maintained—indeed, where they can earn a Nobel Prize—is deftly painted by the 30-year-old Klamer, a Dutch economist who was goaded into journalism by his brother, a radio interviewer and theater-lover. "He said it was crazy to think that I could understand what they were writing about merely by reading them. I defended my strategy, but realized of course that he was right. To truly understand economics it is necessary to understand the human dimension."

Klamer set out with tape recorder, crisscrossing the country, armed with his inside knowledge of the debate and a lively curiosity about how economics is really done. The results are real conversations about ideas, and not a little story-telling in between. In talks with his 11 economists, who constitute perhaps an emblematic quarter of the most efficacious thinkers working in the field today, Klamer developed a fascinating glimpse at the basic fact of life in economics, as in baseball or any other game, the inequality of talent: in economics, there are teachers, researchers, econometricians, and at the very top of the trade, there are theorists, a comparative handful of men conducting a conversation among themselves.

Thanks to the competition between university departments, the pecking order among these fellows is constantly sorting out—a little like free-agents in baseball. The best are the most sought-after. Thus Harvard tried to hire John Taylor and Thomas Sargent; MIT tried for Sargent and Robert

Lucas. "Listening to Lucas, it's clear why everyone wants to talk to him, to talk about him. The man has a powerful mind. It is intellectual charisma," says Klamer.

The book traces the social history of the New Classicals. For example, there is the moving story, told from two points of view, of how after achieving the first big breakthrough into "rational expectations" with Robert Lucas, Leonard A. Rapping, disillusioned over Vietnam, quit high economics on principle and moved to the University of Massachusetts to teach radical economics. "You could think of it as a football player who suddenly decides that football is not his cup of tea and tries another game . . . . It was an awful experience," Rapping tells Klamer. "Rapping was always much more interested than me in being where the action was," says Lucas.

Again and again, the theme of the book seems to be the incommensurability of two different points of view. "When an economist gets mad, he says, 'I don't understand you.' So here are some of the most brilliant people in the world saying to equally brilliant people, 'I don't understand you,' " says Klamer.

The only truly angry line in the book is Robert Lucas on MIT's Robert Solow. He just makes jokes, says Lucas. The best line in the book belongs, predictably, to Solow. He says most communication between economists nowadays takes this form: "I went to Grantchester today," says one. "That is funny, I didn't," says the other.

Solow says, "Suppose someone sits down . . . and tells me that he is Napoleon Bonaparte. The last thing I want to do is to get involved with him in a technical discussion of cavalry tactics at the battle of Austerlitz. . . . Now Bob Lucas and Tom Sargent like nothing better than to get drawn into technical discussions, because then you have tacitly gone along with their fundamental assumptions; your attention is attracted away from the basic weakness of the whole story. Since I find that fundamental framework ludicrous, I respond by treating it as ludicrous—that is, by laughing at it."

Klamer says, "I think that the Neo-Keynesians are very constrained by the rules that are set up in a neoclassical conversation. New Classicals exploit those rules much better than Neo-Keynesians." Solow agrees. To him, the New Classical economics is simply the "third reincarnation of monetarism," with wider appeal to young economists than it would otherwise have because it is "technically sweet."

As Klamer sees it, the difference between good economists and not-so-good economists is a difference in the degree of passion they bring to their task. "When you talk with these guys, all of whom have a good record, you sense that they feel very strongly, and therefore they are very persuasive.

But what you get so clearly from these conversations is that they believe—believe passionately—that they are on the right journey, on the right track. Therefore, they don't really talk about what they've done, they speculate about what's ahead, about what they think is promising. That is how they try to convince you that you have to follow them."

NOVEMBER 20, 1983

The Woody Guthrie of Economics

To hear Seymour Melman tell it, this is America's 23d consecutive wartime Christmas. It was in 1961, he says, that "the permanent war economy" emerged as the dominant feature of the modern world, under President John F. Kennedy.

Seymour Melman is the Woody Guthrie of economics. Like Guthrie, who heard Irving Berlin's song "God Bless America" and decided to write "This Land is Your Land" as an alternative anthem, Melman has spent a lifetime creating an alternative to the conventional wisdom about defense spending.

In the conventional wisdom, weapons spending hardly matters—as long as it is conventionally financed, by taxes. Defense as a percent of gross national product can be high, as it was in the mid-1960s, and the economy may run well. Or spending can be very low, as it was in the mid-1970s, and the economy will run poorly. The fiscal and monetary variables are what matter most. Defense, like any other industry, melts away in the great systems of simultaneous equations which comprise economists' models.

In Melman's world, the military-industrial complex is a major and devastating force. In a series of books on what he calls "Pentagon capitalism" and seminars on "conversion" from a military to a peacetime economy—including a lively group in Massachusetts—Melman has in the course of 25 years become the leading economic spokesman for the antiwar movement. In a new book, the Columbia University professor assigns the blame for America's eroding competitive position in world markets—especially in machine tools—to its addiction to a heavy defense budget.

Melman's life and work form a remarkably coherent whole. He was born

Dec. 30, 1917, a month after the Russian revolution, and his hopes are those that were characteristic of the time. A City College of New York graduate, he was politically active, and spent a year in Palestine in 1941. After military service, he started out researching industrial issues for The Conference Board, a business research organization. "I found that research came easily," he says.

After a doctoral dissertation on the rise of administrative overhead in manufacturing activity, Melman turned to productivity research, and produced a mid-1950s study called *Dynamic Factors in Industrial Productivity*. Meanwhile, he began looking into verification processes for disarmament. He's been looking into both issues ever since.

One result of his early work was a trip to Russia. He presented his work on machine tools; at one point a controversy arose: immediately there was a split, "right down the lines of the dove-hawk position," he says. "It was a very important lesson to me.

"Looking back, it seems clear that the dividing line was in 1961," says Melman. "It was there that they escalated the military budget in a way that was undreamt of before. They also propagated guns and butter ideology. There was a major military, ideological, organizational change. They began to use the military budget as a Keynesian tool.

"I started, in my innocent way, looking into what happened to firms that do business with the Pentagon. I found that they usually get into very big trouble." He assigns subsidiary blame to business school gurus who teach short-term profit maximization. His most ambitious summary to date is *Profits Without Production*, published earlier this fall.

Melman's book hasn't been received especially well; even *Publishers Weekly* panned it. The reception is surprising, since the book is dense, closely reasoned and packed with detailed new material. A central allegation, for instance, is that work complexity is a key to productivity, and that the Japanese grew far ahead in learning how to make machine tools that are interesting to the workers who have to operate them. Although the scene-setting chapter on the machine-tool industry was published in *Technology Review*, MIT's alumni magazine, *Profits Without Production* has so far stirred up surprisingly little discussion.

One of the reasons for this, of course, is Melman's tendency to preach to those who are already converted. An interesting example of his style is an early study, done 20 years ago for the Senate Judiciary Committee, on the impact of patents on research, a monograph that produced a great fight among patent lawyers and the research community.

Melman reported that the patent system was an impediment to the general process of industrial research. "The effort to place property rights on knowledge was fundamentally flawed and was at the core of the manifestly undesirable condition of endless loss and litigation. Under modern conditions, we found that groups of people are inevitably involved in research . . . . How do you assign property rights to one person, or as is nowadays fashionable, to three or four people? What about all the supporting staff? I really went to the heart of the matter, in the attempt to put the property rights on knowledge," he remembers.

The trouble is that Melman's discovery that patents were holding up the growth of knowledge came just in the middle of perhaps the greatest burst in the growth of science in the history of the human race. Moreover, a few years later, the distinguished economic historian Douglass North put his stamp on long-term history by arguing that the rise of the West could be explained largely in terms of its determination to provide incentives to the production of intellectual property—180 degrees the opposite of Melman's conclusions. "I haven't been in touch with him," says Melman.

Something of the same sort operates with respect to Melman's larger work. Mainstream economists tend to dismiss him as something less than persuasive—his overall positions simply don't square with the facts, they say. "His statements would carry more weight if they were put in a larger picture," says George Brown, defense economist for Data Resources Inc. in Washington. But noting Melman's testimony before Congress last week, Brown adds: "He is sharp; he is a scientist, for sure. But his is not the dominant view." In short, Melman is the Woody Guthrie of defense economics.

DECEMBER 25, 1983

The Bear
in My Closet

MY DAUGHTER WORRIES THAT THERE IS A BEAR IN THE CLOSET. THAT IS UNREALISTIC, I tell her. There is no bear in the closet. The problem is Robert Reich. I confess that I am afraid that when I open my closet, Robert Reich will jump out and begin to expound on the way to get America moving again.

Reich, 36, a Phi Beta Kappa from Dartmouth College, a genuine whiz kid, was catapulted to fame from the unlikely position as policy planning and evaluation director at the Federal Trade Commission. Before that he had worked for Robert Bork in the U.S. Solicitor General's Office for two years. Nice work, the kind reserved for the brightest kids, but not the sort likely to make you a household word, much less an expert on the world economy.

Yet today Reich seems to be everywhere, with an oeuvre that consists of half a book, a piece in the *Harvard Business Review*, another in *Foreign Affairs*, and a slew of opposite-editorial newspaper columns. He has been running a widely attended seminar at the Kennedy School of Goverment at Harvard University through the autumn. Staffers from the offices of Walter Mondale and Senators Edward M. Kennedy and Gary Hart have shuttled in and out.

His new book, *The Next American Frontier*, is circulating in galleys. Leslie Wayne, writing in *The New York Times*, assured readers that Reich had "gained a wide following among both businessmen and liberal politicians with his intriguing prescriptions for what ails our economy."

Reich promises nothing less than the "new Democratic alternative" that everyone has been looking for, "an economics of production, not protectionism," as pundit Anthony Lewis calls it. It would be realized through the exercise of the existing array of government guidance: tax credits, subsidies, tariffs, licenses, insurance and loan guarantees. "I'd bet the family fortune that industrial policy is going to be the central issue of the 1984 campaign," says MIT economist Lester Thurow. "He's a leading proponent of it."

So what has he got? Well, Reich offers a curious mix of BCG + PPE, of the kind of hotshot managerial strategism that is associated with the Boston Consulting Group and classical, free-trade economics he learned as a Rhodes scholar doing philosophy and political economy (PPE) at Oxford. (He learned consulting from his Rhode Island sidekick, Ira Magaziner, with whom he wrote *Minding America's Business: The Decline and Rise of The American Economy*.)

If the B-School/Law School perspective seems an unlikely mix for a would-be new Keynes, it is strangely compelling, if only because nobody else had the nerve to do anything like it before. Who else do you know who will recite the long, sorry story of the steel industry—and then tell you things would have gone much better if only the FTC had been given more and broader power?

Moreover, Reich has a wonderful profile. He is a natty dresser. He has good manners and a wonderful sense of humor (he says of his 4-foot-11 stature that he used to be 6 feet tall, but that government service ground him down.) He is a brilliant teacher. He has a handsome, accomplished wife (she's a professor at the Harvard Law School.) He takes things seriously—from policy to drama. (Indeed, he's explained to interviewers that he won his wife by producing a play for which he was certain she would try out—and then casting her as the leading lady.) He is kind to children.

His fellow lawyers like him. "He's the kind of guy who can be very smart without making an ass of himself," says Jack Fuller, editor of the editorial page of the *Chicago Tribune* and a former colleague.

But suddenly Reich has become a trifle overexposed, and the knives are out. His critics call him "the lesser Thurow" because of his emphasis on American comparative advantage in high-technology industry, a "zero-sum socialist" for his interest in government intervention. Confederates think he is bafflingly unclear about just what sort of measures he thinks are needed. Friends say he has promised too much. Even his mentors agree, that Reich has got his profile up a little too high for his own good. Like the sorcerer's apprentice, having started the publicity machine, Reich cannot now turn it off.

(Indeed, when asked last week to to sit for a profile, Reich artfully declined. He said: "I don't want to reduce the incentive to others to espouse views which we hold in common," he said. It may have been the first time Reich ever failed to consent to an interview. In the old days, he wrote me letters inviting me to come to Washington; they fell off in avidity as I failed to show up.)

It is a fact that Bob Reich is sometimes mixed up with another product of the Yale Law School, Charles Reich, the former professor who wrote *The Greening Of America* a dozen years ago. Reich 2, like Reich 1, employs a brand of facile analysis, not quite tied to the big ideas of the time, that seems eminently common-sensical on first reading, then melts away, sometimes into nonsense, on closer examination. He writes with textbook certitude about problems no one else seems to have solved, and discovers tragedies where no one else even knew they existed.

For example, when he writes, as he did in *Minding America's Business*, that with respect to unemployment, "in the 50 years since the onset of the Great Depression, the United States has experienced only 13 'normal' years—that is, years in which the country was neither at war nor in a major economic slump," you're not sure whether he understands that there has been a Cold War that has served as a terrific stimulus to the economy since

1945, that the number of jobs has increased to more than 100 million from 57 million since then, and that in any event the world has passed through perhaps the greatest binge of wealth creation in human history.

Likewise, when he writes, as he did last week, that the problem with the economy is that no one trusts each other, that plant closings, hostile take-overs, bank embezzlements, voluntary marketing agreements and the pro-liferation of lawyers can be curtailed if only we abandon "cowboy capitalism" in favor of a reaffirmation of mutual commitment to fair treat-ment all around, Reich sounds more like a celebrant of good school spirit than a serious economic analyst.

In any event, he is full of well-informed thoughts on what's wrong with the steel industry, but silent on issues like how he would take government out of the postal business into electronic mail. He is full of thoughts on the shortcomings of businessmen, but silent on the failings of bureaucrats. Perhaps the problems are solved in his new book; Walter Mondale is said to have read it. But the galleys haven't reached the bookbinders.

What Reich lacks is a dependable power base. His appointment at the Kennedy School is as a lecturer, "which usually isn't forever," a colleague notes. True, Reich has good relations with Democratic politicians—he consulted to Adlai Stevenson's campaign in Illinois, to Michael Dukakis's in Massachusetts—but he is not nearly so solid with those on the profes-sional left, who admire his facility even as they worry about his commitment to their ideals. "He is not nearly so up front about his values as is Lester Thurow," says Bennett Harrison, an MIT professor who is co-author of *The Deindustrialization of America.*

Unlike economists John Kenneth Galbraith or Robert Heilbroner, Reich has developed no underlying structure to his work. Unlike Thurow, he has no band of brothers to attest to his competence in economics. "He knows a lot of little things," says an economist familiar with his new book, "and he is very smart, but he is quite out of his depth."

Probably his most significant affiliation so far is with the *New Republic* magazine. As one of a circle of analysts around editor-in-chief and pub-lisher Martin Peretz—others include Morton Kondracke, Robert Kuttner, Mark Green and Michael Kinsley—Reich helps define one of the poles of "neo-liberalism," such as it is. Like Daniel Yergin or Richard Goodwin, he occupies a position somewhere between a policy-intellectual and a jour-nalist.

This much is clear: unlike Charlie Reich, who drifted off into good times in California, this Reich is serious. He'll be around. He works hard, mends fences, keeps cool. And most of all, of course, he is wildly popular. When I called the Harvard University information number, the operator said with some surprise: "I have had three calls in a row for him." Sure enough, when I rang through, the line was busy.

DECEMBER 5, 1982

Trust-Buster in the Idea Business

ANYONE WHO COMES IN CONTACT WITH MODERN TECHNICAL ECONOMICS KNOWS THAT IT is highly mathematical. The style can be daunting, and those without an unusual knack for the highest mathematics don't go far as theorists. The trouble is that mathematical competence does not lead necessarily to greater relevance; indeed, the case is often just the opposite.

Now a conservative and highly skilled mathematical economist has challenged even the rhetoric of mathematics itself. Donald N. McCloskey of the University of Iowa and the Institute for Advanced Study at Princeton University has sparked a widespread debate about the methods that economists follow by suggesting that economics open itself to literary and other forms of criticism.

According to McCloskey, mathematical sophistication is the modern-day equivalent of turn-of-the-century mastery of Latin and Greek among cultured persons in England; that men and women master the vocabulary not because it confers any special insight, but to show that they can lead; that like the white laboratory coats of physicians, equations are often used simply to intimidate those who are expected to take the advice that is offered.

To laymen, he recommends unrelenting scrutiny of the language of economists; to economists themselves, he recommends a year or two of post-graduate field work with businessmen and better manners among themselves, and to the arbiters of economic science known as "methodologists," he counsels a descent "from the frigid peaks of scientific absolutism to the sweet valleys of anarchic rhetoric." At the very least, he says, economics "should officially open itself to a wider range of discourse."

He says his skirmish is part of the wider revolt against modernism. In painting, in architecture, in physics and even mathematics itself, he says, modernism is dead. "I'm simply an arbitrageur of ideas."

McCloskey, 41, is a faculty brat. His father was a professor of government at Harvard University who made a specialty of the Supreme Court; his mother was an opera singer who sang with Sarah Caldwell in her early days. First at Harvard College, then as a graduate student there, he took up economic history under the great Alexander Gerschenkron.

"Gerschenkron was a tremendous model as a scholar. He knew Greek, he knew mathematics, he wrote criticism, he did statistical history, but as far as supervising, well, he didn't really do that; our conversations were all about the prospects of the Boston Celtics." McCloskey's dissertation, "Economic Maturity and Entrepreneurial Decline: British Steel 1870–1913," was about the sort of barriers that Americans now put up against Japan. He left Cambridge for a job at the University of Chicago in 1968.

Did he fit into the somewhat regimented view of the "Chicago school economists?" Yes, says McCloskey, "I'd call myself a member of the Chicago school. I believe in price theory, I believe that peasants are rational, I believe that the present state of conversation in economics is pretty good. But I'm not ready to put people to the torch over their willingness to share those beliefs."

Something quite like that is what happened to McCloskey at Chicago, however. After publishing a paper on the international gold standard in the 19th century that was sharply contested by Milton Friedman, McCloskey found himself stopped in his tracks. Given tenure in 1975 but not promoted to full professor, he finally quit Chicago for Iowa City in 1980. There he has been chairman of the department, written an intermediate text, done further work on the gold standard and started a project in medieval agricultural history.

But it was a deeply-felt article in the *Journal of Economic Literature*, entitled "The Rhetoric of Economics," that struck the responsive chord. "I have a file drawerful of correspondence about it," he says. "I was stunned. In this age of sensory overload, it's remarkable that people pay attention to anything. But so many people have come forward with something to say," he says.

Now McCloskey is completing a book that extends the argument. He was the star of a little conference last weekend at Middlebury College; he is the host of a great big conference on "The Rhetoric of the Human Sciences" in Iowa City late this month, which in turn is starring MIT's Thomas S. Kuhn.

The burden of McCloskey's argument is as follows: any method at all is a mistake. The realm of Method lies somewhere between the common rules of discourse ("don't shout, pay attention, be reasonably open-minded; explain yourself when asked; don't resort to violence in aid of your ideas") and the tools of the trade (regression analysis, equilibrium equations) that are largely homegrown within a field.

"This Methodology tells us what Science is; it orders us to be Objective; it mandates Quantification; it segregates Ought from Is. Altogether it has a schoolmarmish tone, lurching occasionally toward inquisition. When it is not slapping wrists it is seizing heretical non-scientists and burning them at the stake." It should be done without, says McCloskey, who embraces the anarchic theorizing of Paul Feyerabend, a philosopher of science best known for his claims that Galileo faked his supporting evidence.

Harsher critics of Feyerabend, such as the economist Mark Blaug, have written off him and his followers as advocates of "flower power" and "dadaism," whose chief methodological claim is that "anything goes." And McCloskey, who is not above closing a seminar with a few rhetorical choruses of a classic Wobbly folk song like "I Dreamed I Saw Joe Hill," has come in for his share of criticism, too.

For example, in a soon-to-be published reply to his paper, Bruce Caldwell and A.W. Coats of the University of North Carolina charge that he has little to say about why scientists prefer one theory to another, about how they tell good rhetoric from bad. "Far from being dead (as McCloskey claims)," they say, "methodology has dramatically increased its scope in recent years."

McCloskey is philosophical about controversy, a Chicago-School economist who is a prophet of tolerance. Last week, after an intense discussion, he tumbled on a phrase that nicely encapsulates his current role. "I want to be an antitrust person in the marketplace of ideas." Then, switching metaphors with the skill one expects of a man who described Chicago's Gary Becker as "the Kipling of the economics empire," he continued, "I want others to enlist in the army of rhetorical criticism of economics. We're going to submit all these swear-words to scrutiny. Is it really so bad to be anecdotal? Political? Inconsistent?"

True, McCloskey has not exactly called into question the most fundamental tenet of science—don't knock it unless you have something better to put in its place. Nor is he likely to dissuade economic theorists from their fondness for the purest mathematics. But somewhere around the edges of his science, he is making room for the legitimate practice of an old tradition. Economic criticism is becoming a legitimate part of the conversation.

MARCH 18, 1984

Too Little Knowledge:
Too Much Leverage

WITH THOUSANDS OF KIDS TRUDGING BACK TO THE CLASSROOM, IT IS SOBERING TO recall that there is almost no discipline in which the distinction between the realm of the textbook and the real world is more fruitful than in economics. With the accuracy of forecasting under scrutiny in the *Wall Street Journal*, in *Time*, in the *Harvard Business Review*; with the continuing strength of the dollar a universal puzzlement, is there anything for the kid to write home about?

Well, yes, according to Andrew M. Kamarck. Part of the problem is that too much is expected of a field that is still in its youth, he says. A World Bank official who spent more than 40 years in the field, Kamarck is the author of a fine book that should be tucked into each concentrator's book bag—at least all those who are headed for honors. Published last year by Basil Blackwell in England, it is being issued as a paperback there, yet here remains tucked in obscurity as a University of Pennsylvania hardcover edition, with no paperback in prospect.

The gravamen of the book is that economics is a fine guide to investigations of the world, as long as it is not pushed too far—but that it is regularly pushed too far. The trick is to forever remember that the map is not the territory—and that it is the territory, not mapmaking, that is of the greatest interest. What *Economics and the Real World* really amounts to is a careful survey of 40 years of literature on measurement error. Literally scores of complicated and difficult papers are each digested in a single lucid paragraph or two, and strung together in graceful chapters as by an old sergeant teaching jungle lore to a bunch of green lieutenants. The book amounts to a manual for applying common-sense windage in nearly every situation.

To pick an example is thus to trivialize the book. Nevertheless, consider an aspect of Gross National Product. "Because of the way we measure GNP," Kamarck says, "It is impossible to improve productivity of government, since we measure output by the wages and salaries paid the government workers. If it turns out that a job mailing social security checks that formerly took 10,000 workers now takes 1,000, you don't show that as an increase in productivity; instead, it turns up as a decrease in GNP."

The book is best, however, when dwelling on the mathematical foibles that beset economists. Whether sorting out the problems of encoding data for computers or writing about the rounding-off of numbers, Kamarck is completely at home in a world in which a little knowledge is all he's got, dangerous mainly when he thinks it's a lot. Indeed, an appendix on significant digits, meaning a scientific technique for indicating the degree of precision to be attached to numbers, employed by every physical scientist in the world and ignored by virtually every economist, is worth the price of the book alone.

This focus on epistemological economics puts Kamarck in a line that includes Adolph Lowe, Sidney Shoeffler, T.W. Hutchison, but that inevitably recalls Oskar Morgenstern, whose book *On the Accuracy of Economic Observations* remains the classic. Is a new book needed? "I wanted to bring Morgenstern's book up to date, as it were," says Kamarck. "And I was trying to add something. What I was trying to do is show that there are a whole series of problems where we have not been able to develop good concepts, concepts that have been able to handle economic reality."

To be sure, *Economics and the Real World* is not a complete tour of the horizon; there is no entry on Bayseian statistics, for example, and Kamarck notes there are a number of new mathematical techniques which may help economics escape some of its straitjackets: by supplying a role for history to a demand function, for instance; or by dealing with the problems of aggregation and disaggregation that plague economists by classifying some entities in "fuzzy sets."

"I'm not enough of a mathematician and I don't want to commit that much time to the project," says the economist. "I've got a lot of other things that I want to look into."

Kamarck, 69, has kept track of the literature on measurement problems throughout a long career, first at Harvard in the 1930s, then at the Federal Reserve Board, then the Treasury Department, the Allied Control Council in Italy and Germany. In 1950, he moved to the World Bank, where he started both the economics department and the Economic Development Institute, which trains government officials from around the world. He lives now in Brewster, Mass., on Cape Cod, travels little except up to Harvard University once a week to sit in on seminars as a fellow of the Institute for International Development. His wife paints, manages a successful gallery in Orleans.

Not surprisingly, Kamarck is most vibrant on problems arising from the process of world development, yet the class of problems that receives the least attention in the book are those that stem from growing global interdependence. "I mention the fact, for example, that our measurements of monetary supply are getting more and more difficult. For instance in M1, we include U.S. currency. But there are countries—Poland is one, Israel is another—where U.S. dollars are the real currency, and the local currency is a, well, something residents have to contend with, but not really money. So what is the relevant money supply?"

Or take the strength of the dollar. "Nobody, as far as I can see, has come up with a very good explanation of what is happening, except that clearly, what is happening is some kind of inflow of capital. Well, the trouble is, we just don't have very good statistics on the movement of capital. This is something that's important to us, but it's important for the world as a whole, too.

"Yet compare the amount of money that we're spending in order to make it possible for astronomers and physicists to learn more about outer space; marvelous. But we don't spend a fraction of that on trying to improve our understanding of these problems . . . worse, the present administration in Washington is cutting back."

Kamarck is somewhat pessimistic about the direction of technical economics. He writes, "The drift . . . away from consideration of real problems towards scholasticism is apparently an almost irresistable temptation in academia in all subjects. Career pressures to publish or perish encourage work on articles that emphasize technical sophistication of technique rather than time consuming laborious work on real-world problems." Yet he acknowledges the existence of a large technological sector, where trained researchers sift through numbers on behalf of banks, investment houses, government agencies, newspapers and the like; and he offers several concrete suggestions of techniques designed to keep economists from becoming too inward-looking, so-called "Delphi surveys" in which opinions are sought and scrutinized, and "working parties" composed of diverse specialists.

In the end, Kamarck's tough-minded willingness to confront the limitations of economics becomes a revelation of strength, not a confession of weakness. The discipline he scouts out has little in common with the maturity and the comforting precision of the natural sciences, but it is a long way up from sociology.

SEPTEMBER 16, 1984

Never Mind
the Second Law

THE CURRENT ARGUMENT ABOUT THE FATE OF THE EARTH IS NOT EXACTLY CHARAC-
terized by its narrowness or precision. One day a new report says global
warming is under way and all but irreversible. Another report speculates a
tanker full of iron filings in the southern ocean could fertilize enough algae
to rival the biomass of the Amazon rain forest—and so roll back the greenhouse effect. In the spring Congress passes a $30 billion Clean Air Act; in
the summer a soil scientist ventures that $500,000 a year would be enough
to lime every lake in New York and New England sufficiently to restore
their habitability to fish. The great division of opinion among those who
concern themselves with planetary affairs often seems to be between a sense
of bottomless despair and one of boundless efficacy.

This conflict is apparent in the recent works of a pair of leading lights of
opposing camps. Herman Daly, a Louisiana State University professor who
has for several years been serving as chief environmental economist of the
World Bank, has with co-author John Cobb published *For the Common
Good: Redirecting the Economy Toward Community, the Environment and a
Sustainable Future.* And Julian Simon, a University of Maryland professor
who for 20 years has been among the most effective critics of the full-
throated environmentalists, has published a collection of his popular articles, reviews and talks, called *Population Matters: People, Resources,
Environment and Immigration* as well as a more scholarly tome, *The Economic Consequences of Immigration.*

Daly and Cobb, economist and theologian, offer a relatively comforting
and familiar version of what life should be all about. They flirt with calling
for a "return to socialism," but settle instead on the Catholic Church
critique of socialism and capitalism, with its emphasis on the person as a
member of a community. (Both writers are Protestants.) "The scale of
human activity relative to the biosphere has grown too large," they write;
the enemy of sustainability is growth. They devote an appropriate amount
of effort to deflating the elaborate rhetoric of growth. The first quarter of the

book is a critique of neo-classical economics. A substantial appendix presents an alternative to GNP or growth accounting.

Much flows out of this, and some of it is sophisticated economics—the discussion of the kind of national tax system that would be conducive to a steady state makes fascinating reading, as do discussions of the illusive concept of the ecological "carrying capacity" of particular regions of land. But as gentle and genteel as is the Daly-Cobb critique of our highly individualistic society, it is not altogether clear that they have envisioned a persuasively better way. "We are glad that China's leaders saw the error of laissez-faire individualism, and we hope for a reversal of recent trends in the United States," they write at one point. Also on their agenda—highly managed trade, regional decentralization and the resettlement of the countryside by the family farm. These are all in some sense desirable goals, but perhaps Daly and Cobb underestimate the importance of achieving them by consensus. Or perhaps that is precisely the point of their concluding chapter on religious vision.

Simon, on the other hand, has little use for the concept of limits. He quotes the physicist Freeman Dyson approvingly: "Boiled down to one sentence, my message is the unboundedness of life and the consequent unboundedness of human destiny." And the chronicle of Simon's jousts with doomsayers over one issue after another makes for illuminating reading. He's crossed swords with practically every environmental prophet in America during the past 20 years—over disappearing farmland, global famine, vanishing wildlife, illegal aliens, population policies and the rest. He's won far more battles than he's lost.

On balance, I think I prefer Daly. We don't need more permissions—to multiply our numbers, to greatly alter our environment, to diminish the species population of the Earth, to divide our labor ever more intricately—nearly so much as we need warnings that there are environmental limits somewhere and that we are surely reaching them. Never mind the Second Law of Thermodynamics; to live harmoniously with nature seems to be one of the truly universal human imperatives, as intuitively obvious in South America as it is in Asia, North America and Africa. Surely the preservation and conservation of the ecosystem will become ever more important during the unprecedented knitting-together of the nations of the world during the next 50 years.

But let the last word on the subject belong to Julian Simon. His point, after all, is that whatever we need to do, can be done. It is true that more people increase demands on the global system, and so disturb it more, he says. But more people also have brought about better understanding of the system and greater ability to bend it to our will. "The difference is between a world of 10,000 people many millennia ago, who inadvertently disturbed little and could not intentionally alter much, and as we are many billions now, who disturb much but who can purposefully alter even more."

AUGUST 26, 1990

Against the Weapons Biz

SO GORBACHEV HAS GONE HOME. SOME 4 PERCENT OF THE WORLD'S NUKES ARE headed for the scrap heap. Meanwhile, Star Wars seems to have been the quiet winner of last week's negotiations: the Americans and Russians apparently agreed to let each other quietly go ahead developing space weapons while they work on their long-range missile pact.

Is there any "peace dividend" in all this? Might there instead be a further "space race spinoff" from Star Wars? Or is it possible that the world might actually face a slowdown if the superpowers are able to get along better and do without their "military Keynesianism?"

These questions about the mainsprings of economic growth are so far beyond the present-day capacity of economics to answer them—even to venture crisp hypotheses—that only the boldest are tempted to ask and answer them. They tend to be the old and wise and daring (John Kenneth Galbraith is a prime example) or the young and passionate and daring (Tom Riddell of Smith College is typical of the latest generation of defense economists who are working in the explicit service of peace.) But no one has been more energetic in thinking about the economics of war and peace than Walter Isard, who is today a professor at Cornell University.

Thirty years ago, while at the University of Pennsylvania, Isard launched a spinoff of economics he called regional science, a discipline that since has found a respectable place in many universities. Like many successful entrepreneurs, Isard wasn't content with just one success: some years ago he set out to found a discipline of "peace science." As a result, a dozen sessions at the American Economic Association meetings in Chicago later this month will be given over to the discussion of topics like build-downs (as opposed to build-ups) and general equilibrium modelling of changes in world military expenditures. And if these techniques haven't yet been imported to the sophisticated discourse of arms control, they represent a start on a truly disciplined conversation about the economic consequences of international tension.

In a telephone interview last week, Isard said, "This round is really only a small round. The real significance lies in the fact that it represents a turn around in the U.S. attitude and perspective. These major steps that will be taken will cause other problems, economic problems, job losses in various regions of the United States, but I'm optimistic that we can plan ahead various kinds of offset programs to minimize any negative reaction."

"One of the key factors is the fact that they've been able to work out monitoring and inspection procedures. This has always been the real trouble point before. I can foresee that major steps can be made. It won't be easy, but it can be done."

Another influential thinker is Kenneth Boulding, a University of Colorado economist and former American Economic Association president who has been publishing works on disarmament since 1960. From his cabin in the Rockies, Boulding last week discussed the Euromissile treaty.

"It is rather unprecedented. I'm hopeful about it. I'm rather pleasantly surprised by Mr. Reagan. I confess I haven't had a very high opinion of him in the past. But I must say, I think the role captured the man, shall we say. He really rose to the needs and virtues of his office. Of course the whole thing could still go wrong in the Senate.

"Star Wars, of course, is much more difficult because they don't know anything about it, do they? It's just literally pie in the sky. As I've often said, it's like trying to shoot the bullet that the cowboy just fired at you instead of the cowboy. There is a very widespread opinion in the scientific community that it's nonsense.

"It could easily be very destabilizing, do you see, because it isn't a defensive weapon. It's not like armor, is it? It's like a better pistol. I thinks it's crazy, there's no other word to describe it. On the other hand, it is a recognition that what one might call conventional national defense has really broken down. We've got to find mutual security by other means, just the way we have in Canada. We've got to turn Russia into Canada. It's not easy but it's by no means impossible because it pays off so well. It pays off just enormously, so there's at least half a chance of it happening.

"We've had a spreading stable peace in the world since the middle of the 19th century. It began in Scandanavia, really. It spread to North America, starting about 1870. We got it in Western Europe after the Second World

War; I don't think the French and the Germans are going to fight each other are they? So the next thing is how to get it with the Russians. Then to spread it to the Third World, that's the really difficult thing.

"We don't have any real conflicts with the Russians at all; there are no boundary conflicts, they don't really want Alaska, I don't think. We don't have any economic conflicts at all; the better off they are, the better off we are, there's no question about it. It should be fairly easy, but nobody quite sees how to do it."

There are those, of course, who fear that war or the threat of it often has been a major contributor to economic growth—though not always to the growth of the warrior nations. One scholar who set himself to the task of examining the record was John U. Nef, the great University of Chicago scholar who in 1950 published *War and Human Progress: An Essay on the Rise of Industrial Civilization*. In the just-published *The New Palgrave, A Dictionary of Economics*, Colin Clark, an economic historian of great distinction, describes Nef's findings "on the ominous subject of whether the world could have made the same progress, economic and social, without the stimulus of war."

Clark writes, "It was only war, in the physical sense, not merely international tension, which brought about the principal developments in the European metal trades; and the same might be said of the side-effects of the American Civil War. Keynes said that war was 'a great sifter, bringing the right men to the top.' In present times it would be hard to deny that our extraordinary progress in all branches of electronics would have been at the same pace without the continuous stimulus of military demand."

But last week Boulding took issue with Clark (and perhaps came closer to the spirit of John Nef's original argument.) "I take the opposite view completely. War is an interruption, it's a brain drain. The current sort of mild decay of American productivity—it's not disastrous, but it's certainly noticeable—is very much a result of the war industry. I've often said that engineers who should have been designing autos in Detroit are designing missiles for the military. There's a very severe brain drain.

"This sort of thing has never paid off for an imperial power. The way to get rich is to stay home and mind your own business, like the Swedes or the Danes. They got much richer than the French or the English in the 19th century. It's absurd to think that you get rich by exploiting people, any more than you get rich by mugging. You get rich by producing things other people want. The military spin-off effect is easily exaggerated. Just look at light-water reactors; I don't think we ever would have done anything as stupid as that if we had done it in peace-time," Boulding said.

Isard concurs: "It may not have occurred in electronics, but it would have occurred in other areas. Take the whole area of housing construction. We're still using outmoded methods. Or take the aeronautics industry. Right before the war, this was the hot thing; the war effort shifted resources out of aeronautics; before the the war there was all this talk about having big air trains; the war effort was the damper on those big-think R&D efforts."

Did it really? Or did the life-or-death competition for technological supremacy that was chronicled so brilliantly earlier this year by author Richard Rhodes in the year's best book, *The Making of the Atomic Bomb*, actually result in more peace rather than less under today's nuclear umbrella? Does war-like competition help or hinder economic progress? There are no models that can resolve these issues; there are only great historians.

Meanwhile, despite the hopeful tone in Washington last week, the reality seems to be that the United States and the Soviet Union are still locked in a struggle for the upper hand. This is what American conservatives are so mad about. Don't trust the Russians, they say. As William Safire put it last week, they remain "a puissant force in this world that does not wish us well."

He may be wrong; they may be no more a natural enemy than Canada. But there is thus more than enough mutual distrust to assure that competition will continue for the foreseeable future between the military Hertz of the modern industrial world and its Avis.

DECEMBER 13, 1987

Medicine
for Hurry Sickness

WHAT DOES IT MEAN TO HAVE *ENOUGH* TIME? EVERYONE CONNECTED WITH THE WORLD of business has felt its shortage—even in August, when the entire world seems to be running at a slower pace.

A good place to do a little thinking about time is *The Metronomic Society: Natural Rhythms and Human Timetables* by Michael Young. It's an August kind of book—ruminative, writerly, difficult—about the clock systems with which we are born and those that govern the industrial system that we have created and the changing balance between them. It offers some useful insights into the life of everyone who works for a living. Michael Young is an English analog to Daniel Patrick Moynihan, a brilliant academician who has wound up in politics. (He's Lord Young now, a member of the House of Lords.) If you had read his anti-utopian novel *The Rise and Fall of the Meritocracy, 1875–2025* when it was first published in 1957 you would have had a greatly increased appreciation of global politics—and of the universal significance of China's Cultural Revolution—ever since.

To begin with Young makes a distinction between cyclical and linear time, between the constant repetition of what there has been before and a continuous occurrence of the new, between time viewed as a circle and time viewed as a strung-out line. It's the straight-line view that dominates industrial societies, Young says—the story of growing political and cultural integration, technological progress, social evolution—but we ignore the cyclical dimension at our peril.

This cyclical dimension is not simply the daily rising and setting of the sun, the monthly circuit of the moon around the earth, nor the yearly cycle of the seasons. Young delves into the new field of chronobiology to report the latest discoveries of the oscillations that govern the human body. He scouts the extent to which our genetic systems lead us to reproduce the past. He dwells on the role of memory, habit and custom in preserving what we already know. He notes that language, itself, is a kind of a cycle, always changing but preserved mainly by constant repetition.

(Oddly enough, for a man who spent the last 25 years studying the family, he gives very little attention to the place of the reproductive cycle in modern industrial society. This is especially surprising in view of the extent to which child-care issues have suddenly moved close to center stage in American politics.) Against this tendency to repetition, Young sets the "metronomic pulse" of the modern world. He writes, "Years have been divided into equal days, days into equal hours, hours into equal minutes, minutes into equal seconds, seconds into equal nanoseconds; these are the beats of our metronomic society."

Ever since the first street lights were installed on London's Pall Mall in 1820, the human race has been engaged in a "hundred years war against nature" whose purpose was to obliterate all those natural clues of light and temperature that trigger cycles. But following historians like Lewis Mumford and David Landes, Young identifies the clock as the real tyrant of the modern age. Today, people are required to work around the clock, to synchronize their efforts in different time zones, to relentlessly hedge the future in the present, all in the name of economic progress, but the "homogenization" of time has come at a very high price.

Perhaps the most painful consequence of the rise of strictly linear time has been what others have called the "time famine." People who were alienated from their natural propensity to cycles find that a rising standard of living means more and more choices—and less and less time to distribute among the possibilities. As material goods proliferate, the cost of leisure time soars—measured, that is, in terms of what could have been earned if the time had been spent in work, instead. Young writes, "Dr. Johnson, when he saw the lovely furniture, the books, and beautiful women around the famous actor David Garrick, said, 'Davey, Davey, this must make death very terrible.' " We are not all Garricks, as Young notes, but each of us has more to see, to do, to enjoy than we have time.

What is wanted in these circumstances is not necessarily the instinctive response of the economist—to assign every activity a shadow price and let the market do the rationing. Nor is it the "nonchalant indifference to the passage of time" of the premodern peasant. As Young says, we cannot return to the world that was lost. But rather what is indicated is some greater looseness in the presence of the inevitable passage of time. More attention to the sunrise and sunset, to the seasons, and to the natural rhythms of life; less attention to strictly linear careers. "If we would let the sense of time refer to something besides being on the dot, and always knowing where the dot is; if we would leave more room for spontaneity; if more of us would let the future move into the present without grasping at it, with more presence of mind, the time famine could begin to abate."

In a short epilogue, designed to illustrate the better world he imagines, Young offers a glimpse of a morning in the life of a fisherman. The skipper of a West Country trawler wakes, looks out the window, taps the barometer, and postpones the decision of whether or not to put to sea. He makes a cup of tea. He considers the tides, the migration habits of the fish, the prices they might fetch in the market—and decides to go ahead.

You don't have to be a fisherman to recognize the wisdom of what Young is saying. The more people pick their own rhythms, the better the chance is that they will pick the right ones. Not all days—or months—are created equal, as any denizen of the month of August knows.

AUGUST 21, 1988

Building
Pandaemonium

COMPARED TO ALL THE INK SPILLED ON GEORGE ORWELL, HUMPHREY JENNINGS HAS not attracted much attention. Yet, like Orwell, Jennings was a classic English character of a certain sort. His parents were crafts movement followers of William Morris and John Ruskin, also of Gurdjieff; he himself was the product of a good but eccentric public school that emphasized literature and drama—and that threw him out for failing to join its war games. Like Orwell, he was a superb publicist for England during World War II.

But where Orwell worked in journalism on the great news stories of his day, Jennings worked in film, or at least film-like images. His documentaries, *Listen to Britain, Fires Were Started* and *Diary for Timothy*, were as successful at galvanizing opinion at home as were Edward R. Murrow's broadcasts abroad, and they made him famous. But Jennings' work of 13 years, a dozen red notebooks comprising hundreds of passages from literature and his notes thereon, all describing the impact of machines of all sorts on daily life in England over several centuries, were unpublished when he died in 1950—at 43, in an accident in Greece.

Now—thanks to a collaboration between Jennings' granddaughter, Mary-Lou Jennings, and a distinguished editor, Charles Madge—those commonplace books have been carefully assembled and published as *Pandaemonium: The Coming of Machines as Seen by Contemporary Observers*. The resulting 350 carefully organized and indexed pages are a little like those early time-lapse photographs of a man running, each frame still and apart on the page but altogether telling a riveting story. Divided into four parts—"Observations and Reports, 1660–1729"; "Exploitation, 1730–1790"; "Revolution, 1791–1850"; and "Confusion, 1851–1886"—*Pandaemonium* gives an always vivid, never very coherent sense of what it was like to live in times that, seen from a distance, are even more stirring than the war. The title is from Milton's verses on the building of the industrial city of Pandaemonium, "the high Capital of Satan and his peers."

The selections are about equally distributed between jubilation and horror. An early anatomist narrates the vivisection of a mare. A farm servant describes his sub-human diet: "Ay, no man knows what he can do till he's put to it," he says. Josiah Wedgwood wistfully abandons his passion for geology for "the forming of a jug or teapot." Sherlock Holmes performs a blood test and claps with glee at the results. Betty Higden prepares to drown herself in the Thames in Dickens' *Our Mutual Friend*. If William Blake had made a movie of the Industrial Revolution, this is what it would look like; nearly every scene finds some direct counterpart in modern life.

A fitting companion to *Pandaemonium*, a kind of continuation of the story by other means, is to be found in Robert Howard's book, *Brave New Workplace: America's Corporate Utopias—How They Create New Inequalities and Social Conflict in Our Working Lives*. Howard is an Amherst College graduate and a Cambridge writer; his witness stems from the same impulse as that of Jennings, his sense that things have gotten out of hand. But his story has to do with computers and corporations and the way they have changed the character of modern work. They've disenfranchised workers of their skills, he says, tilted the labor-management steeply in favor of the bosses, and, in general, just made things worse. What's needed is much more social control of technology—as in Europe, where computer terminals sometimes remain shrouded even after they have been installed.

Much of what Howard has to say is already familiar to readers of David Noble, Larry Hirschhorn and Harley Shaiken, but he writes a lively and graceful magazine style, covering the issues thoroughly, and when he zeroes in on what is one of the most fascinating issues of the day, job design, he has much of his own to add. Participatory job design, on the shop floor and in the office, is an idea whose time is coming, under pressure of increasing competition. But whether making lathes, airplane engines and computer terminals "user-friendly" is the stuff of which social revolutions are made is open to doubt.

The thing about both *Pandaemonium* and *Brave New Workplace* is that neither gives much sympathy to understanding the reasons why industrial development has succeeded so completely, or why it is so widely thought to be a good thing. That sort of thing is usually delegated to the economists. But both books are excellent goads to thinking about the history of work. And that is something that the economists usually leave out.

NOVEMBER 24, 1985

A Son Charts
His Own Course

THERE WAS A RUMPLED MAN IN THE NEXT SEAT, AND AS THE PLANE CLIMBED INTO THE air and the passengers spread out their work it became clear that he was an economist, none other than the legendary monetarist Harry Johnson, who could write two papers during a trip across the Atlantic. The youth allowed that he, too, was an economist, a graduate student at Yale University, James Galbraith by name.

Johnson's eyes lit up. "You wouldn't," he said, "by any chance," the smile spreading as he continued the interlocutory, "be the son," the boy bracing for the inevitable recognition, "of the president of the Bank of Montreal?"

In fact, of course, James K. Galbraith is the third and youngest son of Harvard University's John Kenneth Galbraith—Jay-me to his friends. At 32, he is a veteran of 10 years of work on Capitol Hill, the last four of them as the quietly influential deputy director of the staff of the Joint Economic Committee, where supply-sider Bruce Bartlett is chief of staff. Galbraith's job was letting people in to testify, keeping them out, writing legislation, commissioning and receiving reports, and in general helping Congress make its will known, first to itself, then to the policymakers.

Now, with the new Congress coming back to town, Rep. Lee Hamilton (D-Ind.) is moving up from the joint committee to the Intelligence Committee, and Rep. Gillis W. Long (D-La.) is moving into the vice chairman's office with his own staff man (not an economist), so Galbraith is moving out. He's taken a job as guest scholar at the Brookings Institution, has started a book and is looking for teaching jobs.

"This is the first time in four years that I haven't had to preface a conversation with a reporter by saying that this is all off the record," he noted.

Of his famous father, Galbraith said, "The only courageous stance is unreserved praise. Anything else would be a sign of insecurity." Sure enough, for a recent retrospective session on the author of *The New Indus-*

trial State and 20 other books, he wrote about his father, "Galbraith's professional colleagues have taken a long time and circuitous road to arrive where he stood before the void which is an economics pertinent to the modern corporation. The essence of that void is the economic underdevelopment of a theory of power."

True, Galbraith's own economics are somewhat more technical than his father's, but on most policy matters they are of a single view. As a doctoral student at Yale, the neoclassical tradition bore down on him, though predictably he headed for William Parker, the historian there. And he married Lucy Ferguson, the president of the Economics Club when he arrived; she is an applied micro theorist, more at home in the down-to-earth issues of rail transportation than in the stratospheric reaches of macroeconomics.

Galbraith's own thinking now runs more to the problems of deindexation, a policy he sees as a Democratic alternative to very tight money. He said, "Republicans ran in 1984 on a platform of no more high interest rates; but the word inflation wasn't even in the Democrats' vocabulary. Unless they find ways to make stable prices their issue, too, I don't think that Democrats can hope to compete in the future."

The trick, therefore, is to negotiate nearly everyone out of their cost-of-living allowances, bit by bit. "The way you do it is to move to discretionary adjustments in the CPI (Consumer Price Index), just as there used to be in the federal system, when Congress used to vote increases, usually every two years. There was something to be said back at the beginning of the 1970s for automatic increases, but when you're getting inflation out of the system you want to get people back to writing contracts in which they do not anticipate rising prices," he said.

But how is this different from Martin Feldstein's proposal to change the cost-of-living formula for Social Security benefit adjustments to changes in the consumer price index minus 3 percent? "All the difference in the world," said Galbraith. "Feldstein's plan would reduce the real level of benefits, whereas I am interested in preserving their real value. Mine is a macroeconomic tool; his is a budget-cutting device."

Galbraith's emphasis on the problems of achieving stable prices clearly reflects the work he began 10 years ago under then-Rep. Henry Reuss to forge a congressional relationship with the Federal Reserve system. "It started out, with Arthur Burns, as basically a relationship of contempt, flowing from Constitution Avenue to Capitol Hill. Burns would come up, puff on his pipe and intimidate the members of Congress.

"Under Henry Reuss' leadership, in the transition from Arthur Burns to William Miller to Paul Volcker, through the refinement of the regular process of oversight hearings, it is now possible to get a serious, intelligent dialogue going. It's very hard work, but it can be done," he said.

"When we started out in 1975, it took from 10 o'clock in the morning until 4:30 or 5 o'clock in the afternoon to get Arthur Burns to answer the simple question: What's the relationship of monetary growth to nominal GNP? We had to ask seven or eight times before he finally answered it. But we established the precedent that he would answer it, and in 1977 we put it into the law that the Fed must disclose what they believe is 'the central tendency.' So now we have some sense of what the Federal Reserve thinks is going to happen so that we can look back in an oversight way and see whether in retrospect the forecasts they were making were sensibly based or not.

"This process had its real climax in the summer of 1982. I'm not saying that we single-handedly forced the Fed to abandon its targets in time to avert a crash, but we certainly were able to make our views known to them, in a timely and forcible fashion."

Galbraith probably still isn't anywhere near the economic—as opposed to the political—mainstream. But his competence in the language of economists makes him attractive to politicians seeking to figure out where the tricky currents lead. Would-be presidential contenders chat him up; the invisible college of potential advisers to Democratic administrations acknowledges his legislative leadership. He cuts a certain figure, as they say.

Robert Kuttner, the widely-followed dogmatist of the left, put it this way: "Galbraith is one of the few under-40 left-liberal economists playing in the policy game, and the Joint Economic Committee was one of the few forums in Washington. He's terrific, and if we had 50 more like him we'd have a real policy debate."

JANUARY 13, 1985

On the Issue
of the Whole and Its Parts

WHAT DO WINE, COMPUTERS, CITIES, COMPANIES AND ECONOMIC ORGANIZATION IN general have in common? The answer is that they come in varying degrees of complexity.

This aspect of things has had a long existence in the twilight zone of discourse; telephone company ads, for example, have dwelt for years on the complexity of the modern communications system; the Boston Consulting Group has done a good business recently advising corporations on how to adjust the complexity of their product lines and management structures to changing situations. Indeed, the term at times has threatened to become a weasel-word of the first magnitude.

Now, however, scattered bands of scientists in diverse fields are on the verge of turning the concept of complexity from a barrier to understanding to a useful tool. In a prescient but little-remarked book called *Coping with Complexity*, aimed at extending its formal analysis to fields as diverse as job design, decision rules and organizational structure, the German theorist Hans-Werner Gottinger wrote in 1983:

"The starting point is the recognition that complexity is a well-defined concept in mathematics (e.g. in topological dynamics), computer science, information theory and artificial intelligence. But it is a rather diffuse concept in other fields, and sometimes it has only descriptive value, or even worse, it is used only in a colloquial sense."

It is this that is slowly beginning to change.

"Unless you've been unconscious for the last year, you know that a very great deal is going on." The speaker was Margaret Wright of Stanford's Operations Laboratory, and she was talking about developments in the field of linear programming, the optimal arrangement of complex systems. But she might just as well have been surveying all the fields on the boundaries between economics, applied mathematics and computer science. When the Econometric Society meets in Cambridge tomorrow, it will be in a spirit of catch-up to its younger sib, the Mathematical Programming Society, whose members met here a week ago.

The fact is that economists, having dined out for two centuries on their ever-deepening analysis of equilibrium (meaning the counterpoise of opposing forces), are slowly broadening their studies to include methods associated with the analysis of complexity (meaning the arrangement of parts to form a whole). That is to say that, among other things, economists are seeking to make ever-better friends with methods of linear programming, the preeminent allocative tools of the visible hand of management, the things you reach for when the market isn't there.

It was three widely separated men pondering the allocation of resources in the turmoil surrounding World War II who came up with linear programming. The Dutch physicist-turned-economist Tjalling Koopmans was thinking about carrying cargo in ships; a young American researcher named George B. Dantzig was thinking about equipping and training the Air Force; and it was later discovered by Koopmans that a Russian scientist named Leonid Kantorovitch had hit upon some of the same ideas in the Soviet Union in 1939. For a while after the war, the body of techniques they developed were identified by the less technical name of "activity analysis"; gradually it became more widely known as operations research.

Koopmans and Kantorovitch shared the Nobel Prize for economics in 1975; Dantzig was left out because he was not an economist. But in the view of many it was he who made the most far-reaching contribution, for it was Dantzig's idea to firmly connect planning methods with computers.

A few years ago, Dantzig wrote, "If anyone were to ask me what my greatest achievement was, I would say it was the realization that the planning problem (for all its complicated ground rules, apparent exceptions and variety of ways of stating the technology and the interrelations between activities and items) could for the most part be encompassed into one simple system—the linear program." Earlier this month, at a dinner honoring Dantzig, Harvard economist Robert Dorfman recalled with laughter the difficulty he has teaching Dantzig elementary economics. "I could never get him to take marginal productivity seriously—thank goodness."

For solving his linear program, for achieving the best possible arrangement of a set of resources under the circumstances, Dantzig came up with a procedure for disciplined trial-and-error search—an algorithm—that he named the simplex method. Privately, he described the approach as "climbing the beanpole," after the intuitive geometry derived from its graph. It promised a way to manage things—companies, armies, activities of all sorts—that were quickly getting out of hand.

When Dantzig invented the simplex method, computers were in their infancy and the algorithm was "a goal rather than a calculation that could be performed," as Robert Dorfman says. But over the years, computers and applied math have grown considerably. Computing power has been increased by incredible proportions, and the the environs of the "beanpole" has become a multidimensional polygon called a polytope—an abstraction that planners spend their adolescent years learning to handle.

It's the approach to the polytope that's now the center of a lively concern in linear programming. The simplex method goes around its outside, checking each corner, turning this way and that, moving on each time in the direction of a better solution. The process takes many steps, and the steps take time. These increase dramatically with the difficulty of the problem, but the method produces highly reliable answers.

The new method, announced last fall amid great hoopla, promised to bring into range a far more complicated range of problems—those with 5,000 variables and more. Its analytic underpinnings are sound enough; everyone agrees it's a breakthrough. But hardly anybody understands how the 28-year-old Indian scientist named Narendra Karmarkar gets the extraordinarily fast and precise results he claims. The Karmarkar method starts in the inside of the polytope, then uses a technique called projective geometry to warp the whole structure, again and again, in effect changing the shape of the polytope, over and over, until the best solution is achieved. The technique smacks of the geometry of relativity theory; it is not for the typical liberal-arts dilettante. But it could dramatically cut the number of steps necessary to reach an answer—if it works.

Whether he turns out to be father of a new field of problem-solving or just another footnote in the history of applied mathematics, Narendra Karmarkar has stimulated an extremely useful reexamination of the deep underpinnings of linear programming. But even before he came along, it was clear that computational complexity has relevance to economics, high and low.

Yale University's Herbert Scarf, who organized a session at the Econometric Society on complexity, says, "We know that computational methods, algorithms for solving problems in economics, have to do with economic theory. That's an old notion, from (Paul) Samuelson and Koopmans. They knew there was a connection between market mechanisms and computational procedures. But these new discoveries are terribly interesting. I think this stuff bears on how complex are the problems that a firm is meant to solve, for example." Thus, slowly but surely, social scientists are reaching out to acquire ideas from mathematicians and computer scientists that may prove useful in their fields. Next year, for example, a number of computer scientists interested in complexity theory will meet and mingle with a lot of mathematical economists in a big session at Berkeley organized by Gerard Debreu and Stephen Smale.

So what? Who cares, when they've got bills to pay, about events taking place far out on remote frontiers? The answer is that the way we think about the world is changing, deep down, perhaps more than at any time in the past 300 years. You can expect the results to catch up with daily life some years from now. In *Frontiers of Supercomputing*, mathematician James Glimm has written:

"Computers will affect science and technology at least as profoundly as did the invention of the calculus. The reasons are the same. As with the calculus, computers have increased and will increase enormously their range of solvable problems. The full development of these events will occupy decades, and the rapid progress which we see currently is a strong sign that the impact of computing will be much greater in the future than it is today."

AUGUST 18, 1985

Telling the Wants
from the Wanters

Thank God, those fresh spirits gathered down from Granite
Hills and from green peaceful valleys by their own wills,
to the carnival of spindles and looms and iron arms,
heaving with their titan best, are nonetheless, but more
beautiful, while pure, they stand up and vindicate the
sacredness of Toil. They are not called by imperious wants.
—*New York Daily Tribune*, "Visit to Lowell," describing
an influx of young women into the work force in 1845

Well, after a hundred years or so of wondering, men finally know what it is that women want. They want to work. Since 1950, the percentage of married women in the work force has risen from less than a quarter in 1950 to nearly a half today. The trend is continuing, perhaps even accelerating.

But why do they want to work?

Seen through the lens of conventional economics, the occupational history of women presents a history of personal choice.

If women are entering the work force in greater numbers today, it is because they prefer to, because their earning power is greater than in the "shadow wage" attached to their work as mothers. They've always had the choice; it is just that formerly the price wasn't right.

If today they are paid 60 cents on the dollar of what men earn, on average, it is either because the work they do is worth less to others intrinsically, or because discrimination has "crowded" them into particular occupations and created artificial gluts.

According to this economic view of things, there is no vital difference between men and women. Each are sovereign consumers, and if families are less important today than formerly, it is—as economist Gary Becker says—because the marketplace can provide many of their advantages more efficiently: "Market insurance is used instead of kin insurance, market schools instead of family schools and examinations and contracts instead of family certification."

According to Marxists, however, the story of working women—and of the rest of life—has much more *Sturm und Drang*. It is a matter of periodic revolutions in production technology and in consciousness itself (changing preferences, economists might say) and it is a subtle episode in this process in which we are caught up today.

According to this view, women don't work because they want to; they work because they are psychologically forced. Like men, they are victims of an economic system that robs them of the fruits of their labors, but unlike men, they have suffered from a special class of discrimination. They have been victims of a sexual division of labor, forced by culture, not nature, to raise the children they have borne and to keep house.

At the heart of this debate, then, are rival conceptions of the essential nature of men and women: economists see people as self-aggrandizing, selfish, maximizing; Marxists see them as relatively plastic, easily fooled, slow to fight for their rights—but rather relentless once they do.

The issue comes up because a new interpretation of women's historical experience appears this month, part of a recent effusion of historical scholarship from Boston. There was Michael Piore's history of migrant workers, *Birds of Passage*; Bennett Harrison and Barry Bluestone's history of economic growth and abandonment, *The Deindustrialization of America*; Rosalind Williams' book on the origins of mass consumption psychology in 19th-century France, *Dream Worlds*; even Alfred Chandler's *The Visible Hand*, a history of corporate organization.

Now Julie Matthaei, an associate professor of economics at Wellesley, has written *An Economic History of Women in America*. The book is not exactly conventional Marxism, nor conventional economic history either. Matthaei hasn't been piling up new data on women in county courthouses around the country, but she doesn't cut corners with the existing literature. The book is a labor of many years, a work that has to be taken seriously. It maybe is a bit more architectonic than most, but still valuable for the story it tells.

According to Matthaei, it was only during the 19th century that the home and economy emerged as separate spheres. Before that, the rigors of colonial life had enforced a certain solidarity on families; men and women were differentiated, but not highly: women could work without becoming pale imitations of men.

But with the advent of the Industrial Revolution, family life became a vocation for women, no different in principle from the "callings" of men, and the ideal woman thus was separated from economic life. This evolution depended on a "cult of domesticity," propagated in books and pamphlets. Matthaei cites a passage from the *Cyclopedia of Domestic Economy*, written in 1857: "As it is the business of man to provide the means of living comfortably, so it is the province of women to dispose judiciously of those means, and maintain order and harmony in all things. On her due performance of her part rests the comfort and social peace of the home."

At the very moment that this "cult of domesticity" was flowering, however, Matthaei notes that there was a great increase in the number of single women in the labor force, especially in New England. How come?

The author says it was partly because of the way the New Englanders thought of their children, partly because of the extent to which they'd go to keep their homemakers out of the labor force, and partly because the concept of femininity required the subordination of self to one's family.

For Matthaei, ideas are much of the story. The fact that married women kept getting pregnant all those years had little to do with the state of birth-control technology; it was a matter of the conception of women, not the fact of conception. The fact that women worked had little to do with changes on the "supply," or sellers', sides in the 19th century; it owed to a change on the part of buyers' psychology of demand.

This was "consumerism," which set in motion the massive in-migration of women to the work force that is going on today. It is this continuing feminization of the work force that Matthei calls a "contradiction" which now threatens to destroy capitalism.

How? Her analysis goes something like this: Capitalism sets up a "perpetual gnawing neediness, and ignores other areas of self-fulfillment, particularly in the political area." It draws people away from family life, and as more people are drawn into the work force to fill these needs, the family breaks down. The sexual division of labor disappears.

But since capitalism is built on hierarchy and patriarchy, this end to traditional occupational stereotypes itself will bring change in the system, she says. Qualitative changes of personalities, male and female alike, will result. "Women are learning from men not to live through their children, men are learning from women that competition with others is self-destructive and unproductive," she says.

Is this what Marxist eschatology has become? Matthaei agrees that hers is a vision that will never compare to the thrill of singing *The Internationale*. But she adds, "We need some vision. We have none now except to talk about falling apart, or staying the same. To extend history into the future, the little kinds of quantitive change the economists are talking about really don't suffice. We have a chance to invent the future. It is up to us to take it."

OCTOBER 31, 1982

In Which John Kenneth Galbraith Goes Soft on the Corporation and Has Tea . . .

FOR 30 YEARS, THE GREAT FIGURE IN AMERICAN INSTITUTIONAL ECONOMICS HAS BEEN John Kenneth Galbraith. Ever since he published *American Capitalism: The Concept of Countervailing Power*, it has been to Galbraith, not to the mainstream, that many people turned for interpretations of the changing economic landscape.

Again in *The Affluent Society* and *The New Industrial State*, he painted a picture of a historically evolving economic system composed of contending organizations that people found hugely compelling when compared to the austere explanatory principles of high theory, or the nuts-and-bolts magnitudes of econometric models.

Now, the Cambridge philosopher has a new book out called *The Anatomy of Power*, and guess what? Galbraith has gone soft on the corporation.

"Maybe. Well, yes. I think that's probably true," he said in an interview last week.

In Galbraith's earlier books, big companies tended to be founts of almost untrammeled power. They could sell anything to anybody. They simply figured out what they wanted to do next—and did it. Now all this has changed.

"In a world of the United Auto Workers, in a world of the consumer protection movement and in a world of hundred-million vehicle recalls, one has difficulty presenting General Motors as an all-powerful ogre. This is a manifestation of the dialectic of power. In the book, I say that this is the way power is countered by those who sell their labor and by those who buy the product. General Motors learned something when it organized that crusade against Ralph Nader's personal life."

Perhaps they learned something, too, from the Japanese?

"Ah yes, I think maybe I should have added that. As compared with 20 years or 25 years ago, before the advent of the Japanese, Detroit looked more formidable than it does today."

It is quite an interesting admission from a fellow who has spent his life focusing attention on the economic role of corporations. But then, as he says, things have changed, partly as a result of his own efforts. "Once economic instruction is perceived not as the reality but as guidance away from the reality, its conditioning value is, not surprisingly, impaired," he writes. At 75, Galbraith is a literally towering figure, a bit like Nehru or Martin Luther King, an inspirational leader first and foremost, a symbol of progressive resistance to the established order. Yet his reputation rests on his books. There are 23 of them now, but *Anatomy of Power* is only the fourth to be completed with uninterrupted concentration in the Galbraiths' winter home in Gstaad, Switzerland. (The others are *The Affluent Society*, *The New Industrial State* and *Money*.)

Now the author is hoisting himself to go out on tour. "St. Mark himself would go on the *Today* show, or else the Gospel would be ignored," he says.

In the book, Galbraith writes that the power of modern business is still considerable, "but it cannot be supposed that it rivals" the power of the great capitalist firm in the age of high capitalism. He explains, "With the rising living standards, increasing levels of affluence, the power associated with the sellers of goods becomes less formidable, for the reason that the goods themselves become less urgently significant. If one looks over the publications of Consumers Union, you find detailed and sometimes slightly indignant complaints about the shortcomings of 500 stereo sets. I don't find myself sharing this deep concern. I'm glad that the organization exists, but I'm no longer weeping over the person who buys a slightly inferior Jacuzzi."

Then too, the state has emerged as a power in its own right. What has replaced the marketing corporation at the top of Galbraith's list of dangerously untrammeled organizations is the weapons industry. He devotes increasing time to arguing for arms control.

"Modern society deals with power not by dissolving it but by erecting an opposing position of power—that I've never doubted and it has been on my mind ever since I wrote *American Capitalism*. It is present in this book, but when I wrote that 30 years ago, I had an unduly optimistic view of the equilibrium that results that I no longer hold. It could have been a manifestation of youthful optimism.

"The defense establishment deploys all of the instruments of power. . . .

It has an enormous control over the process of social conditioning. The one thing it doesn't have is the strong personality. Nobody any longer knows the names of the heads of the services. To a very substantial extent, the secretary of defense is a synthetic personality. He owes his distinction to the organization he heads. Once he disappears from the organization, he's never heard from again, and I think it's fair to say that, in the case of quite a few past secretaries of defense, that is not something to be regretted. When Caspar Weinberger leaves office he will descend into the obscurity for which many people figure he was intended."

Is the book going to be read around the profession with any more enthusiasm than *The New Industrial State?* "Less. This is a book that could not be confined to economics, in the way which modern economics seeks to exclude everything that isn't associated with pecuniary motivation and the ultimate competitive equilibrium. It would be hard to bring this book within the mathematical framework of modern economics. As Joan Robinson said, I was never a very good mathematician, so I had to think. This is the least pure of pure economics."

Galbraith said he had just signed a contract for a history of economics, "not a history of economic thought, but of economists and economic thought. I'll try to write it so it is interesting to read, to deal fully with the absurdities of some of the people and of some of the ideas, to show also how the ideas were part of the times."

Midway through the interview last week, Galbraith unconsciously displayed a bit of his own. As he sat in the library of his big brick home, he turned to the photographer, who was present snapping away. "Here, put away those cameras and serve this tea here while we talk." It was simply the habit of command, acquired long ago.

The photographer, a woman, hesitated between being embarrassed and appalled. Had it been anyone else in the world who had asked her to serve tea, surely she would have said something, or perhaps walked out. Instead of leaving, however, she hung on, waiting for Galbraith to serve the tea himself, then listened with rapt attention to the voice that, like a cello playing a Bach suite, rose and fell as he told stories in the late afternoon. He was, after all, the symbol of much in which she believed.

NOVEMBER 1, 1983

Why Do We
Work So Hard?

THERE IS IN AMERICA TODAY A SENSE OF FLUIDITY, OF SHIFTING PLATES, OF OLD
positions being abandoned and new ones being taken up. This is not just
the routine working of the business cycle; it stems from the abrupt and
surprising ending of the 50-year Cold War. It helps matters that a presidential election is at hand. Politics sharpens talk, hastens the evolution of
successful positions. But deep down, durable new viewpoints still have
long gestations.

One of the most striking visions to emerge in many years is to be found
in a new book called *The Overworked American: The Unexpected Decline of
Leisure*, by Harvard University economist Juliet B. Schor. Her idea is that
Americans—as opposed to Europeans—are caught in an insidious cycle of
working and spending, and that it is the legitimate task of government to
help them slow the motion of this "squirrel cage."

Sound like a pipedream? Well, possibly. But the hunch here is that *The
Overworked American* may be the most evocative call for political change to
appear since *The Affluent Society* was published by John Kenneth Galbraith
in 1958. Schor's book is not simply an intuition based on summer vacations
in Europe but rather a thoroughly researched and analytically reasoned
investigation, the first of its sort. It is precisely the sort of position around
which the Left can begin to reform its ranks.

That the left needs to regroup seems beyond doubt. With the collapse of
the experiments in central planning, the democratic left in the United
States has retreated to a variety of positions, none very commanding. There
are Greens, who want to slow growth because it is dirty and wasteful, and
Mercantilists, who want to manage trade because they say that business
executives and consumers cannot be trusted. There are even a few mild
Communards, who want to dramatically redistribute wealth in the name of
fairness.

There is a mainstream faction, too, that wants to follow the Republicans
where they have led: to a recognition that markets are the only way to

organize complex modern societies and integrate them into the international order. This mainstream Democratic position holds that the party can oversee not only America's participation in this international market system better than the Republicans can, but that Democrats can better maintain the infrastructure of American mixed capitalism, as well, because they understand it so well.

But it requires only a moment's thought to recognize that none of these positions is sufficiently deeply grounded in the appreciation of a more decent, compassionate and humane world that is the hallmark of the Left to be able to command widespread assent. And you have only to look at the collection of earnest young men who came of age during the Vietnam era and who are now contending for the Democratic presidential nomination to realize that, even without a vision, the Democrats are not yet ready to govern.

It is in these circumstances that *The Overworked American* is worth thinking about. At a time when we're worried so much by joblessness, it may seem churlish to ask, why do Americans work so hard? But according to Schor, the two are not entirely unrelated.

For the past 20 years, Schor writes, the amount of time Americans spend at their jobs has risen, year after year. The annual increase has been small, she says: about nine hours. But it adds up. Already, American working hours are back where they were in the 1940s. Nor is it just blue-collar workers who have felt the speed up. Housewives are working longer hours. So are most professionals. Schor writes: "Financiers used to keep bankers' hours, and lawyers had a leisured life. Now bankers work like doctors, and lawyers do the same." She quotes one corporate chief executive, "People who work for me should have phones in their bathrooms."

Proof that this is a mainly American situation can be found in Europe, Schor writes. American and European working hours moved in tandem for a century, she says, and then after World War II diverged. They've been marching to different drummers ever since. Today, the differences are large: U.S. manufacturing employees work 320 hours a year more than their counterparts in West Germany and France, the equivalent of two months work.

Why is this happening? Well, Schor gives short shrift to the 1973 climacteric in productivity that preoccupies most economists. Instead, the answer she gives is that it is a built-in tendency of capitalism to create "long-hour jobs." She hints darkly at the old Marxist concept of the "reserve army of the unemployed." She devotes many pages to showing that the quality of working life in the Middle Ages, with their frequent feast days, was better. She may be right. But she is sure to spark a hundred worthwhile arguments.

For the fact is that an increasingly competitive world has nearly everybody working harder than they ought. Most Japanese are on a six-day-a-week schedule, and half don't take their allotted vacations. Koreans still work three Sundays out of four. Schor describes a 1989 letter to 300 business leaders advocating a shorter work week that failed to elicit a single favorable response. Indeed, one executive wrote, "My view of the world, our country and our country's needs is diametrically opposite to yours. I cannot imagine a shorter work week. I can imagine a longer one both at school and at work if America is to be competitive in the first half of the next century."

How to reconcile these conflicting views? Through politics, naturally. It doesn't take a rocket scientist to see that these wealth-getting races have as their mainspring the competition for status, among neighbors, among nations—or to recognize that there is a self-defeating dynamic that can quickly set in, as at a football game, when one person stands to get a better view, forcing all those behind to clamber to their feet.

The great reduction in working hours that occurred between the mid-19th century and the 1920s came about as a result of union organizing and political action. After a 20-year-or-so hiatus, it is time to begin the lobbying process again. The reason that the Europeans hold onto their leisure in the face of mounting competition from the Asians is that they prefer to preserve it—through the acceptance of a variety of tradeoffs between material well-being and spare time.

You don't have to buy all of Schor's arguments to recognize that she has hit upon an absolutely fundamental point. Industrial societies choose how to take the gains from their increasing productivity. Either they prefer more goods and services, or they prefer more leisure, or some broad combination of the two. The choice is, in some broad sense, up to consumers, individually and collectively.

Schor writes, "We could now reproduce our 1948 standard of living (measured in terms of market goods and services) in less than half the time it took in 1948. We actually could have chosen the four-hour day. Or a working year of six months. Or imagine this: Every worker in the United States could now be taking every other year off from work, with pay."

One of the tasks of the Left in the coming decades is surely to turn this stunning insight into a political program. The West is rich enough for now. In the next leg, we should address our poverty of time.

A Voice from
the Economic Left

Is Italy a harbinger of the wave of the future? Michael Piore thinks so.

To be sure, until he popped up last week on the MacArthur Foundation's "genius list," the 43-year-old Piore was not obviously a man to be reckoned with. A labor economist at MIT, he is "not disciplined enough to be an economic historian," says a colleague. He certainly doesn't write the polished little mathematical exercises in econometrics that fill the technical journals. Nevertheless, when Piore turns out an idea, it is a doozy. He is, by common consent, one of the brightest and most penetrating thinkers writing on the Left.

The striking thing about Italian economic organization, says Piore, is that despite the obvious muscle of a few giant enterprises like Fiat and Olivetti, a large share of the nation's output comes from small firms. There is "a vast network of very small enterprises spread throughout the villages and small cities of central and northeast Italy, in and around Bologna, Florence, Ancona and Venice," he says. It is these enterprises that accounted for "a new wave of Italian growth" in the 1970s, he says.

Four out of five Italian firms employ fewer than 500 workers; 40 percent of all job holders work for firms with fewer than 100 persons. Small companies account for 35 percent of dollar value of exports. Why? Well, part of the reason is tax laws and government regulation. Firms smaller than 15 persons are virtually unregulated. Another part of the reason is that small-scale enterprise is somehow built into the Italian character.

But a substantial part of the explanation may be that a deep change in the economic logic of the times is taking place. Where, for more than a century, mass production and a high degree of specialization marked by long production runs dominated the international marketplace, now "batch processes" involving the manufacture of relatively few items at a time, may be the preferred form of economic organization—thanks largely to the computer, Piore says.

In a new book due in the fall from Basic Books—*The Second Industrial*

Divide, written with MIT political scientist Charles Sabel—Piore lays out his argument.

He says he finished the manuscript last week, just before he was handed his $216,000, 5-year MacArthur grant. "If I hadn't already finished it, I don't know how I would have lived with an award like this. It makes you feel like something enormous to justify it," Piore said. Nevertheless, the grant was more than welcome, he added; his plan had been to spend the rest of the term applying for increasingly scarce grant money to support his work.

Piore says: "The argument of the book is that to get out of the current economic crisis, you've got to do one of two things: either develop institutional structures which accommodate this new technology (and we try to describe what those structures might be); or, in the second alternative, we might be able to develop institutions that would permit a revival of mass production, which would require the regeneration on an international scale of the institutions which are analogous to those which regulated the balance of the domestic economy."

In the first instance, he says, a marriage of Italian-style economic organization and computer-driven manufacturing might provide the basis for an overhaul of the international economic order. In the second instance, new forms of control of the world economy—a strengthened International Monetary Fund or General Agreement on Tariffs and Trade, an international minimum wage law, stronger unions—would be necessary to extend the world market for mass-produced goods.

Piore "would seem to be a perfect recipient of a MacArthur fellowship," MIT's Paul Samuelson said last week. "He is very bright and he is somewhat resistant to the mainstream." Boston College economist Barry Bluestone said, "He basically represents the modern institutional tradition. Michael Piore has kept that tradition alive more than anybody I can think of. He is constantly exploring the conditions in labor markets, often shedding distressing light on structural conditions."

John Dunlop, Harvard's celebrated labor economist, for whom Piore wrote his dissertation, said, "He has an original mind that crosses over many fields. He is not the conventional economist of our time, being much more interested in institutional aspects of labor markets.

"For example, he became interested in illegal aliens a few years ago," said Dunlop. "That turned into a very interesting book on migrant workers, *Birds of Passage*. Now he is interested in Italy and in the French approaches to some of these issues. That is the sort of identification of problems that characterizes his work."

And Stephen Marglin, a Harvard economist who is somewhat to the left of Piore, said, "I think he's terrific. He does very innovative work. I'm glad that the McJigger people heard of him."

Piore had a good start in the life of public issues. His father was director of the Office of Naval Research for a time, then became vice president for research of IBM Corp. His mother, a health economist, has a long record as an activist in public health care and welfare. He himself spent the 1960s in the civil rights movement, and has done a good deal of public policy work ever since—including serving as an adviser to the government of Puerto Rico. "He lived a year in San Juan—before it was chic," says Peter Doeringer, his collaborator and long-time friend.

Doeringer says Piore is the kind of economist who will make the most of the no-strings-attached MacArthur money. "He is a super-macro economist, almost a philosophical economist, whose catholic interests transcend the boundaries of sponsored research. Five years to think about what he wants will mean a great deal to him."

Still, whenever one person gets a fat prize like the MacArthur fellowship, the natural inclination is to stop to wonder, why him and not another? Why not, say, Doeringer, with whom Piore pioneered the theory of dual labor markets for rich and poor. Why not, say, Charles Sabel, his co-author of *The Second Industrial Divide*? "Oh, but I've got one," said Sabel, meaning a MacArthur grant. "I've had it now for more than a year."

FEBRUARY 19, 1984

Questing for the "Bionomic Perspective"

THERE'S NOT MUCH DOUBT ANY LONGER: WITH THE PLUNGING OF THE LEADING indicators Friday, the fifth decline in a row, the United States is in the recession we've been waiting for since the mid-1980s.

What a curious word "recession" is. Especially when it's used to mean the kind of widespread, mutually reinforcing decline in expectations and results that we associate with the business downturn.

Recession of what? Of the division of labor, presumably, to recall an old-fashioned name given to the phenomenon that today we denote by the catch phrase, "the economy." In the course of a normal business cycle, we say that the economy recedes a little after a period of growth, cutting here, pruning there, before expanding to some greater, more complex articulation of the possibilities.

Cutting? Pruning? It is not surprising that when the talk turns to economic growth and decline, the metaphors turn biological. Philosophers at least since St. Paul have compared the organization of the world of work to the organization of the human body—some members of the church are active as its head, said Paul, others are its hands and feet. And Alfred Marshall, the great Victorian codifier of economics, yearned for the day when its analogies would be borrowed from biology instead of physics.

A century after Marshall expressed that wish, it's finally coming true. In the attempt to link economic and biological ideas, there's the usual dispersion of points of view. There are outsiders eager to make their marks on professional economics. And there are insiders who meet with varying degrees of success and pursuing their intuitions.

Take Michael Rothschild, for example, a one-time trouble-shooter for the Boston Consulting Group. This writer's economics-as-evolutionary-biology theories are arguably inspired from Bruce Henderson himself. The business world remembers BCG founder Henderson as the man who gave it cash cows, dogs and stars as symbols of types of companies—a typology Henderson devised in the process of fanning the flames of the 1970's mania for conglomerates.

But Henderson, now at Vanderbilt University, would rather be remembered as a thinker who called attention to the similarities between business and biological competition. "Evolution determines who survives and who is crowded out—in business just as surely as in the jungle," he wrote in a *Harvard Business Review* article a year ago that was presumably a preview of a long-awaited book.

Now Rothschild has beaten his teacher to the punch. In *Bionomics: The Inevitability of Capitalism*, Rothschild has spun a fascinating mixture of war stories from corporate battles, biological analogies and anecdotes from the history of technology. It's not economics exactly; it aims more to be engaging reading than to alter reproduceable results. Nor does it represent economics itself altogether dependably; Rothschild thinks that economists have ignored the famous "learning curve," when what they have really done is to file it under various other headings, including "convexities," after the way that mathematical functions representing increasing returns to scale look when graphed.

And in trying to answer all the Big Questions—"How did Japan grab world leadership from the United States?" and "Why did America lose the War on Poverty?"—it dissipates its force. But Rothschild's book is still probably the best case yet made for the biological analogy, what the author calls "the bionomic perspective." Potentially it is, he says, an infinitely-adjustable macroscope, "an instrument for the mind's eye, able to scan the panorama of the global economy or zoom in on its finest details."

A somewhat less ambitious attempt to deal with the history of technology as an evolutionary process is to be found in the last chapter of Joel Mokyr's book *The Lever of Riches: Technological Creativity and Economic Progress.* Noting that Richard Nelson and Sydney Winter were in 1982 the first economists to adopt evolutionary models to economic change, Mokyr makes a strategic modification: instead of letting firms be the unit of analysis, as Nelson and Winter did, why not let specific techniques be the "species?" Square-rigged sailing vessels, movable type and the Newcomen engine are the real mutations, Mokyr argues, and much can be gained from differentiating between macro-inventions, which change the way work itself is organized, and micro-inventions that marginally improve products and processes, he says.

As usual, however, it is deep inside the discipline that the real inroads probably are being made. At various interdisciplinary think-tanks, such as the Center for the Advanced Study of Behavioral Science at Stanford University and at the Sante Fe Institute, economists are chowing down with biologists with some regularity—and the results are as esoteric as they are interesting. The Hoover Institution's Thomas Sargent, for example, is using genetic algorithms to impose some texture on the concept of rational expectations. And, in a little new book of lectures, *Game Theory and Economic Modeling*, David Kreps of Stanford University reports that theorists have become very interested in modeling learning processes, as a means of talking about what determines "the rules of the game."

It will be years—decades, most likely—before these new beginnings in borrowing from biology come together to give a better understanding of the overarching processes of economic growth. The current recession will be a distant memory. But with profits plunging and unemployment rising, it's somehow comforting to know that there is still plenty of progress in economic understanding to be made.

DECEMBER 30, 1990

Species Goldbug,
Genus Crank

His partner stole his mailing list after a bitter quarrel, he says, so after nearly 20 years on lower Fourth Avenue in New York City, he packed up and moved to Boston.

He had grown up in Providence, gone to college at Harvard, liked New England, and found it home. So he and his newsletter moved into the laundry room of his sister's and brother-in-law's suburban home in Lexington.

Now Howard S. Katz is Boston's own goldbug, and he will bend your ear telling you why a gold standard is the Jeffersonian thing to do. "Gold is naturally a liberal issue," he says.

"The biggest propaganda victory that the bankers scored was getting people to believe that gold was a conservative issue." This is Katz' gimmick, and he is perhaps the only person in the world who propounds the idea. According to his publisher, Katz is "one of the most brilliant minds of our time," but his publisher works out of Suite 31B at 160 E. 38th St.

"I work behind the scenes with many of these conservatives and I can assure you that they stab gold in the back at every opportunity, even while they are publicly pretending to support it. Thus the liberals, who should be supporting gold, are scared away, on the premise that, if the conservatives are for it, it must be bad," Katz says.

But doesn't nearly everyone agree that a sudden adoption of the gold standard would cause an incalculably great depression, with millions of the poor thrown out of work and millions of the rich ruined financially? Wouldn't it be, as one European banker puts it, like putting a car into reverse at 150 mph?

By way of reply, Katz draws little boxes locating just about any personality you can name in a matrix of his own devising—conservatives here, liberals there, authoritarians here, socialists there. He hasn't much talk about cataclysm.

Katz is a shining example of the species "goldbug," of that fascinating genus, the money crank. A goldbug, in other words, is someone who is reminded of gold by everything he sees.

As goldbugs go, Katz is very clear and focused. His books, *The Warmongers*, *The Paper Aristocracy*, *Honest Money Now*, show a steady development of his views; in fact by now, they have a nearly seamless quality. His monthly newsletter, *The Goldbug*, keeps up a running commentary on the public discussion of gold, often casting up sharp insights.

Indeed, on a few topics, Katz is better than fellow goldbugs James Dines or Julian Snyder or James Sinclair, because he is a little less slick, less investment-oriented, a little more attuned to the economic and political implications of his ideas.

Katz doesn't joke much, and his manuscripts are full of striking peculiarities. In his book *The Warmongers*, for example, he makes much of a routine letter that he fished out of a wastebasket in which Wassily Leontieff asks ITT Corp. to fund a scholarship. He explains how a "paper aristocracy," meaning the rich, has taken over the world, using the Trilateral Commission as their vehicle. And he dwells at length on how the bankers contrived World War I to facilitate their plot to destroy the gold standard.

When he is described as being a crank, he rallies a fellow expert to tesify in behalf of the acceptability of his views. She is a radio talk-show hostess who once refereed a debate between Katz and a Harvard professor. Says Katz: "If the world is proper in its orb, the Harvard professor should have made hash of the crank, right . . . ? People without titles are ipso facto cranks, even when they are right."

Katz became chairman of a Committee to Establish the Gold Standard in 1972, and since then he has seen the return-to-gold moment blossom and fade. With the appointment of a U.S. Gold Commission a year ago, he and other goldbugs looked forward to a serious debate on the merits of their program.

But now, Katz writes: "Hopes for a positive report from the gold commission are quietly going down the drain. This is not because of the successful attacks of the paper money forces. It is because of a disgraceful and cowardly betrayal on the part of people who represent themselves as pro-gold."

The villains of Katz' story are Alan Greenspan and libertarian Hans Sennholz. He accuses them of sabotaging the return to gold by saying there might be a problem if it were undertaken at once.

For example, Sennholz told the Gold Commission in November that "it is futile to discuss the return to the gold standard or the use of gold in our monetary system as long as the federal government suffers large budget deficits. The government needs an elastic paper standard that can be stretched to finance . . . a total federal sector deficit of more than $150 billion a year."

To Katz, this doesn't make sense: why balance the budget, he asks, "before we can have a gold standard? Why not have some other requirement, such as: we must have a bald Secretary of State, or we must have a Supreme Court Justice who digs the Beatles . . . ? One of our purposes in advocating a gold standard is to create a political climate in which the budget would be balanced." But what about the crash that would ensue? It just isn't a topic for consideration in Katz' talk, a little like the "transition" in Marxist talk. After the conversion, after the revolution, everything will be great, the story goes. Men will be honest, money sound and peace will obtain throughout the world.

Here's the way Katz put it in a recent issue of his newsletter:

"We have argued repeatedly that the adoption of a gold standard would radically reduce corporate profits, and we regard this as a desirable end. If a thief is operating in a neighborhood, then the successful action of police in catching him will sharply reduce his income."

And what about the unemployment that would result from the bankruptcy of the Fortune 500? What about the injustice of wiping out all those shareholders who own a few shares of AT&T? What about those workers who depend on pension plans backed by corporate profits?

Katz is unswayed. He says: "Unfortunately, the most persuasive argument for bank paper money is the chair of economics at a prestigious university endowed by a banker. The occupant of this chair then spouts the banker line and heaps ridicule on the gold standard. Since very few people understand monetary economics, who are they to dispute the distinguished professor?"

So he operates now out of his sister's house in Lexington, writing amid washing and drying machines built by the corporations he reviles. He files his papers on the staircase. He writes and his little newsletter takes its place in the mail along with a thousand others.

FEBRUARY 7, 1982

Is There Life
Before Death?

CAN THERE BE AN ADULT IN BOSTON WHO HASN'T COMPLAINED OF NOT HAVING ENOUGH time for the holidays? There is writing to friends, making phone calls, going to parties, dealing with children, husbands, wives, parents—to say nothing of shopping for gifts. As Walter Kerr once wrote, "Isn't it odd that a century which should, by all rights, be the most leisurely in all history is also known to be, and condemned for being, the fastest?"

That money shouldn't buy happiness is grist for novels aplenty, and a fair amount of pop psychology, ranging from good to bad to awful. Yet not very much effort has been devoted to formally thinking through the problems of mixing consumption and time to maximize happiness, what Schlomo Maital calls "the King Kong of social science questions." Under the heading of affluence, there is John Kenneth Galbraith's *Affluent Society*, but it is mainly about the role of government in making life pleasant. There are Fred Hirsch's *Social Limits to Growth*, and Robert Frank's *Choosing the Right Pond*, but these are focused mainly on the competition for status. So what about happiness itself? Why doesn't money buy more of it?

For those who habitually look to economists for guidance, the starting point is John Maynard Keynes, of course: He foresaw the possibility of a world of too much leisure, in which "a general nervous breakdown" would be a threat. The problem would be "to spread the bread thin on the butter—to make what work there is still to be done to be as widely shared as possible. Three-hour shifts or a 15-hour week may put the problem off for quite a while."

Well, it hasn't worked out that way—not yet, anyway. People still bang away, with shorter work weeks, longer vacations, but they are just as hungry for more. Tibor Scitovsky, a Hungarian expatriate based at Stanford, has argued that consumers habitually choose short-term "pleasure" over long-term "comfort," insuring their general distress. In *The Joyless Economy*, he described a society that produced too much and consumed too little. And then there is Staffan Burenstam Linder. In his book, *The Harried*

Leisure Class, he says the problem is that we don't budget time nearly as well as we budget money.

Linder is an interesting man. A well-born Swede, MIT PhD, professor at the Stockholm School of Economics, he has been active for 20 years as vice chairman of Sweden's Conservative Party, a distinctly minority group with views not unlike those of an Eisenhower Republican. Still in politics as a member of the Swedish Parliament, Linder has been edging back to economics. His book on the rise of the nations of the Pacific basin is coming out next spring —he believes they are the wave of the future. But it is *The Harried Leisure Class*, a slim, thoughtful meditation that he wrote nearly 20 years ago "to map the changes that (economic) growth will cause in the way we spend our time," that is remembered, especially in holiday season.

The central problem, according to *The Harried Leisure Class*, is to realize that spending money entails spending one's time, too, and to act accordingly. The proliferation of goods and services has made for a continually declining quality of information about them. Impulse purchases take up a larger fraction of the budget; costs associated with searching for a desired object have grown. Who hasn't spent a day searching for some well-remembered childhood toy, a bongo-board, say, or a pair of stilts?

Meanwhile, the amount of time devoted to cultural pursuit will diminish in relation to consumption activities, as goods become cheaper and time more expensive. "More goods will not increase the pleasure derived," he writes, "but will actually decrease it," a matter that is demonstrated to his satisfaction in the complicated algebra that he mercifully confines to an appendix.

Among the striking consequences of abundance, Linder notes, are modern attempts to leverage consumption—to push up the yield in goods consumed per unit of time. The circularized Christmas letter is one example of this tendency, he says; the widespread devotion to banquets, conventions and cocktail parties is another, for at them "one devotes oneself to the simultaneous consumption of food and people." The danger is that one ends up with all acquaintances and no friends, Linder writes, for "to be the only guests at dinner is normally considered less flattering than to be invited with many others." Yet perhaps the most ubiquitous symbol of this need to leverage experience is the camera: "Cameras have made it possible to raise the goods intensity of many pursuits. It is easy to understand why love is so vulnerable to competition, if we reflect that we are spending time on only one person and cannot even take photographs of the occasion."

In an interview in his offices at the Swedish Rikstag earlier this month, Linder shrugged, "I've forgotten all the algebra—it took me six months to learn it. But the book stands up in many respects, doesn't it?" He was philosophical about the direction politics had taken since he first entered Parliament in 1968. The Social Democratic party, which has governed Sweden pretty much without interruption since the Great Depression, has seen its most powerful tenets of belief wither, he said. "It is an enormously important, powerful machine, without much of a message. These machines can do wonders for the short run, but in the long run I'm not so sure you can do so well without a message."

Talk about the "consumption maximum," the dreamy state of affairs envisaged by John Stuart Mill that dominated the final chapters of Burenstam Linder's book, seemed quite beside the point. With Sweden busily computerizing everything in sight, with a new $25,000 base-price Saab about to go into the showrooms, with demand rising for holidays in the tropics and a sixth week of summer vacation, and the real possibility looming of a general strike for higher wages, it seemed silly to spend much time imagining, with Mill, "the best state for human nature . . . in which, while no one is poor, no one desires to be richer, nor has any reasons for fear of being thrust back, by the efforts of others to push themselves forward."

Instead, the lines that Linder quoted in *The Harried Leisure Class* from the journalist Marya Mannes will do:

> . . . Yourself, be still—
> There is no living when you're nagging time
> And stunting every second with your will.
> You work for this: to be the sovereign
> Of what you slave to have—not
> Slave.

DECEMBER 22, 1985

part six

NEIGHBORS

Much More than
Just a Common Scold

WHAT TO MAKE OF JANE JACOBS? THE LADY IS FAMOUS FOR HER WORK ON WHAT makes a successful city, and for more than 20 years, she has been a source of inspiration to opponents of superhighways, suburban malls and bulldozer-driven "urban renewal" programs with low-cost housing for the poor. It is she who most forcefully framed the need for small shops, diverse neighborhoods and dense networks of economic activity—all that is purely local in economic life.

Now Jacobs has struck out ambitiously with a principles of economics, called *Cities and the Wealth of Nations*. The book has created a big stir in culture's main ring: two excerpts from it were printed in the *Atlantic Monthly*, one in the *New York Review of Books*. But, nevertheless, it is being privately dismissed as "screwball" by specialists in economics. Jacobs is a splendid stylist, a fine analyst, but above all, she is a person working outside a discipline. Perhaps she is the first writer since Lewis Mumford to really make a go of it.

At the heart of the book is the contention that cities, not nations, are the engines of economic progress, and that economists' wholesale failure to recognize this "fundamental reality" dooms their efforts to triviality. She writes, "Once we remove the blinders . . . and try looking at the real economic world in its own right rather than as a dependent artifact of politics, we can't avoid seeing that most nations are composed of collections or grab bags of very different economies, rich regions and poor ones within the same nation."

To be sure, development economics is not the proudest, shiniest profession outside of which to find oneself. Beginning perhaps 40 years ago, the high-tech field of "growth economics" split off from it, all mathematical and neoclassical, leaving development economics a poor cousin concerned with the real world. And while growth economics becomes more and more esoteric, development economics languishes, at least in the fancy universities, as an untidy area in which the differences between nations and other practical matters are discussed. True, there are many departments of urban studies, planning and architecture, full of original minds. But in development economics, there is simply not the same buzzing hive of first-rate minds as in other fields, or even as once there was 30 years ago.

In three books published over a span of 20 years, Jacobs has done her best to create an alternative approach to our understanding of how economic development proceeds. The work speaks for itself. Jacobs not only doesn't give interviews freely; her publicist doesn't even call back to say she doesn't give interviews. But over time, she has left a long trail of fact and opinion, and one overriding fact about her dominates all the others. She has relatively little use for most experts, though she is an expert herself. In the past, it was architects and city planners who drew her scorn. This time it is the economists.

To choose between competing theories in economics is "bootless," says Jacobs. Economics is a "fool's paradise," she says; what's needed now is a wholesale re-thinking of the field, a trip "back to reality." This is presumably not the way to build a following among the 100,000 or so professional economists at work in the world today, many of them very smart people, who are laboring away to understand the same problems on which Jacobs dwells. Charles Kindleberger, one of the senior authorities in the field, says, "All of us hate these autodidacts. We are in the business of teaching people, and we want them to learn our stuff, not make it up." But the notions in Jacobs are so fresh and compelling, that those interested in the topic must welcome her anyway, despite her contempt for their efforts.

Born Jane Butzner in 1916 in Scranton, Pa., Jacobs worked first as a reporter for the *Scranton Tribune*. Indeed, the Scranton of those year— booming, every year adding new products to its export mix, new amenities to its public life—seems to have served as model for much of what has come after. But at a certain point, she decamped to New York to seek her fortune. In 1944, she married an architect, Robert H. Jacobs Jr., and had three children.

It was working as an associate editor at *Architectural Forum*, a widely followed trade journal, that she began to have influence, but only with the publication of *The Death and Life of American Cities* that she became a major force. At a time when New York planner Robert Moses was attempting to tear down most all of what was at the time called "Hell's Canyon"— the century-old manufacturing area between Canal and Houston Streets in Manhattan—to make a crosstown superhighway, Jacobs was writing about the need for diversity, the virtues of decentralization and the self-improving characteristics of vital cities. Moses' highway was not built, at least in part because of Jacobs' book, and Hell's Canyon is, of course, today the rich SoHo district of Manhattan, living testimony to the power of her insights.

Jacobs' work has had great effect over the years, especially with architects, planners, developers and the like. Indeed, it wouldn't be far-fetched to call her the Mother of Rousedom, for it was her intellectual blueprint which architect Ben Thompson intuited and developer James Rouse executed over and over again in almost every Eastern seaport city, beginning with Quincy Market. But her decentralist doctrines haven't penetrated far into developmental economics. Albert Hirshman, the premier figure of the field (and a man of extraordinary fecundity himself), says, "I liked her first book very much, and I see that she has been developing along similar lines ever since." But she isn't required reading, he says, even though Jacobsian doctrines are finding their way into practice.

"Take all the work that has been going on about shanty towns in Latin America, for example," said Hirshman in a telephone interview. "There has been a certain amount of literature not by economists but by sociologists about rehabilitating instead of relocating these slums, for a slum in Lima is very different from a slum in New York. These are very similar ideas . . . they have had influence on World Bank planning. They know all about these ideas, and they have given up putting a lot of money into low cost housing and they are putting a lot of money into what they call sites and services."

Economists, when they stop to think about it, see Jacobs mainly as a woman intent on reinventing the wheel. Mancur Olson, for instance, a University of Maryland professor who has been writing for several years on why national economies grow in different ways, says, "She has got a strange sort of inductive discovery of the market in her new book, and even, I think, in *The Economy of Cities*, which has come with the most complete innocence of economics as a discipline. In a way she argues for the market without knowing it. Now she mixes it up with all sorts of ideas about cities which are not really to the point and some ideas about import-replacement which are simply confused and with a general slander against economic theory because in fact she doesn't understand it. But I think she has some extremely valuable insights, and I think we should value them all the more because she came by them on the strength of her own observation."

Other economists think that it is not the market but something else that she has discovered, and that she is a great deal more than a common scold. Peter Albin, director of the Center for the Study of Systems Complexity at John Jay College at the City University of New York, is one such. Albin says that in her emphasis on the intermediate constituents of economic life—cities, villages, regions, industries—that Jacobs is talking about a completely different dimension of things than the one in which economists are accustomed to operate.

"She takes account of what I would call the complexity variable. She sees cities as multilayered units with much redundancy, and with adaptive capacity," he says. What he means is that cities are lists of different kinds of firms, and sometimes they can be invisible and geographically far-flung. "I think she should be looked at more seriously by economists, as the source of a structural theory of technical change, where the word "urban" is less important than underlying terms like complexity, redundancy, thresholds and the rest. I don't think there are comparable dynamic structural change theories anywhere in the literature."

JUNE 3, 1984

Thomas Kuhn: Paradigm Gained—and Lost

WHOSE NAMES WILL BE CARVED ON CLASSROOM BUILDINGS IN THE FUTURE? YOU COULD argue that the most successful social scientist of our age is a mild-mannered physicist-turned-historian named Thomas S. Kuhn. He is the man who contributed the word "paradigm" to the modern vocabulary.

But what a lot of indignities Kuhn has endured on his way to immortality! It's been 43 years since his ideas occurred to him as a Junior Fellow at Harvard, 28 years since he published them as a recondite monograph in the International Encyclopedia of Unified Science under the title, *The Structure of Scientific Revolutions*, 10 years since he sought stoic obscurity by moving from Princeton University to MIT.

Now Kuhn's concepts are at the center of an intriguing flap over ideas at the White House. More or less coincidentally, they were on the cover of *Newsweek* magazine and the top of the editorial page of the *Wall Street Journal*, at least implicitly.

Not bad staying-power for a concept whose first appearance in a *New Yorker* cartoon was in 1974. Not good noteriety for a high-minded, hard-mannered scholar who once told the *Washington Post's* Jim Lardner that he feels more comfortable with his critics than with his fans.

Before Kuhn adopted "paradigm" for use in the study of the history of science, the word was familiar mainly as a term from grammar lessons. It meant an example, a pattern of usage, as in the conjugation or declension of a verb: I go, I went, I have gone. Paradigms were the almost-unconscious rules that helped you learn to speak a language.

After the 1962 publication of *Structure*, however, the word paradigm came to mean something bigger and more complicated than a mere example. It meant the constellation of subtle institutions and beliefs surrounding any dominating example of successful scientific research.

Thus a science in the stage before a paradigm was established resembled free play among smart people, Kuhn said; maybe there would be good questions about phenomena and maybe not, but almost anyone aspiring to wisdom was entitled to a view. Once a paradigm was established, however, an infant science would begin to take on new shape and definition; an organized set of questions would emerge, as would a small community of investigators to answer them.

To be accepted as a paradigm, a theory must seem better than its competitors. That is, it must win an intimate election among scientists. But once accepted, it had an astonishing ability to weld together a community of scientists. It held on though great shakings, then collapsed swiftly and completely—but only when a new paradigm appeared to replace it.

Within a few years, logicians had identified 22 subtly different shadings of meaning in the word paradigm in Kuhn's book. Professional students of his work retreated into departments of history and philosophy of science. But the basic idea remained that there were fundamentally two types of change in knowlege: slow, steady, incremental change, or "normal" science, as Kuhn called it, which was the usual order of the day; and sharp, discontinuous transformations of worldview, "revolutions" or paradigm shifts, which occured rarely but with great significance.

Sound a little like Karl Marx for the life of the mind? Well, yes, actually it does. The idea of punctuated equilibrium—of one dispensation lasting for a long time, then giving way quickly to another long-lasting regime—was profoundly troubling to the conservative world of science history. But from the moment of its appearance, Kuhn's book was enormously influential with persons outside the field. Within a few years it began to pass hand-to-hand among undergraduates and high school students. At the end of the 1960s and the beginning of the 1970s, it was the very hottest intellectual book around. More than half a million copies have been sold, in 16 different languages.

One of those students into whose hands the book fell was a gangly Evanston, Ill., schoolboy named James P. Pinkerton. Paradigm is in the news today because Pinkerton, now a 32-year-old deputy assistant to George Bush, says there is a new one—a new free-market antibureaucratic Republican tradition that is bidding to replace the New Deal as the dominant political matrix in the United States.

Pinkerton is in the news today because Office of Management and Budget Director Richard Darman attacked him obliquly in a recent speech: "The problem with all these New Thises and New Thats is that, however seriously intended, they can be little more than slogans. They are necessarily abstract."

Indeed, the controversy over whether there is or is not a new political paradigm reveals all the weaknesses of the term. It is almost impossible to pin down exactly what is meant—at least in real time. "Informed pragmatic idealism" is Pinkerton's description of his stance, which he says rests on five principles: decentralization, market forces, empowering the poor, an emphasis on choice, and sheer practicality. And whereas scientific revolutions are resolved almost instantly in seminar rooms and among journal referees, political revolutions generally require elections to work their way—and there is not another one of those until 1992.

Still, there's something similar to this analysis of paradigm change to be found in the current fracas over the discovery of the "politically correct," or PC, point of view in the universities today. The rap here—heard last week from as disparate sources as liberal *Newsweek* magazine and the conservative editorial page of the *Wall Street Journal*—is that a creed, a set of beliefs emphasizing the levelling of hierarchies and elevation of multicultural diversity, has taken over on many of the nation's campuses.

The dim view of the politically correct is that it is enforced by faculty members, aging rads who are refighting in the lecture halls the battles they failed to win 20 years ago on the nation's streets. The hopeful interpretation is of a sorting-through and integrating function that is precisely what is required to create a common culture in a newly complicated world.

What is unmistakable is the extent to which the NP and PC world views fail to come to grips with one another. Talk about incommensurability! What happens when paradigms compete is the very essence of the story of Kuhn's landmark book. One by one, disputants try each set of ideas on for size, he says; they judge them by their power to explain. They "vote" by shifting professional allegiances to one paradigm or another. In the end, one point of view triumphs and the other slips into obscurity as the textbooks are rewritten.

None of this pop political analysis is what Thomas Kuhn intended. He's spent much of the last 20 years fleeing from the widespread popularization of his ideas. But the fact remains that *The Structure of Scientific Revolutions* is one of the very finest books of the 20th century, a luminous and surprising picture of science as a metaphor for society. Reading it pays off in some unexpected ways.

DECEMBER 23, 1990

A Noble Story of Technological Change

DIGITAL VS. ANALOG ARE HARDLY WORDS THAT INFLAME THE PASSIONS THE WAY *Liberté! Egalité! Fraternité!* once did, but they describe the opposite poles of a technological revolution that is hardly less far-reaching in its effects than the political tide that swept the world at the end of the 18th century, or the "mechanical philosophy" whose advent marked the dawn of modern science in the 17th century.

Digital and analog refer to alternative techniques for the control of machines: electronic vs. mechanical, control by numbers vs. control by motion, push-buttons and keyboards vs. rotary dials and gauges. Seemingly dry stuff. But the effects of choosing one method or the other as a general principle of design go far beyond the outward appearance of computers and telephones, down to the very roots by which work is organized.

Take machine tools, for example. These modern day descendants of the plane and the auger are used to drill, hone, mill, saw and otherwise cut (and never mind those tools that simply shape) the highly specialized types of metal from which modern machines from airplane engines to gyroscopes are built. For a time at the end of World War II, machine tools hesitated at the fork between analog and digital control.

Then, along with the fledgling automatic computing business, the industry veered sharply off on the road to digital control, which required a sharp division of labor between programmer of the machine and its operator. So the skilled machinist, who could have instructed the machine and run it with analog techniques, was no longer needed in large numbers in the digital age. Where once a single person had run a turret lathe, suddenly there were two, the operator and the person who wrote the tape.

David Noble, 39, curator of industrial automation at the Smithsonian Institution, sets all this out in a book, *Forces Of Production, A Social History of Industrial Automation*. Noble, in an attempt to paint technological change as something other than the inevitable triumph of science, finds that a managerial drive for power over workers is at the heart of the process, and his interpretation of events is a red flag to those who see history as more complicated than a conspiracy of one class or another. Indeed, most of those who were there say that Noble's construction of events is not the correct one. But the book is crammed with the most interesting detail, illuminating heretofore dark corners of our times. It may not be the right story, but it is certainly the relevant story, a narrative of what Noble calls "the drive toward complexity" played out at its most local level.

Noble is a Florida kid who came up the hard way. He acquired his interest in technology from politics, specifically from Students for a Democratic Society, and worked his way slowly through the University of Rochester graduate school in history while working as a lab technician in genetics labs at Tufts, Rochester and Purdue. In 1977, he published *America By Design*, a history of technological changes in the chemical and electrical industries. "*Forces of Production* is a logical outgrowth of that book," he says. "I wanted to show how managerial choices operated in a certain way even in the things that seem the most unlikely. If anything is given, it should be machine tools, right? I mean, my God, these are machines!"

Noble succeeds in illuminating the landscape of technical choice—up to a point. The quest for low-cost production, he argues, often had less to do with manager and engineers' decisions than their collective fear of labor unrest. Automation, in the form of numerically controlled tools, offered a way to "de-skill" many factory techniques and turn labor more into a commodity. With sustained aid from the U.S. Air Force, the inventors of numerical control techniques married computers to cutting tools in processes of unwarranted complexity—and deflected what would have otherwise been a golden age of labor, in which master machinists would attain the status of premier violinists.

What's wrong with that? Well, the evidence of de-skilling is very thin, at best, and Noble never makes any attempt to describe the outcome of the process he limns. Then, too, there are very few dollar signs in Noble's book; he has relatively little sense of what things cost, and no interest in accounting. He says, "There is reasonable doubt that all this investment in automation has paid off in profitability. These things are ambiguous." Maybe; but there is no attempt to show it.

So the real problem with *Forces of Production* is its pervasive sense of advocacy. "Dave Noble argues like a lawyer, not a scholar; he makes up his mind, then proves the case," says a colleague. For all the talk of illumination in the book, it is never clear that Noble understands human motivation, at least as the ordinary well-informed citizen understands it. The result, as one wag put it, is that some of the book is like four-star cuisine, and some of it is like garbage, and for most people, there is no way to tell the difference.

It is a shame, for on one subject, Noble is especially interesting, and that is the MIT nexus, where the military and the industrial establishments mix and mingle with the scientific. Noble dwells on one particular story.

It was a Michigan businessman and manufacturer of helicopter rotors named John Parsons who was among the first to invent numerical controls, but he lost control of his invention after he hired an MIT lab working on the problem to serve as contractor. According to Noble, MIT scientists viewed Parsons as a promoter, an amateur, a country rube, and they simply stole the concept from him in the name of professional science, before bending it to the services of the ruling classes. It is a story vaguely reminiscent of one told recently by Joel Shurkin, in *Engines of the Mind*, in which engineers at the University of Pennsylvania's Moore school lost out to IBM in the race to develop a marketable computer. It may be so, but to build history around the might-have-beens of such priority disputes is shaky business.

Did this searching scrutiny of MIT have something to do with the fact that Noble was not offered tenure, and so was sent packing this spring from the university in which he taught for a decade? Noble thinks so. He had, of course, been a prominent gadfly throughout his time at MIT, challenging the administration often, most memorably over its decision to accept a large gift with some strings to establish the Whitehead Laboratories. But many faculty members opposed the Whitehead, and there is no shortage of staff critics of MIT's close ties to government and industry who haven't been chastened or banished.

Noble says, "I was fired by MIT. The central reason, so far as I can tell, was this book. Because of the way I write about MIT, especially the way MIT stole the idea from John Parsons . . . I don't know whether it was institutional coverup or what, but given my academic standing, it's something of a scandal. It's a classic adademic freedom case. I'll probably be taking MIT to court."

But anyone who is familiar with the glut of good young academicians in the world today knows that it is simply not correct to describe Noble as having been "fired"; there are some awfully good people not getting tenure these days. It is true that neither MIT nor its Program in the History of Science, Technology and Society seem to have agonized over the decision to pass him by; but he landed on his feet, in a good job at the Smithsonian Institution. And *Forces of Production* was published last week by Knopf, which is generally regarded as America's premier publishing house.

Indeed, this dubious understanding of his personal situation is emblematic of the flaws colleagues find in Noble's larger interpretation of the evolution of "the permanent war economy" in the year's after World War II. Like his fellow Knopf authors Barry Commoner and Seymour Melman, he is a combative, even truculent man, often at odds with his peers; recently, he has caused a stir with an article in the quarterly *Democracy* called "In Praise of Luddites." ("The Luddites were very sophisticated people often," he says.) As a result, he says, "I've been somewhat sidelined, even as far as the major U.S. unions are concerned." But he notes with pride that he's been invited to keynote address at a major Canadian labor conference.

No matter, really: at the Smithsonian Institution, Noble will continue to be a major contributor to the debate over the history of the division of labor. But it won't be peaceful there, either. Noble's first exhibit, entitled "Automation Madness," starring the robot R2D2 from the movie *Star Wars*, has just been canceled.

JUNE 17, 1984

Francis Reintjes:
Reconstructing an
Engineering Revolution

ONE OF THE BIG MYSTERIES OF POST-WAR AMERICAN INDUSTRIAL HISTORY IS THE machine-tool business. Its powerful metal-working machines are the basis of any industrial economy. They shape metal in the myriad forms of the modern, everything from auto fenders and airplane wing components to tiny valves and gears. Today they are increasingly controlled by computers, through numbers. Indeed, numerical control was invented more or less simultaneously with digital computers in the late 1940s and early 1950s.

But where American companies pioneered in computers and today dominate most world markets for them, US machine-tool companies have been soundly beaten by the Germans and the Japanese. That loss of leadership, in turn, has cost the rest of American industry dearly, because numerically controlled tools are at the heart of the quick design changes and short production runs that are the secret of Japanese success in, say, automobiles. The defeat in numerical controls makes the more widely-publicized case of consumer electronics—televisions and VCRs—look like strategic small potatoes.

What went wrong?

For some years the dominant theory among historians of technology has been that the machine-tool business was a casualty of the Cold War and the military-industrial complex. The Air Force bankrolled the advent of numerical control because it knew that helicopter rotor blades and supersonic jets' wings would require new manufacturing methods—an undisputed fact. The design complexity required in the early days for these sophisticated tasks was so great that it scared away the majority of users and suppliers of machine tools, or so the story goes. This skein of analysis owes the most to David Noble, a social historian now teaching in Toronto whose *Forces of Production*, published in 1984, is a landmark of critical interpretation.

But now an MIT professor, who was instrumental in the development of numerical control, has taken a crack at the story. J. Francis Reintjes, long-time director of the Servomechanisms Laboratory, was so angry about not being interviewed by Noble for his book (the fractious Noble sued him for defamation, among other things, for mentioning the fact to colleagues!) that he sat down to write one of his own. He has published *Numerical Control: Making a New Technology* (Oxford). If it is not exactly easy reading, it is a considerably fuller and more just-minded account than Noble's.

Reintjes' theory is that it was the conservatism of owners and managers in the machine-tool industry that caused them to be slow to perceive the competitive necessity of staying on top of computer-control methods. Survivors in an industry that is highly cyclical—machine tools last a long time, after all, and owners can always defer a decision to replace them until business turns up—the big companies had little incentive to invest in far-reaching research-and-development projects, while little ones couldn't afford to. They had many reasons to go on controlling their tools the way they always had, the way a sewing machine operator controlled a sewing machine—by the eye of a machinist, standing at a bench when it was practicible, by pattern or a cam, or by other means when it was not.

Surely this has the ring of truth. A well-established and hugely successful industry such as the machine-tool business may have had little incentive to reinvent itself at the height of its prosperity—or even to look abroad, where others may be doing it instead. Such complacency is the key to what happened to American steel and to American automotive manufacturing.

Reintjes even publishes the guest lists of a key MIT conference called in 1952 to demonstrate a numerically-controlled milling machine, and of three intensive two-week courses on numerical control for corporate engineers held in 1954, 1955 and 1957. All the blue chip companies are there: Cincinnati Milling Machine, General Electric, General Motors, Norton, Carborundum, Rockford Machine, Giddings & Lewis, Warner & Swasey, National Automatic Tool. Thus American industry can't say it wasn't warned. "You can only stay in the game so long if people aren't interested," says Reintjes of MIT's efforts to interest the companies in its applications.

Reintjes says he wrote his book as a kind of case study in how government-sponsored, university-based, industry-led research and development can work. "I would say the Air Force got a heck of a lot for about $1.5 million," he says. "They got what we call the 'elephant tools,' the enormous machines necessary to demonstrate to the aeronautical industry that this was the way to go. It's just too bad that it wasn't enough for the rest of American industry. They needed the Japanese to do it for them."

To be sure, there are plenty of tantalizing questions that Reintjes' book doesn't answer, or even address. Much has been made of the place in the history of numerical control of engineer John Parsons, for example. He was a brilliant Michigan machinist who first got the Air Force, then MIT, into the numerical control business in the summer of 1949 with a contract to build a planer mill driven by information from IBM punch cards. Reintjes sheds a good deal of light on Parsons' relationship with MIT, but has little to say about Parsons' subsequent career as a businessman. (Parsons promises his own book.) Nor does he have much to say about how the evolving "systems approach" of Jay W. Forrester influenced the early approach of the Servomechanisms Laboratory to the problems of numerical control.

But then it is scarcely reasonable to expect a researcher so thoroughly steeped in the culture of MIT as Reintjes to shed much light on that culture, except indirectly. This "book is not the stuff from which motion pictures are made," he writes in a brief preface. "It contains no comedy, intrigue, drama nor confrontations, because there were none. The story is unfolded with no artificial coloring." This is perhaps the single most (inadvertently) revealing observation in the book.

The fact is that the history of technology is, like the history of nearly everything, fairly packed with comedy, intrigue, drama and confrontation. It just happens that scientists and engineers aim to minimize these artifacts of human behavior in the name of their attempted dispassionate search for truth. It is for this reason that we should be grateful for the university-based discipline of the history of technology, which has grown up in the shadow of the great Lewis Mumford, who died last year at 95. Mumford knew that the lives of engineers could be as illuminating as their textbooks, that their works produced "revolutionary takeovers" as dramatic and far-reaching as more obviously political events. (The life and works of Mumford himself get a good going-over in an interesting new collection of essays edited by Thomas and Agatha Hughes, *Lewis Mumford, Public Intellectual.*)

One of these days a gifted historian of technology is going to tackle the extraordinary transformation that was imagined so successfully at MIT by a handful of engineers in the years during and just after World War II that goes under the banner of the digital revolution. Then it was just a glint in a few eyes; today it is intercontinental ballistic missiles and facsimile machines and ZIP codes and airplanes that "fly by wire." In the 20th century, it is often engineers, not poets, who are the "unacknowledged legislators of the world."

JULY 21, 1991

America:
Democracy to
Bureaucracy?

IN ITS FIRST HUNDRED YEARS, AMERICA WAS AN AGRICULTURAL NATION WITH MORE horses than people, and it was considered a worthwhile novelty to roll a slogan-decorated ball 12-feet high from Boston to New York to Philadelphia for a political convention. Today, executives making the same trip carry cellular telephones in their briefcases in order to carry on their business from stalled airplanes waiting at the end of runways, and television covers the conventions from beginning to end.

Does this modern age of ours constitute a whole new ball game in terms of the institutional governance it requires? A number of interesting writers think so.

Take John Lukacs, for example. Or Michael Stewart. One frames the issue in terms of international interdependence. The other wonders whether modern complexity means that we've grown beyond democracy. But both argue that we have entered a fundamentally different regime, quite different from the one in which the Founding Fathers operated.

John Lukacs is a man who does history the old-fashioned way: he writes it. Surrounded by annalistes and cliometricians, modern professional historians of all persuasions, Lukacs has diligently digested the past and regurgitated it in English, in 11 books over nearly 40 years, while living in rural Chester County splendor in Phoenixville, Pennsylvania. He largely eschews numbers, at least financial ones: he has written 404 pages of history of America and the world in the 20th century with just 14 dollar signs (by my count)—fitting enough to a man who views economics as "the most widespread idiocy of the 20th century." If the result sounds a little like an up-to-date Henry Adams, well, it is up to date, and deeply interesting. At one juncture, Lukacs hammers down a point about the Europeanization of America by observing that most American wildflowers—

buttercups, daisies, clover, Queen Anne's lace, even the common dandelion—are European immigrants, too. Only asters, goldenrod, milkweek, cranesbill and a few others are truly native.

The central premise of *Outgrowing Democracy: A History of the United States in the Twentieth Century* is that time and technology have transformed the nation from a democratic order to a bureaucratic state. What's the difference? The primacy of the individual has given way to the primacy of the corporation, he says, and the democratic order called forth certain civic virtues that no longer have much of a place in the technological present. He quotes the poet Randall Jarrell, "I think that George Washington would be extremely afraid of traffic on the Merritt Parkway, but I think that we would be afraid of George Washington."

Like others, Lukacs sees the period between the Mayflower and World War I the equivalent of the golden age of Greece, with a tragi-comic afterglow lasting from 1895 to 1955, when American civilization was both urban and urbane. "But by the mid-1950s the mental attitudes, the inclinations, procedures, aspirations and the very language of a government bureaucrat were not one whit different from that of a college administrator or foundation official or corporation executive," he writes. (So much for the painstaking efforts of the Harvard Business School's Joseph Bower and others to differentiate between two cultures of public and private management.) The result is the end of the Modern Age, nearly 500 years dominated by Enlightenment, and the beginning of something new.

In Lukacs' mind, inflation is the central metaphor of our times, but he says that the impulse to the debasement of values came not from the Federal Reserve system but from the real creators of the 20th century: Henry Ford, Woodrow Wilson, the publicist Edward Bernays. "The inflation of society grew before the inflation of money, the inflation of circulation before the inflation of traffic, the inflation of verbal communications before the inflation of physical communications. The increase of money was a consequence rather than a cause."

Lukacs is only the most recent in a long line of analysts stretching back to Max Weber, Jakob Burckhardt and beyond, who have found a key to understanding in the increasing specialization of the workforce. A similar analysis was volunteered recently from anthropologist Marvin Harris. In an interesting little book called *America Now: The Anthropology of a Changing Culture*, published two years ago by Simon & Schuster, the Columbia University anthropologist wrote that "since the end of World War II, the United States has become a bureaucratized and oligopilized country, oriented more to people-processing and information-processing than to the production of goods. What was once a decentralized manufacturing society has become a centralized service and information-processing society. And equally important, what was once a society where women stayed home to work has become a society where women leave home to work."

Even University of Chicago historian William McNeill, who has probably written more and better sweeping histories than any other man alive, is feeling a little gloomy along these lines. In his Charles Edmondson historical lectures at Baylor University, now published as *The Great Frontier: Freedom and Hierarchy in Modern Times* McNeill speculates that the role of the market and individual choice is apt to diminish in the United States over time.

"A complex, differentiated, flow-through economy, staffed by diverse religious and ethnic groups who are united more by propinquity than by any obvious cultural uniformity, probably requires management by some kind of power elite," he writes. The history of the frontier, McNeill says "shows that the rewards of interdependence and exchange are too great to be foregone. But interdependence implies social hierarchy and management based on some mix of compulsion and incentive."

Historian Lucas' prescription against the terrors of the bureaucratic—in social science and history as well as everyday life—is history itself. "Outside the airport of Orlando, Florida," he writes, "the road sign has two arrows. One points to Disneyworld, the other to the Kennedy Space Flight Center. Under the latter arrow are these words: THIS WAY TO REALITY. No: The way to reality lies within us, within and not outside the bounds of our mother earth; within our historical consciousness, which is nothing else but our consciousness of ourselves, potentially drawing on inexhaustible essences, including the inexhaustible wisdom of the past."

Just the opposite tack has been taken by Michael Stewart. Whereas Lukacs thinks that economics is bunk and that only history is real, Stewart starts from economics—fair enough from a member of the faculty of University College and author of a widely admired volume on Keynes who has worked as an economist in the British Treasury, the Cabinet Office and 10 Downing St. His theme, a familiar one among economists nowadays, is that nations' policy decisions now have global effects in a world increasingly tied together by trade.

What is interesting about Stewart's argument in *The Age of Interdependence* (MIT Press, $15) is the assertion that separate policies, which are reasonable on their own terms, when taken together, have a distinct deflationary bias because of the perverse logic of international capital flows: policies of low inflation and high unemployment are reinforced by big capital inflows. Hence, the history of the early 1980s, in which American monetary stringency (and fiscal profligacy) has been rewarded with huge flows of foreign investment—at the expense of much economic growth that would have been otherwise possible.

Given this interdependence, Stewart sees two possible strategies, to de-link or to coordinate national policies. De-linking, a policy often associated with the applied economics group at Cambridge University, requires both important controls and exchange controls to buffer the national economy against events elsewhere, he acknowledges. It probably would work fairly well for some nations, but not for many. If Japan and Germany were to opt out of the world economy, he says, world trade would dry up, and nearly everyone would be worse off.

In the end, Stewart says, the industrial countries must become much more sophisticated about the spatial and temporal effects of their disparate policies, and learn to pull together. More and better summit meetings, better organized supra-national agencies like the International Monetary Fund and the Organization for Economic Cooperation and Development are all part of the answer.

The class of programs on which Lukacs and Stewart and Harris and McNeill are working was identified years ago in a paper called "The Governance of Complexity," by Eugene B. Skolnikoff. Now more an administrator than a working scholar—he is head of the center for International Studies at MIT—Skolnikoff summarized the circumstances surrounding economic growth and asked, "Is man capable of designing social institutions that will be able to govern a world of incredibly growing complexity and scale without sacrificing values important to the society?" Maybe, he answered; but political breakdown due to hypercomplexity was the more likely alternative.

So more professionalization? Or less? It is the really interesting question.

JULY 8, 1984

A Knack for
"Thick Description"

IF THERE IS A SINGLE WORD THAT SEEMS TO DESCRIBE THE SECRET OF SUCCESS IN business it is "differentiation." Differentiation is what everybody everywhere tries to do to their products: to make them different from and better than the products of their competitors, to achieve a secure place in customers' affections—and a secure niche in the economic world.

Consultants try to show businessmen how to achieve prosperity this way, but for obvious reasons they prefer to keep what they really know about the art between themselves and their customers. The prince of differentiation, the man who has published more and been more widely read on the subject than any other, is a 58-year-old Harvard Business School professor named Theodore Levitt.

Levitt didn't start out as a scholar of business. In fact he was teaching economics at the University of North Dakota in 1955, headed for Europe on a Fulbright scholarship to study German co-determination, when a partner in the Chicago law firm of Kirkland & Ellis read a piece he had published in the *American Economic Review* and asked him to help out in the antitrust defense of Standard Oil of Indiana. "I'm the enemy, I'm not on your side," he told the lawyers. They replied, he says: "We've been hiring our friends and we keep losing in the courts. We thought we would try something different."

So Levitt set up shop in Chicago, doing the most uneconomical things. "To understand what was going on in retail pricing, I started driving all around the Midwest. I did massive studies of different cities—Chicago, Des Moines, Indianapolis, Rockford. We read the price of every pump in every gas station on a single day and put it all on the map—this was before computers—to show how variable prices were. I spent a lot of time chewing the fat with jobbers and retailers to find out how things worked.

"In the process of doing that as an economist, I'd write memos to executives I had gotten to know about what was going on out in the field. In one case, I wrote a long memo suggesting a major shift in the way in which they opted to market retail gasoline, the kind of stations they ought to have, what their location strategy ought to be, how many stations they should have. After a while they said: 'It looks like you can be more valuable to us on that side of the business than on the other.' "

When the Amos Tuck School at Dartmouth College offered him a job, he stopped over in Boston on the way. He phoned Gilbert Bursk, then editor of the *Harvard Business Review*, where he had been publishing. Bursk said: "Don't take a job until you've talked to the administration here!"—and Levitt has been at Harvard ever since.

In a book just out—*The Marketing Imagination* (The Free Press, $16.75)—Levitt writes about marketing and the corporate purpose, then applies his principles to a variety of subjects. Among his arguments is that the multinational corporation is tottering on the brink of extinction, soon to be replaced by the global corporation.

What's the difference? The multinational simply operates to a lot of different countries, Levitt says, adjusting at relatively high cost to local conditions, whereas the global corporation treats the whole world as a single market. A shining example of such a global approach, he says, is McDonald's, which sells the same hamburgers on the Ginza in Tokyo that it does on Washington Street in Boston.

Levitt polishes his pieces to a considerable brilliance. (Most of the chapters in his book appeared first in the *Harvard Business Review*.) "In the last 20 years I've never published anything without at least five serious rewrites. I used to keep a record of it. I've got deep rewrites up to 12. It's not to change the substance so much; it's to change the pace, the sound, the sense of making progress, even the physical appearance of it. Why should you make customers go through the torture chamber? I want them to say 'Aha!' " The result is that Levitt has won the awards given annually to the best single article in the *Harvard Business Review* four separate times—twice as many times as anybody else.

Despite a strong overlay of systemic thinking, there is not very much of the economics textbook left in Levitt. He says he thinks that technical economics is "grievously on the wrong track and it has been for many, many years." A "clubby insularity" permits it to thrive, so "people of enormous talent and capability are wasting their gifts on things that are unimportant and irrelevant."

In his own field of "marketing science," things are not much better, he says. "There is an overwhelming and malignant tendency to work on trivial things," and "an obsessive quest for academic recognition." A happy exception, he notes, is Columbia University economist Kelvin Lancaster, who has tried to bring the formal study of product variety to economics. "He's really terrific, but the economics profession doesn't pay any attention to him. Harvard's Harvey Liebenstein, too. But the mainstream of the profession has passed them by.

"I've been reading a marvelous book by anthropologist Clifford Geertz, called *Local Knowledge*, in which he argues for something he calls 'thick description.' There's a constant leitmotif of interpretation inside the description—that's why he calls it thick description, it's interpretive. Thick description is a style of analysis I'd love to see cultivated in our field and other fields of social science. There is one problem with doing that—you really have to know everything about everything. I remember the first thing of Geertz's I ever read was "Notes on the Balinese Cockfight," a very long piece, and after I read it, I couldn't tell you what I knew, but I sure as hell knew it.

"That's the thing about thick description. It gets systemic, it becomes part of your gut, and I'd say that is one of the things about our teaching at the business school. It gets inside of people's cognitive sytems in a way that they're not necessarily aware of, but it's there and it never goes away."

OCTOBER 23, 1983

The Conference Room as the Symbol of the Times

IT IS SAID TO BE THE "AGE OF INFORMATION"—AS OPPOSED TO BRONZE, IRON, WHEAT, steam or any other thing. Investigators are trying all the time now to nail down precisely what this means, so far without conspicuous success. Clearly, it is not enough to say that today we have computers. But each stroke adds a little to our understanding of what it means to live in a time whose symbol is (as Daniel Bell has succinctly put it) not the smokestack but the conference room.

Take, for example, James R. Beniger's *The Control Revolution—Technological and Economic Origins of the Information Society*. Published last year, the book is the latest in a long series of attempts to parse the essence of modern times. A table listing proclamations of modern socioeconomic transformations published since 1950, spills over two pages and identifies all the familiar names—Kenneth Boulding, Milovan Djilas, Michael Young, Walt Rostow, Peter Drucker, Daniel Bell and John Kenneth Galbraith—as well as a host of interesting but less-well-known writers.

Beniger singles out economist Fritz Machlup as the first scholar to attempt to measure the size of the sector engaged in "the production and distribution of knowledge." He ascribes central significance to the analyses of Harvard historian Alfred Chandler of the evolution of the mechanisms of administrative control—management committees, bookkeeping and reporting systems as well as new processes that grew up in industry after industry starting in the 1830s. And he takes pains to locate his ideas of programming and control in the context of larger systems of thought, notably population and molecular biology.

What emerges with unmistakeable clarity from Beniger's historical chapters on mass production, distribution and consumption is the folly of treating the information sector as a recent arrival. Indeed, a dominating graphic early in the book shows the information sector swelling to more than 25 percent of the civilian work force—while agriculture shrinks to less than 25 percent—sometime during the 1920s. Today, information production dominates the American economy at something like 45 percent of the whole; services account for 30 percent; industrial products about 22 percent, and agriculture a mere 3 percent.

Beniger writes, "The Information Society has not resulted from recent changes . . . but rather from increases in the speed of material processing and of flows through the material economy that began more than a century ago. Similarly, microprocessing and computing technology, contrary to currently fashionable opinion, do not represent a new force only recently unleashed on an unprepared society, but merely the most recent installment in the continuing development of the Control Revolution."

Alas, as is often the case, Beniger's attempt at synthesis—in this case, to show that the history of all life can be seen in terms of the information flows necessary to maintain increasing complexity, lacks a certain persuasive force in the rest of the academic establishment. Glenn Porter, the distinguished historian of technology, likened the more general chapters of the book to "attending about four dozen academic cocktail parties in a row." (Or, perhaps, to the mid-1960s social science general education course at Harvard College in which Beniger's great adventure began.)

Certainly the book's biological metaphors lack the wonderful "if . . .

then" quality of formal economic models. But if the book is an intuition rather than a blueprint, it is a contagious one; more and more scholars are being drawn to the history of science, technology, business and the work of "development" in general. The trail of the patterns there is hot. Beniger's key insight, the growing "systemness" of society, is a fact no less important for not yet being fully understood.

SEPTEMBER 6, 1987

Lessons from the Game of "Life"

Savez-vous the game of Life?

If not, pop into a computer research facility, says Peter Albin, and ask if Life is played there. The answer will be yes, he says.

Then ask if it is played on the machines themselves, if programs exist for putting the figures of the game up on screens.

The answer will be yes again, says Albin, "but guarded—since the next question—'How much time gets wasted here on the game of Life, any-way?'—will confirm all your doubts and misgivings about the inefficiency of the system."

The game of Life is a harmless-seeming diversion in which cell-like configurations, with names such as "blinkers," "clocks," "toads," and "gliders," and governed by a few simple rules, are born, grow and die on graph paper or CRT screens.

It was invented in the late 1960s by John Horton Conway, a celebrated English pure mathematician, and popularized by Martin Gardiner in his column in *Scientific American* in 1971. Since then, like one of its little configurations, it's become a closet enthusiasm of thousands of scientists and computer buffs, peaked, and fallen off. Fallen off, that is, in all but a few minds—including that of Albin.

Albin is a City University of New York economist who has built the ideas underlying Life—called automata theory—into a mathematics capable of dealing with the trickiest dimension in economics, that of complexity. When Albin watches the forms of Life drift across his computer screen, he sees not the little electronic configurations of a game, but the basic shapes of the life histories of neighborhoods, of companies, of nations.

Complexity? There is nothing hard about the idea, at least intuitively. New York is more complex than Boston, Boston is more complex than Worcester, Worcester is more complex than Maynard, and Maynard is more complex than New Marlboro.

But is New Marlboro more complex than Tyringham? And just how complex is Tyringham, anyway? If the idea of degrees of complexity is to have meaning, it should be capable of measurement. It is not now. To differentiate between cities, you might as well use the Yellow Pages— something Jane Jacobs said more than 20 years ago. "Classified telephone directories tell us the greatest single fact about cities," wrote Jacobs, "the immense numbers of parts that make up a city, and the immense diversity of those parts."

The measurement of complexity is where Albin comes in. Try to bend the conventional tools of economics to the task, he says, and they don't serve. The system of equations used to describe a small city looks about the same as that used to describe a complex one; the model of an industrial nation looks indistinguishable from one of an underdeveloped country.

"In the literature of economics," said Albin, "structure and complexity are poorly defined concepts which are invested with weight and magical significance and are assumed to be well understood." They aren't, he adds, noting there is no analytical or descriptive category devoted to complexity the way there is to, say, productivity or economic activity, no statistical index to measure complexity as it waxes and wanes.

But how? It helps to think of the economic system as a big computer, Albin says; after all, computer scientists are well along in their attempts to describe the complexity of their designs. The problem in economics thus is akin to the problem of describing an advanced IBM 370 system computer in comparison to simpler versions and also in comparison to predecessor models in the 7000 series or 650 series, Albin says.

With that in mind, he proceeded to devise a series of applications in economics of the theory (of automata) behind Life. Life's advantage was that it was highly visual, whimsical, interesting. Automata theory's advantage was that it was rigorous and beautiful, as befits one of the final projects of mathematician John von Neumann. Since his work was published posthumously in the mid-1960s, it has become the foundation discipline in abstract computer science, of linguistics, of mathematical logic, says Albin.

Yet it scarcely has made a dent in economics. Albin's papers find ready homes in systems journals, but, generally speaking, economics journals have rejected them on the grounds they are "not economics."

When Albin, 46, attended his 25th reunion at Yale last week, he looked back on a career that conveniently broke just about in the middle, in 1968, when he went to Cambridge University. He was trained at Princeton by, among others, Burton Malkiel, and worked at various neoclassical topics, mostly in welfare economics, until he hit Cambridge. Even then, he later wrote, "It took some years for me to realize the power of the tradition and the style of work which derive from and extend Keynes' original insights into the driving forces of capitalism."

If chewing the fat with James Meade, Joan Robinson and Nicholas Kaldor softened him up, it was in fact his first encounter with the game of Life in *Scientific American* that finally caused him to drift away from the neoclassical tradition and into the study of complexity. He recalls, "Life forms could be made to behave like populations grouped into towns or village . . . similar forms could be grouped into capital goods and other artifacts. . . . With a bit of ingenuity, one could combine the elements to form an intriguing world apparently filled with social interactions, threshold phenomena, environmental effects and evolutionary or adaptive phenomena.

"I am concerned with technical change, with understanding technical change," says Albin, "and, in the end, my politics amount to a kind of Keynesian socialism." In his 1978 book *Progress Without Poverty: Socially Responsible Economic Growth*, he took notions he had developed earlier of a "dual economy," one for the rich, another for the poor, and spun out the policy conclusions of his economic analysis in a call for economic planning.

Meanwhile, he has been no stranger to the real world. At one time or another, he has played on the edge of expert class bridge, Go and chess. He was a founding partner of the Unicorn Group, a hedge fund that now manages around $100 million—successfully enough to consistently rank in the top one percent of those whose performance is monitored by the Becker organization, a ratings service.

Indeed, Unicorn is so tangibly of the real world that a couple of years ago it got smacked with a suit by the Labor Department for its stewardship of the Central States Teamsters' Pension Fund. There has been no movement one way or the other in the suit.

What happens next? Albin has a carefully laid-out research program, hamstrung somewhat by the fact that the City University of New York's John Jay College is hardly a first-rate economics department. It may be the best place for a dangerous innovator, but Albin's work is beginning to move beyond its early stages into a genuine network of fellow researchers. He is accorded much more attention in Europe than in the United States, partly because Europeans have recognized more quickly than their American counterparts the wide range of applications of Albin's work possible in tinkering with workers' productivity.

"I am working now on the direct observation of work," he says. "Understanding and being able to measure the complexity of work performed with a turret lathe is a necessary step to understanding technical change in general. And of course understanding the complexity of work means I can break it down into its component operations; I can do things that [Frederick Winslow] Taylor never dreamed of."

"The point of being in a discipline is that you don't say that this is like that and that is the end of it. There are very stringent rules of analysis which must be obeyed. There is a great deal of work to be done."

So the analysis of complexity, like regional science, like operations research, like managerial economics and the rest of the business school disciplines, is taking up a position on the fringes of the discipline of neoclassical economics, in the interstices between departments of knowledge. Together, these disciplines superficially resemble nothing so much as guerrilla forces encircling a frontier town. One day they hope to simply walk into town and take over their target, with scarcely a metaphorical shot being fired.

JUNE 2, 1981

How Long Did
Mass Production Last?

ONE THING MOST PEOPLE CRAVE IS A NOTION OF THEIR PLACE IN THE SYSTEM. IN THE play *Our Town*, the minister sends a letter to "Jane Crowfut, The Crowfut Farm, Grover's Corners, Sutton County, New Hampshire, United States of America, Continent of North America, Western Hemisphere, The Earth, the Solar System, the Universe, the Mind of God"—knowing that she needs to know her address. So it is with the economic system, except that our concern with it usually involves the further questions: What happens next and what might we do to change it?

People are forever coming forward with answers, of course, from news magazines that announce that computers mean people won't go to the office any more to popular books designed to help you classify whatever mega-trends in which you may be caught up. Two unusually interesting books have surfaced in the last year, however, both having to do with the organization of work.

Michael J. Piore and Charles F. Sabel provoked a wave of interest last year when they linked the spread of computers with something they called "The Second Industrial Divide." The industrial world was at a historic crossroads, they argued in a book by that name, and instead of more dreary mass production in big factories, the future could hold a return to craftsmanship, in tiny shops like those of Italy or East Cambridge, amid a vivid entrepreneurial socialism whose ideal form they called "yeoman democracy"—if only people were willing to press for it.

About the same time, David F. Hounshell published a remarkable study of the events that Piore and Sabel, somewhat casually, brevetted first industrial divide. *From the American System to Mass Production, 1800-1932*, was published by the Johns Hopkins University Press but nevertheless sold briskly through two printings—thanks partly to the sheer beauty of the photo-filled volume. It is due out in paperback this fall.

Together, the two books focus attention not only on the particular arguments involved, but on the existence, quite apart from technical economics, of a community of people interested in the rules of the economic game and how they change. What professional economists have in common is their view of the economy as an intricate system of interdependent forces in balance; what these other scholars share is a sense of patternment not quite so mechanical: call it the study of history of the division of labor.

Piore and Sabel, two MacArthur Foundation fellows with "genius grants" that relieve them from much of their ordinary Massachusetts Institute of Technology teaching load, operate far closer to the popular sphere than does historian Hounshell. They portray the economic history of the 19th century as essentially a struggle between two ways of doing things, as mass production vs. craft economies, as long production runs and big markets vs. artisans shops serving highly differentiated markets with batch production, like the Solingen knife works. In this battle, mass production won completely, they say; it was as victorious in the realm of ideas as in the realm of practice. Craft production became discredited, "a practice without a name, by definition incoherent."

The computer now offers a rare chance to reverse the tide, according to Piore and Sabel, by permitting manufacturers to continually rearrange the parts of their production processes—workers and their tools. The trick now is to revive the lost craft system, to give it a new name ("flexible specialization") and a lot of government subsidies to get it started. There is no hidden dynamic of historical evolution, they write, there is only choice. They spin a vision of flattening hierarchies, of spun-off business units and thriving worker cooperatives.

Because of the emphasis on public policy, *Fortune* magazine attacked *The Second Industrial Divide* as "the latest case for planning," while the *Harvard Business Review* noncommitally plugged it as a book that every businessman should read. Some of Piore's and Sabel's prescriptions were immediately incorporated into platform statements by a few of the more adventurous Democrats. Nobody campaigned on Hounshell's ideas, but then Hounshell, an historian of technology, employs a far more orthodox approach.

An electrical engineer from Southern Methodist University in Dallas, Hounshell worked five years for an electrical contractor before going back to school in the mid-1970s to become a historian. Today, at 35, he teaches at the University of Delaware and is curator of technology at the Hagley Museum in Wilmington, Del. "It was something of a gamble," he says. It was worth it. Hounshell's mass-production system took a long, long time to replace existing methods of manufacture, and then just as it succeeded most brilliantly, with the Model T Ford, it spiked and fell back. Where Piore and Sabel tend to make references at key points to philosophers such as Proudhon and Marx, Hounshell's is a thorough history of firms. He follows the introduction of the idea of fully interchangeable parts from French and American armories, where the adoption of the practice was driven by government wishes and where expense was no object (rather like semiconductors a century later), through its subsequent development in the manufacture of clocks, sewing machines and reapers, to the bicycle business.

It was in the 1890s, in the early years of mass-market bicycling, in the unlikely precincts of Chicago's Western Wheel Works, that Hounshell found that the stamping of parts from sheet metal replaced drop-forging, ushering in the age of true interchangeability. Why Chicago? Why Western? Because the company's mechanics were johnnies-come-lately to the trade, Hounshell discovered; they weren't steeped in the metal-working traditions of the New England armories. Their press-formed hubs weren't as good as machined Yankee hubs, it was true, but they cost a lot less and they fit a lot better. That, he says, was the real end of the "American system" of hand-finishing machined parts and the beginning of the system of mass production. What was left was for Henry Ford to introduce the assembly line.

Hounshell's book is interesting partly because of its implications for the existence of a clearcut "Second Divide": Ford's vision of universal mass production was a cul-de-sac, he argues. Ahead lay an era of flexible mass production, stressing out-sourcing, model changes and a far more variegated work force. What General Motors' Alfred P. Sloan, Jr., called "the laws of the Paris dressmakers" took over, Hounshell says, and in any event, the era ended with World War II. "The specter of the atomic bomb removed mass production from its central place in the American consciousness and forced the nation and the world into the nuclear age."

Thus the preoccupation with mass production that ran from Diego Rivera's murals to Charlie Chaplin's movies was just one more high-culture fad, in historian Hounshell's view. "Whenever we see the introduction of a new technology, there is a tremendous, widespread fascination with it, often charged with utopianism," he said in an interview last week. "We had it with the division of labor, with steam, with electricity, with nuclear power. It was that way with mass production when it was at its zenith in the 1920s. It is that way with computers today."

JUNE 23, 1985

Frank Talk
About Class
from ... Granola Valley?

BENJAMIN DEMOTT IS ANGRY ABOUT AMERICA'S PRETENSE THAT IT IS A LARGELY classless society. The author, who writes as well as you would expect the Mellon Professor of Humanities at Amherst College to write, lives in a lovely stretch along the Connecticut River known as Granola Valley, where the ratio of tax-and-tuition-and-inheritance-funded intellectuals to production workers may be as high as it is anywhere in the country except Washington. An aura of make-believe suffuses the apple orchards there.

A few years ago, DeMott's daughter spent two years living in Muncie, Ind., to make a documentary about blue-collar high school kids there—a kind of inside version of *Sex, Lies & Videotape*, as it turned out. The heads of Xerox Corp. and the Public Broadcasting System, having funded the documentary, refused to air it, on grounds that it disparaged the kids. So the film, titled *Seventeen*, went instead to theaters, where it received lavish praise from reviewers. Now, DeMott has written a book, *The Imperial Middle: Why Americans Can't Think Straight About Class* (Morrow), to gain revenge on those corporate sponsors who didn't share his daughter's vision of class and to enlarge upon his own, as he explains in an extraordinary acknowledgement at the end.

And what a book! Intensely personal, suffused with a father's rage at mistreatment of a daughter ("Because they lacked knowledge of American working-class life . . . they had to hang the messenger, had to call my daughter a liar."), *The Imperial Middle* argues relentlessly that there are social situations from which there is no way out, that assimilation and upward mobility are often a public relations smokescreen and that 15 minutes of genuine "talkback"—from the likes of Jake LaMotta, Bruce Springsteen, Richard Pryor, Gary Gilmore—are worth 1,000 hours of Cosby show reruns. You can't make apples into oranges, he seems to say.

The entire book is dominated by this distasteful anecdotal image, which appears in its first pages: "Ten years ago, at Amherst College where I teach, a black freshman named Gerald Penny went down the hill with his classmates during orientation to take a compulsory swimming test. Rows of larking students—mainly children of affluence—dove one after the other into the pool, filling the lanes. Penny dove in with the others and, not knowing how to swim, drowned. The college's Black Cultural Center now bears Penny's name." The publisher says that the picture that emerges from the book is of a nation tragically out of touch with itself.

As interesting as DeMott's book is, there's a certain impracticality about it—a massive indifference to the ways by which people learn to swim, or accidents happen, or persons are saved or not saved, the ways by which, in other words, things actually get done. DeMott is, for example, relentless in his assertion that occupation is not class, yet is greatly incurious about what occupations mean, or how they have changed over the years. For example, at a certain point, he tells this joke: "There was this star and director discussing a new starlet on the set and:

"Director: She's Polish.

"Star: Polish? Who says?

"Director: Gotta be. She's sleeping with the writer."

Notes DeMott, "Most ethnic jokes consist of class insult, ethnically masked."

But if you look more closely about what this joke is about, it turns out to be the distribution of power among occupations. You could almost say it is a joke about corporate consciousness, about the difference between inside and outside, between full-time and part-time, between staff vs. free lance. Its point is that directors and producers are powerful, that writers are not. But surely that's not a matter of class?

An alternative to DeMott's analysis might be to actually begin to make a map of the evolution of the American economy and society, of who works for whom, under what circumstances, and of what their work conveys in the way of social mobility. Olivier Zunz, an historian of the annaliste school, trained at the Sorbonne, who now teaches at the University of Virginia, offers a good example of how this task proceeds. In a new book, *Making America Corporate, 1870-1920* (University of Chicago Press), Zunz relates how America gave up its Jeffersonian self-image as a nation of yeoman farmers for the model of corporate organization that obtains today.

The straw man in Zunz's account is that famous critic, C. Wright Mills, leader of a generation of critics who saw white-collar workers as "passive prisoners in a system they did not attempt to change." Mills had said in the

1950s that American history of the last century "seems to be a series of mishaps for the independent man." And certainly a generation of novelists, playwrights and sociologists has embroidered this familiar picture: American executives as acted-upon but not acting, existing without beliefs, living only to sell, political eunuchs, in short, and victims of a sick society.

Far from it, says Zunz. Starting with railroads, the early executives didn't so much react to a system as design one. They saw themselves as diminishing the role of class, not enhancing it. Workers in those early corporations were defined by occupation, not lineage—though the DuPont family held on into the 1970s.

Whether creating organization charts by trial and error, building skyscrapers, dispatching salesmen to far territories, or hiring clerks, white-collar managers believed they were off on a mission from God. They were not simply Yankees hiring immigrants, but rather tinkerers and theorists and willing architects, who built the modern corporate state, and they changed it in many ways not yet fully understood. "To the old 19th-century dualisms of rich and poor, city and country, they added new dichotomies of bigness and smallness, hierarchy and independence, homogeneity and diversity."

Today, even after a decade of battering in the 1980s, corporate organization is still the pervasive social mode in America, not the only form of organization, but still the dominant one. Indeed, corporate vs. noncorporate, big business vs. little business, has been the axis of much of the fiscal politics of the last decade. How these economic issues will play out in the future is far from clear. But certainly they will have as much to do with who gathers around that swimming pool at Amherst College as do questions of class.

NOVEMBER 11, 1990

On the Economic Significance of Noam Chomsky

HERE'S AN INTERESTING LITTLE TEST: WHICH OF THESE SYLLABLES MIGHT BE PART OF words found in an unabridged dictionary of English, and which might not?

Flib. Slin. Vlim. Smid. Fnit. Vrig. Plit. Trit. Brid. Blim. Tnig. Bnin.*

Chances are you got them right. The really interesting question is how you knew.

Since you've never seen these syllables before in anything resembling this form, you didn't check them off against all the real words you know and separate the candidates for nonsense. You therefore must know some general principle that tells you whether any arbitrary sequence of sounds is or is not a well-formed syllable of English.

Just because you cannot say what the rule is doesn't mean you do not know it. As Massachusetts Institute of Technology professor Morris Halle says—he is the author of this example—people know lots of things without being conscious of the fact.

For example, he writes, "Major league ball players must surely have knowledge of parabolic trajectories, for each time they catch a ball they must somehow calculate such a trajectory. But no one is likely to conclude that baseball players have explicit knowledge of Newton's Laws of Motion, that they can solve differential equations or even that they can do simple sums." Like the knowledge of parabolic trajectories possessed by ball players, says Halle, knowledge of syllable onsets is largely implicit—but that doesn't make it any less real.

---

* (The answer is that a vlim, fnit, vrig, tnig and bnin would not be found; the others would. The rule, for those who like such things, is that English syllable onsets containing two consonants are composed of "p t k b d g f th" followed by "l r w" or of "s" followed by "p t k m n l w." This is easy enough to put in a computer.)

Welcome to the world of linguistics, where the task shared by an expanding corps of specialists is to scout out those unformulated but knowable laws of language. It's a world that Halle helped create, not least by hiring Noam Chomsky to teach with him at MIT, then building the world's best linguistics department around him.

Chomsky is the man who, with the publication of a single set of lecture notes in 1957, transformed the study of language from an old-fashioned habit of collecting and comparing different languages—sometimes looking for an *Ursprache*, a mythic mother tongue from which all languages are descended—to the very cutting edge of cognitive psychology.

That is to say, he demonstrated conclusively, across a broad front, that these regularities in the human language faculty existed, no less than the laws of motion. By asking, how does a mind know a language? How does it acquire its knowledge? Chomsky and Halle and others showed that answers to these questions were rooted in knowable biological facts: the shape of the mouth, the physics of sound, the physiology of the brain, the mechanisms of natural selection, the deep structure of grammar. Linguistics from 1957 on, therefore, has mainly been about elucidating the hidden basis of nature's hardwiring of one sort or another. And, of course, where hidden order undergirds casually-observed surface behavior, usually there is money to be made.

There cannot be a man in Cambridge harder to get a handle on than the 63-year-old Chomsky (he lives in Lexington, spends much time in Wellfleet). When Jeremy Campbell wrote *Grammatical Man*, his brilliant exposition of the revolution in information theory, he steered clear of the MIT linguist to a surprising extent. Social science citation counts show Chomsky to be the most influential psychologist of the 20th century—well beyond Sigmund Freud.

Yet, Chomsky is still not quite at the center of a field that either has or hasn't overturned philosophy, having long since conquered a major part of psychology. One reason is his scientific style, a relentless pushing of propositions to their extremes. Another is the protective coloration of Chomsky's strong personal politics, which are well to the left of those of Fidel Castro. Nothing has changed his lifelong conviction that America is what is wrong with the world.

In contrast, in science, Chomsky has changed his mind three times about crucial issues in structural linguistics, and there are rumors of an impending fourth. This is not especially surprising, for the conversation of science proceeds in a much more orderly fashion than political discourse. As Chomsky says: "You have to understand more, but maybe know less."

Linguistics has been racing ahead in recent years, into realms of computer science, cognitive psychology, neuroscience. Today you're as likely to meet a linguist in an artificial intelligence laboratory as a computer scientist, a cognitive psychologist or a neuroscientist. The point is that we are getting a handle on what it means to think—and what it means to adapt computers to the process. Ahead lies the realization of dreams like machine translation, object-oriented search (meaning machines that do the reading for you) and numerical analysis.

And therein lies the economic significance of the brief 35-year story of modern linguistics. One moral is conventional, and has to do with location. It's a commonplace that the abandoned textile mills of New England provided a friendly home to digital electronics companies, which were looking for bargain space. In a somewhat similar way it is surely significant that it was linguistics that moved in when radar moved out of MIT's famously ramshackle Building 20 to posher quarters.

The other point is more subtle. There is a school of thought that says diffusion of new knowledge is accomplished best by the presence of financial incentives at every stage. Certainly, MIT is a brilliant example of how this can work. Department by department, from chemical and electronic engineering to biology, it has been responsible for astonishing economic gains. And what is not diffused by profit can be blown by puff, MIT's fabled Media Lab being the prime example.

The exception is linguistics. It, too, is responsible for many new jobs. It may be too much to say that when International Business Machines Corp. made its first move into parallel processing by entering into a collaborative research agreement with Thinking Machines Corp. of Cambridge last week, it was because Cambrige was the capital of the investigation of thought. But in a certain sense, the mountain had come to Mohammed.

For in linguistics the mechanism has been subtlety, importantly different. For Chomsky and Halle, there are no founder's shares, no scientific advisory boards with their enormous fees. Indeed, the second page of Chomsky's book on the media grouses, "Copyrights are required for book production in the United States. However, in our case it is a disliked necessity." But Chomsky has been chosen to give the Killian Lecture at MIT this fall; Halle is in Paris this week to accept an exalted scientific prize. "Their riches are elsewhere," says the poet Naomi Chase, Halle's friend.

SEPTEMBER 29, 1991

The Odyssey
of George Lodge

IT WAS A GOOD DAY ON WHICH TO VISIT GEORGE LODGE. THE NEWSPAPERS WERE FULL of symbols flying off events.

President Ronald Reagan was on the stump describing America's "spiritual reawakening," inveighing against promiscuity. Gary Hart was on a roll as the candidate of "new ideas." Paul Tsongas was saying: "I did not think it was going to happen in the Democratic party until 1988, but it is happening right now." Meanwhile, Standard Oil of California was gobbling up Gulf Oil Corp., the Japanese were increasing their stake in an important American computer manufacturer (Amdahl Corp.) and a big California chip manufacturer, National Semiconductor, was indicted for selling untested chips to the Defense Department.

George Cabot Lodge, of course, is the son of one of Massachusetts' best known politicians, the man who lost to Edward M. Kennedy in Kennedy's first race for the U.S. Senate. Today he is the Harvard Business School's expert on ideology, a student, he says, of the ideas that have a formative effect on communities, and why they change and how they change. He teaches everything from Teilhard de Chardin to Sam Huntington to everyone from first-year students to advanced management program executives.

"I have a strong ambition to make ideology into a reputable academic discipline instead of a bag of junk—the confusing imprecise thing that it is now, where people talk about Right and Left and liberal and conservative and nobody knows what it means," he says.

Instead of the familiar Left-Right distinction, Lodge sees a dichotomy between communitarian values and individual ones. Individual values—he calls them "Lockean" after the 17th-century philosopher with whom they are closely identified—are the familiar ones of the Federalist Papers, the Constitution, the Declaration of Independence. This "traditional ideology" stresses equality of opportunity, the primacy of property rights, the efficiency of competition, clear limits on the role of the state, and a high degree of specialization, Lodge says.

This constellation of traditional values is being replaced by a "new ideology," Lodge says, which stresses equality, consensus, community needs over individual rights and something he calls "holism," which is the opposite of specialization. Where the traditional view stresses equality of opportunity, Lodge says, the other stresses equality of result: One gives everyone an equal start; the other seeks to achieve an equal finish, even if it means issuing "lead belts" to the best performers.

The key to Lodge's system is his sense that a "Great Transition" from one regime to another is "proceeding vigorously in the 1980s." He doesn't spell out very much about the nature of the cycle, but at one point he likens the present day to the "similar blight of upheaval, confusion and corruption" four and five centuries ago as "medieval communitarianism gave way to individualism in Europe."

(Lodge says he himself is not a proponent of the transition to communitarianism from individualism—"The old creed is, I should say, as dear to me as to anyone," he writes—but rather merely a witness to historic inevitability.)

In fact, Lodge's views have a great deal in common with those of Pitrim Sorokin, a Harvard sociologist whose ideas about a many-century cycle of alternating cultural styles dominated the social relations department of Harvard University when Lodge was a student there. "Sorokin made a very great impression on me," he says. "I took his courses, and when I went to Washington (to become assistant secretary of labor for international affairs) I corresponded with him and even had him down to talk once.

"I think what I've got here is a way of understanding what happens, of making some order of it. Otherwise, you listen to Reagan make speeches and you might be led to think that we were actually going back to the traditional ideology, that government was really going to get off our backs—unless you were to ask yourself what was happening. The reality, of course, is that government is bigger than ever.

"We are torn in so many ways between the old hymns and the new realities. What I am suggesting is that if we would compose some new hymns to go with the new realities they wouldn't seem so terrible and they would make all of our lives easier. We wouldn't have so much schizophrenia."

What kind of new hymns, then? Lodge says we should look to the model of Japan and seek to strengthen government control of the national economy. "Somebody has got to be thinking strategically and integratively," he says. He locates himself firmly in the line of those who argue that the United States needs more collective industrial planning to strengthen its international competitiveness—fellow businessmen Felix Rohatyn, Peter Peterson, Irving Shapiro, as well as Robert Reich, Ezra Vogel, Lester Thurow and many others.

In a new book, Lodge has settled on the metaphor of disease to describe the views of those who disagree with him. "The American Disease," he says, "is a pathological condition, deriving from a severe developmental crisis, characterized by the denial of reality and the inability to develop solutions to the problems being forced upon the community by a new and unfamiliar environment." It resembles, he says, "the ailment of a troubled adolescent whose grief at growing up causes him to deny reality, or to cope with it through wishful thinking or a regression into immature, counterproductive behavior."

"It's a pernicious sort of a thing, not a hopeless malady, but it is terribly expensive. In a larger sense, this is the British Disease—it took them so damn long to realize what had happened to them. If you look at Britain in the 1920s, when the pound was very overvalued, you see that the British banks were very glad to have it that way. In the meantime their ability to compete was deteriorating because they weren't putting enough money into investment."

So who is suffering from the American Disease? Reaganites, mostly, at least according to the analysis. Lodge snorts, "He talks about Americans standing tall while we're being clobbered by the Japanese, the Taiwanese, the South Koreans, Hong Kong and Singapore in any line of endeavor in which they clobber us. It's just a question of where they want to aim the gun."

Is it really so bad as that? Is the communitarian revolution really so inevitable as Lodge thinks? The usual quarrel with his argument is that liberal values—the "traditional ideology"—may be much more durable than he thinks. After all, as interpreted by political columnist Robert Healy last week, Gary Hart's surprising strength in the primaries means that "what is happening is a real revolution in the Democratic Party, in which the leaders are saying there is something to the Reagan revolution, but we can do it better."

Time will tell. In any event, George Cabot Lodge has made a very long journey from that '62 Senate race against Kennedy. Then he was a Republican, the son of Henry Cabot Lodge, full of good intentions, whose fate seemed to be in politics. Today, he is still a registered Republican (he was John Anderson's vice presidential candidate in Massachusetts and Maine), but last week Gary Hart's people asked for a copy of *The American Disease.* Once a candidate, he is now an adviser to candidates. It is a position, arguably, of greater power.

MARCH 11, 1984

Robert Nozick and the Zigzag of Politics

BACK IN 1975 ROBERT NOZICK WAS, BRIEFLY, FAMOUS. THE (THEN) 36-YEAR-OLD Harvard University professor made the pages of *Newsweek, Forbes* and *The New York Times* with the publication of a tome called *Anarchy, State and Utopia*—a forceful argument against nearly all forms of government coercion, including redistribution by taxes.

As a precocious bigfoot among his colleagues in academic philosophy, Nozick was something of a novelty, throwing his weight against the temper of the times instead of pursuing with other philosphers ever more desiccated forms of thought. That put him in a class of people, along with Jamie O'Conner, George Gilder, Martin Feldstein, Janos Kornai and James Buchanan, who fomented the tax revolt along a broad ideological front. The trouble with socialism, Nozick would say, is that it prohibits capitalist acts among consenting adults.

Fifteen years later, much has changed—including Nozick. What had been controversial in the 1970s became conventional in the 1980s. The wave of changing sentiment that brought Margaret Thatcher and Ronald Reagan to office swept on to Europe, including Scandinavia, most of the Third World, China, Eastern Europe and even Russia. Today deregulation is the watchword of the world. Meanwhile, Nozick is back, too, with some second thoughts about his earlier attack on the right of the state to coerce people to do good.

His new book, *The Examined Life*, consists of 27 meditations, ranging from "Dying" to "Love's Bond" to "Giving Everything Its Due." To some, it is high-brow Harold Kushner; to others, philosophically adroit Garrison

Keillor; to others still, a distillation of wisdom to put on the shelf next to Marcus Aurelius, Montaigne and Samuel Johnson. Whatever the case, the book has a claim on the attention of those interested in the spirit of the times in which we live, for toward its end, in an essay called "The Zigzag of Politics," he writes: "The libertarian position I once propounded now seems to me seriously inadequate." Why? "Because," he writes, "it did not fully knit" more closely into its fabric "the humane considerations and joint cooperative activities" for which the theory had room.

What does this mean? It means the welfare state may be a good idea after all, as an expression of humankind's solidarity with the needy. It's not enough that government have a particular purpose, he writes—it must have a symbolic meaning, too.

What changed? Well, from the beginning, Nozick was never quite in sync with the New Conservatism, culturally speaking: He was uncomfortable with Ayn Rand–style libertarianism and *National Review* politics, he says, and the symbolic neglect of social concerns of the early Reagan years made him uneasy. So he eschewed the think-tank celebrity and stuck close to Harvard.

After an intervening book, *Philosophical Explanations*, he turned to writing his meditations on how to live, and so, at least tangentially, to politics. Olin and Scaife Foundation funding gradually dried up as the work progressed; he finished writing *The Examined Life* on a National Endowment for the Humanities fellowship.

Nozick shrugs at not being involved with an intellectual gang, but notes that the costs of continuing to speak his mind are real. He writes: "Once having pigeonholed people and figured out what they are saying, we do not welcome new information that would require us to re-understand and re-classify them, and we resent their forcing us to devote fresh energy to this when we have already expended more than enough in that direction already!"

Presumably what will keep the liberals from pecking him to death is that his theorizing is still exceedingly sharp, his writing program is still unfolding, his second act still looms up ahead.

The new book takes some positions that contrast sharply with the old one. For instance, there is the "subtraction rule" he proposes in his essay, "Parents and Children." Nozick doesn't want to rule out parental bequests to children; they are legitimate expressions of caring about them, he says. But great wealth cascading down the generations doesn't appeal. So, he asks, why not have taxes that would insure that a bequest would last only one lifetime. People could pass only what they earned, not what they inherited. For example: If they inherited $1 million, and saved $500,000, they bequeath only the money they made. Perhaps this would be an accounting nightmare with economic consequences that might be difficult to predict. But it's an interesting suggestion, philosophically speaking, from the man who once wrote: "Individuals have rights and there are certain things no person or group may do to them" without violating their rights.

Indeed, Nozick cobbles up his own zigzag course toward truth to a full-scale vision of public life. Suppose that there are multiple competing values that no political viewpoint can completely encompass, he says: liberty and equality, love and justice, efficiency and fairness, solidarity and individuality, each entailing a fairly complete political program: save the whales, a chicken in every pot.

Each political party will select some goals from the list to represent and rank them differently, while giving lip service to all the other possible goals. Some party will gain the ascendancy and go on to build a "record of accomplishment," while the loser searches for a new act.

"The electorate I see as being in the following situation," Nozick writes: "Goals and programs have been pursued for some time by the party in power, and the electorate comes to think that's far enough, perhaps even too far. It's now time to right the balance, to include other goals that have been, until recently at least, neglected or given too low a priority, and it's time to cut back on some of the newly instituted programs, to reform or curtail them. . . .

"The electorate wants the zigzag. Sensible folk, they realize that no political position will adequately include all of the values and goals one wants pursued in the political realm, so these will have to take turns. The electorate as a whole behaves in this sensible fashion, even if significant numbers of people stay committed to their previous goals and favorite programs, come what may. For there may be a significant swing bloc of voters that will shift to new goals and make the difference—that the least-ideologically committed voters may determine an election is abhorrent to the view that wishes politics to institute one set of principles, yet desirable otherwise—and in any case, a new generation of voters will appear on the scene, ready to seek a different balance, eager even to try something new."

To be sure, "The Zigzag of Politics" is not much more than a fragment. Nozick, who makes no prediction about the timing of such shifts, says little about the scale on which they take place. There is little about how a generation experiences a transformation of its commitment, not even much about the experience of commitment itself. But then that is not very surprising; Nozick's is a private life, not a public one: He's a man not especially enmeshed in his times. But zigzag is a far more appealing metaphor than cycle. The image of humankind forever tacking toward a desired destination is more persuasive than the vision of it "turning back" toward earlier truths.

Meanwhile, Nozick doesn't rule out the possibility of some day sidling up on another book on political philosophy. He plans to teach one Harvard course (on rationality) with Amartya Sen next year, another (on varieties of knowledge) with fellow New Yorkers Stephen Jay Gould and Alan Dershowitz. His independence as a political philosopher remains one of his principal gifts. "People put a megaphone in front of your face and they expect you to speak only while it's there, and they take it away if they begin to disagree. There's something wrong with that." Thus 15 years on, Nozick remains one of the most valuable early warning systems around, reversing the usual order of things: Having been conservative in youth, he's becoming more liberal with age.

JANUARY 14, 1990

"Somebody's Got to Take the Responsibility!"

FOR THE LAST FEW DAYS, WASHINGTON HAS BEEN A BEEHIVE OF BEHIND-THE-SCENES activity. Bankers and Treasury aides from all over the world have descended on the city to prepare for the annual meeting of the International Monetary Fund and the World Bank that begins tomorrow. No big surprises are expected.

Indeed, the worst seems over. Threatened not once but three or four times with collapse during the Great Recession of 1981–83, the international monetary system was saved not by dramatic government intervention, but by hard work among commercial bankers' steering committees and borrowers' counterparts, and nimble central banking in Washington and

Basel. This year's meetings will be far less dramatic affairs than those of the last few years, notably 1978 and 1979, when the ticking started; or 1982, when the seriousness of the debt bomb was just beginning to be apparent.

The question has arisen repeatedly: Can the world really hope to continue to work in this decentralized fashion? Or must there be some hegemonic leader? The question was put forcefully by Charles Kindleberger at the end of his book about the Great Depression, in which he argued that there must be one strong leader in the world to prevent such things. It was put even more forcefully by the actor George C. Scott at the end of the movie *Hospital*. "Ah, hell," he said, before returning to his job as an administrator, "Somebody's got to take the responsibility."

One of the people who currently has most to say about these matters won't be in Washington this week. Much light has been shed in recent years by discussion about the theory of international cooperation, full of fancy terms like Prisoner's Dilemma, collective action, the Coase theorem, moral hazard. Robert Keohane, 42, of Brandeis University has pulled it together in a much ballyhooed book about the international political economy called *After Hegemony*.

The book is well-tailored, forceful—a "system-level theory," as they say—closely argued, full of assumptions, tightened then relaxed, with something of the atmosphere of a sweet-smelling, wool-carpeted weight room at the Princeton Club of New York. It is built on three chapters of firm analysis of events since World War II, and has the Kissingeresque willingness to deal with the world as it is that we have come to expect from really political scientists—only this time with an economic twist. It is aimed at people outside the academic world.

Keohane says you can't always hope to live in "Pax Britannica" or "the American Century"—and that world order can be quite stable without a single dominant leader. He says that quality of information available to leaders and their firmness of commitment are the keys to living in an increasingly interdependent world.

Wars create leaders, Keohane says, and the first 15 or 20 years after World War II, the United State was the hegemonic leader of the world. But hegemony generates growth, and growth generates interdependence, and interdependence generates conflict, and hegemony ends.

Keohane divides the world between realists, who think perpetual conflict is the rule, and institutionalists, who stress cooperation in an interdependent world. He's pretty much of an institutionalist, stressing the usefulness of international agreements and agencies from the Organization for Economic Cooperation and Development to the UN Commission on Trade and

Development, and the likelihood that no one dominant world leader can emerge without another major war.

But what about the world monetary system? Paul Volcker seems to have played the take-charge guy with pretty good results. Isn't the relative success of the Federal Reserve System at bringing down inflation an indication that the hegemonic spirit is alive and well and working on Constitution Avenue?

Keohane says, "I think our leadership there is the result of the particularly central role of the dollar. The U.S. position is much more important in money than in trade. It is not as strong even in money as it was in the 1940s and the 1950s, when the United States could make rules and everyone would accept them, but it still is able to follow its own rules.

"The striking thing is the reversal that has taken place. In 1978 and 1979, it appears that the United States was having to conform to others' wishes more. The two packages of policy measures that were taken in the fall of 1978, then in 1979, both appear to have been prompted by complaints at the IMF meetings by others. Now we have at least a temporary reversal of that. But in the future there will be a period of dollar weakness for sure, and then we will become more susceptible to the influence of others than we are now.

"There is no interest in the Reagan administration in anything that smacks of policy coordination. What is striking to me is the extent to which the administration has had to move into supporting the IMF, even though it came into office with contempt for international policy coordination, with contempt for development economics and contempt for the IMF in particular. Yet it spent a lot of its capital in the fall of 1982, putting through its IMF support bill. It had a lot of opposition, it twisted a lot of arms, for the liberal Democrats were skeptical of the measure as a bank bailout, the conservative Republicans were opposed to it as being a measure of internationalist bankers. But the IMF is such an important organization that they had to go along with it, even though their ideologies were opposed."

Keohane says that the serious problem today is not with the fund, but rather with the institutions that mediate world trade. "There's no doubt that GATT [the Geneva-based General Agreement on Tariffs and Trade] is in very serious trouble. There is a decay going on there at a rather alarming rate. Still, we have a tendency to view protectionism as synonymous with discord, and liberalism with cooperation, but that's not what we're seeing right now. What we're seeing instead is voluntary protectionism. The textile agreement is the best example of that, where the United States and the Europeans cooperate, as well cooperate with some of the LDCs who already have a stake in the market, to divide up that market—it's a cartel kind of agreement. If you look at the Japanese-American auto agreement, I do not believe the Japanese are really opposed to that, because Japanese manufacturers collect tremendous scarcity charges, and they are making out like bandits.

"What we've seen in the last 10 years is that the institutional structures are a lot stronger than we thought they were. There is a lot more resilience. In the press, everything is falling apart all the time, but there has been real strengthening in the oil regime, meaning the rules of the game and the institutions by which they are administered, in the debt regime. If the forecasts are right, the institutions are likely to strengthen further, and the debt problem is likely to improve. If the dollar falls soon enough, even the trade regime may get better," he says.

SEPTEMBER 23, 1984

Rebuilding Beirut

BACK IN THE MID-1980S HARVARD LAW SCHOOL EARNED THE SOBRIQUET "THE Beirut of American law schools" when it fell to civil war over how to teach its students about the law and who should teach them. Within its faculty, a band of neo-Marxists known as "Crits" attacked from the Left, while "law and economics" acolytes of Milton Friedman and others of his ilk charged from the Right (mostly off-campus), squeezing the large, proud and decidely un-theoretical middle. Voices were raised and civility declined, as the amorphous controversy was fought out in an endless series of faculty meetings (and the gossip after), which routinely brought out the worst in the smartest people. The situation turned melancholy after one of the school's best men, conservative Paul Bator, decamped to Chicago, denouncing the bitter Cambridge atmosphere, and then a few years later died.

One of the raised voices belonged to a moderate teacher of corporate law named Robert Clark, and in due course, Harvard president Derek Bok last year picked Clark to serve as dean. Clark had beaten up on the antics of the critical legal studies group (that professors ought to work a month a year as janitors was among the Crits' planks). He had pummeled their highly polemical teaching style. (Crits are "anti-everything," he said, "anti-law, anti-business, anti-capitalism, anti-technology.") But otherwise he took their scholarship seriously. Clark, 45, is now undertaking to restore a liberal viewpoint to the school, both administratively and through scholarly argument. It is a Herculean task.

Consider. Though the faction that has garnered most of the the ink over the years at Harvard is the Crits, far more significant inroads into the kinds of law that Harvard teaches have been made in the past 20 years by the law and economics movement. This intellectual fashion, involving the precise application of economic theory to legal situations, grows to an astonishing extent out of the work of Ronald Coase, an 80-year-old Englishman who may yet live to win a Nobel Prize for having fathered much of the deregulatory movement. Working out of the University of Virginia, then Chicago (where Aaron Director had lured him), Coase first persuaded economists of the applicability of economic analysis to legal situations, and they in turn persuaded law professors and eventually judges. By the early 1980s Harvard graduates were having to argue before the likes of Richard Posner and Frank Easterbrook, immensely influential appellate judges in Chicago who were leaders in the new field. By the mid-1980s most questions of accident law and of corporate governance—meaning takeover battles—were couched in terms of law and economics.

Through most of the diffusion of the law and economics movement, Harvard stayed on the sidelines; after all, the new fashion had a distinctly Chicagoan tinge. To be sure, the law school added three economists to its faculty, the foremost of whom is Steven Shavell. It hired many others who were conversant with the new ideas, like Robert Clark. But mostly it stuck to its tradition of selecting the best common-law lawyers it could find to teach the law as a field unto itself, a matter of respect for history and institutions. Instead, it was the Harvard Business School that hired away the University of Rochester's Michael Jensen, guru of the new shareholders' rights interpretation of merger-and-acquisition law.

Against this steady march of ideas the Crits had relatively little to offer serious scholars, much less to practicing lawyers. For example, one of the critical studies movement's leading lights, Duncan Kennedy, advised students to use "sly, collective tactics" to "confront, outflank, sabotage or manipulate" senior partners within their firms. At its worst, the Richard Rorty-style relativism of the Crits is facile, shallow and nihilistic. At its best, as in Roberto Unger's three-volume *Politics, A Work in Constructive Social Theory*, it is deeply original and illuminating social criticism, in the tradition of Lewis Mumford and Karl Marx. But the truth is that much of the law school controversy in the mid-1980s had to do simply with the Crits' attempt to break out of their secure beachhead on the faculty. As with the similar fracas in Harvard's economics department a decade earlier, once the Rads were decisively contained, the shouting died down.

Meanwhile, however, the law and economics movement seems to have crested as well, having reached, perhaps, the limits of its ability to inform. In a new and much-discussed article in the *Chicago-Kent Law Review*, Yale professor Robert Ellickson, himself once a leading light of the L&E business, writes: "In general, law and economics is no longer growing as a scholarly or curricular force within the leading American law schools." He cites a variety of informal indicators of the trend: The number of economists among tenured faculty of the four leading law schools—Stanford, Chicago, Harvard and Yale—has stabilized at 11 persons among 183 professors; law and economic articles appearing in leading student law journals are down to around 25 percent, from around 33 percent in the first five years of the 1980s. "Compared to a decade ago, law and economics is less often seen as an intellectual tide with which every scholar must come to terms, but rather as a technical sideshow that a young professor may now spurn with little professional peril."

Moreover, Ellickson says, the action in that specialty has turned to bringing culture and human frailty to economic models that portray human beings as entirely rational, citing the work of scholars such as Amos Tversky, Robert Frank and Herbert Simon. Such a gradual enriching will constitute an "improvement" more like that of moving to Kepler from Copernicus than like an abrupt "shift" in perspective, as to Copernicus from Ptolemy, according to Ellickson. But in the same issue, Richard Posner offers a rejoinder, accusing Ellickson of having "magpie" tendencies, and of adding "bells and whistles" that may "stop the analytic engine in its tracks." It may be true, Posner says, that landlords may permit long-time tenants to renew their leases at below-market rates because of "cultural considerations," as Ellickson says; it may also be that there is an economic reason for the custom, that long-term tenants are "good" tenants, that they impose fewer costs, and so deserve a discount.

It's here that Robert Clark comes in. Quite aside from having written the leading textbook on corporate law, Clark is the possessor of an extraordinarily sharp and broad philosophical mind, capable of slugging it out with, say, Richard Posner or Roberto Unger. A seminarian who studied for the priesthood at Maryknoll College, he did a philosophy degree at Columbia instead—comparing the social science philosophy of sociologist Talcott Parsons to that of psychologist B.F. Skinner—before becoming a lawyer. An avid musician, he stays up late composing on a synthesizer. But mostly he is a legal scholar, and during a talk to the Harvard chapter of the Federalist Society last week, he described the book he intends to finish "as soon as I can get rid of this deanship." Not surprisingly, the "Morals and Markets" project involves an attempt to compare infrequently-examined religious and social systems of organizing human societies alongside more frequently analyzed market and legal systems of control. "I tend to think that what needs to be done is to incorporate some of the techniques of religion in other spheres, the educational and the legal, rather than to have some global revival."

Clark's idea, of course, is to contribute another little bit of framework for the stance that until recently was called without hesitation "liberal"; to work out the relationship between the individual and his or her community without asserting the absolute primacy of either. His is just part of a movement arising in response to the vast success of the economic approach to human behavior. This movement is going forward along a very broad front, mostly in the universities, and it is here, not in the wise-guy polling operations of the most recent presidential campaign, that a new and more widely acceptable version of the basic American mind-set will emerge.

Nor do you have to wait for Clark to finish writing to see where it is going in the law. The *Yale Journal of Law and Literature*, for example, was founded last year specifically to battle the influence of law and economics. Its goal: "to restore to legal studies a proper place for the question of values."

Meanwhile, seven months into Clark's deanship, the Harvard Law School is enjoying a simmering cease-fire. His principal technique for keeping the lid on seems to be to hold fewer faculty meetings—just two last fall—down sharply from the earlier rate. The idea may be to limit the temptation of some of the best minds in America to slash and parry, like the cockfights of the bad old days. After Clark terminated a public-interest law placement program within the school, many students were furious for weeks. And something like a fifth of his audience quietly walked out when he began to discuss religious values during his talk last week. The Beirut of American legal education may be rebuilding, but it is still a school enjoying a truce, not peace itself.

FEBRUARY 11, 1990

A Philadelphia Story

In his classic tale of two cities, E. Digby Baltzell pursues a sharp distinction between "Puritan Boston and Quaker Philadelphia." The religious convictions of the founders of the two American colonies produced cultures that have differed with a clarity that might be hoped for from a controlled experiment, Baltzell said.

Even after 300 years, Philadelphians tended to be egalitarian, anti-authoritarian, visually-inclined and "virtuously materialist." Bostonians were hierarchical, intellectual, literary and action-oriented. Baltzell quoted a friend who had lived in both places: "The people in Boston all want to be chiefs, while in Philly they are all content to be Indians."

This distinction between acting and being is worth keeping in mind when it comes to thinking about where the human tribe is coming from and where it is going. If you have an autumn reading project in mind, a good place to start is with *American Genesis: A Century of Invention and Technological Enthusiasm* (Viking, $24.95) by Thomas P. Hughes. It is hard to exaggerate the merits of this 500-page volume: It is deeply knowledgeable, beautifully written and handsomely produced. It is the summa of the University of Pennsylvania's premier historian of technology, and there is no more absorbing chronicle of how Alexander Graham Bell, Thomas Edison, Elmer Sperry, the Wright brothers, Nikola Tesla, Lee de Forest, Reginald Fessenden and countless lesser lights began the transformation of American culture, before giving way to the more systematized efforts of corporate labs, and eventually government research and development programs.

Yet there is something troubling about Hughes' book, too, and it has to do with the uniquely Philadelphia angle on its subject. Hughes is a technological pessimist, something more than a professional doubter or skeptic. He regards technology as a paralyzing influence on modern life—often a terrible mistake, in fact. That makes him the ultimate supply sider. In his fascination with the inventors and financiers that build these big systems—automotive and electrical systems, for example—he overlooks consumers and the myriad decisions they make to buy or not to buy. The result is a curiously one-sided account of how economic "progress" unfolds.

The book is a great guide to what Hughes calls the modern era of technology, which is the period, say, from the invention of the light bulb to the end of World War II. But Hughes is an unreliable witness to those years, largely because he is one of those for whom the Challenger disaster and Chernobyl meltdown loom larger than the story of the computer and the rise of DNA.

Certainly the eight essays that constitute *American Genesis* are worthwhile for anyone interested in what happened to the America of Washington, Adams, Franklin, Hamilton, Jefferson, Madison and Monroe. Excellent scholarly history of American business and technology has been produced in the last 20 years, and Hughes knows it all.

In "A Gigantic Tidal Wave," Hughes limns the generation of independent inventors who got things started—men for whom "hunt-and-try was to hypothesize and experiment in the absence of theory." In "Choosing and Solving Problems," he describes technologists as working across a broad and continously changing front, much like soldiers in an army during World War I, with breakthroughs here and laggard sectors there. "Inventors and generals are seldom without problems to solve," he says.

It is in "Taylorismus + Fordismus," that Hughes' most penetrating insights turn up. And that's where the limitations of his view also show through most clearly. This infuriating essay describes the extent to which the Soviet revolutionaries were influenced by technological wonders wrought in America. He quotes Lenin—"the combination of the Russian revolutionary sweep with American efficiency is the essence of Leninism"—explaining the rush to build enormous dams, steel mills, truck factories, and he describes the Nazis' attempt to marry American methods of production with good old-fashioned "soulful" German values.

One would have thought, however, that the Soviet Union offered a nearly perfect example of Hughes' theories about where big systems come from and how they work. If large systems were all that were required, then surely the Soviet Union would have succeeded in its grand economic ambitions. Yet, Hughes is oddly incurious about where things went wrong. He notes that Chicago electricity magnate Sam Insull could have told the Soviets a thing or two about the management of consumer demand. But, otherwise, he makes little of the political conditions that stifled transfer of technology from the American companies to the Soviet Union. So American tractor designs weren't very good at plowing deep Russian soil; why was it that nobody adapted them?

After a chapter on the adoption of American modernism by artists and architects, Hughes zeros in on the further evolution of giant systems that began in the United States with the Great Depression and World War II. But the results are disappointing. He picks two "systems," the Tennessee Valley Authority and the Manhattan Project, and tells their stories well enough. But he fails to persuade the reader that the addition of the government to the systems' equation was the last step in assuring their all-but-"unbreakable momentum." Indeed, when it comes to post-war technology, Hughes has surprisingly little interesting to say. For him, "momentum is almost everything."

The systems whose origins in the 19th century he has studied have matured, grown large and rigid, and now resist further change. Citing works by Lewis Mumford, Theodore Rozak and Jacques Ellul, Hughes speculates that only a sea change in human values, amounting to a religious conversion, will break the hold of the great systems and usher in an age of small-scale, decentralized, flexible and relatively autonomous production units. "With the demise of the large systems, so characteristic of modern America, a post-modern era would arise," he writes.

Is this what technological post-moderism is all about, then? The counter-culture? The greening of America? The *Whole Earth Catalog*? Alas, probably not. You have to ask yourself how it is that a University of Pennsylvania historian of modern American technology has next to nothing to say about the momentous developments that began with the invention of the modern electronic computer at Penn's Moore School of Engineering during World War II. Today, computers and related information services make up something like over 10 percent of American Gross National Product. They are quintissentially American. And they are providing the technological underpinning for the revolution in decentralization that we all presumably await. But Hughes has only this to say about them. "Celebrating industrial revolutions, was, and is now, an American pastime . . . . Recently there has been talk of a computer or information revolution."

In the end, then, it is probably going to be some Bostonian—Harvard's Daniel Bell, say (who established the term "post-industrial" and connected it firmly with computers), who will begin to write the history of technology in the last 50 years. In the meantime, Hughes has provided a vivid specimen of the Philadelphia view of an ultra-democratic world in which there would be only Indians and no chiefs.

AUGUST 27, 1989

A Visual
Strunk and White

PEOPLE WHO USE NUMBERS LOVE CHARTS. THAT'S ALL THERE IS TO IT. NUMBERS, after all, are the essence of any really good and unarguable story. A felicitous representation of them gives more punch than the best-written narrative. Even a bad chart is sometimes better than none.

God knows Edward Tufte loves numbers. He is a Yale professor who teaches both political science and statistics. Four years ago he wrote a very influential book called *Political Control of the Economy* in which he argued for the existence of an election-dominated political cycle that drives the more familiar business cycle. His idea of fun is trying to make a simple mathematical model that predicts congressional elections.

On the other hand, compared with his colleagues, Tufte ("Tuf-tee," he says) likes his numbers relatively simple. He plots them on the plane, performs very simple regression analyses of one or two variables instead of dozens. The penchant for simplicity makes him very attractive to newspapermen.

Tufte, 41, set out 10 years ago to write a principles of graphic design—not a textbook exactly, but a catalogue of the very best things that could be done, together with some thinking about what makes them the best. "Statistical graphics are the only place where art and science come together in a meaningful way," he says.

The result is *The Visual Display of Quantitative Information*, a $34 coffee-table book about chart-making—"a celebration of data graphics," he says. "The model was Strunk and White," says Tufte, naming the classic little book on clear writing—*The Elements of Style* by William Strunk and E.B. White.

"Clarity, clarity, clarity. You can't draw well unless you respect the reader. That's the whole point. The philosophy of the book is that good visual communications work is like good writing. Clarity in design and complexity in information are what count—just the opposite of the modern world."

Why did it take so long? "I never had the words. I looked around for a long time for language. Artists are hopeless. When they write about themselves, it's so murky; Paul Klee is good, but the others are difficult. Finally I found architects. They have a lot of straight lines, there are science and technology in the field, so in many ways, the book underneath is sort of a secret architecture book."

A year ago, Tufte was finally ready to go to press. But nobody would produce the book the way he wanted. So he published it himself, taking a year to finish.

From a distance, Tufte's venture looked riskier than it probably was. He borrowed from his local bank against the equity in his house. (The bank told him it was the second-most unusual loan they had ever made; the first was money to buy an elephant for a circus.) "The full investment came to about $100,000—that's a lot of money relative to me."

Expensively printed on fancy paper, *The Visual Display* is a picture book of do's and don'ts that owes as much to Robert Venturi's *Complexity and Contradiction in Architecture* as to Strunk and White. Frederick Mosteller, Harvard's leading statistician, called it "a landmark book, a wonderful book." John Tukey, perhaps the most original number-cruncher of the age, described it as a "tour de force." Yale's design chief Alvin Eisenmen called it "a revolution in graphic technique." And Herbert C. Morton described it in his review in *Science* magazine as "ambitious, innovative and idiosyncratic."

A fair part of *The Visual Display of Quantitative Information* is taken up with historical review. Here are such things as a 19th-century map of London showing the spread of cholera from a bad water pump, and the great 18th-century balance-of-payment charts of William Playfair, cheek by jowl with a map of the galaxies and an elegant French railroad timetable.

(There are 12 pages of color, but in general Tufte doesn't trust it: it's too complicated. Someday he may add a chapter on it, he says.)

The book's centerpiece is a map drawn in 1869 by a French engineer named Charles Joseph Minard to describe the advance on and retreat from Moscow by Napoleon's army. It seems to show a giant river stretching from Paris to Moscow; beneath it is an ever-diminishing creek. "It may be the best statistical graphic ever written," says Tufte. Here is the way he explains it.

"Beginning at the left on the Polish-Russian border near the Nieman River, the thick band shows the size of the army [422,000 men as it invades Russia in June 1812]. The width of the band describes the size of the army at each place on the map. In September, the Army reached Moscow, which was then sacked and deserted, with 100,000 men.

"The path of Napoleon's retreat from Moscow is depicted by the darker, lower band, which is linked to a temperature scaler and dates at the bottom of the chart. It was a bitterly cold winter, and many froze on the march out of Russia. As the graphic shows, the crossing of the Berezina River was a disaster, and the army finally struggled back to Poland with only 10,000 men. Also shown are the movements of auxiliary troops, as they sought to protect the rear and the flanks of the advancing army.

"Minard's graphic tells a rich, coherent story with its multivariate data, far more enlightening than just a single number bouncing along over time. Six variables are plotted: the size of the army, its location on a two-dimensional surface, direction of the army's movement and the temperature on various dates during the retreat from Moscow.

"Minard made the graphic because he was antiwar," says Tufte. "It wasn't because he was an engineer or a statistician. It's more powerful than *Guernica* [the famous antiwar mural painted during the Spanish Civil War by Pablo Picasso] because it evokes the pain of war, in a very precise way, telling what happened to whom, where."

Tufte's book is selling well. "I took a little course in junk mail in New York. I mailed 50,000 flyers out, to statisticians, cartographers, a lot of doctors. I took out ads in *Scientific American* and *The New Yorker*," he explains. You can get the book only from the author at Cheshire Press, Box 430, Cheshire, Conn. 06410

Priced at $34, the break-even point was at 2,900 copies, he says. Everything after that is gravy. He printed 5,000 copies and is about to go into a second printing. So that puts him around $70,000 to the good—so far. A French translation is in the works.

Self-publishing isn't for everyone, Tufte says. It is a very risky undertaking. But in this case, it seems entirely fitting, for Tufte is a man who is autocratic even by the standards of the academy. "It's a very important thing to me, to be free of editors and assistant deans—mice studying to be rats—all that paraphernalia with which most every enterprise in the modern word is afflicted. All that chicken stuff, for this moment, is gone. Occasionally I drive the road and I hear Frank Sinatra singing, 'I did it my way,' and, you know, I want to shake my fist."

OCTOBER 23, 1983

Astronomers, Ragpickers and J. Maynard Keynes

EVERYBODY REMEMBERS JOHN MAYNARD KEYNES' FAMOUS WINDUP AT THE END OF HIS *General Theory of Employment, Interest and Money.* The great English economist wrote in 1935, "The ideas of economists and political philosophers, both when they are right and when they are wrong, are more powerful than is commonly understood. Indeed the world is ruled by little else. Practical men, who believe themselves to be quite exempt from any intellectual influences, are usually the slaves of some defunct economist. Madmen in authority, who hear voices in the air, are distilling their frenzy from some academic scribbler of a few years back."

Was there ever a more scintillating—or self-interested—boast of the significance of one's own work? The remarks are surely the greatest all-time, all-purpose blurb ever penned, serving to justify the attention paid to thousands of books (and, of course, to this column, which often concerns those books and their authors).

But was Keynes right? In the 20th century we've become accustomed to professional economists working away in splendid isolation from the rest of us with their blackboards, computers and their deductive Great Truth of general equilibrium, enforced by maximizing rational individuals. They seek to persuade us that they are universal social scientists, that however hazy we may be about our motives and intentions, beneath our muddled views there is an objective reality that can be grasped only through their formal models. Every once in a while, some new group of economists comes forward to tell us that they've figured out some new institution—the family, say, or education, or elections, or discrimination or status. Meanwhile they continue wrangling among themselves about how best to manage the economy.

Over the years an opposite tack has been taken by Stephen Gudeman, a University of Minnesota anthropologist. Gudeman first went to Panama to study the rural economy in the late 1960s. He has been there and in Colombia off and on ever since, talking to peasants, doing what he calls "the imaginative and hard work of learning about others' lives." The result is three remarkable books that weave back and forth between conversations with peasants and high economic theory—and not just the latest neoclassical jazz, either, but all the roads-not-taken of technical economics. You're as likely to encounter Francois Quesnay as Karl Marx or John Stuart Mill, as likely to meet Piero Sraffa as Keynes. More attention is lavished on the views of the Gogo and Bemba and Bisa tribes of Africa than on German, American and Japanese styles of corporate organization; more weight is given to careful listening to what people say than to the application of mathematical tools devised by astronomers to human affairs.

Gudeman's vision is fairly radical. There is no demonstrably superior "hard science," in his scheme of things, no objective truth. He draws no sharp lines between amateur and pro, between scientist and crackpot, as economist Milton Friedman would have us do. Instead, for Gudeman, there is only a rich collection of models and metaphors that are elaborated in a series of "conversations" among living folk. The high conversations are interesting, but so are the low, and the ideas flow clumsily back and forth between. Just as there are "voices in the air," Gudeman says, there are "voices on the ground"—and the stubborn fact of their continuing existence requires "a new look at the communities in which models are made." Philip Mirowski of Notre Dame University has dinged economists for borrowing most of their metaphors from physical scientists; now comes Gudeman to take them to task for ignoring the large stock of metaphors that they have inherited from common speech.

In his latest book, *Conversations in Colombia, The Domestic Economy in Life and Text*, Gudeman distinguishes between two fundamental forms of economic organization, the "house" and the "corporation." Each is modeled after a quite different and distinct idea, he says. The corporation is organic, the house is mechanical; one is naturally given, the other is humanly constructed. The corporation is a relatively recent invention. The house is a folk institution of long standing, a source of ideas to economists from Aristotle to Marx, but still little understood. Its style of organization can be seen in the Roman villa, fundus or praedium; in the manor, the great estate, and the hacienda. A house has no balance sheet, no assets and liabilities; it is not susceptible to economic cycles, because the whole idea is a distancing from the intentions of others. The key difference between a house and a corporation has to do with "making savings" instead of "making money": What's hoarded for a rainy day among members of a household becomes invested for growth by the owners of a corporation.

In recent centuries, corporations have been picking up shares at the expense of houses, to say the least, and not just in the industrialized nations of the world, according to Gudeman. But that doesn't mean that they are gone, or that an understanding of how they work can be conveniently dispensed with. "The recipes of domestic economy, including ways to be thrifty and the art of home baking that used to be so avidly taught in land-grant universities are the remnants of this once-vibrant way of life. In the United States 'fast foods' sold by corporations and bought in the market have replaced the slow foods that used to be prepared in pots on the stove, but the house economy is still alive in many parts of Latin America today."

So? Well, in the end, what Gudeman offers is a different way of pursuing economic development, by listening first instead of immediately giving advice. "Rather than using the various forms of power—from monetary control of capital to the writing of texts—that subjugate and exclude these other voices, rather than offering prescriptions for 'deepening capital' or raising agricultural productivity through doses of technological improvement (such as the Green Revolution), we might try to develop an 'appropriate economics' that would expand the community of conversationalists by drawing upon the work of both," laymen and pros.

And where would that lead? Well, one of the haunting images in Gudeman's book is that of the rag-picker, the hunter after the flotsam-and-jetsam of modern industrial life. There are thousands of persons, after all, who make lifelong careers of picking through Mexico City's garbage dumps, day after day, searching out scraps to recycle and use. "Old rubber tires are recycled into sandals, discarded plastic sheeting becomes a windbreaker and raincoat; distant forests are used for firewood, leftover grass by the roadside becomes pasture for animals." This is the house organization doing what it does best, Gudeman says, putting remainders to use—and understanding its principles is vital to bettering the lot of those who now live bleak lives on the periphery of markets.

JUNE 17, 1990

Reflections
on "Belindia"

IT IS TWO YEARS SINCE THE EVENTS WERE SET IN MOTION THAT QUICKLY LED TO THE
fall of the Berlin Wall—the fall of communism itself—in the autumn of
1989. We appreciate better than we did then how easy it is to tear down,
how difficult it is to build up.

Now the first really incisive accounts of these global developments are
beginning to appear. They are making it even clearer how truly momentous
these events are on the one hand—and how great the risk is they will
disappoint, on the other.

Take *Democracy and the Market*, by Adam Przeworski, which has just
been published by the Cambridge University Press. This razor-sharp little
book by a cosmopolitan University of Chicago political scientist is part of
a remarkable series of studies on rationality and technical change at whose
heart is the theoretical perspective of the "multiple self;" a self that loves
justice as well as economic gain.

It warns that there will be nothing automatic about the integration of
Poland, Czechoslovakia, Hungary, Yugoslavia, Romania and Bulgaria into
Western Europe. It holds out the possibility that, as the nations of Eastern
Europe rush to create capitalist institutions, their new democracies will
come to resemble the chronically poor and divided economies of Brazil,
Argentina or Chile.

Przeworski quotes a Brazilian businessman: "Our businessmen think
communism has failed. They forget that our capitalism is also a monstrous
failure."

Forget geography for a moment, Przeworski says, and put Poland in the
place of Argentina, Hungary in the place of Uruguay.

"You will see states weak as organizations; political parties and other
organizations that are ineffectual in representing and mobilizing; economies
that are monopolistic, overprotected and overregulated; agricultures that
cannot feed their own people; public bureaucracies that are overgrown;
welfare services that are fragmentary and rudimentary.

"And will you not conclude that such conditions breed governments vulnerable to pressure from large firms, populist movements of doubtful commitment to democratic institutions, armed forces that sit menacingly on the sidelines, church hierarchies torn between authoritarianism and social justice, nationalist sentiments vulnerable to xenophobia?

"The bare facts are that Eastern European countries are embracing capitalism and they are poor. . . . One can expect they, too, will confront all the normal problems of the economics, the politics and the culture of poor capitalism," he writes.

"The East has become the South."

There is, in fact, some reason for hope here, and Przeworski puts his finger on it: It is that a few chronically hamstrung nations have successfully made the transition to democratic market-oriented economies, knit extensively into the international division of labor.

Few remember, for example, that it was Spain that led the world in the parade to economic and democratic liberalization that, 15 years on, still has no commonly accepted name.

It was in 1976 that Spain put aside the legacy of its bitter civil war and began a decisive metamorphosis into a modern European industrial democracy. "The future is not written, because only the people can write it," Adolfo Suarez, the prime minister who managed the transition, told the Constituent Assembly.

Przeworski writes: "In only 15 years, Spain has succeeded in irreversibly consolidating democratic institutions; allowing peaceful alternation in power; in modernizing its economy and making it internationally competitive; in imposing civilian control over the military; in solving complicated national questions; in extending citizenship rights, and in inducing cultural changes that made it part of the European community of nations."

Isn't that precisely what everybody wants for the newly emerging democracies?

Yet Spain, as Przeworski notes, is a "miracle," one of only a handful of nations to have escaped from the dynamics of poor capitalism since World War II. France and Italy were earlier winners. Portugal and Greece are struggling to match the Spanish achievement. Turkey still has a chance. Taiwan and South Korea may yet succeed. Mexico is the most hopeful new experiment in democratic and economic liberalization.

But many other nations—indeed, most others—are stuck in the unhappy state that has been described as "Belindia," that is typical of, say, Brazil. For a fortunate few at the pinnacle of the economic pyramid, the state of affairs resembles Belgium; for the rest, it is India that provides the template, with its staggering unemployment, low income and slow growth.

What makes the sort of cooperation and restraint that leads to economic growth possible in one time and place and so very difficult in others? Why did the *Federalist Papers* read so persuasively in the 13 American colonies and why do they sell so poorly today in Yugoslavia? These are among the most pressing questions in all political and social thought today.

Meanwhile, the Eastern European nations tend to look down their noses at Latin American countries, Przeworski writes. When they look across the southern Atlantic, they see Joseph Conrad's world of military juntas, coups, landed oligarchies, populist movements, authoritarian religious orders, jungles and beaches.

But Conrad was a Pole, after all. And Przeworski writes, "I know many a Polish village where Gabriel Garcia Marquez would feel right at home; I hear the allure of the tango to the Polish ear; I have sensed on my shoulders the weight of hundreds of thousands of people propelling me to kneel before a sacred image of the Virgin Mary, the Queen of Czestochowa and the Tiranita of Santiago del Estero.

"And can you imagine a Western European parliament that, facing an agenda of several pieces of fundamental economic legislation, would plunge into a debate about whether a cross should be placed on the crown of the emblematic eagle?"

AUGUST 18, 1991

The Kennedy School Tries Again

THE KENNEDY SCHOOL OF GOVERNMENT AT HARVARD UNIVERSITY, WHICH SAYS IT wants to fix Russia, is in something of a predicament itself. It is not as messed up as the Soviet Union, not by any means; it's more like England, say, or Italy. It is a toss-up which of these underachieving powerhouses will be running smoothly first.

The Kennedy school was rocked this spring when Robert Putnam quit as dean after two increasingly difficult years. His predecessor, founding dean Graham Allison, the one who now wants to fix Russia as part of a "Grand Bargain," was forced into an early return to the professorial life by Harvard president Derek Bok.

Allison had been spectacularly successful raising money for buildings— but more than a little inattentive to ethical details, pinning a medal on Attorney General Edwin Meese, trying to name the school's library for South African gold king Charles Englehard, selling officers bursar's cards to rich Texans in return for big gifts.

The school's opulent buildings sprouted in the old rail yard along the Charles River like brick mushrooms; so did the conviction that the school was somehow missing its academic opportunities. That was presumably why Bok turned to Putnam, Yale-trained, an undisputed star of high academic political science from Harvard's government department, with a mission to make the school great through purification.

But in a wrenching demonstration of the gulf between analytic skill and political acumen that is at the root of the ever-normal Kennedy school identity crisis, Putnam crashed. He demonstrated little interest in raising money, serving as faculty interlocutor, glad-handing politicians or any of the other myriad acts of ingratiation and discipline that a successful deanship requires. Other Harvard deans have done worse; biologist Phil Sharp, tabbed for president of MIT, didn't even try. Putnam left, he explained with conviction, because he preferred to do his research.

At heart of the turmoil is the question, what exactly is the Kennedy school supposed to do? The institution evolved slowly out of a graduate school for civil servants and diplomats that was established with Lucius Littauer's money and Felix Frankfurter's brains during the early days of the New Deal—until it was renamed for the fallen president in 1968. Then, a newly-inaugurated Harvard president Derek Bok in the early 1970s decreed in a burst of enthusiasm that it would establish "nothing less than a new profession"—a school dedicated to excellence in government.

The Kennedy school's real competitors, therefore, are not so much smaller-scale versions of itself (like the Woodrow Wilson School at Princeton, the public policy school at the University of Maryland, the LBJ school at the University of Texas at Austin) as the other institutions that bid for influence over government—law schools and business schools, as well as old-line think tanks like the Brookings Institution and the Hoover Institution. It's these organizations that the Kennedy school hasn't quite caught up to—much less a discipline-based international magnet like the London School of Economics.

Why? Well, it's not for lack of excitement. With more than 700 degree candidates entering annually, and a constant stream of mid-career executives coming through, the Kennedy school, with its roughly 80 full-time professors, has become a highly profitable operation for Harvard University—at the cost of being disparaged occasionally by its competitors as a diploma mill. With its continual stream of visitors from Washington, the provinces and abroad, it is one of the livelier centers of university life in Cambridge.

And certainly its faculty has plenty of stars—economists Dale Jorgenson and Richard Zeckhauser, poverty specialists David Ellwood and Mary Jo Bane (Glenn Loury has been raided by Boston University), arms control specialists Joseph Nye and Paul Doty, science policy adviser Lewis Branscome, lawyer-journalist Robert Reich.

But just across the river is an institutional reminder that the Kennedy school hasn't yet quite found its niche. The Harvard Business School is far from perfect; it can be argued that more than once, it missed a march: in Europe after World War II, for example. But in some indefinable way, the B-school is truly on top of the corporate world in a way that the Kennedy school isn't in the realm of administration. Part of the answer may simply be competition—the B-school has a lot of it, and the Kennedy school doesn't. Part of it may simply be that in a fundamentally capitalist world, business and law are the superior disciplines.

Now there is a lot of talk about who will be the Kennedy school's new dean. One rumor has it that Harvard's new president, Neil Rudenstine, wants to appoint an outsider at the B-school, so he'll do the same at the Kennedy school for the sake of symmetry. Another has it that among the leading candidates are the insiders like Herman "Dutch" Leonard and Alan Altschuler. Meanwhile, Albert Carnesale, a well-liked nuclear engineer who is the school's academic chief, is acting dean—and many professors hope he'll get the job for keeps.

But whoever is selected as dean, what's really going on is that the school's senior faculty is aging fast and must be replaced. The remarkable collection of scholars who were recruited in the 1960s in the name of JFK included Richard Neustandt, Harvey Brooks, Howard Raiffa, Thomas Schelling, Frederick Mosteller, Don K. Price, Ray Vernon, John Dunlop, Jack Montgomery, John Meyer, Ernie May and Francis Bator—not an easy gang to replace.

Indeed, when the faculty voted recently to make an offer to monetary economist Jacob Frenkel of the International Monetary Fund, John Dunlop quit the school in a huff. Frenkel took the presidency of the Bank of Israel instead, and second choice Robert Lawrence of the Brookings Institution, a specialist in industrial policy, was embarrassed. These are the choices that, in the next few years, will determine whether the Kennedy School of Government moves forward or falls back.

JUNE 16, 1991

What Do Corporations Want?

CORPORATIONS, WHICH WERE AT ONE POINT IN THE 1970s PAINTED AS BEING ON THE defensive (chief Nixon adviser Herb Stein said: "We need a businessman's liberation movement") have been pretty clearly on the attack recently. Journalist Elizabeth Drew, in her little book, *Politics and Money*, has called attention to the way old-fashioned patronage has given way to Political Action Committees (PACs) and new corporate clout.

Now a Boston University sociologist named Michael Useem has extended the argument, finding that emerging shared concerns of giant corporations are dominating politics, instead of the old style of "every firm for itself."

"Transcorporate leadership," he says in *The Inner Circle* is the coming thing.

"Most business leaders are not part of . . . this inner circle," he writes, "but those few whose positions make them sensitive to the welfare of a wide range of firms have come to exercise a voice on behalf of the entire business community." He means "business statesmen" such as Du Pont's Irving Shapiro and General Electric's Reg Jones—both retired now.

To be sure, Useem notes, scholarly opinion about how big business works its political will "could hardly be more divided." Some see a socially cohesive "national upper class." Others, like Daniel Bell, see very few issues on which the managerial elite is unified.

Useem, a sociologist who spent the 1970s gazing at the other side of the coin—he studied the youth movement—decided to look into rising corporate unrest. For a year he poked around in government document rooms. Then, with the aid of a National Science Foundation grant, he undertook a lot of interviewing of 150 business leaders on both sides of the Atlantic.

As a result of these talks, he concluded that the 1980s have meant a somewhat greater significance for organizations like the Business Roundtable, the Committee for Economic Development, the Council on Foreign Relations, the Conference Board, the National Chamber of Commerce, the National Alliance of Businessmen and, in England, the Confederation of British Industry. Meanwhile, trade associations, composed of companies in particular industries, have faded into the background, he argues—not very convincingly.

Moreover, Useem found a kind of intermediary organization on the way to the stewardship of such organizations: interlocking directorships, which create "a special form of social organization within the business communities of both America and Britain, an inner circle whose unique qualities equip corporate leaders to enter politics on behalf of consensually arrived-at classwide interests rather than narrow, individual corporate interests.

"Business interests in the 1970s had two problems: declining profits and rising regulation. So business leaders set out very self-consciously to turn that around. It was not so much different from what other groups had done during the 1960s."

The real event of the late 1970s, Useem says, was "not a tax revolt, but a profit revolt." He states that the "average corporate pretax profit rate," which in the late 1940s was 12 percent—of assets, he says—declined in the late 1970s to 6 percent or 7 percent. "This is what really brought out this Inner Circle. They were feeling the pinch not just in terms of taxes, but in terms of government and social regulation as well."

Useem assigns special significance to the rise of the public executive. "To say that this is a new era may be overstatement, but a decade ago companies were saying stay out of politics, stick to business and don't talk to reporters, and now they are saying just the reverse."

How do you identify a member of the Inner Circle? Well, ask if he went to an exclusive prep school: 15 percent of his "core" inner circle, or those with three or more major directorships, did. Or look to see if he's in the Social Register: one out of five of the multiboard directors are there. Or here is still another tip: "Ask whether the executive has taken an active part in programs designed to introduce business-oriented curricula into the schools." The clincher is to ask if he has ever had a government appointment.

In the end, it is nothing less than a third stage in capitalist development that has taken place. "Institutional capitalism" has succeeded "managerial capitalism," which in turn had replaced family capitalism.

Well, maybe. But there are a multitude of factors that are not captured in the account that Useem gives. Not surprisingly, they have to do with what economists teach. What is missing is any sense of how winners and losers eventuate, of how the competitive environment, between companies, between entire industries, shapes the responses of businessmen.

So those looking for a quick glimpse of the machinery by which the nation's economic fate is governed will still do better with *The American Establishment* by Leonard and Mark Silk and with *Winning and Losing on the Corporate Battlefield* by Paul Solman and Thomas Friedman—both around in paperback—than with Useem's book.

But there is no question about it, the relationships that Useem scouts exist and are highly interesting and important. The "power elite" of C. Wright Mills is alive and well and living in sociology.

FEBRUARY 5, 1984

"The Cumulated Complexity of a Coral Reef"

IF WE LEARNED NOTHING ELSE DURING THE 1970S AND 1980S, IT IS THAT IN A certain broad and deep fashion, economics works. If the price of oil goes up, then people demand less oil, the supply of it increases as producers come forward eager to sell what they've got, and the price of oil comes down again—all because individuals, left to their own devices, tend to choose what is best for themselves. There were lots of fine points to be learned along the way, but the experience of OPEC had the force of a giant experiment.

Therefore it was a distressing exhibition that was staged last week by Massachusetts politicians. There was Gov. Dukakis writing President Bush urging him to put the government into the oil business, Sen. John Kerry and Rep. Ed Markey slamming big oil companies in stagey hearings on Capitol Hill, Attorney General Jim Shannon threatening to sue every oil man in sight. There were intricacies of pricing policies to be mastered and explained, but these fellows weren't interested: They commission a congressional investigation and offer to take over the industry every time there's a price spike. (Remember last winter, when the weather was bad? Prices fell nearly as quickly as they rose.)

Worse, Markey took pride in conjuring up one of Jack Kennedy's less-fine hours as president—when he browbeat U.S. Steel chairman Roger Blough over his decision to raise steel prices to improve his margins in 1962. It was a widely shared conviction then—by Kennedy, Blough and union leaders—that steel somehow enjoyed immunity from the laws of supply and demand, that prices could be set as well by politicians at their press conferences as by businessmen, that nearly wrecked the American steel industry a decade later, by depressing its rate of investment in new, more competitive technology.

Significantly, the latter-day Kennedys themselves—especially Joe, who made something of a career in the oil business, were wisely silent last week about the complicated workings of the market.

The education of the politicians is going to come soon enough at the polls. Indeed, in Michael Dukakis' case, it already has. But that's the easy part. What about the rest of us, especially the students in the schools? The quest for a better, deeper understanding of the worlds in which we live is taking place in precincts far removed from politics. One major venue is the American Sociological Association, which meets next week in Washington.

For about 150 years sociology has flourished in Europe and America as kind of an academic alternative to economics. If you didn't like big business and the direction things were taking in the modern world, you could always turn for solace to the heirs of Karl Marx, Emile Durkheim and Max Weber.

There you would find critical stances, ranging from mild to militant, whose shared principal concern was for the ways in which social environment affects the individual: alienation, anomie, the psychology of the mob and all that. There was not much attention to the other way around, the effect of individual decisions on the social order, not even in Weberian studies of bureaucracy, but never mind. Generations of some of the smartest people around had built an elaborate gym in which to pump intellectual iron, and afterward you could use your degree for something else.

In the last 20 years, however, sociology—all of sociology—has begun to wear a little thin. For one thing, it ran into ever-more blind alleys. The great abstract ziggurat of structural-functionalism erected at Harvard over the course of decades by Talcott Parsons is the prime exhibit here: It offered plenty of systems and subsystems, but rarely a glimpse of real life.

For another, the collapse of the governments of Eastern Europe has left a segment of the field discredited, exposing it for the meretricious mumbo-jumbo that it is. For still another, economists for 20 years have been moving in on the sociologists' turf—perhaps most memorably when Gary Becker began discussing children as "durable consumer goods." The sociologists are now on the eve of a great battle, one that promises to have reverberations far beyond the chalky precincts.

This boundary-crossing is detailed in an excellent new book by Richard Swedberg, *Economics and Sociology*, (Princeton University Press, $12.95). This isn't the first time we've been blessed with a European sojourner in a technical economic community. Arigio Levi in the early 1970s captured the state of play in macroeconomics in *Journey Among the Economists*; Arjo Klamer did the same in the 1980s with *Conversations with Economists*. Now Swedberg, an assistant professor of sociology at the University of Stockholm, has weighed in with 17 interviews with leading lights of various political persuasions. The result makes fascinating reading, at least for students.

Thus here is Jon Elster, whose book *Ulysses and the Sirens* introduced the notion that individuals sometimes find strange ways to resist temptation in everyday life. Here is Mark Granovetter, the Stony Brook sociologist who has focused attention on the importance of certain kinds of social networks with a book called *Getting a Job*. Here is Harrison White, the peripatetic Columbia University scholar who has worked brilliantly all around the edges of economics for 30 years. Here is Neil Smelser, the journalist who became Talcott Parsons' sidekick, then inheritor. Here, too, are the remarkable economists who have moved their methods into new terrain: Gary Becker, Kenneth Arrow, George Akerlof, Oliver Williamson, Amartya Sen, Mancur Olson, Thomas Schelling, as well as grand old men of the controversy like Daniel Bell and Robert Solow.

Most of the thinkers in Swedberg's book offer little insights, glimpses of how people might calculate about this class of problems or that. One who doesn't shrink from theorizing on the grandest scale is James S. Coleman, the University of Chicago sociologist. The publication this fall of his *Foundations of Social Theory* is conceivably the most important thing to happen in sociology in 50 years.

To begin with, Coleman is no shrinking violet. His report on the effect of segregation in education was used by many—including him, for a while—as a brief for busing. A later study demonstrated conclusively the white flight to the suburbs that followed, concluded that parochial schools did a better job than public ones, and came out for a system of educational vouchers. For the last 10 years or so Coleman has been one of the leading lights in the movement to end (or at least diminish) the opposition between economics and sociology. With economist Gary Becker he has run the Chicago workshop that has been the Mecca of all those seeking a broader truth.

Now he is determined to sum it all up with a grand theory, in the tradition of Marx, Weber and Durkheim. The title self-conciously echoes the title with which a young Paul Samuelson transformed economics in 1947. Whether Coleman ultimately succeeds or not, he's certain to set the agenda for many years to come.

The hinge on which the book turns is the theory of "rational choice." Sociology has always been good at examining the influence of the social setting on the individual, Coleman says, but it's been downright poor at moving the other way. This "micro-to-macro" problem can be solved simply by assuming that people in general act in a purposeful way—not, perhaps, quite as simply as the "utility-maximizers" of economic fame, but in a generally coherent and meaningful fashion. People who buy and sell oil are rational choosers; so are parents who send their children to school. This simple assumption provides the bridge to economics.

But it's not just individuals who act, Coleman says, especially in the modern world; institutions play an increasingly important role, and any good theory of society will have a major place for these corporate actors. Contemporary societies are not cumulative and accreted, according to Coleman. They are "constructed," instead. Contemporary societies "are more like modern cities of skyscrapers and tenements than like the honeycomb of dwellings on the island of Mykonos or the cumulated complexity of a coral reef."

"Just as the constructed physical environment which has replaced that of nature for much of our lives requires its architects, constructed social organization requires its architects. These will be the social scientists of the 21st century," Coleman writes. And their tasks will be not merely to build and supervise markets, but to repair the cities, reinvigorate the schools and restore viability to the fundamental institution of the family.

He's probably right, and there is much consolation in that. Where the social scientists go, the politicians are bound to follow. Coleman's book represents the intellectual journey through our times of an immensely clever and powerful mind. It's going to be around a lot longer than the current crop of Republicans. For Democrats, the moral of the story is: Come to terms!

AUGUST 12, 1990

part seven

PRACTITIONERS

The Reflective
Practitioners

THE HARVARD BUSINESS SCHOOL IS GETTING CLOBBERED AGAIN, AND NO WONDER. IT accepted a $30 million gift from retiring Securities and Exchange Commission chairman John Shad and some friends to teach ethics, but meanwhile has been systematically lopping off its ethics teachers, declining to grant tenure to its top three specialists in as many years, as reported by Michael Kranish.

Shad, of course, is the man who has been threatening to send a number of investment bankers in jail for insider-trading; several of the miscreants are graduates, as he is, of the nation's best-known business school. The veteran former chairman of E.F. Hutton is clearly apalled by much that has happened on Wall Street in the 1980s, during his governmental watch. Harvard has no clearly-formulated plans of how to spend the enormous windfall, however, which amounts to a tenth of its total endowment. There is talk of videotaping corporate chieftains talking about their ethical dilemmas for broadcast by satellite around the world. Nevertheless its deans talk about "The Shad Program" as if it already exists.

It is necessary, however, to say a word in defense of the B-School.

Harvard has a unique place in American business education. Other schools have niches: they specialize in teaching finance, or educating the inheritors of wealth, or turning out "quants" or training managers to be engineers and vice versa. Harvard works at something at once more diffuse and more ambitious. It just wants to be The Best.

This means that Harvard aims—not always with success—at attracting the very best students among those with a raft of choices and then sending them out into the world as the exemplars of managerial competence. It wants them to be the best-equipped minds on the block—spiritually as well as technically. In a way, this is comparable to aspiring to instill "Celtic Pride" in its graduates, or to being "the Goldman Sachs of graduate business education." It is a laudable target, often missed, yet hit frequently enough to make credible the claim of Harvard—and arch-rival Stanford and perhaps the Wharton School of the University of Pennsylvania—to the title.

First-year students take a common curriculum, based on extensive case studies. The idea is to ground every graduate's knowledge in a good general business education. Few other schools require such a common core; elsewhere students specialize from the very beginning. Even fewer competing schools depend mainly on the historical studies on which Harvard relies for its main diet of instruction; most simply hand textbooks to their students, full of general principles, and then send them out into the world. Harvard says that its case studies, in which there are no right answers, develop the beginnings of wisdom and not mere technical skill.

The key to the program is passionate, low-key teaching by most of the faculty. Ask a B-school professor involved in the MBA program how it is going, and you'll suddenly find yourself talking about his teaching experiences, of all things, instead of his research interests. Watch his lunching habits for a week and you'll find he spends more time talking to other teachers about their students than to those who share his interests in the outside world.

This is in stark contrast to what goes on at the university across the river. At Harvard College and the graduate schools, teaching usually takes a back seat to research. And indeed, who has been beating up on the business school but university president Derek Bok? In a major criticism several years ago, Bok argued that the professors across the river should teach more theory and fewer cases; their students risked becoming disconnected from the rest of the intellectual world, he wrote. Last week he reiterated his dissatisfaction; the school wasn't teaching enough ethics, he said.

An eloquent case for a B-School-style education is to be found in *The Reflective Practitioner* by Donald A. Schoen. An MIT professor, Schoen looks at how practitioners in five professions go about solving problems through a process he calls "reflection-in-action." He concludes that such practitioners—at least the best of them—depend on the same kind of deep instinctive knowledge as baseball pitchers and jazz musicians. They are better off in graduate school practicing a great deal under intensive supervision than studying textbooks on the theory of the curveball and workbooks on the sense of swing.

Smart people are easy to come by at Harvard. Finding professors who are very smart and whose primary dedication is to the kind of day-in-day-out teaching in which the Harvard Business School specializes is not an easy task. This is, at least in part, the gate at which the discontinued ethicists were turned away. They wanted to specialize in ethics; Harvard wanted them to teach business to first-year students as well. Two were women; the business school has a demonstrated predilection to tenure men. (In fact, the two ethicists who were considered for promotion taught extensively in the school's MBA program; the school decided not to promote them on other grounds.) The point is, however, that the faculty has stuck by its version of "the Product," meaning the quality of the education they give; now they are taking their lumps from a small corps of academic entrepreneurs.

To be sure, the B-School is vulnerable to criticism. It is the victim of its own hype, not the Tokyo University of the business school world, but one voice among many. But at its most distinctive, it is a clear and worthwhile and often even beautiful voice in education, every bit as well-qualified to teach ethics as the SEC or Derek Bok.

APRIL 8, 1987

Why the "Greenhouse Plan" Fell Through

A DOZEN YEARS AGO, A BRIGHT YOUNG STUDENT NOT LONG OUT OF COLLEGE TRIED TO organize politically the faded little industrial city of Brockton, Mass. Ira Magaziner and some friends were fresh from having restructured the curriculum at Brown University, 25 miles away, and the idea was to galvanize and then take over the city. Brockton mostly ignored them, and after a year or so, Magaziner went to work for the Boston Consulting Group, the corporate consulting firm famous for its whiz-kids.

Last month it happened again—only this time it was the faded little industrial state of Rhode Island that rebuffed his efforts. Magaziner had teamed up with the big banker in town, Terry Murray, chairman of Fleet Financial Group. Together they made big plans—a quarter billion dollars to be spent by a junta of labor, business and pols on various economic development programs, all specifically exempted from the administrative sunshine laws. Magaziner rounded up a lot of endorsements ("Everybody from the Republicans and Democrats to the Association of Retired People and Vietnam Vets") and spent two years building a nearly universal consensus among opinionmakers that his "Greenhouse Compact" was exactly what Rhode Island needed to engender a high-tech renaissance.

The proposal was defeated 4-1.

What went wrong? Magaziner says that part of the answer is that there was a sudden wave of revulsion against state government in Rhode Island. At the last moment, for example, the Democratic leaders of both the House and the Senate appointed themselves to the commission that was to allocate the funds, signaling to many that the process would be driven by politics as usual. Then the mayor of Providence resigned, after being convicted of beating up the alleged boyfriend of his estranged wife, a felony. Finally, on the morning of the election, recalls Magaziner, "the building commissioner was led away in handcuffs. It was reported that he was going to have been a Democratic poll watcher that day."

Moreover, there was well-organized opposition, both from the Right and the Left. Indeed, the whole Brown economics department opposed the plan. Associate Professor Allan M. Feldmann stumped nearly every night against the Greenhouse, arguing that it was an expensive and inefficient way to stimulate development. His colleague George Borts says, "Even for Brown University, where a lot of the money was to have been spent, it was a bad idea. Why should we pay $250 million to get $30 million back?" And the left-wing group viewed the plan as a subsidy for big business.

To many people, however, the issue was simply taxes. Magaziner's task force insisted the program would pay for itself in jobs created, but opponents remained skeptical, even after Data Resources Inc. produced studies (late in the game) which they said bore out the Greenhouse analysis. Rhode Island's tax burden is already somewhat higher than the rest of New England, according to most measures; many voters said they feared it would go higher. "Our polls were telling us that we were ahead by a two-to-one margin until two weeks before the election. Then everything turned around."

To others, however, the vote on the Greenhouse Compact was a referendum on that class of political prescriptions known as "industrial policy," that until recently, at least, have been identified with Democratic presidential candidates. "Only a tiny fraction of Rhode Islanders know what industrial policy is," says Brown University economist Borts. "What they saw was a powerful commission made up of the biggies, the big union leaders, big businessmen, big bankers, big politicians, who were going to take a lot of tax money and make decisions about how to spend it." Says economist Feldman, "Ira is a very persuasive man and I think he just convinced the state's leaders that this is a good idea."

As a persuader, Magaziner goes a long way back. As a college freshman in 1965, he undertook to reorganize the entire university, and succeeded in restructuring the curriculum by the time he was a senior. ("It was a pretty comprehensive program," he says, "it would take a while to explain it.") Professor Paul Maeder, who as deputy provost at the end of the 1960s was one of Magaziner's principle allies, describes the student leader as having had "tremendous charisma." Maeder continues, "Ira was a very stabilizing influence, because he absolutely disclaimed violence."

(A Brown graduate cracks that "there's a Magaziner Plan everywhere he goes. I understand he wrote a report on his own fetal monitoring when he was in the womb, and that his mother gave birth to both the report and him. He's that precocious.")

Today, Magaziner is perhaps best known for his collaboration with Robert Reich, the John F. Kennedy School of Government guru who has been touted by Walter Mondale as the sage with the key to the next election. Magaziner and Reich met at Oxford, then wrote *Minding America's Business*, a lively brief for government industrial policy which exists, they argued, whether the government acknowledged them or not. It was therefore the responsibility of government to plan for businesses, to pick winners and losers among them, and to structure incentives accordingly. Even many conservatives liked the book. George Gilder, for example, says it is the best book yet written on planning.

It is economists who don't approve of Magaziner's vision. As Rhodes Scholars at Oxford at the end of the 1960s, Magaziner and Reich were well known as outsiders to the circle of hotshot technicians that included Harvard University's Michael Porter, Martin Feldstein and Michael Spence who had been there at roughly the same time. "I went through a reading program, not a formal degree," says Magaziner. "I'm a business strategist. We base our approach on corporate strategy rather than pure economic theory. We treat it as something other than a zero sum situation. . . . Economists don't like that." Telesis, the Providence consulting firm he formed when he left the Boston Consulting Group after six years there, has grown to 51 professionals from an initial six persons, with offices in Paris, Melbourne and Munich.

"If you try to do things that are significant, that make a big change—the thing we did at Brown was a big thing, and it really did make a change—if you try to do these things, you can bobble them," says Magaziner. "If you think about the Olympic diving contests, say, where you have a choice about the complexity of the dive you're going to take: if you always take safe dives, you won't do badly. On the other hand, you never achieve very much. If you try a really hard dive, you may fall on your face completely, but sometimes you'll do something that you can really be proud of."

Much is now being made of the national implications of the defeat of the Greenhouse Compact in Rhode Island. Magaziner doesn't see the defeat of the Greenhouse as having much to do with the national planning issue because, he says, the program he proposed for Rhode Island was so much more narrow and less powerful in its instruments than the big national program he envisages. He says, "A good national program would have a trade policy, a tax policy, a monetary policy, a whole range of things we couldn't undertake in Rhode Island."

For the nation, then, the moral of the story is one thing. For Magaziner, it's another. "I'm going to spend the next couple of years trying to understand a lot more about the political process," he says.

JULY 1, 1984

Of Kings, Cabbages and Robert Reich

AN IMPORTANT NEW BIOGRAPHY HAS APPEARED OF J. PIERPONT MORGAN, THE MAN whom Lincoln Steffens called "the boss of the United States." It is *The Morgans: Private International Bankers*, by Vincent P. Carosso (Harvard University Press, $65); it chronicles the lives of father Junius and son J.P. from the beginnings of the family's fortune in Hartford and Boston to Pierpont Morgan's eventual humiliation in Washington at the hands of the Pujo Committee's investigation of the "money trust" in 1912.

Along the way, it illuminates politics, international finance, industrial innovation and high society and trans-Atlantic yachting in the cockpit of the Second Industrial Revolution—a cataclysmic integration of the global economy of which Morgan himself was a principal beneficiary and victim. It puts to rest an earlier judgment that if Morgan had simply broadened his base, he would have become America's greatest businessman.

Morgan exemplified the private banking tradition of the 18th century, and was "the last of his kind" writes Carosso, a distinguished professor of history at New York University. It was entirely fitting that he should have died in 1913, when the Internal Revenue Service and the Federal Reserve System took hold and put an end to his world. The book is a beauty, but it won't be widely read. Business history is in, well, in eclipse.

The fascinating story of why you don't read more of it is laid out in a new book by Stephen Sass, *Entrepreneurial Historians and History: Leadership and Rationality in American Economic Historiography, 1940–1960* (Garland Publishing Co., $40). The book itself, a dissertation, may be of interest mainly to historians and economists. But the story it tells is of far wider interest, for it concerns the American self-consciousness, the way we see ourselves—and in particular, the way we think of businessmen and labor leaders and the giant organizations they head.

The story Sass tells with great delicacy goes something like this in crude form: Until the Depression, there was not much university interest in systematic narratives of business history. Moral philosophers of the better mousetrap like Ralph Waldo Emerson gave way to writers on the fringes of economics like Thorstein Veblen, Charles Beard and Werner Sombart. Meanwhile, marginalist economics—with its vision of a world as a gigantic machine of consumers and producers in intricate counterpoise and equilibrium—took the social sciences by storm.

But starting in the 1920s, two clear strands emerged in business history, both of them at Harvard, each identified with its founder, Edwin S. Gay and Norman S.B. Gras. A member of the Department of Economics, Gay was co-director with Wesley Clair Mitchell of the National Bureau of Economic Research; he was in tune with the spirit of the time. The economic historians he trained were go-along guys who quickly moved on to other universities to become the leadership of the profession.

But at the Harvard Business School across the river, Gras sought the high ground opposite. Searching for "a theme worthy of almost epic treatment," he settled upon the entrepreneurial spirit as the key force in economic life, and, in essence, seceded from economic history to found a separate field of business history, with its own journals, agendas and research center. Too many of his students were quickly enough writing company histories for public relations departments; but others, including Gay's student Arthur Cole, were ready to take over the tradition of, as Cole wrote, "the analysis of business and economic evolution in terms of the 'disruptive, innovating energy' " of innovators and entrepreneurs.

So Cambridge became for 20 years the center of entrepreneurial history. At the business school's Center for Research in Economic History and elsewhere, scholars including Alfred Chandler, David Landes, Richard Wohl and Hugh Aitken worked on the development of a great analytical framework to explain the rise and import of industrial capitalism; across the river, Joseph Schumpeter weaved a vision of economics in which the entrepreneur was the central figure.

This was, of course, a sort of supply-side economics in subtle and genteel form—as opposed to the economists' "neoclassical synthesis," with its emphasis on government management of aggregate demand, that was coming up like the sun from MIT and Harvard across the river. Entrepreneurial historians were for a time clearly arrayed against neoclassical economists, writes Steve Sass: They offered competing visions of the economic process along a broad and potentially well-defended front.

But Cambridge was also home to a group of scholars who together would create the "new" economic history—or "cliometrics," as it gradually became known in the newspapers. There was not much place for the entrepreneur in the world of fully-maximizing rational decision-makers that was represented by the new econometric models of the cliometricians. John Meyer and Alfred Conrad published a revolutionary study of the economics of slavery in the pre–Civil War South: it turned out that those planters knew what they were doing after all; slavery was profitable, ideas about the natural order and civil rights had little to do with it.

In time, Harvard scholars Alexander Gershenkron and Simon Kuznets threw their considerable weight against the entrepreneurial historians' idea that individuals had a significant impact on outcomes. Schumpeter died. And in a crowning blow, Robert Fogel argued forcefully that even the advent of railroads—whose financing with European capital was Pierpont Morgan's signal achievement—really didn't make very much difference in American growth. Meanwhile, Talcott Parsons was leading sociology—the other possible ally of business history—in a different direction.

In the face of such competition, the Center for Research in Economic History, which had been the institutional bastion of the entrepreneurial historians at Harvard, foundered. The Rockefeller Foundation stopped its funding, the Harvard Business School gave up its leadership in what Sass calls the central task, "raising live moral issues and placing them in historical context." The fruits of that flowering are still among us, in the persons of Chandler, Landes and Aitken—hardly a less distinguished crew than the more familiar figures of the Nobel Economics Prize winners. There is even a promising set of embers smoldering at the Harvard Business School, in the form of new generation of talented young historians around Chandler, led by Pulitzer Prize winner Tom McCraw.

But outside, there is not much. The shabby little insurrection that was supply-side economics is itself history now. True, university historians across the country are starting an encyclopedia of business history that has got some press. But it is not the same as the deeply-rooted effort that was undertaken at the Harvard Business School; it lacks the subtlety to go up against an entrenched discipline like economics. It is true, too, that a Henry Ford miniseries is about to air on Channel 56. An interest in entrepreneurs is in the air.

In the meantime, we get by with less deeply-grounded work. Robert Reich's new book, *Tales of a New America*, is in the bookshops. It too is a kind of entrepreneurial history, an interesting attempt to go beneath the surface of conventional narrative forms in order to devise new ones. He identifies four "core parables" that dominate American political life: The Mob At the Gates (about immigration); The Triumphant Individual (about individual enterprise); The Benevolent Community (about attempts to ease poverty); and The Rot at the Top (about public and private bureaucracy); and he offers—less than convincingly—The Teamwork Society (collective endeavor) as an alternative.

As a kind of counterweight, John Silber's 1986 Commencement Address is still making the rounds—most recently reprinted in *Reason* magazine. It is, of course, firmly in the tradition of moral philosophy. His theme is that we need our heroes. "The genius of democracy is this," he writes, "We are all a dime a dozen and we are all magnificent."

Meanwhile, however, in the universities, a solid discipline built around the history of technology has taken root. The field of the history of science has made dramatic gains. And business history is experiencing something of a revival. The newest generation of historians are at work in libraries with "fire in their eyes," in Sass's phrase. His next project, an institutional history of private pensions, will appear in due course.

MARCH 29, 1987

Why Oxford
and Cambridge Want
B-Schools

THE BUSINESS MAGAZINES ARE ABOUT TO PUBLISH THEIR ANNUAL DIRECTORY ISSUES. The *Fortune* and *Forbes* tabulations of the 500 biggest companies come out once a year, and require big statistical staffs equipped with PCs and awesome software to keep them going. The result is a pretty accurate map of American capitalism, in which industrial organizations appear (as Fernand Braudel once put it), as "a succession of different altitudes, like a relief map."

But what about the patterns that lurk behind the changing figures, which differ greatly from decade to decade? When you glance back, it is sobering to see the names of firms that once numbered among the top 10: Bethlehem Steel, Anaconda Copper, International Harvester, Armour, Swift, U.S. Rubber, Midvale Steel and Ordnance. It is equally interesting to note that many of the companies that were at the top of the heap 70 years ago are still there.

But remember, the magazines still keep tabs mainly on American firms. What are the chances that the lists will be dominated by Japanese companies when the surveys go global, as eventually they must? Or that big corporations will have been replaced altogether by a swarm of tightly focused little entrepreneurial firms?

The best place to look for thoughtful answers to these questions are the business schools, which have come a long way since the first was established in 1880—at the University of Pennsylvania—to educate the scions of rich families. For a time, their pedagogy consisted of what historian Stephen Sass described as "an extended form of business journalism." But in the last 50 years, they have evolved quite a bit.

Today, for all the derision their graduates suffer, B-schools are probably the most exciting centers of self-understanding, at least in connection with money and competition, that the university has to offer society at large. How much they have to offer their students is another question. University-based critics like Hawaii's Robert Locke and McGill's Henry Minzberg (and of course not a few business leaders and media mavens) have bashed away at B-schools' pretensions to a "science" of management. The formal systems they teach are often a disaster; the kids they recruit often do better on tests than as leaders in the field.

Yet the B-schools continue to flourish. Their applicants are among the brightest in the pool. Their graduates get good jobs. Their professors command high salaries. Through their alumni, the deans knit their schools into industrial structures around the world, where the money is to be found for further growth and development. The economics departments of universities with good business schools have pulled away from schools without them. (Harvard and Stanford vs. Princeton, for example.)

When Stanford last month hired Michael Spence, Harvard's principal academic dean, to head its B-school, it was striking testimony of the ability of business schools to command the very cleverest academic talent in the world. It's for these reasons that Oxford and Cambridge in England are belatedly scrambling to get into the act with start-up schools of their own—a move they disdained when it was formally broached in the 1960s.

The publication next month of a pair of books from a pair of Harvard gurus, Alfred Chandler and Michael Porter, affords a glimpse of the view from this world. Still the best B-school in the world by a comfortable margin, despite 25 years of increasing competition, Harvard has plenty of world figures to offer: Robert Merton in finance, Michael Jensen in corporate control, Robert Kaplan in accounting, Theodore Levitt in marketing, and Samuel Hayes in investment banking.

But Chandler and Porter are special, more prominent, operating with a grander sweep, painting the evolution of the economy as a whole. Theirs is the world of the Standard Industrial Code, of the industrial constellation, and of history. And their convictions, especially Porter's, are regularly trumpeted to the business elite around the world by London's *Economist* magazine. They write at the pinnacle of the world capitalist system, about the pinnacle, for the pinnacle.

Chandler, 72, is the better-known of the pair, something of a heroic figure for his long-time stand in favor of history as central to the study of business. A Harvard sailing teammate of John F. Kennedy, editor of the presidential papers of Dwight Eisenhower, Chandler began his "historical theory of big business" with *Strategy and Structure* in 1962, then published *The Visible Hand* in 1977. With *Scale and Scope: The Dynamics of Indus-*

trial Capitalism, published this month by Harvard University Press, the work is complete.

Porter, 43, comes across as more nearly resembling Buckaroo Banzai than the president of anything. A star college golfer, one-time aerospace engineer, consultant to big companies and sometime rock-band manager, he has taught at the business school since he was 26. His fame had rested on two extremely popular books of corporate strategy, *Competitive Strategy* and *Competitive Advantage.* With the publication next month of *The Competitive Advantage of Nations* (The Free Press), Porter moves into the arena of prescribing to governments. His advice: let competition reign supreme.

As analysts, Chandler and Porter have much in common. Each book is based on a series of long-term multinational case studies, and each takes account of the microeconomics of particular industries. Yet each author strives to see his subject matter whole, his view informed by theory but not entailed by it. The two studies dovetail naturally, with Chandler the historian being somewhat backward-looking, concerned with the 30 years after World War II, while economist Porter is forward-looking, concerned about the future. Chandler emphasizes the internal reasoning that impels firms to build far-ranging managerial hierarchies; Porter emphasizes ways in which the external environment in which firms must operate shapes their destiny.

But what's the bottom line? Both writers conclude that success stems from sticking to the businesses that you know best. Chandler, in particular, emphasizes the virtue of being the "first mover," that is, of pre-emptively investing heavily in production, marketing and distribution networks on a global scale in order to blow away rivals. Big companies may be out of fashion at the moment, he says, but their logic is enduring. Meanwhile, Porter preaches competition and rivalry at every juncture. Protection, subsidy, joint production agreements, R&D consortia and other forms of bureaucratic administration almost never work, he says; the only sure way to stay in business is to remain competitive. The trick is to understand your strengths and act on them.

APRIL 22, 1990

About Commitment

I see that my life was determined long ago
And that the struggle to escape from it
Is only a make-believe, a pretence
That what is, is not, or could be changed.

THESE WORDS ARE FROM *THE COCKTAIL PARTY*, BY T.S. ELIOT, BUT BUSINESS managers and students of their choices will recognize a truth that applies to companies as well. Many an executive has come to grief trying to make his company into something it could not be. There is plenty of caution (and solace) from playwrights and poets, but no place to turn in the literature of business economics.

Until now. Pankaj Ghemawat, the youngest professor ever tenured at the Harvard Business School, has generalized the role of history in business decisions, and put it in the lingo in which corporate managers are nowadays taught to think.

It boils down, he says, to the notion of commitment, meaning the ways in which earlier choices constrain later ones. In *Commitment*, a remarkable new book, he puts under a microscope the kinds of large, irreversible investments that companies occasionally must make or not make as part of their daily life, and finds that they are the very essence of strategic thinking.

The popular literature of business is full of stories about these choices, and not surprisingly: They make for great suspense. *The Fanciest Dive*, Christopher Byron's wonderful story of Time Inc.'s cable TV magazine disaster, is a prime example; so is Nucor's bold gamble with a new continuous casting machine as described in *American Steel* by Richard Preston; or Salomon Brothers' experiment in positioning as described in *Liar's Poker* by Michael Lewis. But these big, literary case histories have their limits. If you favor a more analytic viewpoint, you cannot do better than to read this book.

In fact, people don't generally read books like *Commitment* on their own. Somewhere between technical economics articles in journals and the trades, books like these often make their way as teaching texts, intended mainly for MBAs in training, consultants and business practitioners. Occasionally they can be enormously influential; witness Michael Porter's 1980 *Competitive Strategy*, which more or less took the intellectual high ground away from the consultants like the Boston Consulting Group, Bain & Co. and McKinsey & Co., who had occupied it throughout the 1960s and 1970s.

Commitment is the newest of this ilk. Given its rock-solid foundation in the literature of the industrial organization, chances are that it will dominate thinking in the business schools for many years to come. What with George Bush, Nicholas Brady and Mikhail Gorbachev planning to establish an American-style business school in Moscow, and with leading companies of every nation locked in battle on a global scale, this venue presumably is more important than ever. It's a relief that the quality of its thinking is rapidly improving.

Ghemawat identifies four key areas in which commitment is an overriding factor: He calls them lock-in, lock-out, lags and inertia. Boeing spent so much on the 747 that at an early point, its investment greatly exceeded the company's net worth. That's lock-in, he says. Reynolds Metals decided to close its costly old alumina refinery at Hurricane Creek, Ark., which meant that it was out of aluminum manufacturing in America for good— lock-out. Coors' decision to sell its beer nationally involved committing to a strategy for a decade, before key advertising economies could be expected to pay off—such lags are longer and more common than expected, Ghemawat says. General Motors went on building big cars far longer than was good for it because that's what it knew how to do—inertia is a better explanation for this failure than "culture."

Commitment strategies show up in surprising ways. Sam Walton's genius rests on knowing how to open his Wal-Mart stores in towns that are big enough to support one discount store but not two, Ghemawat notes. Likewise, the practical effects of airline deregulation were quite different from what had been expected because of commitment factors, he adds.

"Contestable entry" doctrine had supposed that it was enough that other firms could enter the business against existing air carriers, once the formal barriers to entry were removed, to cut profits from their artificial highs. And sure enough, new airlines sprung up overnight; even Brockway Glass opened an airline in the early days of deregulation—for a few months. Then factors like hub-and-spoke efficiencies and giant computerized reservation systems came into play, sending the interlopers running for cover, while particular companies in the industry, instead of seeing their margins shrink, emerged as more profitable than ever.

Even Coca-Cola's decision to make a quick, highly visible switch to new formula in order to have it all over the country in time for the 99th anniversary of the old one in 1985 was an example of the importance of commitment—in a backhanded way, according to Ghemawat. If Coca-Cola had shown a little more appreciation for the value of flexibility—flexibility being the opposite of commitment—they might not be hiring superagent Michael Ovitz to polish up their image today.

Sound reasonable? It is, profoundly so. The picture of the strategic business decision-maker that emerges from *Commitment* bears a much closer resemblance to the great business heroes of the past than to the global poker players of the game theorists. These optimizers, who spot a Cournot-Nash equilibrium faster than you can blink an eye, have been the vogue in doctrines of industrial organization through much of the 1980s, at least in the classroom. But in Ghemawat's world, there will be less talk about the players' card-counting, and much more thinking about their circumstances and character.

Indeed, the brightest hope arising from the new attention to history and commitment in business schools may be that it will offer some sustained refuge from the steady stream of fads that have plagued business strategy for the past 30 years. "The important thing is to figure out which choices are critical and to devote extra attention to trying to get them right," Ghemawat concludes. That was the poet Eliot's advice, too, as he continued in *The Cocktail Party*:

> The self that can say "I want this—or want that"—
> The self that wills—he is a feeble creature;
> He has to come to terms in the end
> With the obstinate, the tougher self; who does not speak,
> Who never talks, who cannot argue;
> And who in some men may be the guardian—
> But in men like me, the dull, the implacable,
> The indomitable spirit of mediocrity.
> The willing self can contrive the disaster
> Of this unwilling partnership—but can only flourish
> In submission to the rule of the stronger partner.

SEPTEMBER 22, 1991

Preachy Inventors,
Inventive Preachers

AMERICANS DO SO LOVE AWARD CEREMONIES. THE TRADITIONAL DINNER AFFORDS AN opportunity to celebrate the fact that life is organized in leagues, and not just big leagues, either, but an almost infinite gradation of relatively small competitive universes arrayed roughly according to seniority. A good example of the phenomenon was the Entrepreneur of the Year ceremony held in Boston last week.

As a ritual, it was far from perfect. It was the first year the contest had been held; not even the categories were clear. The entrants were far from a comprehensive selection of company-builders at any particular stage of development, and whole pigeonholes remained virtually empty; the authors of recent leveraged buyouts stayed away from the contest in droves, for example, rather than run the gantlet of salesmen that celebrity surrounding new wealth requires.

And of course there was a touch of self-interest in the very act of bestowal. The local contest was organized as part of a national roundup by the Big Eight accounting firm of Arthur Young, which sells accounting services to start-ups in particular, and *Venture* magazine, which sells subscriptions. That's not the same as when the Swedish Academy of Sciences weighs in with its view. And in a misplaced attempt to connect themselves to the larger world beyond the P&L, the organizers even enlisted this columnist as a judge, along with half a dozen better men from the business education and venture capital communities.

Yet when all was said and done, the ceremony was utterly fascinating, and not just because of the winners. The room was full of extraordinary people; as in professional baseball, even the losers were winners beyond the ability of everyday duffers to imagine. New England always has been rich in inventors, business starters. The current crop is no exception. What is astonishing is the range of creativity.

Take Richard Brooks. A Northeastern basketball star of the late 1950s who majored in chemical engineering, he tried out for the Celtics and didn't make it. So he went to work for Badger Engineering, Arthur D. Little, then spent 20 years at Polaroid. Frustrated, Brooks quit in 1981 to found a specialty chemical company. Today, Chemdesign Corp., based in Framingham, employs 125 people, had sales last year of $14 million.

Or consider Thomas Flatley, who founded the Flatley Company in 1959, nine years after emigrating from County Mayo, Ireland. Today Flatley's empire includes hotels, hospitals, TV stations, shopping centers and 6,000 apartments. He is almost wealthy, but he is also widely admired for his persistent innovation—in everything from child-care to day-care for Alzheimer's disease victims—and his ability to still run the firm out of his vest pocket.

High tech? Boston cardiologist Paul Zoll invented the temporary noninvasive pacemaker—you put it on the chest instead of in it—and hired Rolf Stutz to help him make and market it. Stutz had a product within 11 months, and a profitable and growing company, ZMI Corp., within two years. Bill Frusztajer, who emigrated from England in 1956, took a little longer to build BBF Corp. into a $100 million electronics company. John White led the management buyout of Haemonetics Inc. from a big hospital supply company; today the little company, which specializes in the recycling of human blood, is healther than ever as a result. And Patrizio Vinciarelli, a physicist who left Princeton's Institute for Advanced Study to found Vicor Corp., has been growing rapidly by the most familiar strategy, offering a better mousetrap—in his case, power converters that regulate the flow of electricity that goes into sensitive machines.

To be sure, there were not many entrants in the kind of basic industrial processes that were the source of American economic strength in the late 19th century. And beer manufacturers, packagers of popcorn and lubritorium founders attracted much favorable attention. For the snobbish, it was hard to get to excited about the achievement of real estate entrepreneur of the year Philipe Grande of Williamstown, who buys land by the mile and sells it by the yard—even if he does it better than anyone else.

The same thing goes for Jerry Ellis, the founder of Building 19, the salvage specialist; his nine bargain outlets, where you can buy almost any discarded object you can imagine, are perfect targets for critics of the service economy. But you have only to look at the career of Sharon P. Cavanaugh to see how much preparation and hard work such entrepreneurial success requires. She worked 13 years on the fringes of the Quincy Market business before founding Peacock Papers in 1982. And the fact remains that retail and service and development companies spread an awful lot of satisfaction. They are vital parts of a vibrant economy.

There were other awards, including several in the "masters" category: triple-founder John Poduska, Kenneth Olsen of Digital Equipment, a special award for the Small Business Association of New England, venture capitalist Peter Brooke. Brooke, just off an airplane from England, was flushed with pleasure. "If there was a man on the street in London who hasn't given me a buck to invest in start-ups, I'd like you to find him," Brooke exulted. He told the crowd, "You do what you do because you have to do it. It's your destiny."

Paul Theroux, the writer, has described his book *The Mosquito Coast* as being about "the two noisiest contenders in American life, the inventive preacher and the preachy inventor." New England is full of well-known inventive preachers—think of Robert Reich, David Brudnoy, Martin Feldstein, Arnold Relman, George Gilder, Lester Thurow, Ray Shamie and Michael Dukakis, to name just a few. But it is also full of preachy inventors, and it was fitting that last week they should have had their day.

JUNE 21, 1987

The Case of a Supersonic Reactor

ARE THERE A LOT OF GREAT IDEAS OUT THERE LANGUISHING FOR LACK OF SUPPORT? To put it slightly differently, are there things that giant corporations, those extraordinary engines of change, could be doing but aren't? The internal combustion engine that runs on water, the miracle fiber of the movie *The Man in the White Suit*: these are the stuff of myth, but more what about the gray areas? Are there a lot of worthwhile things not undertaken because they are too risky or too slow to pay off?

It is an interesting question. Consider the case of Moshe Alamaro.

To begin with, Alamaro has two strikes against him. He talks excitedly, with a heavy accent, about his "supersonic reactor," which he says not only is worth billions of dollars as an antidote to world poverty, but which also represents a whole new approach to chemistry. So at first, he sounds like a candidate for the guy who sits next to you at the patent office, talking wildly about the perpetual motion machine he has in that big paper-wrapped box on his lap.

Alamaro, 36, has certain things going for him, however. He's an aeronautical engineer, trained at the Technicon in Israel, with a record of solid engineering work behind him. His grasp of basic science is good, and senior scientists are willing to take time to talk with him, even though he has no advanced degree. He has mastered the delicate mix of assertiveness and willingness to be provisionally contradicted that is essential to good talk. He has been offered a job teaching at Tufts University; he has no lack of opportunities to earn a living as an engineer, in the United States or in Israel.

Most important, he's got an idea that is highly interesting, particularly to specialists in Third World development. It's a proposal for the manufacture of transportable reactors which turn air into nitrogen fertilizer—that's what green plants do, after all—wherever electricity is relatively plentiful. Alamaro's reactors could be trucked around to farmers' fields beneath the great dams of Africa and Asia—whenever they could be guaranteed power at a discount because of excess capacity—a "special" situation that routinely occurs every time new capacity is added.

These portable machines could run at night; they could be turned off whenever they were not needed; they would virtually eliminate storage costs. Alamaro's plan is technically simple, safe, and ineffably sweet: It is the ideal small-is-beautiful tool for Jane Jacobs-style development practices, the perfect thing to do while waiting for the cities to come to the dam. Moreover, the method is historically-proven; it was the dominant technology in Norway in the first 30 years of the century, until cheap oil shouldered it aside.

Alamaro had his inspiration in 1978, while working on high-powered convection lasers for cutting, welding—like his reactor system, a plasma process. It was, of course, a time when it looked as though oil prices might go on rising forever—making the transportable reactor scheme far more attractive than in a regime of relatively low oil prices. But Alamaro thinks he knows how to make the Norwegian process (named the Birkeland and Eyde process after its inventors) even more efficient—if he can get air flowing into his reactor at supersonic speeds, through a combination of nozzles; and if he can recycle the lost kinetic and thermal energy as electricity. If so, the process is competitive even at today's prices.

All this has been looked at by competent authorities, and it is at least an open question, at best a promising possibility. That it exists only at the intersection of plasma physics, process engineering, public finance and agricultural economics doesn't make it any easier to think about. Yet, in a six-year odyssey, Alamaro has shown his plans to one company and one lab after another—often encouraged, but never funded. At last he has found his way to the world of venture capital—and decided to try to do it himself.

This might be less interesting but for all the emphasis these days on the entrepreneurial process. Take George Gilder's new book, for example, *The Spirit of Enterprise*, which is about to be a big noise in September, as a Book of the Month Club alternate, and a ringing paean to Reaganomics. The Tyringham sage has set down some truly fascinating war stories from recent economic history, tied together in the kind of frame tale more readily associated with, say, John Barth, than with writing on economic topics.

One of Gilder's central propositions is that the best schemes often seem the ones furthest removed from practicality. "Entrepreneurs everywhere ignored the suave voices of expertise . . ." he writes. "Confronting the perennial perils of human life, the scientific odds against human triumph, the rationalistic counsels of despair, the entrepreneur finds a higher source of hope than reason, a deeper well of faith than science, a farther reach of charity than welfare."

The star of the book is Micron Corp., a semiconductor company built in Boise, Idaho, of all places. (It went public last month at $14 a share and is now selling at more than $25.) But there is a waste-management innovator, a frozen french-fry magnate, a Canadian prospector and a Cuban computer king—all battlers against long odds before they struck it rich. The problem is that many of these lonely quests don't pay off—and to tell only the successful stories can be misleading.

Which brings us back to Alamaro. Over the fast few years, he's learned to navigate the shoals skillfully, yet nobody has bitten. He's shown his ideas to the Energy Lab at MIT, to NASA, to the Tennessee Valley Authority, to the plasma division of Westinghouse Corp., to giant fertilizer firms, to the invention management program at Arthur D. Little and to the Stanford Research Institute—in short, every place you can readily think of. (Curiously, perhaps significantly, it was the TVA that was most negative.) In the process, he's learned much about the etiquette of presenting a new idea, partly by taking a course in enterprise management at MIT. "If you had seen me six years ago, well, I could hardly sit still," he says with a rueful smile. And he has developed a network of helpful, but not necessarily hopeful advisers. Still, so far Alamaro has uncovered only possibilities—and instead of coming closer, they seem to be receding. To be sure, he's presenting his plans to MIT alumni-run "start-up clinics" in Cambridge and New York this autumn. And he's discussing investments with various Boston and San Francisco venture capital firms. The problem is that it is assured markets that are needed, even more than technical know-how, and Alamaro is more a laboratory investigator than a promoter. He plans to become a businessman "just temporarily," he says, adding, "I have looked for a long time for a company that would pay me to tinker with my equation." So his business plan really boils down to putting together just enough of a company to be absorbed into a larger corporation. He's a prime example of the raison d'etre for Herztein's Law of Venture Capital: bet on the man, not the idea.

Isn't this the sort of thing for which governments exist? Alamaro's product obviously meets a need: in countries with poor roads, far removed from big fertilizer plants, transportation can be four times the cost of production. Perhaps this is the very sort of thing for which the National Technology Foundation is being created as the applied science clone of the National Science Foundation. Yet the fact is that governments themselves, embarrassed by the range of choices that are offered to them, are seeking more and more often to tie their investments to the market, through joint ventures of all sorts.

So Alamaro is looking for someone with a very particular angle of vision, international in scope and deeply patient. Oil prices are going up again some day. The manufacture of reactor vessels should be attractive to governments of nations with excess shipbuilding capacity—the Baltic countries, for instance, or Japan or Korea. It would only take one resolute backer, his advisers say, adding that he isn't asking for very much. So the verdict is far from in on the case of the supersonic reactor.

The moral is that the invisible hand of competition cannot be counted on to produce tearless results. Every would-be entrepreneur has to live deep down with the recognition that there is a 4-in-5 or 7-in-8 or 9-in-10 chance that he will fail. The answer to the initial question seems to be that, yes, there is a lot of interesting technology around that just can't be brought into general use quickly: you can dry hay, box fish, grow mushrooms in your cellar, even floss teeth and save billions of dollars—but it is devilishly hard to get people to implement these changes.

Whatever the sorrow, though, you can't watch these human salmon swimming upstream without wondering about the incentives that make them do it, without admitting that the supply-siders, especially George Gilder, have made some very interesting and important points. Alamaro himself notes that "technology transfer from defense research to the economy is not what it should be. This is an extremely peaceful idea, for example, but all the relevant technology is military. The only diffusion force is free enterprise. That is a far more powerful factor here in the United States than in Israel or in Europe, where profit is something of a dirty word."

JULY 15, 1984

In Praise of a New Hero

LAST WEEK EXXON CORP. REPORTED HAVING MADE THE LARGEST PROFITS OF ANY American corporation in 1986, more than rivals IBM Corp. and General Motors Corp., even though the price of oil halved at the beginning of the year. To be sure, 1986 earnings were down over the year earlier, but they were still impressive by industry standards.

How did they do it? Well, at one level it had to do with lags: the company says that "downstream operations bid better than upstream," meaning that retail prices fell slower than wholesale costs and so consumers paid—not through the nose, but just enough to keep the company in glowing good financial health. So in a larger sense, Exxon's superior performance comes from the kind of adroit and tough-minded management—the "leaning of Corporate America" in the phrasemakers' dictionary—that is probably at the heart of the current binge of marking-up in value of corporations in the stock market.

Perhaps as responsible as any other executive for Exxon's current prosperity is Jack F. Bennett, an acerbic Georgian by way of Yale and Harvard University (a doctorate in money and banking). Except for four years off in the early 1970s as Paul Volcker's deputy (and eventual replacement) as deputy for monetary affairs at the Treasury Department, he's been at Exxon since 1955. His title is a relatively unfamiliar one: chief financial officer.

CFOs are all the rage these days, the targets of advertisers, the darlings of analysts, beneficiaries of the kind of mild celebrity beyond the confines of their industry that was reserved in the '70s for strategic planners or for "conglomerateurs" in the late 1960s. They are seen as occupying a position nearly as strategically important as that of the chief executive officer himself. It is CFOs, after all, who plot tactics as their companies seek to prosper in the newly-integrated world capital markets. They raise money, cut costs, cut deals, and, in general, practice what MIT's Mel Horwitch has dubbed "post-modern management," meaning they constitute seemingly contradictory aims in a single coherent program.

Last fall, *Institutional Investor*, a kind of fan magazine for big-time money managers, surveyed analysts and came up with the 10 most admired CFOs in the country, and the top CFO in each of 30 industries. Several were from Boston. James Osterhoff of Digital Equipment made the top 10; the former mechanical engineer was credited with achieving a miracle on DEC's financial side since coming over from Ford Motor Co. two years ago. Also cited were Polaroid's Harvey Thayer and Gillette's treasurer Milton Glass (CFO Thomas Skelley was busy saving the company from raiders). But it was Exxon's Jack Bennett who was described as the "senior statesman" of corporate finance.

It was Bennett, for example, who conceived the $7 billion buy-back of Exxon stock that has raised the price of Exxon shares dramatically. Other oil companies spent their extra cash acquiring competitors at premium prices; Bennett figured his own shares were the real bargain. It wasn't altogether obvious. Even so canny an investor as Warren Buffet sold out his significant Exxon position in the early $60s; the stock has since soared to over $80. Of the original "seven sisters," only two—Exxon and Royal Dutch Shell—are left. The other rich and independent international oil companies that seemed to rule the world at the beginning of the 1970s are today no better than cousins. Some of them even married out of the family.

It was Bennett, too, who systematically de-accessioned the companies that Exxon had bought during a diversification binge in the late 1970s (purchases that he helped to arrange). Remember when Gulf Oil tried to buy the circus at the height of the OPEC zaniness? Exxon had taken some flyers in non-oil businesses, too: computer companies, a "black box" designed to make electric motors run more efficiently. But the new businesses didn't match the profits of the old, and the corporate garage sale culminated last month in the disposition of Reliance Electric Co. for a relatively favorable price.

Bennett even sold the building housing Exxon's Rockefeller Center headquarters to the Japanese last month. "It's a fine building, very profitable," he said. "It's just that the Japanese were willing to pay such a high price that it just wasn't going to earn enough of a return at that price to want to keep it."

So what worries Bennett? Not surprisingly, he says it is the government he frets about most. Take Secretary Baker's jawboning of the dollar since the Plaza Agreement of 1985, which he describes as the deft execution of bad policy. "I don't think you should be trying to run policy by signaling things. . . . The government is so damned disruptive when it takes these steps. It's unnecessary. People worry a lot about business cycles, and they're important. But most of the disruption that hits the market is clearly government-created."

Another case in point is inflation, Bennett says. He gives his friend Paul Volcker much credit for subduing the worst of the process, but worries that the battle has already been lost. "They haven't kept the ratchet working," he says. "Another thing: they ought to come out each day and say what they've done, instead of three months later or whatever it is. It's a little bit like prices in a company. If it changes frequently, it's not big news, but if you hold up and make big changes after six months, you stir up the animals. I have a little bit of that feeling about the Fed."

Indeed, it is chasing these little imperfections that gives Bennett his major challenge. "People used to talk about the interest rate and what it was in Germany or the U.S. In a sense, there's only one world interest rate now, but of course because it's expressed in different currencies it's a little different, but it's really only one rate, one market. We're always looking for a niche to borrow cheap, and one way or another, we usually find something. Hell, I spend half my time chasing around the world, looking for a way to exploit some obstacle or another that a government has put in my way."

FEBRUARY 1, 1987

A Man of Girders
and Concrete

THERE WERE OYSTERS AND HIGH EXCITEMENT: IT CLEARLY WAS NOT AN ORDINARY dinner. Robert Seamans, who had overseen much of the American race to the moon, and Jay Forrester, who had invented computer core memory, addressed the group between courses. Telegrams poured in from U.S. presidents and foreign heads of state. The astronaut and the lady consultant seated next to each other could scarcely keep their enthusiasm for each other from taking the normal course, to the mild discomfiture of the senior Japanese businessman across the table. It was a warm April night last spring.

In the audience, venture capitalist Gen. George Doriot, Boston University president John Silber, economist Lester Thurow and a hundred other luminaries sat patiently while British Steel's Ian McGregor droned on interminably about the history of schemes to tunnel under the English Channel, each one of which was slightly different from the one before. By the time the main speaker was introduced it was 11 P.M. The lady consultant was glassy-eyed and the astronaut was asleep. As one man staggered to the bathroom, he said, "No doubt about it, this was a macro-event."

Indeed it was. It was the founding dinner of the American Society for Macro-Engineering, a professional organization dedicated to building projects of all sorts, as long as they are very large and complex. The fellow who had called it all together was Frank P. Davidson, a 65-year-old Concord man, a would-be Christo whose media are girders and concrete.

Technically Davidson is an MIT researcher, the head of the Systems Dynamics Steering Committee and the founder of its Macro-engineering Group. More to the point, says a friend, "He is an intellectual Elsa Maxwell. He puts people together who otherwise never would meet."

Davidson came by his interest in big engineering projects through his family. His father, commissioner of the water supply for New York mayor Fiorello LaGuardia, built the world's longest tunnel, a conduit for drinking water from the Delaware Water Gap to Manhattan. As a well-connected

23-year-old, young Davidson petitioned Franklin D. Roosevelt to establish Camp William James, a legendary Civilian Convervation Corps operation in Tunbridge, Vt., but he is best known for a long and enthusiastic effort on behalf of "The Chunnel," a name he coined.

He became interested in the idea of a tunnel from England to France during a stormy passage of the Channel with his family in 1956. He recalled 19th-century attempts to drive a tunnel beneath the water that were thwarted by British fears of a French invasion. He wrote to the Suez Canal Co. "to see if that maiden aunt' of investment companies was interested in joining some young Americans in reviving the channel tunnel project."

It was; a study group was formed (with the cable address "Chunnel") and Davidson spent the next quarter-century flogging the on-again, off-again project. "After 26 years, the old girl is alive again. We almost began construction in 1974, but for a late-night cabinet-meeting . . . ."

Davidson is not an engineer but a lawyer. A key fact is that he has plenty of money. In a book making the rounds now, (*Macro, a Clear Vision of How Science and Technology Will Shape Our Future*, William Morrow and Co.,) he writes: "In a way I suppose macro-engineering could be recommended as a hobby to people who have reached a position in life where their bread and butter is taken care of, and who would like to make some major contribution to human progress. Large projects, like small ones, need champions and sponsors."

The call to MIT came after engineering professor David G. Wilson read an article Davidson published in 1970 called "Macro-engineering, a Capability in Search of a Methodology" and invited him to give a seminar. When it worked out, Davidson folded up his upper Fifth Avenue law practice and moved in with Jay Forrester, the electrical engineer turned world-planner, former Boston Mayor John Collins and the rest of the Systems Dynamic Group. He has been there ever since, pushing his ideas to faculty, students, money men and engineers.

It is mostly through the American Association for the Advancement of Science that Davidson has gone about building an audience for his macro-engineering group. Papers prepared for a series of meetings have been published as a quartet of books. Last spring the society was founded, with an impressive board of directors, including George Kozmetsky, dean of the Graduate School of Business at the University of Texas; Sherwood L. Fawcett, chairman of Battelle Memorial Institute; Cordell W. Hull, chief financial officer of Bechtel Corp.; and Nancy Wardell of Boston's Institute for Corporate and Government Strategy.

As Davidson talks, the ideas fairly tumble from him in long lists. He pulls out charts and old prints, a transatlantic tunnel-bridge across Iceland and Greenland, a picture of London Bridge when it was new. The ideas he likes best are basically low-tech, he says, tunnels and dams, channels and housing projects, floating islands and dirigibles.

To be sure, there is a pronounced "humanistic" flavor to the group. It isn't everywhere that The Committee for the Study of Success of the Oliver Wendell Holmes Institute can expect so favorable a hearing. Colleagues in the more established fields at MIT, like the operations research program and the economics department often display a gentle scorn for the projects that grow out of the Systems Dynamics Group. But on that count, Davidson is philosophical. "My hunch is that the first graduate program in macro-engineering will be established on the West Coast, not the East," he says.

NOVEMBER 27, 1983

New Thoughts on Liquidity

THERE ARE A LOT OF PEOPLE WHO, IN WORKING THROUGH AN EXAMPLE FOR A CLIENT, come up with a fairly useful tool, and then build a business around it. One such cottage intellectual is Harry Ernst of Arlington, and his story tells something about both the rewards and the terrors of life outside the system of organized production of knowledge that forms such a big part of the economy.

Ernst, 62, is a former Tufts professor (his bachelor's degree came from Boston College, his masters from Boston University and his PhD from Harvard). But in 1965 he left Tufts to found his own firm. "I always had ideas of model building in my head, and to tell you the truth, I didn't like teaching all that much. I loved the seminars, the bright kids."

Over the years Ernst's firm has been largely supported by Boston's Pneumo Corp., a big manufacturing company with a hammerlock on the market for jet plane landing gear and a side interest in the grocery business. "Gerry Fulham [Pneumo's chairman] told me: 'It's your job to keep me from falling off a cliff.'"

One day Ernst hit upon an idea that he thought was an especially effective early-warning device. "I remember the day as if it was yesterday; it was January 1980," says Ernst. "I'd been trying to tear apart the Pneumo balance sheet, to see it through an economist's eyes instead of an accountant's. Suddenly I saw a way to make a snapshot."

What Ernst saw was that a balance sheet, with its columns of offsetting assets and liabilities, has a way of disguising the most interesting truths about a business, by treating profits as something stored up, put safely away like so many nuts. All the equity in the world won't help you if there is no cash in the bank on payday. Ratios of all sorts are used by businessmen to gauge the trend of cash on hand relative to their obligations.

The key to Ernst's insight was that inventory should be thought of as a physical asset instead of a financial one; it was true you could sell it off in a hurry to raise cash, but if you did, you would be out of business. Better to move the value of your inventory out of the category of "working capital," where it could lead to a false sense of security.

So Ernst began recasting the balance sheet in terms of growth and liquidity categories instead of assets and liabilities. In this way, Ernst found he got a clearer picture of the relationship between financial and physical assets. And by charting annual changes in liquidity as a percent of sales against assets, he found he could generate a curve. He called it "the operating curve." He says, "A picture, a convincing chart, is worth a lot."

Such a device is most useful if you can merchandise it or give it away, and preferably both—that is, if you can publish it and persuade others of its usefulness, while keeping the deepest insights to yourself. Ernst, a manly man who smells of shaving soap and gives the impression of someone you could trust to undertake a combat mission, began calling on firms to explain himself and his product. And he set out to write it down. This month it was finally published in the *Harvard Business Review* as "New Balance Sheet for Managing Liquidity and Growth."

He had a lot of help. William White, a finance professor at the Harvard Business School, took him under his wing—mainly because he retained a dramatic image of a younger Ernst. "I was a caddy and worked all through my teens at Winchester Country Club," White explains. "Harry was a star golfer. He carried his own bags, though he played golf by himself. He was the seniors' champion for a bunch of years. He was a loner there, too, but he was a hell of a good golfer.

"When I first saw Harry, he was angry. All his baggage from life was in the article, and often in only tangential ways. And when I figured out what he was driving at, I found that it wasn't too different from what other people had said, and that it made sense. So I said, 'It's a great idea, but it's not your idea, but that doesn't mean you can't write an article about it.' He worked so hard. He called the *Business Review*'s bluff, in effect, and they hired an editor who worked with him, and now the piece is in the *Review*."

Indeed it is. The material is still fairly hard, not so clear as Ernst had hoped. There are brief narratives of the histories of Digital Equipment, IBM, Prime Computer, Kennametal Inc., Chrysler Corp. and Compugraphic Corp. There are many of the beautiful graphs and charts at which the *Business Review* excels. There are new definitions and concepts, and near the end of the article some hints of what close study of the operating curve can tell a company about itself and its competition. "I can scarcely believe it took four years."

But what to make of it? The *Boston Globe* asked a couple of well-known analysts—former professors of finance or accounting and both at the top of their trade—who were generally accepting; neither was overwhelmed. The first one said, "There are all kinds of pro forma projections around capable of telling people when they've been growing too fast. This one might be useful for helping operating executives get a gut feel for the liquidity of their company. But my image of the thing is that it is a couple of charts, sort of Exhibit 7, a sloping line and a way of looking at the data. It is not a new equation or a new skill. But as the Boston Consulting Group showed, a couple of good strong 2 by 2 arrays and the concept of the learning curve can take you a good long way in helping managers to understand what they're doing."

The second one said, "It is a little bit elaborate, in the sense that you could have come up with the same kinds of cash flows in different ways. But as far as a discipline that people can look at and see, and say, 'Gee, I've got a cash pattern that is different from my earnings pattern,' that's useful. All the financial analysis you traditionally see looks at accrual earnings rather than cash flow, and any kind of a device that puts attention on cash is useful."

Ernst's article reminded both experts of work done years ago under the heading of "sustainable growth."

In short, Ernst has paid a penalty for being off on his own, in the sense that he has not learned much about what others have done. On the other hand, he has gotten a good sense of what businessmen worry about and how they think. So what has he got? The same intensity. A diminished bundle of frustrations. Big plans for new software, new models, new applications of his tool. And a kind of immortality.

Those reprints from the *Harvard Business Review* last forever.

MARCH 25, 1984

When Businessmen
Turn Preachers

IN THE 15 YEARS SINCE OPEC SO FORCEFULLY ROLLED BACK THE LIMITS OF THE permissible, there has been an enormous proliferation in types of political activity on the part of members of the business community. Eclipsing the familiar old figure of the business statesman, who spoke from offices atop the lofty spires of corporate America—Reg Jones, say, Crawford Greenewalt, or "Engine Charlie" Wilson—(and leaving aside the recent generation of loud-mouthed, book-writing self-promoters like Lee Iacocca, T. Boone Pickens, Felix Rohatyn, George Soros and Donald Trump), the most interesting new model on the scene has been the business activist.

Consider a few examples of the extraordinary range of activities: there is Ervin (Pete) Pietz, who has used the fortune he made inventing shock mounts for Barry Wright Co. to bankroll primary school education in economics. Ray Stata took time out from Analog Devices to co-found the Massachusetts High Tech Council. Bernie O'Keefe left EG&G to proselytize against the nuclear arms race. David Packard, co-founder of Hewlett-Packard Co., presided over innumerable blue-ribbon commissions; John Young, who took over from him as chief executive of the company, created the three-sector Council on Competitiveness. The late William Casey (the lawyer-spy) and Lewis Lehrman (Riteway Drugs) created think tanks (The Manhattan and Lehrman Institutes), whence have issued a stream of high-powered polemics. Ray Shamie sold his Metal Bellows Corp. and took up office-seeking, rebuilding the Republican party in Massachusetts. John D. MacArthur (the insurance tycoon) and Thomas Lord (another antivibration wizard) took up prize-giving; Arnold Beckman and Edwin Whitehead are scientific instrument magnates who endowed big research institutes. An Wang is famous for cultural and educational good works. George Hatsopoulos, the thermodynamicist who founded Thermoelectron Corp., has found his way to economist Dale Jorgenson and the concept of the cost of capital and introduced them to discussions of international competitiveness; he has also taken up with the Federal Reserve system as chairman of one of its regional banks.

All these men have been efficacious; with the exception of Hatsopoulos, perhaps none has been more so than Ralph Landau, whose forum has been national technology policy. In this wonderfully jumbled pyramid of businessmen-turned-activists—more narrowly, as a specimen of the businessmen-turned economic preacher—it is Landau who has operated nearest anonymity—and just possibly is closest to the top of the heap of boffins, wazirs and all others who seek to advise princes. As vice president of the National Academy of Engineering, with adjunct appointments at Harvard and Stanford universities (where he funded centers for the study of technology and public policy), Landau has for much of a decade brokered a dialogue among engineers, economists and high-tech businessmen. In the last few months, the talk has paid off by achieving a surprisingly widespread consensus among professionals about the nature of the problems facing the next president of the United States.

"He was clearly a very good chemical engineer—I was on the panel that awarded him one of the first national medals of technology," says Edwin Mansfield, a University of Pennsylvania professor who is one of the nation's leading specialists on the economics of innovation. "He came rather later in life to matters involved in economic policy, and brought an enormous amount of vitality and interest. Economists are forever looking over the shoulders of engineers—or at least they ought to be. So it's good to have engineers like Landau looking over the shoulders of economists. If such a person is foolish enough to think that he knows everything, that can be an embarrassment to everyone. But he is too smart to do that."

As a young man, Landau had the good fortune to arrive at MIT in the 1930s, when chemical engineering there was at its zenith. Indeed, few people realize what a remarkable stream of ideas—and earnings—were forthcoming from that department, which celebrated the 100th anniversary of its founding yesterday with a day of talks and banquets. World War I—with its abrupt end to American dependence on German chemistry—had given a tremendous stimulus to the field, and during the 1920s and 1930s MIT sent a continuous stream of graduates to found the petrochemical departments of Esso Oil (later Exxon) and Standard Oil of Indiana. Arthur D. Little grew rich consulting to the chemical industry, and so did Landau and hundreds of others.

After spending the war years helping build the Oak Ridge uranium plant for M.W. Kellogg Co., Landau struck out on his own and built a series of key patents and innovations into a fortune from the manufacture of propylene oxide, one of those little segments of an American chemical industry that, taken as a whole, even today (with oil prices plummeting) rivals computers, aerospace, or telecommunications as a contributor to manufacturing GNP. Landau steadily grew his Halcon International Group until the economic turbulence of the 1970s forced him to sell out to his partner, Atlantic Richfield Co.: "In 1980, with the prime rate at 21 percent, we were paying all our cash flow to the banks." Newly rich but greatly distressed, he headed for the library. "I became an academic economist to find out what happened to us at the height of our success."

In June, Landau boiled down what he had learned into a *Scientific American* article that began, "U.S. economic growth can be enhanced by improving workers skills, supporting research and development and encouraging investment in capital that applies to technological innovations." Big deal, you say, everybody knows that; but the triumph of Landau's reconnaissance is that before he began, everybody didn't agree on the extent to which the growth of productivity turned on investment in education and state-of-the-art technology; it was the province of a few technical economists at the frontiers of growth theory.

Naturally, it wasn't Landau alone who raised the national consciousness to its present fever pitch of awareness about the changing competitive climate. Indeed, events often outraced analysis. Today, nearly every thinking person who pretends to seriousness in the national debate over national economic policy begins with the observation that the national savings rate is too low and that the easist way to increase it is to stop borrowing so much money to finance government operations.

Still, it's not every student who gets to publish his homework in *Scientific American*—precisely because the scientific standards of peer review require that statements be acceptable as fact, not opinion, by the overwhelming majority of specialists in the field.

Landau wrote: "A prudent macroeconomic strategy for long-term growth would include a tight fiscal policy (aimed at lowering interest rates and stabilizing the value of the dollar) and a tax system that encourages investment rather than consumption. (Changes in the U.S. regulatory and legal systems to cut down on wasteful lawsuits would also help.) Probably the most important prerequisite is that capital in all its forms, including the capital required for improved education, training and research and development, should be abundant and cheap; it should also incorporate the most efficient technology available. Above all, this means pursuit of policies that encourage high rates of savings, since it is from the savings pool that a nation's money for capital investment is drawn."

It says something that the *Scientific American* article that the Republican Landau produced, with the extensive assistance of one of George Bush's top economic advisers (Michael Boskin) was all but indistinguishable from a *Science* article that appeared about the same time by George Hatsopoulos, co-authored with Michael Dukakis' principal economist, Lawrence Summers. For that matter, their proposals differ little from the White Paper on "investment economics," whose framers include Nobel laureate Robert Solow, Sloan School dean Lester Thurow and Harvard's Robert Reich, that is scheduled to be released next week by Rebuild America, a coalition of Democrats.

Thus for one shining moment, economists—who are so often chided for their inability to agree on anything—have agreed, for practical purposes, on everything, and so have the the cream of the crop of entrepreneurial businessmen who are among the objects of their study.

OCTOBER 9, 1988

Tom Peters: Between Arrogance and Terror

IT WAS A PUBLISHING PHENOMENON OF A RARE ORDER. BROUGHT OUT IN 1982, WITH the world in deep economic recession, the book was expected to sell 6,000 copies or so. Instead, *In Search of Excellence* was a blockbuster, with 44 hardcover printings totaling 1.4 million copies, and another 1.6 million copies in paperback—the best-selling volume in its publisher's long history.

Why? Well, presumably businessmen were tired of being slugged with Japan as No. 1; U.S. unemployment was pressing 10 percent; clearly readers were ready for an account of what was right with America. And that's exactly what a pair of McKinsey & Co. management consultants, authors Thomas Peters and Robert Waterman, Jr., gave them. There were vivid stories of how companies like IBM, Hewlett-Packard, Johnson & Johnson and even McDonald's hamburger chain had prospered, by observing eight key principles for success.

Inevitably, the sniggers set in. Seafirst Corp., the big Seattle bank that was among Bob Waterman's clients, went broke. *Business Week* magazine did a cover story called "Oops," chronicling reverses suffered by others of Peters and Waterman's best examples. The *Harvard Business Review* teed off on *In Search of Excellence* for being—shudder—anecdotal and insufficiently grounded in scholarly research.

But the book stood up and continued to sell. It made Bob Waterman merely famous, for McKinsey partners are encouraged to publish but not to pocket; all royalties go to the deliberately staid firm. But it made Peters, who quit the company, both famous and rich: McKinsey agreed to take the royalties on the first 100,000 copies alone.

Now Peters, 42, is back with a new book, *A Passion For Excellence*, this time with another co-author, Nancy Austin. He is now not so much an author as a small company. He runs seminars, makes audio visual tapes, markets a calendar, baseball caps and T-shirts, and runs a summer camp called The Skunk Camp. Last week he was in Boston, touring.

The new book consists mainly of answers to questions that were raised about the first book, a kind of sweeping-up exercise. "After the first book was published, I drifted very quickly into seminars. You'd be amazed at what good questions people ask," says Peters. For example, one chapter of the new book—"No Such Thing as a Commodity"—popped out in response to the question, "How were we ever swept away so completely by the idea of the learning curve?"

Time and again, Peters and Austin stress the strictest standards of quality control as the key to continuing success. Thus, Walt Disney's triumph rests on knowing how to keep theme parks clean, and candy baron Forrest Mars is seen hurling poorly wrapped candy against the boardroom wall.

A Passion for Excellence spares some time for smaller companies, is full of cute stuff and contains many more good war stories. But it is not an event of the same magnitude as the first book. *Fortune* magazine scooped parts of it; the critical reception has been restrained but respectful. Peters says, "This is the second iteration and last."

That raises the question, what does Tom Peters do next? There is no going back to McKinsey, that's for sure. He has his own little consulting firm, but it is not like the old days. He makes a lot of speeches, and he has spent a lot of time taping inspirational talks on corporate leadership.

("We literally had to decide between pricing a particular tape at either $29.95 or $1,100," he says. "It depends on who we try sell it to. The training people get mad as hell if you go down-market on them, for the same reason that centralized management information services don't like the personal computer.")

But the big thing at the moment is his Skunk Camp, a four-day workshop for executives. The name derives from Lockheed Corp.'s famous "skunk works," an out-of-channels group of improvisational engineers charged with cutting red tape and coming up with new products.

The logical place for Peters now would be a business school; that's how he was trained. But what fine school is going to have a guy who is so routinely given to the violation of scholarly norms in the name of readability? "I'm giving a lot of thought to what to do next," says Peters. "What I've decided is that the natural state of man alternates between arrogance and terror."

JUNE 2, 1985

The Second Draft
of History

THE BRIGHT IDEA CAME TO HIM ONE DAY IN CHICAGO. "I WAS READING BRUCE CATTON on the Civil War. He reconstructed events of the day by reading the newspapers. And I said to myself, How come newspapers can be primary source material 100 years later? That was before I heard newspapers described as 'the first draft of history.' "

"My epiphany was when I went down to the out-of-town newspaper stand and bought about 50 papers, and one afternoon and into the evening I looked at the *Witchita Eagle* and the *Seattle Post-Intelligencer* and I saw what happened in all the city councils and the zoning boards. I learned so much in one day that I thought, my God, if I can systematize this . . .' "

And so he did. Today John Naisbitt is the proprieter of a prosperous Washington firm and the author of a prodigiously successful book called, *Megatrends: Ten New Directions Transforming Our Lives*. The book is built on Naisbitt's analysis of files compiled by dozens of assistants who clipped hundreds of local newspapers over a 10-year period and sorted them into various categories.

Naisbitt's chief trend, father to all the rest: "We are in a megashift from an industrial economy to an information economy." That makes Naisbitt a kind of a corporate Alvin Toffler; i.e., he goes out on a limb, much farther out than econometric forecasters or corporate planners, to interpret the present and predict the future.

Toffler, of course, is a major prophet of the "human potential" movement. *Future Shock* was an advertisement for "the premature arrival of the future." His *Third Wave*, which is billed as "the book that makes sense of the exploding eighties," describes "a genuinely new way of life based on diversified renewable energy sources; on methods of production that make most factory assembly lines obsolete; on new, nonnuclear families; on a novel institution that might be called the electronic cottage; and on radically changed schools and corporations of the future."

Somewhat similar are Naisbitt's *Megatrends*. Megatrend No. 5, for example, is: "Our centralized structures are crumbling." Megatrend No. 6 is: "We are reclaiming our traditional sense of self-reliance, after four decades of looking to institutions for help."

Megatrend No. 8 is: "We are moving from hierarchies to networking; the computer is smashing the pyramid." Megatrend No. 9: "The North-South shift in the United States is real and irreversible for the foreseeable future." And megatrend No. 10 is: "We no longer live in an either-or, chocolate-or-vanilla world; people have demanded and are getting a multitude of choices."

But there are significant differences between the two visions of the future. For one thing, Naisbitt is a bit of a conservative. "Al drives me crazy with his made-up words. And we have a very different prism. My prism is very pro-business. I've worked in business all my life."

For another, the clipping of newspapers on a very large scale is a genuinely interesting way to get data, sometimes called "content analysis." (Moviegoers will remember that it was content analysis in which Robert Redford was engaged in the scenes that began the movie thriller *Three Days of the Condor*.) Naisbitt's book, like Toffler's, makes for sometimes fascinating reading.

"We're drowning in information, but we're starved for intelligence, for meaning," says Naisbitt. "But people don't have much patience for what they have to work for. So we do all this content analysis, not because we are that interested in newspapers. What we are interested in is local behavior, and nobody comes close to chronicling local change like newspapers. There are local events that are so insistent you've got to put it in the papers. That is what we are looking for: insistent events."

For Naisbitt, who is out on the hustings touting the paperback edition of the book, the new-found celebrity is a refreshing change after a long life writing anonymously for others. "I've been a special assistant to so many people for so long that the only way to become a principal was to start my own company," he says.

Naisbitt, 55, began his career by writing speeches for the chairman of Eastman Kodak, then moved to IBM, before beginning a series of tours in Washington—as personal assistant to Francis Keppell, then to Health, Education and Welfare Secretary John Gardner. He turned out a book on student protest called *Right On!*

It was in 1968 that he founded his firm, in the first of many incarnations called Urban Research Corp (it is now Naisbitt Associates). He merged briefly with Yankelovitch Skelly White Inc., the polling outfit, "and then demerged." His current associate is Mike Evans, supply-side econometrician. Together, they plan to write a newspaper column, dislodge the Dow Jones Index with a new high-tech Naisbitt-Evans Index. "It's all been bumpy," Naisbitt laughs, "but now I've finally got it right.

"People keep describing me as a consultant," he says, "but I am not. I never was. I only forecast social trends. It was Lyle Spencer—he was the founder of Science Research Associates, the smartest man I've ever known—who told me when I was his special assistant that 'consultants are like dentists. They only make money when they are on their feet.' "

Hence the leverage built into Naisbitt's present-day operation. A handful of corporate clients foot the bill for Naisbitt's 150-person newspaper clipping operation. Then there is the book—900,000 hard cover copies sold, 2 million paperbacks printed. Then there is a newsletter ($98 a year) to update the book. And soon there are going to be megatrend partners (not franchises, he says) in a dozen nations around the world.

Naisbitt's vision of the future has called forth a certain amount of criticism. Not everybody is impressed by his impressions of the coming age. Murray Weidenbaum, President Ronald Reagan's first economic adviser, took a poke at him recently for being unnecessarily vague. And Harper's magazine memorably described his firm last fall as "Naisbitt's clip joint."

The criticism rolls off his back, of course. "I talked to Tom Peters the other day," Naisbitt said, referring to an author of another million-selling business book, "And I told him, I've figured out why his *In Search of*

Excellence and *Megatrends* have done so well. It is because people already knew what was in them. It validated what they already knew—and that's a very powerful effect."

Naisbitt was born and reared in a little town in southern Utah called Glenwood—"about 300 people, and they were all my relatives." It is the reason for his success, he says. "I knew I wanted to get out of where I was, so I joined the Marine Corps. I can't tell you how little I knew about the world. So when I saw it for the first time, I really saw it. That innocent eye has served me well."

FEBRUARY 26, 1984

Coupon-Clipper Economics

PAUL HAWKEN WAS JUST 21 WHEN HE STARTED EREWHON, A HEALTH FOODS RETAILER in Cambridge, in 1967 with $500 in cash. He built it into a big little business, sold it in 1973, moved to California from Boston and undertook a series of turn-arounds, "to see," he says, "if I really knew something about business."

He did. When he decided that the mesquite charcoal that one little company sold to restaurants was an ingredient instead of a fuel, he doubled the price, and also doubled the demand. Suddenly a charcoal stove was a status symbol. You can't go into a California restaurant without being offered mesquite-flavored chicken, mesquite-flavored fish.

Today Hawken runs Smith and Hawken, a beautiful little mail-order tool business with $5 million in sales. "What I'm good at is seeing how markets change. I could probably start a conceptually sound business a week," he says, "but I lose interest after a certain point. I don't have an instinct for the jugular."

He's also good at talking about how businesses work. Some years ago, he got to talking with then-Gov. Jerry Brown about economics at a party. The conversation lasted until 5 A.M., he says. The result was a series of position papers he prepared for the California governor to use in the Iowa debates. But the debates were canceled because of the Iranian hostage crisis, and the papers went on the shelf, until Stewart Brand, editor of the *Coevolution Quarterly* (and *Whole Earth Catalog* founder,) persuaded Hawken to publish them in that counter-culture journal. The series struck sparks; the result is a book, *The Next Economy: What To Do With Your Money and Your Life in the Coming Decade.* Hawken was in town last week, talking about the paperback edition.

The burden of the book is that the world economy has turned a decisive corner into something new. "The mass economy is being replaced by an economy based on the changing ratio between the mass and information contained in goods and services," he writes.

"Mass means the energy, material and embodied resources required to produce or perform a service. The mass economy was characterized by economies of scale, by many goods being produced and consumed by many people. The informative economy is characterized by people producing and consuming smaller numbers of goods that contain more information. What is this information? It is design, utility, craft, durability and knowledge added to mass. It is the quality and intelligence that make a product more useful and functional, longer-lasting, easier to repair, lighter, stronger and less consumptive of energy." In other words, Hawken has seen the future and it is Erewhon, Smith and Hawken Tools and L.L. Bean.

Hawken has been around Stanford Research Institute International with James Ogilvy, and the concept of an information-based economy came easily to mind. He had even turned out a book called *Seven Tomorrows*, with Ogilvy and Peter Schwartz. It was later that he became convinced that something had changed. "I was talking to Peter Schwartz of Royal Dutch Shell—it is the second largest company in the world, and he was its strategic planner—and suddenly the pattern of industrial organization of the last 100 years seemed extraordinarily clear to me.

"It was like looking at a template, like putting on glasses that permitted one to see the infrared spectrum. I began reading voraciously in the business press; everything I read confirmed the usefulness of the concept of looking at things in terms of the information embodied in it." How do you measure embodied information? "It isn't easy, but it can be done," says Hawken.

Much of *The Next Economy* hasn't worn very well. The material on OPEC, for example, makes it clear that Hawken thought along with most of the rest of the race that oil prices can only go up. And in his thinking on "The Long Contraction," Hawken seems to have viewed the industrial world as somewhat closer to collapse than it subsequently turned out to be. In any event, he kept telling his readers to stay liquid as possible, throughout the period of the great bull market in equities in that began in 1982.

But other aspects of the book seem prescient. Before General Electric began marketing its home appliances on the basis of their repairability, for example, you could hear about it from Hawken. And his thought on what he calls "disintermediation"—borrowing a term from the world of finance to describe the process of cutting out the middleman—is exceedingly interesting. His speculations about the nature of current changes in economic reorganization put him in a corner with Robert Reich of the John F. Kennedy School of Government at Harvard University, and Michael Piore of MIT and others who believe that a dramatic turn has occurred toward more intimate modes of production.

How sanguine can you be about a sage who tells you that his high-quality pitch forks and beautifully made watering cans from England are somehow more significant harbingers of change than Pepsi commercials or the newest development in away-from-home wiping tissues? Michael Melford, the Cambridge lawyer, calls it "coupon clipper economics"—that is, good for the rich who can afford the best, irrelevant to nearly everybody else.

It doesn't bother Hawken, who's already at work on another book, to be called *Corporate Courage*. It's about "what corporations really are and how they function," says Hawken. It will open with a history of their development from what he calls "the original sin"—the invention of limited liability in the last century.

"I learned my lesson at Erewhon, the hard way, very early on," says Hawken. "One day a customer came into the Newbury Street store and said, 'How do you know these products are really as pure as you say they are?' I started to reassure him, and then I thought, 'Paul, what are you saying?' So I began investigating my suppliers, going out to their farms, and what I found was outrageous. Half of them were lying to me about not using chemicals. In the end I had to put the entire system together myself.

"Pillsbury Corp. makes some things I don't think are very healthy. But the people who run the corporation up in Minneapolis are upright, decent, hardworking, intelligent citizens of good will. People who run health food stores are often as not the worst sleazos and scum. Just because a guy is in an alternative business doesn't mean he's good or bad. It is a function of the system."

APRIL 22, 1984

How One Company Died

THERE'S SOMETHING DEEPLY SATISFYING ABOUT WHAT MAGAZINE WRITERS CALL "COM-pany stories." Corporations are the units in which much of economic evolution unfolds, after all; most of us work in or around one. *Forbes, Fortune, Business Week, Barron's, Inc.* magazine, *Financial World* and *OTC Review:* all thrive by chronicling the ups and downs of collectivities on which you depend for some vital product.

But the conventions of magazine journalism are one thing; scholarly histories of enterprises that are clearly great (in restrospect) are another. In between, there is not much room for accounts that chronicle the life histories of firms in real time and in satisfying detail in order to illuminate the landscape of our working lives—though occasionally, some outsider will wander on to the scene, usually to be utterly buffaloed by the corporate bosses who flatter him with access, as when an *Esquire* contributing editor pronounced Sears, Roebuck to be in glowing good health a couple of years ago in *The Big Store.*

An exception is *When the Machine Stopped: A Cautionary Tale from Industrial America,* by Max Holland (Harvard Business Review Press). It is a strangely gripping narrative of the war history of a small but distinguished West Coast machine tool company that made the headlines, briefly, in 1983, when its conglomerate owners accused the Japanese of conspiring to do it in. Similar companies all over New England were meeting with similar fates during those years, and Holland has produced an account that will be recognizable to anyone connected with an industry that was once among America's very strongest.

Says no less a figure than Alfred Chandler, dean of American business historians: "I found this book hard to put down. It is one of the most important and well-written sagas of an American industrial enterprise that I have read for a long time. . . . It includes almost every aspect of the opportunities and challenges facing, and the inadequacies of, American industry since 1945."

When the Machine Stopped is the story of Burg Tool Manufacturing Co., later Burgmaster Corp., a Los Angeles maker of machine tools founded in

1944 by a Czech immigrant with an itch to bend metal. Fred Burg tumbled on an extremely bright idea—why not put a rotating turret holding six or eight different tools on top of a drill press, just like a lathe?

He tried without success to sell it to the best corporations in the business. So with some $5,000 of his sister's money and a lot of dedication, Burg formed an enterprise that by the 1950s was growing smoothly, generating its own capital, branching out aggressively into promising new technologies on the strength of its own tough-minded research and development work. It sent some of the first numerically-controlled (that is, computer-compatible) tools into the field in the mid-1950s.

But by the mid-1960s, the market was changing. The Burg family, which ran the company, sold out to Buffalo-based Houdaille Industries. On paper, the merger looked great. But the West Coast firm soon lost its competitive edge, just as a Japanese competitor, Yamazaki Tool, began a determined bid for American customers. Stagnation followed in the 1970s, followed by a bid in 1979 to reinvigorate Houdaille by initiating one of the first management leveraged buyouts, designed—it was said—to make the company's bosses more reponsive to the discipline of the market.

It was too late. Crippled by rising interest bills and battered by the soaring dollar, Burg's tool business crumbled, while Houdaille turned to Washington for protection against what had become a flood tide of Japanese imports.

Denied protection under its novel complaint to the U.S. trade representative—it said that its own inattention to fundamentals over the years was the fault of the scheming Japanese, who had secretly subsidized an industry cartel—Houdaille began stiffing suppliers, automatically marking down all invoices by 5 percent. Finally, in October 1985, Houdaille pulled the plug on what was left of the company. After 40 years, the enterprise that Burg had founded was out of business.

Holland's book makes fascinating reading because of its utter fidelity to significant detail. This is, in part, the result of a deeply personal commitment: the writer's father worked for Burg for 29 years. The larger conclusions of his study, confined to an epilogue, are not so persuasive. They represent the fairly standard diagnosis of the American malady by the analytical Left: What killed Burg was a case of managerialism, followed by an overdose of greed; military Keynesianism robbed the little company of vitality while permitting bigger firms to overfeed. (Why did this same military Keynesianism cause the firm to flourish for its first 15 years?)

But these convictions—they may in good part be quite valid, but they have in no sense been proved, or even very closely argued—in no way mar Max Holland's story. The story of Burg Tool Manufacturing Co. is an obituary that almost anyone who is interested in business can read with real pleasure.

MARCH 5, 1989

Acknowledgments

No writer gets anywhere in this world without a great deal of help from editors. James Michaels first assigned me to cover economics at *Forbes* magazine. Robert Phelps gave me an all-important second lease on life at the *Boston Globe*. It was Lincoln Millstein who enabled me to begin writing a column, Hank Gilman under whom it became what I did, Steven Pearlstein who brought it to the *Washington Post* for a time, Jack Fuller who put it in the *Chicago Tribune*, where it still appears. Without Richard Pennington and his associates in the wonderful *Globe* library I would be lost. Without the bold and wry Peter Dougherty, I wouldn't even be here, as I am, in print. But of course the ultimate editors are one's closest friends, and over the years Mark Feeney, Laurence Minard, Elizabeth Bailey, Hope Tompkins and Charlotte Harrison have provided the essential baseline of daily talk, before and after, against which these columns were conceived. I am endlessly grateful to each.

Mostly, however, I must thank the economists and their critics on whose activities I have reported over the years, men and women of every persuasion who seek to understand the forces that produce the ever-changing human division of labor. Though often particular persons did not agree with particular points, nearly always they kept talking to me, believing that in the final analysis, as a friend once put it, I am a flack for them.

Not quite, or so I hope. But among a thousand such informal guides, I must single out this particular friend, Charles P. Kindleberger. It was he who spotted me when I was lost, and with characteristic directness and good cheer, pointed me in the right direction, not once but many times. He is, however, no more to blame for the views expressed in this book (or even complicit in them) than might be a professional mountain climber who had spoken occasionally of the pleasure of his craft to a passing hiker—no matter how moving or enthusiastic he had been.

Index of Names

518 | Index